T0310896

Technology Platform Innovations and Forthcoming Trends in Ubiquitous Learning

Francisco Milton Mendes Neto
Rural Federal University of Semi-Arid, Brazil

A volume in the Advances in Educational
Technologies and Instructional Design
(AETID) Book Series

An Imprint of IGI Global

Managing Director:	Lindsay Johnston
Production Manager:	Jennifer Yoder
Development Editor:	Monica Speca
Acquisitions Editor:	Kayla Wolfe
Typesetter:	Christina Barkanic
Cover Design:	Jason Mull

Published in the United States of America by
Information Science Reference (an imprint of IGI Global)
701 E. Chocolate Avenue
Hershey PA 17033
Tel: 717-533-8845
Fax: 717-533-8661
E-mail: cust@igi-global.com
Web site: http://www.igi-global.com

Library of Congress Cataloging-in-Publication Data

Technology platform innovations and forthcoming trends in ubiquitous learning / Francisco Milton Mendes Neto, editor.
    pages cm
  Includes bibliographical references and index.
   ISBN 978-1-4666-4542-4 (hardcover) -- ISBN 978-1-4666-4543-1 (ebook) -- ISBN 978-1-4666-4544-8 (print & perpetual access) 1. Mobile communication systems in education. 2. Educational technology. 3. Distance education. 4. Education--Effect of technological innovations on. I. Mendes Neto, Francisco Milton, 1973-
  LB1044.84.T43 2014
  371.33--dc23
                              2013020685

This book is published in the IGI Global book series Advances in Educational Technologies and Instructional Design (AE-TID) (ISSN: 2326-8905; eISSN: 2326-8913)

British Cataloguing in Publication Data
A Cataloguing in Publication record for this book is available from the British Library.

For electronic access to this publication, please contact: eresources@igi-global.com.

Advances in Educational Technologies and Instructional Design (AETID) Book Series

Lawrence A. Tomei
Robert Morris University, USA

ISSN: 2326-8905
EISSN: 2326-8913

MISSION

Education has undergone, and continues to undergo, immense changes in the way it is enacted and distributed to both child and adult learners. From distance education, Massive-Open-Online-Courses (MOOCs), and electronic tablets in the classroom, technology is now an integral part of the educational experience and is also affecting the way educators communicate information to students.

The **Advances in Educational Technologies & Instructional Design (AETID) Book Series** is a resource where researchers, students, administrators, and educators alike can find the most updated research and theories regarding technology's integration within education and its effect on teaching as a practice.

COVERAGE

- Adaptive Learning
- Collaboration Tools
- Curriculum Development
- Digital Divide in Education
- E-Learning
- Game-Based Learning
- Hybrid Learning
- Instructional Design
- Social Media Effects on Education
- Web 2.0 and Education

IGI Global is currently accepting manuscripts for publication within this series. To submit a proposal for a volume in this series, please contact our Acquisition Editors at Acquisitions@igi-global.com or visit: http://www.igi-global.com/publish/.

Titles in this Series

For a list of additional titles in this series, please visit: www.igi-global.com

Technology Platform Innovations and Forthcoming Trends in Ubiquitous Learning
Francisco Milton Mendes Neto (Rural Federal University of Semi-Arid, Brazil)
Information Science Reference • copyright 2014 • 317pp • H/C (ISBN: 9781466645424) • US $175.00 (our price)

Advancing Technology and Educational Development through Blended Learning in Emerging Economies
Nwachukwu Prince Ololube (University of Education Port Harcourt, Nigeria)
Information Science Reference • copyright 2014 • 301pp • H/C (ISBN: 9781466645745) • US $175.00 (our price)

Packaging Digital Information for Enhanced Learning and Analysis Data Visualization, Spatialization, and Multidimensionality
Shalin Hai-Jew (Kansas State University, USA)
Information Science Reference • copyright 2014 • 349pp • H/C (ISBN: 9781466644625) • US $175.00 (our price)

Cases on Communication Technology for Second Language Acquisition and Cultural Learning
Joan E. Aitken (Park University, USA)
Information Science Reference • copyright 2014 • 611pp • H/C (ISBN: 9781466644823) • US $175.00 (our price)

Exploring Technology for Writing and Writing Instruction
Kristine E. Pytash (Kent State University, USA) and Richard E. Ferdig (Research Center for Educational Technology - Kent State University, USA)
Information Science Reference • copyright 2014 • 368pp • H/C (ISBN: 9781466643413) • US $175.00 (our price)

Cases on Educational Technology Planning, Design, and Implementation A Project Management Perspective
Angela D. Benson (University of Alabama, USA) Joi L. Moore (University of Missouri, USA) and Shahron Williams van Rooij (George Mason University, USA)
Information Science Reference • copyright 2013 • 435pp • H/C (ISBN: 9781466642379) • US $175.00 (our price)

Common Core Mathematics Standards and Implementing Digital Technologies
Drew Polly (University of North Carolina at Charlotte, USA)
Information Science Reference • copyright 2013 • 364pp • H/C (ISBN: 9781466640863) • US $175.00 (our price)

Technologies for Inclusive Education Beyond Traditional Integration Approaches
David Griol Barres (Carlos III University of Madrid, Spain) Zoraida Callejas Carrión (University of Granada, Spain) and Ramón López-Cózar Delgado (University of Granada, Spain)
Information Science Reference • copyright 2013 • 393pp • H/C (ISBN: 9781466625303) • US $175.00 (our price)

www.igi-global.com

701 E. Chocolate Ave., Hershey, PA 17033
Order online at www.igi-global.com or call 717-533-8845 x100
To place a standing order for titles released in this series, contact: cust@igi-global.com
Mon-Fri 8:00 am - 5:00 pm (est) or fax 24 hours a day 717-533-8661

Editorial Advisory Board

Table of Contents

Section 3
Context-Aware Learning Objects for U-Learning

Detailed Table of Contents

Section 1
Virtual and Augmented Reality Technologies Applied to U-Learning

Chapter 1

One of the methods of teaching that has brought significant contributions to the field of education is augmented reality. This technology transformed learning into a more motivating, enjoyable, fun, and interesting activity. This chapter contributes an augmented reality application for mobile devices that complements and supports the learning of geometric figures. The application, called AGeRA, consists of a geometry book and software capable of reading special markers inserted into the book's content. When this book is placed in front of the camera of a mobile device, 3D objects, sounds, animations, and other interactive elements leap from book pages making learning more fun and exciting. Preliminary tests were made with teachers and students and showed good acceptance of the application to support the teaching of geometry.

Chapter 2

This chapter describes ARIS, an open source tool for creating educational games, narratives, and field research activities on mobile devices. The tool is the result of years of design-based research into educational gaming, design pedagogy, and place-based learning. It has been used in a variety of educational contexts from after-school game-design workshops to university-level language courses. Deeply committed to open and democratic education, the project invites involvement at all levels and continues to innovate as a community of users matures.

Avatars are virtual agents or characters that graphically represent users within virtual environments. Avatars can be implemented in three-dimensional (3-D) virtual environments for training purposes. While there are promising findings indicating that avatars can enhance the learning experience, conclusive and generalized evaluations cannot be made at this time. The effectiveness of these virtual agents in a learning context remains an open question. The purpose of this chapter is to present background information on the definitions and use of avatars in e-based, virtual learning environments and to address the applicability of avatars to ubiquitous learning (u-learning). This chapter examines the available empirical research on the effectiveness of avatars in facilitating social interactivity, motivation, and collaborative learning in 3-D environments. Finally, this chapter provides suggestions for future studies on the design of avatars in both e- and u-learning.

Section 2
Mobile and Context-Aware Learning

The ever-increasing use of mobile devices allied to the widespread adoption of wireless network technology has greatly stimulated mobile and ubiquitous computing research. The adoption of mobile technology enables improvement to several application areas, such as education. New pedagogical opportunities can be created through the use of location systems and context-aware computing technology to track each learner's location and customize his/her learning process. In this chapter, the authors discuss a ubiquitous learning model called LOCAL (Location and Context Aware Learning). LOCAL was created to explore those aforementioned pedagogical opportunities, leveraging location technology and context management in order to support ubiquitous learning and facilitate collaboration among learners. This model was conceived for small-scale learning spaces, but can be extended in order to be applied to a large-scale environment. Initial results were obtained in a real scenario, attesting the viability of the approach.

Mobile learning environments are human networks that afford learners the opportunity to participate in creative endeavors, social networking, organize and reorganize social contents, learner-created cognitive space, and manage social acts anytime and anywhere through mobile technologies. Social interaction with mobile technology is very different from Computer-Mediated Communication (CMC) or Web 2.0 networking technologies. Effective mobile interaction focuses on social-context awareness by integrating location-based technology, which is unique to mobile technology, not easily found in other types of commuting. This chapter proposes a model for mobile social presence consisting of four dimensions: enriching social context-awareness, managing location-based communication, personalizing multi-layered interactivity, and optimizing digital and social identities. Under each dimension there are a few suggested strategies or tips to assist educators in integrating them into their mobile instructions to enhance the mobile-social presence of learners.

    Francisco Miguel da Silva, Rural Federal University of Semi Arid, Brazil
    Francisco Milton Mendes Neto, Rural Federal University of Semi Arid, Brazil
    Aquiles Medeiros Filgueira Burlamaqui, Federal University of Rio Grande do Norte, Brazil
    João Phellipe Freitas Pinto, Rural Federal University of Semi Arid, Brazil
    Carlos Evandro de Medeiros Fernandes, Rural Federal University of Semi Arid, Brazil
    Rafael Castro de Souza, Rural Federal University of Semi Arid, Brazil

Interactive Digital Television (iDTV) has facilitated and expanded the communication and interaction in activities of knowledge acquisitions, entertainment, and recreation in the distance learning field. This new way of teaching and learning has been called t-Learning. In this context, the Learning Objects (LOs) have an important role in assisting in the electronic courses' development. Due the fast progress of e-Learning, some efforts toward standardization have appeared in order to enable the reusability of educational contents and interoperability among systems, and one of these standards is the Sharable Content Object Reference Model (SCORM). Therefore, the main goal of this work is to present an extension of SCORM aiming to adapt it to improve the search and navigation of LOs with educational content for t-Learning. This is done through an authoring tool named T-SCORM ADAPTER, which is able to apply this extension in a fast and efficient way.

    Sílvio César Cazella, Universidade Federal de Ciências da Saúde de Porto Alegre, Brazil
      & Universidade do Vale do Rio dos Sinos, Brazil
    Jorge Luiz Victória Barbosa, Universidade do Vale do Rio dos Sinos, Brazil
    Eliseo Berni Reategui, Universidade Federal do Rio Grande do Sul, Brazil
    Patricia Alejandra Behar, Universidade Federal do Rio Grande do Sul, Brazil
    Otavio Costa Acosta, Universidade Federal do Rio Grande do Sul, Brazil

Mobile learning is about increasing learners' capability to carry their own learning environment along with them. Recommender Systems are widely used nowadays, especially in e-commerce sites and mobile devices, for example, Amazon.com and Submarino.com. In this chapter, the authors propose the use of such systems in the area of education, specifically for the recommendation of learning objects in mobile devices. The advantage of using Recommender Systems in mobile devices is that it is an easy way to deliver recommendations to students. Based on this scenario, this chapter presents a model of a recommender system based on information filtering for mobile environments. The proposed model was implemented in a prototype aimed to recommend learning objects in mobile devices. The evaluation of the received recommendations was conducted using a Likert scale of 5 points. At the end of this chapter, some future works are described.

Section 3
Context-Aware Learning Objects for U-Learning

Chapter 8

Bruno de Sousa Monteiro, Federal University of Pernambuco (UFPE), Brazil
Alex Sandro Gomes, Federal University of Pernambuco (UFPE), Brazil

With the popularization of mobile devices and access to Internet, there has been an intense growth in ubiquitous learning products and studies. How does this effectively impact learners' (not just students') and teachers' daily lives? This chapter presents a literature review on ubiquitous learning, highlighting the impacts of this paradigm on the educational practice, seeking to combine this paradigm with social learning theories. Finally, the authors describe the extension of a social learning service called Redu, whose development is guided by the flexibility of pedagogical models, self-regulated learning, and by supporting the context, allowing a ubiquitous learning experience.

Chapter 9

Laura E Sujo-Montes, Northern Arizona University, USA
Shadow W. J. Armfield, Northern Arizona University, USA
Cherng-Jyh Yen, Old Dominion University, USA
Chih-Hsiung Tu, Northern Arizona University, USA

Ubiquitous computing is opening new opportunities for learning. Researchers and philosophers are still debating what learning theory best explains computer ubiquitous learning. Meanwhile, as it has happened many times throughout history, individuals with disabilities are not able to benefit from such advances until late in the adoption curve. This chapter discusses (a) several learning theories that have the potential to explain computer ubiquitous learning, (b) uses of computer ubiquitous learning for and by individuals with Down syndrome, and (c) a new emerging model for computer ubiquitous learning.

Chapter 10

Kamal Taha, Khalifa University of Science, Technology, and Research, UAE

Most problems facing Distance Education (DE) academic advising can be overcome using a course recommender system. Such a system can overcome the problem of students who do not know their interest in courses from merely their titles or descriptions provided in course catalogues. The authors introduce in this chapter an XML user-based Collaborative Filtering (CF) system called CRS. The system aims at predicting a DE student's academic performance and interest on a course based on a collection of profiles of students who have similar interests and academic performance in prior courses. The system advises a student to take courses that were taken successfully by students who have the same interests and academic performance as the active student. The framework of CRS identifies a set of course features for every academic major. The authors experimentally evaluate CRS. Results show marked improvement.

Chapter 11

Justin A. Wolske, Caseworx, Inc., USA & New York Film Academy, USA

The author looks at the recent drivers that have changed the ways authors and audiences share stories, first by looking at the landscape in art and entertainment, and then by analyzing how these drivers are affecting education. Inspired by his own work as a film and new media producer and his recent foray into educational media, the author isolates four different factors for consideration: (a) the falling price and rising accessibility of digital image acquisition, (b) the Internet as a cheap and instantaneous distribution platform, (c) the evolving ways in which audiences are accessing and consuming content, and (d) increased interactivity between storyteller and audience. By analyzing both the entertainment and education industries, the author predicts that storytelling—a dormant educational tool through much of the 20th century—will become a centerpiece of future educational models. Furthermore, he asserts that storytelling itself must radically change to accommodate this new discourse.

Section 4
Use of Intelligent and Pedagogical Agents for Improving Collaboration in U-Learning

Chapter 12

Kleber Jacinto, Rural Federal University of Semi Arid, Brazil

Francisco Milton Mendes Neto, Rural Federal University of Semi Arid, Brazil

Cicília Raquel Maia Leite, State University of Rio Grande do Norte, Brazil

Kempes Jacinto, Federal University of Alagoas, Brazil

Accessibility means free access to content and services, regardless of one's physical and cognitive limitations, maximizing the user's aspect of hardware and software platform independence. Providing this access is a technical issue more than an ethical issue because the characteristics and limiting standards of accessibility are widely known but little used by software engineers, developers, and content producers. Although there is a specific set of standards and legislation to address these difficulties, accessibility is still far from being a priority among developers and content producers. One of the challenges for ubiquitous teaching, in the present and near future, is building tools to support the creation of accessible learning objects, in compliance with current and future standards. This chapter concerns accessibility standards and points out technological ways to enable the creation of support tools in order to minimize accessibility flaws.

Chapter 13

Demetrio Ovalle, Universidad Nacional de Colombia – Campus Medellín, Colombia

Oscar Salazar, Universidad Nacional de Colombia – Campus Medellín, Colombia

Néstor Duque, Universidad Nacional de Colombia – Campus Manizales, Colombia

The need for ubiquitous systems that allow access to computer systems from anywhere at anytime and the massive use of the Internet has prompted the creation of e-learning systems that can be accessed from mobile smart phones, PDA, or tablets, taking advantage of the current growth of mobile technologies. The aim of this chapter is to present the advantages brought by the integration of ubiquitous computing-oriented along with distributed artificial intelligence techniques in order to build student-centered context-aware learning systems. Based on this model, the authors propose a multi-agent context-aware u-learning system that offers several functionalities such as context-aware learning planning, personalized course evaluation, selection of learning objects according to student's profile, search of learning objects in repository federations, search of thematic learning assistants, and access of current context-aware collaborative learning activities involved. Finally, the authors present some solutions considering the functionalities that a u-learning multi-agent context-aware system should exhibit.

Chapter 14

Adriano Pereira, Universidade Federal de Santa Maria, Brazil

Iara Augustin, Universidade Federal de Santa Maria, Brazil

Emotions play a very important role in the learning process. Affective computing studies try to identify users' affective state, as emotion, using affect models and affect detection techniques, in order to improve human-computer interactions, as in a learning environment. The Internet explosion makes a huge volume of information, including learning objects data, available. In this scenario, recommendation systems help users by selecting and suggesting probable interesting items, dealing with large data availability and decision making problems, and customizing users' interaction. In u-learning context, students could learn anywhere and anytime, having different options of data objects available. Since different students have different preferences and learning styles, personalization becomes an important feature in u-learning systems. Considering all this, the authors propose the Affective-Recommender, a learning object recommendation system. In this chapter, they describe the system's requirements and architecture, focusing on affect detection and the recommendation algorithm, an example of use case, and results of system implementation over Moodle LMS.

Chapter 15

Jocelma Almeida Rios, Instituto Federal de Educação, Brazil

Emanuel do Rosário Santos Nonato, Universidade do Estado da Bahia, Brazil

Mary Valda Souza Sales, Universidade do Estado da Bahia, Brazil

Tereza Kelly Gomes Carneiro, Universidade Estadual de Ciências da Saúde de Alagoas, Brazil

The Internet has permitted some changes that may not have been foreseen on its initial design. We started to constitute friendly or professional interactions, and it eventually enabled the emergence of collaborative actions that resulted in cognitive processes in unusual ways, that is, that take place without the physical presence of those involved but with the effective participation of everyone involved in a broad and democratic approach, constituting a collective intelligence. In the professional world, these interactions can turn into significant gains to developed activities. This chapter reviews relevant findings concerning the cognitive aspects related to the knowledge construction developed under the collaborative work approach in Learning Management Systems (LMS). When working collaboratively in a LMS, the subjects engage in cognitive processes mediated by hypermedia resources that potentially have positive impact on their ability to construct, sense, and/or produce knowledge, to the extent that these resources dynamically dialogue with the already markedly multimodal human cognitive ability. In order to support the analysis, the authors present the relationship between cognitive processes and hypermedia and their influence on knowledge production in an LMS. They also present two experiences developed in Moodle, which showed the possibility of using such resources for people prone to collaboration, resulting in a continuous design optimization of the mentioned course.

Preface

Distance Education (DE) is a growing mode of teaching and learning. The developments of computer networks, the improvement of the processing capability of personal computers, and the advance of multimedia technologies, among other factors, contributed to the creation of this scenario. However, despite consisting of an effective teaching method, distance education still presents some challenges, including the need for a pedagogical and computerized support appropriate to the characteristics of each person. This support is possible through the process of making the teacher a facilitator, no longer the main source of information but instead driving the learning process.

One of the ways to provide DE is through the use of mobile devices. This modality is known as Mobile Learning. This way of providing education allows students and teachers to take advantage of the resources offered by mobile technologies. One of these benefits is the possibility to access, view, and provide content irrespective of time and location. However, even with the benefits offered by mobile learning, we should consider the particular characteristics of each student, including the resources of which he holds. This is necessary not only to provide content that meets the needs of students but also to provide content in an appropriate way regarding the constraints of mobile devices since they have distinct and limited resources.

In this context arises the concept of context-aware environments. This kind of environment fits the user, considering information provided by the selfsame user beyond that captured dynamically from his interaction with the learning environment. This learning modality based on context-aware and mobile environments is called Ubiquitous Learning. The increasing use and diffusion of Web technologies and the ubiquity of educational tools has provided breakthroughs in learning environments. Students should no longer be treated in a homogeneous way. A ubiquitous learning (or u-learning) environment provides students with a teaching method that would not be possible in a conventional Web-based course. A u-learning environment may be understood as a context-aware mobile learning environment, providing the most adaptive content for learners. Context awareness describes a paradigm in which the context of a user is considered to define his profile. There is no consensus about the definition of "context." This one is specific of the application and the desired intention, requiring the identification of functions and properties of the individuals' domains.

This book covers subjects related to u-learning. U-learning generally refers to learning supported by technology, performed anytime and anywhere. So, u-learning occurs when learning does not have a fixed location, or when students take advantage of mobile technologies. Some authors consider it as an evolution of the concept of *mobile learning* (m-learning). In this sense, the idea of ubiquity in the learning process provides valuable contributions to thinking about *invisible learning*, which by nature is dependent of the student context. A major contribution of adoption of ICT in everyday life is the extension of pre-established limits of what is traditionally known as learning spaces. In other words, technology is opening new possibilities to convert other spaces into learning spaces.

These new opportunities represent a new educational paradigm because they enable anybody to produce and disseminate information so that learning can occur at any time and space. In other words, learning occurs not only in the classroom, but also at home, at work, in the courtyard, in the library, in the museum, at the park, and in daily interactions with others. For example, through mobile devices, the learner is able to interact with the environment, by capturing images, sounds, videos, and location information. That ability to capture information in different contexts motivates the students to create new learning situations through interactions with the environment.

This book has as overall objective to clarify the new technologies, applications, and studies in the u-learning area. It intends to help students, teachers, and researchers obtain a larger understanding of both the potential of the related new technologies and the trends that are being followed to make u-learning more effective. The successful implementation of u-learning is not a trivial task. The accumulated experience and know-how of the researchers, who have invested time and effort in study in the attempt of solving problems in this area, are, therefore, important success factors. This book shares this know-how with other researchers, students, and interested professionals. We intend to show the current trends, practices, and challenges faced by designers of u-learning environments. These include theoretical assumptions, empirical studies, practical implementations, and case studies. In the end, the readers should have a clear notion about which is the actual stage and which are the future tendencies in this area.

This book is very valuable to researchers and teachers working in both computer-supporting learning and traditional learning environments. It is also useful for scholars, academics, researchers, educators, students, beginners, and experts with interest in the e-learning research area. Given its depth and breadth of coverage, this book is also of interest to a wide audience of researchers in the fields of education as well as computer science. It is helpful for scholars and business professionals entrusted with implementation of mobile, interactive, and flexible learning environments. The major scholarly value of this book is to provide a general overview of the studies on non-conventional technologies for computer-supporting learning and its applications, as well as a notion of the recent progress in works in this area. This overview can support future academic studies with the background provided by the experts in this book. In addition, it points out to scholars what they should do (best practices) and should not do (bad practices).

In relation to the contribution to information science, technology, and management literature, one important improvement that is provided by this book is the discussion of new methodologies, technologies, and approaches being used in u-learning and their advantages and challenges. The topics covered in this book, which include the current best practices in u-learning, can also stimulate the implementation and the use of related technologies in an academic and industrial context. In addition, this book serves to highlight some of the most important gaps in the development of u-learning support tools, patterns of development, and so forth.

We can find in the specialized literature many publications discussing the use of ubiquitous and pervasive computing. However, to the best of our knowledge, there is no literature that gives guidance on the future trends in this area and its maturity level in the educational perspective. This book fills this gap by gathering recent studies in this area.

Computer-supporting learning is a genuinely interdisciplinary area that strives to create a better comprehension of the requirements of the learning process that is mediated by a diverse set of computer technologies. Therefore, this book is addressed to a wide audience, including researchers and students, educators and industrial trainers interested in various disciplines, such as education, cognition, social and educational psychology, didacticism, and, mainly, computer science applied to education.

Four sections compose this book. Section 1 covers virtual and augmented reality technologies applied to u-learning. The traditional e-learning tools do not meet the specific requirements for all kind of training. This is due to the constant need of practicing and evaluation of acquired knowledge. The use of the Virtual Reality (VR) improves the e-learning environment, which is defined as a high-end user-computer interface that involves real-time simulation and interaction through the stimulation of multiple sensorial channels such as visual, auditory, tactile, smell, and taste. A VR system comprises a computer-generated three-dimensional representation of a real or imaginary environment, called virtual environment, and peripherals such as visual display and interaction devices are used to create and interact with the Virtual Environment (VE). Unlike other instructive systems, interaction with the VE occurs in real-time and the user experiences, presence, and/or immersion, that is, feelings of being inside the virtual world. Objects within the environment can display real world behavior.

Virtual reality systems have been applied for education, training, and entertainment purposes in the areas of medicine, military, architecture, safety training, flying simulators, and video games. This type of instructional system has been used in different domains where conventional training methods are expensive, complex, or dangerous. The concept of Augmented Reality can be defined as an interface based on computer-generated virtual information with the user's physical environment perceived through technological devices. In the context of learning, Augmented Reality aligns with the theoretical framework of situated learning, as students build connections between their lives and their education by adding a contextual layer. In addition, when operated in conjunction with mobile devices, it positions itself on the border between formal and informal learning, contributing to the evolution of an ecology of learning that transcends the educational institutions and increases the potential for just-in-time learning.

Section 2 covers concepts related to mobile and context-aware learning. Some authors define context as information consisting of properties that combine each other to describe and characterize an entity and its role as a computer-readable form. The location is crucial to the context of the student in an environment for ubiquitous learning. However, the context includes more than just the location. A wide range of context factors combine themselves to form a context definition. Almost all information available at the moment of interaction can be seen as contextual information, among which stand out: 1) the various tasks required from users; 2) the wide range of devices that combine to create mobile systems with associated infrastructure services; 3) resource availability (e.g. battery status, screen size, network bandwidth, etc.); 4) resources in the neighborhood (e.g. accessible devices and servers); 5) the physical situation (e.g. temperature, air quality, brightness level, noise, etc.); 6) spatial information (e.g. location, orientation, velocity, acceleration, etc.); 7) time information (e.g. time of day, date, season, etc.); and 8) physiological measures (e.g. blood pressure, heart rate, respiratory rate, muscle activity, etc.).

Section 3 covers topics related to context-aware learning objects for u-learning. Due the fast progress of e-learning, some efforts to standardize have appeared in order to enable the re usability of educational contents and interoperability among systems. A relevant concept in relation to the content of teaching and learning in the field of distance education is the Learning Object (LO). LOs have an important role to assist in electronic courses' development. According to the Learning Technology Standard Committee (LTSC) of the Institute of Electrical and Electronics Engineers (IEEE), a LO is defined as any entity, digital or non-digital, that may be used for learning, education, or training. LOs are considered information blocks and present the following features: 1) reusability – reusable several times in different learning environments; 2) adaptability – adaptable to any teaching environment; 3) granularity – pieces of content, in order to facilitate its reusability; 4) accessibility – easily accessible on the Internet to be used in many locations; 5) durability – possibility to be used continuously, regardless of technological change; 6) interoperability – ability to operate through a variety of hardware, operating systems, and browsers (i.e. effective exchange between different systems).

Section 4 focuses on the use of intelligent and pedagogical agents for improving collaboration in u-learning. To improve the effectiveness, or even the autonomy of computational learning tools, some techniques of Artificial Intelligence (AI) have been employed. Due to some of their abilities, such as behavior guided by goals, reactivity, reasoning, adaptability, learning, communication, and cooperation, Intelligent Agents have become very popular in computer-supported learning environments. An intelligent agent is any entity which may receive information about the environment by means of sensors and act in that environment by the performers rationally – in the other words, in a correct way and tending to maximize an expected outcome. An autonomous agent set that cooperates to solve a problem that is beyond the capacity of a single agent is considered a Multi-Agent System (MAS).

Francisco Milton Mendes Neto
Rural Federal University of Semi Arid, Brazil

Section 1
Virtual and Augmented Reality Technologies Applied to U-Learning

Chapter 1
Interactive Books in Augmented Reality for Mobile Devices:
A Case Study in the Learning of Geometric Figures

Ana Grasielle Dionísio Corrêa
Universidade Presbiteriana Mackenzie, Brazil

ABSTRACT

One of the methods of teaching that has brought significant contributions to the field of education is augmented reality. This technology transformed learning into a more motivating, enjoyable, fun, and interesting activity. This chapter contributes an augmented reality application for mobile devices that complements and supports the learning of geometric figures. The application, called AGeRA, consists of a geometry book and software capable of reading special markers inserted into the book's content. When this book is placed in front of the camera of a mobile device, 3D objects, sounds, animations, and other interactive elements leap from book pages making learning more fun and exciting. Preliminary tests were made with teachers and students and showed good acceptance of the application to support the teaching of geometry.

INTRODUCTION

Evolution of mobile devices such as laptops, Personal Digital Assistants (PDAs), mobile phones and tablets led to emergence of a new field called Mobile Computing. According to

DOI: 10.4018/978-1-4666-4542-4.ch001

Guan et al (2011), Mobile Computing is treated as a new computing paradigm that enables users to manipulate digital information remotely from anywhere and at any time. It is a concept that involves processing, mobility and communication through wireless network, which eliminates the need for users to be always connected to a fixed network structure.

Mobile applications demand for support of these technologies. Therefore, new solutions and services have grown exponentially with development of devices. Currently it is possible to find a variety of applications in various areas of knowledge, eg, economics (Giridher et al, 2009), banking (Ciurea, 2012), medicine (Merdes; Laux, 2002), education (Kun et al, 2011), among others. In particular, in education, the use of mobile devices for teaching and learning has expanded the area of computer education creating a new concept called "Mobile Learning" or "M-Learning" (Wei, Liqiang, 2011). This new educational paradigm enables the learner to access content and interact with teachers and classmates from anywhere.

One main factor for the spread of mobile devices in education can be explained, in a first analysis, by the significant number of users in all age groups (Mishra, 2009), (GSMA, 2010). According to Benedek (2012, pp.17), it is estimated that in 2013 there will be 4.5 billion mobile phone users worldwide using entertainment services, community information and social networking. The low cost of the devices and mobile services, in comparison with the values of computers and Internet services, increased demand for applications to support teaching and learning (Lane et al, 2010). The teacher should look to expand his/her potential for teaching and learning, since such devices are meant for communication between users, i.e. send and receive calls and messages.

Besides the low cost, technological developments in mobile telephony has enabled the development of increasingly powerful mobile devices, with greater processing power, multimedia features and loads of sensors such as compasses, accelerometers and cameras (Lane et al, 2010). These device characteristics caused the spread, in large-scale, of augmented reality applications (Olsson; Salo, 2011). This technology makes it possible to integrate the real world with 3D virtual elements (Azuma et al, 2001); which can arouse the learner's curiosity and so makes the learning process more attractive, fun and motivat-

ing (Fotouhi-Ghazvini et al, 2009), (Balog et al, 2007), (Shelton, Hedley, 2002).

For all these reasons, this paper presents the research and development of an educational augmented reality application for mobile devices called AGeRA. This is an interactive book with augmented reality for teaching and learning of geometric figures. When looking at the book, it seems like other conventional books. However, when the book is placed in front of a camera on a mobile device, 3D objects, sounds, animations, textual explanations and other interactive elements, leap from its pages. These features added to the physical book can increase student interest and motivates them to explore the topics presented, thus enhancing learning.

Besides this introductory section, the chapter provides, in section 2, benefits of mobile learning, and discusses how mobile computing can be used as a teaching resource in the classroom. Section 3 presents the concepts and fundamentals of augmented reality technology and brings a study of papers that show the development of books created with augmented reality. In Section 4 we present the methodology of the AGeRA application development, detailing the choices of topic, target audience, functional requirements, interaction design, content covered in the book and the results of tests with users (students and teachers). Finally, in section 5, the main conclusions of this work and proposal to future works are presented.

MOBILE LEARNING

Use of mobile devices in education provided a new educational paradigm, called M-Learning, since no more learning occurs in formal locations like classroom (Wei; Liqiang, 2011). Particularly for children, it offers many opportunities for students to work their creativity, while at same time it becomes an element of motivation and collaboration.

This definition is consistent with the idea of pervasive learning "*In essence, pervasive learning concerns the use of a technology the apprentice has in his/her hands to create learning situations more meaningful and relevant, authored by student*"(Zanella et al, 2007, p.2). Furthermore, these types of devices utilize open platforms, allowing deployment of low cost educational applications with potential for expansion and replication in several places (Lane et al, 2010).

Vision of mobile computing is that of portable computation: rich interactivity, total connectivity and powerful processing, strong search capabilities, powerful support for effective learning and performance based assessment (Quinn, 2000). Its advantages is that a user can use it while on the move due to ubiquitous devices that makes mobile learning to be more considered as anytime, anywhere learning. The information can be accessed in any location; it is informal and formal learning. Mobile Learning ties the world together to encourage collaboration and communication.

Table 1 shows the evolution of mobile learning from the 19780's to 2000's. These include the telephony operation, generation and networks used in the mobile development. It really shows that mobile learning is upgrading and new technologies are invented.

Experts are concerned to provide a learning environment that always makes available to users the most current information possible. Thus, M-Learning emerges as an important alternative education and distance learning, where can be highlighted the following objectives (Marçal et al, 2005):

- Resources to improve student learning through task execution, ideas annotation, searching for information on Internet, record facts through digital camera, sound recording, access to podcasts of classes and lectures among other existing features.
- To provide access to educational content anywhere and anytime, according to device connectivity.
- To increase the possibilities of access to content, increasing and encouraging the use of services provided by an educational institution.
- To expand group of teachers and learning strategies available through new technologies that support classroom and distance learning.
- To provide means for developing innovative methods of teaching and training using new computing and mobility resources.

Currently, most children grow handling different technologies. This ability allows these children access to an unlimited universe of knowledge and information. According to the Center for Research on Information Technology and Communication (CETIC 2012), in Brazil, about 47% of children and adolescents between 9 and 16 years old have access to Internet every day or almost every day. Around 45% have a mobile device, and of those, 21% have a mobile device with Internet access.

AUGMENTED REALITY

Augmented Reality is a technology that enables to mix virtual objects generated by computer with a real environment, generating a mixed environment that can be viewed through any technological device in real time (Azuma et al, 2001). The main characteristics of an Augmented Reality system are: a) real-time interactivity, b) use of 3D virtual elements, c) mix of virtual elements with real elements.

Table 1. Mobile development

	1980S	1990S	2000S
Telephony	Analog Calls	Mobile communication Simple messaging	Smartphone's
Generation	1G-Analog Cellular telephony	2G-Digital Mobile communication	3G-wideband Mobile communication
Networks	Cellular Networks	Digital networks	IP Data Networks

Augmented reality has emerged from research in virtual reality. According to Burdea and Coffet, (1994), virtual reality environments make possible total immersion in an artificial three-dimensional world. This way, the user can explore and manipulate imaginary virtual worlds as if it was being part of him. Images generated by computer seem to be natural size and scenery modifies starting from the user's interaction with the virtual world. If environment incorporates three-dimensional sounds, then user is convinced that the orientation sounds change naturally in agreement with his/her orientation inside the environment. The immersion in a virtual world can be provided through specific technology (Burdea; Coffet, 1994): head-mounted displays (HMD), devices of optical tracking, force-feedback data gloves and joysticks that allow the user to navigate inside a virtual world and to interact with virtual objects.

From the appearance of virtual reality, there was always a separation between real and virtual world. However, technological progress has made possible to mix real environment and virtual worlds (in real time) originating a new concept denominated mixed reality (Kirner & Tori, 2006b). Unlike virtual reality that transports the user inside of virtual world, mixed reality propitiates the incorporation of virtual elements in real environment (the user maintains the presence sense in real world) or it transports real elements for virtual environments complementing the environment. When there is predominance of real over virtual, the environment is characterized as augmented reality; therefore the real environment is enlarged ("augmented") with addition of three-dimensional objects. To the opposite, when there is predominance of virtual over real, the environment is characterized as augmented virtuality; therefore real physical objects are captured in real time and inserted in simulated environment by computer.

Augmented reality presents a great advantage on augmented virtuality: allows transport of virtual objects to the real world providing new interaction possibilities to individuals with serious problems

of fine motricity (ability) and global motricity (agility). In this case, that the user can manipulate virtual objects happens in a natural way, dragging or touching an object with his/her hands or with his/her feet, without necessarily using devices of interaction or adapters. In case of augmented virtuality or even of virtual reality, training is necessary to use devices as mouse, keyboard, joystick or other technological devices. Many times, that need generates indifference, fear or even individual's incapacity in interacting with virtual environment.

Regarding the hardware of augmented reality, it's needed a common computer equipped with a display device (HMD, video monitor, screen or projector) and an image capture device (video camera or webcam). Ideal equipment for viewing the augmented reality environment is HMD with a processor, and navigation devices such as Global Positioning System (GPS), forming what could be understood as a helmet capable of capturing images, processing them and showing them to user in real time (Azuma et al, 2001). The helmet with these technologies is expensive and still with restrict use.

In relation to development software, it is necessary to use an Application Programming Interface (API) that uses augmented reality technology. The best known API is ARToolKit, but there are several other tools, such as NyARToolkit, ARtag, OSGART, Sudara, all based on ARToolKit. In this project we used NyARToolkit: an Object-Oriented Programming port aimed at Java 3D, JOGL, Android, SilverLight, C#, and C++.

Figure 1 shows the basic cycle of ARToolKit execution. Initially, the real world image is captured by a video input device (a). Captured real image (b) is transformed into binary image (c). This image is analyzed to find square regions (d). Then, ARToolkit calculates the position and orientation of camera relative to the square region seeking to identify specific figures, called markers (e). When the marker is recognized, ARToolkit verifies which virtual object is associated with it

Figure 1. Basic cicle of ARToolkit

(a)   (b)   (c)   (d)   (e)   (f)   (g)

(f). Finally, the ARToolkit calculates the exact point the virtual object must occupy in the real world and executes the superimposition of images returned to the user the visual combination of real world and virtual object (g).

In a simple application for Desktop, the user must point the marker to the camera so that it captures the image and transmits to the computer software. Software, in turn, will create the virtual object associated with this marker and show this virtual object on video monitor. While in a desktop application the user manipulates the marker; on a mobile device application the user manipulates the device itself with camera pointed at marker. Below there are some examples of the use of augmented reality with focus on Education.

EVOLUTION OF AUGMENTED REALITY DEVICES

In 1968 Ivan Sutherland, an American computer scientist and Internet pioneer, said that "*the fundamental idea behind the three-dimensional display is to present the user with a perspective image which changes as he moves*" (Suthterland, 1968). Based on this, there are four display techniques used for augmented reality applications:

- Head-Mounted-Display (HMD).
- Personal Digital Assistants (PDAs).
- Tablet.
- Smartphone.

First of all the HMD, one might say as a archetype, was invented in 1966 by Sutherland himself. A HMD combines a helmet with a visor being, at least in part, paraboloid (Mostrom, 1975). The visor and a projection apparatus are fixed on the helmet (Mostrom, 1975). By means of a specific configuration of reflective surfaces any virtual object can be produced "*within the field of view of the person wearing the helmet*" (Mostrom, 1975). In a nutshell: HMDs obtain an enhanced view of the real environment by superimposing 3D computer generated objects into the real world view (Rolland; Fuchs, 2000). About 30 years after Sutherland's path breaking work in 1997, Azuma distinguishes between optical see-through and video see-through HMDs (Azuma, 1997). Optical see-through HMD's are based on optical combiners being placed in front of the user's eyes (Azuma, 1997). To avoid, that the users view is obstructed, these combiners are particial transmissive (Azuma, 1997). In contrast, video see-through HMDs capture the real world view with two cameras being mounted on the helmet (Emiliy et al, 1993). Until the images reaches the users eyes the virtual objects are placed electronically into the real worlds view (Rolland; Fuchs, 2000).

The second major technology used for augmented reality applications are handheld devices like tablet pcs, PDAs or mobile phones (Figure 4). In this paper we define handheld augmented reality just like Figure 2d.

Wagner (2007) does: "*We define handheld AR as a setup, where the user holds the mobile device actively in his hand*". Besides the fact that the screen containing the virtual content is handheld rather than head worn, which results in the great advantage of mobility, handheld AR differs from

Figure 2. Form factors of mobile augmented reality systems: (a) traditional "backpack" computer and HMD, (b) Tablet PC, (c) PDA, (d) Mobile phone (Wagner, 2007)

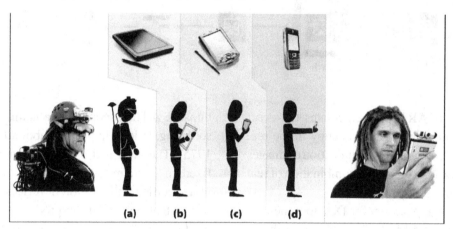

HMDs in several key distinctions. In contrast to the HMDs, handheld devices are ubiquitous and often abundant. The screen of a handheld device is directly connected to its input device (Billinghurst; Henrysson, 2006). Unlike HMDs, handheld devices *"are typically used only for short periods of intensive activity"* Billinghurst; Henrysson, 2006).

MULTIMEDIA INTERACTIVE BOOK WITH AUGMENTED REALITY TO LEARNING

Development of books potentiated with augmented reality is addressed in literature through reports of experiences, highlighting the work of: (Billinghurst et al, 2001), (Oliveira; Kirner, 2007), (Maier et al, 2009), (Costa; Kirner, 2010), (Gutierrez et al, 2010), (Okawa et al, 2010), (Kirner et al, 2012).

Billinghurst et al (2001) are pioneers in development of books potentiated with augmented reality . Authors created the Magic Book, where user can read the book content in the traditional way, flipping through its pages, without any additional technology. However, if you look through the pages with an augmented reality display (display

connected to a hand held computer Desktop), users can view 3D objects coming out of the pages and enriching the contents presented. Just like the Magic Book, several other educational books potentiated with augmented reality were also created for desktop computers, they are:

- **LIRA (Oliveira; Kirner, 2007):** Helps to increase visual, audible and tactile capabilities of children with special needs. Traditional book was augmented with features capable of stimulating the senses of children through songs and animations issued by virtual three-dimensional objects.
- **Increased Chemical Reactions (Maier et al, 2009):** Proposes to help students to understand and learn chemistry, enabling to inspect molecules from different viewpoints, to control interaction between molecules and to observe chemical reactions.
- **LIPRA (Costa; Kirner, 2010):** Presents basic aspects of a game of chess as: names of parts, movements, catch and checkmates. Each of these topics is discussed in a separate topic in the book. At the end, book provides some exercises so that users can test their knowledge.

- **AR-Dehaes (Gutierrez et al, 2010):** Designed to help students to visualize, perform tasks and understand complex concepts of space engineering, such as surfaces, planes, corners, projections, etc.
- **SOLRA (Okawa et al, 2010):** Presents a solar system with interactive augmented reality using features of images, animations, sounds and interactions with multiple markers to facilitate knowledge acquisition in the context of the structure and behavior of the Solar System for educational use.
- **GeoAR (Kirner et al, 2012):** Designed for teaching and learning of geometric shapes, as recommended in the contents of elementary school mathematics. To use the book GeoAR, you must have a webcam connected to your computer and a video monitor. The content covered in the book GeoAR comprises the following topics related to geometry: rectangle, square, triangle, classification of the triangles according to their sides, classification of the triangles by their angles, trapezoid, pentagon and circle.

These innovative technological approaches allow a rich end user experience concerning sensorial stimuli, allowing for an enjoyable simultaneous interaction with the content (e.g. reading, hearing and display of static images and moving in 3D virtual models through augmented reality), thus enhancing the learning process.

The use of augmented reality applications mentioned so far are of use for desktops or notebooks which limits the user to a restricted space for the equipment. Multiple handsets and PDAs, tablets and iPads are capable of supporting a system based on augmented reality because they have a good processing power. This way you can use the camera's own device to capture the real environment and also use the display device itself with the virtual objects added. Researches on books potentiated with augmented reality for use with mobile devices are recent:

- **Children's Literature (Galvão; Zorzal, 2012):** Authors created a children's book of a Bible story. Stories are enriched with detection of rapprochement between two markers resulting in specific animations and sound effects, such as music, voices and storytelling.
- **Coloring Book (Clark et al, 2011):** Created for students to interact, to create and to express themselves through painting three-dimensional designs created by the user.

Some companies like Digital Tech Frontier and Sesame Workshop are combining augmented reality with toys and other children's books. These companies argue that the augmented reality helps children's learning, and at the same time keeping them entertained for longer time.

E-SPECIFICATION, DEVELOPMENT AND AVAILABILITY OF AGERA

To create AGeRA application, a specific development process was defined, compliant with principles of software engineering (Figure 3). The specifics of application and the technology of augmented reality were considered. Process follows a targeted approach to prototyping, where versions of the application are being constructed and evaluated, until a prototype that meets user requirements is obtained.

As shown in Figure 2, AGeRA application development comprises the following steps:

- In step Needs Assessment a research was carried out on teaching and learning methods of geometric figures geared for children.
- In Requirements Analysis phase a survey of requirements that needed to be developed was conducted . In this step were also defined the technologies used for develop-

Figure 3. AGeRA development methodology

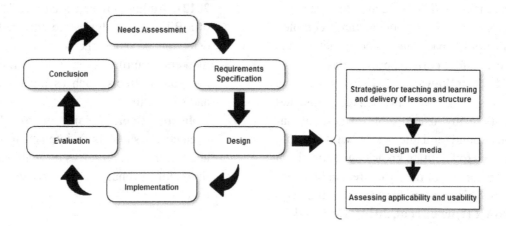

ing AGeRA (environments and development libraries).

- In step Design a teaching and learning strategy of geometry was chosen and set a structure for implementing the lessons. Then, the design of printed media was created. Based on proposed activities in print, was made a planning application usability testing.

- In the stage Implementation use-case, class and sequence diagrams were created. With the complete conceptual modeling, a functional prototype was created to validate requirements.

- In step Evaluation a valuation methodology was defined, questionnaires were developed to collect data on users. These questionnaires were applied to students and teachers to assess applicability and usability of the application. After data collection, analyses of results were made.

- In step Conclusion final remarks on this work are made.

NEEDS ASSESSMENT

First the user profile was defined: elementary school students (1st to 5th year) that are learning matters pertaining to the sense of location, recognition of images, manipulation of geometric shapes, spatial representation and establishment of properties as specified by Parâmetros Curriculares Nacionais (PCNs). National Curriculum Parameters (Brasil, 1998) – specify how education should be conducted of Ministry of Education.

Then, a search was created to verify and analyze what are the difficulties that students of lower grades of elementary school have in the process of differentiation between spatial and planar geometries. We conducted a theoretical study about development of geometric thinking, considering the knowledge stage in which the child is, to be able to relate with practice in classroom (Fazza 2008).

It is known that geometry is present in various fields of human life, whether in civil constructions, nature elements or manipulable objects of everyday. School, as a formation agent, should give children access to this knowledge, in order that they understand and interact with the same world where they live. Therefore, Fazza (2008)

Figure 4. Sample page from AGeRA Book

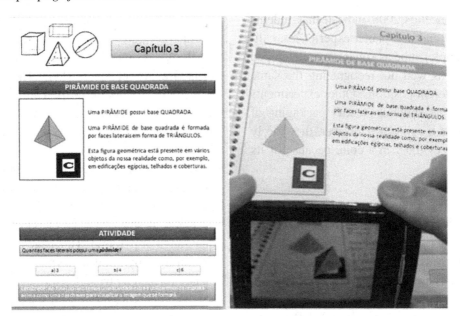

recommends that teachers develop activities that provide the establishment of spatial relations in objects, like:

- Recognition of plane geometric figures (circle, triangle, square and rectangle) and their relationship with other objects present in every day.
- Recognition of non-planar geometries (spheres, pyramids, cubes and parallelepipeds) and their relationship with other objects present in every day.
- Perception of three-dimensionality in non-planar geometries, as well as the similarities and differences that exist between them.
- Classification of figures as plane or non-planar geometries based on criteria stipulated by students, explaining orally what are these criteria .
- Disclosure orally the relation and differences that exists between the plane and non-planar figures.

Smole et al (2003) present examples of activities that exploit the properties of objects:

- Conduct activities related to arm and disarm objects that help establish inverse relationships.
- Group objects by similarity and, at the same time establish differences relationships. Children should compare objects around them depending on its physical qualities. They may discover the same properties, such as color, texture, flavor, if used to eat, dress, among others. Manipulate objects of the same shape but different sizes, and verbalize what was made.

With the geometric objects (cylinder, cone, pyramid, prism, cube and sphere):

- Conduct exploratory activities and displacements.
- Plan activities so that the group works simultaneously with geometric and everyday objects that have the shape of the first.

Reports of teacher's experiences in early grades (Vasconcellos, 2008) indicate that students confuse plane and non-planar experiences, calling, for example, cube as square, parallelepiped as rectangle, as well not recognizing the same figures in different positions. Other experiments have shown that children identify packaging of a glue stick as a cylinder. However, they rarely recognize the cylinder in a coin, because of its small height.

REQUIREMENTS SPECIFICATION

Based on the needs assessment for learning Geometry and research involving educational systems with augmented reality, it was possible to establish the functional requirements of the AGeRA:

- Allow viewing and manipulation of geometric models in real time.
- Allow solving math challenges with issues related to geometric figures.
- Allow individual and collaborative work.
- Have low cost for dissemination in public schools.
- Have high availability to be easily acquired by students and teachers.
- Interface should be simple with minimal detail and easy to understand.
- Allow tangible and intuitive interaction.

As hardware requirements, AGeRA application needs a mobile device equipped with camera and Android OS.

INTERACTION DESIGN AND CONTENT ADDRESSED

The stage of interaction design involved design of media (printed book prototype and augmented reality application) and study of teaching strategy. This strategy depends on the order and manner in which contents are exposed and treated. For this, we created a book, here called Print Media, with content on geometry, specifically about geometric figures.

Book is designed to be used together with augmented reality application (Digital Media) capable of reading the markers inserted into the book content. These markers generate three-dimensional geometric elements. This type of functionality, feature of books with interactive augmented reality represents a paradigm that maintains the use of books in their traditional form, along with the enrichment afforded by technology.

Figure 4 shows a page of book related to a quadrangular pyramid. This page contains information about pyramid: a) has a square base, b) side phases formed by triangles form, c) examples of similar objects of everyday life where the pyramid is present. At the end of the page, a question is posted to the user: how many sides has a pyramid? User must choose one of three response options. Book shows the 3D design pyramid drawn on 2D plane, but the user can use the mobile device to view 3D model of the pyramid. This enriches the learning.

Book has one marker to page. Each page presents a planar geometry as part of a non-planar geometric figure. For example, a cube is formed by squares; parallelepiped is formed by rectangles, prism is formed by triangles, and so on. The following geometric elements are treated: square-cube, rectangle-parallelepiped; triangle-prism, triangle-pyramid, triangle-cone, circle-sphere, cylinder-circle. Besides 3D models, animation and sound scripts were included to enhance interactivity. For example, when 3D object appears on screen, a sound effect is executed and, if user "touches" on 3D object, then it starts spinning on the screen. Each page has an activity for the user to choose a correct answer. Extra exercises were also created, where user can compare pairs of geometric figures and make a reflection on the similarities and differences between them (Figure 5). Moreover, there are also issues with open spaces so user can write what each question asks.

Figure 5. Example exercises of AGeRA book

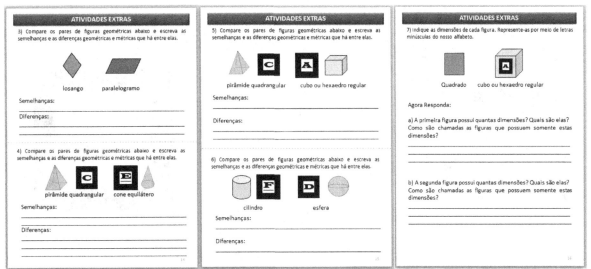

At the end of book it's provided a set of puzzles involving some geometric figures discussed in book. Goal is to analyze images of everyday objects and try to identify geometric figures studied are present in those figures. For this, book has a page containing a set of card markers used in previous activities. Each letter present inside the marker corresponds to a geometry studied. This page can be detached from the book and the user must cut cards to form small pieces. This activity is divided into three steps: 1) cut the cards to form parts markers, b) analyze the pictures of the book with everyday objects, c) paste cards on grid answers in correct sequence (Figure 6).

If the assembly of puzzle is correct, the image of Android mascot in 3D is shown to user. Mascot is animated at sound of a really fun soundtrack (Figure 7). Answers of the exercises in book, including open questions, are available on the last page of book.

DEVELOPMENT AND TECHNOLOGIES

Figure 8 shows the relationship between technologies used in development of AGeRA.

Below is a brief description of these technologies:

- **Eclipse:** Development environment used to develop applications in Java programming language.
- **Java Development Kit (JDK):** A set of utilities that let create systems for Java platform. It contains the entire necessary environment for creation and execution of Java applications, including Java Virtual Machine (JVM), Java compiler, Java APIs and other utility tools.
- **Android Software Development Kit (SDK):** Is the process by which new applications are created for the Android Operating System. Includes a comprehensive set of development tools, debugger, libraries, a handset emulator based on QEMU, documentation, sample code, and tutorials.

Figure 6. End exercise of AGeRA book

Figure 7. Mascot of AGeRA book

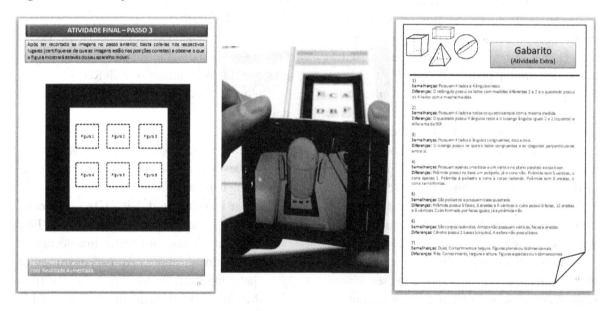

- **Java Bindings for OpenGL (JOGL):** Used for loading and rendering 3D objects. Uses Java 3D to create a 3D virtual world by means of functions that let load 3D models into the application. It is necessary to use the library Java Media Framework (JMF) to enable and build multimedia applications.

- **NyARToolkit:** Is the port of ARToolkit in Java. It is used to create augmented reality application: find a video capture device, makes the capture of frames, does all the processing of images for recognition markers, uses JOGL libraries for manipulating 3D objects and mix them with the real world.

Figure 8. Technologies used in development of AGeRA

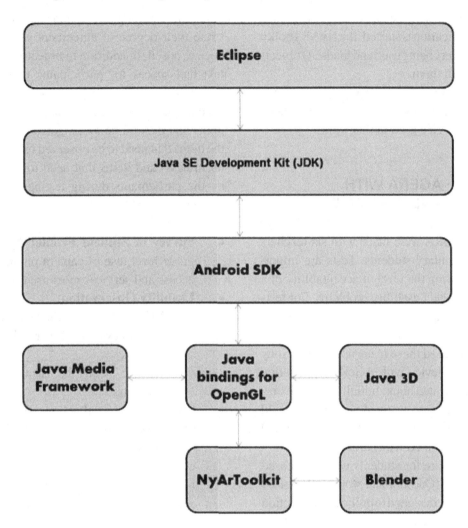

- **Blender:** Tool used for creating 3D models.

Initially a study about installation and configuration of NyARToolkit library in a conventional computer was done. It was necessary to study and understand the characteristics of major classes of NyARToolkitAndroidActivity.java file. In this file is located InitScene() method where you can make the object instance that defines Animation-Object3d control frames, position and scale of geometric objects. NyARToolkit supports up to three types of 3D file formats: a) OBJ (Geometric Object), b) MAX_3DS (3D Studio Max) and

MD2 (Model Format). In this project we used the md2 file format due to familiarity with Blender tool that supports import and export files in this format. 3D models were placed within the folder res/draw of NyARToolkit to be loaded into the application by manipulating the class InitScene(). Textures of 3D model were separated and placed in the folder res/drawable of NyARToolkit.

Files relating to markers were created and pasted into folder res\raw so that the NyARToolkit also be loaded into the application. Marker relative to the cube, for example, has been renamed pattcubo. Each marker is associated with a 3D object. It uses a list where there is an association identifier marker with the identifier of 3D model. When the application is started, the NyARToolkit reads the markers being used and loads 3D objects associated with them.

AGeRA is designed for Android 2.1 mobile phone, as this is a version supported by Smartphone Sony Xperia device used in this work.

TESTES OF AGERA WITH TEACHERS AND STUDENTS

Tests with AGeRA were made with six teachers and five elementary students. Tests are important for measuring the level of acceptability of a software and detect usability problems. For tests two satisfaction questionnaires were designed to assess the applicability and usability of AGeRA. In the tests we used these materials: a mini Sony Xperia mobile device with AGeRA application installed, and printed book. Initially a demonstration of application use was made so students could meet the augmented reality technology. Figure 9 shows tests performed with students.

A questionnaire for students was built based on QUIS method (Questionnaire for User Interface and Satisfaction), designed to probe the interaction of satisfaction and usability aspects. The questionnaire for teachers was built based on Likert scale, with statements made by the respondent. It measured the degree of agreement and disagreement

regarding the questions of questionnaire. Respondents chose among five options that best demonstrate their degree of agreement with what has been exposed. In addition to objective questions, text had spaces for participants to write their opinions.

For data collection, it was necessary to identify items that need to be investigated (user profile), the items that need to be observed (efficiency and usefulness) and items that need to be evaluated by the participants during testing (expectation about the result):

- **Survey of Student Profile:** Age, gender, grade level, use of camera phone, Internet access and services most used on mobile.
- **Usability Observation:**
  - **Effectiveness:** Completed the task.
  - **Efficiency (User Effort):** Understood the task.
  - **Utility:** Can be used to learn geometry.
- **Satisfaction Evaluation (expectations about the results):** Fun (amused), interest (would use again), attractiveness (aroused curiosity when the instructor was presenting the augmented reality technology), aesthetically appreciable interface (nice), pleasure (is happy, angry or frustrated), easy (easy use and easy to learn how to use).

Figure 9. Tests of AGeRA with teachers and students

RESULTS OF EVALUATIONS WITH TEACHERS

Mean age, 35 years of which 3 are women and 2 are men, 100% have a camera phone and Internet access. Among the most used services on mobile, beyond phone calls, include: access to social networks and posting photos on the Internet. 100% of teachers completed the task without interference from instructor. 100% of teachers agreed that AGeRA is suitable for use in teaching Geometry. 80% of teachers agreed that the interaction with virtual objects enhances the activity and allows students to feel motivated and challenged to solve the problems posed. 100% found the book attractive to work with students, 80% agreed that the AGeRA is easy to use and easy to learn to use. In the open questions, some teachers said the AGeRA has potential for use in other disciplines such as Arts and Physical.

RESULTS OF EVALUATIONS WITH STUDENTS

Mean age, 12 years of which 3 are boys and 3 are girls. 83,33% do not have their own cell phone, but they use their parents' and already carry a cell phone to school. 100% have used camera phone to take pictures and play. 80% completed the task without intervention from the instructor. Just game was needed to help the instructor to clarify the aim of puzzle game. 100% found fun to learn geometry with application AGeRA. 83,33% of students would use it again on other occasions to show colleagues and brothers. 66,67% liked the design of printed book. 100% said they were satisfied with use of AGeRA, 66,67% found it easy to learn geometry with the AGeRA.

FUTURE RESEARCH DIRECTIONS

We intend to increase the content of geometry subject discussed in the book, for example, include formulas to calculate the area and volume of solids. We are developing an evaluating AGeRA´s contribution to the process of teaching students, by following them in classroom with the help of a teacher of the area. This review could be performed from random separation of students into two groups: one group would have lessons with the help of AGeRA and the other group would have the same classes, but without the aid of AGeRA. After this step, the two groups were assessed for knowledge obtained from the classes. Finally, with the support of specialists, a study was done to identify whether there was some progress in the students who used the system as a support tool during lectures.

For this, we are reshaping the questionnaires and raising hypotheses to be investigated. From the hypotheses we will elaborate issues and define a scale of assessment to be used. We intend to offer the app for free in the Androids App Store.

CONCLUSION

Computer graphics have become much more sophisticated, looking all too real. In the near future the researchers plan to make the graphics on the TV screen or computer display and integrate them into real world settings. This new technology called augmented reality, further blur the line between reality and what is computer generated, improving what we see, hear, feel and smell.

Augmented reality has a vast field of exploration in various areas of knowledge, contributing significantly in education. It´s provides a great potential in the creation of interactive books, allowing an interaction intuitive and easy to adapt. It allows users to have a vision and expanded the enriched environment. It´s possible to enrich the information conveyed by the author of book with use of multimedia and three-dimensional objects. In this context, this work presents the development of AGeRA, an interactive book in augmented reality for mobile devices capable of supporting and supplementing learning geometry, especially of geometrical figures.

A preliminary usability evaluation of AGeRA was carried out with six teachers and five elementary students. They were exposed to a simple task to interact with AGeRA, content in augmented reality context, and they answered a satisfaction questionnaire related to the task. We have concluded that the AGeRA enhanced features impact on learning process:

- Adding visualization to a standard text book about Geometry will enhance its value as an educational material.
- Visualized text is easier to understand, and thus learning process will be fostered.
- Audio-visual content is more attractive and fun than standard text books.
- Adding visualization features to a standard text book creates a new media concept and possibilities, resulting in completely new educational instruments.
- A very intuitive and easy to use authoring tool will allow for unlimited creativity during educational material preparation.

Summarizing, AGeRA can bring benefits to teaching and learning of geometry, it provides greater interest and curiosity on part of students. Besides the fun, the AGeRA has provided digital inclusion, given that none of the users had previously interacted with augmented reality technologies. It was observed that the tests with augmented reality had great acceptance for educational use in mobile devices.

ACKNOWLEDGMENT

This research paper could not have been written without the support of students of: André Tahira, João Ribeiro; Rodrigo Kitamura and Tiago Yuzo. Acknowledgments to Ramona Straube for reviewing this text.

REFERENCES

Azuma, R. T. (1997). A survey of augmented reality. *Teleoperators and Virtual Environments*, *6*(1), 1–10.

Azuma, R. T., Baillot, Y., Behringer, R., Feiner, S., Julier, S., & MacIntyre, B. (2001). Recent advances in augmented reality. *IEEE Computer Graphics and Applications*, *21*(6), 34–47. doi:10.1109/38.963459.

Balog, A., Pribeanu, C., & Iordache, D. (2007). Augmented reality in schools: Preliminary evaluation results from a summer school. *International Journal of Social Sciences*, *2*(3), 184–187.

Benedek, A. (2009). *Notes on the perspectives of media convergence and the new learning paradigm*. Paper presented at the Meeting of the LOGOS Open Conference New Technology Platforms for Learning Revisited. Budapest, Hungary.

Billinghurst, M. N., & Henrysson, A. (2006). Research directions in handheld AR. *International Journal of Virtual Reality*, *2*(1), 51–58.

Billinghurst, M. N., Kato, H., & Poupyrev, I. (2001). The MagicBook - Moving seamlessly between reality and virtuality. *IEEE Computer Graphics and Applications*, *21*(3), 6–8.

Brasil. (1998). *Secretaria de educação fundamental: Parâmetros curriculares nacionais*. Matemática: Ensino de quinta a oitava série.

Burdea, G., & Coffet, P. (1994). Virtual reality technology (2ª Ed.). Washington, DC: Wiley-IEEE Press.

CETIC. (2012). *Centro de estudos sobre as tecnologias da informação e da comunicação*. TIC Kids Online Brasil 2012 - Pesquisa sobre o Uso das Tecnologias de Informação e Comunicação no Brasil.

Ciurea, C. (2012). The development of a mobile application in a collaborative banking system. *Informatica Economică, 14*(3), 86–97.

Clark, A., Dunser, A., & Grasset, R. (2011). *An interactive augmented reality coloring book.* Paper presented at the meeting of the IEEE International Symposium on Mixed and Augmented Reality (ISMAR). Basel, Switzerland.

Costa, R., & Kirner, C. (2012). *Livro interativo de xadrez potencializado com realidade aumentada.* Paper presented at the meeting of the Workshop de Realidade Virtual e Aumentada (WRVA). São Paulo, Brazil.

Emiliy, J. P. R., Edwards, K., & Keller, P. K. (1993). Video see-through design for merging or real and virtual environments. In *Proceedings of the Virtual Reality Annual International Symposium*, (pp. 223-233). VR.

Fetch. (2012). Retrieved September 11, 2012, from https://itunes.apple.com/us/app/fetch!-lunch-rush/id469089331?mt=8

Fotouhi-Ghazvini, F., Earnshaw, R. A., Robison, D., & Excell, P. S. (2009). *Designing augmented reality games for mobile learning using an instructional-motivational paradigm.* Paper presented at the Meeting of the IEEE Conference on CyberWorlds. Singapore.

Galvão, M. A., & Zorzal, E. R. (2012). Aplicações móveis com realidade aumentada para potencializar livros. *Revista de Novas Tecnologias na Educação, 10*(1), 1–10.

Geiger, C., Schmidt, T., & Stocklein, J. (2007). *Rapid development of expressive AR applications.* Paper presented at the meeting of the IEEE International Symposium on Mixed and Augmented Reality (ISMAR). Nara, Japan.

Giridher, T., Kim, R., Rai, D., Hanover, A., Yuan, J., & Zarinni, F. … Wong, J.L. (2009). *Mobile applications for informal economies.* Paper presented at the meeting of the IEEE International Multiconference on Computer Science and Information Technology. Mragowo, Poland.

GSMA. (2012). *mLearning: A platform for educational opportunities at the base of the pyramid.* Retrieved September 20, 2012, from http://www.mobileactive.org/files/file_uploads/mLearning_Report_Final_Dec2010.pdf

Guan, L., Ke, X., Song, M., & Song, J. (2011). *A survey of research on mobile cloud computing.* Paper presented at the Meeting of the IEEE International Conference on Computer and Information Science. Sanya, China.

Gutierrez, J. M., Saorín, J. L., Contero, M., Alcañiz, M., Pérez-Lopes, D. C., & Ortega, M. (2010). Design and validation of an augmented book for spatial abilities development in engineering students. *Journal Computers & Graphics, 34*(1), 77–91. doi:10.1016/j.cag.2009.11.003.

Kirner, T., Reis, F. M. V., & Kirner, C. (2012). *Development of an interactive book with augmented reality for teaching and learning geometric shapes.* Paper presented at the meeting of the Conferência Ibérica de Sistemas e Tecnologias de Informação. Madrid, Spain.

Kun, G., Zhisheng, L., & Xu, O. (2011). *Technical analysis of mobile learning application in high education.* Paper presented at the meeting of the IEEE International Conference on Computer Science and Education. Shanghai, China.

Lane, N. D., Miluzzo, E., Lu, H., Peebles, D., Choudhury, T., & Campbell, A. T. (2010). A survey of mobile phone sensing. *IEEE Communications Magazine, 48*(9), 140–150. doi:10.1109/MCOM.2010.5560598.

Maier, P., Kinlker, G., & Tonnis, M. (2009). Augmented reality for teaching spatial relations. *International Journal of Arts & Sciences.*

Marçal, E., Andrade, R., & Rios, R. (2007). Aprendizagem utilizando dispositivos móveis com sistemas de realidade virtual. *Revista Novas Tecnologias na Educação, 3*(1), 1–7.

Merdes, M., & Laux, G. (2002). Towards mobile computing in transplantation medicine. *Mobile Computing in Medicine, 1*(2), 131–142.

Mishra, S. (2012). *Mobile technologies in open schools: Commonwealth of learning 2009.* Retrieved September 20, 2012, from http://www.col.org/SiteCollectionDocuments/Mobile_Technologies_in_Open_Schools_web.pdf

Mostrom, R. N. (1975). *Head mounted displays.* New York: Honeywell, Inc..

Okawa, E. S., Kirner, C., & Kirner, T. G. (2010). *Sistema solar com realidade aumentada.* Paper presented at the meeting of the VII Workshop de Realidade Virtual e Aumentada (WRVA). Porto Alegre, Brazil.

Oliveira, F. C., & Kirner, C. (2007). *Uso do livro interativo com realidade aumentada em aplicações educacionais.* Paper presented at the meeting of the IV Workshop de Realidade Virtual e Aumentada (WRVA). Porto Alegre, Brazil.

Olsson, T., & Salo, M. (2011). *Online user survey on current mobile augmented reality applications.* Paper presented at the meeting of the IEEE International Symposium on Mixed and Augmented Reality (ISMAR). Basel, Switzerland.

Quinn, C. (2000). *MLearning, mobile, wireless: In -your- pocket learning.* Retrieved December 05, 2012, from: http://www.linezine.com/2.1/features/cqmmwiyp.htm

Rolland, J. P., & Fuchs, H. (2000). Optical versus video see-through head-mounted displays: Medical visualization. *Presence (Cambridge, Mass.),* 287–309. doi:10.1162/105474600566808.

Shelton, B., & Hedley, N. (2002). *Using augmented reality for teaching earthsun relationships to undergraduate geography students.* Paper presented at the meeting of the IEEE International Augmented Reality Toolkit Workshop. Darmstadt, Germany.

Suthterland, I. (1968). A head-mounted three dimensional display. In *Proceedings of the AFIPS Fall Joint Computer Conference.* ACM.

Vasconcellos, M. (2008). A diferenciação entre figuras geométricas não-planas e planas: O conhecimento dos alunos das séries iniciais do ensino fundamental e o ponto de vista dos professores. *Zetetiké-Unicamp, 16*(30), 77–106.

Wagner, D. (2007). *Handheld augmented reality.* (PhD thesis). Graz University of Technology, Graz, Austria.

Wei, Z., & Liqiang, S. (2011). *Mobile-learning (m-learning) apply to physical education in colleges.* Paper presented at the Meeting of the IEEE Conference on Circuits, Communications and System. Wuhan, China.

Chapter 2
ARIS:
An Open-Source Platform for Widespread Mobile Augmented Reality Experimentation

Chris Holden
University of New Mexico, USA

David J. Gagnon
University of Wisconsin, USA

Breanne K. Litts
University of Wisconsin, USA

Garrett Smith
University of Wisconsin, USA

ABSTRACT

This chapter describes ARIS, an open source tool for creating educational games, narratives, and field research activities on mobile devices. The tool is the result of years of design-based research into educational gaming, design pedagogy, and place-based learning. It has been used in a variety of educational contexts from after-school game-design workshops to university-level language courses. Deeply committed to open and democratic education, the project invites involvement at all levels and continues to innovate as a community of users matures.

INTRODUCTION

ARIS consists of both an authoring tool as well as an iPhone application that work together to create mobile, locative, narrative-centric, interactive experiences: i.e. augmented reality games.

DOI: 10.4018/978-1-4666-4542-4.ch002

In a nutshell, augmented reality couples virtual data or representations with real world locations and contexts. This can be accomplished in many ways via the various affordances of mobile devices and their ecologies of use. A decade ago, the idea was somewhat abstract, but today the concept is a commercial commonplace (e.g. SCVNGR, Layar) even to the point of not being billed as such (Foursquare creates a game world that sits on top of the real one). As a design response to a number of theories and examples from various disciplines of learning science, curriculum studies, media studies, contemporary social media and game design, ARIS serves a complex continuum of user-designers including artists, teachers, students, administrators and researchers. This user base has found interesting ways to use it in a different capacities ranging from a rapid prototyping tool for interactive stories to a mobile scientific data collection tool. Consequently, ARIS has attracted significant funding from partners to continue to provide a free resource and further develop the platform.

In this chapter, we offer a glimpse into the affordances and constraints of ARIS, as a free and open source mobile educational design platform. We have broken it down into four main parts. First, we describe the ARIS platform and its design, including the intellectual, social, and technological climates within which it was conceived. Second, we dig deeper into the complexities of the tool itself outlining our design goals, its features, and the general ethos of openness that permeates our efforts. Third, we describe the community that has emerged and grown around ARIS, and the expanding relationship that has developed between ARIS users and developers. Fourth, we provide a few use cases as illustrative examples of what ARIS is capable of. We will, then, provide a quick picture of the challenges ahead in these areas of mobile learning and the directions this project is heading next.

BACKGROUND

ARIS was conceived through a unique fusion of intellectual, social, and technological contexts that shaped its formation and development in meaningful ways. In this section, we briefly outline some of these major influences and offer a foundational description of the ARIS platform and essential vocabulary to describe its use.

INTELLECTUAL CONTEXT

At the time of ARIS' inception in 2008, both the constructionist and multiliteracies movements were well underway and had gained a great deal of traction in educational contexts, particularly in the form of games (Eisenburg & Buechley, 2007; Gee, 2003; Ito et al., 2008; Kafai & Resnick, 1996;). This, combined with the increasing adoption of new media among young people (e.g. the Internet, mobile devices, social networking, micro-blogging, and video-sharing), offered a fertile ground in which to plant the ARIS platform. Researchers were recognizing that the nature of those media provide a window into how people think and learn (Gee, 2003; Kozma, 1991; McLuhan & Lapham, 1994; New London Group, 1996), and were looking for ways to leverage them to create new learning opportunities.

Mobile technologies, in particular, showed promise in shaping how we think about learning and the design learning of environments. In addition to its rising ubiquity, mobile technology has fundamentally changed how people go about their day-to-day activities and relate to their surroundings (Squire, 2009; Squire & Dikkers, 2011). Additionally, in the spirit of situated learning theory (Brown, Collins, & Duguid, 1989; Lave & Wenger, 1991), the natural integrative characteristics and large-scale impact of mobile technologies reveal a need to makes sense of mobile. As a result, scholars began pointing to a requisite in higher education and education writ large: to innovate around mobile technologies (Johnson, Levine, Smith, & Stone, 2010).

With this movement, educational researchers examined a number of transformative uses of mobile technology, and one of the most promising is augmented reality (e.g. Squire & Klopfer, 2007), where virtual data or representations are coupled with real world locations and contexts. In this early research, a number of scholars probed how location-aware mobile devices may be used to engage a unique form of educational video games (Klopfer, 2008). This line of research has not only developed ideas for how to create more meaningful educational experiences, but also made progress toward understanding how mobile technologies make other pedagogical advances practically possible; for example, problem-based (Barron, Schwartz, Vye, Moore, Petrosino, Zech, Bransford, et al., 1998) and place-based learning have proven difficult to instantiate within traditional classroom settings, but show promise through mobile technologies. Specifically, a variety of mobile learning designs, such as environment simulation (Klopfer & Squire, 2008), design literacy (Mathews, 2010), and scientific literacy and argumentation (Squire & Jan, 2007), have demonstrated favorable results.

Yet, like a lot of inspiring educational research in this area, this innovative academic research was somewhat limited in scope and has spread far more slowly than the vast cultural changes brought about by modern technologies. To understand what new, undiscovered capabilities mobile offers for teaching and learning requires broad experimentation around the basic functionality of mobile devices.

Therefore, we joined the effort to create software and pedagogy that has the capacity to have a transformative effect and is capable of scaling in new ways. In the case of mobile learning, we need a way for the masses to begin exploring the educational affordances of using mobile technology to restructure our relationship with place. Additionally, we believe that mobile has inherent technological affordances and ecologies of use that are capable of generating new types of learning environments and interactions worth exploring.

SOCIAL CONTEXT

Constructionist theorists (Harel & Papert, 1991) talk about the *"collaboration through the air"* that happens in the incubation phase of design-based learning environments; ARIS is a product of such collaboration. Hence, on a more pragmatic and personal level, we want describe the social context in which ARIS was conceived. At the University of Wisconsin–Madison, David Gagnon began the idea of ARIS to teach art history in the context of a museum. The project developed the first iteration of ARIS as a class project in Dr. Kurt Squire's educational game design course. Much of what ARIS represents is a direct result of being incubated in an environment where others were working to explore and examine the affordances and constraints of mobile technologies in education.

Relationally speaking, the conception of ARIS was heavily influenced by relationships with the Games+Learning+Society research group and MIT who were working together to build augmented reality games. In addition, many of the scholars who have helped shape ARIS from the beginning were also part of a local group of researchers at the University of Wisconsin-Madison, called Augmented Reality Games on Handhelds (ARGH), who were simultaneously experimenting with mobile technologies. This cross-pollination of projects via individual scholars remains a defining characteristic of ARIS development.

Another aspect of the relational context that surrounded ARIS' development is more practical. David Gagnon worked directly with faculty, instructors, and educators at the University of Wisconsin-Madison to design learning experiences through simulations and games.

TECHNOLOGICAL CONTEXT

Just a year before the ARIS project began, Apple released the first iPhone (Honan, 2007). This release fundamentally altered the future for mobile learning, as the iPhone included video recording, GPS, near-ubiquitous internet, etc. capabilities all in one device. Compiling all of these capabilities into a single device opened the door to designing with deeper and richer mobile learning technology.

It is important for us to give a nod to the timing of this breakthrough, because of how profoundly it affected the development of ARIS.

TERMINOLOGY

Before we dig into the nooks and crannies of the ARIS platform, we want to establish a common discourse with our readers. ARIS is a platform with many complex parts, and over time we have developed a vocabulary around the tool tailored to its unique characteristics. Thus, in this section, we layout this terminology to build a shared understanding and effectively communicate the macro- and micro-level intricacies of ARIS.

First, there are different levels of 'designing' in ARIS: the developers and designers of the platform and the designers of individual ARIS games. In this chapter, we distinguish these levels by referring to those who actually build the platform ARIS as *designers* and referring to those who build games in the ARIS editor as *authors*.

Next, when we refer to *players* of ARIS, we are describing those who are users of ARIS games. Many players rarely see the ARIS editor and, rather, engage with ARIS on the client-level playing 'games. We use the term *game* to describe the "designed experiences" (Squire, 2006) authors create in the ARIS editor for players to play on the client. While games studies has developed substantially since the conception of ARIS, it is important for us to note that not all games in ARIS fit the definition of "game" that game studies scholars propose. Instead, we use the term game broadly to mean designed experiences, including all manner of locative tours, situated documentaries, geo-narratives, field research activities and so forth.

Lastly, and more broadly, we use the term *users* to encompass both the authors and players of ARIS. The need for this term highlights the fact that ARIS allows for people to engage in many of the design activities around this platform. Put differently, it is not uncommon for a single individual could be an *author* of one game and a *player* of another game, while at the same time contributing to ARIS as a *designer*.

THE SOFTWARE TOOL

Goals

Our main goal with ARIS is to mainstream experimentation with the creation and play of mobile augmented reality games and activities, largely across a variety of learning contexts from classrooms to museums to the great outdoors. So, we want the authoring tool to be as easy to use as possible by teachers, students, and researchers alike. We want the client, by leveraging the device's ability to connect to and make sense of the outside world, to provide a powerful and transparent means of interacting with these game worlds. Finally, ARIS is not intended to be a finished product, but something that grows out of communication surrounding its own use. Accordingly, we want ARIS to expand and deepen the repository of viable mobile learning experiences by drawing from growing bank of use cases to steer its growth, development, and our own understanding of how mobile technologies and augmented reality can be used to achieve learning goals.

ARIS itself is very much a product of the iterative process of design-based research (Brown, 1992; Design Based Research Collective, 2003). We've specifically designed ARIS as a prototyping tool by offering users a simple on ramp to quickly design games and activities and get them working in a rough form. Not only does this jump start the iterative design process, but it also allows for early playtesting, so that something can be learned from real-world use. Novice authors can get a simple narrative-based game playable in less than an hour and a data collection style activity for even as fast as one minute for a data collection style activity.

Partly we have been interested in this because we really enjoy making augmented reality games and want to share that joy as broadly as possible. But this project is also motivated by several converging threads of educational thought and research, many questions whose answers seem to lie within enabling large-scale, grass roots experimentation with the creation and play of mobile augmented reality games.

FEATURES

The ARIS platform consists of a web-based editor (see Figure 1) for authoring games, an iOS client app (see Figure 2) for players to interact with games, and a server (LAMP) running in a cloud-based environment with which both the editor and iOS client communicate (see Figure 3). In this sense, ARIS games are "server-based", not requiring additional actions to become published.

The client provides players with access to play any games that have been authored by anyone using the editor. Players can look for games near their current location, by popularity, or by title search.

The main interface of the client is organized by several tabs. *Quests* is used to give the player

contextual information about what they have done and what they can do next, the *map* displays a player's location, a rendered map, and the locations of game objects. Other tabs include a *decoder* (QR codes, bar codes, manual entry), player *inventory*, player *attributes*, and the *notebook*.

The player navigates through game play either using the *map*, *decoder* or a combination. Most commonly, the map is used for outdoor games, while the decoder is used for indoor games. When the map is used, game objects will appear on the map according to the requirements set by the author of the game. When the decoder is used, the game objects are displayed in the actual environment as a QR code for players to scan and, similarly, their interaction is based on the requirements set by the author of the game. Furthermore, as part of gameplay, players unlock new *quests* that give them goals to complete in the game. Quests often include visiting certain characters in the game or adding specific items to the player's inventory, but can be much more complex.

Figure 1. ARIS web-based editor in which authors create games

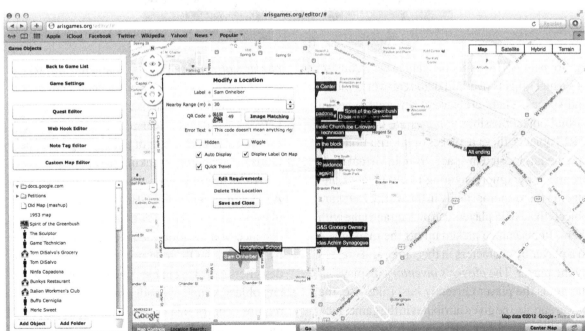

Figure 2. ARIS iOS client application where games are accessed by players

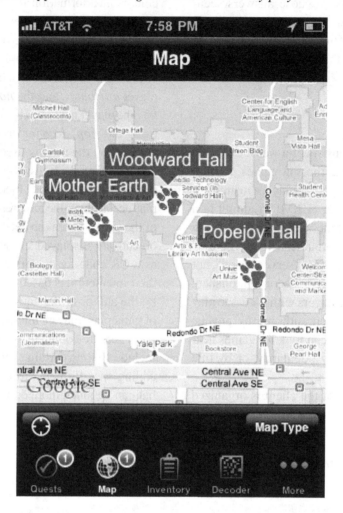

So in an ARIS game, the game space consists of virtual objects overlaid onto real-world places and spaces. There are several different types of virtual object possible. *Plaques* are the simplest ARIS objects; they are pieces of information (text and media) located in space. Simple virtual tours are made by simply creating a few plaques and placing them appropriately in the world. *Items* are objects that ARIS players can pick up and take with them. Items can be picked up off the map, given to a player by characters in the game, and created by the player. The *player's inventory* displays all the items the player currently has. Likewise, the player can also be given attributes in the game, such as health, experience, etc, which is logged in the *player's attributes*. Finally, characters afford virtual dialogue with players via a "hub-and-spoke" method similar to that used in games like Mass Effect. Characters can also interact with player's inventories in these bits of dialogue, giving them items or attributes, or taking them away.

All of the plaques, characters, and items in ARIS games can be linked to real world locations; players can access them by being within a specified distance of a location (detected through GPS) or by scanning a QR code with the decoder. Game designers can also enable "quick travel" mode for any object, which overrides the location-specific requirements of that object, so that the player can interact with it from afar.

Figure 3. Current ARIS platform architecture

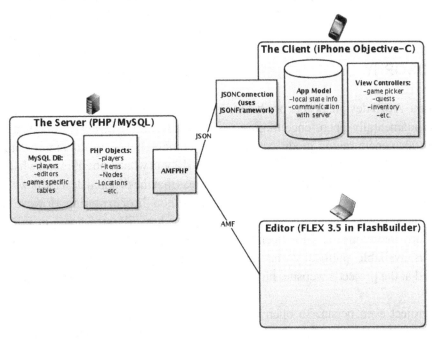

In addition to these core objects (plaques, characters and items), there are several features that allow for more complex games. First, the fact that ARIS is server-based allows games to become multiplayer virtual worlds, where interactions by one player in the game can affect other players. For example, items can be limited in number, where one player picking up an item may make it unavailable to another player. Players can also trade items with each other, allowing for the creation of virtual economies.

The *notebook* feature takes the idea of a shared virtual world in another direction. It allows players to create and share video, photo, audio and text content with other players of the same game. It is used to create data collection activities where the emphasis is on players' interactions based on what they discover and document in the world rather than what has been created for them by the author.

There are also features that allow for further variety in design using these basic objects. Rather than objects being placed individually at locations, authors can create items or characters that *spawn*, appearing within a specified radius of a player

or given location at a specified rate. In this way, authors can create games where players' options are determined algorithmically. Authors also have the ability to create their own *custom maps* that appear or change during the game, overlaying Apple's iOS maps. This allows fictional or informational backdrops to the designed game world to be created and even to change in response to player actions. In a similar vein, *panoramic views* that overlay custom digital information onto the physical space when looking through the camera afford camera-based augmented reality without requiring the authors to have much technical skill.

Finally, authors can create HTML5-based web applications and place them at a location within the game, like any other object. With this feature, authors are not limited to creating game content via the ARIS editor. With a bit of programming skills, authors can design any web-based content and embed it into the game directly. This includes mini-games, simulations and even programs that manipulate the way ARIS functions. Not only does this allow for authors to create any kind of interactive content, it also affords the possibility for custom, high-end game production using ARIS as the base.

OPEN PHILOSOPHY

A core value of the ARIS designers is to produce a tool that is fundamentally open, encouraging not only use but also encouraging modification and customization. The MIT licence was selected for most parts of the software, allowing anyone to "use, copy, modify, merge, publish, distribute, sublicense, and/or sell copies of the Software" as long as any copy maintains the same licence. The live code is available publically and the location is posted at the project's website, http://arisgames.org.

Before the project even began, an open approach was chosen for two reasons. First, it encouraged members of the team to invest their time out of only intellectual or creative motivations, by shutting down any potential for profit to come. This has a side effect of silencing disputes of "who did what" before they even begin. Since the building intellectual property of the project can be used by anyone, it does not close the door to profit by consultation or additional customization.

Second, choosing an open licensing model encourages participation by other people and groups that have similar interests. A key feature of ARIS for many collaborators and funders is that they know that their contribution will extend beyond their own project. Open licensing lends a sense of trustworthiness to the project that wouldn't be present if it was closed. Possible contributors would wonder why they are working for someone else's profit.

USER COMMUNITY

The two year process of moving from a closed group of scholars doing design experiments (Brown, 1992) into a platform with an active audience also meant moving the focus from serving the interests and curiosities of the original designers of ARIS into the support and nurturing of a community using ARIS to conduct their own investigations. This move is actually quite efficient from a research standpoint: Authoring an augmented reality game takes quite a bit of work. Crowdsourcing that work among a community of designers should result in more data being generated about what is possible and what is favorable in areas that the original designers would have never even thought of exploring. However, as each ARIS author has different goals in mind, supporting divergent visions and facilitating communication among them has proven to be a very interesting and challenging aspect of building this platform. This "opening up," focusing on a broader audience and facilitating their desires is also the likely reason the project is still active today.

So how did the author community grow? Early on, the community began through word of mouth about a few one-off projects run by close friends of ARIS designers. Particularly important in this regard was the *Mentira* project, which was the first classroom curriculum designed and implemented with ARIS. In the summer of 2010, at the same time that these one-off projects begin to bear fruit, the platform became much easier to use and install on a mobile device. A website was created that explained the project and provided links to start using it. It's perhaps no surprise that a specific focus on helping others start using the software is what allowed ARIS to gain traction, but it was nevertheless a big and somewhat rare step for software originally designed as educational research. It's also no surprise that we needed to do more to help people wrap their heads around AR games and get them in the driver's seat.

At that time, much of ARIS' publicity was through conference presentations, including hands-on workshops, stories from ARIS users, and playable demo content. The abstract promises of creating augmented reality were gradually replaced with concrete, shared experiences with the tool and its use. For example, *Dow Day*, a situated documentary built on the ARIS platform by Jim Mathews, was developed in ARIS around this time and became an iconic example of what the tool is capable of producing. In it players role play as journalists on the scene for famous anti-war protests in Madison, WI in October of 1967. Also at this time, users of the platform ended up joining the team to help design ARIS, greatly influencing the direction and usability of the iterations of the tool since.

As we made ARIS visible and usable, we looked for ways to broaden the user base and connect users to each other. A big early push in this direction was the 2011 ARIS Global Game Jam. Inspired by the IGDA's Global Game Jam, the designers hosted a ARIS game creation event over three days that was open to the public, distributed across multiple locations, and coordinated through a set of common objectives and videoconferencing software.

Private industry, museums, educators, game designers, and the generally curious gathered to have fun, learn from each other, and quickly iterate some of the most creative ideas mobile has seen. Over the course of three days, more than 100 participants from four countries and 11 states created 127 games; 19 of which were showcased in the closing ceremony. We averaged 5,000 hours of total development time worldwide in making new mobile experiences. Participants ranged from teams of middle school and high school students to professors.

This was an encouraging success. We learned that there is broad-based interest in experimenting with mobile through an augmented reality toolkit, and many of the participants continued to use ARIS and got involved with the project generally. As a result of this game jam, a more cohesive ARIS community was born.

Over the last two years, we have created additional resources to introduce people to ARIS and to give them meaningful access to it's features. Numerous tutorials, software documentation and various usage scenarios have been created in ad-

dition to a myriad hands-on design workshops facilitated by core users. Transparent, public project management tools (see lighthouseapp. com and pivotaltracker.com) monitor the developers' progress (adding features and squashing bugs), and allow users to report bugs and request features. The most important tool, however, is the threaded discussion through ARIS Games Google Group. This group functions as a unique platform for users-designer interactions. Users ask troubleshooting questions, share their games, and make connections with other users around common interests. ARIS designers are actively involved in this discussion community, and use it to inform immediate and future developments.

The result of all these new supports and forms of activity is an accelerating pace of adoption, communication, diversity, and sense of community around ARIS. At the time of writing (January, 2013) ARIS has 3,582 registered authors, 10,155 players, and 4,725 games. For an updated count, see http://arisgames.org/server/stats

AUDIENCE AND USES

ARIS is, above all else, a tool for experimentation. Authors, whether researchers, educators, artists, or students, bring to the platform their own backgrounds, including notions about their content areas, their experience designing for others, the context of use for their eventual designs, and a host of other intentions and bases of knowledge. ARIS is a tool for them to take who they are and what they are interested in, and play with those ideas in a situated context of interactions, mediated through - in part - a mobile device.

So what kinds of designs does ARIS aim to afford? Although variety is the intended rule, there is a personality and history to the kinds of games ARIS was made to build. For example, ARIS is a narrative-centric tool because its development was driven in its formative years by narrative-thinking scholars. The initial designs of ARIS hold close to ideas that not only do games of all types provide a means for producing new forms of narrative (Salen and Zimmerman, 2003; Jenkins 2002), but that a primary method of meaning making relies on the narrativization of experience sequences into mental schemata (Bruner, 1991; Polkinghorne, 1988). Coupled with an array of inspiring narrative mechanics present inspired by games like Oblivion, LA Noire and the Walking Dead, ARIS feels like a tool for telling stories.

Since ARIS is aimed at audiences with all these aspirations, but no assumed technical background, it creates a stage for broad experimentation. As the user base continues to grown, ARIS designers are not just designing for users, but are designing for *different types* of users.

Educators remain one of the largest groups of ARIS authors. We identified with, and in many cases were ourselves, teachers who saw new educational possibilities to link course content and the outside world using modern technologies, but lacked the budget or technical background to implement forward thinking ideas for learners. ARIS has become a tool to facilitate the gap between inspiration and act for these educators.

The two most important respects in which the design of ARIS supports experimentation for this important audience are the ease of use of the authoring tool for novice users and simplicity of deployment. Maintaining a simple, easy-to-use authoring tool targeted at non-programmers means most educators can begin creating games in the ARIS editor immediately. Coupling this with the community support provided by the Google Group, provides an on-ramp for novice users to see themselves as producers in a technology advance environment.

ARIS games are not only simple to make, but simple to deploy. Because they are authored directly from the ARIS editor to the ARIS app, authors do not need to submit them for approval to the App Store, nor do they individually require developer's licenses. Games do not require publication of any sort really; as soon as they are made,

they can be played via the client. Even if we were not operating within Apple's walled garden, we would still want to avoid the technical hurdles of more complicated forms of deployment to maintain broad experimentation opportunities.

These steps toward simplicity, initially undertaken to enable educators as experimenters, have inadvertently opened ARIS up to another audience of authors: *youth*. Today, a significant portion of ARIS authors are middle and high school age children. They use ARIS in afterschool and summer programs as a design tool and sometimes even pick it up to use on their own in absence of any formal context.

Of course, the ease of use and deployment designed for educators aids in this additional use, but there seems to be other factors involved in making ARIS game design available to young people. In part, this could be that ARIS does not reek of school, either in the way that the authoring environment is designed or in the rhetorical goals of design: ARIS is used to *make games*, not *complete assignments*. So, when young people get their hands on it, they approach it as a medium through which to reproduce their favorite games and movies or to tell stories about their lives. It can become for them a vehicle of expression. Moreover, the use of ARIS by rather large numbers of young people is likely a result of the rise of maker culture and its co-option by facilitators to create meaningful technologically-based design activities for young people. To these facilitators, the affordances of ARIS that make it a desirable tool are somewhat similar to what we have seen for educators who are using ARIS to make games themselves.

Another indication that this platform expands beyond the scope of traditional education is the use some *artists* are making of it. Place and mobile are areas of active experimentation within communities of artists, and many have used ARIS to this end. For artists, the technical barriers to entry are less of a concern than with many of our other audiences, but still a likely reason for rather frequent adoption of ARIS.

Researchers also use ARIS to produce Design-Based Research (DBR) experiments. Following Ann Brown (1992), researchers often seek to understand processes and environments of learning by producing artifacts and studying their use and further development in situ. This use typically overlaps classroom use, with the distinction usually being not the creation or use, but the goals and further products of that creation and use. Design-based researchers hope to improve their ideas about how learning works and how to best support it through the development of interventions. The earlier work in mobile augmented reality we discussed above is DBR, and in a summary report (Dunleavy et al, 2009) complexity and expense of implementation were seen as the major reasons preventing further experimentation. ARIS hopes to have an impact here by making it cheap and easy for researchers to use it to design their experimental interventions and gather data about learners' participation.

Finally, as we briefly mentioned above, ARIS is itself a form of DBR. By creating a tool for people to experiment broadly with, we can begin to see the contours of what is possible and profitable in a variety of educational contexts in relation to mobile technologies and considerations of local place. In addition to building the tool that enables the experiment, we also must devise methods for communicating our ideas to and with all of our users and find ways to gather data about, summarize, and discuss implications of use cases. For this use, features that define the ARIS community rather than the software itself will be the most important for this experiment to be a success.

USER SUPPORT

As soon as ARIS was being used by more than it's creators, documentation became a primary method of supporting new users. Originally,

members of the ARIS design team established a free online wiki space and crafted a number of short pages that explained the main features of the system. Another approach was to create a few short screencast videos and post them to youtube.

The first substantial documentation was produced by an ARIS author-turned-designer. This is a publicly available Google document that contains images of every screen within the system and descriptions of every feature. The document is updated as soon as new features are added or changes are performed, mostly by a small number of ARIS designers but sometimes by authors themselves. Though other technologies and methods are constantly discussed, this simple, low-cost solution has proven very functional.

A second, professionally produced documentation has more recently been produced by a University teaching and learning program that required a more stable and visually appealing document to distribute to the instructors they were consulting with. As expected, this document serves as a fantastic entry point to the software, but is by nature not as comprehensive or up-to-date as the live manual.

The other main form of software support is facilitated by an online discussion group and mailing list. The request to join the group is made by the automated email upon registering to become a content author and a pitch is done in workshops and on the website. Dozens of discussion threads are active every month and often questions posted by users are answered within mere hours or even minutes, though some requests do take days or even go unanswered. The group supplements the documentation with human opinion and interaction around personal goals.

A recent development in support is that an increasing number of workshops are being offered by ARIS users themselves. Until recently, ARIS designers and developers were the only people presenting ARIS at conferences and local trainings, however, ARIS users have begun sharing their experiences and stories with the tool on similar public platforms.

A final support model is that of paid, private support. Though options are limited at this time, a few consulting firms are offering ARIS consultative services for design, debugging and educational integration. This may continue to grow into a future ecosystem of paid support similar to what the moodle community has so brilliantly fostered over the last decade.

SOFTWARE DEVELOPMENT

Unlike the diversity seen in game authorship and community support, Software development has remained centralized despite the intentions of the designers. To date, a little over a dozen developers have contributed to the project, all of which have been located at the University of Wisconsin - Madison's central IT department. While a few of these developers have been short-term volunteers or unpaid interns, the vast majority of work has happened by paid staff and students. A variety of educational research grants and specific projects have paid for these development hours.

Educational research grants have been both large and small. While the first funder, the University of Wisconsin - Madison's ENGAGE program, contributed only a small amount of seed funding, it was able to bring ARIS to a state where it was attractive by larger groups such as MacArthur Foundation and the Pearson Foundation. One of the advantage of these donors is that they have provided funding for experimentation into both high risk features, but also the expensive fundamental infrastructure that individual projects don't care to support.

Specific ARIS game projects have also been a large source of development funding. It is becoming a more common story that individual projects begin using ARIS as a prototyping tool and realize that a few new features or bug fixes would make a big difference for their project. Since it is often

much less costly to spend a few thousand dollars on development than to start from scratch, ARIS is able to improve through the small investments of numerous projects.

CASE STUDIES

Mentira: ARIS as an Interactive Storytelling Platform

Mentira, mentioned briefly above as the first ARIS game to actually be used as part of classroom instruction, is an example of ARIS being used to author an interactive story. In this case, it is a murder mystery, historical fiction set in an old neighborhood of Albuquerque, NM. The setting, personalities, language, and other themes are locally situated, but as they say, the names and events are completely made up. Players join one of four families, each with a different personality and background, and must work together to solve an 80 year old murder.

HISTORY IN OUR HANDS: ARIS AS A MIXED REALITY EDUCATIONAL PLATFORM

History in Our Hands is the mobile game extension of a 15,000 square foot exhibit in the Minnesota History Center that, at the time of this writing, is being beta tested and scheduled for public release in October of 2013. The goals of the project are to use emerging technologies for 21st century digital learners (Jenkins, 2002) and to redesign the field trip experience to extend more deeply into the classroom.

During early brainstorming, ARIS was used as a prototyping tool. This allowed museum designers to rapidly create interactions with historic characters and artifacts, then embedding them into the exhibit for playtesting using QR codes. This phase was so successful, ARIS was chosen as the final production platform, specifically embracing and refining features that allow the mobile game to communicate with physical exhibit components.

The game begins with a group watching a short video and being handed devices. They take a photo of themselves and enter an in game username, then are given a number of "quests" that involve interacting with different areas of the exhibit. The overall theme of the game is to learn how to thrive in different places and time periods of Minnesotan history.

In the Iron Mine component, players are given the task of making a living wage by drilling holes for dynamite, loading and detonating dynamite, then prodding at the ceiling to check for cave-ins. To drill, the players scan a QR code next to one of four physical drills in the space, then press the trigger of the drill, which rumbles and makes a drilling sound. If they drill to the correct depth, they are award a small sum of money. Along the simulated rock wall a bit further, players load rubber dynamite sticks into the wall, watching lights on their mobile light up in real time as each hole is filled. A countdown begins to clear the area, then a push on the handle of a plunger triggers the explosion and rewards the player with their payment. If anything was done out of order, the player is told they were injured and loses their bank. Further along, the players scan the code to become a backman, the person responsible for testing the recently exploded rock for safety. Here they prod a metal rod up into the ceiling and listen for cracking sounds or small pebbles dropping. If they prod again, their impatience results in injury. If they wait, they are able to keep prodding safely and avoid injury.

In the Fur Trade, players scan QR codes attached to a number of physical artifacts including pelts, cast iron kettles, fabrics, etc. They are then prompted to choose their role, a hunter or a trader. Each role is able to continue to harvest their own items (pelts for hunters and goods for traders) by simply scanning the codes, but have a quest to obtain a number of the other role's items. To do

so, they have to trade with one another by selecting the items they are offering and physically bumping phones together to complete the transaction.

At the end of their experience, ARIS provides a web page to the teachers to use back in class, the Web Back Pack. This page shows the progress made by each of the students, characters they met, items they collected, media that was produced. This information can be used in the classroom to launch ongoing conversations about their experience and the periods of history it represented.

MOBILE QUEST: ARIS AS A YOUTH-ACCESSIBLE GAME DESIGN TOOL

Mobile quest is a week long program offered in both New York and Chicago by the Quest to Learn schools and the Institute of Play. The program aims to increase design and systems thinking in 6th graders by playing and designing mobile, location-based games.

During the first few days of the program, the participants learn about game design using a number of analog tools. As they move into the second half, ARIS allows them, without programming experience, to translate their ideas into playable software. In the classroom, they work to draft their stories and craft their media into formats ARIS accepts. After they have produced their designs, they go outside and try out the ideas on the mobile device.

At the end of the week, each team shares they mobile games with the other teams and with their parents, creating a public space around the design work they have accomplished.

UW MADISON FOLKLORE 100: ARIS AS A FIELD ETHNOGRAPHY TOOL

In Folklore 100, Introduction to Folklore, students are exposed to the core values and practices of the field. In many ways, the goal of the course is to provide students with a fresh view the people, events and culture of their environment through practicing methods of ethnographic research. This fundamentally requires work done outside of the classroom environment.

During the first few weeks of class, a number of concepts such as Identity, Tradition, Folk Art, etc. were discussed as entry points into phenomena that exists within a community. These concepts were entered into ARIS as notebook "tags" and players were tasked with finding examples around campus. Each student used ARIS to record photographs, audio clips and, short videos that were manifested one or more of these attributes. They also explained the media with a short text note and then geotagged it with the location it was recorded.

During and following the fieldwork, all of the player created information was aggregated to a web page that allows for filtering the content based on tags, locations and authors. This content was then used by a subset of the class as source material to create their own ARIS games.

FUTURE RESEARCH DIRECTIONS

This is an exciting time for the ARIS platform. Several new mechanics and design elements have been recently completed or are in progress, allowing prolific game types and interactions, which were once thought to be impossible. Currently, there are three new directions being pursued: camera-based augmented reality, a design process conscious editor and continued community development.

Following commercial augmented reality, we are currently designing an entirely new version of the ARIS client that integrates camera-based augmented reality. This technology allows virtual objects in ARIS to be superimposed with the video stream from the camera, visually mixing the physical and virtual together. The effect is quite striking. When done properly, the mobile device acts as a magic window of sorts, allowing the player to see additional parts of the world that are invisible to the naked eye.

The main advantage of integrating camera-based augmented reality will be for indoor games that are able to place visual markers (printed images that are detected by the software to represent something virtual) in the environment. Our hope is that, by generating a high fidelity visual effect, players will more easily comprehend the the existence of virtual objects in their space. The primary risk is that the effect will be slightly off, having the opposite effect of drawing attention to the technology in a distracting way.

Based on author feedback with the original ARIS editor and the emergence of new technologies, a complete rewrite is scheduled for the tool in the short term. While many of the changes will be purely cosmetic or minor refinements to the user interface, this is also an opportunity to design a tool that encourages authors to use ARIS to it's full capacity. For example, one of the keys to producing a good game in ARIS is to provide clear goals and timely feedback as they move toward those goals. This is often as simple as reminding the authors to create introductory content and create quests that highlight goals and progress. There may be elegant ways for the editor to guide novice authors into best practices while remaining flexible and experimental for those that intentionally want to try something different.

Developing the decision making and communication capacity of the community has become a larger and larger opportunity for growth. As more players and authors use ARIS, the amount of information generated and features requested also grows. It is no small task to create systems that encourage feedback from users, manage and consolidate it into something actionable and provide a mechanism for identifying the best investment of resources. Our short-term goal is to form an advisory board of users that have large investments into the tool. Another goal of ours is to develop new ways of decentralizing the software development process whether through encouraging crowdsourced financial investments or helping other locations form their own development teams.

CONCLUSION

In closing, ARIS is a remarkable project that brings together cutting edge technology, situated and game-based learning theory, and a commitment to openness and democratic participation into a tool that invites playful exploration as well as high end production. The strength of the project has been in its ability to continue serving an audience of non-programmers that would otherwise not be able to participate in the kinds of mobile, locative design activities ARIS creates. Although we're really proud that we've helped as many people as we have to find new ways to tell stories and interact with their worlds, the myriad of future possibilities keep the project from ever growing stale.

REFERENCES

Barron, B. J. S., Schwartz, D. L., Vye, N. J., Moore, A., Petrosino, A., & Zech, L. et al. (1998). Doing with understanding: Lessons from research on problem- and project-based learning. *Journal of the Learning Sciences*, 7(3/4).

Brown, A. L. (1992). Design experiments: Theoretical and methodological challenges in creating complex interventions in classroom settings. *Journal of the Learning Sciences*, 2(2), 141–178. doi:10.1207/s15327809jls0202_2.

Brown, J. S., Collins, A., & Duguid, P. (1989). Situated cognition and the culture of learning. *Educational Researcher*, 18(1), 32–42. doi:10.3102/0013189X018001032.

Bruner, J. (1991). The narrative construction of reality. *Critical Inquiry*, 18(1), 1–21. doi:10.1086/448619.

Design-Based Research Collective. (2003). Design-based research: An emerging paradigm for educational inquiry. *Educational Researcher*, 5–8.

Dikkers, S., Martin, J., & Coulter, B. (2011). *Mobile media learning*. ETC Press.

Dunleavy, M., Dede, C., & Mitchell, R. (2009). Affordances and limitations of immersive participatory augmented reality simulations for teaching and learning. *Journal of Science Education and Technology*, 18(1), 7–22. doi:10.1007/s10956-008-9119-1.

Eisenberg, M., & Buechley, L. (2007). *Pervasive fabrication: Making construction ubiquitous in education*. Paper presented at the Fifth Annual IEEE International Conference on Pervasive Computing and Communications. New York, NY.

Gee, J. P. (2003). *What video games have to teach us about learning and literacy*. New York: Palgrave Macmillan. doi:10.1145/950566.950595.

Harel, I., & Papert, S. (1991). *Constructionism*. Norwood, NJ: Ablex Pub. Corp..

Honan, M. (2007). Apple unveils iPhone. *Macworld*. Retrieved January 2010, from http://www.macworld.com/article/1054769/iphone.html

Itō, M., Horst, H., Bittanti, M., Boyd, D., Herr-Stephenson, B., & Lange, P. G. et al. (2008). *Living and learning with new media: Summary of findings from the digital youth project*. MacArthur Foundation.

Jenkins, H. (2002). Game design as narrative architecture. In P. Harrington & N. Frup-Waldrop (Eds.), *First Person*. Cambridge, MA: MIT Press. Retrieved from http://www.web.mit.edu/cms/People/henry3/games&narrative.html

Johnson, L., Levine, A., Smith, R., & Stone, S. (2010). *The 2010 horizon report*. Austin, TX: The New Media Consortium.

Kafai, Y. B., & Resnick, M. (1996). *Constructionism in practice: Designing, thinking, and learning in a digital world*. Mahwah, NJ: Lawrence Erlbaum Associates.

Klopfer, E. (2008). *Augmented learning - Research and design of mobile educational games*. Cambridge, MA: MIT Press.

Klopfer, E., & Squire, K. (2008). Environmental detectives - The development of an augmented reality platform for environmental simulations. *Education Tech Research*, *56*, 203–228. doi:10.1007/s11423-007-9037-6.

Kozma, R. B. (1991). Learning with media. *Review of Educational Research*, *61*(2), 179–212. doi:10.3102/00346543061002179.

Lave, J., & Wenger, E. (1991). *Situated learning: Legitimate peripheral participation*. Cambridge, UK: Cambridge University Press. doi:10.1017/CBO9780511815355.

Mathews, J. (2010). Using a studio-based pedagogy to engage students in the design of mobile-based media. *English Teaching: Practice and Critique*, *9*(1), 87–102.

McLuhan, M., & Lapham, L. (1994). *Understanding media: The extensions of man*. Cambridge, MA: The MIT Press.

New London Group. (1996). A pedagogy of multiliteracies: Designing social futures. *Harvard Educational Review*, *66*(1), 60–92.

Polkinghorne, D. (1988). *Narrative knowing and the human sciences*. New York: State University of New York Press.

Salen, K., & Zimmerman, E. (2003). *Rules of play: Game design fundamentals*. Cambridge, MA: MIT Press.

Squire, K. (2006). From content to context: Videogames as designed experience. *Educational Researcher*, *35*(8), 19–29. doi:10.3102/0013189X035008019.

Squire, K., & Dikkers, S. (2011). Amplifications of learning: Use of mobile media devices among youth. *Convergence: The International Journal of Research into New Media Technologies*. DOI 10.1177/1354856511429646

Squire, K., & Jan, M. (2007). Mad city mystery: Developing scientific argumentation skills with a place-based augmented reality game on handheld computers. *Journal of Science Education and Technology*, *16*(1), 5–29. doi:10.1007/s10956-006-9037-z.

Squire, K., Jan, M., Matthews, J., Wagler, M., Martin, J., & DeVane, B. (2007). Wherever you go, there you are: Place-based augmented reality games for learning. In B. Sheldon, & D. Wiley (Eds.), *The Educational Design and Use of Computer Simulation Games* (pp. 265–296). Rotterdam, The Netherlands: Sense Publishing.

Squire, K., & Klopfer, E. (2007). Augmented reality simulations on handheld computers. *Journal of the Learning Sciences*, *16*(3), 371–413. doi:10.1080/10508400701413435.

Chapter 3
Avatars in E- and U-Learning

Raymond Szmigiel
Penn State University, USA

Doris Lee
Penn State University, USA

ABSTRACT

Avatars are virtual agents or characters that graphically represent users within virtual environments. Avatars can be implemented in three-dimensional (3-D) virtual environments for training purposes. While there are promising findings indicating that avatars can enhance the learning experience, conclusive and generalized evaluations cannot be made at this time. The effectiveness of these virtual agents in a learning context remains an open question. The purpose of this chapter is to present background information on the definitions and use of avatars in e-based, virtual learning environments and to address the applicability of avatars to ubiquitous learning (u-learning). This chapter examines the available empirical research on the effectiveness of avatars in facilitating social interactivity, motivation, and collaborative learning in 3-D environments. Finally, this chapter provides suggestions for future studies on the design of avatars in both e- and u-learning.

INTRODUCTION

Background Information

The term "avatar" has entered into common usage in both the popular vernacular and in professional circles due to the increasing popularity of mass multi-user online role-playing games (MMOR-PGs) such as World of Warcraft and online virtual environments such as Second Life in the late 90s

and early 2000s. With conservative estimates placing the number of MMORPG users at over 14 million, the private sector has started to recognize the potential of virtual online environments in streamlining many business procedures. Following IBM's venture into Second Life in 2007, companies such as Wells Fargo, Accenture, and BP have created virtual meeting spaces for training, product demonstrations, and awareness-raising events. The U.S. Naval Undersea Warfare Center (NUWC) employs avatars in multiple virtual world environments to facilitate training and work

DOI: 10.4018/978-1-4666-4542-4.ch003

teams. In addition, many universities and colleges now have virtual campuses. It is predicted that just under one billion users worldwide will have an avatar within a 3-D virtual environment by 2017. As a result, the use of avatars has become a topic of discussion among learning professionals (Chou, 2009; Gartner Group, 2007; Gutl, Chang, Kopeinik, &Williams, 2009; Korolov, 2009; Lemon & Kelly, 2009; Second Life Education, 2010; Shein, 2010; StrategyAnalytics, 2008; Takahaski, 2010; Twining, 2009; Vasileiou & Paraskeva, 2010; Wyld, 2010).

For the purposes of this chapter, an avatar is defined as a user-created digital representation whose appearance and behavior resembles that of a human (Yee, Bailenson, & Ducheneaut, 2009) and who represents the learner's presence in a multi-user virtual environment (MUVE) (Bailenson, Swinth, Hoyt, Dimov, & Blascovich, 2005). In general publications, the term avatar, within the context of learning, is sometimes loosely defined as a visual representation of a learning agent within a MUVE (Hew & Cheung, 2008; Salmon, 2009). The learning agent could be either a real person or a computer application. This definition would include the sub-classification of embodied agents, or computer-controlled representations providing help, assistance, and instruction in MUVEs. The two, however, are fundamentally different in principle; therefore, avatars will be, in this paper, classified as distinct from embodied agents.

Though avatars and embodied agents are both integral components of interactive virtual environments, their operating mechanisms are fundamentally different. A person or user controls the former while a computer program uses the latter as a conduit to convey information to the user (Bailenson, Merget, Schroeder, & Yee, 2006; Vasileiou & Paraskeva, 2010). Currently, in a MUVE or a "metaverse" (Davis, Murphy, Owens, Khazanchi, & Zigurs, 2009, p. 91), learners can create an avatar that allows them to interact with other avatars or even embodied agents within

the environment (Lemon & Kelly, 2009; Jones, Morales, & Knezek, 2005; Warburton, 2009).

While immersive environments with avatars have proven popular outside the business world, their acceptance within the business community has been limited (ASTD, 2010). Erica Driver, of the ThinkBalm analyst firm, notes that avatars and virtual worlds are in the early adopter (Rodgers, 2003) stage as an enterprise tool (Shein, 2010). Beyond Second Life, there are enterprise virtual worlds such as ProtoSphere, OLIVE, Open Simulator, 3-D Wonderland, Active Worlds, and vPresence (Rosen, 2010). The use of avatars in 3-D virtual worlds still has a way to go before being fully accepted for training or learning purposes. There are several reasons: lack of management buy-in, cost, insufficient technological infrastructure, a video game image, a trend towards mobile devices, and questions about effectiveness. Moreover, the response among colleges and universities has also been hesitant (Davis et al., 2009; Bessiere, Ellis, & Kellogg, 2009; Young, 2010).

RESEARCH PROCESS

In order to provide a detailed examination of the available research, the researchers employed the research method of an integrative literature review. The utilization of embodied agents and avatars in e-learning dates back slightly more than a decade, and much of the early research, beginning in the late 1990s, focused on embodied agents. Since the technology for rendering realistic-appearing avatars was not available to the research community until the middle of this past decade, empirical research on avatars is limited (Bailenson, Merget, Schroeder, & Yee, 2006). An integrated review would bring together the existing literature, analyze it for common themes, and synthesize them into a new understanding of this topic as well as provide suggestions for future investigation (Torraco, 2005). According to Cooper (1982), researchers utilizing this review method make inferences that impact the review's findings in the same way that researchers make inferences when conducting empirical research. Therefore, an integrative research review should consist of five stages comparable to those in empirical research: research question formulation, data collection, data evaluation, data analysis and interpretation, and reporting. (Gutl, Chang, Kopeinik, & Williams, 2009; Dalgarno & Lee, 2010; Edirisingha, Nie, Pluciennik, & Young, 2009; Herold, 2010).

To begin the review process, the research question regarding avatars in e-learning and, by extension, ubiquitous learning was raised: "What does the existing empirical research indicate concerning the effectiveness of using avatars?" This question established the parameters and the general direction for the data collection stage. For the review, research engines and databases such as the ProQuest, ABI/INFORM, ERIC, PsychINFO, and Education Abstracts databases were used. In addition, the ancestry information retrieval technique was also employed which involved checking the references at the end of research articles and identifying previous studies that may have relevant information.

Once the search was completed, content analysis was employed to analyze the data collected and to generate thematic categories (Berelson, 1952; GAO, 1996; Krippendorff, 1980; Weber, 1990). Through the categorization, social interaction, motivation, and collaborative learning emerged as the most common themes. Lincoln and Guba's criterion for generalizability or external validity was also addressed through triangulation, as the use of multiple data sources and multiple investigators can enhance the applicability of a study's findings to other situations (Marshall & Rossman, 1995; Merriam, 1998). However, the integrative literature review method used for this research is not without its limitations. It is possible that some keywords or keyword combinations, that would have produced additional material, were not employed.

AVATARS: USAGE AND EFFECTIVENESS

Using Avatars for Social Interactivity

Since the early 2000s, research has shown that learners can have social interactions with virtual agents and learn within MUVEs (Bailenson et al., 2008; Chou, Chan, & Lin, 2003; Gulz, 2004). Avatars can provide the interactivity through asking questions, guiding instruction, and offering feedback (Moreno & Mayer, 2007). However, there are several issues to consider when employing avatars: social presence, appearance, nonverbal behavior, and socialization.

Social presence refers to the learner's sense of being present or cognitively immersed within the same shared virtual environment (Davis, Murphy, Owens, Khazanchi, & Zigurs, 2009; Franceschi, Lee, & Hinds, 2008; Jarmon, 2008; Thomas & Seeley Brown, 2009). Each learner, through his or her own avatar, can project a new identity and interact with other avatars or even embodied agents in the virtual world. He or she then forms connections with his or her real world identity through reflection and self-analysis (Edirisingha, Nie, Pluciennik, & Young, 2009; Lemon & Kelly, 2009; Warburton, 2009).

Sense of presence is affected by a number of representation factors such as appearance, fluidity of movement, and behavior time-delay (Davis et al., 2009). The verisimilitude of an avatar in its representation of its user is a key factor in the quality of interaction and copresence (Yee, Bailenson, & Ducheneaut, 2009). Users can personalize their avatars through changes to their avatar's body, age, and clothing permitting learners to express their personality and experiment with their identity in the learning environment. At the same time, they are also able to maintain anonymity through a limited set of provided names or by creating a new name (Davis et al., 2009; McArthur & Baljko, 2009; Yee, Bailenson, & Ducheneaut, 2009).

An avatar's appearance also enables other learners, through their avatars, to develop impressions of the learner. However, there is a potential downside to avatar appearance: social stigmatization in the virtual world. McArthur and Baljko (2009, p.1) cited an Eastman Kodak Technical Paper (Neustaedter & Fedorovskaya, 2008) which documented that a Second Life inhabitant who keeps the default appearance of his or her avatar and does not customize it is judged to be a "newbie" and therefore becomes less desirable in a social interaction. Studies by Banakou, Chorianopoulos, and Anagnostu (2009) and O'Brien and Murmane (2009) confirmed this finding. The former did note, however, that the importance of avatar appearance can vary depending on whether the interaction is professional or personal.

In 2009, McArthur and Baljko conducted a study that examined "employee" avatars (p. 1) and compared them to "personal" avatars (p. 1). They defined the employee avatars as a virtual representation of a company or organization for the purpose of interacting with others in a virtual environment. The researchers noted that learners may create and maintain more than one avatar or identity in a virtual world such as Second Life. Just as a dress code at work may require one to appear and behave differently than when at home, this same separation of identity can occur in the virtual realm due to an organization's corporate policy or, as the researchers refer to it, the "appearance code" (p. 2). Veteran learners, who have mastered the avatar creation interface in the virtual world, tend to view the new learners as lacking in social interaction skills. In turn, the newbies feel pressure to modify their employee avatar appearance to increase their sense of social acceptance in the virtual environment. McArthur (2010) suggests that the default avatar or one whose appearance is constrained by corporate governance is stigmatized since the general population of a virtual world like Second Life perceives it as an intrusion or threat to the existing social order. These researchers express concern that the corporate personnel responsible for establishing governance regarding virtual worlds may not be familiar with this stigmatization. The resulting corporate policy could create a disparity between the appearance code's intent and its actual impact within a virtual world.

In addition to appearance, behavioral realism impacts presence. Each avatar should not only "hear" what the other says, but take note of the latter's facial expression and body stance. Verbal communications need to be complemented with nonverbal behavior so that the social interaction's emotional context is conveyed. Franceschi, Lee, Zanakis, and Hinds (2009) point out that previous human psychological research indicates that both physical and behavioral activities convey information beyond what is provided verbally. If the observer notes a discrepancy between verbal and non-verbal communication, he or she tends to give more weight to the latter. Facial expressions are particularly critical since they convey emotions, agreement/disagreement, and comprehension/confusion. Eye contact and gazing provide clues about where the speaker's or listener's attention is directed at a particular moment. Body posture and orientation can indicate whose turn is it is to speak and who is welcome in the conversation. Franceschi et al. (2009) assert that instructional designers and educators need to understand the connection between these cues in the virtual world and in the real world. When designing an activity for the virtual world, designers and educators should use cues that are easily recognized to avoid creating a confusing and adverse impact on the sense of presence (Gerhard, Hobbs, & Moore, 2004; Moreno & Mayer, 2007; Yee, Bailenson, Urbanek, Chang, & Merget, 2007).

In much online training, these non-verbal behaviors are not available for viewing. Through the use of virtual worlds, learners can manipulate their avatars to express themselves nonverbally as well as verbally. This can enhance their learning experience as well as strengthen the knowledge transfer through the use of these multiple modes of communication. Furthermore, the ability of the user's avatar to interpret both the verbal and non-verbal cues from other avatars influences the former's ability to behave in a socially expected and realistic way (Davis et al., 2009; Franceschi et al., 2009; McArthur, 2010)

The importance of behavioral realism cannot be understated. Bailenson et al. (2005) found that visual and behavioral realism must match to create a high social presence and that a mismatch between the degrees of realism produces results worse than a general lack of realism. The variability of an avatar's appearance can influence its nonverbal behavior. Yee et al. (2009) go further and argue that a learner's ability to change his or her avatar's appearance influences his or her perception of how to behave in the virtual world. The researchers referred to this as the "Proteus effect" (p. 17). In 2007, Yee and Bailenson found that users in more attractive avatars conformed to the expectation that more attractive people are friendlier and more extroverted. Their research found that even a small change in the avatar's form can lead to significant changes in user behavior and interaction in the virtual environment. These researchers provide tentative evidence that the Proteus Effect on virtual world behavior can carry over, at least initially, to one's real world behavior (Baylor, 2009; Yee et al., 2009). Ersner-Hershfield, Bailenson, and Carstensen (2008) and Fox and Bailenson (2009) followed up this study with their own that supported the virtual world-real world connection. A theoretical implication is that anonymous nature of the virtual world can be used as scaffolding to promote enhanced self-perception that might linger into the real world where anonymity is no longer present.

Together, these personality characteristics make online socialization possible. Alterations in appearance, behavior, or both can strategically impact the quality of socialization with other avatars (Yee et al., 2009). Before knowledge construction can take place in a collaborative group, the learners must attain a mutually agreeable

level of intimacy and trust. Intimacy requires that the learner develop a sense of belonging as well as a comfort level which allows them to express visual social cues and non-verbal cues. Trust is not easily developed in many virtual teams since face-to-face interaction, which provides people with the opportunity to see each other and to observe each other's non-verbal communication, is lacking. The ability to visually identify the other parties enhances the development of the sense of belonging as well trust. In real world face-to-face interactions, non-verbal cues are harder to control since they tend to be automatic and are not normally planned out. In MUVES, avatars enable individuals to control both their appearance as well as the behavior (verbal and non-verbal) in a way not possible in real world (Davis et al., 2009; McArthur 2010). As a result, they can create their online image, manage their non-verbal behavior, and achieve a mutual sense of trust that facilitates group communication. (Campbell & Uys, 2007; Edirisingha et al., 2009; Franceschi et al., 2008; Franceschi et al., 2009; Hussain, Nakamura, & Marino, 2011).

Even with face to face interactions within a virtual world, the issue of anonymity can impact the level of trust. As Lastowka and Hunter (2006) and Boellstorff (2008) note, there is a commonly held notion that the virtual identity does not necessarily duplicate real identity. The learner's ability to modify his or her avatar's appearance has positive or negative consequences. Anonymity in the virtual world can allow the learner to experiment with his or her virtual identity using an idealized or a completely different version of him or herself that is not possible in the real world. Yet this very same anonymity can also inhibit a learner since he or she may not trust the identity of other avatars involved in an interaction. In addition, the avatar's behaviors in the virtual world may not coincide with those of the human operator in the real world. Finally, the previously noted ability to control non-verbal cues can be used to mask the operator's true feelings. The end result is that the level of trust needed for socialization and exchange of knowledge is not achieved (Campbell, 2009; Davis et al., 2009; Gunkel, 2010; Gutl, Chang, Kopeinik, & Williams, 2009).

Using Avatars to Enhance Motivation

A learner's decision to undertake an online course can be motivated by professional need, personal interest, or a desire to have fun. However, e-learning has long been plagued by a significant number of learners who choose not to complete such courses for a variety of reasons including work/family issues, financial problems, or time constraints (Angelino, Williams, & Natvig, 2007; Tyler-Smith, 2006). Since motivation strongly correlates with the successful completion of e-learning, avatars are one possible solution to the drop out problem.

In reviewing the current literature regarding the effectiveness of avatars, the published studies address all or part of several commonly-cited motivational theories or models. The latter include: Keller's ARCS (attention, relevance, confidence, and satisfaction) model (1987, 2000; Keller & Suzuki, 2004), Bandura's (1997) Social Cognitive Theory (SCT), Weiner's Attribution Theory (1974), the Expectancy-Value Theory (Eccles & Wigfield, 2002; Wigfield, 1994), the Goal Theory (Elliot & Dweck, 1988), Wlodkowski's Time Continuum Model (1985), Deci and Ryan's (1985, 2000) Self-Determination Theory (SDT), and Yee's (2007) MMORPG study. It should be noted that only Yee's research occurred after the advent of avatars and virtual worlds. Together, these theories or models provide a framework for analyzing the existing research findings.

Several recent studies indicate that learners find e-learning programs with avatars more engaging at the beginning of the course (Lemon & Kelly, 2009; Omale, Hung, Luetkehans, & Cooke-Plagwitz, 2009) due to their animated and interactive qualities. However, the novelty of the avatar's presence is not enough to sustain learner motivation throughout a course. Avatars can help sustain motivation by creating cognitive dissonance, prompting the learner to reflect on the material just covered, guiding the learner through a problem-solving exercise, or serving as a counterpart in a role-playing simulation (Borthick, Jones, & Wakai, 2003; Gulz, 2004; Moreno & Mayer, 2007). This ability to engage learners and maintain their motivation is characteristic of the attention condition of Keller's ARCS model (Keller 1987, 2000; Keller & Suzuki 2004) which indicates that attention can be attained through the use of novel tactics. The level of engagement in the learning activity, within the virtual world, is a critical factor in developing the learner's sense of presence, mentioned in the previous section. Whereas the engaged learner has a heighten sense of presence, the disinterested learner will fail to feel psychologically immersed (Franceschi, Lee, Zanakis, & Hinds, 2009).

Once the learner's attention is gained, the learner needs to understand the significance of the new knowledge or skill as well as to determine how it relates to his or her objectives and how it fits in with his or her prior knowledge. Coffman and Klinger (2007) and Bessiere, Ellis, and Kellogg (2009) indicate that the clearer the connection between the virtual learning activity and learner's goals or objectives, the more motivated that the learner will be regarding the virtual environment and the learning content. Edwards, Dominguez, and Rico (2008) point out that, through learners' own avatars and/or with the help of embodied agents, learners can view demonstrations and participate in simulations of real-world tasks set within learning contexts that closely resemble their real-world environment. However, Herrington, Reeves, and Oliver (2007) emphasize that, in the learning context, the cognitive authenticity of the activity is more critical to learning effectiveness that the physical resemblance to the work environment.

In these studies involving virtual worlds, the importance of the connection between the learning and the learner's goals reflects the relevance condition of Keller's ARCS model (1987, 2000; Keller & Suzuki, 2004), the Goal Theory (Elliot & Dweck, 1988), and the beginning phase (attitudes and needs) of Wlodkowski (1985) Time Continuum Model. By relating the knowledge or skills to short-term, measureable, and intrinsic goals or needs that can be achieved and are tied to the learner's prior knowledge, relevance can be enhanced (Hodges, 2004).

If the learner's attention can be gained and relevancy is established, the next step is to build his or her self-assurance when it comes to using the new knowledge or skill. One way to appeal to the learner's self-assurance is through demonstrations of a relevant role model successfully completing the task. An avatar, representing a trainer or mentor, can present such a role model. Upon viewing the demonstration, the learner may feel more at ease with performing the task on his or her own (Gulz, 2004). The use of virtual worlds for the training of soldiers or surgeons is an example that addresses both relevance and self-assurance. By participating as an avatar, such learners can acquire and practice new skills in a realistic, but safe environment, until they are confident in their ability to execute the task.

Keller (1987, 2000) refers to the building of self-assurance through the confidence component of his ARCS model. This involves helping the learner develop a positive expectation regarding the outcome of a task and providing opportunities for success. Bandura (1997) refers to this condition through his concept of self-efficacy or a person's attitude regarding how well he or she can perform a task. Self-efficacy is as important as actual ability and directly correlates with the learner's eventual satisfaction (Cocea and Weibelzahl, 2006). Wlodkowski (1985) and Deci and Ryan (1985, 2000) both address confidence through their concept of competence, while Yee (2007) refers to it through his concept of achievement.

Critical to the above confidence-building tasks or activities is that the learner can credit his or her success or failure to his or her own ability and not to external forces or fate. This consideration ties in with Weiner's (1974) Attribution Theory. The focus of such activities should be on outcomes that are within the learner's ability to control. If success or failure is perceived as being beyond his or her control, then the learner will lose motivation to continue or complete the lesson. Deci and Ryan (2000) point out in their Cognitive Evaluation Theory that learners must feel that their performance is not only competent, but also self-determined, in order to increase intrinsic motivation.

If the learner becomes more proficient in using the new knowledge or skill, he or she should be feel more satisfied or have a more positive response to the learning experience. The learner then should be more inclined to continue with the learning activity. Unfortunately, satisfaction has not received significant attention in the literature on avatars. While some researchers (Gulz, 2004; Laffey, Lin, & Lin, 2005; Moundridou &Virvou, 2002) all indicate that avatars may increase learner motivation overall, they do not offer findings that specifically address satisfaction.

Satisfaction makes up the final component of Keller's (1987, 2000) ARCS model. He states that satisfaction with the current learning module or course enhances the learner's motivation to continue with it. Keller makes reference to two types of satisfaction that can occur within this condition. Intrinsic satisfaction involves the learner receiving some form of self-fulfillment and the possibility of applying the newly gained knowledge or skill in a productive context. Extrinsic satisfaction entails the learner's receipt of compensation, rewards, or public recognition. In Keller's ARCS model, the two forms are not mutually exclusive. Rather, Keller states that some forms of extrinsic satisfaction, such as public recognition, can complement intrinsic satisfaction, such as a sense of accomplishment. Eccles and Wigfield (1994, 2002) address this through the Expectancy-Value Theory. This theory holds that the more value the learner places on the outcome, the more likely he or she is to continue the behavior. Hodges (2004) notes that the learner's confidence or self-efficacy significantly influences this expected value. In his study of MMORPG players, Yee (2007) found that social interaction influences satisfaction. This is based on Maslow's (1943) Hierarchy of Needs in which human interaction occurs after individuals satisfy their physiological and safety concerns. Deci and Ryan (2000) referred to this as "relatedness" (p. 64) or the need to feel connected in their Basic Psychological Need Theory. Edirisingha, Nie, Pluciennik, and Young (2009) suggest that social interaction in MUVEs may facilitate increased satisfaction, but they note that little empirical study has been published on this topic.

Using Avatars for Collaborative Learning

In the earlier section on social interactivity, the focus of the research studies was on how appearance and behavior impacts the learner's sense of social presence and socialization within a virtual world. Much of the early research on avatars, as well as embodied agents, addressed this individual sense of immersion. However, since the middle of the last decade, some research articles have broaden the research scope to include the collaborative experience where multiple avatars help each other learn (Maldonado et al., 2005; Maldonado & Nass, 2007; Franceschi, Lee, Zanakis, & Hinds, 2009).

Social presence is defined as the learner's sense of being cognitively immersed in a virtual environment (Davis, Murphy, Owens, Khazanchi, & Zigurs, 2009; Franceschi, Lee, & Hinds, 2008; Jarmon, 2008; Thomas & Seeley Brown, 2009). As researchers have begun investigating multiple avatars in MUVEs, the term "copresence" has been used in the research literature. There is no consensus on a definition (Davis et al., 2009). In fact, Shen, Khalifa, and Yu (2006) and Bailenson and Yee (2008) consider the two terms synony-

mous. Gerhard, Hobbs, and Moore (2004) and Schroeder (2006) define copresence as a sense of being among others in a virtual environment. Finally, Monahan, McArdle, and Bertolotto (2008) and Franceschi, Lee, and Hinds (2008) explain copresence as a visual perception of others within the virtual environment. Given the lack of a singular definition, researchers have not achieved consensus on how to measure copresence.

Nevertheless, the visualization of a learner through his or her avatar, as highlighted in the social interactivity section, promotes the face-to-face interaction considered critical to facilitating copresence as well as collaborative learning. It also enables a community of practice to coordinate roles and tasks as well as internalize norms and processes within it. Each member of the learning community must be accountable for his or her own role and assignments and must be able to trust the others to fulfill their roles and tasks; otherwise, the community's objectives are not attained. Beyond factors such as appearance and non-verbal behavior, the use of instant messaging, voice chat, a shared environment, and shared objects further enhances the learner's sense of immersion within a virtual community of practice (Davis et al., 2009; Franceschi et al., 2008).

Gerhard et al.'s (2004) research indicates that there is a direct correlation between copresence and presence in virtual environments: as the learner's sense of copresence with other learners increases or decreases, the learner's sense of presence also increases or decreases. By adding additional avatars to the learner's avatar, both the sense of copresence and presence rise. In addition, Laffey et al. (2005) note that copresence is a significant factor influencing a learner's favorable or unfavorable perception of an online course and his or her motivation to continue with the course. Copresence also facilitates a social learning context. In addition, Vygotsky (1978) noted that learning has a social/cognitive duality. First, learners bring their own perspectives to a social interaction and negotiate mutually acceptable knowledge. Subsequently, this knowledge is cognitively internalized and personalized within each learner. Vygotsky further asserted that the social and the cognitive mutually support each other through the Zone of Proximal Development (ZPD). The Zone is defined as the distance between what the learner can currently do on his or her own and what he or she could possibly do with assistance from a superior or more experienced colleague (Borthick et al, 2003). The learner, a new member of a community of practice, works in tandem with a more experienced member to solve a problem or execute a task that the former could not initially do alone. Eventually, he or she is able to perform the above action without assistance, having internalized the knowledge or skill (Borthick, Jones, &Wakai, 2003; Dickey, 2007; Edwards, Dominguez, & Rico, 2008; Gulz, 2004; Gutl, Chang, Kopeinik, & Williams, 2009; Laffey et al., 2005; Laffey, Lin, & Lin, 2006; Oliver & Carr, 2009; Prasolova-Farland & Divitini, 2003).

Wenger's (1998) theory asserts that knowledge is the result of humans working together in a social context and actively learning through practical application. Knowledge or skill is measured through the learner's performance of a socially valued activity. Novices begin on the periphery of the community of practice with easy tasks and work with the more experience members to take on more difficult tasks in what Wenger termed legitimate peripheral participation. As the newcomers increase their competency, they assume more central and valued roles in the community. This reflects an inbound learning trajectory, one of Wenger's five trajectories of participation in a community (Borthick et al., 2003; Chou, 2009; Oliver & Carr, 2009).

The utilization of avatars makes possible social learning within virtual environments. Learners, through their own avatars, can join with other avatars to establish the aforementioned community of practice. Instead of passively absorbing knowledge, the learners can work with and learn from each other within a virtual social context.

Experienced members, through their avatars, or an embodied agent can assist new learners with improving their performance through scaffolding (Gutl et al., 2009) or in what Parscal &Hencmann (2008, p. 1) characterize as a "cognitive apprenticeship." Twining (2009) observes that, in virtual worlds, the socio-cultural model views knowledge as being shared across a network of avatars instead of residing separately in each one.

This practical application of knowledge within the social context can be viewed as an example of situated learning. As apprentices to more experienced members of the virtual community of practice, the learners initially are exposed to a variety of simple situations to achieve a basic comfort level with the community. As noted above, this is the beginning of the learner's inbound trajectory. However, Thomas and Seeley Brown's (2009) research indicates a "learning inversion" occurs between the traditional model of learning and situated learning within virtual worlds. The traditional model consists of a two-step process: 1) "learning about" and then 2) "learning to be" (p. 5). Thomas and Seeley Brown note that, in virtual worlds, learners learn to be before they learn about. Instructional designers and educators need to adjust for this inversion when developing learning experiences in virtual worlds.

Together copresence and social learning create a collaborative learning environment. Research reveals that learning in a collaborative environment results in increased achievement, improved problem solving and critical thinking, and greater motivation when compared to individual and competitive learning environments (Campbell, 2009; Franceschi et al., 2008; Maldonado et al., 2005; Parscal &Hencmann, 2008). Steinkuehler's (2004) study and Dickey's (2007) analysis of MMORPG players found that new players rose from novice to expert through their interaction and collaboration with veteran players. Through their avatars, the novices practiced and enhanced their ability to evaluate and resolve game situations by way of communication with and feedback from their fellow players. Dickey points out that MMORPG role-playing games promote communication, collaboration, and critical thinking similar to what instructional designer and educators are seeking in virtual learning environments. Second Life allows similar role playing for learning purposes. An example could involve managers of company, under consideration for executive leadership positions, joining the senior management team in Second Life. Through authentic scenarios, guided discussions, and decision making simulations, the executives can facilitate the managers' development of the knowledge and skills required for advancement to senior leadership positions. This follows the guided activity principle (Mayer, 2004) in which avatars can, through guiding a learner's cognitive processes, increase his or her learning.

With collaboration, critical thinking, and problems solving considered crucial 21st-century skills, virtual worlds provide an environment well suited for applying them. Within such worlds, learners can safely test various responses to a scenario in much more realistic settings to understand and reflect on the consequences. As a result, learners can be more creative in their decision making, view situations from multiple perspectives, and more deeply reflect on their actions (Yu, 2009). Thus, within these collaborative environments, Maldonado et al. (2005) and Baylor (2009) state that avatars generally assume one of three roles: instructor, colleague, or peer. In terms of the instructor, the nature of the role has evolved from the classic lecturer to a guide or tutor. The colleague is usually a more mature and knowledgeable co-worker or student. In contrast, the peer normally has equal or less knowledge than the learner. According to Maldonado et al. and Baylor, the instructor, as an avatar, can demonstrate a task, prompt discovery learning, or encourage reflection on newly acquired knowledge. In the role of the colleague, the avatar can mentor the learner by providing feedback during simulations. Finally, in the role of the peer, avatars can pose questions or make requests for assistance. This prompts the

learner to share what he or she has learned and to demonstrate his or her grasp of the newly acquired knowledge or skill.

Using Avatars in Ubiquitous Learning

During the same time frame as avatars and virtual worlds, ubiquitous learning has evolved. It is not entirely new concept having drawn interest from researchers as far back as 2000. Its origin dates back even further to Mark Weser, a researcher for XEROXPARC, who came up with the term "ubiquitous" in the 1980s. In 1993, he described a "third wave" of computing where individuals interacted with multiple computers. Eventually, this "one-to-many" relationship was applied to learning. Ubiquitous learning involves each learner interacting with multiple mobile devices. (Chen, Chang, & Wang, 2008; Jones & Jo, 2004)

While initial interest in ubiquitous learning was modest, the evolution of ubiquitous or mobile devices such as smart phones and tablets has greatly increased the interest level in recent years. The idea of anytime, anywhere learning is beginning to be realized; however, it will take time for its potential to be fully realized, similar to avatars. Initial forays into ubiquitous learning have produced uneven results as instructional designers and educators try figure out how and when to adapt existing materials and courses to this new type of learning. For instance, attempts to use existing e-learning on the new mobile devices have, at times, produced less than stellar visual results (Chen, Chang, & Wang, 2008).

Although the above-mentioned concept of anytime, anywhere learning has been commonly used to describe ubiquitous learning, researchers have yet to come up with a mutually agreeable definition for the term. Throughout the last decade, various researchers (Chen, Kao, Sheu, & Chiang, 2002; Chui, Kuo, Huang, & Chen, 2008; Casey, 2005; Hwang, 2008; Lyytinen & Yoo, 2002; Ogata & Yano, 2004) attempted to put forth such a definition. Although they were not completely successful, these researchers have each contributed to a definition that is still evolving. Drawing from all these prior efforts, Yahya, Ahmad, and Jalil (2010) defined ubiquitous learning as a type of learning that occurs within a ubiquitous computing environment which results in the learner receiving customized knowledge when and where it is needed. A ubiquitous computing environment consists of embedded sensors and interfaces that allow the learning environment to be context-aware and the learning to be customized based on the learner's particular circumstance at that moment. The context awareness is regarded as a key quality that marks ubiquitous learning as the next step in a continuum that began with e-learning and evolved with mobile learning (Liu & Hwang, 2010).

Yahya et al. (2010) also summarized the main characteristics of ubiquitous learning: 1) Permanency: whatever is created during a learning session is not lost when it ends; 2) Accessibility: learning can be self-guided since learner can access information from anywhere; 3) Immediacy: information is available at any time; 4) Situation of Learning Activities: learning can occur within an authentic environment; and 5) Adaptability: the correct information is provided based on the learning context. Some or all of the previous research studies referenced the first four characteristics, but only recently was the fifth characteristic, adaptability, added. According to the researchers, adaptability, along with context awareness, is what differentiates ubiquitous learning from mobile learning.

Although avatars and virtual worlds cannot emulate all the above characteristics of ubiquitous learning, they can provide permanency and situated learning activities. When a person logs out of a virtual world, his or her avatar is no longer active. However, the virtual world itself can remain operational, allowing for objects that were created to remain in existence for future use. Within the last five years, virtual world developers have been

working on enabling people to use their avatars in multiple MUVEs. This would offer them the ability to present a consistent appearance across difference virtual environments should that be desired (Davis, Murphy, Owens, Khazanchi, & Zigurs, 2009; Schmeil & Eppler, 2008).

Beyond permanency, research papers on both avatars and ubiquitous learning draw upon constructivism and social learning as a theoretical foundation for how learning occurs within virtual and ubiquitous learning environments. As documented earlier in the collaborative learning section, avatars allow individuals to create virtual communities of practice where they can progress from novices to experts through progressively more challenging exercises. Virtual worlds also allow such exercises to take place within settings that closely simulate real world contexts. Knowledge and skills are gained and shared within a social learning environment. Jones and Jo's (2004) research indicates that ubiquitous learning environments also support constructivism since learners are developing knowledge within a social learning context. Instead of simply absorbing knowledge through a class lecture, learners are discovering knowledge through interactions with other learners in real-world situations. Furthermore, in social contexts, the key to success is not merely possessing information, but also know where to find it when it is needed. As with virtual worlds, the knowledge exists in a communal network and not with any one member of the community of practice (Yahya, Ahmad & Jalil, 2010; Yang, 2006).

Instructional designers and educators need to carefully think through the application of avatars within ubiquitous learning environments. Clearly, they are not appropriate for every learning context. There is a learning curve, in terms of educating some learners on how to function as an avatar within a virtual world, which needs to be factored in when including this option within a ubiquitous learning strategy. In addition, the visibility of a virtual world on mobile devices needs to be considered. Depending on the level of detail the learner needs to see, displaying a virtual environment on a tablet may produce acceptable visual results.

CONCLUSION AND FUTURE RESEARCH DIRECTIONS

The effectiveness of avatars remains an unanswered question at this time. Avatars can provide the social interaction missing in most e-learning. They can be customized in appearance and in behavior. But trust issues regarding appearance and behavior need to be considered when creating trainings for MUVEs. The research so far also supports part or all of several motivational models and/or theories, especially when it comes to establishing the relevance of the training or building the learners' self-assurance regarding a new skill. The concept of copresence, which multiple avatars make possible, allows social learning to occur within MUVEs. Virtual communities of practice can be developed that allow knowledge to be socially constructed and for learners to advance from novices to experts. Avatars and virtual worlds can play a role in ubiquitous learning; however, the criteria for their utilization need to be very carefully developed and applied.

In order to realize the aforementioned benefits of avatars and virtual worlds, instructional designers and educators need to move beyond merely designing learning tasks similar to those used in training rooms and class rooms. Instead, they have to start choreographing full learning experiences involving collaborative practice, mentoring, and apprenticeships. This will require a significant initial commitment of time and effort to create the virtual environments and to equip the instructional designers and educators with a new skill set. They first need to learn how to function within a virtual world before they can begin to create learning experiences for trainees or students. Furthermore, instructional designers and educators have to factor in time for the learners to acquire the necessary

proficiency with the virtual environment before the latter can embark on a learning experience (Campbell, 2009; de Frietas, Rebolledo-Mendez, Liarokapis, Magoulas, & Poulevassilis, 2009; Gutl, Chang, Kopeinik, & Williams, 2009)

Despite the generally positive findings, the research literature has identified several issues that limit the ability to generalize the results. One is the relative lack of empirical studies. A second issue is that some research studies were based on small sample sizes according to the researchers themselves (Edirisingha, Nie, Pluciennik, & Young, 2009; Gerhard, Moore, & Hobbs, 2004; Gutl et al., 2009; Hung, Kinzer, & Chen, 2009). Third, the amount of time that learners utilized an avatar was limited in many studies. Consequently, more empirical studies are needed.

Furthermore, as discussed earlier in the chapter, social presence and socialization are both critical for social interactivity as well as collaboration among avatars. Edirisingha et al.'s (2009) pilot study focused on how social presence and socialization can be developed in MUVEs. However, they state that research into the nature and the properties of social presence and subsequent socialization is still in the beginning stage. Another area of social interactivity that bears further investigation is appearance. Ersner-Hershfield, Bailenson, and Carstensen (2008), Yee and Bailenson (2007), and Yee, Bailenson, and Ducheneaut (2009) found that how individuals appear in virtual worlds can impact their verbal and nonverbal behavior, with these alterations also impacting their real world behavior. However, very little empirical research exists documenting the extent of the impact over prolonged period of time (Baylor, 2009). A series of studies or a longitudinal study would enable a researcher to track such behavioral changes over multiple interactions within the virtual environment. In addition, the Yee et al. (2009) study showed tentative evidence that even short-term experience in a virtual environment can produce an observable behavioral difference in the real world. However further study, especially in terms of long-term participation in virtual worlds, is need to determine whether the Proteus Effect has a long-term implications.

Another topic of investigation surrounds the issue of utilizing multiple avatars within training. In the section on collaboration, Maldonado's (2005) and Baylor's (2009) research suggests that learners benefit from multiple virtual agents taking on different roles during a simulation. Yet there are four studies (Davis, Murphy, Owens, Khazanchi, & Zigurs, 2009; Kluge & Renly, 2008; Lim, Nonis, & Hedberg, 2006; Omale, Hung, Luetkehans, & Cooke-Plagwitz, 2009) suggesting that multiple agents cause learners to spend too much time socializing and not enough time on the cognitive part of the training. Additional studies could examine whether there are an optimum number of avatars for training so that the social and cognitive parts of the learning balance themselves out.

More research could examine how leaders develop within virtual communities of practice. In the section on collaborative learning, an example was provided where executives work with managers to develop their future leadership skills. Given the ability to change appearance and control nonverbal behaviors beyond what is possible in the real world, researchers could study whether and how the manipulation of appearance and behavior influences which virtual community members ultimately attain leadership positions. Davis et al. (2009) question whether physical and behavioral cues commonly used to influence group members in the real world are the same in the virtual world or are there new cues that have developed within the latter? Finally, researchers would look at how avatars and virtual worlds can be integrated into ubiquitous learning environments. A review of the research literature on both subjects did not reveal any existing studies that address the utilization of avatars as a component of a ubiquitous learning strategy. Therefore, this would be a new area of research that would bring together two previously disparate topics.

In conclusion, this chapter has shown that avatars can facilitate a learner's sense of presence and socialization in a MUVE and of copresence within a virtual community, can enhance a learner's motivation to continue learning, and can promote collaborative learning. In addition, avatars do have the potential for being included in a ubiquitous learning strategy. While the existing research has some methodological limitations, it also has uncovered several issues for further investigation. As noted in the introduction, the enthusiasm for virtual worlds in both the business and educational areas has been tempered some since IBM made news in 2007 with its own island in Second Life. The effectiveness of avatars within MUVEs is only one factor influencing the acceptance of this new Web 2.0 technology as a training tool in corporations and higher education. However, its perceived effectiveness does play a role in how readily senior management or educational administrators buy into the virtual world technology and how willing they are to budget money for its implementation.

REFERENCES

American Society for Training and Development. (2010). *The rise of social media: Enhancing collaboration and productivity across generations*. Retrieved on February 3, 2011 from http://www.astd.org/Publications/Research-Reports/2010/2010-Rise-of-Social-Media

Angelino, L. M., Williams, F. K., & Natvig, D. (2007). Strategies to engage online students and reduce attrition rates. *The Journal of Educators Online, 4*(2), 1-14. Retrieved on October 14, 2011 from http://www.thejeo.com/Archives/Volume4Number2/Angelino-Final.pdf

Bailenson, J. N., Merget, D., Schroeder, R., & Yee, N. (2006). The effect of behavioral realism and form realism of real-time avatar faces on verbal disclosure, non-verbal disclosure, emotion recognition, and copresence in dyadic interaction. *Presence: Teleoperators and Virtual Environments, 15*(4), 359-372. Retrieved September 30, 2009 from http://www.mitpressjournals.org/doi/pdf/10.1162/pres.15.4.359

Bailenson, J. N., Swinth, K., Hoyt, C., Persky, S., Dimov, A., & Blascovich, J. (2005) The independent and interactive effects of embodied-agent appearance and behavior on self-report, cognitive, and behavioral markers of copresence in immersive virtual environments. *Presence: Teleoperators & Virtual Environments, 14*(4), 379-393. Retrieved on May 15, 2011 from http://vhil/stanford.edu/pubs/2005/bailenson-copresence.pdf

Bailenson, J. N., & Yee, N. (2008). Virtual interpersonal touch: Haptic interaction and copresence in collaborative virtual environments. *Multimedia Tools and Applications, 37*, 5-14. Retrieved on July 25, 2010 from http://vhil.stanford.edu/pubs/2007/bailenson-mm-VIT-CVE.pdf

Bailenson, J. N., Yee, N., Blascovich, J., Bell, A. C., Lunbald, N., & Jin, M. (2008). The use of immersive virtual reality in the learning sciences: Digital transformation of teachers, students, and social context. *The Journal of the Learning Sciences, 17*, 102-141. Retrieved on August 10, 2010 from http://www.life-slc.org/Bailenson_etal-immersiveVR.pdf

Banakou, D., Chorianopoulos, K., & Anagnostou, K. (2009). Avatars appearance and social behavior in online virtual worlds. In *Proceedings of the 13ᵗʰ Panhellenic Conference on Informatics* (pp. 207-211). Corfu, Greece: IEEE Computer Society. Retrieved on January 29, 2012 from http://ebookbrowse.com/avatars-appearance-and-social-behaviors-in-online-virtual-worlds-pdf-d266139551

Bandura, A. (1997). *Self-efficacy: The exercise of control*. New York: Freeman.

Baylor, A. L. (2009). Promoting motivation with virtual agents and avatars: The role of visual presence and appearance. *Philosophical Transactions of the Royal Society of London. Series B, Biological Sciences*, 3559–3565. doi:10.1098/rstb.2009.0148 PMID:19884150.

Berelson, B. (1952). *Content analysis in communication research*. Glencoe, IL: Free Press.

Bessiere, K., Ellis, J. B., & Kellogg, W. A. (2009). Acquiring a professional 'second life': Problems and prospects for the use of virtual worlds in business. In *Proceedings of the 27ᵗʰ International Conference Extended Abstracts on Human Factors in Computing Systems* (pp. 2883-2898). New York: ACM. doi: 10.1145/1520340.1520416

Boellstorff, T. (2008). *Coming of age in second life: An anthropologist explores the virtually human*. Princeton, NJ: Princeton University Press.

Borthick, A. F., Jones, D. R., & Wakai, S. (2003). Designing learning experiences within learners' zone of proximal development (ZPD), enabling collaborative learning on-site and online. *Journal of Information Systems, 17*(1), 107-134. Retrieved on October 12, 2009 from http://www2.gsu.edu/~accafb/pubs/JISBorthickJonesWakai2003.pdf

Campbell, M. (2009). Using 3-D virtual worlds to teach decision-making: In same places, different spaces. In *Proceedings ASCILITE*, (pp. 104-109). Auckland, New Zealand: ASCILITE. Retrieved on March 7, 2011 from www.ascilite.org.au/conferences/auckland09/procs/campbell-m.pdf

Campbell, M., & Uys, P. (2007). Identifying factors that influence the success of ICT in developing a learning community: The CELT experience. *Campus-Wide Information Systems, 24*(1), 17–26. doi:10.1108/10650740710726464.

Casey, D. (2005). U-learning = e-learning + m-learning. In G. Richards (Ed.), *Proceedings of the World Conference on E-Learning in Corporate, Government, Healthcare, and Higher Education 2005* (pp. 2864-2871). Chesapeake, VA: AACE. Retrieved on October 17, 2012 from http://www.editlib.org/p/21634

Chen, G. D., Chang, C. K., & Wang, C. Y. (2008). Ubiquitous learning website: Scaffold learners by mobile devices with information-aware techniques. *Computers & Education, 50*(1), 77-80. Retrieved on October 16, 2012 from http://www.cbit.soton.ac.uk/multimedia/PDFs/Ubiquitous%20 learning%20website%20 scaffolding%20learners%20by%20mobile%20devices%20with%20 info-aware %20techniques.pdf

Chen, Y. S., Kao, T. C., Sheu, J. P., & Chiang, C. Y. (2002). A mobile scaffolding-aid-based bird watching learning system. In *Proceedings of IEEE International Workshop on Wireless and Mobile Technologies in Education (WMTE'02)*, (pp. 15-22). IEEE. Retrieved on October 18, 2012 from http://www.csie.ntpu.edu.tw/~yschen/compapers/bird/pdf

Chiu, P. S., Kuo, Y., Huang, Y., & Chen, T. (2008). A meaningful learning based u-learning evaluation model. In *Proceedings of the Eighth IEEE International Conference on Advanced Learning Technologies*, (pp. 77-81). IEEE. Retrieved on October 14, 2012 from http://ieeexplore.ieee.org/xpl/login.jsp?tp=&anumber=4561631&url=http%3A%2 F%2Fie eexplore.ieee.org%2Fxpls%2Fabs_all.jsp%3Fanumber%3D4561631

Chou, C. C. (2009). Virtual worlds for organizational learning and communities of practice. In U. Cress, V. Dimitrova, & M. Specht (Eds.), *Learning in the Synergy of Multiple Disciplines (LNCS)* (Vol. 5794, pp. 751–756). Berlin, Germany: Springer. doi:10.1007/978-3-642-04636-0_79.

Chou, C. Y., Chan, T. W., & Lin, C. J. (2003). Redefining the learning companion: The past, present, and future of educational agents. *Computers & Education, 40*, 256–269. doi:10.1016/S0360-1315(02)00130-6.

Cocea, M., & Weibelzahl, S. (2006). Motivation - Included or excluded from e-learning. In D. Kinshuk, G. Sampson, J. M. Spector, & P. Isias (Eds.), *IADIS International Conference on Cognition and Exploratory Learning in Digital Age, CELDA 2006* (pp. 435-437). Retrieved August 1, 2010 from http://www.easy-hub.org/stephan/cocea-celda06.pdf

Coffman, T., & Klinger, M. B. (2007). Utilizing virtual worlds in education: The implications for practice. *International Journal for Social Sciences, 2*(1), 29-33. Retrieved September 26, 2010 from http://www.akademik.unsri.ac.id/download/journal/files/waset/v2-1-5 1.pdf

Cooper, H. (1982). Scientific guidelines for conducting integrative research reviews. *Review of Educational Research, 52*(2), 291–302. doi:10.3102/00346543052002291.

Dalgarno, B., & Lee, M. J. (2010). What are the learning affordances of 3-D virtual environments? *British Journal of Education Technology, 41*(1), 10-32. Retrieved on January 15, 2012 from http://edtc6325teamone2ndlife.pbworks.com/f/6325%B Learning%Baffordances%Bof%B 3-D.pdf

Davis, A., Murphy, J., Owens, D., Khazanchi, D., & Zigurs, I. (2009). Avatars, people, and virtual worlds: Foundations for research in metaverses. *Journal of the Association for Information Services, 10*(2), 90-117. Retrieved on January 29, 2011 from http://kmcms.free.fr/virtualworlds/AvatarsPeopleandVirtualWorldsFoundationfor-ResearchinMetaverses.pdf de Freitas, S., Rebolledo-Mendez, G., Liarokapis, F., Magoulas, G., & Poulovassilis, A. (2009). Learning as an immersive experience: Using the four dimensional framework for designing and evaluating immersive learning experiences in a virtual world. *British Journal of Educational Technology, 41*(1), 69-85. Retrieved on July 4, 2011 from http://www.sussex.ac.uk/Users/gr20/BJET(2010).pdf

Deci, E. L., & Ryan, R. M. (1985). *Intrinsic motivation and self-determination in human behavior*. New York: Plenum. doi:10.1007/978-1-4899-2271-7.

Deci, E. L., & Ryan, R. M. (2000). Intrinsic and extrinsic motivations: Classic definitions and new directions. *Contemporary Educational Psychology, 25*, 54–67. doi:10.1006/ceps.1999.1020 PMID:10620381.

Dickey, M. (2007). Game design and learning: A conjectural analysis of how massively multiple online role-playing games (MMORPG) foster intrinsic motivation. *Educational Technology Research and Development, 55*, 253–273. doi:10.1007/s11423-006-9004-7.

Eccles, J., & Wigfield, A. (2002). Motivational beliefs, values, and goals. *Annual Review of Psychology, 53*, 109-132. Retrieved on September 24, 2010 from http://www2.csdm.qc.ca/SaintEmile/bernet/annexes/ASS6826/Eccles2002.pdf

Edirisingha, P., Nie, M., Pluciennik, M., & Young, R. (2009). Socialization for learning at a distance in a 3-D multi-user virtual environment. *British Journal of Educational Technology, 40*(3), 458–479. doi:10.1111/j.1467-8535.2009.00962.x.

Edwards, P., Dominguez, E., & Rico, M. (2008) A second look at second life: Virtual role-play as a motivational factor in higher education. In K. McFerrin et al. (Eds.), *Proceedings of Society for Information Technology and Teacher Education Internationial Conference 2008* (pp. 2566-2571). Chesapeake, VA: AACE.

Elliott, E. S., & Dweck, C. S. (1988). Goals: An approach to motivation and achievement. *Journal of Personality and Social Psychology, 54*(1), 5-12. Retrieved on September 26, 2010 from http://www.ncbi.nlm.nih.gov/pubmed/3346808

Ersner-Hershfield, H., Bailenson, J. N., & Carstensen, L. L. (2008). *A vivid future self: Immersive virtual reality enhances retirement saving*. Chicago: Association for Psychological Science.

Fox, J., & Bailenson, J. N. (2009). Virtual self-modeling: The effect of vicarious reinforcement and indentification on exercise behaviors. *Media Psychology, 12*, 1-25. Retrieved on October 12, 2011 from http://www.stanford.edu/~bailenso/papers/fox-mp-selfmodeling.pdf

Franceschi, K. G., Lee, R. M., & Hinds, D. (2008). Engaging e-learning in virtual worlds: Supporting group collaboration. In *Proceedings for the 41st Hawaii International Conference on System Sciences*, (pp. 1-10). IEEE. Retrieved on February 16, 2011 from http://www.computer.org/comp/proceedings/hicss/2008/3075/00/30750007.pdf

Franceschi, K. G., Lee, R. M., Zanakis, S. H., & Hinds, D. (2009). Engaging group e-learning in virtual worlds. *Journal of Management Information Systems, 26*(1), 73–100. doi:10.2753/MIS0742-1222260104.

Gartner Group. (2007). Gartner says 80 percent of active internet users will have a second life in the virtual world by the end of 2011. *Gartner Group*. Retrieved on June 1, 2010 from http://www.gartner.com/it/page.jsp?id=503861

Gerhard, M., Hobbs, D. J., & Moore, D. J. (2004). Embodiment and copresence in collaborative interfaces. *International Journal of Human-Computer Studies, 61*(4), 453-480. Retrieved on October 5, 2009 from http://www.geomobile.de/fileadmin/docs/IJHCS-Paper.pdf

Gulz, A. (2004). Benefits of virtual characters in computer-based learning environments: Claims and evidence. *International Journal of Artifical Intelligence in Education, 14*(3), 313-334. Retrieved on September 22, 2009 from http://hal.inria.fr/docs/00/19/73/09/PDF/Gulz04.pdf

Gunkel, D. J. (2010). The real problem: Avatars, metaphysics, and online social interaction. *New Media & Society, 12*(1), 127-141. Retrieved on December 26, 2011 from http://commons.lib.niu.edu/bitstream/10843/13147/1/real_problem_preprint.ped

Gutl, C., Chang, V., Kopeinik, S., & Williams, R. (2009). Evaluation of collaborative learning settings in 3D virtual worlds. In *Proceedings of the International Conference of Interactive Computer Aided Learning*, (pp. 6-17). Vienna: iJet. Retrieved on May 17, 2010 from http://dx.doi.org/ijet.v4s3.1112

Herold, D. K. (2010). Mediating media studies - Stimulating critical awareness in a virtual environment. *Computers & Education*, 791–798. doi:10.1016/j.compedu.2009.10.019.

Herrington, J., Reeves, T. C., & Oliver, R. (2007). Immersive learning technologies: Realism and online authentic learning. *Journal of Computing in Higher Education, 19*(10), 65-84. Retrieved on May 18, 2010 from http://ro.uow.edu.au/edupapers/27/

Hew, K., & Cheung, W. (2008). Use of three-dimensional (3-D) immersive virtual worlds in K-12 and higher education settings: A review of the research. *British Journal of Educational Technology, 39*(6), 959–1148. doi:doi:10.1111/j.1467-8535.2008.00900.x.

Hodges, C. (2004). Designing to motivate: Motivational techniques to incorporate in e-learning experiences. *The Journal of Interactive Online Learning, 2*(3), 1-7. Retrieved August 1, 2010 from http://www.ncolr.org/jiol/issues/PDF/2.3.1.pdf

Hung, K. H., Kinzer, C., & Chen, C.-L. (2009). Motivational factors in educational MMORPGs: Some implications for education. In Z. Pan et al. (Eds.), *Transactions in Edutainment (LNCS)* (Vol. 5940, pp. 93–104). Berlin: Springer. doi:10.1007/978-3-642-11245-4_9.

Hussain, M., Nakamura, B., & Marino, J. (2011). Avatar appearance and information credibility in second life. In *Proceedings of the 2011iConference*, (pp. 682-68). Seattle, WA: ACM. doi:10.1145/1940761.1940868

Hwang, G.-J. (2006). Criteria and strategies of ubiquitous learning. In *Proceedings of the IEEE International Conference on Sensor Networks, Ubiquitous, and Trustworthy Computer (SUTC '06)*, (pp. 72-77). IEEE. Retrieved on October 13, 2012 from http://ieeexplore.ieee.org/xpl/login.jsp?tp=&anumber=1636255&url=http%3A%2F%2Fieeexplore.ieee.org%2Fxpls%2Fabs_all.jsp%3Fanumber%3D1636255

Jarmon, L. (2008). Pedagogy and learning in the virtual world of second life. In P. Rogers, G. Berg, J. Boettcher, C. Howard, L. Justice, & K. Schenk (Eds.), *Encyclopedia of Distance and Online Learning* (2nd Ed.). Retrieved on February 12, 2011 from http://research.educatorscoop.org/Leslie_Jarmon_Second_Life.pdf

Jones, J. G., Morales, C., & Knezek, C. G. (2005). 3-dimensional online learning environments: Examining attitudes toward information technology between students in internet-based 3-dimensional and face-to-face classroom instruction. *Educational Media International, 42*(3), 219-236, Retrieved on June 1, 2010 from http://www.informaworld.com/smpp/content~db=all~content=a714023310

Jones, V., & Jo, J. H. (2004). Ubiquitous learning environment: An adaptive teaching system using ubiquitous technology. In R. Atkinson, C. McBeath, D. Jones-Dwyer, & R. Phillips (Eds.), *Beyond the comfort zone: Proceedings of the 21ˢᵗ ASCILITE Conference* (pp. 468-474). ASCILITE. Retrieved on October 16, 2012 from http://www.ascilite.org.au/conferences/perth04/procs/jones.html

Keller, J. (1987). Strategies for stimulating the motivation to learn. *Performance & Instruction, 26*(8), 1–7. doi:10.1002/pfi.4160260802.

Keller, J. (2000). *How to integrate learner motivation planning into lesson planning: The ARCS model approach.* Retrieved on September 26, 2009 from http://mailer.fsu.edu/~jkeller/Articles/Keller%202000%20ARCS%20Lesson%20Planning.pdf

Keller, J., & Suzuki, K. (2004). Learner motivation and e-learning design: A multinationally validated process. *Journal of Educational Media, 29*(3), 229–239. doi:10.1080/1358165042000283084.

Kluge, S., & Riley, L. (2008). Teaching in virtual worlds: Opportunities and challenges. *Issues in Informing Science and Information Technology, 5,* 127-135. Retrieved March 7, 2011 from http://proceedings.informingscience.org/InSITE2008/IISITv5p127-135Kluge459.pdf?q=forming-learning-connections

Korolov, M. (2009). Virtual meeting rush. *Treasury & Risk*: Retrieved on September 22, 2009 from http://www.treasuryandrisk.com/Issues/2009/September%202009/Pages/Virtual-Meeting-Rush.aspx

Krippendorf, K. (1980). *Content analysis: An introduction to its methodology.* Newbury Park, CA: Sage.

Laffey, J., Cho, M.-H., Hsu, Y.-C., Huang, X., Kim, B., & Lin, G. Y. Shen, ... Yang, C.-C. (2005). Understanding computer mediated social experience: Implications for CSCL. In T. Koschmann, D. Suthers, & T. W. Chan (Eds.), *Computer Supported Collaboration Learning 2005: The Next 10 Years, Proceedings of the International Conference on Computer-Supported Collaborative Learning 2005* (pp. 617-621). Taipei, Taiwan: International Society of the Learning Sciences.

Laffey, J., Lin, G. Y., & Lin, Y. (2006). Assessing social ability in online learning environments. *Journal of Interactive Learning Research, 17*(2), 163–177.

Lastowka, F. G., & Hunter, D. (2006). Virtual worlds: A primer. In J.M. Balkin & B.S. Noveck (Eds.), *State of play: Law, games, and virtual worlds,* (pp. 13-28). New York, NY: New York University Press. Retrieved December 27, 2011 from hci.stanford.edu/courses/cs047n/readings/virtual-primer.pdf

Lemon, M., & Kelly, O. (2009). Laying second life foundations: Second chance learners get first life skills. *Same Places, Different Spaces: Proceedings Ascilite Auckland 2009,* (pp. 557-565). ASCILITE. Retrieved on December 24, 2009 from http://www.ascilite.org.au/conferences/auckland09/procs/lemon.pdf

Lim, C. P., Nonis, D., & Hedberg, J. (2006). Gaming in a 3D multiuser virtual environment: Engaging students in science lessons. *British Journal of Educational Technology, 37*(2), 211-231. Retrieved on August 9, 2010 from http://edithcowan.academia.edu/documents/0011/5264/BJET__Lim__Nonis___Hedberg_2005_.pdf

Lincoln, Y., & Guba, E. (1985). *Naturalistic inquiry*. Beverly Hills, CA: Sage.

Lui, G.-Z., & Hwang, G.-J. (2010). A key step to understanding paradigm shifts in e-learning: Towards context-aware ubiquitous learning. *British Journal of Educational Technology, 41*(2), E1–E0. doi:10.1111/j.1467-8535.2009.00976.x.

Lyytinen, K., & Yoo, Y. (2002). Issues and challenges in ubiquitous computing. *Communications of the ACM, 45*(12), 63-65. Retrieved on October 14, 2012 from citeseerx.ist.psu.edu/viewdoc/download?doi=10.1.1.135.3184.pdf

Maldonado, H., Lee, J.-Y., Brave, S., Nass, C., Nakajima, H., Yamada, R., et al. (2005). We learn better together: Enchancing elearning with emotional characters. In T. Koschmann, D.Suthers, & T. W. Chan (Eds.), *Computer Supported Collaborative Learning 2005: The Next 10 Years, Proceedings of the International Conference on Computer Supported Collaborative Learning 2005* (pp. 408-417). Taipei, Taiwan: International Society of the Learning Sciences. Retrieved on November 11, 2009 from http://www.stanford.edu/~kiky/publications.html

Maldonado, H., & Nass, C. (2007). Emotive characters make learning more productive and enjoyable: It takes two to learn to tango. *Educational Technology, 47*(1), 33-38. Retrieved on November 11, 2009 from http://www.stanford.edu/~kiky/publications.html

Marshall, C., & Rossman, G. (1995). *Designing qualitative research* (2nd ed.). Thousand Oaks, CA: Sage.

Maslow, A. H. (1943). A theory of human motivation. *Psychological Review, 50*, 370-396. Retrieved on September 30, 2010 from http://mcv.planc.ee/misc/doc/filosoofia/artiklid/Abraham%20H.%20Maslow%20%20A%20Theory%20Of%20Human%20Motivation.pdf

Mayer, R. E. (2004). Should there be a three-strikes rule against discovery learning? *American Psychologist, 59*, 14-19. Retrieved on November 13, 2010 from http://apps.fischlerschool.nova.edu/toolbox/instructionalproducts/edd8124/fall1/2004-Mayer.pdf

McArthur, V. (2010). Professional second lives: An analysis of virtual world professionals and avatar appearance. In *Proceedings of the International Academic Conference on the Future of Game Design and Technology*, (pp. 231-235). doi:10.1145/1920778.1920814

McArthur, V., & Baljko, M. (2009). Outsiders, interlopers, and employee-identified avatars. In *Proceedings of the 12th Annual International Workshop on Presence*, (pp. 1-8). Retrieved on July 24, 2011 from http://astro.temple.edu/~tuc16417/papers/McArthur_et_al.pdf

Merriam, S. (1998). *Qualitative research and case study applications in education*. San Francisco, CA: Jossey-Bass Publishers.

Monahan, T., McArdle, G., & Bertolotto, M. (2008). Virtual reality for collaborative learning. *Computers & Education*, 1339-1353. Retrieved on October 5, 2009 from http://squidguts.org/Portfolio/Subj_use_Technology/virtual_reality.pdf

Moreno, R., & Mayer, R. (2007). Interactive multimodal learning environments. *Educational Psychology Review, 19*(3), 309–326. doi:10.1007/s10648-007-9047-2.

Moundridou, M., & Virvou, M. (2002). Evaluating the persona effect of an interface agent in a tutoring systems. *Journal of Computer Assisted Learning, 18*(3), 253-261. Retrieved on October 3, 2009 from http://74.125.155.132/scholar?q= cache:mCpgtGyN3KgJ:scholar.google.com/+E valuating+the+Persona+Effect+of+an+Interf act+Agent+in+a+Tutoring+Sysem&hl=en& as_sdt=2000

Neustaedter, C., & Fedorovskaya, E. (2008). Establishing and maintaining relationships in a social virtual world. *Eastman Kodak Technical Report 344195F*. Retrieved October 10, 2011 from http://clab.iat.sfu.ca/uploads/Main/VirtualRelationships.pdf

O'Brien, L., & Murnane, J. (2009). An investigation into how avatar appearance can affect interactions in a virtual world. *International Journal of Social and Humanistic Computing, 1*(2), 192-202. Retrieved October 10, 2011 from http://inderscience.metapress.com/content/ g8267g163k347466/

Ogata, H., & Yano, Y. (2004). Context-aware support for computer-supported ubiquitous learning. In *Proceedings of the 2nd IEEE Workshop on Wireless and Mobile Technologies in Education*, (pp. 27-34). IEEE. Retrieved on October 15, 2012 from http://140.115.126.240/mediawiki/images/e/ e9/Content_Awareness.pdf

Oliver, M., & Carr, D. (2009). Learning in virtual worlds: Using communities of practice to explain how people learn from play. *British Journal of Educational Technology, 40*(3), 444–457. doi:10.1111/j.1467-8535.2009.00948.x.

Omale, N., Hung, W. C., Luetkehans, L., & Cooke-Plagwitz, J. (2009). Learning in 3-D multiuser virtual environments: Exploring the use of unique 3-D attributes for online problem-based learning. *British Journal of Educational Technology, 40*(3), 480–495. doi:10.1111/j.1467-8535.2009.00941.x.

Parscal, T., & Hencmann, M. (2008). Cognitive apprenticeships in online learning. In *Proceedings of the 24th Annual Conference on Distance Teaching & Learning*, (pp. 1-4). Retrieved October 21, 2011 from http://pdf.aminer.org/000/270/204/ tool_mediated_cognitive_apprencticeship_approach_for_a_computer_engineering_course.pdf

Prasolova-Forland, E., & Divitini, M. (2003). Collaborative virtual environments for supporting learning communities: An experience of use. In *Proceedings of 2003 International ACM SIGGROUP Conference on Supporting Group Work* (pp. 58-67). New York: ACM. Retrieved on October 5, 2009 from http://delivery.acm. org/10.1145/960000/958170/p58-prasolova forland.pdf?key1=958170&key2=9426969521&c oll=GUIDE&dl=GUIDE&CFID=65999580& CFTOKEN=24982540

Rogers, E. (2003). *Diffusion of innovation* (5th ed.). New York: Free Press.

Salmon, G. (2009). The future for (second) life and learning. *British Journal of Educational Technology, 40*(3), 526–538. doi:10.1111/j.1467-8535.2009.00967.x.

Schmeil, A., & Eppler, M. (2008). Knowledge sharing and collaborative learning in second life: A classification of virtual 3-D group interaction scripts. *Journal of Universal Computer Science, 14*(3), 665-677. Retrieved on February 20, 2011 from http://oaj.unsri.ac.id/files/jucs/ jucs_15_03_0665_0677_schmeil_oaj_unscri.pdf

Schroeder, R. (2006). Being there together and the future of connected presence. *Presence (Cambridge, Mass.), 15*(4), 438–454. doi:10.1162/ pres.15.4.438.

Second Life Education. (2010). *Academic organizations in second life*. Retrieved from http:// edudirectory.secondlife.com/

Shein, E. (2010). Avatars rising in the enterprise. *Computerworld.* Retrieved on April 20, 2010 from http://www.computerworld.com/s/article/9174873/Avatars_rising_in_the_enterprise

Shen, K. N., Khalifa, M., & Yu, A. Y. (2006). Supporting social interaction in virtual communities: Role of social presence. In *Proceedings of the Twelfth Americas Conference on Information Systems,* (pp. 4461-4469). Retrieved on May 15, 2011 from citeseerx.ist.psu.edu

Steinkuehler, C. A. (2004). Learning in massively multiplayer online games. In *Proceedings of the 6th International Conference on Learning Sciences,* (pp. 521-528). Retrieved on November 5, 2009 from http://delivery.acm.org/10.1145/1150000/1149190/p521steinkuehler.pdf?key1=1149190&key2=4767589521&coll=GUIDE&dl=GUIDE&CFID=64891945&CFTOKEN=50934250

StrategyAnalystics. (2008). *Virtual worlds projected to mushroom to nearly one billion users.* Retrieved on June 1, 2010 from https://www.strategyanalytics.com/default.aspx?mod=PressReleaseViewer&a0=3983

Takahaski, D. (2010). Free realm hits 9M players, closing in on World of Warcraft. *Gamebeat.* Retrieved on August 18, 2010 from http://games.venturebeat.com/2010/03/05/free-realms-hits-9m players-closing-in-on-world-of-warcraft/

Thomas, D., & Seeley Brown, J. (2009). Why virtual worlds matter. *International Journal of Learning and Media, 1*(1), 37-49. Retrieved on April 3, 2011 from http://johnseeleybrown.com/virtualworlds.pdf

Torraco, R. J. (2005). Writing integrative literature reviews: Guidelines and examples. *Human Resources Development Review, 4*(3), 356-367. Retrieved on April 3, 2011 from http://docseminar2.wikispaces.com/file/view/Literature+review+paper_Torraco.pdf

Twining, P. (2009). Exploring the educational potential of virtual worlds - Some reflections from SPP. *British Journal of Educational Technology, 40*(3), 496–514. doi:10.1111/j.1467-8535.2009.00963.x.

Tyler-Smith, K. (2005). Early attrition among first-time learners: A review of factors that contribute to drop-out, withdrawal, and non-completion rates of adult learners undertaking elearning programs. *Journal of Online Learning and Teaching, 2*(2). Retrieved September 18, 2009 from jolt.merlot.org/Vol2_No2_TylerSmith.htm

U.S. General Accounting Office. (1996). *Content analysis: A methodology for structuring and analyzing written material.* Washington, DC: GAO.

Vasileiou, V., & Paraskeva, F. (2010). Teaching role-playing instruction in second life: An exploratory study. *Journal of Information, Information Technology, and Organizations, 5,* 25-50. Retrieved on March 3, 2011 from http://jiito.org/articles/JIITOv5p025-050Vasileious431.pdf

Vygotsky, L. S. (1978). *Mind in society: The development of higher psychological processes.* Cambridge, MA: Harvard University Press.

Warburton, S. (2009). Second life in higher education: Assessing the potential for and barriers to deploying virtual worlds in learning and teaching. *British Journal of Educational Technology, 40*(3), 414–426. doi:10.1111/j.1467-8535.2009.00952.x.

Weber, R. P. (1990). *Basic content analysis.* Cambridge, UK: Cambridge University Press.

B. Weiner (Ed.). (1974). *Achievement, motivation & attribution theory.* Morristown, NJ: General Learning Press.

Wenger, E. (1998). *Communities of practice: Learning, meaning and identity.* Cambridge, UK: Cambridge University Press. doi:10.1017/CBO9780511803932.

Wigfield, A. (1994). Expectancy-value theory of achievement motivation: A developmental perspective. *Educational Psychology Review, 6*(1), 49–78. doi:10.1007/BF02209024.

Wlodkowski, R. (1985). *Enhancing adult motivation to learn.* San Francisco, CA: Jossey-Bass Publishers.

Wyld, D. (2010). A virtual explosion or SNAFU is always better than a real one: Exploring the use of virtual worlds for simulations and training… and developing the leaders of tomorrow. In M. Iskander, V. Kapilla, & M. Karim (Eds.), *Technological Development in Education and Automation* (pp. 73–78). doi:10.1007/978-90-481-3656-8_15.

Yahya, S., Ahmad, E. A., & Jalil, K. A. (2010). The definition and characteristics of ubiquitous learning: A discussion. *International Journal of Education and Development Using Information and Communication Technology, 6*(1). Retrieved on October 17, 2012 from http://ijedict.dec.uwi.edu/viewarticle.php?id=785

Yang, S. J. H. (2006). Context aware ubiquitous learning environments for peer-to-peer collaborative learning. *Educational Technology & Society, 9*(1), 188-201. Retrieved on October 15, 2012 from http://library.oum.edu.my/oumlib/sites/default/files/file_attachments/odl-resources/4479/context-aware.pef

Yee, N. (2007). Motivations of play in online games. *Journal of Cyber Psychology & Behavior, 9,* 772-775. Retrieved on September 24, 2010 from http://www.cblt.soton.ac.uk/multimedia/PDFsMM09/MMORPG%20motivation%20for%20playing.pdf

Yee, N., & Bailenson, J. N. (2007). The proteus effect: The effect of transformed self-representation on behavior. *Human Communication Research, 33,* 271-290. Retrieved June 22, 2010 from http://dx.doi.org/doi:10.1111/j.1468-2958.2007.00299.x

Yee, N., Bailenson, J. N., & Ducheneaut, N. (2009). The proteus effect implications of transformed digitial self-representation on online and offline behavior. *Communcation Research, 36,* 285-312. Retrieved April 23, 2011 from http://dx.doi.org/doi: 10.1177/0093650208330254

Yee, N., Bailenson, J. N., Urbanek, M., Chang, F., & Merget, D. (2007). The unbearable likeness of being digital: The persistence of nonvrebal social norms in online virtual environments. *The Journal of CyberPsychology and Behavior, 10,* 115–121. doi:10.1089/cpb.2006.9984 PMID:17305457.

Young, J. (2010). After frustrations in second life, colleges look to new virtual worlds. *The Chronicle of Higher Education.* Retrieved on May 19, 2010 from http://chronicle.com/article/After-Frustrations-in-Second/64137

Yu, T. W. (2009). Learning in the virtual world: The pedagogical potentials of massively multiplayer online role-playing games. *International Education Studies, 2*(1), 32-38. Retrieved on July 4, 2011 from http://www.ccsenet.org/journal/index.php/ies/article/view/287/362

ADDITIONAL READING

Andrade, A. D., Bagri, A., Zaw, K., Roos, B. A., & Ruiz, J. (2010). Avatar-mediated training in the delivery of bad news in a virtual world. *Journal of Palliative Medicine, 13*(12), 1415–1419. doi:10.1089/jpm.2010.0108 PMID:21091407.

Andreas, K., Tsiatsos, T., Terzidou, T. & Pomportis, A. (2010). Fostering collaborative learning in second life: Metaphors and affordances. *Computer & Education, 55*(2), 603-615. Retrieved on July 4, 2011 from http://dx.doi.org/10.1016/j.compedu.2010.02.021

Annetta, L., & Holmes, S. (2006). Creating presence and community in a synchronous virtual learning environment using avatars. *International Journal of Instructional Technology and Distance Learning, 3*(8), 27-43. Retrieved on July 4, 2011 from http://itdl.org/Journal/Aug_06/Aug_06.pdf#page=31

Brown, E., Hobbs, M., & Gordon, M. (2008). A virtual world environment for group work. *International Journal of Web-Based Learning and Teaching Technologies, 3*(1), 1–12. doi:10.4018/jwltt.2008010101.

Burgess, M., Slate, J., Rojas-LeBouef, A., & LaPrairie, K. (2010). Teaching and learning in second life: Using the community of inquiry (CoI) model to support online instruction with graduate students in instructional technology. *The Internet and Higher Education, 13*(1-2), 84-88. Retrieved on July 4, 2011 from http://dx.doi.org/10.1016/j.iheduc.2009.12.003

Choi, H. (2010). Social learning through the avatar in the virtual world: The effect of experience type and personality type on achievement motivation. In D. Gibson & B. Dodge (Eds.), *Proceedings of Society for Information Technology & Teacher Education International Conference 2010* (pp. 1866-1873). Chesapeake, VA: AACE. Retrieved on July 4, 2011 from http://www.editlib.org/p/33633

B. Cope, & M. Kalantzis (Eds.). (2009). *Ubiquitous learning*. Champaign-Urbana, IL: University of Illinois Press.

El- Bishouty, M.M., Ogata, H., Ayala, G., & Yano, Y. (2010). Context aware support for self-directed ubiquitous learning. *International Journal of Mobile Learning and Organization, 4*(3), 317–331. doi:10.1504/IJMLO.2010.033558.

El- Bishouty. M.M., Ogata, H., Rahman, S., & Yano, Y. (2010). Social knowledge awareness map for computer-supported ubiquitous learning environment. *Journal of Educational Technology & Society, 13*(4), 27-37. Citeseerx.ist.psu.edu 10.1.1.187.8547.pdf

Games, A. I., & Baumen, E. B. (2011). Virtual worlds: An environment for cultural sensitivity training in the health sciences. *International Journal of Web-Based Communities, 7*(2), 189–205. doi:10.1504/IJWBC.2011.039510.

Heiphetz, A., & Woodill, G. (2009). *Training and collaboration in virtual worlds*. Columbus, OH: McGraw-Hill.

Huang, Y.-M., Chiu, P.-S., Liu, T.-C., & Chen, T.-S. (2011). The design and implementation of a meaningful learning-based evaluation method for ubiquitous learning. *Computers & Education, 57*(4), 2291–2302. Retrieved from http://dx.doi.org/10.1016/j.compedu.2011.05.023 doi:10.1016/j.compedu.2011.05.023.

Kapp, K., & O'Driscoll, T. (2010). *Learning in 3D: Adding a new dimension to enterprise learning and collaboration*. San Francisco, CA: Pfeiffer.

T. Kidd, & I. Chen (Eds.). (2011). *Ubiquitous learning: Strategies for pedagogy, course design, and technology*. Charlotte, NC: Information Age Publishing.

Lee, M. J. W. (2009). How can 3-D virtual worlds be used to support collaborative leaning? An analysis of cases from the literature. *Journal of E-Learning and Knowledge Society, 5*(1), 149-158. Retrieved on July 4, 2011 from http://je-lks.maieutiche.economia.unitn.it/index.php/Je-LKS_EN/article/viewFile/300/282

Mancuso, D. S., Chlup, D. T., & McWhorter, R. R. (2010). A study of adult learning in a virtual world. *Advances in Developing Human Resources, 12*(6), 681–689. doi:10.1177/1523422310395368.

Minocha, S., & Reeves, A. J. (2010). Design of learning spaces in 3-D virtual worlds: An empirical investigation of second life. *Learning, Media and Technology, 35*(2), 111–137. doi:10.1080/17439884.2010.494419.

Nelson, B. C., & Erlandson, B. E. (2012). *Design for learning in virtual worlds*. New York: Routledge.

Roche, L., Kurt, C., & Ahrens, S. (2010). An avatar approach to distributed team training for mission operations. *Acta Astronautica, 67*(9-10), 1164-1169. Retrieved on July 4, 2011 from http://dx.doi.org/10.1016/j.actaastro.2010.06.033

Salmon, G., Nie, M., & Edirisingha, P. (2009). Developing a five-stage model of learning in second life. *Educational Research, 52*(2), 169–182. doi:10.1080/00131881.2010.482744.

Smith, M., & Berge, Z. (2009). Social learning theory in second life. *Journal of Online Learning and Teaching, 5*(2). Retrieved on July 4, 2011 from http://jolt.merlot.org/vol5no2/berge_0609.htm

Tsiatsos, T., & Terzidou, T. (2010). Supporting collaborative learning processes in CVE by augmenting student avatars, with nonverbal communication features. In *Proceedings of the IEEE 10th International Conference on Advanced Learning Technologies (ICALT) 2010,* (pp. 578-580). IEEE. Retrieved on July 4, 2011 from http://ieeexplore.ieee.org/xpl/login.jsp?tp=&arnumber=5572557&url=http%3A%2F%2Fi eeexplore.ieee.org%2Fxpls%2Fabs_all.jsp%3Farnumber%3D5572557

Ward, J. (2010). The avatar lecturer: Learning and teaching in second life. *Marketing Intelligence & Planning, 28*(7), 862–861. doi:10.1108/02634501011086463.

Xinyou, Z., & XinWan, O.T. (2010). Adaptive content delivery in ubiquitous learning environment. In *Proceedings of the 2010 6th IEEE International Conference on Wireless, Mobile, and Ubiquitous Technologies in Education,* (pp. 19-26). IEEE. Retrieved on July 4, 2011 from http://ieeexplore.ieee.org/xpl/login.jsp?tp=&arnumber=5476533&url=http%3A%2F%2Fieeexplore.ieee.org%2Fxpls%2Fabs_all.jsp%3Farnumber%3D5476533

Ye, S.-H., & Hung, Y.-C. (2010). The study of self-seamless teaching strategy for ubiquitous learning environments. In *Proceedings of the 2010 6th IEEE International Conference on Wireless, Mobile, and Ubiquitous Technologies in Education,* (pp. 182-186). IEEE.

Section 2
Mobile and Context-Aware Learning

Chapter 4
Towards a Small–Scale Model for Ubiquitous Learning

Jorge Luis Victória Barbosa
University of Vale do Rio dos Sinos (Unisinos), Brazil

Débora Nice Ferrari Barbosa
FEEVALE University, Brazil

ABSTRACT

The ever-increasing use of mobile devices allied to the widespread adoption of wireless network technology has greatly stimulated mobile and ubiquitous computing research. The adoption of mobile technology enables improvement to several application areas, such as education. New pedagogical opportunities can be created through the use of location systems and context-aware computing technology to track each learner's location and customize his/her learning process. In this chapter, the authors discuss a ubiquitous learning model called LOCAL (Location and Context Aware Learning). LOCAL was created to explore those aforementioned pedagogical opportunities, leveraging location technology and context management in order to support ubiquitous learning and facilitate collaboration among learners. This model was conceived for small-scale learning spaces, but can be extended in order to be applied to a large-scale environment. Initial results were obtained in a real scenario, attesting the viability of the approach.

INTRODUCTION

In recent years, there has been a continued research effort in the field of mobility in distributed computer systems. This is mainly due the widespread availability of portable electronic devices (such as mobile phones, handheld computers and net-

DOI: 10.4018/978-1-4666-4542-4.ch004

books) and of interconnection technologies based on wireless communication (like bluetooth and Wi-Fi). This mobile and distributed paradigm is called *Mobile Computing* (Satyanarayanan, 1996; Satyanarayanan et al., 2009; Diaz, Merino & Rivas, 2009). Moreover, the diffusion of wireless communication technologies enables mobile devices to provide computational services in specific contexts (*Context-aware Computing* (Abowd, et al., 1999; Baldauf, Dustdar & Rosenberg, 2007; Hoareau & Satoh, 2009)). Adaptation related research brought the possibility of continuous computational support, anytime, anywhere (*Ubiquitous Computing* (Satyanarayanan, 2001; Weiser, 1991)). In turn, *Location Systems* (Hightower & Borriello, 2001) are enabling the use of this kind of computing in accordance with the physical location of users.

Location, as was shown by Hightower and Gaetano (2001), is an important topic related to mobile and ubiquitous computing. Hightower, LaMarca and Smith (2006) demonstrate that the precision obtainable in today's location methods (such as A-GPS and cellphone antenna triangulation) already allows for the implementation of commercial applications. Moreover, the widespread adoption of wireless hotspots suggests that in the near future this precision will only grow, giving way to *Location Based Services* (Vaughan-Nichols, 2009; Dey et al., 2010).

Based on today's technology, we can imagine a scenario where society would be permeated by mobile devices, always connected to a communication network, and with precise location data always available. The data would be used in order to provide customized services, depending on the physical location, context and the needs of each particular application. In this scenario, ubiquitous computing would be greatly stimulated, as precise location methods would always be available. This will cause a significant impact in education (*Ubiquitous Learning* (Barbosa et al., 2006; Ogata & Yano, 2009)).

To take advantage of ubiquitous computing, a new educational model should finally arise. This model should allow the construction of learning programs related to dynamic information obtainable from the learners' own physical context, establishing links between contexts and pedagogical goals and resources. This will be a key element to facilitate collaboration among learners with related interests. Towards this scenario, several approaches are being researched, like (Ogata &

Yano, 2009; Barbosa, Geyer & Barbosa, 2005; Yau et al., 2003).

In 2002, a university at south of Brazil called Unisinos has proposed a new pedagogical approach to undergraduate courses. This approach is called *Undergraduate Course of Reference* (nicknamed *GRefe*) (Barbosa et al., 2007). GRefes are based on: (1) Learning Programs: a new kind of academic structure oriented to stimulate the integration between thematic course areas; (2) Learning Projects: long duration activities used to amalgamate the knowledge created in the different thematic areas. The GRefes form a strongly-tied, interdisciplinary community where both teachers and learners are encouraged to use the mobile computing infrastructure in their daily activities. We are always seeking for new ways to better explore this infrastructure in the pedagogical processes. As such, the *Mobile Computing Lab* (nicknamed *MobiLab*) at Unisinos has been working on research topics related to the area of ubiquitous computing. One of our main goals was to investigate how mobile devices and location technology could be used to improve learning processes. The high point of this work was the creation of a mobile and ubiquitous learning model powered by mobile computing and location technology, capable of customizing learning and teaching processes by employing contextual information obtained from the environment. This model is called LOCAL (*Location and Context Aware Learning*), and is being tested at our university to support ubiquitous learning. In this sense, we hope to explore pedagogical opportunities through a new technological configuration and a model fine-tuned to support the specific necessities of ubiquitous learning environments.

The chapter is organized in four sections. The second section presents previous work in the area of mobile technology used to create and/or identify pedagogical applications, and how it relates to our work. The third approaches the LOCAL model. The next section shows preliminary test results involving the application of LOCAL in the Computer Engineering GRefe. Finally, last two sections draw future research directions and some conclusions.

BACKGROUND

In the field of mobile applications and infrastructure, user profiles are employed to customize the interaction between the applications and their users. This can be seen in works such as SeLeNe (Rigaux & Spyratos, 2012) and Elena (Simon et al., 2002). However, not all of these employ location technology. Others approach the subject of location technology (like SmartClassroom (Yau et al., 2003) and AmbientWood (Rogers et al., 2005)), incorporating it into an architecture, but don't implement user profiles. We feel that the integration between user profiles, possibly contextualized, and location technologies is key to ubiquitous learning environments; for instance, such integration allows for features like the distribution of contextualized learning objects in a specific location, and the pairing of students relative to their particular interests and current physical location inside a certain learning space. Therefore, we introduced into LOCAL the conciliation between location technology and user profiles. This conciliation is a key point of the LOCAL model.

GlobalEdu (Barbosa, Geyer & Barbosa, 2005) presents a global view of mobile computing technology applied to learning. Its distributed architecture is implemented through the ISAM middleware (Augustin et al., 2004). Though we consider it does not represent a weak point in itself, we believe that the dependence on an external middleware could limit the progress of research. Using an open solution brings an advantage, in the sense of being able to modify the middleware to better adapt to a particular environment's benefit. For example, ISAM empowers GlobalEdu to be used in a large-scale environment (global view). In the case of a small-scale learning environment,

a middleware tuned for performance in a global, distributed architecture could well be going further than necessary to achieve a given goal, spending resources unwisely. Our proposed model is not dependent on a specific communication strategy or framework and, therefore, is not bound to another communication middleware. This gives us the aforementioned benefit of freedom to adapt our communication strategy as we see fit.

Nowadays, the technologies used to establish ubiquitous learning environments can be used to support highly specialized applications. For instance, Japelas (Ogata & Yano, 2009) is a system created with the objective of supporting learning of polite expressions in the Japanese language. The students, porting handheld PCs, are assisted in the identification of the correct polite expressions to be used in a particular context. Japelas uses both location technology and user profiles, but this approach is directed to a specific application. It is our belief that, in order to be wholly useful in a university course scenario, a generic infrastructure should be available. This infrastructure should empower applications with the capability to use location technology as they see fit, in order to improve their particular tasks.

THE LOCAL MODEL: LOCATION AND CONTEXT-AWARE LEARNING

Based on the necessities identified in the last section, we designed a model capable of leveraging user profiles and location technology in order to assist learners in a classroom environment. It facilitates the interaction between the learners and the underlying computer infrastructure. It allows for the delivery of contextualized pedagogical material, adapted to each learner's profile and physical location. It also puts learners with similar goals into contact with each other. In other words, the model acts as a facilitator, stimulating interaction through a novel use of location technology and profiles. This model, which comprehends a small-scale, self-contained mobile and ubiquitous learning environment, is called LOCAL (*Location and Context Aware Learning*). LOCAL is composed by seven subsystems (see Figure 1):

1. **Learner Profiles:** Representing each learner in the system, and storing any information that could be useful to the learning process;
2. **Location System:** Used to determine the physical location of the mobile equipment that each learner carries, to a certain degree of accuracy;
3. **Learning Objects Repository:** Which stores and indexes content related to the teaching process;
4. **Communication System:** Used to route messages in order to establish communication between the different parts of LOCAL, and between the system and its users;
5. **Event System:** Used to schedule tasks;
6. **Tutor:** Which is an analysis engine capable of making user-centric inferences by using the information available in the learner's profiles, as well as location system data;
7. **Personal Assistant:** Which is a mobile application that resides in the user's mobile device and serves as an endpoint to the services offered by LOCAL.

The following sections describe these components in further detail.

LEARNER PROFILES

The learner profiles subsystem in LOCAL stores information about each learner, and provides this information to the other subsystems. This way, the profiles can be used to customize the user's learning process.

In the last few years, the search for standardization of learner profiles has led to several research efforts like PAPI (2012) and LIP (2012). In the scope of ubiquitous learning, profiles allow the exploration of resources based on characteristics of both the learner and the contexts in which he/she interacts. This is underlined in works such as (Barbosa et al., 2006; Nino et al., 2007).

The learner profiles in LOCAL are based on the PAPI standard. The two main reasons behind this decision were as follows:

1. **Flexibility:** The PAPI standard was designed in order to be freely extended, in the sense that its components are optional an can be redefined as needed;
2. **Modularity:** Each profile field and/or section can be handled separately, allowing

Figure 1. The LOCAL architecture

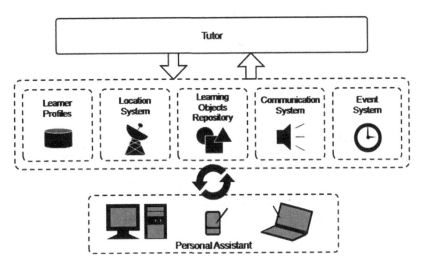

part of the profile to reside in the personal assistant, while another part is tied to each context visited by the user's device.

Each learner profile section can be further specified as either *persistent* or *contextual* (see Figure 2). The persistent data (*Contact, Preferences and Interests*) is stored in the personal assistant, and always accompanies the learner, no matter which context he/she is in. The contextual data (*Relations, Performance and Security*) is associated with the many contexts in which the learner interacts. LOCAL manages both kinds of data, seeking for pedagogical opportunities.

The *Contact* section stores basic user data, such as name, address, phone number and e-mail. The *Preferences* section helps the model to customize the user experience, storing configuration data related to the preferred media type (audio, video and/or text). Also, the learner might suffer from some kind of physical disability. In this case, according to specific disability scenarios, LOCAL can provide the same content in different formats. For example, if the learners of a particular group are following a video tutorial, a transcript would be of particular use to people who are hard of hearing.

The *Interests* section follows the knowledge areas defined in the *ACM Computing Classification System* (ACM, 2012), having a general knowledge area (for example, "Math") and a specific interest topic, in the scope of said knowledge area (for example, "Group Theory"). The specific areas are then classified according to the apprentice's own goals (for example, "to learn" or "to teach"). The *Relations* category stores data which specifies relations with other users in the same context (for example, "student", "teacher" or "researcher"). *Performance* refers to proposed goals and evaluations conducted in a context. *Security* stores credentials (names and passwords) to allow for different access levels in specific contexts.

PERSONAL ASSISTANT AND LOCATION SYSTEM

The personal assistant (PA) is a module which accompanies the learner in its mobile device. It allows users to stay connected to the system, while providing a certain degree of independence. The PA presents the following functionalities:

1. Authentication, keeping track of the learner's connection status.

Figure 2. Organization of learner profiles in LOCAL

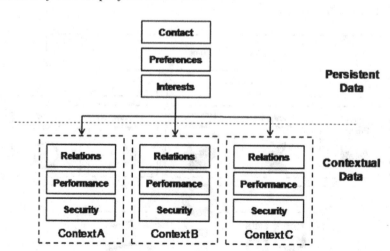

2. Access to the location system, allowing for turning it off at will.
3. Receiving and storing notifications proceeding from the communication system.

The location system used by LOCAL is based on a generic architecture, supporting different methods of determining user's physical locations (Rolim, Sonntag & Barbosa, 2008). The system ties physical location data to symbolic names (contexts). This allows real time mapping of mobile device locations. As the learner authorizes the location system in its PA, it begins to determine the device's location and physical context changes, along with the time and date of such changes. With this data, it is possible to completely track the learner's movements.

LEARNING OBJECTS

Learning objects in LOCAL are made available to learners in accordance with whatever pedagogical opportunities may appear during their interaction with the different contexts (see Figure 3). The

location system keeps the tutor aware of which context the learner is in (step 1). The tutor uses this information, as well as the learner's profile data, to select the objects meeting the learner's goals and the context (steps 2 and 3). The objects meeting these criteria are then forwarded to the learner (step 4). This adaptive process can be started by two events: (1) when the learner enters a new context or (2) insertion of new material at the object repository. The metadata specification for learning objects in LOCAL was made in accordance with the IEEE LTSC (LOM, 2012). The ample acceptance of this standard is underlined in (Rigaux & Spyratos, 2012).

TUTOR: FINDING LEARNING OPPORTUNITIES

The tutor uses profile and location data to find learning opportunities. It can act in two ways: (1) sending learning objects (described in the last section) and (2) stimulating interaction between learners. It uses learner profile data to create

Figure 3. Learning objects management in LOCAL

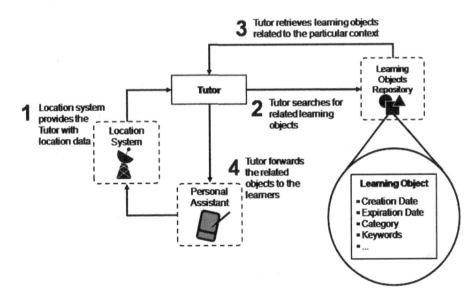

bonds between learners (see Figure 4). There are two interaction forms:

1. Similar interests: the tutor finds learners with similar interests in the same context, and stimulates interaction. This approach can be used in the creation of workgroups in a classroom, for example;

2. Complementary interests: the tutor finds learners with complementary interests. For example, a learner who wishes to learn more about a particular subject is paired along a user who wishes to teach or knows more about it. This way, the tutor can be used, for example, to create pairs of students who complement each other.

COMMUNICATION SYSTEM AND EVENTS

The communication system is used to establish contact with learners, notifying them of new pedagogical opportunities. This system can be controlled automatically, or by an operator using the administrative interface. Users are contacted by textual notifications. The notifications are sent according to profiles, objects, location and event data. The following services are supported:

1. Sending messages to a specific user in the system, wherever he/she is.
2. Sending messages to a specific context (everyone in the context receives the notification).
3. Sending messages to a user, but only if he/she is inside a particular context.
4. Sending messages to all users, regardless of context.

The messages also have an associated date of expiration, delimiting a time interval after which the message loses its validity. Figure 5 shows an example of use for the communication system where, based on the location data (1) and learner profiles (2A), the tutor contacts the learner (3). This can be used to presenting new pedagogical opportunities, for instance. The communication system also supports the creation of events. An event is characterized by a series of properties, including keywords, starting date and location. Events can be defined to a future date, in usual date format (yyyy-mm-dd hh:mm:ss) and have an arbitrary duration. When a message is associ-

Figure 4. Tutor stimulating interaction between two learners

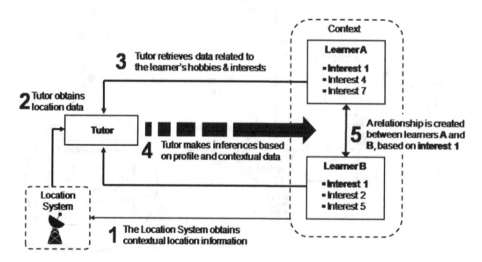

Figure 5. Communication system in LOCAL

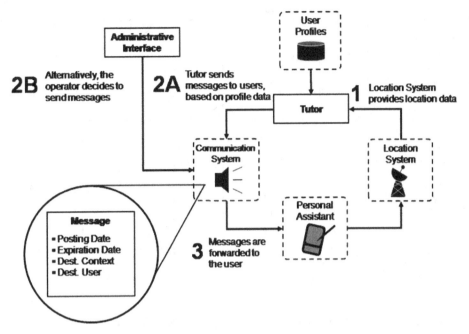

ated to an event, it is up to the tutor to find correspondences, and forward the messages at the appropriate time.

EVALUATION SCENARIO

Our first choice in order to evaluate our proposal was the creation of a small-scale ubiquitous learning scenario in UNISINOS, using LOCAL. The prototype scenario encloses nine rooms pertaining to the Computer Engineering GRefe (Barbosa et al., 2007) and the MobiLab, where LOCAL was developed (see Figure 6). This area is covered by four wireless access points. The Location System (Rolim, Sonntag & Barbosa, 2008) has two parts: (1) a Web Service created in C#, which supplies generic location data and (2) a database which stores context information. The Personal Assistant was developed in C#, using the .NET Compact Framework. The PA runs in iPAQs model hx4700 and tablet PCs model tc1100. It reads potency

information from the four wireless access points and forwards it to the Location System. LOCAL uses this information to determine the location of users' mobile devices. The profiles were implemented using MySQL. Users fill in their contact information using an online tool made in PHP and AJAX technology. This tool can be accessed both in desktops and in mobile devices. The Tutor and Communication System were conceived as modules that perform their tasks without user intervention, and as such, they were both implemented in C# as Windows Services.

FUNCTIONALITY TEST: ACCOMPANYING A LESSON

Our first experiment was a lesson involving ten learners, each carrying a mobile device. The lesson spanned two and a half hours (between 7:30 and 10:00) and involved a debate around the subject "Programming Language Paradigms". All the pro-

Figure 6. LOCAL prototype scenario

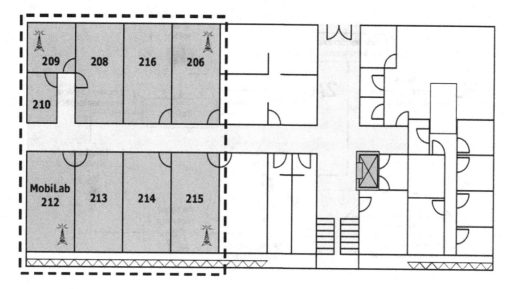

files were previously registered by the attendants (students from the Computer Engineering GRefe). Test results are organized into five moments, and documented in Table 1.

The first moment occurs before the lesson. The professor sets an appointment consisting of a message with the subject of the upcoming debate, as well as a list of online resources. This appointment spans the whole duration of the lesson. This message is tied to room 216, where the debate will occur. The second moment corresponds to the start of the lesson. Seven students enter the classroom, and are promptly detected by the location system. They receive the appointed message.

In the third moment, the professor requests the formation of groups for debating. The groups are then formed according to the similarity between user interests in "Programming Languages". In this particular case, three groups were formed: one (A) with four students interested in Java; the second (B) with two students interested in C# and another one (C) with just one student, interested in C++. The debate starts, where each group presents the pros and cons of each language. At this time, two students come late. Both receive the appointed message, and are also informed about

what group they should participate in. One enters group A, and the other one enters group C.

In the fourth moment, another late student arrives, and receives the appointed messages. However, the debate had already ended, and this student is not directed to any group. The fifth moment occurs after the ending of the lesson. The system registers student attendance via sampled location data. A student is considered present if he/she was in the classroom for at least 60% of the meeting's duration. The last student was considered absent.

The initial technological results proved that it was possible to:

1. Create groups of students via profile and physical location data.
2. Offer a predetermined list of research materials, which can be related to the topic at hand.
3. Automatically handle student attendances in the classroom, based on location data.

Table 1. Accompanying a lesson

Step	Initial Time	Final Time	Actor	Action
1	-	07:00	Professor	Inserts an appointment to be sent between 7:30 and 10:00, to all users in room 216. This appointment accompanies a list of online resources related to the subject to be debated.
2	07:30	07:30	Learners	7 users enter the room (authentication).
	07:30	07:30	LOCAL	Begins tracking user location.
	07:30	07:30	LOCAL	Message system sends the previously appointed message to all users in room 216.
3	08:00	08:10	Professor	Solicits the creation of groups for the debate.
	08:10	08:10	LOCAL	Sends messages, creates groups: A (4 users, Java), B (2 users, C#) and C (1 user, C++).
	08:10	08:30	Learners	The debate starts.
	08:30	08:30	Learners	2 users enter the room (authentication).
	08:30	08:30	LOCAL	Begins tracking location for the 2 last users. Sends appointed message to these 2 users. Informs where they should participate.
	08:30	09:00	Learners	The debate comes to a conclusion.
4	09:00	09:00	Learner	The last user arrives (authentication).
	09:00	09:00	LOCAL	Begins tracking location for the last user. Message system sends previously appointed message to this user.
	09:00	10:00	Professor, Learners	The participants keep exchanging ideas about the debate that was just held.
5	10:00	-	LOCAL	As the location for each participant is evaluated, attendances are registered.

USABILITY TEST: SURVEY

In order to further validate our approach to ubiquitous learning, another experiment was conducted. This new experiment involved a sample consisting of 20 individuals, between teachers and students of the Computer Engineering GRefe. The test was realized into five moments: each moment, a set of four individuals interacted with LOCAL. The following steps were considered:

1. Each participant was given an HP iPAQ hx4700 mobile device, which they used to authenticate into LOCAL.
2. The participants then received suggestions to participate in one of two workshops (based on each learner's profile).
3. The participants were notified whenever a professor they wanted to chat with was available.
4. In the fourth step, LOCAL searched for matches between the subjects' profiles, suggesting learning resources related to their interests.
5. The users were instructed to go to the workshop rooms. LOCAL then made available on the iPAQs the program of the chosen event (per user).

After following these steps, the users were asked to answer a survey that presented questions related to their experience using LOCAL. The questions were roughly based on the concepts proposed by the Technology Acceptance Model created by Davis (1989) and expanded by Yoon and Kim (2007) in a study focused on the acceptance of wireless networks. The TAM considers both perceived usefulness and perceived ease of use as the main influences for the acceptance of a new technology (in the sense of reducing the effort for completion of certain tasks and improving the user's performance). In other words, it models how users come to accept and use a given technology.

In this sense, two groups of statements were defined. The first group related mostly to the aspects of usability, aiming to gauge the overall usefulness of contextual information (as perceived by the students). The second group tried to capture the impressions of the students in relation to the possibility of applying a similar system to the one tested here in a standard classroom setting. Subjects were asked to rate how strongly they agreed or disagreed with a series of statements (shown in Table 2). This evaluation was based on the Likert scale (Likert, 1932), commonly used to gauge the subjects' level of agreement to a certain statement. The scale consists of five points, comprising values between 1 (strongly disagree) and 5 (strongly agree). An answer with the value 3 (indifferent) meant that the user had no particular opinion about that feature. The test subjects could also add comments to their survey

answers, which were used to complement the experiment evaluation.

The relation of statements presented to the test subjects can be seen in Table 2. Several considerations can be made by analyzing these statements.

Figure 7 presents the combined scores obtained in statements 1 through 7, as answered by 20 test subjects. As can be seen, results indicate good acceptance in relation to contextual information, as well as interaction between users and contextual elements. By analyzing these scores we can see how the aspect of usefulness was evaluated by the subjects. There was special interest into the adequate presentation of contextual information, and how the users relate and make use of it. The presence of a location system used to track user location allowed the creation of contextualized services, which were evaluated mostly as positive by the subjects.

The aspects related to the ease of use, focusing on the proposed daily use of the system as learning tool in the classroom, were analyzed through statements 8 to 10. These relate mostly to the usability of the system by the students in a classroom setting. The results in Figure 8 indicate a

Table 2. Statements shown to individuals in the usability test

No.	Statement
1	The notifications you received about the availability of professors could have helped you get answers to your questions quicker.
2	The notifications about events, based on location and your profile data helped you get information relevant to you interests.
3	The notification about the availability of related physical resources in your context made easier the task of finding those same resources.
4	The information you received about users like you, at your location, helped to establish contact.
5	The presentation of content related to events at your location usually brought out items relevant to your interests, improving the experience.
6	The context aware features present in this system make it into a useful learning tool.
7	The system was capable of determining your position with precision.
8	The system improved your interaction with other users in the same location by helping you identify other people like you.
9	This system could be easily used to improve your daily academic activities.
10	This system would be transparently useful in a standard classroom setting.

Figure 7. Contextual information (statements 1 to 7)

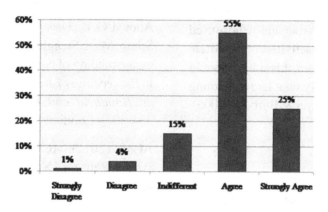

good acceptance by the test subjects. This is a good indication that this system is well fit for daily usage. It should be noted that, in this survey, adaptability aspects were not given a proper analysis. These aspects could be better analyzed if the test involved a heterogeneous sample of mobile devices (desktop PCs, tablet PCs and iPAQs).

FUTURE RESEARCH DIRECTIONS

The prototype and initial results attest the usefulness and viability of our approach, showing that LOCAL could be used in real environments. However, it could use a number of improvements:

1. The pedagogical inferences made by the tutor, as well as the prediction accuracy of the learning objects manager, could be improved.
2. A future expansion of the learner profile system would support a more extensive handling of learner information, enabling us to better match the system to each user's personality and learning style.
3. New tests should be conducted to evaluate our approach using it as a learning tool in a whole, long-term course.

A special point of interest is that this work does not analyze the ethical issues of constantly knowing the user's location. We believe this

Figure 8. Daily usage (statements 8 to 10)

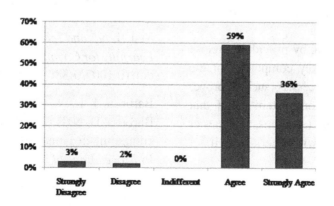

does not constitute a point of special concern, as LOCAL is deployed in a small-scale learning environment and any regions outside of those used specifically in the learning activities of the GRefe aren't mapped at all. That said, this subject should be considered when specifying a larger learning environment (Barbosa, Geyer & Barbosa, 2005).

CONCLUSION

In the field of education, ubiquitous computing has been proving itself as a useful tool, facilitating the interaction between learners and computer systems' infrastructures. This is done through the mapping of the learners' location and user profiles. In this chapter, we tried to show just that, and how ubiquitous computing technologies can be useful in this new scenario. The following general conclusions can be underlined:

1. The use of location technology allows mobile devices to take the learner's location into account in the learning process.
2. User profiles allow the delivery of personalized pedagogical resources. These two points allow the model to offer a customized learning process.

As for LOCAL itself, we saw the following:

1. LOCAL contains the basic modules to support small-scale context-aware learning, empowering learners in a collaborative learning environment.
2. The location system, by providing precise location data, is a key component of the contextualization process. As such, improvements to the location system mean that LOCAL as a whole (and thus, the learner experience as well) will benefit from it.

REFERENCES

Abowd, G. D., Dey, A. K., Brown, P. J., Davies, N., Smith, M., & Steggles, P. (1999). Towards a better understanding of context and context-awareness. In *Proceedings of the 1st International Symposium on Handheld and Ubiquitous Computing* (pp. 304-307). London: Springer-Verlag.

ACM. (2012). *ACM computing classification system*. Retrieved November 5, 2012, from http://www.acm.org/class/1998

Augustin, I., Yamin, A., Barbosa, J. L., Silva, L. C., Real, R. A., & Geyer, C. F. R. (2004). ISAM, join context-awareness and mobility to building pervasive applications. In I. Mahgoub, & M. Ylias (Eds.), *Mobile Computing Handbook* (pp. 73–94). New York: CRC Press. doi:10.1201/9780203504086.ch4.

Baldauf, M., Dustdar, S., & Rosenberg, F. (2007). A survey on context-aware systems. *International Journal of Ad Hoc and Ubiquitous Computing*, 2(4), 263–277. doi:10.1504/IJA-HUC.2007.014070.

Barbosa, D. N. F., Augustin, I., Barbosa, J. L. V., Yamin, A. C., Silva, L. C., & Geyer, C. F. R. (2006). Learning in a large-scale pervasive environment. In *Proceedings of the 2nd IEEE International Workshop on Pervasive Computing (PerEl)* (pp. 226-230). New York: IEEE Press.

Barbosa, D. N. F., Geyer, C. F. R., & Barbosa, J. L. V. (2005). GlobalEdu - An architecture to support learning in a pervasive computing environment. *New Trends and Technologies in Computer-Aided Learning for Computer-Aided Design, 192*, 1–10. doi:10.1007/0-387-30761-3_1.

Barbosa, J. L. V., Hahn, R., Rabello, S. A., & Barbosa, D. N. F. (2007). Mobile and ubiquitous computing in a innovative undergraduate course. In *Proceedings of the 38th ACM Technical Symposium on Computer Science Education* (pp. 379-383). New York: ACM Press.

Davis, F. D. (1989). Perceived usefulness, perceived ease of use, and user acceptance of information technology. *Management Information Systems Quarterly, 13*(3), 319–340. doi:10.2307/249008.

Dey, A., Hightower, J., Lara, E., & Davies, N. (2010). Location-based services. *IEEE Pervasive Computing / IEEE Computer Society [and] IEEE Communications Society, 9*(1), 11–12. doi:10.1109/MPRV.2010.10.

Diaz, A., Merino, P., & Rivas, F. J. (2009). Mobile application profiling for connected mobile devices. *IEEE Pervasive Computing / IEEE Computer Society [and] IEEE Communications Society, 9*(1), 54–61. doi:10.1109/MPRV.2009.63.

Hightower, J., & Borriello, G. (2001). Location systems for ubiquitous computing. *Computer, 34*(8), 57–66. doi:10.1109/2.940014.

Hightower, J. L., LaMarca, A. J., & Smith, I. E. (2006). Practical lessons from place lab. *IEEE Pervasive Computing / IEEE Computer Society [and] IEEE Communications Society, 5*(3), 32–39. doi:10.1109/MPRV.2006.55.

Hoareau, C., & Satoh, I. (2009). Modeling and processing information for context-aware computing: A survey. *New Generation Computing, 27*(3), 177–196. doi:10.1007/s00354-009-0060-5.

Likert, R. (1932). A technique for the measurement of attitudes. *Archives de Psychologie, 22*(140), 1–55.

LIP. (2012). *IMS learner information package especification*. Retrieved November 10, 2012, from http://www.imsglobal.org/profiles/index.html

LOM. (2012). *IEEE/LTSC/LOM. learning object metadata (LOM) working group 12*. Retrieved November 10, 2012, from http://www.ieeeltsc.org:8080/Plone/working-group/learning-object-metadata-working-group-12/learning-object-metadata-lom-working-group-12

Nino, C. P., Marques, J., Barbosa, D. N. F., Geyer, C. F. R., Barbosa, J. L. V., & Augustin, I. (2007). Context-aware model in an ubiquitous learning environment. In *Proceedings of the 3rd International Workshop on Pervasive Learning (PerEL)* (pp. 182-186). New York: IEEE Press.

Ogata, H., & Yano, Y. (2009). Supporting awareness in ubiquitous learning. *International Journal of Mobile and Blended Learning, 1*(4), 1–11. doi:10.4018/jmbl.2009090801.

PAPI. (2012). *IEEE LTSC 1484.2 - Draft standard for learning technology - Public and private information (PAPI) for learners (PAPI learner)*. Retrieved November 10, 2012, from http://www.cen-ltso.net/Main.aspx?put=230

Rigaux, P., & Spyratos, N. (2012). *SeLeNe report: Metadata management and learning object composition in a self elearning network*. Retrieved November 10, 2012, from http://www.dcs.bbk.ac.uk/selene/reports/seleneLRI3.pdf

Rogers, Y., Price, S., Randell, C., Fraser, D. S., Weal, M., & Fitzpatrick, G. (2005). Ubi-learning integrates indoor and outdoor experiences. *Communications of the ACM, 48*(1), 55–59. doi:10.1145/1039539.1039570.

Rolim, C. R., Sonntag, N. B., & Barbosa, J. L. V. (2008). A model for the development of location-aware applications. In *Proceedings of the Brazilian Workshop on High Performance Computational Systems (WSCAD)* (pp. 227-234). Porto Alegre: SBC.

Satyanarayanan, M. (1996). Fundamental challenges in mobile computing. In *Proceedings of the ACM Symposium on Principles of Distributed Computing* (pp. 1-7). Philadelphia, PA: New York: ACM.

Satyanarayanan, M. (2001). Pervasive computing: Vision and challenges. *IEE Personal Communications, 8*, 10–17. doi:10.1109/98.943998.

Satyanarayanan, M., Bahl, P., Cáceres, R., & Davies, N. (2009). The case for VM-based cloudlets in mobile computing. *IEEE Pervasive Computing / IEEE Computer Society [and] IEEE Communications Society*, *8*(4), 14–23. doi:10.1109/MPRV.2009.82.

Simon, B., Miklós, Z., Nejdl, W., & Sintek, M. (2002). Elena: A mediation infrastructure for educational services. In *Proceedings of the WWW Conference*. Budapest, Hungary: IEEE.

Vaughan-Nichols, S. J. (2009). Will mobile computing's future be location, location, location? *Computer*, *42*(2), 14–17. doi:10.1109/MC.2009.65.

Weiser, M. (1991). The computer for the 21st century. *Scientific American*, *265*(3), 94–104. doi:10.1038/scientificamerican0991-94 PMID:1675486.

Yau, S. S., Gupta, E. K. S., & Karim, F. Ahamed, S. I., Wang, Y., & Wang, B. (2003). Smart classroom: Enhancing collaborative learning using pervasive computing technology. In *Proceedings of the II American Society of Engineering Education (ASEE)* (pp. 13633-13642). ASEE.

Yoon, C., & Kim, S. (2007). Convenience and TAM in a ubiquitous computing environment: The case of wireless LAN. *Electronic Commerce Research and Applications*, *6*(1), 102–112. doi:10.1016/j.elerap.2006.06.009.

ADDITIONAL READING

Abowd, G., Mynatt, E., & Rodden, T. (2002). The human experience. *IEEE Pervasive Computing / IEEE Computer Society [and] IEEE Communications Society*, *1*(1), 48–57. doi:10.1109/MPRV.2002.993144.

Abowd, G. D., & Mynatt, E. D. (2000). Charting past, present, and future research in ubiquitous computing. *ACM Transactions on Computer-Human Interaction*, *7*(1), 29–58. doi:10.1145/344949.344988.

Canny, J. (2006). The future of human-computer interaction. *ACM Queue; Tomorrow's Computing Today*, *4*(6), 24–32. doi:10.1145/1147518.1147530.

Dey, A. (2001). Understanding and using context. *Personal and Ubiquitous Computing*, *6*(1), 4–7. doi:10.1007/s007790170019.

Henricksen, K., & Induslka, J. (2006). Developing context-aware pervasive computing applications: Models and approach. *Pervasive and Mobile Computing*, *2*(2), 37–64. doi:10.1016/j.pmcj.2005.07.003.

Jeyaraj, A., Rottman, J. W., & Lacity, M. C. (2006). A review of the predictors, linkages, and biases in IT innovation adoption research. *Journal of Information Technology*, *21*, 1–23. doi:10.1057/palgrave.jit.2000056.

Kukulska-Hulme, A., Sharples, M., Milrad, M., & Sánchez, I. A. (2009). Innovation in mobile learning: A European perspective. *International Journal of Mobile and Blended Learning*, *1*(1), 13–35. doi:10.4018/jmbl.2009010102.

Lewis, M., Nino, C., Rosa, J. H., Barbosa, J. L., & Barbosa, D. N. (2010). A management model of learning objects in a ubiquitous learning environment. In *Proceedings of the IEEE International Workshop on Pervasive Learning (PerEL 2010)* (pp. 256-261). Mannheim, Germany: IEEE.

Lyytinen, K., & Yoo, Y. (2002). Research commentary: The next wave of nomadic computing. *Information Systems Research*, *13*(4), 377–388. doi:10.1287/isre.13.4.377.75.

Lyytinen, K., & Yoo, Y. (2002). Issues and challenges in ubiquitous computing - Introduction. *Communications of the ACM, 45*(12), 62–65. doi: doi:10.1145/585597.585616.

Maturana, H. (2000). *Cognition, science and daily life*. Belo Horizonte: UFMG.

Ogata, H., Yin, C., El-Bishouty, M., & Yano, Y. (2010). Computer supported ubiquitous learning environment for vocabulary learning using RFID tags. *International Journal of Learning Technology, 5*(1), 5–24. doi:10.1504/IJLT.2010.031613.

Piaget, J. (1971). *Biology and knowledge: An essay on the relations between organic regulations and cognitive processes*. Chicago: The University of Chicago.

Piaget, J. (1995). *Sociological studies*. London: Routledge.

Saccol, A., & Reinhard, N. (2006). The hospitality metaphor as a theoretical lens to understand the process of ICT adoption. *Journal of Information Technology, 21*(3), 154–164. doi:10.1057/palgrave.jit.2000067.

Saccol, A. Z., Kich, M., Schlemmer, E., Reinhard, N., Barbosa, J., & Hahn, R. (2009). A framework for design of ubiquitous learning applications. In *Proceedings of the 42nd Annual Hawaii International Conference on Systems Sciences* (pp. 1-10). New York: IEEE Press.

Saha, D., & Mukherjee, A. (2003). Pervasive computing: a paradigm for the 21st century. *IEEE Computer, 36*(3), 25–31. doi:10.1109/MC.2003.1185214.

Sánchez, I. A., Sharples, M., Milrad, M., & Vavoula, G. (2009). Mobile learning: Small devices, big issues. In N. Balacheff, S. Ludvigsen, T. Jong, A. Lazonder, & S. Barnes (Eds.), *Technology-Enhanced Learning: Principles and Products* (pp. 233–251). Berlin: Springer-Verlag.

Schmidt, A. (2005). Potentials and challenges of context-awareness for learning solutions. In *Proceedings of the 13th Annual Workshop of the SIG Adaptivity and User Modeling in Interactive Systems* (pp. 63-68). Saarbrücken, Austria: ACM.

Sharples, M. (2000). The design of personal mobile Technologies for lifelong learning. *Computers & Education, 34*(3-4), 177–193. doi:10.1016/S0360-1315(99)00044-5.

Sherry, J., & Salvador, T. (2001). Running and grimacing: the struggle for balance in mobile work. In B. Brown, N. Green, & R. Harper (Eds.), *Wireless World: Social and Interactional Aspects of the Mobile Age* (pp. 108–120). Berlin: Springer-Verlag.

Tatar, D. E. (2003). Handhelds go to school: Lessons learned. *SRI International Journal Computer, 36*(9), 30–37.

Traxler, J. (2009). The evolution of mobile learning. In R. Guy (Ed.), *The Evolution of Mobile Teaching and Learning* (pp. 103–118). Santa Rosa: Informing Science Press.

Weiser, M. (1993). Some computer science issues in ubiquitous computing. *Communications of the ACM, 36*(7), 75–84. doi:10.1145/159544.159617.

Weiser, M. (1994). The world is not a desktop. *Interactions (New York, N.Y.), 1*(1), 7–8. doi:10.1145/174800.174801.

Yang, S. (2006). Context aware ubiquitous learning environments for peer-to-peer collaborative learning. *Journal of Educational Technology & Society, 9*(1), 188–201.

Yin, C., Ogata, H., Tabata, Y., & Yano, Y. (2010). Supporting the acquisition of Japanese polite expressions in context-aware ubiquitous learning. *International Journal of Mobile Learning and Organisation, 4*(2), 214–234. doi:10.1504/IJMLO.2010.032637.

Yin, C., Ogata, H., & Yano, Y. (2004). JAPELAS: Supporting Japanese polite expressions learning using PDA towards ubiquitous learning. *Journal of Information Systems Education, 3*(1), 33–39.

KEY TERMS AND DEFINITIONS

Learning Objects Repository: Repository used to store content related to the teaching process.

Learning Programs: A new kind of academic structure oriented to stimulate the integration between thematic course areas.

Learning Projects: A long duration activities used to amalgamate the knowledge created in the different thematic areas.

LOCAL: A mobile and ubiquitous learning model powered by mobile computing and location technology, capable of customizing learning and teaching processes by employing contextual information obtained from the environment.

Personal Assistant: Mobile application that resides in the user's mobile device and serves as an endpoint to the services offered by LOCAL.

Tutor: Analysis engine capable of making user-centric inferences by using the information available in the learner's profiles, as well as location system data.

Ubiquitous Computing: Mark Weiser described computer ubiquity as the idea of integrating computers seamlessly, invisibly enhancing the real word. Ubiquitous Computing is an emergent computing paradigm where the user's applications are available in a suitable adapted form, wherever they go and however they move.

Undergraduate Course of Reference: A new pedagogical approach to undergraduate courses based on Learning Programs and Learning Projects.

Ubiquitous Learning: Learning supported by the use of mobile and wireless communication technologies, sensors and location/tracking mechanisms, that work together to integrate students with their environment.

Chapter 5
Building Mobile Social Presence for U–Learning

Chih-Hsiung Tu
Northern Arizona University, USA

Marina McIsaac
Arizona State University, USA

Laura Sujo-Montes
Northern Arizona University, USA

Shadow Armfield
Northern Arizona University, USA

ABSTRACT

Mobile learning environments are human networks that afford learners the opportunity to participate in creative endeavors, social networking, organize and reorganize social contents, learner-created cognitive space, and manage social acts anytime and anywhere through mobile technologies. Social interaction with mobile technology is very different from Computer-Mediated Communication (CMC) or Web 2.0 networking technologies. Effective mobile interaction focuses on social-context awareness by integrating location-based technology, which is unique to mobile technology, not easily found in other types of commuting. This chapter proposes a model for mobile social presence consisting of four dimensions: enriching social context-awareness, managing location-based communication, personalizing multi-layered interactivity, and optimizing digital and social identities. Under each dimension there are a few suggested strategies or tips to assist educators in integrating them into their mobile instructions to enhance the mobile-social presence of learners.

DOI: 10.4018/978-1-4666-4542-4.ch005

INTRODUCTION

Mobile learning environments are human networks that afford learners the opportunity to participate in creative endeavors, social networking, organize and reorganize social contents, learner-created cognitive space (Cornelius & Marston, 2009), and manage social acts at anytime and anywhere through mobile technologies. Social acts that elicit identities, develop awareness (Kekwaletswe, 2007), cement relationships, ensure connections, and promote interactions between and among learners are necessary for interactive learning.

Rather than seeing students' mobile devices as a distracting technology, perhaps teachers can transform mobile devices into learning devices and learning tools. Since we may not have resources to provide each student with a computer. Even if we could, computers are not personalized enough, and are not context specific enough, and are not easily mobilized to enhance learning in disruptive and innovative ways, when compared too mobile technology.

Social interaction with mobile technology is very different from Computer Mediated Communication (CMC) or Web 2.0 networking technologies. Researchers (Koole et al., 2010) are aware of mobile technology and that through human interaction on mobile technology both the user and the technology are shaping each other. Mobile technology connects learners virtually anytime and anywhere while mobile learners utilize it in fairly non-traditional ways to interact with each other (Kukulska-Hulme & Traxler, 2007), such as location-based technology and Augmented Reality (AR) etc. Research has shown that mobile technology has impacted human social relationships (Jones & Issroff, 2007) and interaction both positively and negatively (Rau et al., 2008). Mobile learning is more than just integrating mobile devices and mobile technologies. Mobile learning from an instruction aspect should be integrated from four dimensions: Technology mobile, Learners mobile, Teachers mobile and Instructions mobile.

Mobile social interaction should not just integrate mobile technologies to replicate digital social interaction on computers. Effective mobile interaction is more than a replication of desktop and laptop computing. Effective mobile interaction focuses on social-context awareness by integrating location-based technology, which is unique to mobile technology, not easily found in other types of commuting. With the features of location-based technology or Global Position System (GPS), mobile learners are able to obtain and to enrich their learning context. For example, with these technologies, learners can access online information specifically related to their current location with mobile devices; learners can access their social network friends who are nearby to collaborate their learning tasks; or learners can record the data, such as photos, audio, video, environmental data etc., with embedded geo-location data layer as their learning content and resources. Effective mobile learning design is able to fulfill learning in a more ubiquitous manner, with richer social awareness that is more personalized, and with more meaningful contexts.

MOBILE SOCIAL PRESENCE

Online social presence could be a critical factor to the understanding of social interaction in mobile learning environments. Although Shin & Lowes (2007) preliminarily concluded that active network users did not demonstrate higher social presence in online discussion. Boulos, & Wheelert (2007) & Dunlap & Lowenthal (2009) argued that social network technologies would positively relate to online immediacy and presence. Online social presence should not be overlooked when one ponders integrating mobile learning environments to improve socio-cultural learning.

Online social presence is the degree of feeling, perception, and reaction of being connected by computer-mediated communication (CMC) to another intellectual entity through electronic media (Tu & McIsaac, 2002) and is explained from four dimensions, social context, online community, interactivity, and privacy. Network social presence (Tu, Yen, Blocher, & Chan, 2012) is defined as the degree that network participants engage in creating, maintaining, sharing, connecting social content, digital and social identities, network linkages, and collaborative community.

Mobile social presence is different from online social presence and network social presence in the aspects of control, context-awareness, multi-layers, and location-free digital interactions (Tu, McIsaac, Sujo-Montes, & Armfield, 2012). Mobile social presence is defined as the degree of enriching social context-awareness, managing location-based communication, personalizing multi-layered interactivity, and optimizing digital and social identities to other intellectual beings through mobile technologies (See Figure 1). Mobile technology affords wider and more diversified social interactions and empowers learners to take detailed control of their mobile social presence. Learners are connected constantly and allowed to decide how, when and in what way that they

Figure 1. Online social presence, network social presence and mobile social presence

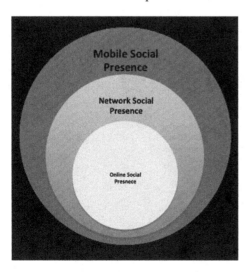

prefer to interact with others; therefore, mobile technology has a greater potential to empower learners to generate higher level of social presence compared to online or network social presences. In fact, from a context-awareness aspect, online social presence and network social presence are more difficult to project when compared to mobile social presence. Learners can interact with others on mobile technology to generate mobile social presence in museums, fields, parks, outdoors, and anywhere away from their desktop or laptop computers. Additionally, mobile social presence generates context richer type of interaction and communication. Like online and network social presence, mobile social presence does not occur without strategic planning and designs. Simply providing learners with mobile devices does not result in an ideal level of mobile social presence. In fact, inadequate integration of mobile technology for learning may result in low and negative interaction and generate low mobile social presence.

How mobile social presence is related to physical social presence? Physical social presence has always been considered paramount; therefore, in the past, educators replicated physical social presence by enhancing virtual social presences such as online and network social presences. Physical and virtual social presences become two separately distinguished entities. In other words, virtual social presences are always the second best to physical ones. With mobile technology's distinguished features, mobile social presence might be a true entity to espouse and to fuse physical and virtual social presences or even encompass both. Mobile social presence truly advances and extends human's physical presence because multiple context-awareness, location-based communication, multi-layered interactivity, and dynamic digital social identities cannot be achieved by physical social presence (Tu, McIsaac, Sujo-Montes, & Armfield, 2012). It should be denoted that mobile social presence is not necessarily higher than physical, online, or network social presences; however, it holds great capacities and capabilities to empower mobile learners.

In early integration with mobile technologies, it is not uncommon that educators used mobile technologies to replicate physical, online, or network social interaction to enhance mobile social presences. Educators should focus on innovative and evolutional instructional strategies by advancing and expanding human capabilities for interactive learning rather than focusing on mobile technologies and devices. Effective mobile learning does not come by default when using mobile technology.

Effective personal control and management is essential; otherwise, it may produce negative results. It is not just the matter of which mobile technologies we have; it is about how we use them innovatively. Innovative mobile interaction does not exclude how learners have been inter-

acting with others. In fact, it is the innovative mobile social interaction that derives from and aggregates multiple dimensions and layers of social interactions to empower human learning. In other words, mobile interaction can be scaled from FTF communication, to email, to creating learning resources, and to multi-dimensional and layered communication.

A MODEL FOR MOBILE SOCIAL PRESENCE

A Model for building mobile social presence (Figure 2) is proposed to assist educators to design effective mobile learning strategies to enhance mobile social presence of learners and instructors. The model consists of four dimensions: Enriching social context-awareness; Managing

Figure 2. Model for building mobile social presence

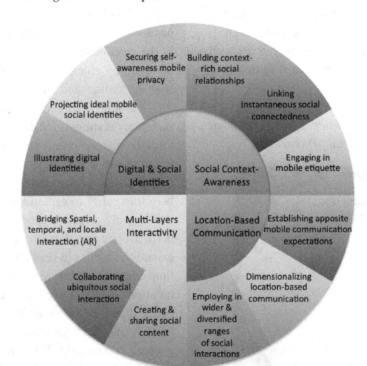

location-based communication; Personalizing multi-layered interactivity; and Optimizing digital and social identities. Under each dimensions, there are a few suggested strategies that will assist educators to integrate them into their instructions to enhance mobile social presence of learners.

ENRICHING SOCIAL CONTEXT-AWARENESS

Building Context-Rich Social Relationships

Mobile social interaction is no longer limited to a location where the computers or laptop computers are located. Constant monitoring of social interaction on mobile devices will increase the levels of awareness and connectedness in social relationships. Mobile learners can decide when, where, and how to interact with others to build context-rich social relationships. Therefore, the communication is more relevant, or context-specific. The mobile communicators can select a wider range of communication types, from e-mail, real-time chat, conferencing systems, to mobile phone calls and SMS. The communication formats are not limited to CMC anymore. The mobile communicators can apply a variety of formats, such as "Like," "tweet," updating their status, updating their digital profile, sharing any content to build context-rich social relationships from one-to-one, one-to-many, to many-to-many interactions. Formats of social interaction can range from as short as one word "Like" to video conferencing. The immediacy can range from instantaneous to asynchronous interaction. A competent mobile communicator should be able to maneuver different mobile devices, mobile communication tools, and mobile interaction formats to build and to enrich social interaction rather than using mobile devices simply for phone calls or to replicate CMC interactions.

Recommended strategies:

- **Use mobile phones for short and immediate communications:** Use mobile tablets to create and to share content and for tasks with more productivity; or use different mobile devices for personally preferred communication tasks to build social relationships.
- **Use different communication tools for different tasks and contexts:** For example use mobile phone call for more immediate or urgent communication; use SMS for short, immediate that allows others to decide when and how to interact; while using e-mail, or conferencing tools for more extensive communications to build social relationships.
- **Select relevant and appropriate communication formats to enrich social interaction:** Such as using Facebook's "Like" or Google Plus' "+"for immediate and simple social interactions for many-to-many interaction; using tweets or updating social status in Facebook or Google Plus to engage in One-to-Many interaction; or using CMC for more traditional social interaction.

Linking Instantaneous Social Connectedness

Using mobile devices for communication doesn't mean that mobile learners should interact constantly. Mobile learners could use mobile devices to "stay on the alert" and "to monitor communication interaction" to increase social connectedness and social awareness, although it is not considered to be as high as level of mobile social presence. However, it empowers mobile learners with flexibility to control their mobile communications rather than being obligated to communicate. Better social connection and social awareness in communication unfolds the perception behind "stay on the alert." It enriches social context when ready to interact, they can have interactions with others via mobile devices. Mobile learners are empowered to manage and to control their interactivity based on their circumstance. Unlike CMC, learners may feel obligated to interact because they have made an extra effort to access desktop or laptop computers and, therefore, feel obligated to interact. Otherwise, they may not have a chance to do so.

Recommended strategies:

- **Based on personal preferences:** Monitor various communication tools on mobile devices, such as phone calls, SMS, E-Mails, social media postings etc.
- **Select context relevant communication format tools to interact:** It is not necessary to apply SMS to interact with SMS communication or to use e-mail to reply e-mail communication. Based on the personal context, one may share e-mail communication on social media, such as Twitter, Facebook, or Google Plus, or use a mobile phone to respond to a SMS communication if necessary for immediate communication.
- **Select a relevant communication format to interact:** Such as using one-to-one e-mail for more personal and extensive communication or retweet any relevant tweets to engage in many-to-many interaction.

Engaging in Mobile Etiquette

Using mobile communication etiquette is critical. Mobile etiquette is more than just virtual and digital communication etiquette since mobile technologies fuse FTF and digital communications. Both physical and virual social relationships are impacted rather than just virtual interaction. Mobile social relationships could be engaging when correct expectations and effective control are exercised in mobile communication. When these devices are not utilized appropriately negative impacts and withdrawing effects could be created. For example, using mobile technology at FTF

meetings could create the feeling by others that the mobile device user is withdrawing because people check and use their mobile technologies frequently during the meetings. This is called "cellular phone prayers" (Tu et al., 2012) because the users constantly look down and work on their mobile devices, creating a feeling of disrespect to other meeting attendees.

Recommended strategies:

- Establish appropriate mobile communication etiquette for both physical and virtual communication.
- Use mobile devices respectfully in the public settings, such as in public location, FTF meetings by honoring the existence of others and not disturbing the physical communication.
- Apply silent or not to disturb modes on mobile devices during FTF communication for any incoming communications and notification on mobile devices to avoid creating a disturbance or embarrassment.

MANAGING LOCATION-BASED COMMUNICATION

Establishing Appropriate Mobile Communication Expectations

Managing mobile communication is based on more than personal preferences. It is critical to communicate and to understand others' communication preferences and expectations. Mobile communicators may use the same mobile communication tools and formats; however, because they have different perceptions for what purposes these communication tools should be used. Knowing the expectations of other mobile users' communication perceptions and preferences is critical.

Recommended strategies:

- Discuss the mobile communication preferences with the persons you intend to communicate and obtain their permission.
- Establish a time line for responding to mobile communication. Although many have mobile devices with them at all times, it is inappropriate to expect others to respond the mobile communications immediately. For example, 24 hours response time during the weekdays, and 1-2 days for the weekends.
- Establish common communication perceptions and protocols with others or group collaborators. It is necessary that collaborators discuss their mobile communication methods. For example: using phone calls for emergency communication, using SMS for urgent communication, using Twitter for reflection sharing, using e-mail for more comprehensive purposes, while using conferencing system for real-time discussions.

Dimensionalizing Location-Based Communication

Location-based technology or geo-location technology enables the enrichment of social interaction (Fitzgerald, 2012) by adding the physical location information to existing personal preferences, digital identities, digital networks, digital collaborations, and interactions. In other words, mobile social interaction is no longer exists in a single dimension. Integrating location-based technology into existing mobile social interaction could lead to innovative location-based learning. For example, in a museum, mobile learners are able to access information about exhibitions and artwork with visual and social information from the museum visitors information sources to enhance social navigation and learning at the museum (Charitonos, Blake, Scanlon, & Jones, 2012).

Recommended strategies:

- Evaluate the availability of location-based technology on mobile communication applications, such as "Check In" feature.
- Integrate location-based technology on mobile communication applications to enhance mobile collaborations by encouraging mobile users to apply the "Check In" feature to support their mobile communication, such as Facebook, Twitter, Google Plus, or FourSquare.
- Evaluate the availability of location-based technology at public locations, such as museums, parks, schools, transportation stations, to access additional information and resources.

Employing Wider and More Diversified Ranges of Social Interactions

Types of interactivity for mobile and network social presences are more diverse than online social presence. Mobile communications can apply diversified tools to communicate, such multimedia channels, voice recognition features, and social networking interaction to communicate and to interact with others.

Recommended strategies:

- **Use Multimedia Communication Channels:** Use different communication channels, such as phone calls, SMS, E-Mail, conference call, audio recording, still camera, video camera to engage in mobile social interaction.
- **Employ Voice Recognition Communication Tools:** Many mobile devices are equipped with voice recognition features to empower users to speak to text or speak to operate mobile devices.
- **Exploit Social Network Communication Channels:** Encourage mobile users to exploit social network sites' "Like" others'

postings, post blog entries, tweet/retweet, create, share multimedia communication content.

PERSONALIZING MULTI-LAYERS INTERACTIVITY

Creating and Sharing Social Content

Creating and sharing content on mobile devices in addition to text-based communication can enhance mobile social presence. In fact, with audio, and video recording features on mobile devices, mobile users can create and share their multimedia content more efficiently than with computers. Once multimedia content has been created, they can be shared by posting to e-mail, SMS, blogs, Facebook and Twitter. Mobile learners can apply multimedia-editing applications to touch and edit photos, audios, and videos. Additionally, the created and shared content can be tagged as an additional layer of information and activity to the communication.

Recommended strategies:

- **Capture Still Photos:** Apply still cameras on mobile devices to snap critical images and share them on communication tools and social network sites. If available, location-based technology can be added to the photos.
- **Record Audio Sound:** Apply audio recording tools on mobile devices to record any sound, soundtracks, or voices and share them through different tools.
- **Catch Video Footages:** Recording video footage to capture critical moments and share them through different tools.

Collaborating Ubiquitous Social Interaction

Creating mobile content can be advanced to the mobile collaboration level to reach ubiquitous interaction. Multiple layers of interactivity can be implemented from either a personal level or a collaborative level. For example, collaborators can utilize musical production applications, such as Garage Band, or presentation application, such as Google Docs, or Prezi, to create presentation content collaboratively for the class presentation.

Recommended strategies:

- **Evaluate the Availability of Collaborative Features on Mobile Applications:** While selecting mobile applications, examine what collaborative features are available and how they support mobile collaboration.
- **Apply Mobile Collaboration to Create Learning Content:** Mobile collaboration can be implemented to enhance face-to-face collaboration. Mobile collaboration can be achieved through prior in-person meetings; therefore, the in-person meetings become more meaningful and can be used to focus on something they couldn't accomplish through mobile technology.
- Share mobile collaborative learning content in conjunction with other mobile networking features, such as location-based technology and social tagging.

Bridging Spatial, Temporal, and Locale Interaction (Augmented Reality)

Augmented reality (AR) is a live, direct or indirect, view of a physical, real world environment whose elements are augmented by computer-generated sensory input to recognize the mobile users' surroundings and to input such elements as sound, video, graphics, or global positioning system

(GPS) data. This feature generally is not found in other computing equipment. When they are, they may not be portable enough to be used in the field. Mobile users will rely on cameras or device sensors as communication tools when AR capabilities are combined with different layers of information, content, and resources for any communication and learning purpose (De Lucia, Francese, Passero, & Tortora, 2012). Many mobile applications have an embedded AR feature while some applications specifically focus on AR features. For example, at a historical site, mobile learners can use mobile devices to aim at certain locations or structures to obtain multiple layers of information about the locations or structures (Griggs, 2011), such as audio and video guides, historical photos showing the progression or evolution of the sites, locations, or structures. Additionally, a rich AR interaction may even include a social layer of interaction, such as other mobile learners' shared contents, resources, thoughts, and reflections. Wikitude app and many museum AR applications are good examples of AR integration.

Recommended strategies:

- **Evaluate Mobile AR Applications:** Not all AR applications are created equally. A few criteria are: location-based technology feature; information accuracy; social networking features; how wide it covers physical spaces; collaborative features; mobile gamification features (earning points or badges); and privacy settings.
- **Design Physical Activities to Integrate AR Application:** It is critical to design physical activities to fuse physical and mobile social interaction and presences.
- **Collaborate through AR Applications:** Effective AR interaction should integrate mobile collaboration. Frequently, AR mobile applications are equipped with mobile collaboration features; therefore, mobile learners can collaborate through AR technology physically and virtually.

OPTIMIZING DIGITAL AND SOCIAL IDENTITIES

Illustrated Digital Identities

Mobile learners should be encouraged in creating, and updating their profiles to maintain and manage their digital mobile identities (Ducate & Lomicka, 2008), such as personal digital profiles. Digital and social identities are the foundations of social relationships. Mobile learners should create and update their digital profiles with personal information, pictures, friend networks, etc. since digital personal information become digital identities.

Recommended strategies:

- **Instruct what Constitutes Digital Identity:** Digital profiles are more than just self-introduction or personal pictures on one social network site. Many learners utilize multiple social network sites to network with other learners. Each social network site has different profile features, personal background, education, hobby, interests, pictures, video, social networks etc.
- **Craft an Ideal Digital Identity:** One should take time to create their digital identities and carefully decide what should be included in the digital profiles and what should not be included. The ideal digital identity should be the created to highlight the way we prefer others to perceive us in both physical and digital worlds.
- **Update your Digital Identity Regularly to Reflect Personal Preferences:** Digital identity is not a one-time task. Mobile learners should update their digital identity regularly to reflect their current identity. An out-of-date digital identity may result in negative personal images and, thereby, interfere with mobile learning. It is highly recommended that ones should review and update their current digital identity regularly.

Project Ideal Mobile Social Identities

Mobile learners communicate, create, and share their mobile communication and mobile content. These digital footprints become part of their digital social identities and are the forms that Goffman (1959) would call "self-presentation," projecting ideal self images. Some mobile learners assume a more active approach by regulating and controlling information in mobile social interaction, such as posting and updating their current status on Facebook, Twitter, replying to the status of others, or blogging about their thoughts, etc. These social interactions become digital mobile footprints and are perceived as digital social identities.

Recommended strategies:

- **Determine Ideal Digital Social Identity:** Ask yourself what you want others know about your digital social identity! An enthusiastic professional? A person with sense of humor? A well-traveled individual? A person knowledgeable in certain knowledge domain?
- **Update and Manage Mobile Social Status:** Update social status on social network sties regularly to reflect your ideal digital social identity by creating, sharing, reflecting and commenting on certain social interactions.
- **Optimize Digital Social Identity:** Sharing the right social interaction with right people rather than sharing everything with everyone. Avoid saying anything that you would not say in a face-to-face context. If there is something that is not appropriate with a certain group of people, likely, it is not appropriate to share.

Secure Self-Awareness Mobile Privacy

Mobile privacy does not come automatically unless learners actively manage it for their digital social identities and digital cognition footprints. Mobile learners likely enjoy the convenient and ubiquitous mobile interaction to create mobile digital and social identities. In fact, they also expressed their digital identities were more social because they have a stronger sense of social awareness and connectedness. All mobile contents and communications are transmitted wirelessly. Mobile privacy requires that learners have an accurate understanding of how wireless technology works.

Recommended strategies:

- **Understand the Potential Risks of Mobile Privacy:** The instructors should explain the potential risks of mobile privacy to mobile learners prior any mobile instructions.
- **Exercise Mobile Privacy:** Discuss and design executable mobile privacy guidelines with mobile learners.
- **Share Personal Mobile Privacy Experiences:** Engage mobile learners in sharing their mobile privacy experiences and ideas with other mobile learners so they maintain a strong self-awareness in mobile interaction.

MOBILE APPS SELECTING GUIDELINES

Mobile LinkageOpen Network Linkage Design Model: Mobile Linkage refers to using "mobile apps" to link to Web 2.0Web 2.0 tools on mobile devices. Mobile Linkage involves more than using an Internet browser to access online information. Specifically, by employing mobile apps, Mobile Linkage focuses on controlling social context-awareness, managing location-based communication, personalized multi-layered interactivity, and optimized digital and social identities.

Mobile information and communication technologies are important enablers of the new social structure. The instructions built within Web 2.0 tools, such as iTunes U, Twitter, Delicious, Facebook, RSS, blogs, Google Apps etc. can be accessed via mobile apps on mobile devices. Mobile learning is able to achieve something that traditional desktop or laptop computers cannot achieve. Mobile Linkage becomes more powerful when mobile devices are equipped with recording, camera, and global positioning system (GPS) technologies.

Mobile apps' general features and designs allow mobile users to access the tools or websites without using a browser. Generally, users can utilize mobile apps to perform whatever features or designs the tools or websites offer. More specific functions for each mobile app may vary, such as log in requirement, free or paid app functions. Tu (in press) suggests the strategies to select mobile apps; to organize mobile apps; to share and to collaborate mobile apps; and to link tools.

To Select Mobile Apps

There are many mobile apps available for different mobile operating systems (OS). Selecting the right apps to support your teaching is critical. Many apps are free, while others range from less a dollar to relatively expensive. Here are a few guidelines for selecting apps to assist you in selecting apps for your teaching and learning.

For any given function, you may find multiple available apps. For example, there are many apps available for Twitter, Facebook, RSS, and e-mail. Try out some different apps to see which best meets your needs. This is especially recommended if the apps are free. You always can delete any unwanted items and add preferred apps.

Use "Review" information to assist you in selecting a right app. All app stores have "Review" information. Generally, they are arranged in five-star review scales. Be sure to read other users' review notes. This is particularly important when the apps are not free, although many apps are inexpensive.

Use "Top Charts" to help you screen for selection of the best apps: Generally, app stores list Top paid apps or Top free apps.

- **Additional Features:** Generally apps have the basic functions you need. Do not overlook the additional features in the apps, such as embedded location-based technology and social networking features for advanced collaboration.

- **Augmented RealityMobile Linkage:** Technology: Augmented Reality (AR): is a live, direct or indirect, view of a physical, real-world environment whose elements are augmented by computer-generated sensory input such as sound, video, graphics or GPS data. This is a feature you don't generally find in other computing equipment. Even you we do, they may not be portable enough to be used in the field. Many apps have an embedded AR feature, while some apps specifically focus on AR features.

Network with people informed about mobile apps to keep up with best new apps.

Allow students to select their own mobile apps as long as their selected apps can be linked to the planned one and can accomplish the same required tasks. Generally, this can be determined through sharing their app activities via social network sites. By allowing students to select their favorite apps you provide them with another effective learning activity.

To Organize Mobile Apps

Since apps can be easily downloaded and many of them are free, they tend to accumulate. Therefore, strategically organizing your apps is necessary. Most mobile OS have multiple pages and folders features. You can organize your apps through the following methods:

- **Page Organization:** Create different pages for apps with similar uses or functions.
- **Folder Organization:** If you prefer less page navigation, apply folder organization feature and organize apps with similar functions or uses into a folder, named with a title that is meaningful to you.

To Share and Collaborate with Mobile Apps

There two types of sharing and collaborating with mobile apps. Within apps, users can share and collaborate on learning activities, and they can also share their apps and collaborate about them.

Share and Collaborate within Apps: Many apps have embedded social networking features that allow you to share and collaborate your app activities within your friends network. For example, within photo apps, you can share the photos on your mobile devices with your network friends by e-mailing them; or you can share the photos with other Web 2.0 tools, such as Facebook, Twitter, and Flickr. The sharing feature can be advanced to collaborative learning by encouraging student groups to share the data or information they gather on their mobile devices. Since many apps have embedded location-based technology, the collaborative data contains other layers of information. Some apps integrate location-based technology to deliver AR functions. Public Broadcasting Service's (PBS) AR mobile app, FETCH! Lunch Rush, overlay computer-generated graphics on top of the physical, real-world environment. It is a 3-D game, which helps children visualize the math problems they are trying to solve. The purpose of this AR mobile app is to use media to nurture children's natural curiosity and inspire them to explore the world around them. See: http://pbskids.org/mobile/fetch-lunch-rush.html

Sharing apps: There are many apps in app stores, and sharing our favorite apps with our network friends is a critical way to learn about the availability of new apps. On your iOS (Internetwork Operation System) device, you can share an app from the App Store directly with your network by finding and clicking on the application you want. Then select "Tell a Friend," which allows you to e-mail your friend with a link to the application. On an Android device, open the Android Market and select the app you would like to share, click "Share this Application" and either e-mail, text, or Facebook message. If you have multiple apps you would like to share, consider using "Applist.me" which allows you share a list of iOS apps with your network friends. It is a free application that you can download to both Mac and Windows computers.

To Link Tools

Effective linkage designs should use mobile apps that link to different mobile devices and tools. Rarely do mobile apps function alone. If you use it alone, consider looking for the ability to link it to different devices or tools to make it more effective.

Same Apps Available on Multiple Devices or Mobile OS: If you use certain apps on certain mobile devices that you use, look for the same apps on your other mobile devices, or on a mobile OS. Most apps are available for different mobile devices and different mobile OS. On Mac computers, there is an App Store that regular computers can download. With the same apps on different devices and computers, you can access the same apps on most of your devices and computers.

Linking Apps to Another Tool: When using certain apps, examine whether the apps have a sharing feature. If yes, you can share the app data with your network friends via E-Mail, Facebook, Twitter, or other popular social network sites.

Linking Apps Data: Apps data and information can also be shared and posted to other Web 2.0

tools. For example, you can post the app data to Facebook, Twitter, Flickr, or Delicious.

Linking to Location-Based Technology: Examine whether the apps have embedded location-based technology which could have potential to apply AR to enhance learning in the more meaningful real-time, context-specific, location-specific ways. When opening an app, the app may ask whether you "Would like to use your current location". If so, you know your app has embedded location-based technology. "For AR apps, search the term "Augmented Reality" in any app store."

SAFETY

Mobile learning safety is very critical to younger learners. While planning effective mobile learning to promote higher mobile social presence, educators should always take the mobile learning safety first. It is important to investigate school or school district's policy for technologies, and mobile devices for learning. Dabbs (2012) suggested five building blocks to ensure the educators have appropriate mobile learning integration for teaching, learning, and connecting with students and parents: Notify parents; Develop a Responsible Use Policy; Establish Classroom Management Procedures; Plan activities with students: and Teach safety and etiquette.

Notifying the parents and involving parents are critical and effective. Mobile learning should involve both students and parents to create ubiquitous learning community. This should include mobile learning ideas, design, and engagements, and how students and parents will use their mobile devices. Develop a responsible use policy process should engage both students and parents and solicit their inputs; therefore, the use policy would be more context specific and more relevant to each individual students and parents. Additionally, the policy should coordinate with the school's or the school district's policy, if any. Establishing

classroom management procedures would ensure the integration is smooth and safe. Since mobile devices are small, lightweight, and requiring different skills, it is necessary the educators should plan the management procedure before any mobile instructions start. It is highly encouraged that teachers can invite both students and parents in planning the management procedures.

Planning instructional activities with students is another effective way to engage students in interactive mobile interaction. Students generally are excited about using mobile devices for learning purposes. Students frequently have creative ideas in using mobile devices. In fact, it could be effective to have one group of students to create mobile learning instructions for other student groups to learn with teachers' supervision.

Teaching mobile learning safety and etiquette should not be omitted. Knowing and practicing suitable mobile learning safety and etiquette is an essential learning skill. It is more than just how to engage in and developing safe and appropriate mobile uses. Students should have knowledge and right attitudes in handling when others not exhibiting appropriate behaviors in mobile learning.

FUTURE RESEARCH DIRECTIONS

The future research directions should distinguish mobile social presence from online and network social presences. The research in mobile social presence should focus on the aspects of personalized control, and location-free digital interaction and avoid replicating online and network social presences to evaluate and to examine mobile social presence. A model for mobile social presence is suggested in this chapter. The future research could apply this model to establish a construct, a framework, or a theoretical framework for mobile social presence rather than borrowing online or network social presence to examine it.

CONCLUSION

Mobile devices for schools are often seen as distractions from classroom learning. If you are unable to eliminate mobile devices from the classroom, then why not creatively integrate them to support teaching and learning? Many students have their own mobile devices already; and mobile devices cost even less for the schools. Therefore, it is likely that all students have access to these devices. Additionally, it is not necessary that all students have devices; they can be used with groups. Mobile learning does not just replicate traditional learning, and should be used in ways that exploit their capabilities. It would not be effective to ask students to complete a written paper on their mobile devices. In such a case, the emerging technology may well become inferior when comparing it to the traditional ones. Tu et al. (2012) argued that doing tasks faster, easier, or more conveniently is an "improvement" for learning. As educators face mobile technology as an emerging technology, we should aim toward "Innovative" and "Revolutionary" mobile learning integrations. We should dwell on what humans could do with mobile technology and what humans could not do without mobile technology.

REFERENCES

Boulos, M. N. K., & Wheeler, S. (2007). The emerging web 2.0 social software: An enabling suite of sociable technologies in health and health care education. *Health Information and Libraries Journal, 24*, 2–23. doi:10.1111/j.1471-1842.2007.00701.x PMID:17331140.

Charitonos, K., Blake, C., Scanlon, E., & Jones, A. (2012). Museum learning via social and mobile technologies: (How) can online interactions enhance the visitor experience? *British Journal of Educational Technology, 43*(5), 802–819. doi:10.1111/j.1467-8535.2012.01360.x.

Cornelius, S., & Marston, P. (2009). Toward an understanding of the virtual context in mobile learning. *Research in Learning Technology, 17*(3), 161–172. doi:10.3402/rlt.v17i3.10874.

Dabbs, L. (2012, October 25). Mobile learning support for new teachers. *Teaching with Soul!* Retrieved November 15, 2012, from http://www.teachingwithsoul.com/2012/mobile-learning-support-for-new-teachers

De Lucia, A., Francese, R., Passero, I., & Tortora, G. (2012). A collaborative augmented campus based on location-aware mobile technology. *International Journal of Distance Education Technologies, 10*(1), 55–73. doi:10.4018/jdet.2012010104.

Ducate, L., & Lomicka, L. (2008). Adventures in the blogosphere: From blog readers to blog writers. *Computer Assisted Language Learning, 21*(1), 9–28. doi:10.1080/09588220701865474.

Dunlap, J. C., & Lowenthal, P. R. (2009). Tweeting the night away: Using Twitter to enhance social presence. *Journal of Information Systems Education, 20*(2). Retrieved March 1, 2010, from http://www.patricklowenthal.com/publications/Using_Twitter_to_Enhance_Social_Presence.pdf

Fitzgerald, E. (2012). Creating user-generated content for location-based learning: An authoring framework. *Journal of Computer Assisted Learning, 28*(3), 195–207. doi:10.1111/j.1365-2729.2012.00481.x.

Goffman, E. (1959). *The presentation of self in everyday life*. Woodstock, NY: Overlook Press.

Jones, A., & Issroff, K. (2007). Motivation and mobile devices: Exploring the role appropriation and coping strategies. *Research in Learning Technology, 15*(3), 247–258. doi:10.3402/rlt.v15i3.10934.

Kekwaletswe, R. M. (2007). Social presence awareness for knowledge transformation in a mobile learning environment. *International Journal of Education and Development using Information and Communication Technology, 3*(4), 102–109.

Koole, M., McQuilkin, J. L., & Ally, M. (2010). Mobile learning in distance education: Utility or futility? *Journal of Distance Education, 24*(2), 59–82.

Kukulska-Hulme, A., & Traxler, J. (2007). Learning design with mobile and wireless technologies. In H. Beetham & R. Sharpe (Eds.), *Rethinking pedagogy for a digital age: Designing and delivering e-learning* (pp. 180–192). Retrieved April 15, 2009, from http://oro.open.ac.uk/9541/

Rau, P.-L. P., Gao, Q., & Wu, L.-M. (2008). Using mobile communication technology in high school education: Motivation, pressure, and learning performance. *Computers & Education, 50*(1), 1–22. doi:10.1016/j.compedu.2006.03.008.

Shin, W., & Lowes, S. (2008). Analyzing web 2.0 users in an online discussion forum. In *Proceedings of World Conference on Educational Multimedia, Hypermedia and Telecommunications 2008* (pp. 1130–1137). Chesapeake, VA: AACE.

Tu, C.-H., & McIsaac, M. (2002). An examination of social presence to increase interaction in online classes. *American Journal of Distance Education, 16*(3), 131–150. doi:10.1207/S15389286AJDE1603_2.

Tu, C.-H., McIsaac, M., Sujo-Montes, L., & Armfield, S. (2012). Is there a mobile social presence? *Educational Media International, 49*(4), 1–15. doi:10.1080/09523987.2012.741195.

Tu, C.-H., Yen, C.-J., Blocher, J. M., & Chan, J.-Y. (2012). A study of the predictive relationship between online social presence and ONLE interaction. *International Journal of Distance Education Technologies, 10*(3), 53–66. doi:10.4018/jdet.2012070104.

ADDITIONAL READING

Ally, M. (2009). *Mobile learning: Transforming the delivery of education and training*. Athabasca, Canada: Athabasca University Press.

Bentley, F., & Metcalf, C. J. (2009). The use of mobile social presence. *Pervasic, 8*(4), 35–41. doi:10.1109/MPRV.2009.83.

Devitt, K., & Roker, D. (2009). The role of mobile phones in family communication. *Children & Society, 23*(3), 189–202. doi:10.1111/j.1099-0860.2008.00166.x.

Huizenga, J., Admiraal, W., Akkerman, S., & Dam, G. T. (2009). Mobile game-based learning in secondary education: Engagement, motivation, and learning in a mobile city. *Journal of Computer Assisted Learning, 25*(4), 332–344. doi:10.1111/j.1365-2729.2009.00316.x.

Jones, A., & Issroff, K. (2007). Motivation and mobile devices: Exploring the role appropriation and coping strategies. *Research in Learning Technology, 15*(3), 247–258. doi:10.3402/rlt.v15i3.10934.

Kim, P., Buckner, E., Kim, H., Makany, T., Taleja, N., & Parikh, V. (2012). A comparative analysis of a game-based mobile learning model in low-socioeconomic communities of India. *International Journal of Educational Development, 32*(2), 329–340. doi:10.1016/j.ijedudev.2011.05.008.

Kim, P., Hagashi, T., Carillo, L., Gonzales, I., Makany, T., Lee, B., & Ga`rate, A. (2011). Socioeconomic strata, mobile technology, and education: A comparative analysis. *Educational Technology Research and Development, 59*, 465–486. doi:10.1007/s11423-010-9172-3.

Knowledge Management System. (2011). Defining mobile learning isn't enough. *Knowledge Management System (KMS) Blog*. Retrieved June 1, 2012, from http://blog.empowerlms.com/index.php/defining-mobile-learning/

Kolb, L. (2011). *Cell phones in the classroom: A practical guide for educators*. Eugene, OR: ISTE.

Kolb, L. (2013). *Help your child learn with cell phones and web 2.0*. Eugene, OR: ISTE.

Lan, Y.-F., & Sie, Y.-S. (2010). Using RSS to support mobile learning based on media richness theory. *Computers & Education, 55*(2), 723–732. doi:10.1016/j.compedu.2010.03.005.

Lorente, S. (2002). Youth and mobile telephones: More than a fashion. *Journal of Studies on Youth, 57*, 9–24.

Nielsen, L., & Webb, W. (2010). *Teaching generation text: Using cell phones to enhance learning*. Hoboken, NJ: Jossey-Bass.

Pachler, N., Pimmer, C., & Seipold, J. (2011). *Work-based mobile learning: Concepts and cases*. Oxford, UK: Peter Lang.

Pimmer, C., Linxen, S., & Grohbiel, U. (2012). Facebook as a learning tool? A case study on the appropriation of social network sites from mobile phones in developing countries. *British Journal of Educational Technology, 43*(5), 726–738. doi:10.1111/j.1467-8535.2012.01351.x.

Ryu, H., & Parsons, D. (2009). *Innovative mobile learning: Techniques and technologies*. Hershey, PA: IGI Global.

Schofield, C. P., West, T., & Taylor, E. (2011). *Going mobile in executive education: How mobile technologies are changing the executive learning landscape* (Research for UNICON). Hertfordshire, UK: Ashridge & UNICON. Retrieved June 10, 2012, from http://www.uniconexed.org/2011/research/UNICON-Going_Mobile_In_Executive_Education-Schofield-Taylor-West-Nov-2011.pdf

Sha, L., Looi, C.-K., Chen, W., & Zhang, B. H. (2012). Understanding mobile learning from the perspective of self-regulated learning. *Journal of Computer Assisted Learning, 28*(4), 366–378. doi:10.1111/j.1365-2729.2011.00461.x.

Sharples, M. (2002). Disruptive devices: Mobile technology for conversational learning. *International Journal of Continuing Engineering Education and Lifelong Learning, 12*(5/6), 505–520. doi:10.1504/IJCEELL.2002.002148.

Ting, Y.-L. (2012). The pitfalls of mobile devices in learning: A different view and implications for pedagogical design. *Journal of Educational Computing Research, 46*(2), 119–134. doi:10.2190/EC.46.2.a.

Traxler, J. (2010). Distance education and mobile learning: Catching up, taking stock. *Distance Education, 31*(2), 129–138. doi:10.1080/01587919.2010.503362.

Tu, C. H. (2004). *Twenty-one designs to build online collaborative learning community*. Westport, CT: Library Unlimited.

Tu, C.-H. (in press). *Strategies for building a web 2.0 learning environment*. Santa Barbara, CA. *ABC-CLIO.*.

Uzunboylu, H., Cavus, N., & Ercag, E. (2009). Using mobile learning to increase environmental awareness. *Computers & Education, 52*(2), 381–389. doi:10.1016/j.compedu.2008.09.008.

Wei, F.-H., & Chen, G.-D. (2006). Collaborative mentor support in a learning context using a ubiquitous discussion forum to facilitate knowledge sharing for lifelong learning. *British Journal of Educational Technology, 37*(6), 917–935. doi:10.1111/j.1467-8535.2006.00674.x.

Wu, W.-H., Wu, Y.-C., Chen, C.-Y., Kao, H.-Y., Lin, C.-H., & Huang, S.-H. (2012). Review of trends from mobile learning studies: A meta-analysis. *Computers & Education*, *59*(2), 817–827. doi:10.1016/j.compedu.2012.03.016.

KEY TERMS AND DEFINITIONS

Augmented Reality (AR): A live, direct or indirect, view of a physical, real world environment whose elements are augmented by computer-generated sensory input to recognize the mobile users' surroundings and to input such elements as sound, video, graphics, or global positioning system (GPS) data.

Location-Based Technology: A mobile technology that allows users to control and to identify physical locations.

Mobile Devices: Compact and handheld devices, such as mobile phones, smartphones, tablets (Android tablets, iOS tablets, Windows tablets etc.).

Mobile Footprint: A digital cognitive and/or social imprint that mobile users engage in directly or indirectly (creating, sharing, modifying, remixing, participating, posting etc.)

Mobile Linkage: A design that refers to use "mobile apps" to link to Web 2.0 tools on mobile devices.

Mobile Social Presence: Definition of Keyword.

Network Social Presence: The degree that network participants engage in creating, maintaining, sharing, connecting social content, digital and social identities, network linkages, and collaborative community.

Online Social Presence: The degree of feeling, perception, and reaction of being connected by computer-mediated communication (CMC) to another intellectual entity through electronic media.

Chapter 6
T-SCORM:
An Extension of the SCORM Standard to Support the Project of Educational Contents for t-Learning

Francisco Miguel da Silva
Rural Federal University of Semi Arid, Brazil

Francisco Milton Mendes Neto
Rural Federal University of Semi Arid, Brazil

Aquiles Medeiros Filgueira Burlamaqui
Federal University of Rio Grande do Norte, Brazil

João Phellipe Freitas Pinto
Rural Federal University of Semi Arid, Brazil

Carlos Evandro de Medeiros Fernandes
Rural Federal University of Semi Arid, Brazil

Rafael Castro de Souza
Rural Federal University of Semi Arid, Brazil

ABSTRACT

Interactive Digital Television (iDTV) has facilitated and expanded the communication and interaction in activities of knowledge acquisitions, entertainment, and recreation in the distance learning field. This new way of teaching and learning has been called t-Learning. In this context, the Learning Objects (LOs) have an important role in assisting in the electronic courses' development. Due the fast progress of e-Learning, some efforts toward standardization have appeared in order to enable the reusability of educational contents and interoperability among systems, and one of these standards is the Sharable Content Object Reference Model (SCORM). Therefore, the main goal of this work is to present an extension of SCORM aiming to adapt it to improve the search and navigation of LOs with educational content for t-Learning. This is done through an authoring tool named T-SCORM ADAPTER, which is able to apply this extension in a fast and efficient way.

DOI: 10.4018/978-1-4666-4542-4.ch006

INTRODUCTION

Nowadays, the appreciation of knowledge influences the way in which people acquire skills by making a particular person search for alternative and flexible ways of learning. According to (Girardi, 2002), this appreciation of knowledge makes that each individual always is looking for new ways to improve and increase their learning level constantly. Having the television as Brazil's most popular media, it appears as a solution for disseminating quality and interactive content.

This happens because of the digitization process, which enables audio and video applications to be executed (Monteiro, Prota, Souza, & Gomes, 2008). The Interactive Digital Television (iDTV) is becoming a reality in the world, due mainly to the advances in telecommunications. The Brazilian government with the development of (SBTVD)2, short for Sistema Brasileiro de Televisão Digital (English: Brazilian Digital Television System) has also contributed to this aspect (SBTVD, 2007).

According to Naidu (2006), e-learning is mostly related to the intentional use of information and communication that are technologically connected in order to benefit the teaching-learning process. In other words, it refers basically to educational process using Information and Communication Technology to mediate both asynchronous and synchronous learning as well as the teaching activities. Naidu (2006) also mentions some other terms that are also used to describe this modality, such as: virtual learning, distributed learning and network-web-based learning.

A major challenge nowadays is the computerized support to this activity. An important point in teaching attendance is the group activity. The students interaction in order to develop some pedagogical task is very important in the learning process (PONTES, 2010). Currently, the advances in information and communication technologies have accelerated the Distance Education development, enabling the use of didactic content structured and more organized. According to Gazzoni et al. (2006), these contents may be available on the Web in different formats, such as: hypertexts, videos, animations etc.

Due to the fast progress of e-learning, many standardization efforts have emerged in order to enable the reusability of educational contents and interoperability among the systems developed (REY-LOPEZ et al., 2009). According to Shih, Yang and Tseng (2011), in order to share and reuse teaching content, many standards have been proposed recently, being Sharable Content Object Reference Model (SCORM) the standard most used for learning content, since that brings in its context many standards of different standardization institutes in many fields of the electronic learning.

Based on this reality, there is the problem in how to adjust educational contents, so as to better support the search and navigation mechanism to make them available in the iDTV platform in order to present an effective and personalized learning. Another problem that arises in this context is how to make the Learning Objects (LOs) become more suitable through their specification in SCORM, aiming at the proper presentation for iDTV.

To fill this gap, this paper proposes an extension to the SCORM standard in order to better support in an effective manner the search, navigation and visualization of LOs with educational contents for t-Learning.

Besides this introductory section, the chapter provides first, a description of the main features of iDTV, Distance Education and t-Learning. Next it presents the definitions of LOs as well as the standards for their development and description. Then, it exposes the details of our proposal and the authoring tool T-SCORM ADAPTER. Following it presents a Case Study with the technologies and languages used, also the final results of tests conducted and an analysis of the results found. After that, it presents and discuss similar approaches. Finally, it draw some conclusions and motivation for future work.

INTERACTIVE DIGITAL AND DISTANCE EDUCATIONAL

It is possible to find in the literature many concepts about Distance Education. In this work, we will use the definition established by the (SEED), short for Secretaria de Educação a Distância (English: Secretariat of Distance Education) of the Ministry of Education and Culture (MEC), in the decree (5.622, 2005). In its article 1st, this decree defines the Distance Education as being:

[...] educational modality in which the didactic-pedagogical mediation in the teaching-learning process occurs with the use of resources along with information and communication technologies, with students and teachers by developing educational activities in places or different times.

Based on this definition, we can present the iDTV as a means of support for distance learning, and with the SBTVD expansion and the interactivity provided by the Ginga middleware, good opportunities show up to the development of educational applications being an innovator in iDTV and characterizing the modality of teaching-learning named as t-Learning.

The e-Learning and t-Learning have different scopes taking into account that e-Learning is highly suitable for a formal education environment.

That is, it is supported by methodologies quite defined to carry out an outline and summary of topics to be covered in an education or training course. t-Learning, in turn, is more appropriate for an informal approach, which al-lows the learning through the entertainment (Pazos-Arias et al., 2008).

As it is shown in Figure 1, the interactivity features represent a great advantage over the traditional television programs, in view of the fact that it makes the learning experience more enjoyable. The interactivity allows among other things, the user should influence the presentation of contents and assesses his knowledge by on-line tests.

LEARNING OBJETCS

A relevant concept in relation to the content of teaching-learning in the field of Distance Education is the Learning Object (LO). According to the Learning Technology Standard Committee (LTSC) of the Institute of Electrical and Electronics Engineers (IEEE), a Learning Object is defined as any entity, digital or non-digital, that may be used for learning, education or training (LTSC, 2002).

According to (Americo, 2010), the LOs are considered information blocks and present the following features: i) reusability - Reusable

Figure 1. t-Learning between pure entertainment and formal education
Source: (Pazos-Arias et al., 2008).

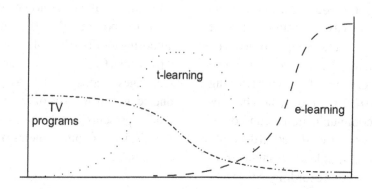

several times in different learning environments; ii) adaptability - Adaptable to any teaching environment; iii) granularity - pieces of content, in order to facilitate its reusability; iv) accessibility - easily accessible on the Internet to be used in many locations; v) durability - possibility to be used continuously, regardless technology change; vi) interoperability - ability to operate through a hardware variety, operating systems and browsers, i.e. effective exchange between different systems.

The efforts for development of standards aiming to the description of LOs may be exemplified by the work of important organizations such as IEEE and the Global Learning Consortium, which have proposed the Learning Object Metadata (LOM) standard (LOM, 2002). The metadata standard LOM allows the LOs be classified, reused and found by searching tools in an appropriate manner. The main elements of LOM are described below:

- **General:** Gather information in general, which describe the LO as a whole.
- **Life Cycle:** Gather features concerning to the history and Status Quo of the LO.
- **Meta-Metadata:** Collect information about the metadata instances.
- **Technical:** Gather the features and the technical requirements of LO.
- **Educational:** Collect the pedagogical and educational characteristics of LO.

- **Rights:** Describe Copyright And Other Restrictions.
- **Relation:** Define the relation characteristics among the LOs.
- **Annotation:** Comments regarding to educational use and information of LO.
- **Classification:** Describe the LO in relation to a classification of a specific system.

The Shareable Content Object Reference Model (SCORM), which has been developed by Advanced Distributed Learning (ADL), is also widely used and describes how the content could be modeled and how the learning management environments should handle such content to make its reuse viable (ADL, 2010).

The standard SCORM content can be distributed to the students by any Learning Management System (LMS), which has to be compatible with SCORM and use the same version of standard (ADL, 2010). Essentially the context description model of SCORM defines a set of metatags and statements to be used in the description files or in the content, aiming for the transfer information to the LMS about the content and the interaction of students with the content.

The Figure 2 shows the SCORM organization as a collection of standards and specifications of other organizations contained or referenced in the model.

Figure 2. SCORM 2004 specification books
Source:[http://www.scorm 2004.fr/]

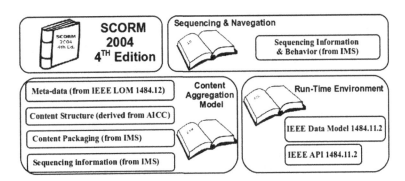

To enable the content aggregation in a format that is easily interpretable and transferable among systems on the Internet, the ADL has adopted the definition of a special file named (imsmanifest. xml), encoded in xml, which describes the different components and resources. It has markers for all the features of the SCORM provided in the configuration files, as well as the locations of the referenced files by these components.

The Figure 3 shows a pseudocode example of imsmanifest.xml.

As it is shown in Figure 3, the imsmanifest. xml starts by defining the language and version of the file. Then it presents the main element <manifest> in which are described the domains that support the entire coding.

The imsmanifest.xml structure is composed by the following elements:

- **<metadata>:** Used in any component of the data model and the content package.
- **<organizations>:** Mandatory in case of Content Aggregation Package.
- **<item>:** Corresponds to an activity of content model.

- **<resources>:** Contains a set of references to the different resources.
- **<files>:** Used to reference the location of archive which belongs to the resource.
- **<manifest>:** In the Content Aggregation, the whole manifest is referenced, or just a few parts of its components.

EXTENSION PROPOSAL OF SCORM STANDARD

The extension of the SCORM standard proposed in this paper has as main goal to improve the support to the search and the navigation making available the LOs for the iDTV platform.

The great advantage of this method is that, it will enable a system to search for information contained in the metadata of the LOs with educational content created specifically for t-Learning within the imsmanifest.xml.

First we start with a scenario in which there is already an LMS working in selecting and distribution of LOs for courses on the iDTV platform regarding to t-Learning context. Then the objective

Figure 3. Structure and pseudocode of imsmanifest.xml

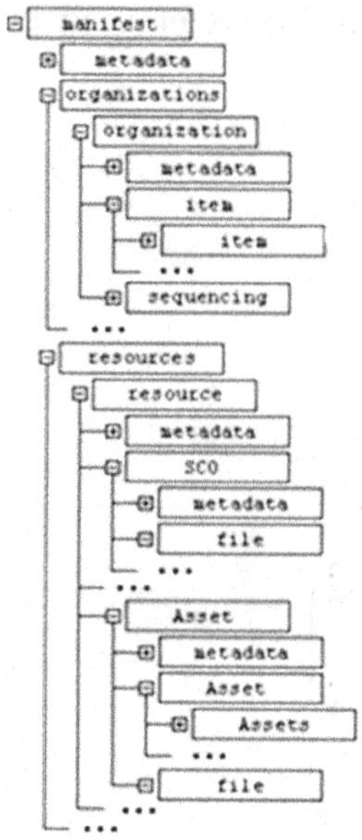

```xml
<?xml version="1.0" encoding="UTF-8"?>
<manifest identifier="ID" version="1.2"
    xmlns="http://www.imsproject.org/xsd/imscp_rootv1p1p2"
    xmlns:adlcp="http://www.adlnet.org/xsd/adlcp_rootv1p2"
    xmlns:xsi="http://www.w3.org/2001/XMLSchema-instance"
    xsi:schemaLocation="http://www.imsglobal.org/xsd/imsmd_rootv1p2p1 imsmd_rootv1p2p1.xsd
                        http://www.adlnet.org/xsd/adlcp_rootv1p2 adlcp_rootv1p2.xsd">

<organizations default="ORG-1">
    <organization identifier="ORG-1">
        <title>Curso</title>
        <item identifier="R_A1" identifierref="A-1">
            <title>Modulo</title>
        </item>
    </organization>
</organizations>

<resources>
    <resource identifier="A1" type="webcontent" adlcp:scormtype="sco" href="index.htm">
        <file href="index.htm"/>
    </resource>
</resources>
</manifest>
```

of this work is to improve the selecting process made by the LMS, adding specific t-Learning information in the metadata of these LOs.

Currently, there is no repository for educational content specific for a t-Learning environment in the international or national context. According to (Bez, 2010), the most part of the LMSs has worked with web content. Then, it is not being possible to convert this content for Digital TV yet. This occurs mainly due to the fact of the navigability between these technologies be different.

The proposed extension contemplates an adaptation of metadata information in the current SCORM standard based on LOM standard. New elements have been proposed in order to give more emphasis to the information of these metadata related to iDTV.

The intention of improving the quality of these metadata, and it is just for, according to the preferences and cognitive characteristics contained in the students' profiles, the LMS can manage in a quickly and efficient manner, to seek and make these LOs available for students in the iDTV platform

New Metadata Model

Metadata, in a brief answer, is defined as data about data, which describe them (semantic and syntactically), and in which is possible to structure and manage the information in different environments (Alves, Kulesza, Silva, Juca, & Bressan, 2006).

It is being proposed in this work, new elements of metadata, where they become child nodes in the main structure of the metadata model of LOM, which SCORM is based on.

With the new elements inserted in the LOM structure, we have twelve categories that make it possible to specify in a more accurate way the LOs metadata with educational content for iDTV. With these new elements added, it will be possible to describe specific information of LOs for iDTV, such as: interactivity level, copyright description, precise description on educational content in digital format, etc.

In Figure 4, it is shown an overview of the new structure proposed to the LOM. In blue, we have the original metadata elements in the LOM structure. In green, we have the new categories

Figure 4. New Structure of LOM for iDTV

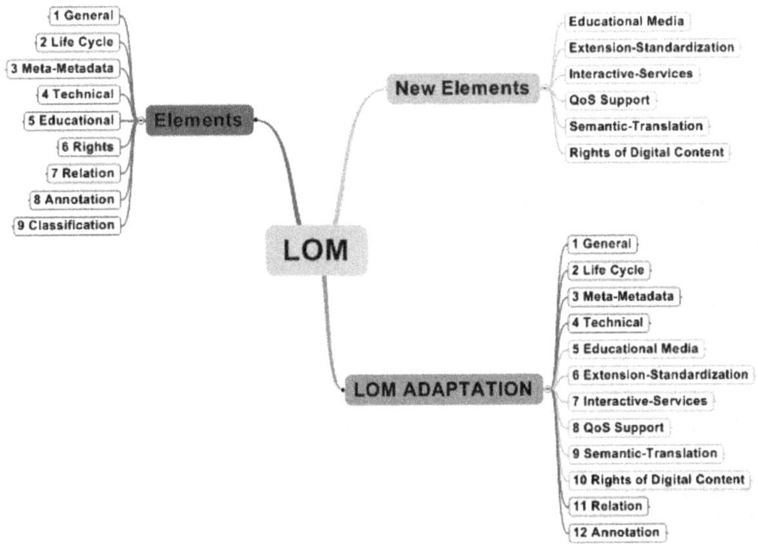

of elements proposed by the extension. Finally, in orange, we have the LOM's adaptation with the new metadata structure.

In spite of the actual LOM metadata structure within the SCORM already includes metadata information for categories such as educational and rights, these categories, as well as the other ones, classify and specify the LOs metadata in a very generic way and these categories do not have fields to treat in a better quality this exclusive information for iDTV.

With the inclusion of these new elements adapted in the structure, we now have twelve categories that allow us to specify in a more accurate way the metadata of the OAs with educational content for TVDi.

With the inclusion of these new elements, it will be possible to describe specific information of LOs for iDTV, such as the interactivity level in which it could describe the system characteristics, since in iDTV this resource may not be available. We also have the description of digital content rights, where, in the case of special particularities, it will

be possible to specify in detail the information on educational content in digital format, among other information.

This adjustment in the categories allows to describe clearer information on the media content with educational and training, in addition to helping any search mechanism to become faster and effective in gathering information directly in the metadata making with these LOS be suitable in a correct way for the specific public.

Figure 5 shows the architecture and how is applied the T-SCORM extension.

As shown in Figure 5, the Vocabulary Creator is in charge of adding the new elements of T-SCORM extension. The new elements shall contain the information relating to the new metadata parameters and inserted in the LOM structure based on SCORM.

The LO must be created and edited according to the specifications of SCORM standard. It has been used in this work the freeware tool Reload Editorfor LO creation and editing.

Figure 5. Architecture of T-SCORM extension

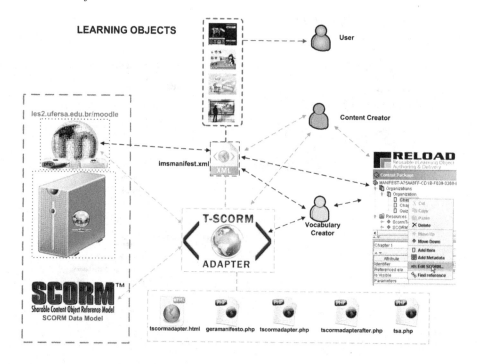

Once edited, the Content Creator for iDTV will compose the LOs in accordance with SCORM. However, the Content Creator will add the new extension using the T-SCORM ADAPTER tool proposed in this paper. This tool will read the imsmanifest.xml file created in the first place.

This will ensure that the T-SCORM extension may be added with the new metadata elements within the LOM structure, improving the classification and the specification of LOs with educational content for iDTV.

After complete such information, the T-SCORM will save the file with the changes related to the new metadata elements, but keeping the original structure (markers and header) of imsmanifest.xml, which is demanding for recognition by the LMS as a SCORM content package

Authoring Tool T-SCORM ADAPTER

To facilitate the process of reading and adding of the T-SCORM extension, it has been developed the T-SCORM ADAPTER tool, which is able to apply the extension proposed within the imsmanifest.xml structure.

In Figure 6, it can be seen that the tool has a friendly interface and easy to use, with the tabs separated in an adequate manner to input the new information in order to compose the new metadata of LOs for iDTV.

The Figure 7 shows a user scenario of the T-SCORM ADAPTER to modify the imsmanifest. xml applying just one element of the extension.

In order to apply the T-SCORM extension, we must follow a sequence of steps. In step 1, you need to create the imsmanifest.xml using the Reload Editor. In step 2, rename the file created to imsmanifest_default.xml and places in the root of .../moodle/mod/tscorm/ where Moodle is installed. In step 3, it is chosen the video resource, which is also a LO with metadata to change. Then, you must fill out the information by scrolling the menu tabs. In step 4, click on Enviar button to finish. The information is saved and automatically inserted, also it creates a final copy of imsmanifest.xml that is created separately, but keeping the original organization structure.

The T-SCORM ADAPTER was developed in PHP and integrated with Moodle. In order to make possible to insert the new metadata categories in imsmanifest.xml, was used the XMLDOM (Document Object Model). It is a standard created by W3C which is specified as an interface for programming applications, in which allows to work with the structure of documents and the goal is to facilitate access to the elements of a document

Figure 6. T-SCORM ADAPTER

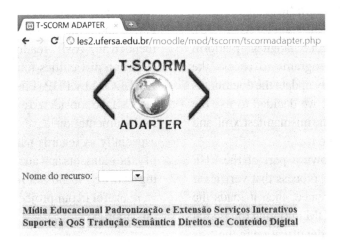

Figure 7. User Scenario of T-SCORM ADAPTER

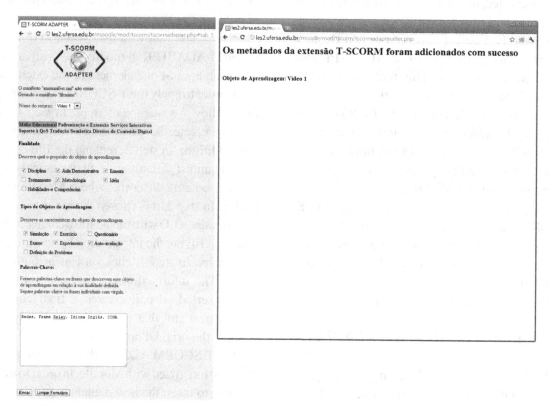

such as tags of an XML file, enabling remove, add or edit its content, attributes and style.

DOM also allows developers to write applications that work properly in all Internet browsers, in addition of Servers on many platforms and even that developers require programming in different languages, the programming model remains.

W3C divided the DOM in different parts (Core, XML, and HTML) and at different levels (1, 2, 3). DOM is a neutral language, i.e., language-platform independent allowing programs to access the databases and dynamically update the documents content. For this project, we decided to use the PHP XMLDOM to load the imsmanifest.xml, and thus we could manipulate it.

In Figure 6, it is shown a part of the PHP code where is started the process that verifies if there is some already created, then it loads the imsmanifest.xml with DOM initiating the search for the videos resources identification in the tags

structure of imsmanifest.xml. Once identified, the resources are loaded in the T-SCORM ADAPTER page, in which the user will apply the information on the new metadata elements of these resources separately.

According to Doyle (2009), besides DOM, PHP uses two more methods to analyze grammatically a XML document, which are: XML-Parser and SimpleXML. The first is most recommended for XML reading, while the second is based on difficulties found in implementing the XMLDOM by PHP (Figure 8). Despite the SimpleXML be considered easier to handle large files, its documentation leaves something to be desired, especially as regards name spaces used to identify the elements and attributes of an XML avoiding conflict. It did not have good examples that were useful in our project, then we did not opt for this approach.

Figure 8. Piece of PHP code using PHP XMLDOM

```php
<?php
    // Verifica se o manifesto já existe
    //Se o manifesto alterado ainda não foi gerado, gerar o mesmo.
    $filename = 'imsmanifest.xml';
    if (file_exists($filename) == 0) {
        echo 'O manifesto "' . $filename .'" não existe';
        echo '<br />Gerando o manifesto "filename" <br />';
        include "geramanifesto.php";
    }
    else{
        echo "O manifesto já existe.<br />";
    }
    ?>
    </p>
<p>Nome do recurso:  <select name="recurso">
    <option disabled="disabled"></option>
    <?php
    // Captura os nomes dos vídeos existentes no imsmanifest.xml
    // Carrega o arquivo XML
    $doc2 = new DOMDocument();
    $doc2->preserveWhiteSpace = false;
    $doc2->load( "imsmanifest.xml" );
    $doc2->formatOutput = true;

    //Armazena uma lista com todos os elementos (TAGS) do tipo 'resource'
    $listaDeRecursos = $doc2->getElementsByTagName( "resource" );
    echo "\n\n";
    foreach($listaDeRecursos as $resourceVisitado){
        $nomeDoVideo = $resourceVisitado->firstChild->firstChild->firstChild->firstChild->firstChild->nodeValue;
        echo "<option>". $nomeDoVideo ."</option>"; //. $nomeDoVideo . "\n\n";
    }
    ?>
```

In Figure 9, it is shown the imsmanifest.xml created with the Reload Editor.

In Figure 10, it is shown the imsmanifest.xml after the metadata addition in <educationalmidia> element edited by T-SCORM ADAPTER.

CASE STUDY

This section describes the technologies and programming languages that were used. In addition of presenting the final results of tests conducted and an analysis of the results found.

RECOMMENDING EDUCATIONAL VIDEOS FOR T-LEARNING ENVIRONMENT

Yin (2005) defines a case study as an empirical research that investigates a contemporary phenomenon within its real life context, especially when the boundaries between the phenomenon and context are not clearly defined.

Babbie (1999) quoted by (Gomes, 2009) complements that a case study search initially the comprehensive understanding of a single case and knowledge generally applicable in addition to the unique case studied, but by itself, a case study does not guarantee this generalization..

As a part of this work, the T-SCORM - Moodle application was designed to present the final results of the recommending videos process with educational content for iDTV platform. It was developed in NCL (Nested Context Language) and Lua. Lua is a script language adopted by middleware Ginga-NCL. The T-SCORM - Moodle was created aiming to work integrated with Moodle, which is charge for a large part in the recommending process.

A virtual machine such as VMWare simulates the operation of Ginga-NCL as if it were operating normally in a set-top box. In the prototype created by this work, we have the T-SCORM - Moodle

Figure 9. Metadata created with the Reload Editor

```
- <resource identifier="V1" adlcp:scormtype="sco" href="media/video/video01.mp4" type="video">
    - <file href="media/video/video01.mp4">
        - <metadata>
            - <imsmd:lom>
                + <imsmd:general>
                + <imsmd:lifecycle>
                + <imsmd:metametadata>
                + <imsmd:technical>
                - <imsmd:educational>
                    - <imsmd:interactivitytype>
                        - <imsmd:source>
                            <imsmd:langstring xml:lang="en">LOMv1.0</imsmd:langstring>
                        </imsmd:source>
                        - <imsmd:value>
                            <imsmd:langstring xml:lang="en">Active</imsmd:langstring>
                        </imsmd:value>
                    </imsmd:interactivitytype>
                    - <imsmd:learningresourcetype>
                        - <imsmd:source>
                            <imsmd:langstring xml:lang="en">LOMv1.0</imsmd:langstring>
                        </imsmd:source>
                        - <imsmd:value>
                            <imsmd:langstring xml:lang="en">Diagram</imsmd:langstring>
                        </imsmd:value>
                    </imsmd:learningresourcetype>
                    <imsmd:language>pt</imsmd:language>
                </imsmd:educational>
                + <imsmd:rights>
                + <imsmd:relation>
                + <imsmd:annotation>
                + <imsmd:classification>
            </imsmd:lom>
        </metadata>
    </file>
</resource>
```

Figure 10. Metadata changed with the T-SCORM ADAPTER

```
- <resource identifier="V1" adlcp:scormtype="sco" href="media/video/video01.mp4" type="video">
    - <file href="media/video/video01.mp4">
        - <metadata>
            - <imsmd:lom>
                + <imsmd:general>
                + <imsmd:lifecycle>
                + <imsmd:metametadata>
                + <imsmd:technical>
                - <imsmd:educationalmedia>
                    - <imsmd:purpose>
                        - <imsmd:source>
                            <imsmd:langstring xml:lang="en">LOMv1.0</imsmd:langstring>
                        </imsmd:source>
                        - <imsmd:value>
                            <imsmd:langstring xml:lang="en">Aula Demonstrativa, Treinamento, Habilidades e Competências</imsmd:langstring>
                        </imsmd:value>
                    </imsmd:purpose>
                    - <imsmd:learningresourcetype>
                        - <imsmd:source>
                            <imsmd:langstring xml:lang="en">LOMv1.0</imsmd:langstring>
                        </imsmd:source>
                        - <imsmd:value>
                            <imsmd:langstring xml:lang="en">Simulação, Exercício, Questionário, Exame, Experimento</imsmd:langstring>
                        </imsmd:value>
                    </imsmd:learningresourcetype>
                    - <imsmd:keyword>
                        <imsmd:langstring xml:lang="en">Redes, Frame Relay, CCNA,</imsmd:langstring>
                    </imsmd:keyword>
                </imsmd:educationalmedia>
                + <imsmd:extensionstandardization>
                + <imsmd:interactiveservices>
                + <imsmd:qossupport>
                + <imsmd:semantictranslation>
                + <imsmd:rightsofdigitalcontent>
                + <imsmd:relation>
                + <imsmd:annotation>
            </imsmd:lom>
        </metadata>
    </file>
</resource>
```

application where will be performed the user authentication process, as well as will be shown the recommendation result of educational videos exclusive to t-Learning environments based on the profile information of the student previously created in Moodle.

The application stars with a video loop on the home screen (see Figure 11). After three seconds, the interactivity icon appears informing that there is an interactive feature ready to be engaged. In this prototype, the interactivity is operated by

<F1> key on the computer keyboard and makes the application pass to the next screen, which is the one for Login and Password.

In Figure 11, it is shown the home screen of T-SCORM - Moodle.

In Figure 12, it is shown the screen requesting Login and Password of the user.

The creating process of the user profile is done through a form created within the LMS Moodle. For this reason, the Moodle 2.0 version was installed and properly configured with Windows

Figure 11. Home screen of T-SCORM-Moodle

Figure 12. Screen requesting login and password

Server 2008 R2 Enterprise, which is physically located at the Software Engineering Laboratory of Federal University of Semi Arid.

It was created the sub-domain [http://les2.ufersa.edu.br/moodle/] making possible the external access in order to perform the tests. In Figure 13, it is shown the Moodle home page.

In Figure 14, it shown the Form T-SCORM - Moodle link, located on top edge left of the screen.

By clicking on the link, the user will be directed to apage which will fill a registry with the information requested on the form as it shown in Figure 15.

In fields of Finalidade, Tipos de Objetos de Aprendizagem, Tipos de Recursos and Disciplinas, the user may choose more than one option. This will ensure that the videos number in the recommendation can be wider.

In Figure 16, it is shown the creating process of a user (TESTE). After the filling, it is necessary to click on the Enviar button.

In Figure 17, it is shown the confirmation screen of the registration done successfully.

Figure 13. Moodle Home Page at the sub-domain [http://les2.ufersa.edu.br/moodle/]

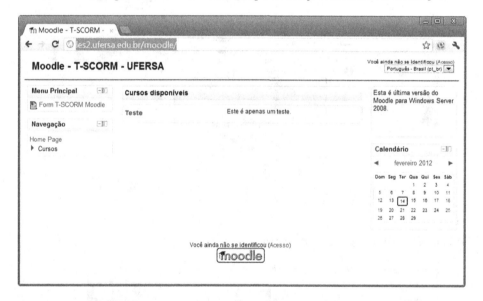

Figure 14. T-SCORM - Moodle link

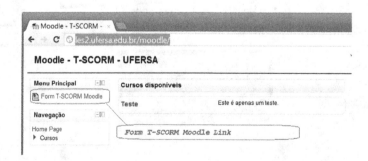

Figure 15. T-SCORM - Moodle link

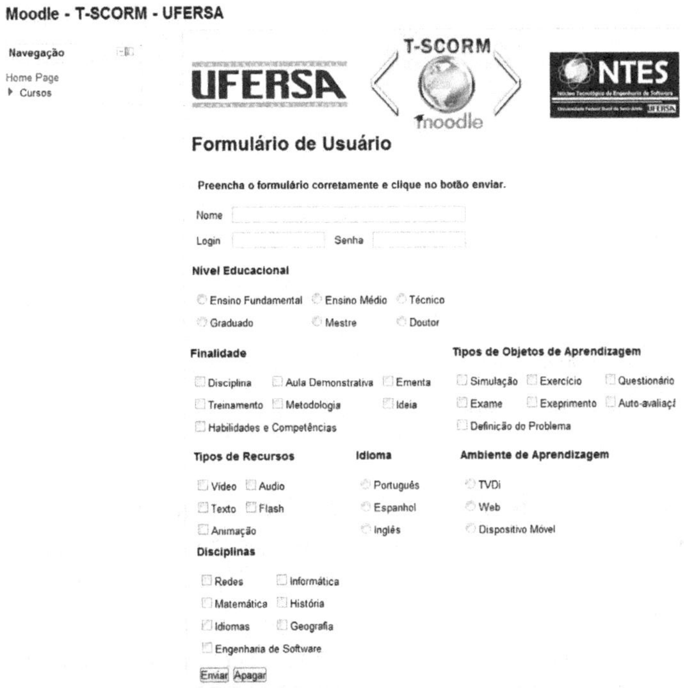

Figure 16. Creating a user (TESTE)

Figure 17. Confirmation screen

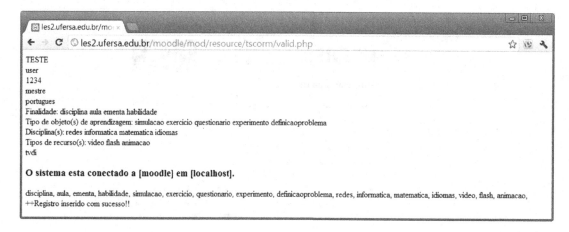

Architecture for Recommending Educational Videos

Now, it will be presented the architecture that will illustrate and explain how is performed the processes of requesting and recommendation of videos with educational content. The videos are already classified and specified in SCORM standard in the imsmanifest.xml structure with T-

SCORM extension properly applied, including the new metadata categories proposed by this work. In Figure 18, it is how this process is performed.

The process starts when the T-SCORM - Moodle application sends an HTTP request: with username and password. In the client-side with the virtual machine, the Lua coding has two functions created: one for sending a requisition with login and password, and other one to receive the

Figure 18. Architecture for recommending process

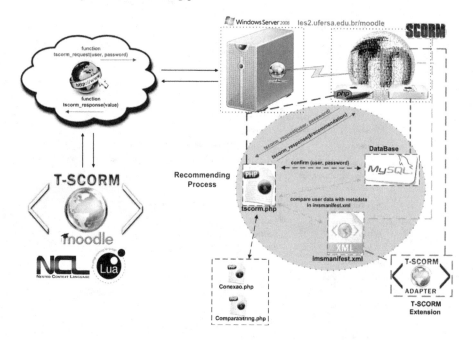

response came from the server-side as the result of the videos recommendation.

In Figure 19, it is shown a piece of the Lua code with the request and response functions.

The process continues when the request reaches the Moodle pointing to the tscorm.php file, and this, in turn, makes the authentication of the login and password in the MySQL Database. In Figure 20, it is shown the piece of code in PHP that performs this task.

Once identified username and password, the process goes ahead, but it is important to remember that the information completed by the user on Form T-SCORM - Moodle are also in MySQL Database. These information are compared with the metadata of the T-SCORM extension applied in the imsmanifest.xml file, which is loaded using the same procedure shown before with the XML-DOM.

In Figure 21, it is shown the piece of code in PHP that performs this task.

The next piece of code chosen was from the field FINALIDADE, in order to exemplify how is done the information comparison, having in mind that all fields of category <educationalmedia> are used as recommendation parameters.

At first, the code reads the tag <educationalmedia>, keeps the reading information in a variable named $finalidadeNoXML, and then, it is checked if any value of this variable is the same as the field FINALIDADE in MySQL database where is the variable $finalidade. In the event of

Figure 19. Request function code

```
dofile('tcp.lua')

HOST = 'les2.ufersa.edu.br';
PORT = 80;
function tscorm_request(user, password)
    return 'GET /moodle/mod/tscorm/tscorm.php?user='..user..'&password='..password..' HTTP/1.0\r\nHost:
end

function tscorm_response(value)
    videos = string.match(value, "<sendrecommendation>(.+)</sendrecommendation>");
    choosed = split(videos, ":");
    answer_semaphore = true;
        coroutine.resume(tscorm_co);
end
```

Figure 20. Code for username and password authentication

```
<?php
        error_reporting( E_ALL );
        $login = $_GET["user"];
        $senha = $_GET["password"];
        include ("Conexao.php");
        include ("ComparaString.php");///
            $conex = new Conexao();
            $conex->open();
            $conex->StatusCon();
            $comparator = new ComparaString();
            $sql = "SELECT * FROM usuario WHERE login = '$login' AND senha = '$senha'";
            $retorno = mysql_query($sql, $conex->getCon());
```

Figure 21. Code for load the imsmanifest.xml file

```php
<?php
    // Carrega o arquivo XML
    $doc = new DOMDocument();
    $doc->preserveWhiteSpace = false;
    $doc->load( "imsmanifest.xml" );
    $doc->formatOutput = true;
```

equality in the information fields, the video resource is recommended and stored in the variable $recommendation, otherwise, the video resource is not recommended

In Figure 22, it shown how is performed the reading information of the user in the MySQL database with metadata of the category <educationalmedia>. All the video resources are visited in the imsmanifest.xml.

In Figure 23, it is shown the final part of the code where are shown the values (in this case, the video resources) that are sent in the variable $recommendation for a recommendation, or not, of videos. Having in mind that there was a comment in this part before where was the piece of code of the recommendation as it is shown in Figure 22.

Figure 22. Code for LOs recommendation

```php
<?php
    foreach($listaDeRecursos as $resourceVisitado){
    //Armazena a posição do nó (TAG) 'imsmd:lom' do primeiro elemento do tipo 'resource'
      $lom = $resourceVisitado->firstChild->firstChild->firstChild;
      $nomeDoVideo = $resourceVisitado->firstChild->firstChild->firstChild->firstChild->firstChild->nodeValue;

        if ( $child = $lom->firstChild ) {
            do {
                if( $child->tagName == "imsmd:educationalmedia") {
                    //Dados dos campos 'FINALIDADE', 'TIPOS DE OBJETOS DE APRENDIZAGEM', 'PALAVRAS-CHAVE' do Banco.
                    //'FINALIDADE' ('imsmd:educationalmedia->imsmd:purpose->imsmd:value'->imsmd:langstring')
                        $temp = $child->firstChild;
                        do {
                            if( $temp->tagName == "imsmd:purpose" ) {
                                $grandSon = $temp;
                                break;
                                }
                            } while($temp = $temp->nextSibling);
                        $temp = $grandSon->firstChild;
                        do {
                            if( $temp->tagName == "imsmd:value" ) {
                                $grandSon = $temp;
                                break;
                                }
                            } while($temp = $temp->nextSibling);
                        $temp = $grandSon->firstChild;
                        do {
                            if( $temp->tagName == "imsmd:langstring" ) {
                                $grandSon = $temp;
                                break;
                                }
                            } while($temp = $temp->nextSibling);

                        $finalidadeNoXML = $grandSon->nodeValue;
                        if($comparator->comparar($finalidade , $finalidadeNoXML)){
                            if($recommendation == ""){
                                $recommendation = $recommendation. $nomeDoVideo;
                                }
                            else {
                                $recommendation = $recommendation. ":" . $nomeDoVideo;
                                }
                            break;}}}
```

Figure 23. Code for sending the recommendation

```php
<?php
    foreach($listaDeRecursos as $resourceVisitado){

        //Armazena a posição do nó (TAG) 'imsmd:lom' do primeiro elemento do tipo 'resource'
        $lom = $resourceVisitado->firstChild->firstChild->firstChild;
        $nomeDoVideo = $resourceVisitado->firstChild->firstChild->firstChild->firstChild->firstChild->nodeValue;

            if ( $child = $lom->firstChild ) {
                do {
                    if( $child->tagName == "imsmd:educationalmedia") {
                        //CÓDIGO REFERENTE A RECOMENDAÇÃO DE VÍDEOS
            } else $recommendation = "0:";
            echo "<sendrecommendation>" . $recommendation . "</sendrecommendation>";
            echo "\n";
?>
```

Tests and Results

For testing and validation of the T-SCORM extension in this work, three users have created their profiles in order to test the recommending process according to their profile features. In Figure 24, it is shown the users that are registered in the Moodle database in the table usuario.

Using a virtual machine with the middleware Ginga-NCL (see Figure 25), we used the T-SCORM Moodle application (see Figure 26) to perform tests with three users.

In Figure 25, it is shown the Virtual Machine with Ginga-NCL.

In Figure 26, it is shown the Virtual Machine with T-SCORM Moodle.

Figure 27 shows requiring login and password and the recommended results for three users: *Carlos, Miguel* and *Diogo*. It is also shown the recommended result for the user *Carlos*.

In the recommendation result for user the Carlos, were compared information that are in the mySQL database in table usuario with the infor-

Figure 24. Users registered in the database for tests

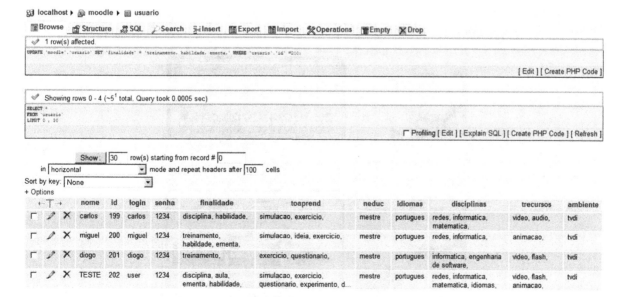

Figure 25. Virtual Machine with Ginga-NCL

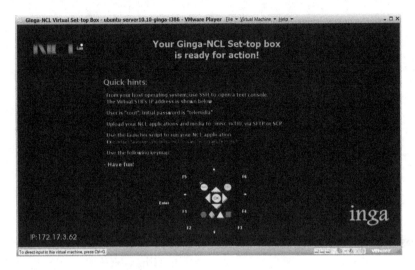

Figure 26. Virtual Machine with T-SCORM Moodle

Figure 27. Recommendation result for a user (Carlos)

mation of the tag <educationalmedia> of ims-manifest.xml file.

The field Finalidade of T-SCORM ADAPTER tool (see Figure 7) corresponds to the node <imsmd:purpose> (See Figure 10) of the tag <educationalmedia>. The value of this tag is compared with the field finalidade (see Figure 24) of the table usuario.

Similarly, the value of node <imsmd:learningresourcetype>, which would be the field Tipos de Objetos de Aprendizagem is compared with the field toaprend. Finally, the field Palavras-Chave, which stores values in the node <imsmd:keyword> is compared with the remaining fields neduc, idiomas, disciplinas, trecursos, ambiente.

Once done the recommendation, some videos in the repository were recommended to the user Carlos, such: Redes I, Redes II, Redes III, Química, Física, Geografia, História, Matemática e Matemática II.

It is possible that not all videos are of total interest for viewing, but analyzing the information in the database, it is likely that videos such as Geografia and História have been recommended because they have in the node <imsmd:learningresourcetype> values such as simulação and exercício in the imsmanifest.xml, which not necessarily makes it an interesting video for a user with computing profile. In this case, the video would not viewed by the user, unless the he may be interested.

The same process is repeated for the next two results of users Miguel and Diogo.

In Figure 28, it is shown the recommendation result for the user Miguel.

In the recommendation result for the user *Miguel*, the videos recommended in the repository were: Redes I, Redes II, Redes III, Engenharia de Software, Engenharia de Software II, Química, Física, Geografia and História. This result seems a little with the recommendation made previously for the user *Carlos*.

However, videos such as Matemática and Matemática II were not recommended.

In Figure 29, it is shown the recommendation result for the user *Diogo*.

Figure 28. Recommendation result for a user (Miguel)

Figure 29. Recommendation result for a user (Diogo)

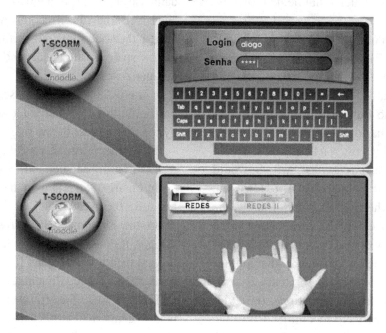

In the recommendation result for the user *Diogo*, only the videos Redes and Redes II were recommended. It is possible to notice in database that only objects with the purpose of treinamento would be chosen, and this has reduced the options for videos recommendation, which in this case were only two.

Analysis of the Results and Conclusions

According to Bates (2003) quoted by (Gomes, 2009), in order to develop a strategy of great range and especially in educational scope, the governments must include the iDTV in this process. In the same way, they should also develop wider strategies for Distance Education considering many solutions offered in the t-Learning area.

The TV has now become a tool which can offer many learning opportunities. Using it in the Distance Education area, the learning can be accomplished in your own residence, which becomes an important factor since many people prefer study at home. Some factors such as the high evasion rate, the precariousness of some public schools and the difficulty of the student in learning content, make the iDTV a fundamental mechanism to entertain, inform and educate the students.

What could be expected in medium term is that the iDTV may increasingly offer possibilities that go beyond the classroom and the means of formal education already known. Taking into account the fact that the TV is a means of communication very integrated with the popular culture, it has a great influence on the population, as well as generates a high expectation in regarding to the quality when using the service.

According to the observations done during the tests and analyzing the results, it has been seen that the users which had more information regarding the choice options in their profiles had an incidence of videos recommendation increased. That is, the less options and preferences the user has, the lower will be the recommendation.

The results lead to the conclusion that the proposal of the T-SCORM extension was considered productive, at the moment that the purpose of this work is to improve the specification and classification of LOs with educational content regarding i to their metadata information compared to the user cognitive information for iDTV. This made the navigation and search processes by LOs in the recommending process would become much more efficient and fast.

Related Work

In (Rey-Lopez et al., 2009), it is proposed an adaptation in the Shareable Content Object (SCO). In the proposed extension, new elements have been introduced in the data model, allowing the objects can request to the LMS information about the user's characteristics and thus, show the content in accordance with such information. At the activity level, new sequencing rules have been created, and making the presented structure to the users depends on their cognitive status and preferences.

The information about these adaptation parameters are obtained starting from a user profile, using inference rules. As a result, courses created

are obtained with the purpose of be personalized before make them available to the user. In Figure 30, it is shown the target scenario of this adaptation.

The focus of our work is different, considering the fact that we are proposing an extension of the SCORM standard directly in the metadata of LOM standard, improving the support to educational content through a detailed specification in how the LOs could be better delivered on the iDTV platform.

(Simões, Luis, & Horta, 2004) introduce a proposal for an extension of the SCORM standard, which allows the modeling of a course related to the entities that surround the LOs and the aggregation content. It is suggested the creation of a new category *Environmental* in the LOM standard in parallel with the current categories.

In Figure 31, it is shown the recursive hierarchy proposed by the authors. The fields for the data may be related to describe, in an arbitrary manner, complex structures that represent modeled entities.

In Figure 32, it is shown a recursive item in the application and its pseudocode.

Figure 30. Target scenario
Source: (Rey-Lopez et al., 2009)

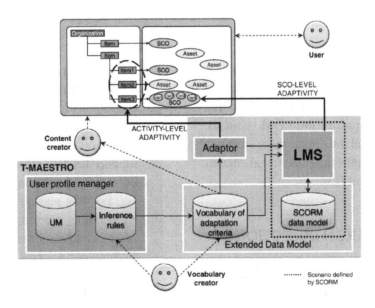

Figure 31. Extension category
Source: (Simões, Luis, & Horta, 2004)

Nr	Name	Description	Variation	Type
10	Environmental	Modeling of the environment where content aggregation is insersed. Describes entities of the courses that has relationship to the learning content.	0 or 1	Container
10.1	Item	Entity belongs to the environmental	1 or more	Container
10.1.1	Type	Type of entity	1	Vocabulary
10.1.2	Value	Value or content of the entity	0 or 1	LangString
10.1.3	Metadate	Metadata that describes the entity	0 or 1	Container
10.1.4	Item	subentity with the same structure of the Item 10.1	0 or more	Container

Figure 32. Application with the recursive item and xml code
Source: (Simões, Luis, & Horta, 2004)

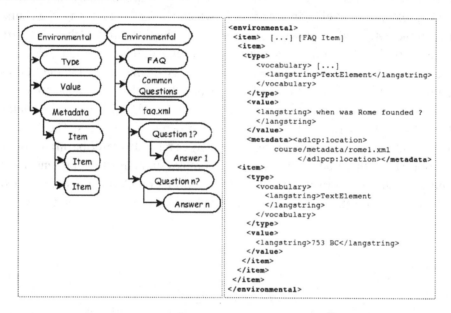

The extension presented in (Simões, Luis, & Horta, 2004) has similarity with the extension proposed in this paper regarding to proposing changes in the structure of the LOM standard. However, our proposal is to create more elements in order to better support the educational content contained in LOs for iDTV.

FUTURE RESEARCH DIRECTIONS

In this Section, before we present the future research direction, we would like to present some contributions of this work.

The main contributions are:

- **Creating an Extension to the SCORM Standard Known as T-SCORM:** The extension includes an adaptation of metadata information of the current SCORM standard based in LOM. This has improved the support for the search and navigation of LOs with educational content for t-Learning. For this reason, it was created a recommending process taking as parameter the information contained in the new metadata categories of the T-SCORM extension in the *imsmanifest.xml* compared the user profile information.

- **Creating the Authoring Tool T-SCORM ADAPTER:** The T-SCORM ADAPTER tool was developed in order to facilitate the process of reading and adding of the T-SCORM extension proposed within the structure of the *imsmanifest.xml* file. This tool makes the addition process of the new metadata in a fast and simple way, i.e., the content creator does not need manually edit the *imsmanifest.xml*. This way, other metadata that were not identified in this work, but which are important in the iDTV area could easily be added.

- **Creating the T-SCORM Moodle Application:** The T-SCORM Moodle application was created to work in integration with *Moodle*. Developed in the NCL and Lua languages, it operates in a virtual machine with the middleware Ginga -NCL, and performs the initial requesting process of videos with educational content with *Moodle*, which receives the requisition, treats and sends it the recommending response that is shown in the video options to be viewed by the user.

As future research directions, the work presented makes room for possible improvements and even innovations for the in applications developed and will certainly create other projects and publishing.

Some of the future work are:

- Review the categories of the T-SCORM extension and seek to improve the information level of the metadata always aiming at the main focus, which is to improve the search and navigation processes for LOs with educational content in the t-Learning platform.
- Implement new features in the authoring tool T-SCORM ADAPTER, e.g., whenever the user select a video resource which will have information added, the form that generates the information will show the last metadata configuration in the *imsmanifest.xml* handled previously. This will be useful to know how are the current metadata configuration and will be much faster for the content creator, in case he wishes only make small changes in the information.
- Creating a dynamic student profile. Currently, the user profile is static, i.e. the user provides the information. In dynamic profile, the information will be captured according to user interaction with the system interface.
- Increase the current videos recommending process taking into consideration, for instance, the relevance order. But for this, the system will identify which videos were most accessed, and it would you rate them depending on the user cognitive characteristics. At first, it could be considered think of using machine learning algorithms in order to improve the classification and suggestions of videos.
- Creating new versions of T-SCORM Moodle, implementing more features for tests in set top boxes and, in the same way, investigate access possibilities with multiple users in real time, with options for evaluations after the presentation of each LO, allowing its use by the community.

CONCLUSION

Along the last decade, it is remarkable growth of the Distance Education by means of excellent results, although it still presents huge challenges. One of these challenges was the spread of the Information and Communication Technology providing infrastructure necessary for the Distance Education has taken a new direction by means of different hardware and software platforms, enabling the e-Learning, i.e., using the Internet for educational purposes.

Following this segment, the iDTV has also been an important factor in the communication and interaction for knowledge acquisition, entertainment and leisure in Distance Education context. This new teaching-learning has context been called t-Learning. In this context, the LOs have an important role helping in the electronic courses development.

The standardization of these LOs was created in order to allow the reusability of educational contents and systems interoperability, being the SCORM standard the most used for educational purposes. One of the major challenges of this work was to study and understand the SCORM, and based on this research, it was notices that it would be possible to create other extension profiles regarding the SCORM.

Thus, the T-SCORM extension was created by contemplating an adaptation of metadata information of current standard based on LOM, improving the support for search and navigation of Learning Objects with educational content for t-Learning.

Some difficulties in the project implementation were considered normal, since they are part of a knowledge process of a new technology. This kind of experience is essential for any development project may be well succeed.

ACKNOWLEDGMENT

The authors thank CAPES for the research scholarships and the financial support provided.

REFERENCES

ADL. (2010). *Advanced distributed learning*. Retrieved from http://www.adlnet.org

Alves, L. G. P., Kulesza, R., Silva, F. S., Juca, P., & Bressan, G. (2006). Análise comparativa de metadados em tv digital. In *SBC Biblioteca Digital* (pp. 87–98). SBC.

Americo, M. (2010). TV digital: Propostas para o desenvolvimento de conteúdos em animação para o ensino de ciências. Tese de Doutorado, Universidade Estadual Paulista, Bauru, SP., Brazil.

Bez, M. R., Vicari, R. M., & Silva, J. M. Carvalho da, Ribeiro, A., Guz, J. C., Passerino, L., ... Roesler, V. (2010). Proposta brasileira de metadados para objetos de aprendizagem baseados em agentes (OBAA). *Revista Novas Tecnologias na Educação, 8*(2), 1–10.

Doyle, M. (2009). *Beginning PHP 5.3*. Birmingham, UK: Wrox Press Ltd..

Gazzoni, A., Canal, A. P., Falkembach, G. A. M., Fioreze, L. A., Pincolini, L. B., & Antoniazzi, R. (2006). Proporcionalidade e semelhança: Aprendizagem via objetos de aprendizagem. *Novas Tecnologias na Educação - CINTED-UFRGS, 4*. Retrieved from http://seer.ufrgs.br/renote/article/viewFile/14141/8076

Girardi, R. (2002). *Framework para coordenação e mediação de web services modelados como learning objects para ambientes de aprendizado na web. (Dissertação de Mestrado). Pontífica Universidade Católica do Rio de Janeiro*. Rio de Janeiro, Brazil: PUC-Rio.

Gomes, F. J. L. (2009). *Explorando objetos de aprendizagem na TV digital: Estudo de caso de alternativas de interação. (Tese Doutorado). Universidade Federal do Rio Grande do Sul*. Porto Alegre, Brazil: UFRS.

LOM. (2002). *Learning object metadata*. Retrieved from http://ltsc.ieee.org/wg12/20020612-Final-LOM-Draft.html

LTSC. (2002). Learning technologies standards committee. *IEEE Standard 1484.12.1*. Retrieved from http://ltsc.ieee.org/wg12/files/LOM_1484_12_1_v1_Final_Draft.pdf

Monteiro, B. S., Prota, T. M., Souza, F. F., & Gomes, A. S. (2008). *Desenvolvimento de objetos de aprendizagem para TVDi*. Fortaleza, Brazil: SBIE.

Naidu, S. (2006). *E-learning: A guidebook of principles, procedures and practices*. New Delhi, India: Common wealth Educational Media Center for Asia (CEMCA).

Pazos-Arias, J. J., López-Nores, M., García-Duque, J., Díaz-Redondo, R. P., Blanco-Fernández, Y., Ramos-Cabrer, M., et al. (2008). *Provision of distance learning services over interactive digital tv with mhp*. Retrieved from http://portal.acm.org/citation.cfm?id=1342427.1342676

Pontes, A. (2010). *Uma arquitetura de agentes para suporte a colaboração na aprendizagem baseada em problemas em ambientes virtuais de aprendizagem. (Dissertação Mestrado)*. Mossoró, Brazil: Universidade Federal Rural do Semi-Árido - UFERSA e Universidade do Estado do Rio G. do Norte - UERN.

Rey-Lopez, M., Diaz-Redondo, R. P., Fernandez-Vilas, A., Pazos-Arias, J. J., Garcia-Duque, J., Gil-Solla, A., & Ramos-Cabrer, M. (2009). *An extension to the adl scorm standard to support adaptivity: The t-learning case-study*. Retrieved from http://portal.acm.org/citation.cfm?id=1460931.14610 76

SBTVD. (2007). *Sistema Brasileiro de TV digital*. Retrieved from http://sbtvd.cpqd.com.br

Shih, W.-C., Yang, C.-T., & Tseng, S.-S. (2011). Fuzzy folksonomy-based index creation for e-learning content retrieval on cloud computing environments. In *Proceedings of Fuzzy Systems (FUZZ)*. IEEE. doi:10.1109/FUZZY.2011.6007516.

Simoes, D., Luis, R., & Horta, N. (2004). Enhancing the scorm modelling scope. In *Proceedings of Advanced Learning Technologies*. IEEE.

Yin, R. K. (2005). *Estudo de caso: Planejamento e métodos 3*. Brazil: Editora Bookman.

Chapter 7
Recommending Academic Papers for Learning Based on Information Filtering Applied to Mobile Environments

Sílvio César Cazella
*Universidade Federal de Ciências da Saúde de Porto Alegre, Brazil
& Universidade do Vale do Rio dos Sinos, Brazil*

Jorge Luiz Victória Barbosa
Universidade do Vale do Rio dos Sinos, Brazil

Eliseo Berni Reategui
Universidade Federal do Rio Grande do Sul, Brazil

Patricia Alejandra Behar
Universidade Federal do Rio Grande do Sul, Brazil

Otavio Costa Acosta
Universidade Federal do Rio Grande do Sul, Brazil

ABSTRACT

Mobile learning is about increasing learners' capability to carry their own learning environment along with them. Recommender Systems are widely used nowadays, especially in e-commerce sites and mobile devices, for example, Amazon.com and Submarino.com. In this chapter, the authors propose the use of such systems in the area of education, specifically for the recommendation of learning objects in mobile devices. The advantage of using Recommender Systems in mobile devices is that it is an easy way to deliver recommendations to students. Based on this scenario, this chapter presents a model of a recommender system based on information filtering for mobile environments. The proposed model was implemented in a prototype aimed to recommend learning objects in mobile devices. The evaluation of the received recommendations was conducted using a Likert scale of 5 points. At the end of this chapter, some future works are described.

DOI: 10.4018/978-1-4666-4542-4.ch007

INTRODUCTION

Nowadays, studies focusing mobility in distributed systems are being stimulated by the proliferation of portable electronic devices (for example, smart phones, handheld computers, tablet PCs, and notebooks) and the use of interconnection technologies based on wireless communication (such as WiFi, WiMAX, and Bluetooth). This new mobile and distributed paradigm is called Mobile Computing (Satyanarayanan, 1996). Moreover, mobility together with the widespread use of wireless communication enabled the availability of computational services in specific contexts – Context-aware Computing (Dey et al., 1999). Furthermore, researches related to adaptation brought the possibility of continuous computational support, anytime and anywhere. This characteristic is sometimes referred as Ubiquitous Computing (Weiser, 1991; Grimm et al., 2004; Saha & Mukherjee, 2003; Satyanarayanan, 2001).

The application of mobile and ubiquitous computing in the improvement of education strategies has created two research fronts called Mobile Learning and Ubiquitous Learning. Mobile learning (m-learning) (Tatar, 2003) is fundamentally about increasing learners' capability to carry their own learning environment along with them. M-learning is the natural evolution of E-learning, and has the potential to make learning even more widely accessible. However, considering the ubiquitous view, mobile computers are still not embedded in the learners' surrounding environment, and as such they cannot seamlessly obtain contextual information.

On the other hand, Ubiquitous Learning (Barbosa, et al., 2007; Lewis, et al., 2010; Ogata, et al., 2010) refers to learning supported by the use of mobile and wireless communication technologies, sensors and location/tracking mechanisms, that work together to integrate learners with their environment. Ubiquitous learning environments connect virtual and real objects, people and events, in order to support a continuous, contextual and meaningful learning. A ubiquitous learning system can use embedded devices that communicate mutually to explore the context, and dynamically build models of their environments. It is considered that while the learner is moving with his/her mobile device, the system dynamically supports his/her learning by communicating with embedded computers in the environment. The opportunities made available by the context can be used to improve the learning experience.

The opportunities are clear but educators need to face some challenges. The greatest challenge with which every educator faces is the organization of content and activities aimed at the development of certain competencies in students. This challenge is intensified when we try to identify and recommend different materials, customized to each student based on individual needs and interests.

This chapter proposes a system to make personalized recommendations of learning objects (LO) using mobile devices, according to students' interests ("tastes" for certain learning objects). Learning objects are understood here as digital learning materials developed in a modular way so that they can be used separately and together - based on an object oriented paradigm (Wiley, 2000). In this sense, a scientific paper, a web page, a simulator, a program of planned questions and answers, all may be considered learning objects.

Among the computational techniques to assist in the search for relevant information, Recommender Systems (Adomavicius & Tuzhilin, 2005) are able to automatically identify contents that are appropriate for each individual based on their characteristics or "tastes", and the relevant content can be acess by a student using a mobile device.

RECOMMENDER SYSTEMS AND LEARNING OBJECTS

There are several applications of content retrieval which try to assist users in identifying items of interest. However, it is common that these applications bring much irrelevant content as result (Adomavicius & Tuzhilin, 2005). Trying to minimize this problem, recommender systems have emerged, focusing on the search for relevant information in accordance with User's own characteristics, as well as certain requirements relating to the items it want to find.

Different techniques are applied in recommender systems to find the most appropriate content for users. In (Sarwar et al., 2000), for example, different algorithms are compared for a recommendation according its accuracy and performance. Here, our focus is the technique of Collaborative Filtering (CF) (Shardanand & Maes, 1995), a technique that is based on information collected about the entire community of users and has already proved suitable for several applications (Herlocker et al., 2004).

With the amount of information available on the Internet easily and quickly, people are faced with a great diversity of options. Often an individual has little personal experience to make choices among various alternatives of content that are presented. In this universe, teachers and students have at their disposal learning objects (LOs), which are modules or units of content designed to support learning with digital technologies (IEEE 2002 apud Coll & Monereo, 2010). They are characterized by the possibility of being adapted, reused, affordable, durable, and can be used on different platforms (Fabre et al, 2003 apud Tarouco et al, 2004). Therefore, the repositories of learning objects assists the teacher in the selection of resources, because they are databases that store the objects to facilitate access and organization. However, there remains the difficulty of choice by the wide availability of options.

According to Wiley (2000), Learning Objects are small instructional components that can be reused numerous times in different learning contexts. Haughey & Muirhead (2005) point out that there are several definitions for the term and some focus on the "object" of the term, while others have emphasized the aspect of "learning".

The authors note that "[...] LOs have no value or utility outside of teaching contexts, its value lies in its application to classroom settings and online environments where teachers may or may not be present" (Haughey & Muirhead, 2005).

According to Haughey & Muirhead (2005), the LOs are designed to help teachers perform the following functions:

- Introduce new topics and skills.
- Provide a reinforcement of existing skills.
- Extending learning through new means for presenting curriculum material.
- Illustrate the concepts that are less easily explained through traditional teaching methods.
- Support new kinds of learning opportunities that are not available in a classroom environment.
- Provide enrichment for highly motivated students.

LOs are appropriate to support learning, because they are interactive features, multimedia and most often built in small modules, making it easy and enjoyable learning process. The LOs are considered facilitators of teaching and learning as they allow to simulate complex events, attracting the attention of students, facilitate planning a lesson, proposes situations related to daily life, bringing the curriculum to student's reality.

To be considered an LO at least four functional requirements must be met (Puustjärvi, 2007):

1. Must be usable in different educational contexts, and therefore reusable.
2. Must be independent of media and learning management system where it is displayed, enabling the interoperability of systems.
3. Should be designed to be combined with other LOs.
4. Must provide appropriate metadata, facilitating a simple search.

The LOs are usually stored in repositories, which allow the indexing of these objects through the metadata, facilitating their recovery and enabling them to be adapted to the teaching context. The register of LOs in repositories is an arduous task and, sometimes, for this reason, this task is not performed properly, as they are normally numerous fields to be filled, for the information about the objects themselves, named metadata.

Therefore, the recommendation systems come assist the user in selecting content. In a typical system of filtering of information people provide recommendations as inputs and the system aggregates and directs to individuals who are considered potential candidates. One of the great challenges of this type of system is to achieve the appropriate mix between the expectations of users (profile) and the items to be recommended, i.e., defining the relationship of interest. In the educational context, one can envision a student being exposed to a lot of LOs seeking assist with their training. In this case, Educational Recommender Systems (ERS) act as information filters transmitting the object that best suits the student meet his learning needs. In fact, recommender systems are highly dependent domain (Santos & Apothecary, 2010), is fundamental to take into account in a ERS participation of educators in their modeling.

Collaborative Filtering

Collaborative Filtering is based on one of the most popular techniques for recommendation and is used in many systems on the Internet (Schafer et al., 2001). The technique is based on the analysis of common preferences in a group of people. The essence of this technique is the exchange of experiences among people who have common interests and have "tastes" for similar items.

In this technique, the contents that may be recommended are filtered based on the evaluations (feedback) made by users on the same items. This evaluation tries to observe the behavior of a group and analyze the similarities between the

"tastes" for items within the group. For each user the technique tries to identify a set of "neighbors" that are so classified because they have similar behavior (Adomavicius & Tuzhilin, 2005). The following subsections deal with the calculation of the coefficient of similarity between two users, the preliminary step of a process of Collaborative Filtering, and the selection of subsets of users with hight similarity, called neighbors, who are considered at the stage of prediction. In this last step, predictions are calculated to indicate how an item is appropriate for a particular user.

Coefficient of Similarity and Prediction Calculation

To calculate the similarity between students, the model presented in this chapter applyies the Pearson's coefficient, which is an approach widely used in Recommender Systems based on Collaborative Filtering (Shardanand & Maes, 1995). This coefficient measures the degree of correlation between two variables, resulting in values between [-1, +1], where the value -1 represents complete lack of correlation between variables, and the value of +1 represents a strong correlation between them. Equation 1 presents the calculation of similarity (Cazella at al, 2008).

$$\text{corr}_{ab} = \frac{\sum i (r_{ai} - \overline{r}_a)(r_{bi} - \overline{r}_b)}{\sqrt{\sum i (r_{ai} - \overline{r}_a)^2 \sum i (r_{bi} - \overline{r}_b)^2}} \quad (1)$$

Since $corr_{ab}$ the correlation of the target user a with a specific user b; r_{ai}: is the assessment that the active user assigned to item i; r_{bi}: is the assessment that the active user b assigned to item i; $\overline{r}_a$ is the average of all evaluations of the active user i, in common with user b, $\overline{r}_b$ is the average of all user ratings b active, in common with the user a.

Once you get the correlation between the opinions of students on certain learning objects, it is possible to calculate the recommendation of an object based on a prediction of how much students appreciate receiving specific recommendation (prediction refers to predict the evaluation this student would give to the learning object, if it had access to it).

The calculation of the prediction is performed independently of the coefficient used for calculating the similarity, since this calculation is performed based on a weighted average of the ratings given by students identified as closest neighbors (individuals who obtained a similarity coefficient less than a predetermined threshold). Equation 2 presents the calculation of prediction (Cazella at al, 2008).

$$p_{ai} = \overline{r}_a + \frac{\sum_{b=1}^{n}(r_{bi} - \overline{r}_b) * corr_{ab})}{\sum_{b=1}^{n}| corr_{ab} |} \qquad (2)$$

$corr_{ab}$ is the correlation of the target student a with particular student b; p_{ai} is the prediction of item i for the target student a; $\overline{r}_a$ is the average of all evaluations made by the target student a for the items which were evaluate by all alike students; r_{bi} is the evaluation that the student b assigned to the item i; $\overline{r}_b$ is the average of all evaluations made by student b in common with the student a.

PROTOTYPE AND EXPERIMENTS

The ubiquitous learning scenario is attractive, but is not easily implemented. We are investigating how to better match people's expectations for such system. In our point of view, ubiquitous learning environments should support the execution of context-aware, distributed, mobile, pervasive and adaptive learning applications.

Since years ago, the mobile computing lab at UNISINOS has been researching ubiquitous computing topics. One of our main goals was the creation of a mobile and ubiquitous learning sys-

tem, called LOCAL (Location and Context Aware Learning). LOCAL utilizes location information and contextual information of learners to aid in the teaching and learning processes. LOCAL is composed by seven subsystems (see Figure 1):

1. **User Profiles:** Which store information related to the users using the PAPI standard (PAPI, 2012.)
2. **Personal Assistant:** Which acts as the system's interface, residing in the user's mobile device.
3. **Location System:** Used to determine the physical position of the mobile devices.
4. **Learning Objects Repository:** Which stores and indexes content related to the teaching process.
5. **Tutor:** An analysis engine capable of making inferences by using the data supplied by the profiles and the location system.
6. **Communication System:** Used to establish communication between the different parts of LOCAL, and between the system and its users.
7. **Event System:** Used to schedule tasks.

The LOCAL model (Location and Context Aware Learning) (Barbosa et al, 2008) (Barbosa et al, 2007) uses location information and context as an aid to teaching and learning. In LOCAL's model a tracking system monitors the mobility of students and, based on their physical positions, explore educational opportunities.

The model RECCOLLABORATIVEMOB (RECommender System based on COLLABORATIVE Filtering for MOBile Device) (Figure 2) uses resources from LOCAL's architecture to enable some features and provides service to LOCAL.

As can be seen in Figure 2, the RECCOLLABORATIVEMOB model consists of:

1. **Recommendation Module:** Responsible for calculating the similarities and definition of

Figure 1. The LOCAL architecture

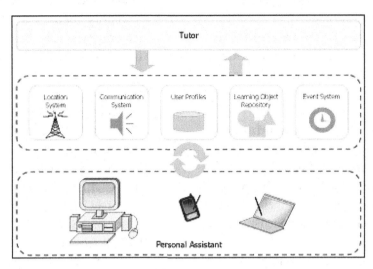

Figure 2. Model RECCOLLABORATIVEMOB

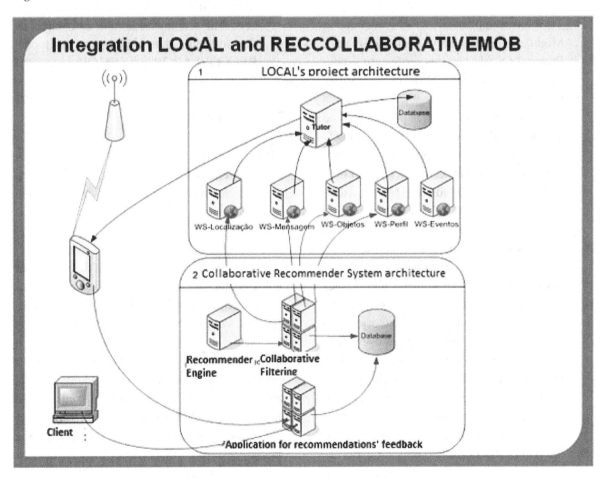

close neighbors, as well as the prediction of items to be recommended;

2. **Collaborative Recommendation:** Responsible for interaction with LOCAL and forwarding the recommendations made to the LOCAL forward the same for mobile devices;

3. **Application to Recommendations' Evaluation:** Application to collect users' ratings for recommended items;

4. **Database:** With the items to be recommended, registered users and their profiles, as well as the evaluations provided by users.

The model described has been implemented and its operation is described below, showing the interaction with the LOCAL's architecture:

1. The tutor recommendation (Recommendation Module) runs as a service on the server's Project LOCAL, and this service runs daily in the evening in search of recommendations for the users.

2. The first time the service is performed, the prototype will calculate the similarity coefficient among all users registered in the system (as described in section 2.1.1) and then will calculate the prediction (as described in section 2.1.1) for all items available to recommendation on the system (in the case of the experiment, these items are scientific papers). After this first run the data related to users' similarity coefficients and predictions are persisted in the database.

3. On subsequent runs of the prototype are made new calculations if any new users, new items, and new items reviews are assessment predicted. Thus, the prototype will check if new evaluations of articles that users have persisted in the database and from these new assessments, the prototype will recalculate the similarity coefficient only for users involved in these new assessments and finally calculate the prediction Items for users.

4. Upon execution of the calculations, both similarity coefficient values as prediction, the prototype will check if any item prediction was made for a particular user, if so, sends the prototype to tutor the LOCAL recommendation of the item intended for user through a Web Service.

5. The tutor LOCAL receive the recommendations resulting from collaborative filtering prototype that implements the model RECCOLLABORATIVEMOB, and after the target user to connect to the recommendation of the project LOCAL's environment he will receive on your mobile device any recommendations available for him.

6. The user connect and identify themselves to the system using a mobile device (HP iPAQ palm), he will automatically receive all recommendations calculated by the prototype that implements the model RECCOLLABORATIVEMOB.

Research Method

Aiming to evaluate the model RECCOLLABORATIVEMOB through the prototype implemented two experiments were conducted with students in the undergraduate program in Computer Engineering at Universidade do Vale do Rio dos Sinos on Database discipline.

The research method applied in this study was experimentation to evaluate the model by using its prototype implemented with a sample of academics. This sample was obtained by convenience, thus becoming a non probabilistic sample, so it should be noted that the results obtained in order to evaluate the model can not be generalized. The sample consisted of 11 volunteers students. To facilitate the evaluation of the model was generated a base of scientific papers related with the database discipline, that is configured as the items to be recommended for future sampling.

The experiment consists in identifying users with similarity of "likes" by predicting which items and new items should be recommended for these users using this for mobile devices and collaborative recommendation technique implemented in the prototype. Users to receive the recommendation were asked to evaluate the recommended items, using a 5 point Likert scale, where a value of 1 represents no satisfaction with the recommendation received and 5 represents total satisfaction with the recommendation received.

Evaluation Metrics

Aiming to evaluate the model became necessary to choose a metric that enabled comparison of the assessment provided by a user to a particular item and the prediction made by prototype. Therefore, we adopted the metric called MAE (Mean Absolute Error) and precision.

With these metrics is possible to verify that the accuracy of recommendations based on the error of prediction. The MAE value for each prediction should be minimized trying a more appropriate recommendation. More formally MAE can be described as: if $\{r_1, ..., r_N\}$ are all real values within the set of ratings assigned by a user to a particular item, and $\{p_1, ..., p_N\}$ are the values of the predictions of ratings assigned by a user to the same item, then the MAE constitutes the ratio of the values of errors between these assessments, $E = \{1, ..., N\} = \{p_1 - r_1, ..., p_N - r_N\}$, according to equation 3:

$$|\bar{E}| = \frac{\sum_{i=1}^{n} |p_i - r_i|}{n} \qquad (3)$$

To calculate the value of MAE was necessary to calculate through the prototype evaluation that the user would possibly be recommended to the article (prediction), and then actually made the recommendation, the target user was asked to rate the article. Based on the difference of these two values for the evaluation (assessment and evaluation predicted real) the MAE is calculated and the result constituting the error of prediction.

In the context of recommendation systems, precision is the ratio of the note given by the user to an item that has been recommended and note the prediction. It was assumed in this experiment that the items recommended are those users that have predictive value greater than or equal to 3 points (on a Likert scale of 5 points). Using this metric, we found that the precision rate of the model implemented.

EXPERIMENTS AND RESULTS

First Experiment: Evaluation of Pre-Selected Items

The first experiment aimed to collect the first evaluations of sampling to allow the application of collaborative filtering, since there were no reviews to allow calculation of prediction. This experiment also aimed to deal with the limitations of the technique of collaborative filtering, the problem of the new user (Schafer, 2001). As informed, was initially selected an initial basis for recommending scientific articles to users sampled. We selected a total of 30 scientific papers and these were distributed to the sampled (the initial distribution of articles was performed with the aid of the teacher of the discipline that these sampled students attending).

Students of the sample initially received the recommendation of some articles to evaluate them. The scoring was done using a tool for this evaluation form, part of the prototype. On average 9 (nine) items were allocated per student. These initial assessments implemented model helped identify the preferences of each user and also helped in enabling the calculation of Pearson's coefficient and future prediction and recommendation (second experiment). After the evaluation of a matrix (students x items) with initial evaluations were generated with a total of 107 evaluations. For reviews, on the interface the 5 points Likert scale was adapted for concepts, so that the evaluation value of 1 corresponded to poor, and evaluation with value 5 corresponded to excellent.

As results of this first experiment can be stated that the percentage of users who actually participated and evaluated the articles stood at 72.72%, and the new user problem was minimized. With these initial assessments could initiate collaborative recommendations.

With the first articles evaluated the implemented model could calculate the similarity between the users who participated in the experiment, using it to calculate the coefficient of Pearson (subsection 2.2). Regarding the distribution of calculated similarities between users sampled showed that 55.81% of the calculated correlations between users correlations are strong, weak correlations are 9.30% and 34.88% of them can not say anything about the similarity between these users. After being computed similarities could start the calculation of the predictions of the items to be recommended to users, starting the second experiment.

Second Experiment: Generation of Predictions

The second experiment consisted in the generation of recommendations based on initial assessments produced by sampled. In this experiment the prototype calculated the prediction articles and forwarded these recommendations to users on their mobile devices.

The implemented model recommended only articles not accessed by those sampled in the first experiment and the prediction value calculated was less than 3 within a 5 point Likert scale. It should be noted that no recommendations were generated for users that have an similarity value less than 0.3 with other users. Once the recommendations were calculated, the sampled were

asked to assess these scientific papers using the application interface (Figure 3).

Table 1 presents the results obtained in this experiment. As can be seen from this table, the model implemented did not generate recommendations for users *U1, U5, U8, U10* and *U11*. These users have not received recommendations because they do not have neighbors with similarity value greater than 0.3 or they had not participated in the first round of evaluations of the first experiment, not allowing in this way, perform the calculation of Pearson's coefficient for these users.

After the predictions were calculated and ratings were provided by the sampled the MAE was calculated. Based on the outcome of MAE, we observed an average difference between the pre-

Figure 3. Application interface to review the recommendations

Table 1. Results of the second experiment

User	Item	Predective Value	Evaluation	MAE	Precision
U_2	18	3	2	1.04	65.79%
U_3	25	3	4	0.61	82.01%
U_4	10	4	3	1.59	65.36%
U_4	16	3	3	0.00	100%
U_6	10	4	3	1.00	75%
U_6	22	3	3	0.55	84.51%
U_7	22	3	2	1.75	53.33%
U_9	10	4	4	0.36	91.74%
U_9	16	3	3	0.00	100%
Average	--	--	--	**0.76**	**79.75%**

dictions made by the model implemented and assessments made by users of 0.76 points. Thus the accuracy of the predictions generated by the model implemented was 79.75%.

Table 1 presents the user, the item code which has been recommended, the predictive value calculated by the model implemented (this predictive value is the value that the user expects to assign for article recommended after reading the same), the assessed value of the real user (this value represents the actual assessment the user assigned to the article recommended after reading have been performed), the absolute error calculated between the two assessments (MAE) and the precision of the prediction made by the model implemented.

FUTURE RESEARCH DIRECTIONS

Research involving the use of Recommender Systems, Mobile Education and Learning are the focus of the scientific community, for example, (Biacalana et al, 2011), (Baltrunas et al, 2012). Some researchers are focused on the use of machine learning techniques (Data mining or Text Mining) to contribute to the process of content recommendation due to the popularity of mobile devices, for example, (Duan et al, 2011), (Venkatraman and Kamatkar, 2013). Below I describe in detail a research focused on Content-based Filtering for a

Mobile Inquiry-based Learning Environment and a Recommender System Based on Competence for Mobile Learning.

Content-Based Filtering for a Mobile Inquiry-Based Learning Environment

Inquiry-based learning is defined as a learning approach guided by the process of making questions by learners themselves (Barret et al., 2005). In this approach, students are asked to make questions about a given theme, as a way to lead them to develop their own investigations about a given topic.

Originated in the 60s, inquiry-based learning emerged as an answer to the limitations of traditional learning methods in which students were required to memorize facts from schoolbooks (Bruner, 1961). Nowadays, inquiry-based learning is seen as an active learning approach in which knowledge is built through the development of experimental and analytical activities (Seol et al, 2011). The research presented in this section focuses on the expansion of the SMILE Project (Stanford Mobile Inquiry Based Learning Environment), whose goal is to allow students to create and share questions and answers related to a given subject (Kim et al., 2011).

The SMILE learning tool enables students to quickly create multiple choice questions and share them with peers using mobile devices. Students can answer and rate each other's questions, subsequently viewing details about the activity, such as the question that obtained the highest rate, the student who achieved the highest score in answering questions accurately, the one who created the highest rated question, among other information. SMILE consists of two modules: a mobile-based application for the students, called Junction Quiz, and an activity management application for the teacher, called the Junction Quiz controller. Originally, none of these tools supported content search on the web as a way to assist students in their investigations. For that reason, a recommendation system has been incorporated to the Junction Quiz interface to enable students to find and use different materials from the web when elaborating their questions and answers.

A small variation on the original SMILE inquiry-based learning strategy has also been proposed here, to allow teachers to propose a general topic of research. For that, the system enables teachers to inform the Junction Quiz Controller a triggering text that can be used by the students to start their questioning process, as depicted in Figure 4.

This text is usually a short introduction to the subject, with basic information to familiarize students to the topic and possibly to some issues that may instigate them in their own question making process. When logging in Junction Quiz, the students have access to the text available, as well as to a text editor to enable them to start inserting their questions and answers. At this moment, the system uses a text mining tool to extract relevant terms from the students' writings, and also of the triggering text, as a way to identify keywords to be used in a web search in order to make recommendations of related contents. The mining method, detailed in Reategui et al. (2011), has been based on the n-simple distance graph model, in which nodes represent the main terms found in the text, and the edges used to link nodes represent adjacency information. The items returned from the web search (articles, books, images, videos) according to the terms coming from the mining tool are then recommended to students as a way to call their attention for the availability of materials they may not be aware of. In addition to recommending items from the web, the recommendation system monitors the materials accessed and used by students, with the

Figure 4. System operation

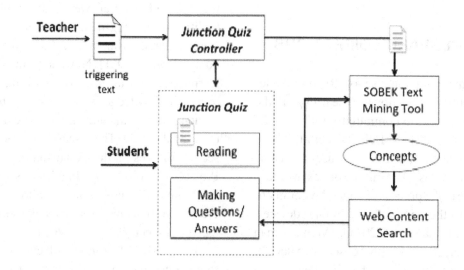

goal of considering this information in new recommendations.

Figure 5 shows a screenshot of the system, displayed on a tablet, in which a student prepares a question about the greenhouse effect, and a recommendation of a related image is presented on the right side of the screen.

Preliminary results have shown that the ability to scan students' writings in the search for related material has the potential to make learners aware of materials they would probably not find/ use if they were to carry out all web searches by themselves using a standard web search tool. Regarding the use of mobile devices to conduct inquiry-based activities, it has been demonstrated that the possibility to take mobile devices to work in different settings, to take pictures and add them to students projects, these and other features can be valuable in promoting learning processes (Seoul et al., 2011).

A Recommender System Based on Competence for Mobile Learning

The concept of competence can be understood as practical intelligence for situations that rely on knowledge and mobilizes, transforms them according to the complexity of the situations (Zarifian, 2002). In this sense, knowledge and skills (know-how) are part of the concept of competence (Fleury & Fleury 2000). Although the recommendation of personalized learning objects is a desirable feature of any educational computer system, regardless of their area of knowledge, our focus of study is the curricula of undergraduate courses in the areas of Information Technology (for example, Computer Science, Computer Engineering, Information Systems). These present a range of disciplines that are distributed throughout the semester according to a set of prerequisites. The caracterization of these disciplines usually lists a series of competences that students should develop during the course. For example, in a curriculum of Computer Engineering, the discipline

Figure 5. Rec quiz screenshot

of Databases may require the student to develop competence in "Multidimensional Modeling". The research presented here is based on this organization and notion of competences. The project aims to facilitate the access to learning objetcts that seem to be more appropriate at certain moment, according to students' features as well as to competencies that need to be developed and distributed in a class planning.

It is possible to find in the literature several definitions for the concept of competency. The Cambridge English dictionary defines it as: "an important skill that is needed to do a job". This definition, however, does not explicit relationships between important concepts such as: skills, issues, knowledge. Other authors enhance the definition: competence can be defined as the set of knowledge, skills and attitudes necessary for a person to develop their roles and responsibilities (Dutra, 2001). Perrenoud (Perrenoud,1999) defines competence as the ability to mobilize a set of cognitive resources (knowledge, skills, information, etc) to address the appropriateness and effectiveness of a variety of situations. In this way the skills are linked to cultural, professional and social conditions.

In all definitions, we can easily see the relationship between the concept of competence and skills (know-how), knowledge and attitudes. Within this research, therefore, the question arises as to how, when and how we can make a recommendation of learning objects that enable students to: build knowledge related to specific issues, develop particular skills related to given contents, develop in students a critical awareness about the importance of competence to understand how and when to use it.

The proposal to address the above issues is to use a recommender system to filter relevant information to the student, and from this information, to select learning objects that are most appropriate in accordance with the competencies to be developed.

The proposed model is shown in Figure 6. The model was designed as a service available on an application server (Cazella et al, 2010). This service is called daily at a predetermined scheadule.

The model proposes the following sequence of steps for its operation (cazella et al, 2010):

1. The teacher plans lessons based on the competencies described in the summary of the course. This provides the learning objects to be used for developing their skills. For example, in the fourth and fifth classes of the discipline of Databases, students should develop the competencie of "developing projections through the use of relational algebra". Secondly, the learning objects that can be used in the development of this competence are listed by the teacher.

2. At the first time the model is applied, the similarity coefficient (Pearson's coefficient) between all users registered in the database is computed. Then, the system calculates the prediction value for all registered contents in the database. In new interactions, only new users, new contents or objects that received new assessments are processed.

3. After the computation of the coefficient of similarity and prediction (subsection 3.1.1), the model makes use of the rules of competencies. These rules are intended to filter the content recommended by the prediction module in order to enable the user to develop certain competencies in a specific period of time. For example, the object related to "developing projections through the use of relational algebra" is recommended to a student as a consequence of his/her similarities with other students that rated the object positively, and because the student is starting to study topics that demand the development of this competency.

Figure 6. Proposed model

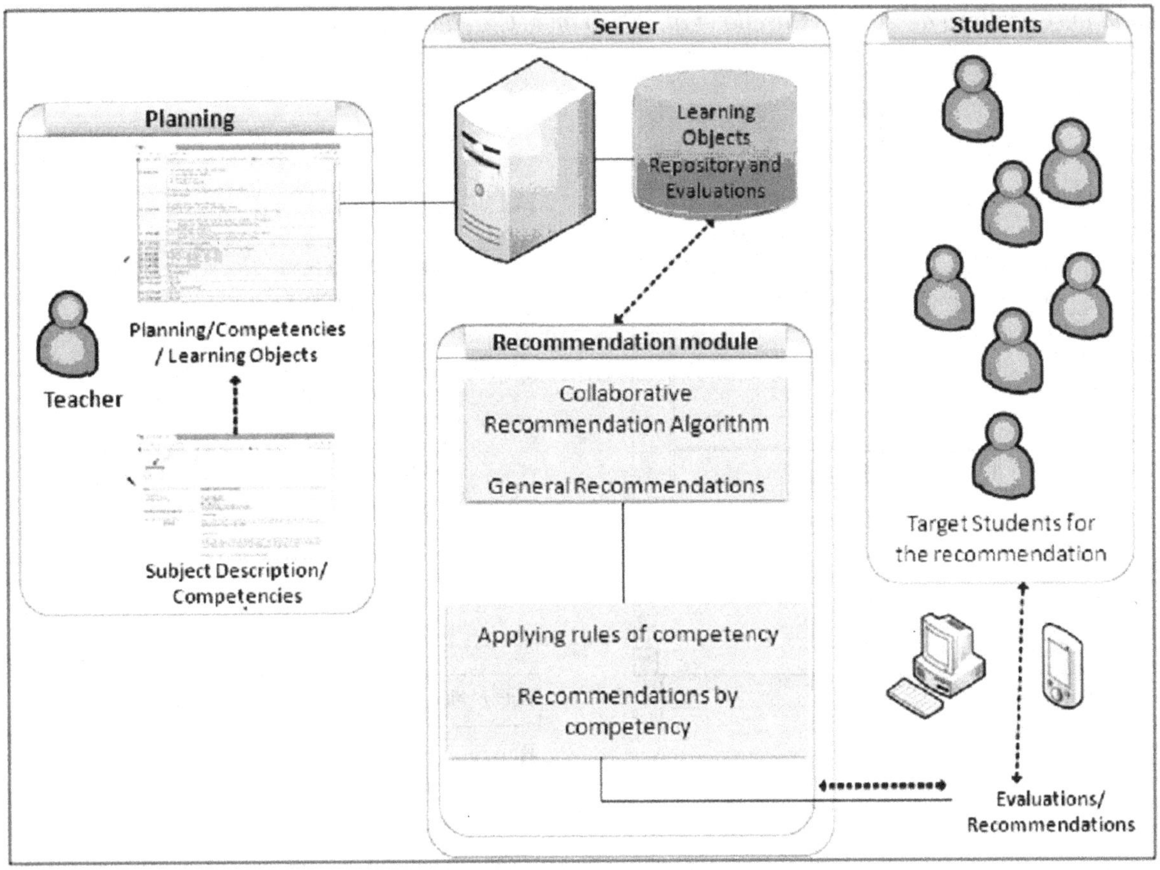

Prototype

A prototype of the model enabled the evaluation. Some students were invited to participate in experiments evaluating learning objects (in this case scientific papers) that were recommended by the system.

The scale used to evaluate learning objects was a Likert scale of 5 points, where the "not rated" is the default option where the user may not want to evaluate the object at that moment, in this case is adopted internally to 0; option "Bad", giving a value of 1; option "Poor", giving a value of 2; option "Good", giving a value of 3; option "Very Good", giving a value of 4; option "Excellent", equivalent to the value 5. A tool for evaluation of learning objects was developed as a web tool that can be accessed by any device that has a browser and have Internet access. For the development of this prototype was used the Java programming language, and the persistence layer was developed using the JDBC API. The database was implemented using MySQL5. Figure 7 shows the interfaces of the prototype PDA (Personal Digital Assistant).

CONCLUSION

This chapter presented a system to make personalized recommendations of learning objects (LO) using mobile devices, according to students' interests. Within the context of mobile learning was presented in this chapter a model for a recom-

Figure 7. (a) Interface access to the prototype on a mobile device, (b) Interface with options for evaluation of papers. More datails about this research and application, as well evolution of this work can be found in (Cazella et al, 2010), (Cazella et al, 2011) and (Cazella et al, 2012).

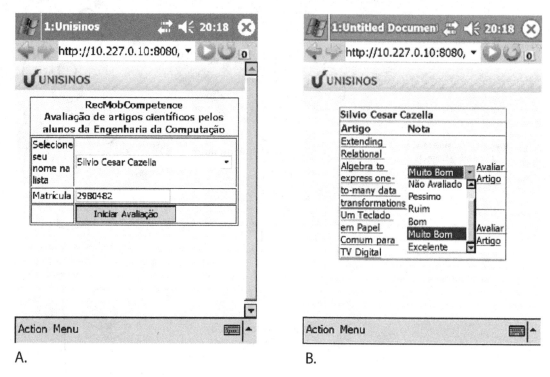

A.

B.

mendation system based on collaborative filtering to recommend items to users through the use of mobile devices. The main objective of the model is to enable a user to receive a recommendation relevant to their learning anytime they start using the system and anywhere due to mobile devices.

The major contribution of this chapter was to present a connection among concepts as Educational Recommender Systems and Mobile Learning. The contribution of study was to add to the model LOCAL a higher degree of quality in the generated recommendations for students. The prediction is based on the recommendations of the users system community's vision. A collaborative filtering technique is transparent to users in the sense that they are aware of how that recommendation is generated, so the user becomes

a developer system and not only a consumer of content generated by it.

A free personalized content recommendation to students, leaving them the initiative to decide which materials are effectively consulted, supports the learning theories that emphasize the importance of the autonomy of learners. As the precision achieved in the experiments using the model proposed and implemented, which was 79.75% in the sample, it was demonstrated that it has achieved a satisfactory result as the prediction. With this model has achieved its goals for this convenience sample, adding quality to the recommendations made for sampled at the same time that these recommendations were sent to their mobile devices through integration of the model RECCOLLABORATIVEMOB with the model LOCAL.

As future research work to be performed, the model RECCOLLABORATIVEMOB could be extended to include the importance of a user's view to aid in the process of collaborative recommendation. We intend to test the system with other types of learning objects to verify if its performance remains satisfactory, using information from the metadata of learning objects to select them according to specific requirements also related to competencies development (e.g. level of difficulty, level of interaction, etc.) and include the relevance of the opinion of a User to complement the process of recommendation.

REFERENCES

Adomavicius, G., & Tuzhilin, A. (2005). Toward the next generation of recommender systems: A survey of the state of-the-art and possible extensions. *IEEE Transactions on Knowledge and Data Engineering, 17*(6), 734–749. doi:10.1109/TKDE.2005.99.

Baltrunas, L., Ludwig, B., Peer, S., & Ricci, F. (2012). Context relevance assessment and exploitation in mobile recommender systems. *Personal and Ubiquitous Computing, 16*(5), 507–526. doi:10.1007/s00779-011-0417-x.

Barbosa, J. L., Hahn, R., Rabello, S. A., & Barbosa, D. N. (2007). Mobile and ubiquitous computing in a innovative undergraduate course. In *Proceedings of the 38th ACM Technical Symposium on Computer Science Education* (pp. 379-383). New York: ACM Press.

Barbosa, J. L. V., Hahn, R., Rabello, S. A., & Barbosa, D. N. F. (2008). LOCAL: A model geared towards ubiquitous learning. In *Proceedings of the ACM Technical Symposium on Computer Science Education* (pp. 432-436). Portland, OR: ACM Press.

Barret, T., Mac Labhrainn, I., & Fallon, H. (2005). *Handbook of enquiry & problem based learning.* Galway: CELT. Retrieved October 10, 2012, from http://www.nuigalway.ie/celt/pblbook/

Barret, T., Mac Labhrainn, I., & Fallon, H. (2005). *Handbook of enquiry & problem based learning.* Galway: CELT. Retrieved October 08, 2012, from http://www.nuigalway.ie/celt/pblbook/

Biancalana, C., Gasparetti, F., Micarelli, A., & Sansonetti, G. (2011). An approach to social recommendation for context-aware mobile services. *ACM Transaction Intelligent. Systems. Technology, 1*(1). DOI = 10.1145/0000000.0000000

Bruner, J. S. (1961). The act of discovery. *Harvard Educational Review, 31*, 21–32.

Cazella, S. C., Behar, P., Schneider, D., Silva, K. K. A., & Freitas, R. (2012). Desenvolvendo um sistema de recomendação de objetos de aprendizagem baseado em competências para a educação: Relato de experiências. In *Simpósio Brasileiro de Informática na Educação.* Rio de Janeiro: Anais do Simpósio Brasileiro de Informática na Educação.

Cazella, S. C., Corrêa, I., & Reategui, E. (2008). Um modelo para recomendação de conteúdos baseado em filtragem colaborativa para dispositivos móveis. *Revista Novas Tecnologias na Educação, 6*(2), 12–22.

Cazella, S. C., Reategui, E., & Behar, P. (2010). Recommendation of learning objects applying collaborative filtering and competencies. In N. Reynolds & M. Turcsányi-Szabó (Eds.), *Key Competencies in the Knowledge Society - IFIP TC 3 International Conference.* Boston: IFIP.

Cazella, S. C., Silva, K. K. A., Behar, P., Schneider, D., & Freitas, R. (2011). Recomendando objetos de aprendizagem baseado em competências em EAD. *Revista Novas Tecnologias na Educação, 9*, 1–10.

Coll, C., & Monereo, C. (2010). Educação e aprendizagem no séc XXI: Novas ferramentas, novos cenários, novas finalidades. In C. Coll (Ed.), *Psicologia da Educação Virtual: Aprender e Ensinar com as Tecnologias da Informação e da Comunicação*. Porto Alegre: Artmed.

Dey, A. K., Abowd, G. D., Brown, P. J., Davies, N., Smith, M., & Steggles, P. (1999). Towards a better understanding of context and context-awareness. In *Proceedings of the 1st International Symposium on Handheld and Ubiquitous Computing*, (LNCS), (Vol. 1707, pp. 304-307). Karlsruhe, Germany: Springer.

Duan, L., Street, W. N., & Xu, E. (2011). Healthcare information systems: Data mining methods in the creation of a clinical recommender system. *Enterprise Information Systems*, 5(2), 169–181. doi:10.1080/17517575.2010.541287.

Dutra, J. S. (2001). *Gestão por competências*. São Paulo: Editora Gente.

Fleury, A. C. C., & Fleury, M. T. L. (2000). *Estratégias empresariais e formação de competências*. Atlas.

Haughey, M., & Muirhead, B. (2005). Evaluating learning objects for schools. *E-Journal of Instructional Science and Technology, 8*(1). Retrieved April 13, 2011, from http://www.usq.edu.au/electpub/e-ist/docs/vol8_no1/fullpapers/eval_learnobjects_school.htm

Herlocker, J. L., Konstan, J. A., Terveen, L. G., & Riedl, J. T. (2004). Evaluating collaborative filtering recommender systems. *ACM Transactions on Information Systems, 22*(1), 5–53. doi:10.1145/963770.963772.

Kim, P., Goyal, A., Seol, S., Dodson, B., & Lam, M. (2011). Pocket school interactive learning ad-hoc network. In *Proceedings of IEEE International Conference on e-Education, Entertainment and e-Management* (pp. 1-14). IEEE.

Lewis, M., Nino, C., Rosa, J. H., Barbosa, J. L., & Barbosa, D. N. (2010). A management model of learning objects in a ubiquitous learning environment. In *Proceedings of the IEEE International Workshop on Pervasive Learning (PerEL 2010)* (pp. 256-261). Mannheim, Germany: IEEE.

Ogata, H., Yin, C., El-Bishouty, M., & Yano, Y. (2010). Computer supported ubiquitous learning environment for vocabulary learning using RFID tags. *International Journal of Learning Technology, 5*(1), 5–24. doi:10.1504/IJLT.2010.031613.

PAPI. (2011). *IEEE LTSC 1484.2 - Draft standard for learning technology - Public and private information (PAPI) for learners (PAPI learner)*. Retrieved August 8, 2012, from http://www.cenltso.net/Users/main.aspx?put=230

Perrenoud, P. (1999). Construir as competências desde a escola. Porto Alegre: Porto Alegre.

Puustjärvi, J. (2007). Syntax and semantics of learning object metadata. In K. Harman, & A. Koohang (Eds.), *Learning Objects: Standards, Metadata, Repositories, and LCMS* (pp. 41–61). Santa Rosa, CA: Informance Science Press.

Reategui, E., Epstein, D., Lorenzatti, A., & Klemann, M. (2011). Sobek: A text mining tool for educational applications. In *Proceedings of the International Conference on Data Mining* (pp. 59-64). Las Vegas, NV: Estados Unidos.

Saha, D., & Mukherjee, A. (2003). Pervasive computing: a paradigm for the 21st century. *IEEE Computer, 36*(3), 25–31. doi:10.1109/MC.2003.1185214.

Santos, O. C., & Boticário, J. G. (2010). Modeling recommendations for the educational domain. In *Proceedings of the Workshop on Recommender Systems for Technology Enhanced Learning* (pp. 2793–2800). ACM Press.

Sarwar, B., Karypis, G., Konstan, J., & Riedl, J. (2000). Analysis of recommender algorithms for e-commerce. In *Proceedings of the 2nd ACM Conference on Electronic Commerce* (pp.158-167). ACM Press.

Satyanarayanan, M. (1996). Fundamental challenges in mobile computing. In *Proceedings of the ACM Symposium on Principles of Distributed Computing* (pp. 1-7). New York: ACM.

Satyanarayanan, M. (2001). Pervasive computing: vision and challenges. *IEEE Personal Communications*, 8(4), 10–17. doi:10.1109/98.943998.

Schafer, J. B., Konstan, J., & Riedl, J. (2001). E-commerce recommendation applications. *Data Mining and Knowledge Discovery*, 5(1-2), 115–153. doi:10.1023/A:1009804230409.

Seol, S., Sharp, A., & Kim, P. (2011). Stanford mobile inquiry-based learning environment (SMILE), using mobile phones to promote student inquires in the elementary classroom. In *Proceedings of IEEE World Congress in Computer Science, Computer Engineering, and Applied Computing*. IEEE.

Shardanand, U., & Maes, P. (1995). Social information filtering: Algorithms for automating word of mouth. In *Proceedings of the SIGCHI Conference on Human Factors in Computing Systems* (CHI '95). ACM Press. DOI=10.1145/223904.223931

Tarouco, L. M. R., et al. (2004). Objetos de aprendizagem para m-learning. In *Anais do Congresso Nacional de Tecnologia da Informação e Comunicação (SUCESU)*. Retrieved September 12, 2010, from http://www.cinted.ufrgs.br/CESTA/objetosdeaprendizagem_sucesu.pdf

Tatar, D. E. (2003). Handhelds go to school: Lessons learned. *SRI International Journal Computer*, 36(9), 30–37.

Venkatraman, S., & Kamatkar, S. J. (2013). Intelligent information retrieval and recommender system framework. *International Journal of Future Computer and Communication*, 2(2), 85–89.

Weiser, M. (1991). The computer for the twenty-first century. *Scientific American*, 265(3), 94–104. doi:10.1038/scientificamerican0991-94 PMID:1675486.

Wiley, D. A. (2000). *Learning object design and sequencing theory. (PhD Tesis)*. Provo, UT: Brigham Young University.

Zarifian, P. (2002). La politique de la compétence et l'appel aux connaissances à partir de la stratégie d'entreprise post-fordiste. *Contribuição ao Colóquio de Nantes*. Retrieved December 13, 2002, from http://www.scoplepave.org/ledico/auteurs/zarifian%20competence%201.htm

ADDITIONAL READING

Adomavicius, G., Sankaranarayanan, R., Sen, S., & Tuzhilin, A. (2005). Incorporating contextual information in recommender systems using a multidimensional approach. *ACM Transactions on Information Systems*, 23(1), 103–145. doi:10.1145/1055709.1055714.

Al-Masri, E., & Mahmoud, Q. H. (2006). A context-aware mobile service discovery and selection mechanism using artificial neural networks. In *Proceedings of the 8th International Conference on Electronic Commerce* (pp. 594–598). New York: ACM Press.

Ansari, A. et al. (2000). Internet recommendation systems. *JMR, Journal of Marketing Research*, 37(3), 363–375. doi:10.1509/jmkr.37.3.363.18779.

Asabere, N. Y. (2012). Review of recommender systems for learners in mobile social/collaborative learning. *International Journal of Information and Communication Technology Research, 2*(5), 429–435.

Balabanovic, M., & Shoham, Y. (1997). Fab: Content-based, collaborative recommendation. *Communications of the ACM, 40*(3), 66–72. doi:10.1145/245108.245124.

Baldauf, M., Dustdar, S., & Rosenberg, F. (2007). A survey on context-aware systems. *International Journal of Ad Hoc and Ubiquitous Computing, 2*(4), 263-277. Retrieved March 06, 2008, from http://dx.doi.org/10.1504/IJAHUC.2007.014070

Billsus, D. et al. (2002). Adaptive interfaces for ubiquitous web access. *Communications of the ACM, 45*(5), 34–38. doi:10.1145/506218.506240.

Burke, R. (2002). Hybrid recommender systems: Survey and experiments. *User Modeling and User-Adapted Interaction, 12*(4), 331–370. doi:10.1023/A:1021240730564.

Cazella, S. C., & Alvares, L. O. C. (2005). Modeling user's opinion relevance to recommending research papers. *User Modeling, 3538*, 327–331.

Cazella, S. C., Reategui, E., & Alvares, L. O. C. (2006). E-commerce recommenders' authority: Applying the user's opinion relevance in recommender systems. In *Proceedings of the 12th Brazilian Symposium on Multimedia and the Web* (WebMedia '06). ACM. DOI=10.1145/1186595.1186605

Foltz, P. W., & Dumais, S. T. (1992). Personalized information delivery: An analysis of information filtering methods. *Communications of the ACM, 35*(12), 51–60. doi:10.1145/138859.138866.

Grimm, R., Davis, J., Lemar, E., Macbeth, A., Swanson, S., & Anderson, T. et al. (2004). System support for pervasive applications. *ACM Transactions on Computer Systems, 22*(4), 421–486. doi:10.1145/1035582.1035584.

Heckmann, D. (2005). *Ubiquitous user modeling*. (Doctor Dissertation). Technischen Fakultlaten der Universitlat des Saarlandes, Saarbrucken, Germany.

Heckmann, D., & Kruger, A. (2003). A user modeling markup language (UserML) for ubiquitous computing. In *Proceedings of the International Conference on User Modeling* (pp. 393-397). Berlin: Springer.

Herlocker, J., Konstan, J., & Riedl, J. (200). Explaining collaborative filtering recommendations. In *Proceedings of the 2000 ACM Conference on Computer Supported Cooperative Work* (pp. 241-250). ACM.

Hoareau, C., & Satoh, I (2009). Modeling and processing information for context-aware computing - A survey. *New Generation Computing, 27*(3), 177-196. DOI= 10.1007/s00354-009-0060-5

Hong, J., Suh, E., Kim, J., & Kim, S. (2009). Context-aware system for proactive personalized service based on context history. *Expert Systems with Applications, 36*(4), 7448-7457. DOI=10.1016/j.eswa.2008.09.002

Kalatzis, N., Roussaki, I., Liampotis, N., Strimpakou, M., & Pils, C. (2008). User-centric inference based on history of context data in pervasive environments. In *Proceedings of the 3rd International Workshop on Services Integration in Pervasive Environments* (pp. 25-30). DOI= 10.1145/1387309.1387316

Konstan, J. A., Miller, B. N., Maltz, D., Herlocker, J. L., Gordon, L. R., & Riedl, J. (1997). Grouplens: Applying collaborative filtering to usenet news. *Communications of the ACM, 40*(3), 77–87. doi:10.1145/245108.245126.

Lisetti, C. L. (2002). Personality, affect and emotion taxonomy for socially intelligent agents. In *Proceedings of the Fifteenth International Florida Artificial Intelligence Research Society Conference* (pp. 397–401). AAAI Press.

Lueg, C. (1998).Considering collaborative filtering as groupware: Experiences and lessons learned. In *Proceedings of the International Conference on Practical Aspects of Knowledge Management* (pp. 29-30). Basel, Switzerland: IEEE.

McDonald, D. W. (2001). Evaluating expertise recommendations. In *Proceedings of the 2001 International ACM SIGGROUP Conference on Supporting Group Work* (pp. 214–223). New York: ACM Press.

McDonald, D. W. (2003). Recommending collaboration with social networks: A comparative evaluation. In *Proceedings of the SIGCHI Conference on Human Factors in Computing Systems* (pp. 593–600). New York: ACM Press.

McDonald, D. W., & Ackerman, M. S. (2000). Expertise recommender: A flexible recommendation system and architecture. In *Proceedings of the 2000 ACM Conference on Computer Supported Cooperative Work* (pp. 231–240). New York: ACM Press.

Middleton, S., Shadbolt, N., & De Roure, D. (2004). Ontological user profiling in recommender systems. *ACM Transactions on Information Systems*, *22*(1), 54–88. doi:10.1145/963770.963773.

Montaner, M. et al. (2003). A taxonomy of recommender agents on the internet. In *Artificial Intelligence Review* (pp. 285–330). Dordrecht, The Netherlands: Kluwer Academic Publishers.

O'Connor, M., Cosley, D., Konstan, J. A., & Riedl, J. (2001). Polylens: A recommender system for groups of users. In *Proceedings of the Seventh Conference on European Conference on Computer Supported Cooperative Work* (pp. 199–218). Norwell, MA: Kluwer Academic Publishers.

Pazzani, M. J. (1999). A framework for collaborative, content-based and demographic filtering. *Artificial Intelligence Review*, *13*(5-6), 393–408. doi:10.1023/A:1006544522159.

Perugini, S., Gonçalves, M. A., & Fox, E. A. (2004). Recommender systems research: A connection-centric survey. *Journal of Intelligent Information Systems*, *23*(2), 107–143. doi:10.1023/B:JIIS.0000039532.05533.99.

Resnick, P., et al. (1994). GroupLens: An open architecture for collaborative filtering of netnews. In *Proceedings of ACM 1994 Conference on Computer Supported Cooperative Work*. Chapel Hill, NC: ACM Press.

Resnick, P., Kuwabara, K., Zeckhauser, R., & Friedman, E. (2000). Reputation systems. *Communications of the ACM*, *43*(12), 45–48. doi:10.1145/355112.355122.

Resnick, P., & Varian, H. R. (1997). Recommender systems. *Communications of the ACM*, *40*(3), 55–58. doi:10.1145/245108.245121.

Resnick, P., Zeckhauser, R., Swanson, J., & Lockwood, K. (2006). The value of reputation on ebay: A controlled experiment. *Experimental Economics*, *9*(2), 79–101. doi:10.1007/s10683-006-4309-2.

Ricci, F. (2011). Mobile recommender systems. *International Journal of Information Technology and Tourism*, *12*(3), 205–231. doi:10.3727/109830511X12978702284390.

Ricci, F., & Rokach, L. (2010). *Recommender systems handbook*. Berlin: Springer.

Riedl, J. et al. (2000). Electronic commerce recommender applications. *Journal of Data Mining and Knowledge Discovery*, *5*(2), 115–152.

Spiliopoulou, M. (2000). Web usage mining for website evaluation. *Communications of the ACM*, *43*(8), 127–134. doi:10.1145/345124.345167.

Terveen, L., Hill, W., Amento, B., McDonald, D., & Creter, J. (1997). Phoaks: A system for sharing recommendations. *Communications of the ACM, 40*(3), 59–62. doi:10.1145/245108.245122.

Wang, T. I., Tsai, K. H., Lee, M. C., & Chiu, T. K. (2007). Personalized learning objects recommendation based on the semantic-aware discovery and the learner preference pattern. *Journal of Educational Technology & Society, 10*(3), 84–105.

Yin, C., Ogata, H., Tabata, Y., & Yano, Y. (2010). Supporting the acquisition of Japanese polite expressions in context-aware ubiquitous learning. *International Journal of Mobile Learning and Organisation, 4*(2), 214–234. doi:10.1504/IJMLO.2010.032637.

Section 3
Context–Aware Learning Objects for U–Learning

Chapter 8
Ubiquitous Technologies and the Emergence of New Learning Experiences

Bruno de Sousa Monteiro
Federal University of Pernambuco (UFPE), Brazil

Alex Sandro Gomes
Federal University of Pernambuco (UFPE), Brazil

ABSTRACT

With the popularization of mobile devices and access to Internet, there has been an intense growth in ubiquitous learning products and studies. How does this effectively impact learners' (not just students') and teachers' daily lives? This chapter presents a literature review on ubiquitous learning, highlighting the impacts of this paradigm on the educational practice, seeking to combine this paradigm with social learning theories. Finally, the authors describe the extension of a social learning service called Redu, whose development is guided by the flexibility of pedagogical models, self-regulated learning, and by supporting the context, allowing a ubiquitous learning experience.

INTRODUCTION

What really matters when dealing with new technologies in education is the unusual didactical mediation introduced by the new technologies. So, far away from representing a simple fad, smartphones and tablets integrated with social networks enable the development of distributed work and learning communities. Through those artifacts, individuals and groups interact productively, communicating and creating new ways of working, teaching and learning. One of the keywords guiding this new way of working and learning is collaboration. The use of these technologies enables, among other things, the exchange of information and experiences among professionals and students by creating environments and communities to interact and learning together. Only those facts should justify the extensive use of this tool as teaching material. However, what justifies the fully didactic

DOI: 10.4018/978-1-4666-4542-4.ch008

appropriation? We follow Anderson (2004), who proposes that emerging interaction styles seems to accommodate new teaching practices, transforming the structure of practices taking place in between the 'poles' of the didactical triangle: the teacher(s), the learner(s), and, the knowledge. Next, we will describe possible situations between these poles, two by two.

Technologies expand the possibilities of the *Teacher-Student* relationships to beyond the school environment and the school teaching time period. Teachers' can structure didactical sequences to present information they consider the most didactically appropriate. The communication can be largely mediated through many media and styles: images, websites, books, educational games, forums, email, and instant messages. Those process are very important to construct empathy between people by transmit the 'shining eyes' and motivations. The remote interactions complement classroom meetings extending the communication possibilities. New forms of communication and new didactic functions are enabled by communication technologies. Thus, teachers and student experiment a rich communication and mediation process. Just to show an example of this unusual experience, let's imagine what can happen when a teacher reuse all the dialogues conducted in a digital forum with a previous group when starting a new class. Technology can plays a role of collective memory and an all series of interpretations and communication phenomena take place. So, technology allows the organization of unusual situations in an intuitive and simplified way. Just to list some others possibilities: coordination of learning communities activities, didactical team extension, formative evaluation, distinct and complementary communication channels, transactional distance improvement using cross platform interaction (Moore, 2002; Tori, 2008), group activity perception and awareness, activity visualization, and cross platform digital communication genres.

Considering the *Teacher-Knowledge* relationships, the possibilities of search and information sharing are almost unlimited. Digital media is flexible and somehow demands a more reflective practice and greater effort to plan what to do. This 'side effect' is seldom considered by designer of educational technologies. Undeveloped practices like sharing knowledge and practices among colleagues are also phenomena to consider. So, informal and peripherals practices, become essential and are legitimated by the structure of the new teaching practices.

Lastly, in the *Student-Knowledge* relationships, we watch the emergency of so many possibilities of self-directed knowledge construction. Apart from lectures and meetings that occur between Teachers-Students in the space of the classroom, colleagues can help each other. The communication between them is intense and quick. The willingness to extensively share information – which former generations had not – promotes a huge set of positive impacts. On the other side, teachers assume roles to guide the construction of the meaning of what students are learning.

Students manage their learning process. The central concepts in this scenario are the metacognitive competences; specifically self-regulated learning ones. Developed students use a greater degree of self-regulation processes - by define their learning objectives and begin to track them - tend to require lower levels of intervention instructor. These students tend to establish rhythms and learning different strategies to achieve their goals. Students who develop these competences can effectively learning from collaboration.

The challenge of the design of collaborative learning environment is to create such adequate digital artifacts to influence the development of learners' competences and thus became unnecessary. We present the system Redu later in this chapter, designed with this intention (Gomes *et al.*, 2012).

In the next section, we conduct a review of the literature on ubiquitous learning, highlighting the impacts that this paradigm causes on the educational practices. Than we describe the virtual environment Redu, whose development is guided by the flexibility of pedagogical models and self-regulated learning. Finally, we suggest an extension to this environment and describe the current efforts to support the context of the learners and to deal with ubiquitous learning situations.

BACKGROUND

The Emergency of New Educational Practices

Recent changes in social organizations, caused by technological advances and popularization of ICT (Table 1), transform the patterns of communication, social relationships, economic activities and leisure, on increasingly accelerated pace (Cobo &

Moravec, 2011; TrendWatching, 2012). Another fact that stands out is the increasing access to Internet through mobile devices. According a report from StatCounter (2012), until October 2012, 12.3% of all accesses worldwide to the Web came from smartphones (Table 2).

In the American context, the overall penetration of ICT (Table 3) and smartphones (Table 4) follow the same trend (Nielsen, 2012).

This growth was also observed among Brazilian people (Table 5 and Table 6) and Brazilian students: among students in elementary and secondary education, 12% use smartphones to access the Internet (CGI.Br, 2011). Also in relation to the Brazilian context, it was found that in 2011 67% of Internet users used it for learning purposes, including, that these practices are also widespread among young users and users with lower family income (Table 7).

Following these trends, the annual Horizon Report (New Media Consortium, 2012) presents a survey of likely emerging technologies that will

Table 1. Penetration of ICT equipment in the world (ITU, 2012)

	2009	2010	2011
Internet	25.6%	29.2%	32.5%
Computer	34.5%	36.2%	38.4%
Mobile Phone	68.2%	77.1%	85.7%

Table 2. Access to the Web from smartphones in the world (StatCounter, 2012)

	October 2010	October 2011	October 2012
Access to the Web from Smartphones	3.8%	6.6%	12.3%

Table 3. Penetration of ICT equipment in the EUA (ITU, 2012)

	2009	2010	2011
Internet	71.0%	74.0%	77.9%
Mobile Phone	89.2%	89.9%	105.9%

Table 4. Penetration of smartphones in EUA (Nielsen, 2012)

	January 2012
Total	48%
Aged 18 to 24 years	62%
Aged 25 to 34 years	66%

Table 5. Proportion of Brazilian households that have ICT equipment (CGI.Br, 2011)

	2009	2010	2011
Internet	24%	27%	38%
Computer	32%	35%	45%
Mobile Phone	78%	84%	87%

Table 6. Proportion of Brazilian people accessing the Internet through mobile, on the total mobile phone users in the last three months (CGI.Br, 2011)

	2010	2011
Total	5%	17%
Aged 16 to 24 years	9%	33%

Table 7. Proportion of Brazilian people using the Internet for education, over the total number of Internet users (CGI.Br, 2011)

	Total Brazil	Rural area	Aged 10 to 15 years	Up to 1 minimum wage
Proportion of individuals using the Internet for education	67%	73%	92%	75%

impact education in the next five years. Importantly, they do not develop in isolation but are correlated and can be developed and adopted jointly. According to this report, in the short term (one year), are the Electronic books and Mobiles; over the medium term (three years), it is anticipated the popularity of Augmented reality and game-based learning, and in the long term (five years) the H and learning analytics.

This perspective motivates the development and adoption of ICTs in educational practices. On the other hand, looking into the future just through the prism of technology can stun our vision and induce distorted to the future prospects. Cobo & Moravec (2011) illustrate the feeling of expectation created on this subject: "When it comes to technology, we tend to treat it as a 'silver bullet' that kills the wolf behind the metaphorical model of education 1.0" (Cobo & Moravec, 2011, p. 66).

Note that it is inevitable to associate the "future of education" to the intensive use of technology, making it an "*inevitable* cliché". So, caution is needed not to follow the path of widespread "Techno-utopia". Based on these and other researchers, it can be said that the mere provision of Information and Communication Technologies

(ICTs) cannot be conceived as a "magic solution" to current problems of education. Although there is no ideal solution that eases this discussion, it is understood that the professionals engaged in the development of Educational Technology should be aware of the risks from extremist views or generalized (Almeida, 2010; European Commission, 2008; Saccol, Schlemmer, & Barbosa, 2011).

Therefore, as it is an area of human application, quite interdisciplinary, the development of educational technology must not only focus on the technical aspects of ICTs, but necessarily also those aspects related to sociocultural context and the didactic-pedagogical aspects:

[...] one of the weakest points identified by different researchers, with regard to these educational modalities, the question is didactic-pedagogic. Do not just have access to new technologies that can be used in combination, it is necessary, above all, know how to use them to facilitate the learning of the subject (Saccol et al., 2011).

As discussed before, the prospect of increasingly dynamic scenarios, and popularization of ICT, there seems to be incompatible with the contemporary educational systems, and some characteristics justify this gap between the skills taught and those required in the professional field; rigid training plans are at risk of becoming obsolete quickly; model teacher-repeater only repeats the contents of a book (in person or virtually), focus on repetition and memorization of content, assessment tests parameterized penalizing the error and omit the reasoning of the learner; difficulty in identifying individual skills, traditional assessments do not provide complete assurance to assess the true individual learning; incorporation of "new technologies" to old teaching practices, and the model of "banking model of education" that prioritizes the accumulation of disconnected contents (Cobo & Moravec, 2011; Freire, 1968; Schmidt, 2010). These characteristics are opposed to synthetic thinking and creative citizens need

in today's society (Robinson, 2010). Also in this sense, Cobo & Moravec (2011) suggest that the focus should be on "how" we learn rather than "what" we learn. Still on the subject, Brown (2008), former chief scientist of Xerox, sums up this concern:

What can we do to improve schools, especially considering the rapid pace of change today? [...] We must find ways to motivate children to embrace change. We must find ways to make them want to learn new things (John Seely Brown, 2008).

In defense of this shift in focus from technology to humans, Azevedo (2009) proposes the adoption of informal learning models, unorganized and not formally defined, which occurs in everyday situations and experiences (often incidentally and non-conscious), as the natural and basic form by which humans learn (Sharples & Taylor, 2005):

Recent efforts seek to reproduce life inside the computer (e.g., virtual worlds, social networks, virtual assistants and knowledge management). However, we enter without merit these initiatives, one must consider that people have a life away from the monitor; continue talking personally, meeting new people, playing sports, seeking leisure options, sharing experiences and discussing several issues (Azevedo, 2009, p. 10).

This issue is originally discussed in the seminal work of Freire (1968, 1977, 1996), which defends the approach to the everyday knowledge acquired. Besides the relation of knowledge to their daily life, curiosity and hence the action of the subject of this reality should also be considered:

Knowledge, on the contrary, requires the presence of the subject curious in view of world. It requires their transforming action on reality. It demands a constant search. It implies invention and reinvention. It calls for critical reflection on each act of knowing, which is recognized by knowing and recognizing themselves thus realize the 'how' of their knowledge and the constraints to which it is subjected his act. [...] There is not possible to dichotomize the man of the world, because there is no one without the other (Freire, 1977, p. 27).

Therefore, it is observed that the different contexts, related to the reality of the learner, open new opportunities for thinking about models more flexible, exploratory, participative learning, based on their own curiosity and motivation of the student (Cobo & Moravec, 2011). However, such changes are not trivial, because the bump industrial paradigm and "banking model of education" so criticized by Paulo Freire, because, "teaching is not to transferring knowledge but to create the possibilities for the production or construction" (Freire, 1996, p. 24).

Finally, the main challenge is merging, in a motivated and efficient way, ICT, learning approach and learner context, to achieve a harmonious integration, as suggested (Chen, Seow, & So, 2010, p. 484), "technology that is used to support learning should be integrated with everyday life in the same way that learning occurs in everyday life: seamlessly".

Ubiquitous Computing and Ubiquitous Learning

The most profound technologies are those that disappear (Weiser, 1991, p. 3).

With these words Mark Weisser introduces the prospect that people and environments would be "augmented" with computing resources to provide information and services, so "invisible" when and where required. Therefore, the use of the expression *ubiquitous computing* originated at Xerox Palo Alto Research Center, within the Ubiquitous Computing Program, led by Weisser. In this project, through ethnographic studies, it analyzed how people actually used the technology, and not as people said to use it. These observations led then reflect less on technical details of the machines and more about its situational use, and, how computers were integrated into the human daily social activities (Weiser, Gold, & Brown, 1999). In this sense, context-awareness in this type of system is essential factor. According to Dey (2001)

Context is any information that can be used to characterize the situation of an entity. An entity is a person, place, or object that is considered relevant to the interaction between a user and an application, including the user and applications themselves (Dey, 2001, p. 5).

However, how to apply this concept? What kinds of equipment are needed? This is feasible? In face these questions, Dey et al. (2011) explored potential devices and technologies that may help to popularize this perspective. They analyzed the user experience with mobile phones through a field study, with 28 participants over a period of 4 weeks, to verify the following hypothesis: "the phone is always close to its owner". The results showed that, when their phones are on, they are within owner arm's reach on 53% of the time, but in 88% of the time they are within owner arm's reach or on the same site of the owner. Therefore, from this finding its possible assume that ubiquitous computing systems can use mobile phones as a means of collecting user data and communicating of information to users at any time.

But, what is the relationship between that concept and the learning field? As discussed by Sharples & Taylor (2005), and other authors already related here, learning is a continuous process that extends throughout life, and may occur at any time or place. The learning phenomenon occurs in a large set of everyday episodes situated by the surrounding social and cultural environment. In this perspective it rises the concept of *m* (or only u-learning) held anytime, anywhere appropriate to the context of the learner. Saccol et al. (2011) define the concept of u-learning:

The u-learning (ubiquitous learning) refers to learning processes supported by the use of Infor-

mation Technology and Communication Mobile and Wireless sensors and location mechanisms that collaborate to integrate learners with their learning context and your surroundings, allowing form networks between virtual and real people, objects and situations or events, so that it can support continuous learning, contextualized and meaningful to the learner (Saccol et al., 2011, p. 28)

Therefore, u-learning generally refers to learning supported by ICT resources. This modality is also characterized by its interdisciplinary nature, origin and the typical computational model. It is directly related to the concepts of m-learning (Sharples & Taylor, 2005), context (Dey, 2001) and different pedagogical approaches (Lave & Wenger, 1991; Wenger, 1998), such as situated learning, informal learning and situated learning, for example.

Regarding other modalities, some authors (Liu & Hwang, 2010; Saccol *et al.*, 2011; Scopeo, 2011) address the u-learning as an evolution of m-learning (mobile learning mediated) and consequently the e-learning (learning mediated computers), as illustrated in Figure 1.

As an example of u-learning project, Chu, Hwang, & Tsai (2010); Hwang, Chu, Lin, & Tsai (2011) propose the construction of mental maps in a context-aware u-learning environment to help students interpret, organize and share their knowl-

edge and discoveries. They conducted quantitative analysis comparing an "experimental group" against a "control group". They observed positive impact on students' motivation and a better students' learning outcomes. The qualitative analysis showed that both teachers and students presented significant difference on motivation and engaged in this type of approach.

Vogel, Kennedy, & Kuan, 2007) developed and evaluated a portfolio of collaborative mobile applications to test its two research questions: "Motivated use of mobile learning applications will positively influence student performance?" and "Mobile learning that applications align with student learning interests will positively moderate performance?". The experiments were conducted with 416 students of an introductory business course. Students who chose to use mobile applications performed significantly better on tests compared with students who chose not to use mobile applications. These results confirm the hypothesis that the motivational factor in the use of mobile applications in the context of learning is directly related to improvement in student performance.

In another experiment conducted by Zaina, Bressan, Cardieri, & Rodrigues (2012), 297 students of Physics I interacted with a recommendation system of learning objects, sensitive to the student's profile. The averages obtained by students who participated in the experiment were imported from the information system of the

Figure 1. Relationship between e-Learning, m-Learning and u-Learning (Liu & Hwang, 2010)

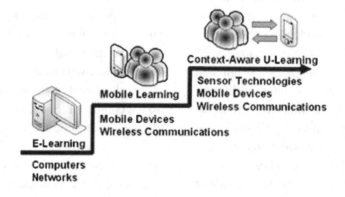

academic institution. The control group, which did not use the tool, achieved overall average of 5.42 while the experimental group had an average of 7.55. These data indicate a significant increase in the use of students who used the context sensitive recommendation system.

Lindemann (2008) also advocates the use of information regarding the student's profile. In this case, to identify learning styles more appropriate. The results inferred on case studies reaffirm the general expectation of the benefits of knowledge on learning styles to educational practices, especially with regard to improving teaching methods, and the upgrading of teacher actions.

ISSUES, CONTROVERSIES, PROBLEMS

ICT at School

The market offers Information and Communication Technology (ICT) designed to meet the needs of general users. The use of computational resources is most obviously characterized by the use of computers and educational software in teaching within a paradigm of epistemic mediation. The practice of teachers and their training back up often using specific devices. With the focus on equipment, laboratories are assembled and then the teachers are led to reflect on whether they can or cannot mediate classes and interactions in that new environment. However, what is easy to do in an office – typing, calculate, organize, scan – may be very complex when performed in front of dozens of students. For numerous reasons ergonomic became unfeasible using digital computing in the school context (Lins & Gomes, 2003). Either because the interfaces provided by the operating systems of the computers are complex or the fact that accommodation in the context of teaching became using complex.

The refraction on the use of digital technologies by teachers is a phenomenon known in many countries (Rosen and Weft, 1995; NCES, 2000; Resnick, 2001; OECD, 2001; Abranches, 2003;

Demetriadisa et al. 2003; Chlopak, 2003). We see today a growing series of studies that show how the use of computers and educational software is still very complex. If we put the problem in another way and imagine that the introduction of technology in the school context does not necessarily mean the installation of computers, but the "computing" in schools (from original term), we may open a new phase of research and development of technologies for teaching. Computing means: communication, computation and representation. A wide range of interactive systems can allow computing and they not necessary depend from computers. Computers are not required in order to have computing at school, which may exist with wooden toys, mobile devices, games and tangible interfaces in general (Szendrei, 1996). That change of perspective is a trend that refers to themes of technology that belong to mobile and ubiquitous technology.

In a research conducted by Baek, Jung, & Kim (2008), in South Korea with 202 teachers, the authors identify factors that influence the decision of teachers to use ICT resources in the classroom. The researchers have identified six factors (Table 8) which influence teachers to use technology in their classroom, in this order of importance:

Due the potential benefits of ICT in the educational context, teachers at all levels should use technology with conscious of its purpose and "truly believe in its effectiveness for learning", but, this idea is not unanimous, how shows the findings reached by these researchers, summarized as follows:

[…] although the majority of teachers intend to use technology to support teaching and learning, experienced teachers generally decide to use technology involuntarily in response to external forces while teachers with little experience are more likely to use it on their own will […] The findings of this study imply that teachers do not pay much attention to raising the quality of learning when they decide to adopt technology, especially as they are more experienced (Baek, Jung, & Kim, 2008, p. 10)

Table 8. Six factors which influenced teachers use technology in classroom (Baek et al., 2008)

Factor	Examples
1) Adapting to external requests and others' expectations	"The Ministry of Education requests that we use technology in the classroom", "It is commonly perceived that good teachers use technology well", "I increase my competence whenever I use technology", and "I might be uncomfortable if I don't use it, because most teachers use it"
2) Deriving attention	"It stimulates the learner's motivation or interest", "It evokes student curiosity", "It is useful to get the students' attention", "Presenting through technology satisfies the students' eyes and ears", and "Students show excitement when new technology is introduced"
3) Using the basic functions of technology	"It is easy to share pictures or movie-clips with other students", "It is easy to share information with other teachers", "It is a convenient way to reorganize or reuse content or material", and "It increases communication with students and parents through the school Web site and Internet community".
4) Relieving physical fatigue	"Technology can substitute for teaching, so it allows me to do routine work", "Displaying video clips in class allows a break from teaching", and "Although initial construction is difficult, once prepared, it makes teaching easy"
5) Class preparation and management	"Information from the Internet can be used for teaching", "It simplifies searching and preparing the subject material", and "It is easy to manage teaching materials". But the item "It allows adjustment of presenting size of visual material for a lecture"
6) Using the enhanced functions of technology	"It is possible to do experiments that are difficult in the regular classroom", "It is possible to simulate experiments that are difficult in the real world" and "Technology provides well-programmed simulations"

About virtual environments and other systems adopted in educational institutions, according to a study conducted by Mülbert & Tecnologias (2011), they analyzed the interaction of students with an LMS. The first finding was that interactions occur much more among student and teacher than student and student. Observing the communication, they observed patterns, organized by categories that reveal the motivations and interests of students to interact in the Learning Management System (LMS), they were: (a) operational questions, content and assessment, (b) initiatives for collaboration, (c) desire for group affiliation, (d) expressions of affection, (e) negotiation and conflict, and (f) desire for privacy and no supervision.

In another study conducted by Patrício e Gonçalves (2010), it examined the impact of using a digital social network, in this case Facebook, the practices of higher education. Although the institution told a LMS to provide information, materials, and encourage the sharing of ideas through forums and chats, it was observed that engagement of students in environment was lower when compared with students whose teachers have adopted Facebook in teaching practice. These findings reinforce that the interactions among students occur primarily by other means or informal environments, not visible by the educational institution.

Although the u-learning environments are innovative and interesting, Chu et al., (2010); Hwang et al. (2011) point out several problems that were identified in practical activities that adopt this approach. One is due to lack of proper learning strategies or tools to guide students in more complex scenarios. In research conducted by (Chen, Lee, Tan, & Lin, 2012), they attempted to analyze the factors that influence the motivation of teachers' pre-service "in Singapore on the use of ICT in the classroom. The data obtained through interviews and ethnography, showed that of the 16 participants, half of them use only slideshows, even though many of them available to devices and software, plus the entire supporting infrastructure. These results imply the urgency of changes in teacher training, ie, we must go beyond the mentality focused on infrastructure for the people-centered mentality.

SOLUTIONS AND RECOMMENDATIONS

Ubiquitous Learning as Social Practices

We follow Figueiredo (2002) in the thought that the future of education is not in the content, but in the contexts that give living (or subsistence) to the content. Therefore, the practical development of communities rich in context (Figure 2) may be a way to become reality that thought:

That is why we believe that the great challenge of the future of the school is to create communities where the rich context of individual and collective learning is built and where learners take responsibility, not only the construction of their own knowledge, but also the construction of collective spaces where learning takes place (Figueiredo, 2002, p. 2).

Given the extensive range strategies and philosophies for creating learning environments, Wenger (1998) argues that it is possible to combine learning theories to guide the learning in learning communities, which are built at the intersection of two main axes that form the Social Theory of Learning (Figure 3).

- **Horizontal:** It shows the tension between theories of social practice (eg, sharing of resources in social systems) and identity theories (eg social formation of the individual and social categories).

Figure 2. Relationship between contents and contexts (Figueiredo, 2002)

- **Vertical:** It shows the tension between theories that emphasize social structure (eg, institutions, norms) and those who favor the action (eg, dynamics, improvisation and activities).

Theories of social practice refer to the production and reproduction of specific forms of engagement within the world, address the activities of daily life and real situations, but also the social systems of shared resources by which groups organize and coordinate their activities, relationships and interpretations.

U-Learning Scenario Example: At home, a student is trying to develop software, but is faced with the problem at the source code that does not work. Then he exposes the error to the virtual community. So an experienced programmer responds with a suggestion to the problem. The student tests the suggested solution solves the problem and provides a complete solution for the community, whose content may also remain available and may be recommended for people with similar interests.

Theories of identity refer to the social formation of self, including the construction of one own identity, e.g., the creation and use of signs belonging and social categories. Therefore, learning is not just the vehicle for the development of practices and integration of new members, but also the development and transformation of identities.

U-Learning Scenario Example: Programmer shares information, tips and help people solve problems on software. The community evaluates the information shared by the programmer and assigns points for each useful contribution. The programmer receives points that allow it to climb in the ranking of most programmers who contribute to the community.

Theories of social structure focus on practices related to institutions, norms, rules, systems and cultural history.

U-Learning Scenario Example: A teacher of a certain educational institution creates activities

Figure 3. Axes of social learning theories according Wenger (1998) (Figueiredo, 2002)

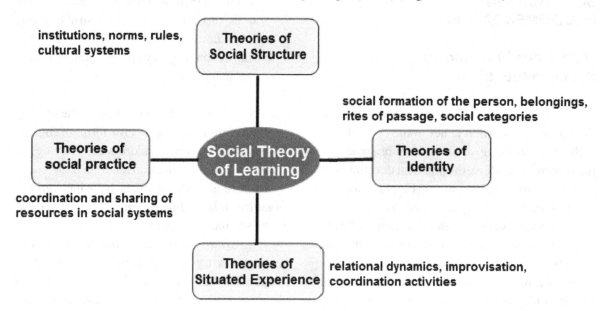

related to the course he teaches, and these activities scattered throughout the city, in the form of "points of interest". Students, when approaching these locations, receive challenges, texts, videos, pictures or can meet others who have gone through the place marked. In this dynamic, the Professor can view and evaluate the interactions of their students.

Theories of Situated Experience: Refer to the action, experience, and local dynamics of everyday life and interactions of people with their environment, improvisation and coordination. Through those practices, learning reproduces and transforms the social structure in which it is held.

U-Learning Scenario Example: A student passes by the city river that is polluted, then take a picture and adds his comments. The picture and comments will be marked at that location, available to the community. Other community members can add new comments and share solutions, based on its experience and expertise to solve that common problem in the community.

Following that approach, in each of these extremes, socially, individuals construct identities, they define rules, organize themselves into

communities, share experiences and resources. So there is a constant flow of ideas and meanings, in a spontaneous way, through the sharing of information.

The importance of sharing is one of the main themes of the book "Where good ideas come from" (Johnson, 2011). In this work, the author argues that many breakthrough discoveries in human history were developed and matured in environments conducive to social interaction and information sharing, for example, the cafes during the Enlightenment, and the Parisian salons during modernism. However, he emphasizes that, currently, these sharing environments increasingly become popular on the Internet, also accelerating the innovation process.

However, which aspects that motivate a person to share information with their peers? Wiese et al. (2011) sought to answer this question through a study with 42 participants in the group that analyzes social, proximity, frequency of sharing and communication. Participants rated their willingness to share in 21 different scenarios based on information from a context-sensitive system. The results show that: (i) self-reported closeness is the strongest indicator of willingness to share; (ii) individuals are more likely to share in scenarios with common information than other kinds of scenarios; and (iii) frequency of communication predicts both closeness and willingness to share better than frequency of collocation.

These results are similar to the thesis advocated by Brian Solis (2010), about social networks. To this author, social networks that have more users are those that enable the creation of a unique identity on the Internet and enable interact with other real followers. The success of a social network depends on its ability to get closer to the real world of each user.

A social network is composed of one or more finite sets of social actors and also the relations established between them. An actor, in turn, can be a person, or a discrete set of people aggregated into a collective social unit, as subgroups, organizations and other groups. Thus, social networks provide the sharing of ideas and values among people and organizations that have common goals and interests. Such environments form a locus, in which aims to build social interaction, collaboration, transformation and sharing ideas around the interests of social actors that compose them (CGI.Br, 2010).

About social network in learning context, several research initiatives aimed to identify the effectiveness of social networks introduced in the context of social practices to the learning process (Abreu, Claudeivan, Veloso, & Gomes, 2011; Melo, 2010). Those works show that social networking environments are ideal to form groups with common interests and to share knowledge, fostering an environment for collaborative learning.

Furthermore, this discussion can't be oblivious to the reality of schools and teachers, because social networks are used by the vast majority of young people. For example, the survey conducted by CGI.Br (2011) analyze the main communication activities by internet users in Brazil: send and receive email (78%), send instant messages

(72%), participating in social networking sites (69%), voice chat programs like Skype (23%), use micro blogging (22%), create or updating blogs or websites (15%), participating in forums or mailing lists (14%). One fact that stands out is the participation of about 83% young aged 16 to 24 years in social networking sites.

Works like (Mazman & Usluel, 2010) propose the use of social networks already established, like Facebook, for example, for purposes of learning. However, social networking environments for specific digital education also follow this trend and are growing in popularity, to mention some: Edu 2.0 (www.edu20.org), Sclipo (www.sclipo. com) Edmodo (www.edmodo.com) and Redu (www.redu.com.br). However, there are insufficient solutions that reflect a gain disruptive to the learning process in relation to existing strategies (Abreu et al., 2011).

Therefore, according definition of context (Dey, 2001), the learner's social network should also be part of context awareness u-learning environments. So, proactive recommendations, u-learning environment feature (Saccol et al., 2011), are not limited to suggest just resources, but also other individuals. In this way, Rodrigues & Júnior (2010) define ubiquitous social networks as an example of systems that arise from the convergence of ubiquitous computing services with online social networks. So, beyond the services available in the physical environment, participants can also discover their social relationships among people who have similar interests and profiles. They may be, for example, socially and physically close (Santaella, 2010).

Following that strategy, Yin, Dong, Tabata, & Ogata (2012) extend this perspective by presenting and testing, with 46 graduate students, a recommendation system of "friends" to problem solving, based on the hypothesis that when we ask for help from others: (i) the closer ("affective"), the easier it is to get help, and (ii) the simplest questions are easier to get help. Another perspective from that convergence is the analysis of the interactions of the participant, for example, through inferences from their behavior in online social network and their location traits (Cranshaw, Toch, Hong, Kittur, & Sadeh, 2010).

In appropriating of these context-sensitive ways to foster sharing and social interaction, Downes (2010) proposes a break with the traditional model of education, claiming that the actions and the productions of the learners feed back into and enrich the environment in order to contribute to the other learners' learning environment, that is, it suggests a strategy of participation rather than retention. The focus is not merely to create a network to situate episodic learning, but rather, to create a network that learns and thus adapts and reshapes itself based on those conversations and interactions. So it is necessary consider learners not only as the subjects of learning (entities that just receive contents) but also as the sources of learning to the whole network. "The things we say, the things we choose to read or view, the things we link to, the people we send messages to - all of these constitute input to the learning network" (Downes, 2010, p. 28).

Social Architecture (Social Educational Platform and Ubiquitous Service)

The social service for learning is provided by a social educational platform accessible through many different software clients and devices. We have already design this service and it is called Redu. The Redu is a social software that represents an environment of learning and teaching that was created from the need to expand the school and provide greater interaction among the actors involved. Thus, students, teachers and institutions are able to make learning a continuous process that goes beyond the school walls.

The Redu supports collaboration, discussion and dissemination of educational content. In this sense, we specify the characteristics of a new concept of teaching platform that extends the user experience in social media and their peers in a social network context for learning. The network has reduced tools (Melo, 2010) capable of providing more intensity s processes for teaching and learning, a greater dynamic in the relationship learner/teacher and learner/learner(s).

The main objective of the project is to design a set Redu of interaction styles, forms of communication and collaboration that can create opportunities to access formal and informal learning (Sefton-Green & Series, 2004). Formal learning takes place in educational institutions that provide diplomas and qualifications recognized by the competent bodies. It is a form of structured learning. Informal learning occurs in everyday life by enriching their knowledge and skills, not necessarily intentionally, sometimes going unnoticed by the individuals themselves. It is a way of unstructured learning that happens without prior planning.

Currently, Redu already provides an API to support applications development and integration with other systems, with support for the following programming languages: Python, PHP, Ruby, Rails and Java. However, considering the increasing penetration of mobile devices and the appropriation of mobile devices in day-to-day life of the population in general, including learners and teachers, we sought to expand the scope of possibilities and Redu features through the integration between Redu and services u-learning context-aware services, currently under development (Figure 4).

Figure 4. Interaction between a digital social network (Redu) and u-learning services

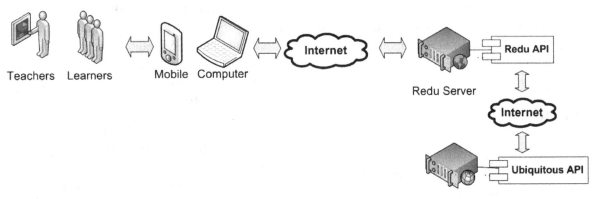

FUTURE RESEARCH TRENDS

We believe in the change of perspective: the focus should not be on the technology but on the humans. In other words, research and development must be directed increasingly to understand the process of appropriation of ICTs by individuals in pursuit of resolving their objectives in an ever faster and easier way. Therefore, our efforts are focused on making digital artifacts increasingly sensitive to the context of the learner, especially of their goals.

We also understand that future developments in u-learning should not be limited by barriers that limit opportunities for learning and knowledge construction, eg, segregating formal and informal learning, or individual and collective learning, or limited by a specific approach learning, when actually learning in practice is "seamless" (Chan, Roschelle, Hsi, & Kinshuk, 2006). Therefore, our view of future trends is that ICTs become increasingly flexible, "by continuity of the learning experience across different scenarios (or environments)", for learners and teachers.

CONCLUSION

New technologies are most of the time presented as solutions to improve the social historical constituted teaching and learning activities. Ubiquitous technologies tend to subvert the normal structure of teaching and learning practices because they inspire the emergency of new paradigms and social organizations at school worldwide. The exploratory activities, and student centered process, the large collaboration peer to peer and the planning and consultant roles assumed by teacher tend to introduce irreversible transformations on the teaching and learning process. Out of the main traditional spaces and practices, teachers and students are involved in a collaborative learning experience when appreciating the problems, objects and artifacts. Different of representing a horizontal innovation for teaching and learning, ubiquitous technologies can be seen as enormous opportunities to create new kinds of learning and socialization process in our societies. We can even imagine a process and technologies co-design, in terms of the overall experience promoted and intended.

Following the motivations from (Figueiredo, 2002), we ask the attention of school leaders, teachers, and software developers to go beyond the traditional centering on content, towards solutions that enhance the community, interaction, activities, contexts, meaning, identity, tasks and shared repertoires, participation, spontaneity and creativity. These are the key components of the future of learning, possible through ICT resources.

REFERENCES

Abranches, S. P. (2003). *Modernidade e formação de professores: A prática dos multiplicadores dos núcleos de tecnologia educacional do nordeste e a informática na educação. Tese de Doutorado.* USP.

Abreu, J., Claudeivan, L., Veloso, F., & Gomes, A. (2011). *Análise das práticas de colaboração e comunicação: Estudo de caso utilizando a rede social educativa redu.* Retrieved from http://www. br-ie.org/sbie-wie2011/WIE-Trilha1/93028_1. pdf

Almeida, M. da G. M. da S. M. E. B. de. (2010). *O cenário atual do uso de tecnologias digitais da informação e comunicação.* Pesquisa sobre o uso das tecnologias de informação e comunicação no Brasil: TIC Educação 2010.

Baek, Y., Jung, J., & Kim, B. (2008). What makes teachers use technology in the classroom? Exploring the factors affecting facilitation of technology with a Korean sample. *Computers & Education*, *50*(1), 224–234. doi:10.1016/j. compedu.2006.05.002.

CGI.Br. (2010). *A evolução da internet no Brasil.* Revista CGI.Br.

Br, C. G. I. (2011). *TIC Brasil: Domicílios e usuários 2011.* Retrieved from http://www.cetic. br/usuarios/tic/2011-total-brasil

Brown, J. S. (2008). *Tinkering as a mode of knowledge production.* Retrieved May 13, 2012, from http://www.youtube.com/watch?v=9u-MczVpkUA

Chen, W., Lee, C., Tan, A., & Lin, C.-P. (2012). What, how and why - A peek into the uses and gratifications of ubiquitous computing for pre-service teachers in Singapore. In *Proceedings of the International Conference on Wireless, Mobile and Ubiquitous Technology in Education*, (pp. 182–186). doi:10.1109/WMUTE.2012.41

Chen, W., Seow, P., & So, H. (2010). Extending students' learning spaces: Technology-supported seamless learning. *ICLS, 1*, 484–491. Retrieved from http://ammonwiemers.com/IdetPortfolio/ articles/Technology Integration/Extending Students Learning Spaces -- Technology-Supported Seamless Learning.pdf

Chlopak, O. (2003). Computers in Russian schools: Current conditions, main problems, and prospects for the future. *Computers & Education*, (40): 41–55. doi:10.1016/S0360-1315(02)00093-3.

Chu, H.-C., Hwang, G.-J., & Tsai, C.-C. (2010). A knowledge engineering approach to developing mindtools for context-aware ubiquitous learning. *Computers & Education*, *54*(1), 289–297. doi:10.1016/j.compedu.2009.08.023.

Cobo, B. A. L., & Moravec, J. W. (2011). *Aprendizaje invisible.* Livro. Universitat de Barcelona.

Cranshaw, J., Toch, E., Hong, J., Kittur, A., & Sadeh, N. (2010). Bridging the gap between physical location and online social networks. *Ubicomp, 10*, 119. doi:10.1145/1864349.1864380.

Creta, G. (2003). *Human computer interaction proceedings.* Hoboken, NJ: Lawrence Erlbaum Associates.

de Azevedo, F. L. B. (2009). *Bora ali tomar um café? Concepção de uma experiência ubíqua de suporte à aprendizagem conversacional no ambiente de trabalho. Mestrado.* UFPE.

de Figueiredo, A. D. (2002). *Redes e educação: A surpreendente riqueza de um conceito.* Conselho Nacional de Educação.

Demetriadisa, S., Barbasb, A., Molohidesb, A., Palaigeorgioua, G., Psillosb, D., & Vlahavasa, I. et al. (2003). Cultures in negotiation: Teachers' acceptance/resistance attitudes considering the infusion of technology into schools. *Computers & Education*, (41): 19–37. doi:10.1016/S0360-1315(03)00012-5.

Dey, A. K. (2001). Understanding and using context. *Personal and Ubiquitous Computing*, 5(1), 4–7. doi:10.1007/s007790170019.

Dey, A. K., Wac, K., Ferreira, D., Tassini, K., Hong, J., & Ramos, J. (2011). Getting closer: An empirical investigation of the proximity of user to their smart phones. *UbiComp*, *11*, 163–172.

Downes, S. (2010). New technology supporting informal learning. *Journal of Emerging Technologies in Web Intelligence*, 2(1). doi:10.4304/jetwi.2.1.27-33.

European Commission. (2008). *The use of ICT to support innovation and lifelong learning for all*. Brussels: Author.

Freire, P. (1968). *Pedagogia do oprimido*. Livro. Editora Paz e Terra.

Freire, P. (1977). *Extensão ou comunicação?* Editora Paz e Terra.

Freire, P. (1996). *Pedagogia da autonomia: Saberes necessários à prática educativa*. Editora Paz e Terra.

Gomes, A. S., Rolim, A. L. S., & Silva, W. M. (2012). *Educar com o redu*. Recife: Editora universitária da UFPE.

Hwang, G.-J., Chu, H.-C., Lin, Y.-S., & Tsai, C.-C. (2011). A knowledge acquisition approach to developing mindtools for organizing and sharing differentiating knowledge in a ubiquitous learning environment. *Computers & Education*, 57(1), 1368–1377. doi:10.1016/j.compedu.2010.12.013.

ITU - International Telecommunication Union. (2012). Retrieved from http://www.itu.int/ITU-D/ict/statistics/at_glance/KeyTelecom.html

Johnson, S. (2010). *Where good ideas come from: The natural history of innovation*. Riverhead.

Lave, J., & Wenger, E. (1991). *Situated learning: Legitimate peripheral participation*. Cambridge, UK: Cambridge University Press. doi:10.1017/CBO9780511815355.

Lindemann, V. (2008). Estilos de aprendizagem: Buscando a sinergia. *Tese (UFRGS)*. Retrieved from http://www.lume.ufrgs.br/handle/10183/15352

Lins, W. C.-B., & Gomes, A. S. (2003). Educational software interfaces and teacher s use. In *HCI International 2003*. HCI.

Liu, G.-Z., & Hwang, G.-J. (2010). A key step to understanding paradigm shifts in e-learning: Towards context-aware ubiquitous learning. *British Journal of Educational Technology*, 41(2), E1–E9. doi:10.1111/j.1467-8535.2009.00976.x.

Mazman, S. G., & Usluel, Y. K. (2010). Modeling educational usage of facebook. *Computers & Education*, 55(2), 444–453. doi:10.1016/j.compedu.2010.02.008.

Melo, C. de A. (2010). *Scaffolding of self-regulated learning in social networks. Dissertação*. UFPE.

Mendonça, A. F., Gomes, A. S., & Montarroyos, E. (2002). *CSCL environment for physics teaching and learning allowing exploratory methodology*. Badajoz: Junta de Extremadura Consejeria de Educación.

Moore, M. (2002). Teoria da distância transacional. *Revista Brasileira de Aprendizagem Aberta e a Distância*. Retrieved from: http://goo.gl/kazuV

Mülbert, A. L., & Tecnologias, C. N. (2011). *A interação em ambientes virtuais de aprendizagem: Motivações e interesses dos alunos. Revista Novas Tecnologias na Educação.* CINTED-UFRGS.

NCES. National Center for Education Statistics. (2000). *Teacher's tools form the 21st century: A report on teacher's use of technology.* Retrieved from nces.ed.gov/pubs2000/2000102.pdf

New Media Consortium. (2012). Horizon report 2012: Higher education ed. book. The New Media Consortium.

Nielsen. (2012). *Survey: New U.S. smartphone growth by age and income.* Retrieved from http://blog.nielsen.com/nielsenwire/online_mobile/survey-new-u-s-smartphone-growth-by-age-and-income

OECD. Organisation for Economic Co-Operation and Development. (2001). Learning to change: ICT in schools. Paris: OECD.

Patrício, M. R., & Gonçalves, V. (2010). *Utilização educativa do facebook no ensino superior.* I Conference Learning and Teaching in Higher Education. Universidade de Évora, Portugal.

Resnick, M. (2001). *Rethinking learning in the digital age.* Retrieved from llk.media.mit.edu/papers/mres-wef.pdf

Robinson, S. K. (2010). *Bring on the learning revolution!* Retrieved May 13, 2012, from http://www.ted.com/talks/sir_ken_robinson_bring_on_the_revolution.html

Rodrigues, P. G., & Júnior, E. P. F. D. (2010). Middlewares e protocolos para redes sociais pervasivas. *Monografia (PUC-RJ).* Retrieved from http://www-di.inf.puc-rio.br/~endler/courses/Mobile/Monografias/09/PauloGallotti_MP4PSN-final.doc

Rosen, L. D., & Weft, M. M. (1995). Computer availability, computer experience and technophobia among public school teachers. *Computers in Human Behavior, 11*(1), 9–31. doi:10.1016/0747-5632(94)00018-D.

Saccol, A., Schlemmer, E., & Barbosa, J. (2011). *M-learning e u-learning: Novas perspectivas da aprendiazgem movel e ubiqua.* Pearson.

Santaella, L. (2010). A aprendizagem ubíqua substitui a educação formal?. *Revista de Computação e Tecnologia da PUC-SP,* 17–22.

Schmidt, J. P. (2010). *Peer 2 peer university.* Retrieved May 13, 2012, from http://vimeo.com/11158136

SCOPEO. (2011). *M-learning en España, Portugal y América Latina.* SCOPEO.

Sharples, M., & Taylor, J. (2005). Towards a theory of mobile learning. *mLearn.* Retrieved from http://www.iamlearn.org/public/mlearn2005/www.mlearn.org.za/CD/papers/Sharples-Theory of Mobile.pdf

Siemens, G. (2006). *Knowing knowledge.* Retrieved from Lulu.com

Solis, B. (2010). *Engage! The complete guide for brands and businesses to build, cultivate, and measure success in the new web.* Hoboken, NJ: John Wiley & Sons.

StatCounter. (2012). *Mobile vs. desktop.* Retrieved from http://gs.statcounter.com/#mobile_vs_desktop-ww-monthly-201010-201210

Szendrei, J. (1996). Concrete materials in the classroom. In *International handbook of mathematics education.* Dordrecht, The Netherlands: Kluwer. doi:10.1007/978-94-009-1465-0_13.

Tori, R. (2009). Cursos híbridos ou blended learning. In *Educação a distância: O estado da arte.* São Paulo: Pearson Prentice Hall.

TrendWatching. (2012). *TrendWatching*. Retrieved May 13, 2012, from http://trendwatching.com

Vogel, D., Kennedy, D., & Kuan, K. (2007). *Do mobile device applications affect learning?* Retrieved from http://ieeexplore.ieee.org/xpls/abs_all.jsp?arnumber=4076377

Weiser, M. (1991). The computer for the 21st century. *Scientific American, 3*(3). Retrieved from http://wiki.daimi.au.dk/pca/_files/weiser-orig.pdf.

Weiser, M., Gold, R., & Brown, J. (1999). The origins of ubiquitous computing research at PARC in the late 1980s. *IBM Systems Journal, 38*(4), 693–696. Retrieved from http://ieeexplore.ieee.org/xpls/abs_all.jsp?arnumber=5387055 doi:10.1147/sj.384.0693.

Wenger, E. (1998). *Communities of practice: Learning, meaning and identity*. New York: Cambridge University Press. doi:10.1017/CBO9780511803932.

Wiese, J., Kelley, P. G., Cranor, L. F., Dabbish, L., Hong, J. I., & Zimmerman, J. (2011). Are you close with me? Are you nearby? Investigating social groups, closeness, and willingness to share. *UbiComp, 11*, 197–206.

Yin, C., Dong, Y., Tabata, Y., & Ogata, H. (2012). Recommendation of helpers based on personal connections in mobile learning. In *Proceedings of the International Conference on Wireless, Mobile and Ubiquitous Technology in Education*, (pp. 137–141). doi:10.1109/WMUTE.2012.32

Zaina, L. A. M., Bressan, G., Cardieri, M. A. C. A., & Rodrigues, J. (2012). e-LORS: Uma abordagem para recomendação de objetos de aprendizagem. *RBIE*, 20.

Chapter 9
The Use of Ubiquitous Learning for Children with Down Syndrome

Laura E Sujo-Montes
Northern Arizona University, USA

Shadow W. J. Armfield
Northern Arizona University, USA

Cherng-Jyh Yen
Old Dominion University, USA

Chih-Hsiung Tu
Northern Arizona University, USA

ABSTRACT

Ubiquitous computing is opening new opportunities for learning. Researchers and philosophers are still debating what learning theory best explains computer ubiquitous learning. Meanwhile, as it has happened many times throughout history, individuals with disabilities are not able to benefit from such advances until late in the adoption curve. This chapter discusses (a) several learning theories that have the potential to explain computer ubiquitous learning, (b) uses of computer ubiquitous learning for and by individuals with Down syndrome, and (c) a new emerging model for computer ubiquitous learning.

INTRODUCTION

John was born on a sunny day in July into a loving home nine years ago. His parents and sister were anxious to receive him as they had decided not to find out his sex. Given that they already had a daughter, John's parents were very happy when they learned that he was a boy. Then the doctor came and delivered the news to John's dad: he had been born with Down syndrome. John's dad response was "just the same. He is beautiful."

Mobile computer and ubiquitous learning has taken off with the advances of technology. It is more common to see a learner using a portable device than to see one with computing technology plugged into a wall outlet and an Ethernet cable to

DOI: 10.4018/978-1-4666-4542-4.ch009

be able to connect to cyberspace. Situated learning/situated cognition, distributed cognition, and contextual learning have being discussed among researchers even before technology became commonplace. However, mobile computer and ubiquitous learning, paired with situated learning and distributed cognition, are rarely read along the topics of special education or Down syndrome.

This chapter discusses how different types of learning (situated, distributed, authentic, lifelong learning), paired with mobile computer and ubiquitous learning, can help children with Down syndrome in particular, and special needs in general, learn in formal and informal environments. Some applications of computer ubiquitous learning will be discussed in the context of Down syndrome and their use by special needs children.

MOBILE AND UBIQUITOUS LEARNING, OR JUST LEARNING?

While some authors consider mobile computer learning to be a synonym of computer ubiquitous learning, El-Bishouty, Ogata, Rahman, and Yano (2010) argue that computer ubiquitous learning is the use of enhanced computing for learning by combining many computers present in the physical environment to be used in an invisible way. On the other hand, Hill, Reeves, and Heidemeier (2000) state that ubiquitous computing is the use of multiple networked computers that offer the ability to have just-in-time, when-needed computing. By extension, the construction of knowledge that happens when using mobile computer devices connected through wireless networks is ubiquitous learning. However, explaining learning takes more than using devices; it requires incorporating a theoretical framework, one or many learning theories and approaches that attempt to explain how the use of these tools mediates knowledge construction. Some of these theories and approaches to learning will be briefly discussed in the following sections.

A THEORETICAL FRAMEWORK FOR COMPUTER UBIQUITOUS LEARNING

More than a decade ago, Spiro, Feltovich, Jacobson, and Coulson (1992) explained constructivism from the cognitive flexibility and situated cognition theories perspectives. They stated that, in constructivism, "one must bring together, from various knowledge sources, an appropriate ensemble of information suited to the particular understanding or problem solving needs of the situation at hand" (p. 64, emphasis added). So, in a way, Spiro and partners connected constructivism (the self-construction of knowledge) with situated cognition. Even longer than that, Brown, Collins, and Duguid (1989) established that learning and acting are indistinguishable from each other because learning is actually a lifelong process that results from actions taken accordingly to situations faced; thus learning can be explained through situated cognition and lifelong learning. They also discussed that for learning to take place, three components need to be present: activity, concept, and culture – elements that are interdependent. Given the interdependency of the three components, it is not possible to understand one of the elements in isolation. As an extension, the use of tools (electronic or otherwise) to carry on an activity has deep implications for learning, as it will be impacted by the culture of the user. Furthermore, lifelong learning, as understood by Sharples (2000), explains the connection between this type of learning and ubiquitous learning when he states that "the abilities, approaches and tools for learning that a person gains from childhood onwards provide a context and resource for learning and performing in later life" (p. 178). Finally, Fischer and Konomi (2005) discuss that the understanding of the interactions between humans and technology can be explained by distributed cognition. That is, distributed cognition provides a theoretical framework to understand how human-technology interactions (what humans do with technology and how these are arranged) happen in a specific environment. The following section will explore each theory in the context of computer ubiquitous learning and children with Down syndrome.

UBIQUTOUS LEARNING AND COGNITION

Constructivism

In many ways, John was born lucky. His father, an educational technology professor at a university, and his mother, a nurse practitioner, understood the power of stimulus and early intervention. John started receiving early intervention therapy, occupational therapy, speech therapy, and physical therapy at 9 months old. He was also very fortunate to have many technologies at home due to his parents' love of new technologies. From early on, John was exposed to a variety of technologies including the early touch screen Tablet PCs (recent versions as well), Palms, Androids (phones and tablets) and i-devices, the Wii, Nintendo DS, the X-Box with Kinect and a Tag Reading System. As a result, John learned to access the devices independently, at will, and as needed.

Much has been written about constructivism, most since the insertion of computing technology into the classroom. However, this approach has existed for several decades and it was the prominent perspective among educators in the '30s and '40s (Rice & Wilson, 1999). The general tenet of constructivism is that each individual constructs knowledge through interpreting his or her own experiences (cognitive constructivism), and that this construction of knowledge is framed by social interaction (social constructivism). Anderson and Dron (2010) argue that there are many models of constructivism but that most of them share specific principles, such as (a) knowledge is built on previous learning; (b) context and tools shape knowledge construction; (c) learning environment

is active and learner centered; and (d) learning is socially constructed and validated. The same authors theorize that social constructivism came more into vogue when many-to-many communications became available through the use of electronic synchronous and asynchronous interactions between student and teacher and student to student. However, Sajadi and Khan (2011) argue that constructivism requires learners to have strong short and long term memory to be able to access previous knowledge; they also need a strong internal locus of control, i.e., motivation, to be in charge of their own learning; finally, they need to be able to reflect on what is learned and what was learned previously so the connection is made and current knowledge is based on previous knowledge. Because of these reasons, some researchers (Moreno, 2004; Mayer, 2004, among others) have questioned the effectiveness of constructivism with children of special needs. Furthermore, given that constructivist teachers facilitate their students' learning through self-guided discovery, students with special needs may feel frustrated if they fail to make the connections between what they are facing with previously constructed knowledge. In this light, Sajadi and Khan (2011) argue that "guided discovery" is a better way to facilitate constructivism, especially for this population of children. In terms of technical use, computing devices need to be user friendly so they fade from the forefront to the background of the learning experience.).

Situated Learning

When John was 5, one of his aunts moved about 1000 miles away. John and his aunt spent a great deal of time together before she left. His family did not want this relationship to be lost because of the distance. Soon after the move, John and his aunt started having periodic video conferences using Skype. John often initiated the conversations by starting his computer, opening Skype, and "calling" his aunt (whether she was available or not). Initially the conversations lasted about half an hour with John and his aunt just talking to one another. Over the last two years the conversations have moved to a newer medium and have taken on new dynamics. Using Google Hangouts, John and his aunt not only talk, but they read together, role play, and share other information from the web. In early conversations, he and his aunt would use "A Story before Bedtime" so that she could read books to him from afar. Both John and his aunt have control of the book and can choose how fast or slow to go through the book, whether she reading it or he telling stories based on the pictures.

Recent research (Jeng, Wu, Huang, Tan, & Yang, 2010; Tan, Lin, Chu, & Liu, 2012) discusses the importance of situated learning in which the context provides support to personalize the learning activity to make it an authentic learning experience. An integral part of situated learning is that it is bound to the situation at hand and construction of knowledge will be impacted by such a situation. Wu, Yang, Hwang, and Chu (2008) explain that situated learning usually takes place within the context of the learning community where the knowledge is used. That is, situated learning is more powerful because it is embedded in a context where applying specific knowledge is authentic and needed, as opposed to use the acquired knowledge in a fabricated situation. Situated learning, when applied to using computer technology with others, explains how computer play can form a community of practice that facilitates informal learning (Sefton-Green, 2004). Situated learning has been identified by many researchers (Jeng, et al., 2010; El-Bishouty, et al., 2010; Hollan, et al., 2001; Vvidis, 2002, among others) as one of the main theories to explain computer ubiquitous learning. In John's case, skills acquired to be able to use Skype, Google Hangouts, and maybe even practice reading and work on speech patterns, represent situated learning where the skills are used within an authentic context.

Beyond the traditional gaming systems, John also uses games on tablets, especially those that require spatial understanding. He initially started by playing Angry Birds (Rovio, 2012a). As he played he would systematically go from level to level trying to earn 3 stars (the highest score per level). Continuing with a similar game, he started playing Shoot the Apple (DroidHen, 2012). This game takes the idea of Angry Birds up a notch by adding obstacles that must be moved and/or avoided to successfully complete a level. He has continued to play games with increasing levels of complexity. Lucky's Escape (Lemon Team, 2012) requires multiple movements and modifications to be successful with level completion. Amazing Alex (Rovio, 2012b) requires John to no longer just create the movement, but to create the path to move along. Finally, he has begun to play with Bad Piggies (Rovio, 2012c) which requires John to develop simple machines to move along paths. The games that John likes to play on these systems require sequencing and scaffolding that are supportive of what John is asked to do in school and outside of school. As John has played these games, he has also progressed in his ability to do daily activities (i.e. making a peanut butter and jelly sandwich).

Dede (2005) discerns that the importance of situated learning lies in part on the issue of "transfer." He defines transfer as "the application of knowledge acquired in one situation to a different situation" (p. 15.5). Situated learning requires learner's immersion in authentic contexts, activities, and assessment coupled with guidance from expert modeling and mentoring (Dede, 2009). Hall and Bannon (2006) report on the design and implementation of computer-supported ubiquitous learning (CSUL). They used CSUL to enhance and personalize children's learning at a museum and how such learning can then be transferred to learning acquired in the classroom. In the same way, when John plays games on his mobile device, he is actually using situated learning to practice and understand difficult concepts taught in the classroom. As John progresses through the levels and the games, he demonstrates greater strength in his ability to use logical reasoning. In the games, John receives immediate feedback and sensory stimulation through sounds, texts, and colors that can increase his motivation. It would not be surprising if John could not grasp the concept of simple machines if they were explained by the teacher in a classroom setting with no other aids as it happens in the games. However, the game makes the difficult concept easier to understand

because he can visualize the principle of a simple machine, besides providing reinforcement of the concept through repetition and practice (Jeng, Lu, & Lin, 2011). Unsurprisingly, Down syndrome children that learn specific behaviors through computer simulations may then transfer them to real-world situations. John's activities described above exemplify many of the characteristics of a mobile learning environment, as described by Chen, Kao, Sheu, and Chiang (2002): urgency of learning need, initiative of knowledge acquisition, mobility of learning setting, interactivity of learning process, situating of instructional activity, and integration of instructional content.

Lifelong Learning

At home John often uses technologies that support the same school goals set by his Individual Education Plan (IEP), but are much less structured. During his first grade year, his parents bought him a Tag Reading System. The Tag system uses a "wand" to play sounds, read the entire book, or read words to the reader. John used this consistently for the first year, having the books read to him and playing the extra sounds related to the pictures. Since that time, he has been less frequent with his use, but still goes back to the books, both having the story read to him through the system and reading the books on his own with parental support.

"Learning is a process of mental and social change over an entire lifetime" (Sharples, 2000. p. 192). Lifelong learning is a way to acquire, act on, and provide knowledge and skills that are necessary to succeed in an ever-changing world.

Although the term "lifelong learning" entered the debate arena right after World War I, the term gained currency in society in the 1990s. Globalization, unstable professional careers, and knowledge as a commodity have brought lifelong learning again to the debate arena (Field, 2000). Lifelong learning usually requires learners to collaborate to solve real-world problems and to play an active role in their own learning (Law, Pelgrum, & Plomp, 2008). As the boundaries and distinctions between formal and informal learning and in-school and out-of-school learning blur, lifelong learning occurs anywhere and at any time. Given that information is so easily acquired, the challenge is not to provide access to it but to provide access to the right information, for the right use, with the right tool for the task at hand. This has paved the way to the concept of context-aware applications. Tan, Lin, Chu, and Liu, (2012) describe these applications as those that provide information relative to the situation at hand to better facilitate the interaction between the user and the environment. For instance, a museum tour that uses handhelds and provides descriptions, cues, and games about the exhibits uses context-aware applications. The advantage of the use of such applications is that it may provide an enhanced real-life learning activity that is more engaging and effective. Context-aware applications eventually fade into the background of the learning experience and become almost transparent to the user.

Computer technology facilitates lifelong learning when the tools it provides are highly portable, individualized, unobtrusive, ubiquitous, adaptable, persistent, useful, and intuitive (Sharples, 2000). For individuals with Down syndrome, a commonly held belief was that their learning plateaus at about the fifth grade level. However, Moni and Jobling (2000) reported that results from longitudinal studies in Australia had debunked that myth. It is in this way that giving access to these types of lifelong learning tools, such as the means to use context-aware applications, to individuals with special needs in general, and with Down syndrome in particular, gain greater importance.

Distributed Cognition

In the school environment, John's logical reasoning is often assessed through mathematics and daily living activities. Outside of school, both of these are continued through homework and daily living, but John's logical reasoning is also evident through his play with technologies. Gaming plays a strong role in his life. It has been used as a motivational tool, and strictly for enjoyment, but it also helps to scaffold John's logical reasoning. For nearly four years John's family has had a Wii and/or an X-Box in the house. Many of the games he plays require a certain level of reading ability for the player to be successful. As John plays the games the first time, his parents will read the instructions or storyline to him. In future play, John will watch the screen and use the written words as clues for what he is supposed to do. If asked about the storyline of the game, he will tell you and lead you through the story and what he is thinking about it.

Distributed cognition emerged as a concept in the mid 1980s (see Schwartz, 2008; and Vvidis, 2002; among others, to learn more on its history). Unlike human cognition, distributed cognition is concerned with cognition that happens not only inside the brain but through the interactions of systems, being those composed of only humans or of humans and machines and not bound by spatial relationships but by usage. In this way, depending on the goals and usage of the tools, subsystems derived from distributed cognition can involve different elements or serve different purposes (Hollan, Hutchins, & Kirsch, 2001). For instance, the games that John plays and how he uses them (or help him) may be totally different than the way other children play them and make use of them. Hollan, et al. (2001) also argue that there are three types of cognitive processes observed in humans (a) processes distributed among members of a social group; (b) processes involving internal and external resources, such as the environment or tools; (c) processes distributed over time where earlier processes may influence later ones. In order to understand computer ubiquitous learning, this section of the chapter will concern itself with the combination of these processes inside the frame of distributed cognition.

Pea (1993) argued that when a tool is used to complete a task, the outcome of the task is always influenced by the use of such tool. If we think of tools as material objects, the environment, or even peers, then it can be said that even Vygotsky's Zone of Proximal Development uses distributed cognition. In such a case, the less able peer has an increased cognition through the able peer and is able to accomplish much more than without the tool, i.e., the able peer (Vvidis, 2002). Fischer and Konomi (2005) expressed that "...wireless and mobile technologies can create exciting opportunities for intelligence augmentation, social creativity, informed participation, and support of unique needs of users in achieving their tasks and engaging in personally meaningful activities" (p. 6). Furthermore, distributed cognition can provide an effective theoretical framework to understand what humans are capable of doing by using the right technology tools. In these terms, distributed cognition should not concern itself only with the use of tools but with the power of human capabilities when those tools are conceived as an extension of the human being (Fischer and Konomi, 2007). Furthermore, distributed cognition, with the use of mobile learning technologies, can help to level the playfield for people with special needs.

Authentic Learning

When John and his aunt are in Google Hangouts, he likes to use Google Effects. As John puts on the "costumes" available in the system, he will play the role of whatever he is wearing; this can include acting like a pirate, The Cat in the Hat and a deep sea diver. Role playing is not limited to the costumes available; at one point his aunt invited him to her house. In the past he would pack a bag and try to walk out the door, but this time he understood that they were playing, and he created his own environment. He still packed his backpack, but this time put it and the computer on a blanket on the floor and pretended to have a flying carpet so that he could fly to her house. Through the creative process he had demonstrated that he had turned a corner to understand that the technology made the conversation available, but not the physical interaction. John and his aunt also use YouTube. Through this tool, not only is he sharing videos with his aunt, but he sings the songs to her. This allows him to practice his speech through singing (a skill that continually needs to be practiced by individuals with Down syndrome).

Lombardi (2007) argues that authentic learning is focused on real world experiences in settings that have not been constructed to teach a specific topic but which happen naturally and are multi-disciplinary in nature. Authentic learning uses the natural way the brain works: looks for connections, practices, and explores new settings. The same author states that authentic learning is important because it involves the use of role playing where the learner takes the place of the expert. Although an authentic learning environment is not the same as an authentic task, the purpose of the latter is to show the relevance and to develop competencies associated with the task that will be useful in the future day-to-day and professional life (Gulikers, Bastiaens, & Martens, 2005). In the case described above, John is embedded in an authentic environment that was not built to teach (Google Hangouts); he is using an authentic task (singing to his aunt); and he is practicing a skill (speech) that will be useful in his present and future life.

Taking the user (or learner) as the focus and unit of learning, authentic learning is the ordinary practices of the culture in which the learner finds him or herself immersed at the time in which learning occurs (Brown et al., 1989). These researchers argue that tool modeling allows others to engage in "peripheral participation." This type of participation allows outsiders to enter a new culture by observing how tools are used within the culture. In this way, the importance of technology modeling by significant adults amounts to cognitive modeling and coaching. The same researchers also stated that tools are understood only through their use, and their use leads the user to better understand and become part of the culture in which such tools are used. If John were using YouTube or Google Hangouts with his friends, these tools would facilitate his integration into that of his regular-developing friends' culture. Given that society and community usually place low expectations on children with special needs and they are tacitly classified as belonging to "a different culture," the use of technology tools by children in this population needs to be closely studied to learn its implications on learning, concept attainment, and social acceptance. Because culture is learned, and because electronic technology is such an integral part of today everyday activities (i.e., culture), educators and caregivers need to model its use for children with Down syndrome and other special needs if they are to become part of the ordinary practices of today's children's culture. Furthermore, Seale (2003) argues that self-esteem and self-concept are highly influenced by the social comparisons that people with disabilities make. Technology can provide children with special needs essential tools to help them develop in a way that they feel fully included in society (Black & Wood, 2003).

Although different types of learning were discussed in this section, the main tenet is that there exist several learning theories that are capable of explaining ubiquitous learning. Along the years, philosophers and researches have come up with different learning theories to explain how learning occurs. Obviously, one theory could not explain all type of learning. In the same way, one theory cannot explain all the learning that occurs in computer ubiquitous learning. However, among many researchers, the consensus is that situated and distributed cognition, peppered with constructivism, authentic, and lifelong learning, provide the theoretical framework that best fits ubiquitous learning.

TOOLS FOR UBIQUTOUS LEARNING FOR INDIVIDUALS WITH DOWN SYNDROME AND OTHER SPECIAL NEEDS

At age 5, John entered kindergarten and was placed in a general education classroom with a one-on-one paraprofessional. 80% of his day was spent in the general education classroom with 20% spent in pull outs including occupational therapy, speech therapy, physical therapy and intensive small group and one-on-one language arts and mathematics work. John continued to receive one-on-one paraprofessional aide, occupational and speech therapy through fourth grade.

The democratic principles of American schooling state that schools must empower all children to effectively function now and in their future (Will, 1986; Peng, Su, Chou, & Tsai, 2009). Mobile learning technology is being investigated and tested as an aid to help students with special needs reach their potential.

Down syndrome individuals are known for demonstrating an "easy going" attitude; in other words, their social development and social learning are their strengths. Development for Down syndrome children used to be measured in terms of IQ. Given that the measure is abstract and does not demonstrate the necessary skills needed at each developmental stage, therapists and educators now use the degree of skills development at each life stage. From this perspective, that is, when focusing on a discrete set of skills, it is known that Down syndrome children develop social and emotional skills almost at the same level as non-disabled children. Social skills and empathy are strengths that will stay with individuals with Down syndrome throughout adult life (Buckley, 2012). As with any child, development in Down syndrome children needs to be a continuous and interactive process and the use of computer mo-

bile and computer ubiquitous learning can foster such development, especially if such technology is used for implicit learning. Vinter and Detable (2008) report that children with Down syndrome respond better to instances of implicit learning than to ones of explicit learning. They define implicit learning as all forms of unintentional learning that is internalized into the individual's behavior. This implicit learning usually comes as a consequence of repeated experiences in which the individual is not told to learn anything. On the other hand, explicit learning requires participants to devote mental and conscious effort to recall the explicit rules and information.

Shuler (2009) explains that there are five key opportunities to use mobile technology for ubiquitous learning. These are (a) anywhere, anytime learning to help bridge school and home environments; (b) help close the digital divide because of its relative low cost; (c) improve social interactions that are needed to be successful in the knowledge economy; (d) integration with larger technologies and learning environments; and (e) ability to support individualized learning as well as social learning. In the following paragraphs, some applications of technology for people with Down syndrome are discussed. It is stated, however, that these technologies may also help individuals with other special needs.

Although very few technology hardware and software have been built exclusively for Down syndrome individuals, new mobile and portable technologies are believed to be especially useful for this population. Even though there is not an extensive research literature on the use of technology by children with Down syndrome, some researchers (Black & Wood, 2003; Moni & Jobling, 2000; Seale, 2001, among others) have discussed some technology applications. Particular computer programs can provide multisensory activities that can be used to help Down syndrome individuals develop social interaction, turn taking, and collaboration that nurture social cognition

Wearable Technology

Advancements in the development of small technology is allowing for much innovation in the field of wearable technology. For instance, Geographic Positioning System (GPS), already embedded into many cellular phones, allows people to locate places and people to locate people. Other wearable technologies already in use are smart clothing (clothing embedded with small pieces of technology for health monitoring) and ID batches that have a tracking device. Other wearable technology, such as visors for virtual reality, have the potential to help Down syndrome children experience activities that otherwise would be difficult to achieve.

Computer Games

John has demonstrated continual growth in his kinesthetic abilities that align to his use of technologies. He often uses the Kinect addition to the X-Box gaming system when he plays games. The Kinect allows for the user to use their physical actions to control the system. John usually plays games that are based on his favorite animated movies that are action oriented with the lead characters engaging in many physical activities. The games follow the storyline of the movies and the player acts as the lead character. This may require the player to run in place, to sneak (walk softly), to kick, to punch, to balance, and to jump. The player receives automatic feedback about their abilities to do each of these activities by passing or failing the level; this has helped John to have greater gross motor control and more confidence to try other physical activities like round offs and hand stands.

The use of computer games can foster the development of social interaction, turn taking, and collaboration that nurture social cognition. Cebula, Moore, and Wishart (2010) broadly define social cognition as the ability to read others and to use appropriate ways of response according to the situation. However, these authors also

argued that goal-directed behaviors are linked to the development of frontal sections of the brain, which is disproportionally reduced in volume in Down syndrome children as compared with the brain of typical development children; this difference may account for the difficulties in the development of socio-cognitive skills in this population of children. On the other hand, Down syndrome children have strong visual and spatial skills and they are considered to be visual learners. Computer technologies that provide a high level of multisensory experiences with vast amount of repetition and visual cues can build the child's sense of accomplishment by experiencing repeated success in learning and, thus, being able to reach self- or educator-stated goals.

Reading

One of the areas in which John receives the greatest support at school is reading. As a 9 year old, he is still at the emergent reader level with full recognition of the letters of the alphabet and their sounds, as well as a growing recognition of many sight words. He is able to successfully read early reader books with images, many sight words and sentences around five words long. At school John has had access to Headsprout (now MimioSprout) to support him with "phonemic awareness, phonics, fluency, comprehension, and vocabulary" (Mimio, 2012). The program was also used at home during the summer between his 2nd and 3rd grade years.

Down syndrome individuals benefit greatly from reading and other literacy activities, especially if they are introduced in the preschool years. Placement of this type of special needs children in inclusive classrooms allows them to reach higher levels of reading than those who are kept in segregated learning environments. Since reading influences the development of speech, language, and memory skills, it is important to emphasize the importance of placement of Down syndrome children in mainstream education. Although Down syndrome children do not develop spoken skills as fast as other children, they use their visual memory skills and may be only about two years behind in their reading and writing skills than children in their cohort (Buckley, 2001).

Language

Down syndrome children have good communication skills through gestures and non-verbal skills due to the delay on the development of speech and language. However, once these children start to produce language, they use it in a meaningful way. Some skills that are difficult to master for Down syndrome children are learning grammar and producing clear speech. The development of speech and language is an essential ability to have because it is linked to the development of thinking, reasoning, and remembering (Buckley, 2000). Although speech and language are one of the most significantly delayed area (many times complicated by hearing impairments that are common in children with Down syndrome), there is a large range of software to promote development in this area, including programs that focus on speech sounds, phonological awareness, sentence comprehension and storytelling which provide a learning environment full with sounds and visual cues and supported by text (Black & Wood, 2003).

NUMBERS AND MATHEMATIC SKILLS

As with the general population, people with Down syndrome vary greatly in their interest for math skills. However, typically, the number skills in individuals with Down syndrome are lower than those in literacy. If taught using the child's strengths, such as visual learning, Down syndrome children follow similar stages of progression as non-disabled children but need more practice at each stage (Bird & Buckley, 2001). There are multiple applications developed for mobile technology

that address mathematical skills. Most of them use sound, color, and images to teach the concepts.

In general, the use of computer devices to help individuals with Down syndrome learn present many benefits. Black and Wood (2003) mention some of the following: provide multisensory experience, the use of non-verbal responses, immediate feedback, errorless learning, self-paced learning, and multiple opportunities for practice, among others.

MOBILE AND UBIQUITOUS LEARNING, OR JUST LEARNING: REVISITED

Weiser (1993), one of the pioneers of ubiquitous computing, discussed that "ubiquitous computing" will be achieved when technology becomes unobtrusive and invisible to the user. Overtime, "ubiquitous computing" has become "ubiquitous learning" maybe because of the pervasiveness of technology in everyday life. Most importantly, technology seems to be getting to the point that Wiser envisioned: to become invisible and unobtrusive to the user. So, one may ask, given the dependence on technology for everyday life, hasn't "ubiquitous computer learning" become just "ubiquitous learning"? When will society understand that learning has almost gone full circle to become again learning and to drop the "ubiquitous computer" part? Based on this argument, a new model of ubiquitous learning is presented in f Figure 1

Ubiquitous learning is offered as the all-encompassing learning. Formal, informal, and distance learning may intersect and overlap, but computer mobile learning and computer ubiquitous learning (Ogata & Yano, 2004) may be used in any of those contexts. Ubiquitous learning, on the other hand, is the umbrella context of learning that is owned by the learner. Peng, Su, Chou, and Tsai, (2009) state that computer ubiquitous learning is learning that happens at anytime, anywhere,

Figure 1. New ubiquitous learning model

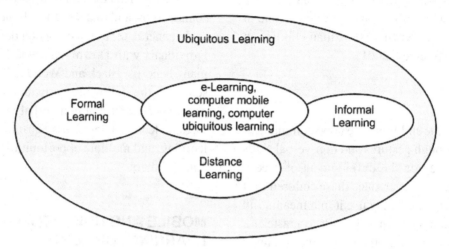

and when needed. Isn't that a general definition of learning, either technology-aided or not? Elliot Soloway stated that "the kids these days are not digital kids. The digital kids were in the '90s. The kids today are mobile, and there's a difference. Digital is the old way of thinking, mobile is the new way" (as quoted by Shuler, 2009, p. 39). Mobile, as Soloway explains, is the new way of learning – and mobile is ubiquitous.

There are still many issues to be resolved before arriving to the point where computer ubiquitous learning can be called only ubiquitous learning. Some of those issues are to identify a stable theoretical framework that explains how ubiquitous learning occurs; there are also the issues of place-bound social norms, differentiated access to mobile technology, physical limitations of small devices, and management of mobile technology in schools – starting by the need to train teachers in its use. All of these issues should not be taken lightly and it may be that Weiser's (1993) vision of unobtrusive technology be delayed for still some years or decades. However, ubiquitous learning (with the implicit use of a technology device) is here to stay and evolve. Educational debates now are still stuck into whether we can use mobile learning in education when they should be focused on how we can use it. It is the hope of these re-

searchers that not-so-distant future debates will not deal with whether computer ubiquitous learning is a more complete form of learning, but will deal with finally dropping the term "computer" out of the term "ubiquitous learning" – by then, computer technologies will really be an extension and augmentation of human beings.

CONCLUSION

Computer mobile learning and computer ubiquitous learning are becoming more pervasive as technology advances. However, children with special needs may be left out of using these advances if parents and educators do not advocate for their use. The same way technology has been increasing human capabilities in general, technologies have the potential to bring individuals with Down syndrome closer to lead a similarly able life as people with traditional development skills. Given the dependency on technology for everyday life activities, computer ubiquitous learning may soon become only ubiquitous learning, which will bring the definition of learning to a full circle. The advancement of this field of education will depend on more research and applications of different existing and new learning theories to mobile and ubiquitous learning.

REFERENCES

Anderson, T., & Dron, J. (2010). Three generations of distance education pedagogy. *International Review of Research in Open and Distance Learning*, *12*(3), 80–97.

Black, B., & Wood, A. (2003). Utilising information communication technology to assist the education of individuals with Down syndrome. *Down Syndrome Issues and Information*. Retrieved from http://www.down-syndrome.org/information/education/technology/

Brown, J. S., Collins, A., & Duguid, P. (1989). Cognition and the culture of learning. *Educational Researcher*, *18*(1), 32–42. doi:10.3102/0013189X018001032.

Buckley, S. J. (2000). Speech, language and communication for individuals with Down syndrome: An overview. *Down Syndrome Issues and Information*. Retrieved from http://www.down-syndrome.org/information/language/overview/

Buckley, S. J. (2001). Reading and writing for individuals with Down syndrome: An overview. *Down Syndrome Issues and Information*. Retrieved from http://www.down-syndrome.org/information/reading/overview/

Buckley, S. J. (2012). *Living with Down syndrome*. Down Syndrome Education International.

Cebula, K. R., Moore, D. G., & Wishart, J. G. (2010). Social cognition in children with Down's syndrome: Challenges to research and theory building. *Journal of Intellectual Disability Research*, *54*, 113–134. doi:10.1111/j.1365-2788.2009.01215.x PMID:19874447.

Chen, Y.-S., Kao, T.-C., Sheu, J.-P., & Chiang, C.-Y. (2002). A mobile scaffolding-aid-based bird-watching learning system. In *Proceedings of the IEEE International Workshop on Wireless and Mobile Technologies in Education* (WMTE'02). Växjö, Sweden: IEEE.

Dede, C. (2005). Planning for neomillennial learning styles: Implications for investments in faculty and technology. In D. Oblinger, & J. Oblinger (Eds.), *Educating the Net generation* (pp. 15.1–15.22). Boulder, CO: EDUCAUSE.

Dede, C. (2009). Immersive interfaces for engagement and learning. *Science*, *323*, 66–69. doi:10.1126/science.1167311 PMID:19119219.

DroidHen. (2012). Shoot the apple. *DroidHen Games*. Retrieved from http://www.droidhen.com/games.html

El-Bishouty, M. M., Ogata, H., Rahman, S., & Yano, Y. (2010). Social knowledge awareness map for computer supported ubiquitous learning environment. *Journal of Educational Technology & Society*, *13*(4), 27–37.

Field, J. (2000). *Lifelong learning and the new educational order*. London: Trentham Books.

Fischer, G., & Konomi, S. (2005). Innovative media in support of distributed intelligence and lifelong learning. In *Proceeding of the International Workshop on Wireless and Mobile Technologies in Education*. Los Alamitos, CA: IEEE Computer Society.

Fischer, G., & Konomi, S. I. (2007). Innovative socio-technical environments in support of distributed intelligence and lifelong learning. *Journal of Computer Assisted Learning*, *23*(4), 338–350. doi:10.1111/j.1365-2729.2007.00238.x.

Gulikers, J. T. M., Bastiaens, T. J., & Martens, R. L. (2005). The surplus value of an authentic learning environment. *Computers in Human Behavior*, *21*(3), 509–521. doi:10.1016/j.chb.2004.10.028.

Hall, T., & Bannon, L. (2006). Designing ubiquitous computing to enhance children's learning in museums. *Journal of Computer Assisted Learning*, 22, 231–243. doi:10.1111/j.1365-2729.2006.00177.x.

Hill, J. R., Reeves, T. C., & Heidemeier, H. (2000). *Ubiquitous computing for teaching, learning and communicating: Trends, issues and recommendations.* Retrieved from http://lpsl.coe.uga.edu/Projects/AAlaptop/pdf/UbiquitousComputing.pdf

Hollan, J., Hutchins, E., & Kirsch, D. (2001). Distributed cognition: Toward a new foundation for human-computer interaction research. In J. M. Carroll (Ed.), *Human-Computer Interaction in the New Millennium* (pp. 75–94). New York: ACM Press.

Jeng, Y., Wu, T., Huang, Y., Tan, Q., & Yang, S. (2010). The add-on impact of mobile applications in learning strategies: A review study. *Journal of Educational Technology & Society*, 13(3), 3–11.

Jeng, Y.-C., Lu, S.-C., & Lin, H.-M. (2011). Using e-learning and situated learning theory: Practical lessons from the vocational special education students. In *Proceedings from the e-Business Engineering (ICEBE)*. IEEE. doi:10.1109/ICEBE.2011.70.

Law, N., Pelgrum, W. J., & Plomp, T. (2008). *Pedagogy and ICT use in schools around the world: Findings from the IEA SITES 2006 study.* Hong Kong: Springer and Comparative Education Research Centre.

Lemon Team. (2012). Lucky's escape. *Lemon Team Game Development and Porting.* Retrieved from http://www.lemonteam.com/app/luckys-escape/

Lombardi, M. M. (2007). *Authentic learning for the 21st century: An overview.* EDUCAUSE Learning Initiative.

Mayer, R. (2004). Should there be a three-strikes rule against pure discovery learning? The case for guided methods of instruction. *The American Psychologist*, 59(1), 14–19. doi:10.1037/0003-066X.59.1.14 PMID:14736316.

Mimio. (2012). MimioSprout early reading. *Mimio.* Retrieved from http://www.mimio.com/en-NA/Products/MimioSprout-Earlyreading.aspx?_id=064914BF5130473EAE50557F1DDE881D&_z=z

Moni, K. B., & Jobling, A. (2000). A program to develop literacy in young adults with Down syndrome. *Journal of Adolescent & Adult Literacy*, 44(1), 40–49.

Moreno, R. (2004). Decreasing cognitive load for novice students: Effects of explanatory versus corrective feedback in discovery-based multimedia. *Instructional Science*, 32(1), 99–113. doi:10.1023/B:TRUC.0000021811.66966.1d.

Ogata, H., & Yano, Y. (2004). Context-aware support for computer-supported ubiquitous learning. In *Proceedings of the 2nd IEEE International Workshop on Wireless and Mobile Technologies in Education* (pp. 27-34). Los Alamitos, CA: IEEE Computer Society.

Pea, R. D. (1993). Practices of distributed intelligence and designs for education. In G. Salomon (Ed.), *Distributed cognitions: Psychological and educational considerations* (pp. 47–87). New York: Cambridge University Press.

Peng, H., Su, Y., Chou, C., & Tsai, C. (2009). Ubiquitous knowledge construction: Mobile learning re-defined and a conceptual framework. *Innovations in Education and Teaching International*, 46, 171–183. doi:10.1080/14703290902843828.

Rice, M. L., & Wilson, E. K. (1999). How technology aids constructivism in the social studies classroom. *Social Studies*, 90(1), 28–34. doi:10.1080/00377999909602388.

Rovio. (2012a). Angry birds. *The Official Home of Angry Birds*. Retrieved from http://www.angrybirds.com/

Rovio. (2012b). Amazing Alex. *Amazing Alex*. Retrieved from http://teaser.amazingalex.com/

Rovio. (2012c). Bad piggies. *Bad Piggies*. Retrieved from http://www.badpiggies.com/

Sajadi, S. S., & Khan, T. M. (2011). An evaluation of constructivism for learners with ADHD: Development of a constructivist pedagogy for special needs. In *Proceedings of the European, Mediterranean & Middle Eastern Conference on Information Systems*. IEEE.

Schwartz, N. H. (2008). Exploiting the use of technology to teach: The value of distributed cognition. *Journal of Research on Technology in Education*, *40*(3), 389–404.

Seale, J. K. (2001). The same but different: The use of the personal home page by adults with Down syndrome as a tool for self-presentation. *British Journal of Educational Technology*, *32*, 343–352. doi:10.1111/1467-8535.00203.

Sefton-Green, J. (2004). *Literature review in informal learning with technology outside school*. Bristol, UK: NESTA Futurelab.

Sharples, M. (2000). The design of personal mobile technologies for lifelong learning. *Computers & Education*, *34*(3), 177–193. doi:10.1016/S0360-1315(99)00044-5.

Spiro, R. J., Feltovich, P. J., Jacobson, M. J., & Coulson, R. L. (1992). Cognitive flexibility, constructivism, and hypertext: Random access instruction for advanced knowledge acquisition in ill-structured domains. *Constructivism and the Technology of Instruction: A Conversation*, 57-75.

Tan, T., Lin, M., Chu, Y., & Liu, T. (2012). Educational affordances of a ubiquitous learning environment in a natural science course. *Journal of Educational Technology & Society*, *15*, 206–219.

Vinter, A., & Detable, C. (2008). Implicit and explicit motor learning in children with and without Down's syndrome. *The British Journal of Developmental Psychology*, *26*(4), 507–523. doi:10.1348/026151007X267300.

Vvidis, I. K. (2002). Distributed cognition and educational practice. *Journal of Interactive Learning Research*, *11*, Retrieved from http://go.galegroup.com/ps/i.do?id=GALE%7CA87079467&v=2.1&u=nauniv&it=r&p=AONE&sw=w.

Weisner, M. (1993). Some computer issues in ubiquitous computer. *Communications of the ACM*, *36*(7), 75–84. doi:10.1145/159544.159617.

Wu, T. T., Yang, T. C., Hwang, G. J., & Chu, H. C. (2008). Conducting situated learning in a context-aware ubiquitous learning environment. In Wireless, Mobile, and Ubiquitous Technology in Education, (pp. 82-86). IEEE.

ADDITIONAL READING

Adomavicius, G., Sankaranarayanan, R., Sen, S., & Tuzhilin, A. (2005). Incorporating contextual information in recommender systems using a multidimensional approach. *ACM Transactions on Information Systems*, *23*(1), 103–145. doi:10.1145/1055709.1055714.

Al-Masri, E., & Mahmoud, Q. H. (2006). A context-aware mobile service discovery and selection mechanism using artificial neural networks. In *Proceedings of the 8th International Conference on Electronic Commerce* (pp. 594–598). New York: ACM Press.

Ansari, A. et al. (2000). Internet recommendation systems. *JMR, Journal of Marketing Research*, *37*(3), 363–375. doi:10.1509/jmkr.37.3.363.18779.

Asabere, N. Y. (2012). Review of recommender systems for learners in mobile social/collaborative learning. *International Journal of Information and Communication Technology Research*, 2(5), 429–435.

Balabanovic, M., & Shoham, Y. (1997). Fab: Content-based, collaborative recommendation. *Communications of the ACM*, 40(3), 66–72. doi:10.1145/245108.245124.

Baldauf, M., Dustdar, S., & Rosenberg, F. (2007). A survey on context-aware systems. *International Journal of Ad Hoc and Ubiquitous Computing*, 2(4), 263-277. Retrieved March 06, 2008, from http://dx.doi.org/10.1504/IJAHUC.2007.014070

Billsus, D. et al. (2002). Adaptive interfaces for ubiquitous web access. *Communications of the ACM*, 45(5), 34–38. doi:10.1145/506218.506240.

Burke, R. (2002). Hybrid recommender systems: Survey and experiments. *User Modeling and User-Adapted Interaction*, 12(4), 331–370. doi:10.1023/A:1021240730564.

Cazella, S. C., & Alvares, L. O. C. (2005). Modeling user's opinion relevance to recommending research papers. *User Modeling*, 3538, 327–331.

Cazella, S. C., Reategui, E., & Alvares, L. O. C. (2006). E-commerce recommenders' authority: Applying the user's opinion relevance in recommender systems. In *Proceedings of the 12th Brazilian Symposium on Multimedia and the Web* (WebMedia '06). ACM. DOI=10.1145/1186595.1186605

Foltz, P. W., & Dumais, S. T. (1992). Personalized information delivery: An analysis of information filtering methods. *Communications of the ACM*, 35(12), 51–60. doi:10.1145/138859.138866.

Grimm, R., Davis, J., Lemar, E., Macbeth, A., Swanson, S., & Anderson, T. et al. (2004). System support for pervasive applications. *ACM Transactions on Computer Systems*, 22(4), 421–486. doi:10.1145/1035582.1035584.

Heckmann, D. (2005). *Ubiquitous user modeling*. (Doctor dissertation). Technischen Fakultlaten der Universitlat des Saarlandes, Saarbrucken, Germany.

Heckmann, D., & Kruger, A. (2003). A user modeling markup language (UserML) for ubiquitous computing. In *International Conference on User Modeling* (pp. 393-397). Springer.

Herlocker, J., Konstan, J., & Riedl, J. (200). Explaining collaborative filtering recommendations. In *Proceedings of the 2000 ACM Conference on Computer Supported Cooperative Work* (pp. 241-250). ACM.

Hoareau, C., & Satoh, I. (2009). Modeling and processing information for context-aware computing - A survey. *New Generation Computing*, 27(3), 177-196. DOI= 10.1007/s00354-009-0060-5

Hong, J., Suh, E., Kim, J., & Kim, S. (2009). Context-aware system for proactive personalized service based on context history. *Expert Systems with Applications*, 36(4), 7448-7457. DOI=10.1016/j.eswa.2008.09.002

Kalatzis, N., Roussaki, I., Liampotis, N., Strimpakou, M., & Pils, C. (2008). User-centric inference based on history of context data in pervasive environments. In *Proceedings of the 3rd International Workshop on Services Integration in Pervasive Environments* (pp. 25-30). DOI= 10.1145/1387309.1387316

Konstan, J. A., Miller, B. N., Maltz, D., Herlocker, J. L., Gordon, L. R., & Riedl, J. (1997). Grouplens: Applying collaborative filtering to usenet news. *Communications of the ACM*, 40(3), 77–87. doi:10.1145/245108.245126.

Lisetti, C. L. (2002). Personality, affect and emotion taxonomy for socially intelligent agents. In *Proceedings of the Fifteenth International Florida Artificial Intelligence Research Society Conference* (pp. 397–401). AAAI Press.

Lueg, C. (1998).Considering collaborative filtering as groupware: Experiences and lessons learned. In *Proceedings of the International Conference on Practical Aspects of Knowledge Management* (pp. 29-30). Basel, Switzerland: IEEE.

McDonald, D. W. (2001). Evaluating expertise recommendations. In *Proceedings of the 2001 International ACM SIGGROUP Conference on Supporting Group Work* (pp. 214–223). New York, NY: ACM Press.

McDonald, D. W. (2003). Recommending collaboration with social networks: A comparative evaluation. In *Proceedings of the SIGCHI Conference on Human Factors in Computing Systems* (pp. 593–600). New York, NY: ACM Press.

McDonald, D. W., & Ackerman, M. S. (2000). Expertise recommender: A flexible recommendation system and architecture. In *Proceedings of the 2000 ACM Conference on Computer Supported Cooperative Work* (pp. 231–240), New York, NY: ACM Press.

Middleton, S., Shadbolt, N., & De Roure, D. (2004).Ontological user profiling in recommender systems. *ACM Transactions on Information Systems, 22*(1), 54–88. doi:10.1145/963770.963773.

Montaner, M. et al. (2003). A taxonomy of recommender agents on the internet. In *Artificial Intelligence Review* (pp. 285–330). Dordrecht, The Netherlands: Kluwer Academic Publishers.

O'Connor, M., Cosley, D., Konstan, J. A., & Riedl, J. (2001). Polylens: A recommender system for groups of users. In *Proceedings of the Seventh Conference on European Conference on Computer Supported Cooperative Work* (pp. 199–218). Norwell, MA: Kluwer Academic Publishers.

Pazzani, M. J. (1999). A framework for collaborative, content-based and demographic filtering. *Artificial Intelligence Review, 13*(5-6), 393–408. doi:10.1023/A:1006544522159.

Perugini, S., Gonçalves, M. A., & Fox, E. A. (2004). Recommender systems research: A connection-centric survey. *Journal of Intelligent Information Systems, 23*(2), 107–143. doi:10.1023/B:JIIS.0000039532.05533.99.

Resnick, P., et al. (1994). GroupLens: An open architecture for collaborative filtering of netnews. In *Proceedings of ACM 1994 Conference on Computer Supported Cooperative Work*. Chapel Hill, NC: ACM Press.

Resnick, P., Kuwabara, K., Zeckhauser, R., & Friedman, E. (2000). Reputation systems. *Communications of the ACM, 43*(12), 45–48. doi:10.1145/355112.355122.

Resnick, P., & Varian, H. R. (1997). Recommender systems. *Communications of the ACM, 40*(3), 55–58. doi:10.1145/245108.245121.

Resnick, P., Zeckhauser, R., Swanson, J., & Lockwood, K. (2006). The value of reputation on ebay: A controlled experiment. *Experimental Economics, 9*(2), 79–101. doi:10.1007/s10683-006-4309-2.

Ricci, F. (2011). Mobile recommender systems. *International Journal of Information Technology and Tourism, 12*(3), 205–231. doi:10.3727/1098 30511X12978702284390.

Ricci, F., & Rokach, L. (2010). *Recommender systems handbook*. Berlin: Springer.

Riedl, J. et al. (2000). Electronic commerce recommender applications. *Journal of Data Mining and Knowledge Discovery, 5*(2), 115–152.

Spiliopoulou, M. (2000). Web usage mining for website evaluation. *Communications of the ACM, 43*(8), 127–134. doi:10.1145/345124.345167.

Terveen, L., Hill, W., Amento, B., McDonald, D., & Creter, J. (1997). Phoaks: A system for sharing recommendations. *Communications of the ACM, 40*(3), 59–62. doi:10.1145/245108.245122.

Wang, T. I., Tsai, K. H., Lee, M. C., & Chiu, T. K. (2007). Personalized learning objects recommendation based on the semantic-aware discovery and the learner preference pattern. *Journal of Educational Technology & Society, 10*(3), 84–105.

Yin, C., Ogata, H., Tabata, Y., & Yano, Y. (2010). Supporting the acquisition of Japanese polite expressions in context-aware ubiquitous learning. *International Journal of Mobile Learning and Organisation, 4*(2), 214–234. doi:10.1504/IJMLO.2010.032637.

Chapter 10
CRS:
A Course Recommender System

Kamal Taha
Khalifa University of Science, Technology, and Research, UAE

ABSTRACT

Most problems facing Distance Education (DE) academic advising can be overcome using a course recommender system. Such a system can overcome the problem of students who do not know their interest in courses from merely their titles or descriptions provided in course catalogues. The authors introduce in this chapter an XML user-based Collaborative Filtering (CF) system called CRS. The system aims at predicting a DE student's academic performance and interest on a course based on a collection of profiles of students who have similar interests and academic performance in prior courses. The system advises a student to take courses that were taken successfully by students who have the same interests and academic performance as the active student. The framework of CRS identifies a set of course features for every academic major. The authors experimentally evaluate CRS. Results show marked improvement.

INTRODUCTION

Currently, Recommender Systems (RS) are widely used in different domains such as E-commerce and digital libraries. In general, recommendation systems suggest items or products, by analyzing what users with similar tastes have chosen in the past. Recently, recommender systems are applied in the e-learning domain in order to personalize learning content. In this process, students are matched with the appropriate learning objects. Students are connected with each other according to their individual interests, skills, needs, and learning goals. A number of research works advocate the use of recommender system in e-learning systems and learning management systems. Calvo (2003) uses recommender system in intelligent learning system. Andronico (2003) suggests educational resources to students through mobile phones. Liu & Gree (2005) provides a framework that selects a list of learning objects that suit students.

DOI: 10.4018/978-1-4666-4542-4.ch010

There are a number of approaches for recommending learning objects. One of these approaches is Content-Based System (CBS) recommend courses to students based on the content of courses and the student's preferences. The approach detects the similarities between courses attributes (such as name, abstract, keywords) and other courses. The student enters a course's attributes and the system recommends courses that have similarities with the active course's attributes. Another approach is Rule Based Filtering. The approach filters courses based on a set of rules to be applied to the student's profile and the system's profile.

There have been a number of works that have addressed on-line automatic advising and predicting student performance in e-learning (Vance, 2004; Khribi, 2007; Thai-Nghe, 2010). Mohamed (2007) provides techniques for on-line automatic recommendations in e-learning systems using the access history of learners. The work of (Vance, 2004) provides a guide to developing e-advising standards for advisees, advisors, and administrators. The work of (Thai-Nghe, 2010) uses recommender system techniques for educational data mining and for predicting student performance.

A DE student may not be able to know his interest in a course from merely its title or from the description of the course provided in the course catalogue. Also, the advisor needs to advise the student to take a course that suits the student's academic performance and skills. Towards this, the advisor needs to consider the performance of students in all his prior courses, which is time consuming. These problems can be overcome using a course recommender system. We introduce in this chapter a type of Collaborative Filtering (CF) system called Course Recommender System (CRS). The system aims at predicting a student's academic performance and interest on a course based on a collection of profiles of students who have similar interests and academic performance on prior courses.

The framework of CRS identifies a set of course features for every academic major. A course feature is a characteristic skill or attribute that a student needs to possess in order to succeed in the course. For example, some of the course features for Computer Science major can be comprehension skills, memorization skills, programming skills, math skills, inferential thinking skills, problem solving skills, application of strategies skills, etc. Students are categorized based on their similarity on course features. Each category (bicluster) includes students who have close academic skills and interests (i.e., course features) in a number of courses. CRS would return to the active student a ranked list of courses that have been rated high by the majority of the members of the cluster, to which the active student belongs. That is, CRS outputs ranked lists of courses, taking into account not only the initial preferences of the active student, but also the ratings of the bicluster, to which the student belongs. The basic idea is that if the students who have the same academic profile as the active student took a course successfully in the past, it is likely this active student will succeed in this course. That is, the underlying assumption is that those who have similar academic performance and interest on prior courses tend to have the same academic performance and interest on future courses. CRS assigns a bicluster to each student user dynamically on the fly. In the framework of CRS, students' characteristics (e.g., biclusters) are inferred *implicitly* by the system without involving the user. That is, the student is not required to reveal the biclusters to which the student belongs. The student is determined whether or not he/she belongs to a bicluster G by matching his/her ratings on course features with the ratings of G. CRS constructs biclusters and also identifies their interests and academic skills *dynamically* on the fly. We developed formal concepts and algorithms that identify the interests and academic skills of various biclusters dynamically on the fly. These interests and academic skills are determined from the interests and academic skills of the biclusters' member users using a group modeling strategy.

BACKGROUND

CF (Herlocker et al., 2004) is one of the successful recommendation tools. It is the process of filtering for information using the opinion of other people. A number of CF algorithms have been proposed. There are two major classes of these algorithms (Breese et al., 1998), memory-based and model-based approaches. Memory-based CF (e.g., (Breese et al., 1998) predicts a user's preference based on his/her similarity to other users in the database. Model-based CF first learns a descriptive model of the user preferences and then uses it for providing item recommendation. The advantage of the memory-based methods over their model-based alternatives is that less parameters have to be tuned. Existing memory-based CF methods, mainly user-based (e.g., (Breese et al., 1998)) and item-based (e.g., (Deshpande & Karypis, 2004)) methods predict new ratings by aggregating rating information from either similar users or items. Given an unknown test rating to be estimated, user-based CF measures similarities between test user and other users. Item-based CF measures similarities between test item and other items.

There have been a number of researches in filtering based on group profiling (Aimeur et al., 2006; Junior & Canuto, 2006; O'Connor et al., 2008; Symeonidis et al., 2008; Tang et al., 2008; Wang et al., 2004). In most of these works, a group is formed based on common interests of its members on an item(s)/features. Symeonidis et al. (2008) proposes to capture the interaction between users and their favorite features by constructing feature profile for users. Users are grouped into biclusters (i.e., *group of users which exhibit highly correlated ratings on groups of items*). Each bicluster acts like a community for its corresponding items. Each bicluster's item features are weighted. The weighted value of feature f for user u $W(u, f)$ is calculated as follows: $W(u, f) = FF(u, f) * IUF(f)$, where $FF(u, f)$ is the number of times f occurs in the profile of user u; and, $IUF(f)$ is the *inverse user frequency* and is calculated as: $IUF(f) = \log (|U|/UF(f))$, where $|U|$ is the *total number of users*; $UF(f)$ is the *number of users in which feature f occurs at least once*. The work of (O'Connor, 2008) describes how a combination of collaborative and demographic filtering can be used to recommend product bundles. It describes how stored data is used to recommend a combination of tourist services. Junior and Canuto (2006) present Caracará, a system for searching and mining information on the World Wide Web, using a dynamic grouping process. Carcará groups Internet users according to their profile. After that, the system makes suggestions of URLs which are likely to be useful for the users of these groups. The work of (Aimeur et al., 2006) creates categories of users having similar demographic characteristics, and tracks the aggregate buying behavior of users within these categories. Recommendations for a new user are issued by applying the aggregate buying preferences of previous users in the category to which the user belongs. In (Wang et al., 2004), the authors present a model for supporting social groups in an Ubicomp environment. There must be consensus between group members in order for a person to be a member of the group.

There have been a number of works that have addressed on-line automatic advising and predicting student performance in e-learning (Vance, 2004; Khribi, 2007; Thai-Nghe, 2010). Mohamed (2007) provides techniques for on-line automatic recommendations in e-learning systems using the access history of learners. The work of (Vance, 2004) provides a guide to developing e-advising standards for advisees, advisors, and administrators. The work of (Thai-Nghe, 2010) uses recommender system techniques for educational data mining and for predicting student performance.

Most current works that address on-line automatic advising suffer the following limitation. When they determine the students having similar rating pattern as the active student, the number of these students is usually much less than the actual number. The reason is that most of these algorithms consider *only* course features rated by the active student and co-rated by other students, and students usually rate only a *subset* of a course's features. We observe that we can account for all students that have similar interests and academic performance as the active student by employing a mechanism similar to *friend-of-a friend* ontology. For example, consider that: (1) student u_x has academic skills on course feature f_i, (2) student u_y has academic skills on course features f_i and f_j, and (3) student u_z has academic skills on course feature f_j. By applying the *friend-of-a friend* ontology, we will find that *all* the three students may have *common* skills. Moreover, these academic skills may include course features other than f_i and f_j, if the three students belong to some common *context*. A context is a set of characteristics that define a group of students based on academic performance on course features. Therefore, we propose grouping students based on their contexts' profiles rather than solely on their rating patterns. If an active student u_x and another student u_y rated *different* course features, but both have similar rating pattern as a group G of students, it is most likely they both have similar interests and academic skills, which are the interests and academic skills of the group G. The interests and academic skills of u_x can be predicted based on the interests and academic skills of the group G. Some of the student members of the group G may have rated course features other than those rated by student u_y.

OUTLINE OF THE APPROACH

Notation 1: Course Feature

A course feature is a characteristic skill or attribute that a student needs to possess in order to succeed in the course.

CRS aims at predicting a student's academic performance and interest for a course based on a collection of profiles of students who have similar interests and academic performance on prior courses. The framework of CRS identifies a set of course features for every academic major.

Students are categorized based on their similarity on course features. Each category (bicluster) includes students who have close academic skills and interests (i.e., course features) in a number of courses. CRS would return to the active student a ranked list of courses that have been rated high by the majority of the members of the cluster, to which the active student belongs. That is, CRS outputs ranked lists of courses, taking into account not only the initial preferences of the active student, but also the ratings of the bicluster, to which the user belongs. The following are outline of the sequential processing steps taken by CRS:

- **Step 1-Categorizing Students into Biclusters:** Each bicluster includes students with similar academic skills and interests. That is, the simultaneous clustering of students and their ratings on course features discovers biclusters, which correspond to groups of students exhibiting highly correlated ratings on groups of course features. This process is described in more details in the section with the heading "*Categorizing students into biclusters*".

- **Step 2- Identifying the Academic Skills of Each Bicluster:** This is done by identifying the bicluster's scores on course features. Based on the weights of a bicluster's member students on course features, each course feature is given a score. This score reflects the importance of the course feature to the bicluster relative to other course features. This process is described in more details in the section with the heading "*Determining the preferences and skills of a bicluster*".

- **Step 3- Identifying the Bicluster of a New Student User:** This is done by matching the student's rating with the biclusters' ratings computed in step 1. That is, the system identifies (*implicitly*) the member students of a bicluster G_x by matching their ratings with the rating pattern of G_x. This process is described in more details in the section with the heading "*Determining a bicluster for student*".

- **Step 4- Ranking and Returning Recommended Courses for New Student User:** This is done using the scores of the bicluster, to which the student belongs. The courses will be displayed to the student user after being ranked based on their features' scores. This process is described in more details in the section with the heading "*Ranking and returning recommended courses*".

CATEGORIZING STUDENTS INTO BICLUSTERS

The framework of CRS identifies a set of course features for every academic major. Students are categorized based on their similarity on course features. Each category (bicluster) includes students who have close academic skills and interests (i.e., course features) in a number of courses. That is, the simultaneous clustering of students and their ratings on course features discovers biclusters, which correspond to groups of students exhibiting highly correlated ratings on groups of course features. Each bicluster includes students with similar academic skills and interests.

A student's ratings on course features are modeled as a set $D = \{(a_1, w_1), ..., (a_m, w_m)\}$, where: a_i denotes course feature i and w_i a weight on a_i. The weight w_i is a value scaled between 1 and 10. A complete set of course features are presented to students to determine their relevance. The system provides the students with a *graphical user interface* (GUI) to reveal their ratings on course features. Table 1 is an example of student's ratings on course features. Let T be a table of student ratings on course features. Let the columns of T represent course features and the rows represent

students. The biclustering technique finds subgroups of rows and columns in the table T that are similar as possible to one another and as different as possible to the rest. Biclustering has been used in many bioinformatics research works (e.g., (Murali & Kasif, 2003)). For the biclustering step, we use the xMotif algorithm (Murali & Kasif, 2003). The algorithm finds subsets of rows and subsets of columns with coherent values (*i.e., subsets of students who have analogous rating behavior*). Each bicluster is defined on a subset of rows and a subset of columns. Two biclusters may overlap.

We now introduce a running example to illustrate some of the concepts in this chapter.

Example 1: Table 1 shows the ratings of fifteen students on ten course features. The rating scale is between [0-10].

DETERMINING THE PREFERENCES AND SKILLS OF A BICLUSTER

The academic skills of a bicluster are determined from the bicluster's scores on course features. Based on the weights of a bicluster's member students on course features, each course feature is given a score. This score reflects the importance of the course feature to the bicluster relative to other course features. We adopt the following strategy for determining these scores:

Each course feature is assigned a score. This score is based on the difference between the number of times the course feature beats other course features (i.e., assigned a higher weight by the members of the bicluster), and the number of times it loses.

Definition 1: A score of a course feature: *Let a* $\succ$ b denote: The number of times the members of a bicluster rated their academic skills on course feature a greater than that of course feature b. Let c(a) denote the score of course

Table 1. Weighted student-feature matrix

	Feature 1	Feature 2	Feature 3	Feature 4	Feature 5	Feature 6	Feature 7	Feature 8	Feature 9	Feature 10
Student 1	7	3	9	2	10	7	9	4	6	8
Student 2	4	7	5	9	4	6	5	3	7	10
Student 3	8	10	4	7	5	3	8	6	2	5
Student 4	6	5	8	3	8	2	7	5	6	8
Student 5	7	8	2	9	4	5	3	4	8	1
Student 6	9	4	5	8	10	6	1	7	2	4
Student 7	5	3	7	6	6	5	10	2	7	5
Student 8	8	2	9	4	3	8	4	6	1	10
Student 9	9	5	8	10	7	1	2	5	3	7
Student 10	10	8	6	4	8	3	6	9	2	3
Student 11	5	7	8	1	9	6	5	3	8	4
Student 12	3	8	6	8	7	4	4	8	10	5
Student 13	8	7	7	2	8	5	6	3	1	8
Student 14	4	8	2	6	5	5	8	10	5	2
Student 15	1	5	7	8	4	9	7	3	8	6

feature a. Given the dominance relation $\succ$ on a set F of course features rated by the bicluster, the score c(a) of course feature "a" equals:

$$|\{b \in F : a \succ b\}| - |\{b \in F : b \succ a\}|$$

The following are some of the characteristics of this scoring strategy:

1. The sum of the scores of all course features is always zero.

2. The highest and lowest possible scores are $(n\text{-}1)$ and $-(n\text{-}1)$ respectively, where n is the number of course features.

We normalize the scores by first adding the absolute of the most negative score to all scores and then normalizing the resulting values.

Example 2: Based on the ratings in Table 1, the "beats" and "looses" of each course feature are shown in Table 2. The symbol "+" denotes that a feature beat a corresponding one (i.e., rated higher by the majority of users), while "-" denotes it lost. For example, *feature 1* beat *feature 2*. A zero means: two features beat each other the same number of times and also lost to each other the same number of times. The raw before the last one in Tables 2 shows the score of each feature computed using the strategy described in Definition 1. The last raw shows the normalized scores.

DETERMINING A BICLUSTER FOR STUDENT

The bicluster of a new student member is determined by matching the student's rating with the biclusters' ratings. That is, the system identifies (*implicitly*) the member students of a bicluster G_x by matching their ratings with the rating pattern of G_x. Let $sim(u_m, G_x)$ be the *similarity* between the ratings of user u_m and bicluster G_x. We measure $sim(u_m, G_x)$ using the *cosine-similarity measure* shown in Equation 1:

$$sim(u_m, G_x) = \frac{\sum_{\forall i \in I} \left((r_{u_m,i} - \overline{r}_{u_m})(r_{G_x,i} - \overline{r}_{G_x}) \right)}{\sqrt{\sum_{\forall i \in I} (r_{u_m,i} - \overline{r}_{u_m})^2} \sqrt{\sum_{\forall i \in I} (r_{G_x,i} - \overline{r}_{G_x})^2}}$$

$$(1)$$

I: Set of features rated by bicluster G_x and *co-rated* by u_m:

c_x: Weight of user u_m on course feature i.

$r_{G_x,i}$: Normalized score of bicluster G_x on feature i.

$\overline{r}_{u_m}$: Normalized *mean* weight of u_m on set I.

$$\overline{r}_{u_m} = \frac{\sum_{\forall i \in I} r_{u_m,i}}{|I|}$$

$\overline{r}_{G_x}$: Normalized *mean score* of G_x on set I;

$$\overline{r}_{G_x} = \frac{\sum_{\forall i \in I} r_{G_x,i}}{|I|}$$

Equation 1 considers *each* feature rated by bicluster G_x and co-rated by user u_m even if the feature was rated by only one student of G_x. Therefore, the equation *may give misleading similarity results*, since some features in set I may not reflect the actual academic performance of G_x. A feature that has been rated very low or by few members of bicluster G_x is most likely rated by a member(s) of G_x who belongs also to another bicluster G_y. Therefore, when measuring the similarity between an active user and G_x, we should consider only the features that reflect the preferences of G_x. That is, we need to consider only the dominant features of G_x (*i.e., the features that have been rated high and by the majority of the members of G_x*).

We adopt the following strategy for determining the set of dominant features for a bicluster. From the set F of all features, the subset F' is the dominant features for a bicluster, if every feature in F': (1) dominates every feature not in F' (*i.e., has a greater score*), and (2) acquires a score greater or equal to a threshold z. For example, recall Table 2 and consider that z is set to "0". Accordingly, the set F' of dominant features for the bicluster would be {*Feature 3, Feature 4, Feature 5, Feature 7, Feature 10*}. We now formalize the concept of dominant features in Definition 2.

Definition 2: Dominant Features for a Bicluster: *Let F be a set of n features and c(f) be the score of feature f. The subset $F' \subset F$ of dominant features with maximal scores for a bicluster is given by: {a∈F: c(a)≥c(b), for all b ∈F} and {c(a) ≥z: (n-1) > z < −(n-1)}*

We adjusted Equation 1 so that only the subset $F' \cap I$ is considered, as shown in Equation 2.

Table 2. Beats/looses, score, and normalized score of each feature based on the ratings in Table 1

	Feature 1	Feature 2	Feature 3	Feature 4	Feature 5	Feature 6	Feature 7	Feature 8	Feature 9	Feature 10
Feature 1	0	-	+	-	+	+	+	-	+	+
Feature 2	+	0	+	+	+	-	-	+	+	+
Feature 3	-	-	0	+	+	-	+	-	-	-
Feature 4	+	-	-	0	-	-	+	+	-	-
Feature 5	-	-	-	+	0	-	-	-	-	-
Feature 6	-	+	+	+	+	0	+	-	+	+
Feature 7	-	+	-	-	+	-	0	-	-	-
Feature 8	+	-	+	-	+	+	+	0	+	+
Feature 9	-	-	+	+	+	-	+	-	0	+
Feature 10	-	-	+	+	+	-	+	-	-	0
Score	-3	-5	+3	+3	+7	-5	+5	-5	-1	+1
Normalized score	0.04	0	0.16	0.16	0.24	0	0.2	0	0.08	0.12

$$sim\,(u_m, G_x) = \frac{\sum_{\forall i \in F''} \left(\left(r_{u_m, i} - \overline{r}_{u_m} \right) \left(r_{G_x, i} - \overline{r}_{G_x} \right) \right)}{\sqrt{\sum_{\forall i \in F''} \left(r_{u_m, i} - \overline{r}_{u_m} \right)^2} \sqrt{\sum_{\forall i \in F''} \left(r_{G_x, i} - \overline{r}_{G_x} \right)^2}}$$

$$(2)$$

F' : Set of dominant features rated with maximal scores by bicluster G_x

F'' : Subset of v_i co-rated by user u_m (i.e., $F'' \subseteq v_i$).

$$\overline{r}_{u_m} = \frac{\sum_{\forall i \in F''} r_{u_m, i}}{|F''|} \quad \text{and} \quad \overline{r}_{G_x} = \frac{\sum_{\forall i \in F''} r_{G_x, i}}{|F''|}$$

From the set F', Equation 2 overlooks the subset $F' - F''$ (*i.e. the subset that has not been cotared by student user u_m*) Therefore, the equation may give inaccurate similarity results. We observe that we can consider user $_{um}$ assigned a weight of zero to each of the features in the subset. The reason is that users usually have either no or very little interest on features they do not

rate. We adjusted Equation 2 to consider the subset $F' - F''$ as shown in equation 3 in Box 1.

$$P = \{F' - F''\}$$

Let F_u be the set of features rated by student user $_{um}$. As a final improvement of the similarity equation, we consider each feature $f_k \in \{F_u - F'\}$, if the weight of bicluster G_x on f_k beat other features' weights at least k number of times, where $k > 0$. However, we need to penalize each expression operand in the equation involving f_k to ensure that it will have a lower impact on the similarity result. Moreover, we need to scale down these expressions appropriately to account for the rank specificity of f_u among the list of features ranked by G_x to ensure that that lower ranked features indeed get higher penalty. Towards this, we *penalize and scale down* each expression operand involving f_u by a factor $decay^{t-1}$, where *decay* is a parameter that can be set to a value in the range 0 to 1. We set the exponent t to account for the rank of f_u among the list of features ranked by bicluster G_x. We adjusted equation 3 accordingly as shown in equation 4 in Box 2.

Box 1.

$$sim(u_m, G_x) = \frac{\sum\limits_{\forall i \in F''} \left(r_{u_m,i} - \overline{r}_{u_m}\right)\left(r_{G_x,i} - \overline{r}_{G_x}\right) + \sum\limits_{\forall j \in P} \left(\overline{r}_{u_m}\left(r_{G_x,j} - \overline{r}_{G_x}\right)\right)}{\sqrt{\sum\limits_{\forall i \in F''} \left(r_{u_m,i} - \overline{r}_{u_m}\right)^2 + |P|\left(\overline{r}_{u_m}\right)^2} \sqrt{\sum\limits_{\forall i \in (F'' \cup P)} \left(r_{G_x,i} - \overline{r}_{G_x}\right)^2}} \qquad (3)$$

Box 2.

$$sim(u_m, G_x) = \frac{\sum\limits_{\forall i \in F''} \left(r_{u_m,i} - \overline{r}_{u_m}\right)\left(r_{G_x,i} - \overline{r}_{G_x}\right) + \sum\limits_{\forall j \in P} \left(\overline{r}_{u_m}\left(r_{G_x,j} - \overline{r}_{G_x}\right)\right) + N}{\sqrt{\sum\limits_{\forall i \in \{F'' \cup F_k\}} \left(r_{u_m,i} - \overline{r}_{u_m}\right)^2 + |P|\left(\overline{r}_{u_m}\right)^2} \sqrt{\sum\limits_{\forall i \in (F'' \cup P)} \left(r_{G_x,i} - \overline{r}_{G_x}\right)^2 + M}}$$

$$N = \sum\limits_{\forall i \in V} \left(r_{u_m,i} - \overline{r}_{u_m}\right)\left(r_{G_x,i} - \overline{r}_{G_x}\right) \times decay^{t-1}$$

$$M = \sum\limits_{\forall i \in V} \left(r_{G_x,i} - \overline{r}_{G_x}\right)^2 \times decay^{t-1}$$

$$V = \{F_k - F'\}$$

(4)

F_k: Set of features that are: (1) rated by G_x, (2) co-rated by u_m, and (3) assigned weights by G_x that beat other features' weights at least k number of times. As *each* new student user is identified by the system as belonging to a bicluster G_x *(using equation 4)*, the current course features' scores of G_x will be re-optimized and re-updated *(dynamically)* based on: (1) the rating of this new user on these course features, and (2) the rating of the other member students of G_x on these course features. That is, the rating of *each* subsequent user would *update* and *optimize* current course features' scores for the bicluster by updating course features' number of beats/looses and scores *(recall Table 2)*.

RANKING AND RETURNING RECOMMENDED COURSES

A student's courses are ranked using the scores of the bicluster, to which the student belongs. The courses will be displayed to the student user after being ranked based on their features' scores. The system ranks recommended courses using a feature-course matrix N. In this matrix, element $N(j, i)$ is *one*, if course C_j requires a student to possess the academic skills of feature f_j and *zero* otherwise. The profile $N(I_j)$ of course C_j is the *j-th* column of matrix N. The score of course C_j is the *summation of the normalized scores* (e.g., recall Table 2) of the course features that C_j requires *(see Equation 5)*

$$Score\ C_j = \sum\limits_{\forall N(f_i, C_j)=1} score f_i \quad (5)$$

The courses will be displayed to the student user after being ranked based on their scores.

Example 3: Table 3 shows an example data set of Matrix *N* for our running example. Element $N(c_j, f_i)$ is one if course *i* requires the student to have the skills of feature f_i and zero otherwise. For example, the score of *Course 1* is the sum of the normalized scores of *feature 2, feature 3, feature 5*, and *feature 9*, which is $0 + 0.16 + 0.24 + 0.08 = 0.48$ (*recall Table 2*). Therefore, the courses will be ranked for the active user as follows: *Course 2, Course 3, Course 4, Course 7, Course 10, Course 8, Course 1, Course 5, Course 6*, and *Course 9*,

SYSTEM ARCHITECTURE

Figure 1 shows the system architecture. Module *BiclusterDeterminer* performs the following: (1) uses the xMotif algorithm (Murali & Kasif, 2003) to identify all possible biclusters that exist because of the similarities among the scores of course features, (2) assigns a folder for each bicluster G_x in the system's database to store information such as the ratings, dominant features, academic skills, and

interests of G_x, and (3) assigns a subfolder within the folder of G_x for each student user belonging to G_x to store information such as the ratings of the student. That is, individual subfolders are associated with G_x folder via file in a file system structure in a two-layer directory tree.

CRS Engine Performs the Following: (1) identifies *implicitly* the bicluster of a new student user by consulting module *BiclusterDeterminer*, and (2) *filters* and *ranks* recommended courses to a student based on the rating of the student as well as the rating of the bicluster, to which the student belongs, and (3) optimizes and updates the ratings of each bicluster G_x based on the ratings of new member students by updating the *Beats-Looses Matrix* and the *Feature-course Matrix* of the bicluster.

EXPERIMENTAL RESULTS

We implemented CRS in Java and ran it on an Intel(R) Core(TM)2 Dup CPU processor, with a CPU of 2.1 GHz and 3 GB of RAM, under Windows Vista. We evaluate CRS by comparing it with (Vance, 2004; Thai-Nghe, 2010) using real-user evaluation conducted by 64 students from the

Table 3. Feature-course matrix

	Course 1	Course 2	Course 3	Course 4	Course 5	Course 6	Course 7	Course 8	Course 9	Course 10
Feature 1	0	1	0	1	1	0	0	1	1	1
Feature 2	1	1	0	1	0	0	1	1	1	0
Feature 3	1	1	1	0	1	0	0	1	0	0
Feature 4	0	0	1	0	1	1	1	1	1	0
Feature 5	1	1	0	1	0	0	1	0	0	1
Feature 6	0	1	0	1	0	1	1	0	0	0
Feature 7	0	0	1	1	0	1	0	1	1	1
Feature 8	0	1	1	0	1	0	0	0	1	1
Feature 9	1	0	1	1	0	0	1	0	1	0
Feature 10	0	0	1	1	1	1	1	0	0	1
Score	0.48	0.88	0.72	0.68	0.48	0.48	0.6	0.56	0.48	0.6

Figure 1. System architecture

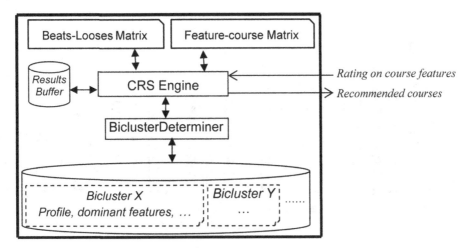

University of Texas at Arlington-USA and Khalifa University-UAE. Each student was asked to: (1) rank and list the courses he/she received at least grade B on, (2) rate the features of these courses and provide them to CRS and to (Vance, 2004; Thai-Nghe, 2010).

MEASURING THE DISTANCE BETWEEN THE LISTS RANKED BY THE STUDENTS AND THE LISTS RANKED BY CRS AND (VANCE, 2004; THAI-NGHE, 2010)

We measured the distance $d(\sigma_u, \sigma_s)$ between each list of courses that a student subject had received at least grade B on after being ranked by the student and the corresponding list ranked by each of CRS and (Vance, 2004; Thai-Nghe, 2010), using the Euclidean distance measure shown in Equation 6.

$$d(\sigma_u, \sigma_s) = \sum_{x \in X} |\sigma_u(x) - \sigma_s(x)| \qquad (6)$$

- s: Refers to the CRS system.
- X: Set of courses.
- $\sigma_u \in [0,1]^{|X|}$: List of courses ranked by student $\succ$.
- $\sigma_s \in [0,1]^{|X|}$: A list ranked by CRS.
- $\sigma_u(x)$ and $\sigma_s(x)$: *Position of course $x \in X$ in the lists σ_u and σ_s respectively (a ranking of a set of n courses is represented as a permutation of the integers 1, 2, ..., n).*

Figure 2 shows the distance results for each of the three methods. We can infer from the figure and the experimental results that: (1) CRS outperforms (Vance, 2004; Thai-Nghe, 2010), and (2) the "closeness" between the lists ranked by the students and the corresponding lists ranked by CRS *increases consistently* as the cumulative number of students increases. This is because after the ratings of *each* student are submitted to CRS, it *updates* and *optimizes* the current ratings of the Bicluster, to which the student belongs based on the ratings of this student. The experimental results revealed the robustness of CRS and its ability to capture the similarities among the interests and academic skills of the students belonging to a bicluster.

Figure 2. Distance between the lists ranked by the students and the lists ranked by CRS

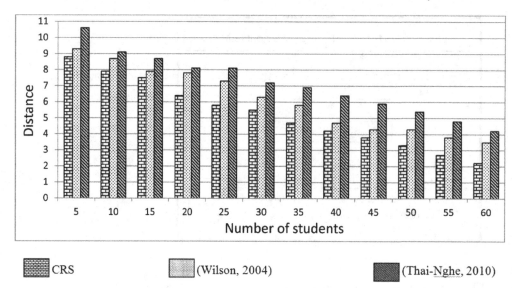

We used z-test (Warner, 2007) to:

1. Determine whether the differences between individual Euclidean distances used in the evaluation of CRS are large enough to be statistically significant.
2. Test our hypothesis on specific Euclidean distances of the population mean.

The z-score is the distance between the sample mean and the population mean in units of the standard error. It is calculated as $Z=(X-M)/SE$ where X is the *mean sample*, M is the *population mean*, $SE=D/$sqrt(n) is the *standard error of the mean* in which D is the *Average Standard Deviation of the mean*, and n is the *sample size*. Table 4 shows the mean (M) of CRS Euclidean distances, and its *Average Standard Deviation* (D) of the mean. As the values of D in Table 4 show, the measured Euclidean distances of CRS did not vary substantially with individual subjects' ratings, because D is computed based on the concept of biclusters, and a bicluster is formed based on the *closeness* of its members' ratings.

Table 5 shows the z-scores for the Euclidean Distances of the system. Using the z-scores, we

Table 4. Average Standard Deviation D of the Mean M

	CRS
Population mean (M)	5.21
Average Standard Deviation (D)	1.8

calculated the probability of a randomly selected subject, whose ranked list and a system's ranked list have an average Euclidean distance equals or less than a sample of mean (X). Column ($D \leq X$) in table 5 shows the probabilities using a sample of three Euclidean mean (D). These probabilities were determined from a standard normal distribution table by using the z-scores as entries. For example, the probabilities for the system to return a ranked list with Euclidean distance $\leq$ 8 is 94%. As the z-scores in Table 5 shows, the distances from the sample mean to the population mean are small. The table shows also that CRS has a very high probability for achieving Euclidean distance equals or less than the sample mean of a randomly selected subject's ranked list.

MEASURING RECALL AND PRECISION OF CRS AND (WILSON, 2004; THAI-NGHE, 2010)

Let: (1) N be the number of courses in a list recommended by CRS, (2) R_n be the number of relevant courses for the student in the recommended list, and (3) R_{ALL} be the total number of relevant courses for the student.

- Recall=R_n/R_{ALL}
- Precision=R_n/N

Figure 3 shows the recall-precision diagram of CRS and (Vance, 2004; Thai-Nghe, 2010). As the figure shows, CRS achieved good recall and precision and outperformed (Vance, 2004; Thai-Nghe, 2010). CRS achieved good precision because: (1) it forms a bicluster based on the rating similarity of its members on the features of courses, and (2) it adopts an effectiveness group modeling strategy and similarity equation. CRS achieved good recall because it considers: (1) *all* dominant course features of a student's bicluster, even if the student did not co-rate some of these

Table 5. Z-Score and the probability of a randomly selected list ranked by CRS that achieved $D \leq X$

Sample of Mean (X)	CRS	
	Z Score	Average Standard Deviation (D) $\leq X$
8	1.55	94%
6	0.439	67%
4	-0.6722	25%

features, and (2) *non-dominant* course features of the student's bicluster, whose assigned weights beat other features' weights at least k number of times[1].

MEASURING EXPLAIN COVERAGE OF CRS AND (WILSON, 2004; THAI-NGHE, 2010)

Explain coverage measures the number of course features that are: (1) rated by a student to a value

Figure 3. Recall vs. precision

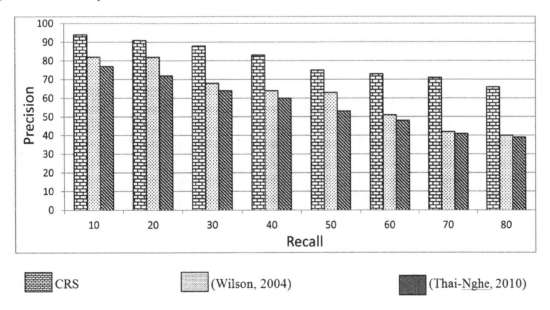

greater or equal to a threshold p, and (2) covered by the features of the courses recommended by a method. We set the threshold p to 5. Figure 4 shows the explain coverage versus the number of course features. As the figure shows, intuitively, the explain coverage of each of the three methods increases as the number of course features increases.

SEARCH EFFICIENCY EVALUATION OF CRS AND (WILSON, 2004; THAI-NGHE, 2010)

We evaluated the *search efficiency* of CRS by comparing its *average execution time* with (Vance, 2004; Thai-Nghe, 2010). We varied the number of students six times in cumulative of 10 students. We computed the *average execution time* for each of the three methods under each of the six cumulative numbers. Figure 5 shows the results. As the figure shows: (1) (Thai-Nghe, 2010) slightly outperformed CRS and (Vance, 2004), and (2) the *average* execution time of CRS

slightly outperformed (Vance, 2004). Overall, the experiment revealed that the execution time of CRS is not expensive considering the *overhead* endured by it to: (1) adopt the *implicit* techniques for determining the biclusters, to which students belong, and (2) filter and rank courses based on the interests and academic skills of students.

FUTURE RESEARCH DIRECTIONS

The smaller a bicluster is, the more granular and specific its interests are. Therefore, we will investigate in future work another class of biclusters called *Multi-Biclusters (MB)* whose size is usually smaller than a bicluster. A MB is composed of an aggregation of students sharing multi interests. Thus, a MB is formed from the *intersection* of two or more biclusters. For example, the *portion* of bicluster B_X who share the interests and academic skills of bicluster B_Y (i.e., the intersection of $B_X \cap B_Y$) forms a MB. The interests and academic skills of a MB are the *union* of the interests and academic skills of the biclusters form-

Figure 4. Explain coverage vs. number of course features

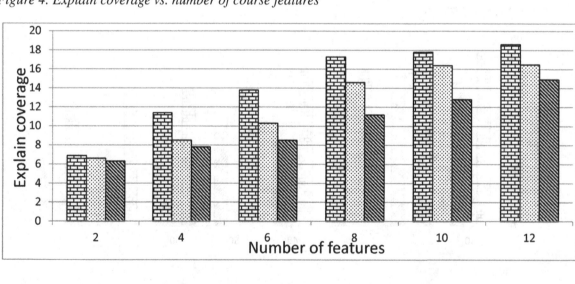

Figure 5. Average execution time of the three methods under six cumulative number of students

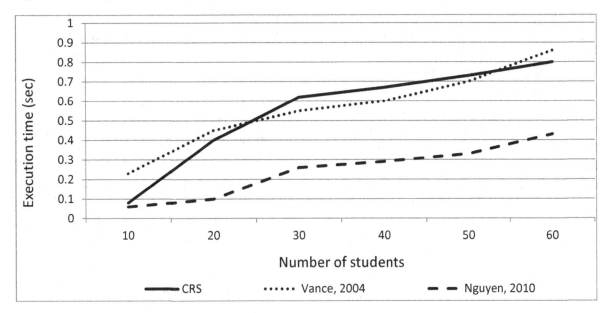

ing it. Thus, the interests and academic skills of a MB are *more specific* than the interests of each of the biclusters forming it. To fine-grain a user's query results, the prospective system should output a filtered and ranked list of courses taking into account the interests and academic skills of the MB, to which the active user belongs.

We will also investigate in the future work how the interests and academic skills of a bicluster can be *initialized* from data acquired from *hard-copy* published studies such as published articles and published studies conducted by organizations or specialized centers belonging to universities.

First, we need to decide on the publications to be used. The more publications used, the more accurate the results are. We need to select ones issued by reputable sources. Interests and academic skills on a course's features obtained from a hard-copy published study are represented as a publication-feature matrix M with entries f_i and P_j. These entries convey the following meaning: publication P_j stresses the importance of feature f_i to course C_x. The rating of publication P_j on feature f_i is the element $M(j, i)$ of matrix M. Element $M(j, i)$ is a Boolean value, where *one* denotes

that publications P_j stresses the importance of feature f_i to the course and *zero* otherwise. That is, the rating $M(P_j)$ of publication P_j is the j-th row of matrix M.

CONCLUSION

In this chapter, we proposed an XML-based Collaborative Filtering (CF) recommender system, called CRS, which overcomes the problems of DE student advising. The system advises a DE student to take courses that were taken *successfully* by students, who have the same interest and academic performance as the student. CRS aims at predicting a student's academic performance and interest on a course based on a collection of profiles of students who have similar interests and academic performance on prior courses. The framework of CRS identifies a set of course features for every academic major. A course feature is a characteristic skill or attribute that a student needs to possess in order to succeed in the course.

CRS would return to the active student a ranked list of courses that have been rated high by the majority of the student members of the bicluster, to which the active student belongs. That is, CRS outputs ranked lists of courses, taking into account not only the initial preferences of the active student, but also the ratings of the bicluster, to which the student user belongs.

We experimentally evaluated CRS using real-user evaluation conducted by 64 students from the University of Texas at Arlington-USA and Khalifa University-UAE. The results showed that the distances between the lists of courses ranked by the students based on their prior academic performance and the corresponding lists ranked by CRS are small. We also measured the recall and precision of the system. The results showed that CRS achieved good recall and precision. It achieved good precision because: (1) it forms a bicluster based on the rating similarity of its members on the features of courses, and (2) it adopts an effectiveness group modeling strategy and similarity equation. It achieved good recall because it considers: (1) *all* dominant course features of a student's bicluster, even if the student did not co-rate some of these features, and (2) *non-dominant* course features of the student's bicluster, whose assigned weights beat other features' weights at least k number of times (in the experiments, we set the threshold k to *number of features*/2). The results showed also good explain coverage. Overall, the results revealed the robustness of CRS and its ability to capture the similarities among the interests and academic skills of the students belonging to a bicluster.

REFERENCES

Aimeur, E., Brassard, G., Fernandez, J., & Mani Onana, F. (2006). Privacy preserving demographic filtering. In *Proceedings of SAC'06*. SAC.

Andronico, A., Carbonaro, A., Casadei, G., Colazzo, L., Molinari, A., & Ronchetti, M. (2003). *Integrating a multi-agent recommendation system into a mobile learning management system*. Academic Press.

Breese, J., Heckerman, D., & Kadie, C. (1998). Empirical analysis of predictive algorithms for collaborative filtering. In *Proceedings of 14th UAI*. UAI.

Calvo, R. (2003). User scenarios for the design and implementation of iLMS. In *Proceedings of the AIED2003 Workshop, Towards Intelligent Learning Management Systems*. AIED.

Deshpande, M., & Karypis, G. (2004). Item-based top-n recommendation algorithms. *ACM Transactions on Information Systems*, *22*(1), 143–177. doi:10.1145/963770.963776.

Herlocker, J., Konstan, J. A., & Riedl, J. (2004). Evaluating collaborative filtering recommender systems. *ACM TOIS, 22*(1).

Junior, M., & Canuto, A. (2006). Carcara: A multi-agent system for web mining using adjustable user profile and dynamic grouping. In *Proc. IEEE/WIC/ACM IAT'06*. Hong Kong, China: IEEE.

Liu, J., & Gree, J. (2005). *Individulaized selection of learning object*. Paper presented at the International Conference on Inelligence Tutoring Systems. Macei-Alagoas, Brazil.

Murali & Kasif. (2003). Extracting conserved gene expression motifs from gene expression data. In *Proceedings of Pacific Symp. Biocomputing Conf.*, (pp. 77–88). IEEE.

Khribi, M.K., Jemni, M., & Nasraoui, O. (2007). Toward a hybrid recommender system for e-learning personalization based on web usage mining techniques and information retrieval. In Proceedings of the World Conference on E-Learning in Corporate, Government, Healthcare, and Higher Education. IEEE.

O'Connor, P., Höpken, W., & Gretzel, U. (2008). Dynamic packaging using a cluster-based demographic filtering approach. In *Proceedings of the International Conference*. IEEE.

Symeonidis, P., Nanopoulos, A., & Manolopoulos, Y. (2008). Providing justifications in recommender systems. *IEEE Transactions on Systems, Man, and Cybernetics, 38*(6).

Tang, L., Liu, H., Zhang, J., Agarwal, N., & Salerno, J. (2008). Topic taxonomy adaptation for group profiling. *ACM Transactions on Knowledge Discovery from Data, 1*(4).

Thai-Nghe, N., Drumond, L., Krohn-Grimberghe, A., & Schmidt-Thieme, L. (2010). Recommender system for predicting student performance. In *Proceedings of the Workshop on Recommender Systems for Technology Enhanced Learning*. IEEE.

Wang, B., Bodily, J., & Gupta, S. (2004). Supporting persistent social groups in ubiquitous computing environments using context aware ephemeral group service. In *Proceedings of the IEEE PerCom*. IEEE.

Warner, R. (2007). *Applied statistics: From bivariate through multivariate techniques*. Thousand Oaks, CA: Sage Publications.

Wilson, V. (2004). A standards framework for academic e-advising services. *International Journal of Services and Standards, 1*(1). doi:10.1504/IJSS.2004.005689.

ENDNOTES

[1]   In the experiments, we set the threshold k to (*number of features*)/2.

Chapter 11
Interactive Storytelling and Experiential Learning:
The Prospect of "Vertical Narrativity"

Justin A. Wolske
Caseworx, Inc., USA & New York Film Academy, USA

ABSTRACT

The author looks at the recent drivers that have changed the ways authors and audiences share stories, first by looking at the landscape in art and entertainment, and then by analyzing how these drivers are affecting education. Inspired by his own work as a film and new media producer and his recent foray into educational media, the author isolates four different factors for consideration: (a) the falling price and rising accessibility of digital image acquisition, (b) the Internet as a cheap and instantaneous distribution platform, (c) the evolving ways in which audiences are accessing and consuming content, and (d) increased interactivity between storyteller and audience. By analyzing both the entertainment and education industries, the author predicts that storytelling—a dormant educational tool through much of the 20th century—will become a centerpiece of future educational models. Furthermore, he asserts that storytelling itself must radically change to accommodate this new discourse.

INTRODUCTION

The prisoners in a maximum security prison had little to entertain themselves with so they told jokes to each other. But they had long since run out of new jokes to tell, so they simply numbered the jokes and yelled out the numbers. A new prisoner hearing "forty-two," "sixty-four," "one hundred eight" being yelled down the hall with raucous laughter following each number asked about what was happening, and it was explained to him. He asked if he could try it, and his cellmate said sure. He hollered "thirty-six," and nothing happened. Next he tried "twenty-seven" and still nothing.

DOI: 10.4018/978-1-4666-4542-4.ch011

The new prisoner finally asked his cellmate what was wrong, and he replied, "You didn't tell them so well" (Schank, 1990).

Our goal for this chapter is to look at the increasingly flexible methods of narrativity in art and entertainment — the cultural cradles for storytelling today — to see how they will affect learning, specifically, experiential learning. Story is critical in learning how to do; it collects and curates experience along themes and demands something from its audience. *Buy Coke. Vote for Sarkozy. Care about Frodo Baggins' journey to Mordor.* Our belief is that the world of education is moving past the centuries-old model of scribbling notes as a uniform, linear lecture is issued forth, and moving back to a millennia-old model of structured discourse, from which an organic, communal cloud of knowledge begins to grow. We believe that a confluence of factors are just beginning to move us past the concept of a person buying into a collective education experience, and into an age where the learning apparatus — technological and infrastructural — becomes supple enough to cater to the specific student's needs and learning objectives. We think non-linear, experiential storytelling will be key to that change, and we will look at some of the most important drivers of that change. We start with technology, and how the free-falling price and near ubiquitous availability of high-level media acquisition is opening up transformative, narrative learning opportunities for educators. We will then look at how cheap, global, instantaneous distribution is allowing disparate audiences to come together to create collaborative narrative and learning experiences, opening up opportunities in addition to challenges of scale and audience learning comprehension. We will see how recent media consumption patterns have had real effects on how people understand story and education. Finally, we will analyze interactivity – the function of technology and distribution and the area

where traditional and new media storytelling bear the least resemblance – to see how educators and students are using gameplay, flipped learning and other groundbreaking practices to stretch the concept of how we learn from stories. By doing so, we hope to demonstrate how one bustling corner of this communication revolution is bringing together two practitioners who need to remain close: the Teacher and the Storyteller.

BACKGROUND: STORYTELLING, EXPERIENTIAL LEARNING AND CASEWORX

Early on in his popular lecture series at UCLA, Mandalay Entertainment CEO Peter Guber routinely asks a question of his audience, mostly graduate students from the prestigious film or business schools. "What business are we in?" he calls out, referring to the one that puts out movies and television for people to watch in theaters or at home. Every year the answers are largely the same, safe choices that underscore an environment where people are still feeling each other out. "The movie business," someone always predictably calls out right before the more sophisticated "entertainment industry." "Content distribution," an MBA student might add. Since it's a large group of really smart people, a clever answer like "popcorn and soda distribution" usually pops up. Like any veteran storyteller, Guber milks this part for maximum effect, and after a pause, he responds. "We are in the transportation business. We are in the emotional transportation business." It's an innovative thought, but it also has the benefit of being true (Guber, 2011). For entertainment media, the job is to take an audience from Emotional Point A and deliver them to Emotional Point B. That's the value proposition. That is a movie's way to fulfill the function of narrative.

For other forms of storytelling, the objective can be slightly different, but they all conform to a central concept. Narratives want you to *do something*. They are a call to action. It's been interesting to watch scholars, artists and executives pick up the buzzword of "interactivity" in our new media age. Story has *always* required interactivity. The interactivity is the audience's choice to take up that call to action. A story's function hasn't really been fulfilled until it's directive is acted upon (or rejected). Though storytelling for entertainment purposes, which serves as a prime example of our industrial age produce/consume way of communicating (ie., sitting rapt around the radio, silently staring at the huge cineplex screen, etc.), is the most prevalent, in many ways it takes the least use of storytelling's considerable powers. Education has a stronger and older claim on the form of narrative. Many of the first coherent stories, which scholars argue appeared around the dawn of civilization were primers on survival. "The early woman would persuade her child from the fire," Arthur Ransome (1909) wrote, "with a tale of how such just another as he had touched the yellow dancer, and had his hair burned and eyelashes singed so that he could not look in the face of the sun" (p. 6). Men narrativized the experience of the hunt to teach adolescent boys of their critical roles. Origination tales were spun to help people come to grips with the seemingly cruel and random vagaries of the landscape. Coming-of-age myths brought boys and girls into adulthood, and pantheons of gods taught us our limits. At their primal level, stories were told so you wouldn't get eaten by the shark, not so you could thrill in watching the shark eating others.

We will briefly look at the history of story, in order to see how it moved into the classroom that we know today. The Warning Example or Origination Story are themselves quite sophisticated, and depended on thousands of years of oral history and ritualized action. The subject is far too broad to do justice here, suffice it to say that narrative shares its DNA with the human-specific instinct to ascribe meaning to the environment around us. As mythology pioneer Joseph Campbell (1990) points out, the human is distinguished not by its

ability to fashion tools (gorillas and other animals share that ability), but that he has the ability to be "susceptible to the allure of beauty which is divinely superfluous. (p. 13)" Campbell points to a tool from the time of *Homo erectus*, a tool about six or eight inches long…"longer that what would be useful," an object given to ceremonial or artistic use. As we move through to *Homo sapien*, he highlights the first two infallible signs of mythological/spiritual activity in burial ceremony and cave bear skull worship. There is no storytelling in these examples, per se, but the necessary seeds of a consciousness that can synthesize the import of reality into an artistic, spiritual and meaningful way are unmistakable. Specialists from ape researcher Daniel Povinelli (Foster, 2002) to new media writer Carolyn Handler Miller (2008) echo this sentiment, calling the ability to construct narrative the fundamental differentiator between humans and other animals.

As humans developed language and culture, the tool of storytelling evolved as well. Famed children's author Ruth Sawyer (1957) describes a pivotal period of narrativity's development:

The first primitive efforts at conscious storytelling consisted of a simple chant, set to rhythm of some daily tribal occupation such as grinding corn, paddling canoe or kayak, sharpening weapons for hunting or war, or ceremonial dancing. They were in the first person, impromptu, giving expression to pride or exhultation over some act of bravery or accomplishment that set individual apart from the tribe. (pp. 45-46)

A critical component of storytelling — and this is also important to understand storytelling's role in education — is the defining of the *self* apart from the group and/or environment. It's is a Hero's journey, not a Heroes' journey that takes place. As Sawyer and many other anthropologists and historians demonstrate, at the root of the storytelling ritual, there is a compulsion to create a central figure who experiences the story. I. You. Gilgamesh. Rostam. Wong Fei Hung. Br'er Rabbit. Neo. The character serves as a sort of cipher into which we pour selected traits, aspirations, fears, skills and destinies. In a well-told story, when the Hero wins, we win. When they lose, so do we. And the lessons they learn are shared with us. The modes of storytelling have changed radically through evolutions in technology, distribution, culture, and economics. These basic structures have not, nor will they ever. Building a narrative is the way we build a scaffolding of meaning around parts of our shared experience, but ingest individually.

Storytelling in the classroom has been around longer than the classroom itself, as oral histories and folklore tales instilled religious, cultural and political identities into the listener. Jackson (1995) goes so far, via an excerpt from philosopher Arthur C. Danto, to posit that, through the transformative power of storytelling, they "actually make us what we are. The are constitutive of our personhood" (p. 12). Post-Enlightenment, story has weaved in and out of fashion as facts and theories were codified, hard sciences moved to a prominent place in the curricula and the number of students swelled, along with the need to dispense information systematically and uniformly. As David Jonassen and Julian Hernadez-Serrano (2002) point out, story took a backseat in academia in the latter half of the 20th century as it became associated more with movies and entertainment; only until the late 1980s was it seen again not only as a powerful descriptive method, but also a way for learners to contextualize and organize information. Since that time, Western education has experienced a renaissance as the use of narrative has spread across many disciplines. Teachers have used it as an evaluation tool (Wood, 1992). Cases have been used to help students understand how to multiply fractions (Barnett, 1991). Clinical psychiatrists use it to build rapport with their patients (Coles, 1989). On so on... As a trend, we see the fruitless veil of "objectivity" lift from many areas of academia — even in the hard sciences — and the rise of multiple perspectives,

the resurgence of subjectivity and a reappraisal of the power of story.

I came to education media from a once little-used path, but one that is more frequently traveled of late. As a film and new media producer, I studied storytelling as an entertainment and artistic vehicle. Attending graduate school at UCLA's School of Theater, Film & Television was an embarrassment of riches, as legendary filmmakers and scholars like Guber, Francis Ford Coppola, Howard Suber, Lazlo Kovacs, Fred Rubin, Robert Rosen, Marina Goldovskaya and countless other producers, directors and writers hammered the craft into us. And after graduate school, I started companies and partnered with others, creating content for MTV, Nike, Reebok, Zippo, Sony, eBay and many other firms around the world. But my drift toward using media as an education platform was driven by a few factors. First, the movie business is changing, and not for the better, which is a function of many of the things we'll be talking about in this chapter. Second, the education business is also changing, though it's fate is much more undecided. Finally, education is a true passion of mine. I am hard-pressed to think of a social problem in our world today that couldn't be helped by easier and cheaper access to quality education, be it schools, tools or networks. And I was seeing a few major trends that were converging to put new paradigms and practices in reach.

Technology has to be at the top of the list. The price point for creating professional-level content is now at a level that makes serving niche education markets viable. Moreover, online distribution platforms allow us to forego the high costs of CD-ROM, DVD or VHS replication, store placement, inventory and shipping. But another important factor is the resurgence of storytelling as a pedagogical tool, as we saw earlier, which lives in a reciprocal relationship with these technological advances. As the ability to tell one's own story becomes easier, the act itself becomes more replicable and valuable as a learning tool.

Finally, the "student" as a concept has evolved. It's a poorly kept secret that the traditional student of days past — the 18-24 year-old who attends a four-year university right after high school — is nowhere near a sufficient description. Today's average student (if one can be defined) lives with a very different set of circumstances: she is likely older, has more family obligations, may be juggling work or a career, is more diasporic, can very well be outside of the developed world…and requires tools and educational infrastructure that support this more fractured learning path.

With this faint sketch in mind, I started to look at areas of education that had a rich history of using stories. I didn't necessarily want to be a "revolutionary" by imprinting the concept of narrative on of top of an area of study that wasn't used to it. I wanted to find a space where I could use what expertise and talents I had to push the tradition forward. When I finally began to understand the use of the case study in business schools, I knew my search was over, for two main reasons. First, for anyone who has not attended business school — including yours truly — the deep history of case studies, at least in the Western sense of business education, was a revelation. Here was a discipline that intuitively appreciated the power of using narrative as a way of practically applying knowledge, and an area of study that adopted educational technology, asynchronous learning and non-traditional students at a pace far above the average. Second, as many in the discipline understand, there is a brewing crisis in business education around the world. Many feel that the thousands of MBAs who pour into the professional world are not equipped to compete or push their employers' aims effectively. One of the areas that is constantly criticized is oral and written communication. Academics and executives agree that students have trouble communicating. One unnamed executive was blunt: "Students need to master the art of storytelling. They must learn to sell their ideas in a powerful, succinct way" (Datar, Garvin & Cullen, 2010, p. 99). So, I saw

an area of study where the concept of storytelling was deeply ingrained, and where students needed help learning to effectively tell their own. That's where Caseworx originated.

As William Ellet (2007) writes in *The Case Study Handbook*, cases are "verbal representations of reality that put the reader in the role of the participant…" Their purpose is "to represent reality, to convey a situation with all its cross currents and rough edges, including irrelevancies, sideshows, misconceptions, little information or an overwhelming amount of it" (p. 13). If you replaced those terms with things like "red herrings," "MacGuffins," "Second Act reversals," and "B stories," you'd be talking about the things writers use in a screenplay to do the same thing. In short, a story…a contextualized and selective presentation of reality for the purpose of gaining knowledge and/or meaning. The case method was developed as a way to provide students with practical, applicable knowledge. It began in other schools, particularly law (Merseth, 1991), but found its way into management studies in the early 20th century. In an ironic twist, faculty members found there was precious little writing and research to help students build their management acumen while on campus. Case studies were developed to fill that gap in knowledge. As is the way today, Harvard University dominated the method, and it was a shrewd example of inter-campus competition that brought it to the Business School. "The Law School training was highly esteemed in influential business circles," Melvin Copeland (1954) remembers, "and that training was effectuated by the use of the case method of instruction. Hence, Dean [Edwin] Gay decided that instruction in the Business School should be patterned on the method used with such conspicuous success in the Law School" (p. 25). Management professionals were brought into class in the 1910s to help dissect business situations, and case development was specifically labeled as research, so as to stay in line with administrative goals (Merseth, 1991, p. 245). As other faculty saw the lively discussions that followed, the method spread quickly and beyond Cambridge, Massachusetts to other business programs. Today, it is more common than not to find not only the U.S.-originated, MBA-style of management education, but also some version of the case method in the business school classroom. They are a cornerstone of the curriculum and a staple of business students' lives. But mechanically, they've changed very little.

My goal with Caseworx is to develop a platform that would transform the paper-based, traditional case study into a multimedia, interactive, immersive experience. By adapting a traditional case study into a documentary-style, video-driven learning module, we can bring the real powers of narrativity to the fore, not only creating a multi-sensory narrative consumption experience, but also a platform where faculty and students learn to author story in a dialectic way with the source material. Our goal is not to interrupt the classroom setting — and any professor or student will tell you that's where cases really comes alive — but to build a better preparatory environment. To build, in essence, a more attractive and inclusive story. When we shot the core documentary for our proof-of-concept for the Caseworx platform in Springfield , Missouri (Petty, C., Still, K., & Prewitt, J.; Wolske, 2012), we covered a small gourmet chocolate maker who had gone to great lengths to make sure his company sourced its raw cacao beans in the most ethical and sustainable of ways. It was a truly compelling story about entrepreneurship, supply chain dynamics and business ethics. It was one thing to read about how he left his law practice to pursue his dream and went all in with his family's nest egg to found the company. It's another thing completely to *see* his almost messianic passion about equity and *hear* the twinges of weary stress in his voice as he speaks about the massive risks he's taken. *Seeing* the chocolate matters. Being able to chart the beans' journey from Davao to Springfield — and to see the logistical and financial hurdles in the way —

is extremely helpful when making management decisions. Regular cases can't do these things.

Case studies haven't really changed in 100 years: it is a result of case publishing industry economics, technological barriers, distribution and consumption hurdles and issues of control, authorship and scholarship in the classroom. Caseworx is an attempt to change that paradigm, and to offer a truly dynamic and responsive learning tool that resonates not only for students in elite programs like Harvard, but for the many millions of distance learners, continuing education students, corporate learners and part-time learners who rely on improving technology to bring quality education within reach.[1] But, this chapter is not about Caseworx. Indeed, we have just begun the journey toward building a company, but whether or not we are successful, a cluster of factors are converging right now that herald a sea change in how we use storytelling in education. It will extend far beyond business schools into hospitals, oil rigs, space shuttles and cubicles. These factors will finally allow powerful educational storytelling into every facet of learning.

IMAGE ACQUISITION

Though image acquisition through video technology has technically been around since the 1930s, cameras didn't have on-board recording capability until the 1980s. But when it arrived many content makers jumped at the chance to abandon expensive film shooting and processing, from independent filmmakers to news organizations to the adult film industry. To capture the revolution that has been taking place in image acquisition technology since the millennium, I offer a personal anecdote. When I arrived at UCLA to begin my MFA, the "24 progressive frame rate" — or, "24p" — was the technology *du jour*. Visual artists were thrilled to have a video format that somewhat approached the photochemical result of film. Companies like Panasonic, Sony and Canon took pains to soften the hard video lines, to bring shallow focus (known as "depth of field") to the image, to "enhance" the image with the slightly stuttered movement that we've grown so accustomed to in movies, to increase the video chip's sensitivity to light, to increase image resolution. The results were seen in cameras like the Panasonic DVX-100 and the Canon XL-2, which gave filmmakers the feeling that they were shooting film at a steep discount. Of course, we were still shooting standard definition images with miniDV tape on cameras that had very limited sensitivity to light and a fraction of the resolution of film…a camera one would be shocked to find inside the walls of a major film studio.

That was in 2003. When I left graduate school in 2008, these cameras were toys. The School was preparing to buy a RED Epic camera, the same camera with which David Fincher would shoot *The Girl with the Dragon Tattoo* (Rudin, Søren, Stærmose & Chaffin, 2011), a 5K resolution tapeless high definition camera that cost less than half of a traditional 35mm film camera. The emergence of ultra-high end HD cameras in the 2000s led to a trickle, then a wave, of Hollywood films captured digitally, from the *Star Wars* prequels (McCallum, 1999; McCallum, 2002; McCallum, 2005) to *Collateral* (Mann & Richardson, 2004), *Superman Returns* (Peters, Singer & Adler, 2006) and *Che* (Bickford & del Toro, 2008a; Bickford & del Toro, 2008b), through to the upcoming *Hobbit* films (Jackson, Walsh, Cunningham & Weiner, 2012; Jackson et al., 2013; Jackson et al, 2014). But the real revolution was happening on the streets around the world, as portable Digital Single-Lens Reflex (DSLR) cameras like the Canon EOS Mark II 5D and Panasonic Lumix delivered superior imagery for under $5,000. Add in ubiquitous HD image-making capability through iPhones, BlackBerries and GoPro's almost disposable line of cameras, and we are looking at a change that is almost terrifying in its speed. Moreover, this does not account for the massive changes that have taken place in media

storage, transfer speeds, editing or visual effects. Companies that had next to no presence in the visual content creation industry in 1985 — Adobe, Apple, Avid, RED Camera Company — are now the tastemakers. When Roger Deakins, possibly the world's most respected living cinematographer, says that video can now produce a better image than film, something major has happened (Holben, 2011, pp. 34-35). And there is no sign of slowing down. So, if we can move from a poor man's approximation of film to images that can compete with the gold standard of Hollywood production in five years, what's next?

This has huge ramifications for content creation, including media education. A few trends are noticeable in this larger wave. First, of course, is cost. We are at a point where a national car commercial could be shot on a camera costing a few thousand dollars, and no one would bat an eye. The dramatic fall in price, which is happening not only in cameras but equipment, data storage and software, gives so many more people access to high-end production capability. Second, user adoption begins at a much earlier age. With powerful computers, advanced software and high-performance cameras within reach, more people can make content more adeptly at an earlier age. What this means is, structurally at least, decent production value is quite possible. The unintentional comedy and poor lighting of educational media in the past was just as much a function of bargain-basement production capability as poor storytelling skills. It's safe to say those times are gone.

What this means is that education content creators can now produce work for reasonable amounts of money that isn't aesthetically separated from what students are used to seeing on their televisions and computer monitors. I can say as a professional that good-looking content demands a respect from the viewer that shoddy production standards cannot. This is backed up by the little research that's been done on the audience's end (Shamir, (2007).[2] But once that threshold is crossed consistently, another obstacle arises. Good production value means high expectations. If it *looks* good, it had better *be* good, and educational content will no longer be shielded, to re-phrase Michael Gerson's words, by "the soft bigotry of low expectations." This is actually the thornier problem: we've all experienced a slickly produced film or television show that failed as a story. The oft-repeated phrase in my industry is "content is king." While that's debatable to an extent, the story and the experience must be ready to meet an audience who is bombarded by top-notch content from movies, commercials and video games. This issue will be attacked from both ends, as laypeople begin to get comfortable with the powerful technical tools at their disposal, and as trained storytellers increasingly see educational content production as a viable way to express themselves. But at least we have moved to a point where high-level production capability is no longer prohibitively expensive or complicated. The impact of this change has yet to be fully felt, but it is hard to overstate.

CHEAP DISTRIBUTION

As difficult as it may be to remember before 2005, cheap, global distribution did not begin with the advent of YouTube, or even the World Wide Web. The real game-changer was the video cassette recorder (VCR).[3] Originally conceived as a time-shifting device — an early Sony ad proclaimed, "Now you don't have to miss *Kojak* because you're watching *Colombo*!" (Greenberg, 2008, p. 2) — the VCR managed to turn programming into a discrete commodity over which viewers had some level of control. Frustratingly, the near hysterical response from Big Media to this 1950s technology[4] has been played out over and again with cases like Napster in the 1990s and Netflix today that presaged intellectual property battles, huge companies suing citizens, the end of "destination television," the degradation of the television ad revenue model and media-rich

social networking and sharing. As Rose (2011) points out, "The fundamental premise of broadcast television was its ability to control viewers — the delivery of eyeballs to advertisers by the tens of millions. ...The funnel is hopelessly, irretrievably busted" (pp. 86-87).

The internet shattered a busted model into pieces. Distribution fundamentally turns on control. Without control, it's a steep challenge to monetize content, to protect assets or to develop and oversee standards. To be fair to large media corporations, these technological advancements really serve as full-frontal assaults on their business models. Litigation is not an outlandish response, and it's usually a lot easier to talk about a massive company being more "nimble" and "creative" than to actually do it. On the other hand, the devastation of the music industry in the early 2000s and the demise of Blockbuster also had an awful lot to do with a persistence toward gouging customers for $20 CDs, considering late fees as a major revenue stream and treating Video-on-Demand (VoD) as an annoying afterthought. Any way you look at it, innovative distribution models are dissolving the pipelines through which large media companies make their profit. There is much more content being created. Several factors are converging to make the content cheaper and evermore available. And users are gaining and demanding more control. Customers are abandoning the networks and the multiplex...that cannot be argued. And the reasons are varied, but inflexibility in the way they deliver content is just as much to blame as cost, quality or some other reason. The stakes are high, indeed.

For the individual consumer, there's a lot of upside right now. The typical American college student could transfer just about any movie in the world to her laptop in less than an afternoon. And even if she is respectful about intellectual property, there is an unfathomable amount of video, music, blogs and *stuff* that she could never even begin to sort through. When Michael Wesch (2008) pointed out in June 2008 that 1.5 million hours of content had been uploaded to YouTube in the previous six months, he also pointed out that it would take the three major US networks 60 years of non-stop broadcasting to reach the same figure. There is incredible choice; moreover, there's the elusive yet very real chance to become not only a local celebrity, but a worldwide phenomenon as Tay Zonday, Antoine Dodson and Keyboard Cat can attest. This new paradigm, the ability to watch just about anything, manipulate it and distribute it globally *and* become the subject as well has come on with breathtaking speed. It's hard to remember that, about 15 years ago, video and the World Wide Web did not mix very well at all.

The world of online video was a pretty barren place well into the 2000s, and there was nothing approaching a business model. The reason was simple: broadband. Or, rather, the lack of deep broadband penetration. Dial-up connections in 14k or 56k were the norm in most 1990s households, and that kind of data rate cannot sustain video watching or downloading. Broadband as we know it was introduced to North America in 1996 (Federal, 2005), but it took consumers some time to catch up to the innovation. But when they did, they did it fast; between 2000 and 2001, cable modem subscriptions jumped 50% in American households (Federal, 2005). As we entered 2012, the United States had over 80% broadband adoption (and still only 36th in the world, in terms of broadband penetration) (Malik, 2012). So, quickly, people were gaining the capacity to upload and view content online that was more than photographs or simple animation. And things would go viral before YouTube and social media sites. But when PayPal alums Chad Hurley, Steve Chen and Jawed Karim uploaded the first video onto YouTube in April 2005, a platform had been created that would easily allow video consumption on a global scale. Moreover, as Wesch (2008) points out, the vast majority of content on YouTube is original. So not only have YouTube, Vimeo, Blip. tv, Funny or Die, Facebook, Twitter and countless other platforms created a multimedia consumption

and marketing portal, they have joined with apps and software like Instamatic, Viddy and iMovie to create a vertically integrated authoring tool.

This clearly goes beyond funny cat videos and into education. Salman Khan is one of those stories that Silicon Valley tech writers fall over themselves to cover.... *A Harvard and MIT-trained investment banker decides to start uploading videos on YouTube to help his nephew in math. He spawns Khan Academy, a "flipped learning" environment where students can use these 7-14 minute lo-fi videos to help them improve in math, science, economics, social science and more, all for free. Teachers bring them into the classroom and watch their students realize their inner trigonometry geniuses. He creates a phenomenon and challenges the very assumptions upon which public education rests in the United States (the end?)* (Thompson, 2011). And Khan Academy is not alone: Engineer Guy, iTunes U, Lynda.com and Google Code University all provide thousands of hours of video-driven educational content across the web, much of it for free or for modest sums. But why is this news? There has never been a shortage of media in education, from 16mm films, VHS tapes to CD-ROMs. But no one is breathlessly writing stories about these companies because they don't alter the underlying dynamics the way Khan & Co. do. This new wave of education media does two major things.

First, it completely re-writes the business economics of a media-rich organization trying to disseminate their content, just as the web did for text driven media a decade before. Salman Khan made most of the videos on his site in his closet with a Logitech headset and a few computer programs. Few do more than that, and the free-falling price of production gear, as we already discussed, puts a watchable end product in reach for even those that want to have a more sophisticated presentation. Second, the instantaneous distribution affects education the same way it affects many other areas. Just as a New Jersey woman can use the power of social media to save a major network show like NBC's *Chuck* from cancellation in a matter of weeks by organizing a march on a Subway sandwich shop (Rose, pp. 194-198), a student can now have virtual one-on-one conversations with those educating him — or those learning alongside him — to surgically target what's holding him back or build on where's he accelerating. This can't happen without a vast, reliable, networked platform that allows instantaneous distribution of ideas *back and forth*. Now that we have a cheap, distributive network that is powerful enough to transmit media beyond text and lo-res images, and to author and send back the same — and instantly, to boot[5] — we can imagine the kind of impact that can have on regular schoolchildren, distance learners, students in developing countries without strong infrastructure and professional trainees on assignment in some far-flung part of the world.

EVOLVING MEDIA CONSUMPTION PATTERNS

With incredible producing power within our reach, and a near ubiquitous high-octane distribution platform, the idea that we consume media differently in this environment is not a large conceptual leap. Rest assured, it is happening. People are watching content differently: different devices, different times and in a different manner. First, let's take a look on a macro level to understand how consumption has changed. Television is still the dominant centerpiece of viewer activity, but platform and time are changing substantially. Online search company Yahoo! And market research firm Interpret (2011) found that online video consumption jumped 33% from 2009 to 2011, with a heavy emphasis on short video clips (74%). However, longer format programming is edging that margin, which stood at 84% in 2009. So, we see two things: (a) a substantial increase and capacity to view, and comfort in viewing video content online and (b) a smaller but noticeable shift

toward longer (and, one assumes, more complex and professional) content.

This trend has been backed up by additional studies. A later study from the Consumer Electronics Association (2012) shows a number of results that support this trend in the US, such as a year-to-year increase in video content consumption (34%) and portable device content consumption (40%). Additionally, the CEA study shows 85% of 18-24 year olds and 70% of 25-34 year-olds multi-tasking while watching video content, and majorities of consumers using laptop computers, desktop computers and smartphones to watch content (62%, 55% and 33%, respectively). Nielsen (2011), the Cable & Satellite Broadcasting Association of Asia (2009), comScore's studies on European (Abraham & Block, 2012) and Latin American (2012) media markets show that, despite serious regional differences, people are globally consuming more video content online, they are using more devices to do so, they are getting acclimated to longer and more sophisticated content online and they are watching it in a more fragmented way with an emphasis on viewer participation. This has real meaning to all content creators, as it warns that simply throwing traditional media online may not be sufficient; at the least, it may not maximize the viewers' experience. Viewers are quickly getting used the rules, aesthetic and behaviors of a new ecosystem, different from television and movie theaters. And content creators would be wise to tailor their offerings accordingly.

As we've seen, educational media has benefitted from greater access to high production value and cheap distribution over the past decade, and there is an expansive collection of educational online video. But what are some of the trends in this niche market, and where will it be headed in the future? The first thing to think about is the time-distortion and de-formalizing of the education window. Back in 1970, Austrian philosopher Ivan Illich (1970) made waves by calling for a deschooling of society, and replacing the top-down global institution with a series of education networks that dispense with the teacher-centered model of industrialized learning. Were he still alive, he might be surprised how technology (not political philosophy) has started to work on the edges toward that goal. Of course, people learn virtually every day they are alive, but the 20th century model of education is rather rigid: compulsory K-12 education with trade schooling or collegiate/graduate education afterward, followed by specialized professional training. This model has fractured as "educational practices have greatly expanded beyond the time-and-place rigidity of fourth-century BC teaching and learning environments" (Bonk, 2009, p. 10). Continuing education really can be continuing now, from learning how to swap out a leaky pipe on one of Demand Media's many video portals to MIT offering almost all of its course curricula free of charge on the Web. In this environment, scanning the back pages of *The New Yorker* for mail-order video series on archeology or philosophy seems even more quaint and rarified than ever. Prospective "students" are now much better able to control education delivery, thanks again to increased accessibility of production and instantaneous, global and easily retrievable distribution. And they are opting to both shorten (faster degrees) and lengthen (continuous learning) the education window, obtain high-level educational materials outside of the establishment and upset the teacher/student dynamic in favor of educational networks and collaborative learning.

Another area to study is curriculum composition; in other words, what are the materials that are being used in class? When mainframes became personal computers, and began to trickle into classrooms in the 1970s and 1980s, it was a major undertaking that almost immediately created a "digital divide" between affluent, white schools who could afford the high cost of the equipment and disadvantaged, minority schools (Anderson, et al, 1984; McPhail, 1985). This imbalance persists today, along racial, gender and geographic axes, but the factors we've been discussing are helping to close it in many places, or at least find a way around

it. Some of this is seen in hardware, as students of all socio-economic stripes adopt (admittedly, at different rates)[6] mp3 players, smartphones, netbooks and laptops that can go far to offset the lack of resources in home districts. But the more expansive efforts are happening on the software side; on one hand, because by now many of even the poorest neighborhoods and school districts around the world have workable equipment that can connect to the Web, and on the other because of the extensive, powerful collaborative networks that are arising from the Web 2.0. Students now have access to an incredibly sophisticated social network that was inconceivable even during the internet's go-go days of the late 1990s. And it is *free*, provided the student can get online at school, at a library, at home, on a phone or via a netbook in the park. Of course, there are administration, bureaucracy, government, academic standards and established culture that will slow the transition, but the scholarship is overwhelming that this kind of access alters the kind of content that teachers use in the classroom, from online video, podcasts, webinars, or YouTube educational channels. These factors are converging to change the raw material of education.

Finally, we look at how these trends have the potential to disrupt the discourse. One of the more interesting ways to view this change is through the case study of "flip teaching." Also known as backwards classroom or reverse instruction, flipped teaching is a form of blended learning in which "students conduct research, watch videos, participate in collaborative online discussions, and so on at school and at home" (Barseghian, 2011), thereby giving educators more time in their classes to focus on one-to-one guidance and coaching. Instead of a lecture occupying to the class time, these always wired students are set loose in a massive field of media-rich information to absorb the initial concepts. The teacher then helps them synthesize and apply it in class. This process clearly predates the rise of broadband and media-rich content online. We can see it in

Eric Mazur's (1991) attempt to use computer simulations of physics basics to guide the student individually through core concepts and using class time to build on that foundation. The concept of the "guide by the side," as opposed to the "sage on the stage" would solidify at the turn of the century under J. Wesley Baker (2000). Jonathan Bergmann and Aaron Sams (2012) would coin the phrase "flip learning," after Sal Khan (2011) would popularize the concept in his TED Talk about Khan Academy. There are many ways to flip a class outside of Khan's videos, and tools like course management systems (CMS) or learning management systems (LMS), Facebook pages, Flickr accounts, Photoshop and Vimeo are just some of the constellation of ways that teachers can leverage the power of the social web to invert the normal dynamic of learning.

We use this example not to necessarily endorse flip teaching or any other pedagogy, but to show that an inflection point has been reached. The environment for quality media consumption and creation has become cheap enough, reliable enough and social enough to foster a more individual relationship between teacher and learner. This was possible among only the most rudimentary of lines in 1995 and impossible in 1985. The changing nature of media now transforms the amount of content we use and make, as well as the way in which we use it.

INTERACTIVITY

We save the subject of interactivity for last, for two reasons. First, interactivity is a function of the trends we've already discussed: the ability to produce, the ability to distribute and the ability to consume. As those points grow/become easier, the the amount of interactivity grows commensurately. Second, with interactivity we can finally return to the role of storytelling (a good storyteller doesn't put the climax in Act I). As we've seen, the world of narrative requires — and has always had — a

degree of interactivity between Teller and Audience. As it grows to the levels now possible, it starts to become a focal point instead of a means to an end. "What the rise of new digital media has done," Arata (2003) writes, "is to widen the focus of interest beyond the object created, to the participation in a process of playing out a multitude of interactions" (p. 219). Now, McLuhan's (1964) famous phrase, "the medium is the message," truly comes to the fore as millions of people can engage in participatory communication with the most famous people in the world, the largest corporations and the most iconic pieces of creative work. What remains to be seen is what ends up being the more culturally and economically viable: the finished product or the global cooperation that went into making it?

Thus far, the level of interactivity discussed has been mainly a result of easier access to production and cheaper, faster ways of dissemination, which has already started to have a marked effect on the way people use media to converse. And this has affected not only education but all types of mediated discourse. But where does it go from here? One area that seems obvious is the increased atomization of media. This topic always reminds me of the landmark Beastie Boys' album *Paul's Boutique* (1989). The album remains legendary not simply because it propelled three white Jews to the pinnacle of hip-hop artistry, but that the group (along with the Dust Brothers) almost single-handedly ushered in an era of sampling that infects youth culture to this day. The album samples over 100 songs from other artists, from Led Zeppelin to Idris Muhammad. And as Dust Brother Mike Simpson points out, the clearance of those songs would be impossible today in the litigious world of music licensing (Tingen, 2005). But even though *Paul's Boutique* could never be replicated, we can see a trendline. Amateur videophiles and audiophiles can record and time-shift songs and television shows in the 1960s and 1970s. Clubhouse DJs team up with bad-boy rappers to sample and bend world-famous music into an entirely new album in late 1980s. Software like Photoshop, Final Cut Pro and ProTools give people incredible power to manipulate pictures and sounds in the 1990s. Today, there is no media that is impregnable in the eyes of the audience. We can smash a finished product into its elements and re-assemble it for consumption by an untold amount of netizens. We can completely alter the meaning of a work—see the impeccable mash-up of Stanley Kubrick's *The Shining* as a romantic comedy trailer (Ryang, 2005)—to the point that the work itself is merely a starting point...and possibly a forgotten one at that.

This level of interactivity has taken us to the sub-atomic level, where we can warp, distort, erase, combine and make our canvas unrecognizable. This has both tremendously exciting and terrifying possibilities, but one prediction that seems plausible is a broad concession and eventual buy-in from Big Media. Content creators will increasingly stop trying to keep their customers from manipulating their product, and focus on creating platforms and content that allow them to do it *more easily*. Think of it as the "media-as-plug-in" approach; why shoot an entire film with Will Smith when you can purchase 20 professionally shot scenes with Smith as the star, to which you can splice together and add music and effects? Hipster superstar Beck is releasing an album this year called *Song Reader* (2012); instead of actual music, he is selling the sheet music for fans to play and record, thus creating a crowd-sourced CD with innumerable combinations. These ideas on are the fringes right now, but they will race toward the center as large media companies relax their grip on the content that whizzes back and forth on Facebook, Renren, Twitter, Instagram, Pinterest and other social media hubs, and they slowly start to understand how to make money on those interactions.

But what does this mean for *education*? When thinking about the future, it's important to remember the problems that are facing us presently:

It is no secret that global higher education...is facing a series of far-reaching crises. Educational institutions everywhere find themselves forced to cope with the explosion in knowledge and information brought by the growth of the Internet, a shift in the roles of public and private educational systems, declining financial support from cash strapped public sources, increasingly rapid development in information and communications technology...a global surge in the demand for higher education and life-long learning, and a growing emphasis on new content delivery approaches. (Zabriskie, 2007, p. 226)

Basically, institutions will have less infrastructure, and will therefore need more powerful learning tools that can cater to a more diasporic, time-shifted student body clamoring for education around the world. It means that the environment is strong for experiential learning, immersive simulations and the further gamification of educational media to get them there. It's also ripe for more sophisticated media: moving from Flash animation to interactive HTML5 platforms; bringing in more live footage to enhance scenario-based learning exercises, delivering and administering user-friendly content authoring tools that allow faculty and students to create media-rich content; and more intuitive LMS platforms that will allow user customization and social media-sourced knowledge to influence the curricula. It will be more privatized. Curricula will be more centralized. Content alone will continue to fall in value, while content embedded in platform-based experiences will rise. And storytelling will continue to build in importance in pedagogical models. As students, we can slip into characters and avatars more easily. We can build universes. We can learn through doing and experiencing in a contextualized, narrativized environment. We can make choices and add input that will send the story careening off into new problem sets and situations. The story — in the classroom and beyond — is no longer about sitting rapt around the storyteller as they weave a tale. It's not even about the ability to change the story from the far-flung cheap seats. It's about the entire, ever-denser ball of interaction, and the value and learning possibilities it promises.

And this brings us to the concept of "vertical narrativity." As media-rich stories become easier to build and tell, and the audience's ears become more receptive to these new ways, the story becomes malleable to the point where linearity is no longer a feature but an option, and narrative is less a line and more a globe. From revolutionary video games like *Grand Theft Auto* to semester-long education sims for learning the periodic table of elements, storytellers are now tasked with a daunting and exciting challenge. They are being asked to step away from the sequence-driven, didactic story, and to construct platforms on which the audience is at least be given the *impression* of total freedom to wander, search, connect and build their own stories from the surrounding particles of content. Again, this is a huge job; critical questions about control, learning objectives, technological equality and user experience cast a major shadow (and deserve their own book). But the potential is too great to turn away. Imagine a learning scenario where a medical resident is placed behind the surgeon's mask. She is begins her story by diagnosing a 35-year-old man with life-threatening cancer. She has to console and counsel this young family. She then takes part in a real-time, hands-on surgical removal of the tumor. If she's successful, she must then navigate her new post as Chief Resident in the hospital, and the HR headaches that involves. If she's not, she may have to muster a defense against a medical malpractice lawsuit. That's not a story one can *tell*. That's a story that must be *discovered*, or to paraphrase statistician Nate Silver, it's a signal that must be pulled from the (artfully constructed) noise. And the platform that holds it must be supple and flexible to hold it together convincingly. That is vertical narrativity. It's a narrativity that encourages the user to dive through instead of follow along, to break apart

the media in front of him, to mash it up, to suffer consequences from his decisions. This requires a new skill set from storytellers that ranges from technological abilities to new ways of telling stories. And we will have many misfires and mistakes along the way. But the successes will move us further toward storytelling's true utility in education and beyond.

CONCLUSION

The aforementioned trends — which may be reaching the shores of art and entertainment first, but will wash over all areas where information is mediated — do not speak to a set of options for education in the 21st century. They speak to a necessity. The way we deliver and receive learning *has* to change. The dominant model we have is not sufficient. There are now too many of us demanding education. The education requirement in the professional world is now too fundamental not to make access to learning a near right. Most people's lives are too demanding to submit to a years-long degree program that is the dominant activity in their day. The way we teach and learn has to change, and it is changing. Returning to the power of storytelling is a big key to that change, and our new-found powers of media authorship and transmission have altered the landscape. What educators must now focus on is developing content and platforms that enhance learning objectives in this new environment. We must prod millennia-old constructs like storytelling to adapt to a model in which the teller does not control things in the same way, or personality of the character changes over time. These are scary requests for storytellers like myself.

But the risks of letting our modes of discourse atrophy because the alternatives are too disruptive is even scarier. We cannot walk away from the potential that these changes promise: reaching billions of people, immersing them in a learning apparatus that can save time, lives and money when they are out the professional world, giving them greater control over the way they express themselves. These possibilities overshadow the challenges before us. It's an exciting time. We no longer need the storyteller to weave a tale around the campfire. That's no longer the only way. We can build one together, one that lives on in ways no one around the circle ever imagined at the beginning, long after the last embers have died out.

REFERENCES

Abraham, L., & Block, B. (2012). Connected Europe: How smartphones and tablets are shifting media consumption. Reston, VA: comScore.

Anderson, R. E., Welch, W. W., & Harris, L. J. (1984). Inequities in opportunities for computer literacy. *The Computing Teacher, 11*(8), 10–12.

Arata, L. O. (2003). Reflections on interactivity. In D. Thorburn, & H. Jenkins (Eds.), *Rethinking media change: The aesthetics of transition*. Cambridge, MA: MIT Press.

Baker, W. J. (2000). The classroom flip: Using web course management tools to become the guide by the side. In J. A Chamber (Ed.), *Selected Papers from the 11th International Conference on College Teaching and Learning*. Jacksonville, FL: Center for the Advancement of Teaching and Learning.

Barnett, C. (1991). Building a case-based curriculum to enhance the pedagogical content knowledge of mathematics teachers. *Journal of Teacher Education, 42*(4), 263–272. doi:10.1177/002248719104200404.

Barseghian, T. (2011, February 5). Three trends that define the future of teaching and learning. [Blog post]. *KQED Mind/Shift*. Retrieved from http://blogs.kqed.org/mindshift/2011/02/three-trends-that-define-the-future-of-teaching-and-learning/

Bergmann, J., & Sams, A. (2012). *Flip your classroom: Reach every student in every class every day*. Eugene, OR: International Society for Technology in Education.

Bickford, L., & del Toro, B. (Producers) & Soderbergh, S. (Director). (2008a). *Che: The Argentine*. [Motion picture]. Los Angeles, CA: IFC Films.

Bickford, L., & del Toro, B. (Producers) & Soderbergh, S. (Director). (2008b). *Che: Guerilla*. [Motion picture]. Los Angeles, CA: IFC Films.

Bonk, C. J. (2009). *The world is open: How web technology is revolutionizing education*. San Francisco, CA: Jossey-Bass.

Boys, B., Brothers, D., & Jr, C. M. (1989). Paul's boutique. [Audio CD]. Los Angeles, CA: Capitol Records.

Cable & Satellite Broadcasting Association of Asia. (2009). *Online video in China, Japan & Korea*. Hong Kong: CASBAA.

Campbell, J. (1990). *Transformations of myth through time: Thirteen brilliant lectures from the renowned master of mythology*. New York: Harper & Row.

Coles, R. (1989). *The call of stories: Teaching and the moral imagination*. Boston: Houghton-Mifflin.

ComScore. (2012, October 17). *Internet users in Mexico watch more than 14 hours of online video to lead as the most engaged audience in Latin America*. [Press release]. Retrieved from http://www.comscore.com/Insights/Press_Releases/2012/10/Internet_Users_in_Mexico_Watch_More_than_14_Hours_of_Online_Video

Consumer Electronics Association. (2012, May 14). *Consumers view video via more platforms, but HDTVs more popular, CEA study finds*. [Press release]. Retrieved from http://www.ce.org/News/News-Releases/Press-Releases/2012-Press-Releases/Consumers-View-Video-Via-More-Platforms,-But-HDTVs.aspx

Copeland, M. T. (1954). The genesis of the case method in business instruction. In M. P. McNair, & A. Hersum (Eds.), *Case Method at the Harvard Business School* (pp. 25–33). New York: McGraw-Hill.

Datar, S. M., Garvin, D. A., & Cullen, P. C. (2010). *Rethinking the MBA: Business education at a crossroads*. Boston: Harvard Business School Press.

DiMaggio, P., & Hargittai, E. (2001). *From the digital divide to digital inequality: Studying internet use and penetration increases* (Working paper). Princeton, NJ: Center for Arts and Cultural Policy Studies, Princeton University.

Ellet, W. (2007). *The case study handbook: How to read, discuss and write persuasively about cases*. Boston: Harvard Business School Press.

Farhoomand, A. F., & Laurie, J. (2006). *FocusAsia business leaders*. [Video series]. Hong Kong: Asia Case Research Centre, Hong Kong University. Retrieved from http://www.acrc.org.hk/focusasia/focusasia_index.asp

Federal Communications Commission. (2005, Nov. 21). *Making the connections*. Retrieved from http://transition.fcc.gov/omd/history/internet/making-connections.html

Finnegan, S. (2012, August 13). *Case study: The importance of production value in new media*. [Blog post]. Retrieved from http://imfinnegan.wordpress.com/2012/08/13/case-study-the-importance-of-production-value-in-new-media/

Foster, D. (2002, June 2). Open the labs and set them free? *Los Angeles Times Magazine*. Retrieved from http://articles.latimes.com/2002/jun/02/magazine/tm-44710

Greenberg, J. M. (2008). *From Betamax to blockbuster: Video stores and the invention of movies on video*. Cambridge, MA: The MIT Press.

Guber, P. (2011). *Tell to win: Connect, persuade, and triumph with the hidden power of story*. New York: Crown Business.

Hansen, B. (2012). *Song reader*. San Francisco, CA: McSweeney's.

Holben, J. (2011). Time bandit. *American Cinematographer, 92*(11), 32–45.

Illich, I. (1970). *Deschooling society*. New York: Harper & Row.

Jackson, P., Walsh, F., Cunningham, C., & Weiner, Z. (Producers) & Jackson, P. (Director). (2012). *The hobbit: An unexpected journey*. [Motion picture]. Los Angeles, CA: Warner Bros. Pictures.

Jackson, P., Walsh, F., Cunningham, C., & Weiner, Z. (Producers) & Jackson, P. (Director). (2013). *The hobbit: The desolation of Smaug*. [Motion picture]. Los Angeles, CA: Warner Bros. Pictures.

Jackson, P., Walsh, F., Cunningham, C., & Weiner, Z. (Producers) & Jackson, P. (Director). (2014). *The hobbit: There and back again*. [Motion picture]. Los Angeles, CA: Warner Bros. Pictures.

Jackson, P. W. (1995). On the place of narrative in teaching. In H. McEwan, & K. Egan (Eds.), *Narrative in teaching, learning, and research*. New York: Teachers College Press.

Jonassen, D. D., & Hernandez-Serrano, J. (2002). Case-based reasoning and instructional design: Using stories to support problem-solving. *Educational Technology Research and Development, 50*(2), 65–77. doi:10.1007/BF02504994.

Krupnick, C. G. (1987). The uses of videotape replay. In C. R. Christensen, & A. J. Hansen (Eds.), *Teaching and the case method: Texts, cases, and readings* (pp. 256–263). Boston: Harvard Business School Press.

Lardner, J. (1987). *Fast forward: Hollywood, the Japanese, and the VCR wars*. New York: W. W. Norton.

Liedtka, J. (2001). The promise and peril of using video cases: Reflections on their creation and use. *Journal of Management Education, 25*(4), 409–424. doi:10.1177/105256290102500405.

Malik, O. (2012, January 30). Global broadband zooms, US penetration is over 80 percent. *GigaOm*. Retrieved from http://gigaom.com/2012/01/30/global-broadband-zooms-us-penetration-is-over-80-percent/

Mann, M., & Richardson, J. (Producers) & Mann, M. (2004). *Collateral*. [Motion picture]. Los Angeles, CA: DreamWorks.

Mazur, E. (1991, January-February). Can we teach computers to teach? *Computers in Physics*, 31–38.

McCallum, R. (Producer) & Lucas, G. (Director). (1999). *Star wars episode I - The phantom menace*. [Motion picture]. Los Angeles, CA: 20th Century Fox.

McCallum, R. (Producer) & Lucas, G. (Director). (2002). *Star wars episode II - Attack of the clones*. [Motion picture]. Los Angeles, CA: 20th Century Fox.

McCallum, R. (Producer) & Lucas, G. (Director). (2005). *Star wars episode III - Revenge of the Sith*. [Motion picture]. Los Angeles, CA: 20th Century Fox.

McLuhan, M. (1964). *Understanding media: The extensions of man*. New York: McGraw-Hill.

McPhail, I. P. (1985). Computer inequities in school uses of microcomputers: Policy implications. *The Journal of Negro Education, 50*(1), 3–13. doi:10.2307/2294895.

Merseth, K. K. (1991). The early history of case-based instruction: Insights for teacher education today. *Journal of Teacher Education, 42*(4), 243–249. doi:10.1177/002248719104200402.

Miller, C. H. (2008). *Digital storytelling* (2nd ed.). Burlington, MA: Focal Press.

Nielsen (2011, June 15). Cross platform report: Americans watching more TV, mobile & web video. [Blog post]. *NielsenWire*. Retrieved from http://blog.nielsen.com/nielsenwire/online_mobile/cross-platform-report-americans-watching-more-tv-mobile-and-web-video/

Orngreen, R. (2004). CaseMaker: An environment for case-based e-learning. *Electronic Journal on e-Learning, 2*(1), 167-180.

Peters, J., Singer, B., & Adler, G. (Producers) & Singer, B. (Director). (2006). *Superman returns*. [Motion picture]. Los Angeles, CA: Warner Bros. Pictures.

Petty, C., Still, K., & Prewitt, J. (2010). Askinosie chocolate: Single-origin or fair-trade sourcing. *Business Case Journal, 17*(2), 16–30.

Ransome, A. (1909). *A history of story-telling: Studies in the development of narrative*. London: T. C., & E. C. Jack.

Rose, F. (2011). *The art of immersion: How the digital generation is remaking Hollywood, Madison Avenue, and the way we tell stories*. New York: W. W. Norton.

Rudin, S., Søren, O., Stærmore, S., & Chaffin, C. (Producers), & Fincher, D. (Director). (2011). *The girl with the dragon tattoo*. [Motion picture]. Los Angeles, CA: Columbia Pictures & Sony Pictures Releasing.

Ryang, R. (2005). *The Shining recut*. Retrieved from http://www.youtube.com/watch?v=sfout_rgPSA/

Sawyer, R. (1957). *The way of the storyteller*. New York: The Viking Press.

Schank, R. C. (1990). *Tell me a story: A new look at real and artificial memory*. New York: Charles Scribner's Sons.

Shamir, J. (2007). Quality assessment of television programs in Israel: Can viewers recognize production value? *Journal of Applied Communication Research*, *35*(3), 320–341. doi:10.1080/00909880701434406.

TED. (2011). Salman Khan: Let's use video to reinvent education. *TED Talks*. Retrieved from http://www.ted.com/talks/salman_khan_let_s_use_video_to_reinvent_education.html

Thompson, C. (2011, July 15). How Khan Academy is changing the rules of education. *Wired Magazine, 19*(8). Retrieved from http://www.wired.com/magazine/2011/07/ff_khan/all/

Tingen, P. (2005). The Dust Brothers: Sampling, remixing & the boat studio. *Sound on Sound*. Retrieved from http://www.soundonsound.com/sos/may05/articles/dust.htm

Wesch, M. (2008). *An anthropological introduction to YouTube*. Retrieved from http://www.youtube.com/watch?v=TPAO-lZ4_hU

Wolske, J. (2012). *Caseworx: Askinosie chocolate*. [Video]. Los Angeles, CA: Caseworx, Inc.

Wood, D. R. (1992). Teaching narratives: A sources for faculty development and evaluation. *Harvard Educational Review*, *62*(4), 535–550.

Yahoo! & Interpret. (2011). Phase 2 of video: Revolution evolution. *Yahoo! Advertising Solutions*. Retrieved from http://advertising.yahoo.com/article/phase-2-of-video-revolution-evolution.html

Zabriskie, F. H., & McNabb, D. E. (2007). E-hancing the master of business administration (MBA) managerial accounting course. *Journal of Education for Business*, *82*(4), 226–233. doi:10.3200/JOEB.82.4.226-233.

ADDITIONAL READING

Bruner, J. (1986). *Actual minds, possible worlds*. Cambridge, MA: Harvard University Press.

Bruner, J. (1990). *Acts of meaning*. Cambridge, MA: Harvard University Press.

Christensen, C. R. (1991). *Teaching and the case method*. Cambridge, MA: Harvard University Press.

Ferguson, W., Bareiss, R., Birnbaum, L., & Osgood, R. (1992). ASK systems: An approach to the realization of story-based teachers. *Journal of the Learning Sciences*, *2*(1), 95–134. doi:10.1207/s15327809jls0201_3.

Jenkins, H. (2006). *Convergence culture: Where old and new media collide*. New York: New York University Press.

Jenkins, H. (2006). *Fans, bloggers & gamers: Exploring participatory culture*. New York: New York University Press.

Koloder, J. L., & Guzdial, M. (2000). Theory and practice of case-based learning aids. In D. H. Jonassen, & S. M. Land (Eds.), *Theoretical foundations of learning environments*. Mahwah, NJ: Lawrence Erlbaum Associates.

Kolodner, J. L. (1993). *Case-based reasoning*. New York: Morgan Kaufman.

Lee, S.-H., Lee, J., Liu, X., Bonk, C. J., & Magjuka, R. J. (2009). A review of case-based learning practices in an online MBA program: A program-level case study. *Journal of Educational Technology & Society*, *12*(3), 178–190.

McConigal, J. (2011). *Reality is broken: Why games make us better and how they can change the world*. New York: Penguin Books.

McEwan, H., & Egan, K. (1995). *Narrative in teaching, learning & research*. New York: Teachers College Press.

McKee. R. (1997). Story: Substance, structure, style and the principles of screenwriting. New York: ReganBooks.

Nolan, A. R. (1927). *The case method in the study of teaching with special reference to vocational agriculture: A case book for teachers of agriculture*. Bloomington, IL: Public School Publishing Co..

Perse, E. M., & Ferguson, D. A. (1993). The impact of the newer television technologies on television satisfaction. *The Journalism Quarterly*, *70*, 843–853. doi:10.1177/107769909307000410.

Polkinghome, D. (1988). *Narrative knowing and human sciences*. Albany, NY: State University of New York Press.

Schon, D. A. (1983). *The reflective practitioner: How professional think in action*. New York: Basic Books.

Snickars, P., & Vonderau, P. (2012). *Moving data: The iPhone and the future of media*. New York: Columbia University Press.

Suster, M. (2012, November 5). Why Silicon Valley and Hollywood don't get each other and who will win the future. [Blog post]. *Both sides of the table*. Retrieved from http://www.bothsideofthetable.com/2012/11/05/why-silicon-valley-and-hollywood-dont-get-each-other-and-who-will-win-the-future/

White, H. (1981). The value of narrativity in the representation of reality. In W. J. T. Mitchell (Ed.), *On narrative*. Chicago: University of Chicago Press.

ENDNOTES

[1]   This is not to say that there have not been attempts at producing multimedia business case studies. There have been numerous attempts and they are on-going, and sometimes quite successful. Harvard Business School Press is again on the forefront of producing multimedia cases, going on tour with Harley Davidson-Motorcycles, or interviewing executives of the Zara clothing brand, or establishing their Leadership Direct module for executive education. Other elite case publishers like Stanford, Darden, Ivey and INSEAD have followed suit.

From Catherine Krupnick (1987) demonstrating how videotaping one's performance can help teachers with their case study delivery, to Jeanne Liedtka (2001) spearheading the production of professional video cases, to the CASEMAKER project at the Copenhagen Business School (Orngreen, 2004), to the Asia Case Research Centre's FocusAsia video case study series (Farhoomand & Laurie, 2006), the prospect of multimedia case studies has long been an area of interest to business educators. The obstacles have been more about execution and delivery than lack of interest or awareness.

[2]   When assessing quality standards in audio visual content, most questions of "production value" are usually laid at the feet of professionals, while blander questions of enjoyment and interest are directed toward viewers. Shamir's (2007) study reverses that trend, and follows how Israeli viewers understand and appreciate the production value of various shows, and how that recognition factors into their enjoyment. He finds that "viewers seem to be sensitive to production value considerations, and that those form a distinct dimension of evaluation. In addition we see that production value also influences people's overall assessment of television programs in terms of interest, enjoyment and quality, and this effect is independent from involvement in the program" (p. 333). One thing that will be very interesting to track through the near future is how the

fast-rising abundance of quick and cheap user-generated content (UGC) will or will not affect viewers' appreciation of production value. New Media cinematographer Sean Finnegan (2012) posted a very thought-provoking case study, in which a poorly-shot music video parody of *The Avengers* movie vastly outperformed a similar parody with much higher production value, in terms of hits and positive comments.

3 To be sure, disruptive media distribution technologies like the phonograph and even the printing press were met with serious anxiety from the establishment, but the VCR is when we see this type of technology - developed by a major corporation, no less - run up against a force as profitable and intractable as motion picture distribution in the 1960-1970s.

4 For a recounting of the infamous "Betamax case" between Sony and Universal, James Lardner's (1987) *Fast Forward* remains the definitive text (pp. 89-121).

5 If anyone doubts the tremendous reflexive speed of our communication hub, spend some time on Twitter and YouTube looking up "Clint Eastwood empty chair" or "binders of women" memes that sprung up during the 2012 U.S. presidential campaign, during which this was written. These are multi-level, participatory, media-rich conversations that were up and running within *minutes* of their utterance. Very different from the virality of, say, the 2004 election, which often required the boost of television or radio to achieve massive numbers (e.g., Howard Dean's scream).

6 Indeed, an important area of study that remains on the digital divide is the distinction between *access* and *use*. As DiMaggio and Hargittai (2001) write, "[a]s access diffuses to parts of the public who were initially excluded, dimensions related to *quality of use* become important bases by which the benefits of the technology are stratified" (p. 4).

Section 4
Use of Intelligent and Pedagogical Agents for Improving Collaboration in U-Learning

Chapter 12
Accessibility in U–Learning:
Standards, Legislation, and Future Visions

Kleber Jacinto
Rural Federal University of Semi Arid, Brazil

Francisco Milton Mendes Neto
Rural Federal University of Semi Arid, Brazil

Cicília Raquel Maia Leite
State University of Rio Grande do Norte, Brazil

Kempes Jacinto
Federal University of Alagoas, Brazil

ABSTRACT

Accessibility means free access to content and services, regardless of one's physical and cognitive limitations, maximizing the user's aspect of hardware and software platform independence. Providing this access is a technical issue more than an ethical issue because the characteristics and limiting standards of accessibility are widely known but little used by software engineers, developers, and content producers. Although there is a specific set of standards and legislation to address these difficulties, accessibility is still far from being a priority among developers and content producers. One of the challenges for ubiquitous teaching, in the present and near future, is building tools to support the creation of accessible learning objects, in compliance with current and future standards. This chapter concerns accessibility standards and points out technological ways to enable the creation of support tools in order to minimize accessibility flaws.

INTRODUCTION

Teaching has long surpassed the physical barriers of the classroom. Distance learning has become a reality, given the popularization of the Internet, especially with the coming of technologies that allow mobility and increase speed of data transmission. By becoming omnipresent, whether in big cities or in the corners of the developing world, the Internet has been recognized as source of information, means for communication, tool of aggregation and improvement of relationships

DOI: 10.4018/978-1-4666-4542-4.ch012

between people, fun, change in culture, and learning environment. This fact is highlighted when we realize that technologies such as 3G and mobile devices, satellite transmission, optic fibers, wireless networks in public and private places, environments such as telecentres or cyber cafes, are increasingly common. From this wide range of possibilities of diffuse, mobile, continuous and interactive access arises the term ubiquitous learning or u-learning (Santos, Lima, & Wives, 2011).

According to data from the International Telecommunication Union (ITU) in 2010, about a third of the 6.8 billion people in Earth have access to the Internet, either from home, on mobile devices, or access points. Even though there are still large distortions between developed and developing countries (only 15.8% of households in developing countries have Internet access, compared to 65.6% in developed countries), to a greater or lesser extent, all countries have been through a strong growth in Internet diffusion (ITU, 2010).

The Web has become not only an agile form of contact between people and knowledge dissemination, but the primary channel of communication between the corporate/government world and the population, as well as a new platform for the development of applications. The Web is no longer just an environment of interconnected documents it is a software publishing space that performs various tasks, from games to the managers of banking accounts and transactions (Puder, 2004).

However to make the content of applications and learning environments available and accessible to all people, even those with physical and intellectual limitations, is a technical and ethical duty still poorly resolved. This chapter will demonstrate aspects of international law involving education and accessibility, and will specially highlight the technical standards that, once followed, collaborate in a positive manner to the construction of accessible learning objects. Finally, we will show an approach on how to address difficulties in meeting accessibility requirements, which involves multi-agent systems and

ontologies, through the use of a tool developed at the Laboratory of Software Engineering of Universidade Federal Rural do Semi-árido.

BACKGROUND

Tim O'Reilly, founder of O'Reilly Media and one of the forerunners of the term Web 2.0, asserts that this new Internet, which provides a platform for "Rich Internet Applications" (RIA), is not a technology, a static pattern, a market niche, but rather, attitudes, concepts and principles which are increasingly dependent on people's interaction. That is, it depends on everyone being able to collaborate, interact and access knowledge (O'Reilly 2007).

This concept incorporates the existence of all kinds of access devices, with non-interoperable hardware and operating system, leaving the applications to concern about compatibility, and it cannot be denied that most of the content on the Web is designed only for desktop computers (Yang & Chen, 2006). Dealing with adaptations or creating specific content with features compatible to a particular device, are the most usual alternatives, although there are situations where the use of mobile devices is still considered infeasible (Trifonova & Ronchetti, 2003).

The use of mobile devices, from cell phones to ultrabooks, through a wide range of devices such as tablets, for teaching actions comprise the creation of learning objects that compensate the weaknesses of each platform, leverage the specific capabilities and are able to motivate students (Oliveira & Medina, 2010). Having these barriers broken, a fundamental concept in u-learning is implemented, Universal Access (Yang & Chen, 2006).

Nonetheless, universality is not to be mistaken with access homogeneity. Even in regions where the Internet is widely used, portions of the population continue to be denied the right to access it, due to form and content characteristics. This denial is commonly entitled exclusion. Exclusion may occur in, essentially, five different ways, namely: i) improper ergonomics; ii) economic exclusion; iii) social exclusion; iv) conceptual exclusion; and v) cultural exclusion (Benyon, Turner & Turner, 2005).

The first refers to exclusion due to improper ergonomics, relates to the physical world and the association between people and the equipment they use to access Internet content. Small keyboards, too sensitive or insensitive mice, the touch screens phenomenon, or screens getting smaller and smaller, are just some examples of the ergonomic issue.

The economic and the social exclusion are two closely related aspects, and their existence is easily verifiable by data from ITU (ITU, 2010). Unfavorable socio-economic conditions prevent the purchase of computers or other technological devices which allow access, or inhibit the very acquisition of the connectivity channel, as it happens in less developed countries. On the other hand, in some countries the population has the appropriate technology, but does not have the freedom to use it, such as in some communist or Islamic countries. In countries like Brazil, despite the attempt to create public policies such as the National Plan for Broadband (Plano Nacional para Banda Larga – PNBL), coordinated by the Ministry of Communications (CGPID, 2010), a lot still depends on initiatives from the population or the private sector so that social and economic barriers may be brought down. Entities from organized civil society, such as the Committee for Internet Democratization (Comitê para Democratização da Internet – CDI), are internationally recognized examples, but lack the coordination and structure of a government to change historical adverse conditions.

Cultural and conceptual exclusions complete the set of the most common forms of exclusion. The cultural incorporates language aspects, usage of unusual communication elements, and even use of a set of inappropriate characters or words. The conceptual comprehends not only layout, organization, colors set, but also technical aspects, such as the use, or not, of animation, the usage of programs as executable scripts in the browser, specific development platforms, browser's compatibility, multimedia technologies, amongst others (Benyon et al., 2005).

The two latter forms of exclusion are the most correlated with accessibility problems in the computational sense. Accessibility is the condition of a given service, in this case, the content of a Web page or service on the Internet, to be ready to meet the needs of people with physical, sensory or cognitive limitations. The legal definition used in Brazil, created by Law 10.098 of December, 2000 (Brasil, 2000) states accessibility as: "possibility and condition to reach for use, with security and autonomy, the spaces, furniture and urban equipment, the buildings, the transportation and the means and systems of communications, by a person with disabilities or reduced mobility". This concept is very similar to that found in other countries which are signatory to international conventions on human rights.

Contrary to common sense, is observed that this group includes children, elderly, illiterates or functional literates (those who attended the early years of school, but cannot understand the written text), people with degenerative diseases of the motor system, not only people considered disabled. The concept of accessibility was created to define the condition of equal use of physical spaces, where everyone can stride along and carry out their activities. Bringing this concept to the virtual world happened naturally. Even Brazilian legislation, usually considered outdated in some respects, already anticipated accessibility to "means of communication" (Brasil, 2000).

These two aspects are also the ones which dependent the most from professionals who build applications for the Web, or even for desktop, whether developers (programmers) or designers (software engineers and architects). Sharing this same idea, the World Wide Web Consortium (W3C) formed commissions to investigate the factors that result in lack of accessibility, this led to the creation of the Web Accessibility Initiative (WAI[1]), which, in summary, establishes minimum criteria for Web pages tools, content and layout to be ready to meet accessibility demands (W3C, 2006).

However, despite clearly defined, these criteria are often overlooked due to many factors, since the educational formation does not usually prepare professionals for this kind of project requirements (Ludi, 2007). These technical aspects are not entirely employed by software engineers, developers, designers and content producers (Spelta, 2009).

Some factors are said to be the reason for this deficiency in employing these technical aspects, such as the lack of technical knowledge (since formal schooling and work market do not have accessibility as an essential requirement), the lack of tools to assist in ensuring accessibility without staff rework, and the distribution of development teams which hinders code verification. Having accessibility as a feature of a product under construction, is not only an ethical and social issue, but also, and primarily, a technical one which affects directly the success of services and the quality of clients relations within these services (Brunet et al., 2005).

Data from the United Nations (UN) report that about 10% of the human population, nearly 650 million people, have some kind of physical or cognitive disability, whether caused by genetic conditions or random incidents, either by age or acquired diseases (United Nations, 2010). Many of these people are in the work market, studying and improving themselves; they are consumers, and potential customers for online services of various natures. Because of their conditions, using services offered through the Web is often simpler than using the same services at physical locations, for they require public transportation, accessibility apparatus (ramps, adapted restrooms, tactile flooring), assistance from others, and sometimes embarrassments (Ritchie & Blanck, 2003).

Given the greater availability of services in the cloud (cloud computing) (Armbrust et al., 2010), making them accessible to all is a challenge where the gathering of techniques and trained professionals can generate satisfactory results. As part of the solution, we can point out the use of tools that integrate with development teams, supporting professionals, reducing their efforts, minimizing the need for input of new knowledge and responsibilities, and helping turning products accessible.

The activities involved in the Software Process occur in such volume that even with a disciplined and qualified team is still complex to deal with distinct documents (requirements, feasibility investigations, project vision, amongst others), different languages (including various diagrams in Unified Modeling Language – UML), and designers and stakeholders diffuse, and at times, conflicting knowledge. Added to this there is the ease of nowadays communication, as this feature allows geographically distributed collaborators to be in different countries or continents and work on the same project.

To add activities related to ensuring accessibility in an already very complex environment, is not a trivial task, because validation tools for accessible traditional content have many limitations, one of them is to allow only the validation of the final product and not that of intermediary artifacts, thus generating rework for the development team. Another limitation consists on the difficulty of dealing with dynamic content, which is not compatible with the speed imposed by technological advances and market demands for more agile applications.

Therefore, the challenge to be faced in the coming years is not only to understand and apply the techniques already documented, but to build and use tools that allow the creation of accessible content and applications to be a natural activity which does not compromise development teams or project costs.

WEB ACCESSIBILITY: TECHNICAL AND LEGAL ASPECTS

Recent data show growing numbers of Internet users worldwide, which doubled from 2005 to 2010, and also divergences between rich and poor countries. Whilst in Africa only 9.6% of the population accesses the Web, in Europe this figure reaches 65%. Whereas in developing countries access to health and nutrition is not yet universal, in countries such as Finland, Spain and Estonia Internet access has been incorporated among citizens basic rights, along with housing and education (ITU, 2010).

These differences have been discussed as digital inclusion and have greater strength in developing countries like Brazil, where a good portion of the population does not possess the financial conditions to manage their essential needs, including their need to access information. The Digital Inclusion portal of the Brazilian Federal Government provides relevant information about government policies and various actions of the third sector concerning this issue (Mattos & Chagas, 2008).

Another aspect consists on the technological limitations, such as connection speed, storage space, processing power, software version (operating system or browser), hardware platform (desktops, mobile, mobile devices, etc.), among other technological limitations. Once again this issue is especially relevant in countries with low Gross Domestic Product (GDP), where technologies are slow to become popular, and is necessary to consider the potential damage or access loss if the application developer always uses the latest technologies (Spelta, 2009). Importation becomes the most common form to acquire technological assets; however taxes on production and imports are constantly seen as villains and prevent widespread access to electronics (Batista, 2010).

Another issue to be discussed is accessibility as to how content is displayed. This is most relevant to software developers, engineers and other professionals who plan and execute Web-based portals and services. But, to meet accessibility demands with technical accuracy, the right choice of platform and appropriate design, is essential to have tools or at least standards that determine technical features which enable access to content (Spelta, 2009).

The first initiatives to create standards for Web accessibility have been established by the Canadian, the American and the Australian governments around the year 1997. In 1998, in the United States, came into force Section 508, a public policy supported by several laws and rules, which required that the electronic and informational technologies from that country's federal agencies were to be accessible to people with special needs.

However, by the year 1999, these standards were not clearly defined and valid for developers. At that point, W3C through working groups established the Web Accessibility Initiative (WAI). Since this initiative the most frequent causes for lack of accessibility in many Web pages was established (Conforto & Santarosa, 2002). In May 1999, the Web Content Accessibility Guidelines 1.0 (WCAG 1.0) was launched and quickly became a worldwide reference in terms of Web accessibility. The current version is 2.0, released on December 11, 2008 (Reid & Snow-Weaver, 2008).

Once standards were established, more and more nations began to create specific standards to address accessibility in communication services. The European Union (EU) countries handle this issue individually since the 90s, but recently EU members began to discuss it collectively, with the eEurope 2002, an agreement signed at Brussels to make public portals in all EU countries handicap-accessible; and the eAcessibility, an initiative launched in 2005 with the audacious goal of getting all telecommunications services, including television, telephone and Internet itself, to become fully accessible by 2010 as a way to promote equal opportunities for European citizens.

Lusophone or Portuguese-speaking countries signed in 2008 the Treaty of Santos, which addresses the commitment of countries such as Brazil, Portugal and Angola, among others, to establish equality standards and laws to benefit disabled citizens, including free access to information, comprising information available on the Internet.

Brazil and 87 other countries are also signatories of the Declaration of Salamanca, produced at the World Conference on Special Educational Needs, held in 1994 in Salamanca, Spain, where governments committed to ensuring inclusive education for their citizens, not referring explicitly to distance learning resources, however, little by little, these nations' educational programs incorporate such concepts to their learning objects (Nakayama, 2011).

Although nations already legislate and W3C worries about the creation of standards for Web accessibility, there is still much resistance to the use of techniques that minimize impacts from lack of accessibility. As a result, there are thousands of Internet pages that cannot be read by elderly, visually impaired, dyslexic or colorblind people, for example. The convergence of real-world services to digital media (such as e-commerce, access to banking services, accountability of income tax specifically in Brazil, etc.), makes these limitations become more apparent and cause severe problems, such as to force paraplegic people to physically go to the bank, when the service could easily be performed over the Internet.

WEB ACCESSIBILITY INITIATIVE: WAI

Working groups involved with the WAI assert that Web accessibility cannot be defined in a punctual manner as it depends on the existence and interaction between various components. Among them are mentioned: i) page content, either in written form or through multimedia resources; ii) browser or another software device that interprets and presents the content to the user; iii) assistive tech-

nologies, which are devices, mainly hardware (as adapted keyboards and mice) and some software (such as screen readers), that help navigating the content; iv) developers (designers, programmers, software engineers, stakeholders, experts that have knowledge of page or application development including people with disabilities) and all who collaborate in the creation of content; v) authoring tools and other tools used in the building stages of a Web site or Web service; and vi) assessment tools to test compatibility between the final product and the established standards (Chisholm & Henry, 2005).

Simply put, they are technical (standards, content and tools) and human (content producers, tool creators, and final users) components.

The relationship between these components may be visualized in Figure 1. Developers should use appropriate authoring tools to build content and validate their artifacts through validation tools or tests made by specific teams, thus obtaining a potentially accessible content. Nevertheless, for the user to really have full awareness of such contents, browsers and other software accessing them should be able to properly read and display them to the user and the assistive tools that must mediate access.

This overview predicts that the content production cycle should go through validation on different platforms with different browsers and assistive technologies, as shown in Figure 2. This cycle should be performed during the content or application building process, but is hardly implemented as routine. The cycle efficiency depends on some factors such as the compatibility of authoring tools, assistive technologies and browsers with the accessibility features that one wants to achieve. It also depends on the easiness to use authoring tools, otherwise the developers will not be interested nor there will be feedback between users and developers, since the multiplicity of platforms and paths through which the user can get to the content makes the tests excessively onerous.

Figure 1. W3C overview on the relationship between components involved in accessibility
Source: www.w3c.org

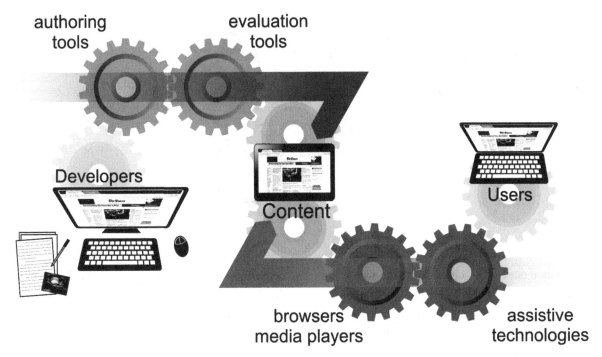

If one or more components fail or if the cycle is not properly promoted, there is high possibility that content does not meet accessibility requirements. This leads to rework from production teams and target audience unhappiness.

In the academic environment, the software construction cycle following the cascade model is inadvisable since the 90s, but its use is still very common among developers, despite the many risks involved, especially the fact that it is usual to get a final product that does not meet specification requirements. Likewise, the cycle proposed by WAI is usually ignored, and validations are not done during development, thus generating products that are unsuitable for accessibility. This deficiency can be handled by using the proposed tool, since Tohossou acts over the artifacts being constructed, performing the incremental iterative cycle, suggested by WAI/W3C, and pointed out by the literature as more effective than the traditional cascade model. Agents acting autonomously and through interaction with developers, lead them to

performing the incremental cycle, improving the artifacts during their construction, and not when finalized.

To define the proposed dynamics, the WAI and its committees created the so called Web Accessibility Guidelines (WAG). They are three large guides: i) Authoring Tool Accessibility Guidelines (ATAG); ii) Web Content Accessibility Guidelines (WCAG); and iii) User Agent Accessibility Guidelines (UAAG).

The ATAG is a guide for authoring tools production to help executers/builders create content compatible with accessibility features. These tools include HTML, text, image, script editors and other elements that will compose pages and services to be published.

Despite the market acceptance of the policies proposed by W3C, which is understandable since large software companies are part of its organization and committees, there are few authoring tools that receive the W3C-WAI seal[2]. Even widespread tools need complements (or plug-ins) to be able

Figure 2. Development cycle with accessibility compatibility
Source: www.w3c.org

to produce accessible content. These tools that meet market demands whilst still compatible with ATAG, depend on the developer's direct knowledge to create accessible content. They do not handle WCAG requirements as mandatory (in fact they are not) and do not encourage users to use WCAG properly. In other words, if the content developer or creator does not have the knowledge, desire or obligation to deal with accessibility concepts, even with the compatible tool, there is no guarantee the content which was created is accessible.

The W3C itself supports the development of a tool in open source software, available for Unix and Windows platforms, called Amaya[3], trying to meet demands for compatible tools.

The expansion of cloud computing services makes new forms of content production arise naturally and frequently. The Content Management Systems (CMS) like Joomla[4], Drupal[5] and Plone[6] are good examples. The CMS allows any user with little or no experience in Web development to build complex Web sites with textual and multimedia elements, commercial, informational and service provider pages, that without due care are potentially non-compliant with accessibility.

The Moodle[7], a widely used platform for e-learning, while providing functionalities and

declaring itself compliant with accessibility standards has many limitations and fails in several tests with end users (Guenaga *et al*, 2004).

The UAAG qualifies tools that present content to users, establishing the characteristics that should be shown to users when multimedia content of a Web page is read. Three challenges are potentially problematic to meeting the UAAG directives: i) integration between different media (PDF or DOC format files, for example, and multimedia platforms such as Adobe Flash[8] or Microsoft Silverlight[9]); ii) integration with assistive tools, such as screen readers and sets of different languages characters (Watanabe & Umegaki, 2007); and iii) multitude of hardware platforms (among them, mobile devices).

The ATAG and the UAAG directly depend on the software production Industry and, subsequently, on market demands. Although internationally accepted standards point to the incorporation of accessibility features, market disputes often lead to unexpected endpoints. The proliferation of mobile platforms such as tablets and smartphones, has brought various operating systems (different manufacturers and versions), and many of their applications to light, built by developers and companies around the world, but sometimes they do not completely meet the UAAG directives. As a result, even if the content is appropriate, hardware and software limitations may impair accessibility.

Finally, the WCAG, whose 2.0 version was released in 2008, demonstrates content compatibility and the way to present this content. The creation of version 2.0 was due to the need to update non-described or non-existing technology at the time of the version 1.0 creation, released in 1999 and unsuited for the current state of the Internet. It is essentially equipped with: i) Principles (perceivable, operable, understandable and robust); ii) Recommendations (providing structure and general scope goals to help authors understand the success criteria and better implement techniques), iii) Success Criteria (testable criteria to allow recommendations to be used, and in order to satisfy one of three levels of compliance, namely A, AA and AAA, where the first is lower and the last higher) and iv) Techniques (set of good practices for formatting, syntax functions and resources usage).

Overall, principles can be summarized by a set of what one may consider advice, non-obligatory expressions, but if taken as starting points, they can help to minimally ensure accessibility. Detailing them:

- Perceptible Principles:
  ◦ Provide text alternatives for non-text content.
  ◦ Provide captions and another alternatives for multimedia.
  ◦ Create content that can be presented in different ways, including by assistive technologies, without losing meaning.
  ◦ Make it easier for users to see and hear content.
- Operating Principles:
  ◦ Make all functionalities available from the keyboard.
  ◦ Provide users with enough time to read and use content.

  ◦ Do not use content that causes seizures (those with convulsive tendencies are strongly sensitive to images and texts that flash or glow fast and periodically).
  ◦ Help users navigate and find content.
- Understanding Principles:
  ◦ Make text readable and understandable.
  ◦ Allow contents to succeed themselves and operate in predictable ways.
  ◦ Help users avoid mistakes and, at the same time, enable their correction.
- Robustness Principle:
  ◦ Maximize compatibility with present and future user's tools.

The success criteria are characteristics liable to be tested, both by automated processes and by humans. There should be awareness that even compatible content with the highest level of compliance (AAA), still will not be accessible to people with all types, degrees, or combinations of disability, particularly in cognitive language and in learning areas.

It is recommended for developers to consider the full range of techniques following the principles and to seek advice from users and other developers on current best practices to ensure that Web content is accessible, because the WCAG is static and technology updates daily. One of the prominently featured recommendations is the inclusion of Metadata (data about the contents) that can help users find content most suited to their needs. This is one of the hallmark features of initiatives related to Semantic Web.

Criteria are measurable or likely to be tested, either by automated testes or ones made by people, for only then documents or applications can be classified as accessible or not, and if accessible, what level of accessibility they have. Thus, there is the possibility to determine which content is suitable for which one of the three compliancy levels

(A, AA or AAA). Some of the commonly assessed factors that define the compliancy level are:

- Whether the Success Criterion is essential (in other words, if the Success Criterion is not met, then even assistive technology cannot make content accessible).
- Whether it is possible to satisfy the Success Criterion under all points of view for a particular site or application (e.g., different themes, content types, types of Web technology).
- Whether the Success Criterion requires skills that can be quickly reached by content creators (i.e. whether knowledge and/or ability to satisfy Success Criteria can be acquired in training).
- Whether the Success Criterion imposes limits on the "look & feel" (if the design is intuitive) and/or function of the Web page (limits on function, presentation, freedom of expression, design or aesthetic).
- Whether there are no alternative solutions to meeting the Criteria.

For each of the existing recommendations and success criteria specific techniques were documented. The techniques have informative features and fall into two categories: those that are of the "enough" kind, i.e., are enough to meet the success criteria, and those of the "advised" kind. The latter go beyond what is required in each of the success criteria and allow authors to have greater compliance with the recommendations. For instance, having a cashier exclusively for seniors is enough, but having seats near this cashier is advised. Some these advised kind of techniques may generate satisfaction greater than that indicated by the testable success criteria.

Specific techniques for specific technologies[10] were mapped. In the WCAG 2.0 version techniques are mapped for documents construction (HTML, XML, CSS and pure Text), for scripting (both from the client side and those executed by the server),

for multimedia content (including SMIL[11], Adobe Flash, Microsoft Silverlight, Adobe PDF) and for rich interfaced applications.

The technical principles described in the WCAG, when applied to the content, are technically traceable, testable and verifiable, either by humans or by software capable of interpreting content. Following this line of thought, there are dozens of validation tools available, some proprietary, but most free and often provided by governments. The W3C itself provides not only validation tools, but allows us to add to the content a link for validation. It also possesses a list of over one hundred validation tools[12]. However, these tools handle validation, but do not encourage the implementation of the iterative incremental cycle suggested by WAI.

In traditional accessibility and validation tools, the final product is evaluated page by page, and in some cases, the effort it takes to exclude non-compliances can be as costly as the initial design (Tanaka & Da Rocha, 2011). The wrong choice of certain techniques or technologies early in the beginning stages of development may lead to needing re-evaluation of the entire project, therefore evaluating accessibility continuously throughout the project, not just at the end, is essential to the final product's success.

The WAI handles Web content, and not only Web pages. Thus, considering learning objects (LO), according to the standards of Institute of Electrical and Electronics Engineers (IEEE) ("any entity, digital or non-digital, which can be used, reused or referenced during technology supported learning" (Committee, 2002)), inside the ubiquitous paradigm also reside in the Internet or Internet based platforms, they constitute content as well and are also subject to the WAI guidelines and its derivatives.

In summary, the WAI standardizes features, as well as the technical and human elements needed to measure and test accessibility, and does so through Guidelines and technical specifications, as illustrated in Figure 3.

Figure 3. WAI-W3C overview
Source: www.w3c.org

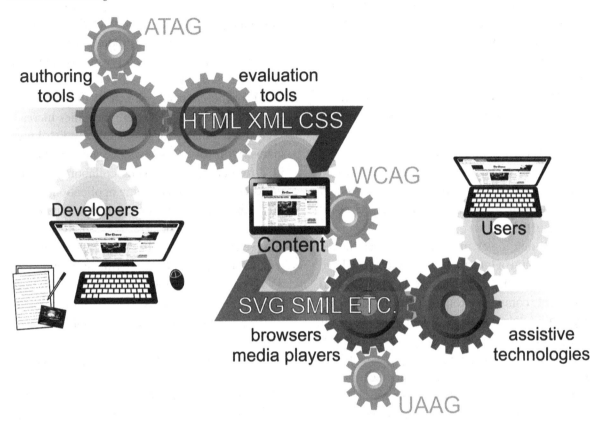

SEMANTIC WEB AND ONTOLOGIES

Another W3C initiative is to allow the Web to no longer be a network of documents only, but become a network of data/information, beginning to deal with meaning. This initiative was named Web Semantics (Berners-Lee & Hendler, 2001; Shadbolt, Hall, & Berners-Lee, 2006). Normally, to computers words are mere sets of characters, especially if they are not part of codes or texts constructed to be interpreted by machines. On the other hand, for human beings, identical words may have different meanings in different contexts, and different words may have the same meaning. Thus, is not trivial for machines to understand the meaning of things. This way, Internet content created by people, but managed by computers, is not indeed understood by the machines. In adding

meaning to the Internet, the Web Semantics seeks to make the content today accessible to people, also accessible to computers, with the most immediate impact on the increase of quality and results of search engines.

On the other hand, adding meaning to textual and multimedia content found on the Web will also provide greater freedom of content when it comes to design dimensions. Graphic design, visual programming, will still continue to have, over time, fundamental importance in the Internet and its growth, but Web Semantics will provide content that is better defined, easier to catalog and locate, easier to understand, and as a result, more accessible to people.

Considering the content's automatic use, in face of computers evolution, they have been used as tools for data manipulation, but always with man's interference when it comes to subjective data manipulation. Thus, has been a challenge for computer scientists to allow computational systems to be able to interpret subjective conditions. Ontologies arise as a concrete and promising technology to address this challenge. According to Uschold and King (1995), ontology is a specification of a conceptualization, i.e., a description of concepts and relationships that exist in an interest domain. Basically, ontologies consist on concepts and relations, and their definitions, properties and restrictions described in the form of axioms, and comprehensible to humans and machines (Uschold & King, 1995).

Thus, ontologies offer a way to handle the representation of information resources, and have become popular, largely because they have as goal to promote common and shared understanding on a given knowledge domain which can be dealt with by people and application software, through a representation vocabulary that captures concepts and relationships in any domain and a set of rules and relations that restrict its interpretation.

The potential use of ontologies to handle the information resources' semantic problem, especially when there are large volumes of information, has been widely explored by Web Semantics and Knowledge Management's research areas, where this problem is clearly crucial. For this reason, ontologies have become the essence of the Web Semantics defined by W3C. In the u-learning context ontologies are already the subject of several studies such as mapping interaction with students (Yang, Huang, Chen, Tseng, & Shen, 2006) or generating specific content for each student (Svensson & Pettersson, 2008).

TOOLS FOR AUTOMATION OF ACCESSIBILITY VALIDATION PROCESSES: A PROMISING VISION

The WAI/W3C predicts an accessible content production cycle which passes through content validation. The diverse tools available today work on the finished product and have difficulties dealing with dynamic content, this generates problems with the finished product, if one or more non-compliance are detected, rework is mandatory and project costs increase.

From another perspective, with the notoriousness and growth of u-learning becomes increasingly more common for geographically distributed teams, with diverse knowledge and specialized in different areas, to work collaboratively on projects for distance learning applications. Most often, these teams are connected through project management tools, social networks, and especially code versions control (CVS – Control Version System, whose best known tool is the SubVersion, or SVN[13]), traditional tools cannot perform this kind of integration with accessibility assurance tools.

These, among other factors, such as lack of technical knowledge when it comes to accessibility standards, have a negative impact on the creation of accessible content. Thus, tools that can interact with users without impacting their activities; that work during construction stages and not on the final product; that are automated and do not have the need for the development team to intervene; that act on clouds and use their features; and that can upgrade themselves to the new realities, new rules and new standards, would be ideal in a world increasingly concerned with accessibility issues.

Some tools are already being designed with this vision and one of them will be presented, so it inspires and theoretically grounds similar initiatives. The tool is called Tohossou and was developed in the Laboratory of Software Engineering of the Computer Science Post-Graduate Program of UFERSA/UERN.

Tohossou is an African divine entity who, according to the tradition of the people living in Ghana and Togo today, protects those born with disabilities. Legend has it that all children born with deformities should be sacrificed, but Tohossou housed them and gave them a normal life, until a great war afflicted the region and the victory only came when Tohossou brought all its protégés to battle. Since then, for these people, those born with different characteristics, far from being a problem, are a sign of good omens.

Tohossou was the name chosen for the Multi Agent System (MAS) created to assist in accessibility support for Web applications, interacting with these applications' project and development team. To fulfill its role, the Tohossou has a number of features which allow it to go beyond today's tools. Above all, it is a MAS where each software agent specialized in a particular activity works collaboratively with the others, often communicating with other agents and system users.

It is a Web application with data storage and agents management executed on the service's server, within the cloud computing vision, not requiring local infrastructure, except for the Internet access, so its use does not overcharge the project nor the development team, by keeping another software or service running and its associated hardware, resources, inputs (electricity, for instance) and secondary activities, among them backup.

The Tohossou was developed using open source software tools. The Yii[14] framework, the PHP[15] language and some of its additional packages, and MySQL[16] relational database were used, with all the benefits of reduced costs, support from the developers community, portability, in addition to facilitating changes, creating plug-ins and other features by third parties, and being possible to integrate it with the other productivity tools of the development team, especially by using Web service integrated to the tool. The interface, despite being within the concepts of Rich Internet Applications (RIA) (Fraternali, Rossi, & Sanchez-Figueroa, 2010), can be considered clean, designed to be able to incorporate new visual elements (logos, texts and agents' graphic representations), to be customize, if so desired, and keep, nevertheless, accessibility features.

Moreover, the Tohossou was developed to communicate to the SVN service used by the team, being able to detect each new artifact inserted in it, perform the accessibility analysis and generate results that will be sent to the project participants. As a result, the team does not need to interrupt their actions to validate codes, or learn new accessibility techniques (or other features that one may wish to validate), because the Tohossou points non-compliances and indicates how to fix it via an e-mail sent to the team, autonomously.

Agents communicate with users, through the Web interface, by e-mail or via Web service, but they also communicate extensively among themselves. For such, the blackboard technique was applied (Li & Hu, 2009), here all agents have access to a portion of memory (or storage space) where they can read and post messages following a predetermined language. In the case of the Tohossou, a set of elementary messages native from the tool was chosen, without causing interoperability problems with other tools, since communication with external elements happens through Web service (and use of XML) and not through the blackboard which is exclusive for the Tohossou agents.

Finally, the Tohossou agents use ontologies as knowledge base. Although it was not designed to autonomously change its ontologies, it was designed to adapt to new ontologies, suggested by users. Hence, not only multiple knowledge domains can be analyzed, as there may be improvement to existing domains.

USAGE SCENARIO

Usage flow of the Tohussou was organized in order to maximize interaction between team members and minimize costs with the integration process of yet another tool to those already used by the team.

The project leader or a team member designated for this purpose registers at the Tohossou through a simple form, which considers the most relevant information to be the user's e-mail. The e-mail is especially relevant because is the primary communication channel between the Tohossou and the users. Upon registration, the new user receives a message with a hyperlink to the so called "register ticket". This ticket is good for 10 days and aims to minimize the possibility of users' unauthorized registrations, therefore only the registrations made by users who click on the link sent to their e-mail will be validated. Consequently, even if a third party performs the registration, only the owner of the e-mail account will be able to validate it. Once validated, the user can log into the tool.

Users must document the work structure and tool interaction. To do so, one must (i) create a project, (ii) assign the project repositories that must be monitored by the agents and (iii) invite users who will receive notifications, as illustrated in Figure 4.

For the project, in addition to name and description, it is requested to inform dates of the project's beginning and end. This information is needed so that agents can understand if the project is active or not, since the lack of updates in the repository is not sufficient criterion to establish that the project is not active and agents do not use their resources on inactive projects.

The registration of repositories occurs through the indication of the Uniform Resource Location (URL) and the login authorized to consult the repository and perform the download of its artifacts. Once registered at least one repository, the Tohossou begins to analyze the repository and use SVN's version management resources to search for more recent and not analyzed versions of the artifacts contained in the repository. Repositories must obviously be within the agents' reach; preferably on the Internet, because if there is more than one repository on a single project, it will not be necessary for them to be physically located at the same site or server.

Project members are invited on the interface itself by indicating name and e-mail. Again the e-mail is essential information because through it guests receive the message with a link to the ticket that frees their registration. The guests receive by e-mail the information that they have been called to participate in the use of the tool and acceptance must be made on a specified page (link in the body of the e-mail). After confirmation, the member starts to receive messages from the communication agent about the progress of the project, especially regarding non-compliance of the code published in the repository. For safety reasons, you can only add to a project via registered invitation of a leader (or creator) of the project.

Having users and repositories registered, the Tohossou agents begin to act and may issue reports and alerts to users and project leaders. The Tohossou's work cycle on a project is limited by the existence of new artifacts in the repository and by the project's end date. The work and register flow of the actors involved in the Tohossou is shown in Figure 5. The details of the Tohossou's agents' actions will be explained in the following sections.

As seen in Figure 5, users (software engineers, developers, stakeholders and other project participants) have little actions and this minimizes learning, facilitates tool integration to the team's work routine and allows everyone to concentrate on aspects inherent to development. They only have the responsibility to read recommendations and implement them at the appropriate time. The intent is for the Tohossou to act as the team's consultant, being able to pass on information to the team with the least possible changes in everyone's work routine.

The project leader also receives through e-mail, sent by the communications agent, which will be explained in the next section, periodic reports on activities concerning the inclusion of artifacts to the repository and on the actions of developers and other project members towards correcting non-compliances.

Figure 4. Project registration structure in the Tohossou

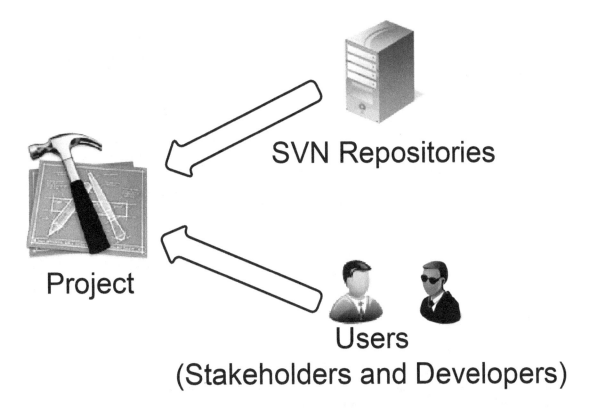

COMMUNITY OF INTELLIGENT AGENTS

The Tohossou consists on a community of agents that detect changes in the environment and perform their actions, communicating with users through the Tohossou's Web interface e-mail and with other agents via a centralized repository of messages (blackboard).

The system has three different types of agents: the Librarian Agent; the Analyzer Agents (there are more than one instance of the analyzer agent, allowing parallel analysis of several artifacts); and the Communications Agent, responsible for contacting users and other systems. Interaction between these agents and the other actors involved (human and other systems) is graphically represented in Figure 6. The white arrows represent data readings; the orange ones, communication

between agents; and the blue one, communication between system and end users.

The Librarian Agent's mission is to access the projects repositories and inform the Tohossou's agents' community if there is material to be validated. The Librarian Agent (i) proactively and periodically accesses repositories searching for file changes, additions or deletions, (ii) builds a library of artifacts and (iii) enumerates amongst them which are subject to validation, which ontologies to be used and which will be or have been analyzed.

The most active components of the Tohosssou's agents' community are called Analyzer Agents. These agents receive the artifacts list of a given project, created by the Librarian Agent, along with the information of what knowledge base must be used, i.e. the Application Ontology. The Analyzer Agent is allocated dynamically and proportionally to the workload, with maximum limit determined

Figure 5. Workflow and actions of each actor in the Tohossou

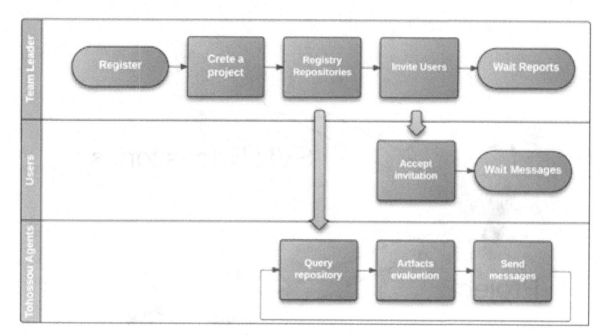

by the capacity of the employed hardware. Each instance of the Analyzer agent takes for themselves one of the artifacts to analyze and communicates this reservation to other agents, so there is no competition or rework and consequently wasted resources. At the end, if there are no more artifacts available for analysis and there are idle agents, they decree the end of their activities, freeing up memory and computational resources. If there are artifacts, they continue to analyze them.

Analyzer Agents were built to adapt to new ontologies that map specific needs of each new project, collaborating with the final product's quality and helping development teams on what they actually need. For such, there is simply the need of an appropriate ontology.

The Communication Agent is responsible for interaction between project participants, either through Web interface, e-mail, and communication with other applications via Web Service. The Communication Agent filters content and keeps users aware of the actions being performed. More-

over, this agent tells users the code's accessibility inconsistencies via e-mail.

KNOWLEDGE BASES

One of the deficiencies found in current content validation tools as for accessibility and is the fact that they do not incorporate all demands, but only those framed in certain patterns, e.g. Section 508 or WAI/W3C. These standards are correct, but do not comprise all faces of accessibility issues, and the tools which use them have the same limitation.

So that the Tohossou did not continue this paradigm, it was determined that its knowledge base was not to be static, but it could be expanded over time. Moreover, that new perspectives and standards were added without the need for reconstruction of the tool or of its agents. The chosen path among the available was the use of ontologies.

For such, the concept of Domain and Application Ontologies was sought out. The Domain Ontologies describe vocabulary and relationships

Figure 6. Basic action scheme of the Tohossou's agents

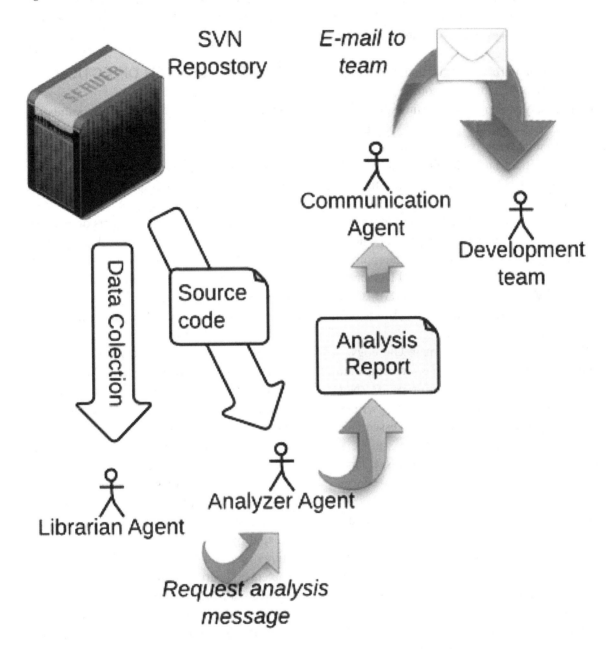

of a given knowledge domain or reality. The Application Ontologies are usually specializations of domain ontologies and determine restrictions, application and even instances of domain individuals (Guarino, 1998).

The artifacts monitored by the Tohossou, whether a Web page or a Java code, are essentially texts, with different syntaxes, different source codecs, different formats, but always a set of characters forming words and sentences. This is the Tohossou's primary domain: texts.

However, each language has specific syntax and semantics which are its own, so that for each language one wishes to encode, an Application Ontology must be created.

For the creation of ontologies there is no single standard or methodology, and some authors have been intensely studying and writing about best practices for creating them. However, some activities are essential to any method: i) defining classes; ii) organizing them hierarchically (taxonomically – sub/superclasses); iii) outlining properties and restrictions; iv) assigning property values; and when necessary, v) creating class instances. For modeling ontology there is no single tool, but the most widely used and referenced in literature is the Protégé[17] maintained by Stanford University School of Medicine (Noy et al., 2003), which was also used in the modeling of the Tohossou's ontologies.

For the creation of the Domain Ontology, a top-down approach was used, i.e., starting from the most generic element to the most specific (Noy et al., 2001). Thus, it was inferred that a written text either a poem or piece of code is essentially composed of characters, be them letters, numbers, kanji (ideograms used to express words in Japanese) or any other which graphically represent an element of the language in use. These, together, form words. The words form sentences that are ultimately organized into paragraphs.

The Application Ontologies were created inheriting the classes of Domain Ontology. For each verification kind, or in this case application, a new ontology must be created to be added to the pre-existing set, expanding the analysis capacity of Analyzer Agents. The need of the ontologies' inheritance and hierarchy is due to the concern of designing dynamic MAS that may evolve over time, expanding validation domains and updating themselves as the norms and standards change. As an example, one can cite the inclusion of specific frameworks validation (Yii, Zend[18], CodeIgniter[19], among others), or specific laws from each country,

as U.S. law Section 508, or any other specific demand that the development team may need.

FUTURE RESEARCH DIRECTIONS

Traditional methods of accessibility validation occur *a posteriori*, requiring refactoring and therefore rework from the development team. Additionally, many teams work collaboratively nowadays and are geographically distributed, relying on code versioning tools, which hinders accessibility validation in code parts of different developers. All of this, together with developers' lack of technical knowledge about accessibility standards, since this information is not a part of most computer science courses' program, complicates the task of ensuring accessibility in projects for Web applications.

As an alternative to this scenario, which culminates in the lack of accessibility in Web content and applications, developers must have, beyond technical and legal knowledge, the moral principle of providing access for all, for this activity requires very drastic changes in culture and without proper tools these changes are difficult.

The construction of support tools is a task that deserves developers' attention because they play an important role in the development cycle predicted by the W3C. The Tohosssou possess features that can be used as a basis for more complete and current tools.

The combination of technologies used is appropriate to the pursuit of full accessibility in Web applications and content. The use of ontologies as knowledge base allows its continuous expansion without the need of the agents' changes, including when facing the challenges of Web Semantics. The inference mechanisms and the level of detail provided by ontologies are suitable for this and other applications.

The natural choice of an implementation language for a tool of this magnitude would normally be Java, but the choice to use PHP and various support packages (e.g., to access the repositories and ontologies) and frameworks (in this case, Yii) is feasible, for in addition to the ease of programming, debugging, and incorporation of new features, PHP is native to the Internet (and so are its main protocols, such as FTP), and incorporates many of the features looked for on a tool inside the Cloud Computing paradigm.

The quality of tool's non-compliance evaluations results with the Tohossou, do not diverge from traditional tools, but present an advantage to be exploited by the others, which is the ability to interact with unfinished artifacts and collaborate within the development cycle and not on the finished products, avoiding the development team's rework. In already completed projects, the benefit is associated with continuous repository monitoring, in case there are any changes.

The next step is to make these tools communicate with users through social networks, via communication agents or other appropriate technology, and also with other communication and collaboration tools on the rise.

The construction of a large volume of application ontologies that allow validation of new rules and standards, permit a greater set of artifacts and projects to be evaluated. There are nowadays a huge number of frameworks for producing Web content, and the majority of them do not explicitly support accessibility, so prior validation as proposed, with the Tohossou, minimizes this lack of support.

CONCLUSION

The accessibility issue should not be treated only from the content standpoint, the rules, standards, and laws are mature, however their application is not. Therefore, is the developers' ethical duty to engage positively, not only in the content construction, but also with the tools that support everyone to handle accessibility, not as a problem but naturally inherent to the egalitarian coexistence among men and women.

Ubiquity enhances the accessibility issues and these may even jeopardize the ability to access everywhere and on as many platforms as possible, finally compromising, ubiquity itself. In this sense, tackling accessibility issues is not limited to creating applications and learning objects for people with disabilities but also creating them for the multiplicity of platforms.

REFERENCES

W3C, W. W. W. C. (2006). *Web Accessibility initiative (WAI)*. W3C.

Armbrust, M., Fox, A., Griffith, R., Joseph, A. D., Katz, R., Konwinski, A., & Zaharia, M. (2010). A view of cloud computing. *Communications of the ACM, 53*(4), 50–58. doi:10.1145/1721654.1721672.

Batista, J. C. (2010). Os efeitos das políticas industriais para o setor de produtos eletrônicos do Brasil. *Revue d'Economie Politique, 30*(1), 112–123. doi:10.1590/S0101-31572010000100007.

Benyon, D., Turner, D. P., & Turner, D. S. (2005). *Designing interactive systems: People, activities, contexts, technologies*. Reading, MA: Addison-Wesley.

Berners-Lee, T., & Hendler, J. (2001). Publishing on the semantic web. *Nature, 410*(6832), 1023–1024. doi:10.1038/35074206 PMID:11323639.

Brasil. 10.098, de 19 de dezembro de 2000., 244 Diário Oficial da União § 1 2 (2000).

Brunet, P., Feigenbaum, B. A., Harris, K., Laws, C., Schwerdtfeger, R., & Weiss, L. (2005). Accessibility requirements for systems design to accommodate users with vision impairments. *IBM Systems Journal, 44*(3), 445–466. doi:10.1147/sj.443.0445.

CGPID. C. G. do P. de I. D. (2010). *Plano nacional de banda larga*. Retrieved from http://www.mc.gov.br/publicacoes/doc_download/418-documento-base-do-programa-nacional-de-banda-larga

Chisholm, W. A., & Henry, S. L. (2005). Interdependent components of web accessibility. In *Proceedings of the 2005 International Cross-Disciplinary Workshop on Web Accessibility (W4A)* (pp. 31–37). New York, NY: ACM. doi:10.1145/1061811.1061818

Committee, L. T. S. (2002). *IEEE standard for learning object metadata. IEEE Standard 1484.* IEEE.

Conforto, D., & Santarosa, L. M. C. (2002). Acessibilidade à web: Internet para todos. *Revista de Informática na Educação: Teoria. Prática, 5*(2), 87–102.

de Oliveira, L. R., & Medina, R. D. (2010). Desenvolvimento de objetos de aprendizagem para dispositivos móveis: Uma nova abordagem que contribui para a educação. *RENOTE, 5*(1). Retrieved from http://seer.ufrgs.br/renote/article/view/14154

Fraternali, P., Rossi, G., & Sanchez-Figueroa, F. (2010). Rich internet applications. *IEEE Internet Computing, 14*(3), 9–12. doi:10.1109/MIC.2010.76.

Guarino, N. (1998). *Formal Ontology in information systems: Proceedings of the first international conference (FOIS'98).* Trento, Italy. IOS Press.

Guenaga, M. L., Burger, D., & Oliver, J. (2004). Accessibility for e-learning environments. In K. Miesenberger, J. Klaus, W. L. Zagler, & D. Burger (Eds.), *Computers Helping People with Special Needs* (Vol. 3118, pp. 157–163). Berlin: Springer. Retrieved from http://www.springerlink.com/index/10.1007/978-3-540-27817-7_23

ITU, I. T. U. (2010). *The world in 2010: ICT facts and figures*. International Telecommunication Union.

Li, S., & Hu, F. (2009). Communication between the RoboCup agents based on the blackboard model and observer pattern. In *Proceedings of the 5th International Conference on Wireless Communications, Networking and Mobile Computing, 2009. WiCom '09* (pp. 1–5). doi:10.1109/WICOM.2009.5304011

Ludi, S. (2007). Introducing accessibility requirements through external stakeholder utilization in an undergraduate requirements engineering course. In *Proceedings of the 29th International Conference on Software Engineering* (pp. 736–743). Washington, DC: IEEE Computer Society. doi:10.1109/ICSE.2007.46

Mattos, F. A. M., de, , & Chagas, G. J. do N. (2008). Challenges for digital inclusion in Brazil. *Perspectivas em Ciência da Informação, 13*(1), 67–94. doi: doi:10.1590/S1413-99362008000100006.

Nakayama, A. M. (2011). *Educação inclusiva: Princípios e representação.* Retrieved from http://www.teses.usp.br/teses/disponiveis/48/48134/tde-07122007-152417/

Noy, N. F., Crubézy, M., Fergerson, R. W., Knublauch, H., Tu, S. W., Vendetti, J., & Musen, M. A. (2003). Protégé-2000: An open-source ontology-development and knowledge-acquisition environment. In *Proceedings of AMIA Annual Symposium.* AMIA.

Noy, N. F., McGuinness, D. L., et al. (2001). *Ontology development 101: A guide to creating your first ontology*. Retrieved from http://er.uni-koblenz.de/IFI/AGStaab/Teaching/SS09/sw09/Ontology101.pdf

Oreilly, T. (2007). What is web 2.0: Design patterns and business models for the next generation of software. *SSRN eLibrary*. Retrieved from http://papers.ssrn.com/sol3/papers.cfm?abstract_id=1008839

Puder, A. (2004). Extending desktop applications to the web. In *Proceedings of the 2004 International Symposium on Information and Communication Technologies* (pp. 8–13). Trinity College Dublin. Retrieved from http://dl.acm.org/citation.cfm?id=1071509.1071512

Reid, L. G., & Snow-Weaver, A. (2008). WCAG 2.0: A web accessibility standard for the evolving web. In *Proceedings of the 2008 International Cross-Disciplinary Conference on Web Accessibility (W4A)* (pp. 109–115). New York, NY: ACM. doi:10.1145/1368044.1368069

Ritchie, H., & Blanck, P. (2003). The promise of the internet for disability: A study of on-line services and web site accessibility at centers for independent living. *Behavioral Sciences & the Law, 21*(1), 5–26. doi:10.1002/bsl.520 PMID:12579615.

Santos, N. dos S. R. S. dos, Lima, J. V. de, & Wives, L. K. (2011). Ubiquidade e mobilidade de objetos de aprendizagem usando o papel como recurso. *RENOTE, 8*(3). Retrieved from http://seer.ufrgs.br/renote/article/view/18067

Shadbolt, N., Hall, W., & Berners-Lee, T. (2006). The semantic web revisited. *IEEE Intelligent Systems, 21*(3), 96–101. doi:10.1109/MIS.2006.62.

Spelta, L. (2009). *Acessibilidade web: 7 mitos e um equívoco*. Retrieved from http://acessodigital.net/art_acessibilidade-web-7-mitos-e-um-equivoco.html

Svensson, M., & Pettersson, O. (2008). Making use of user-generated content and contextual metadata collected during ubiquitous learning activities. In *Proceedings of the Eighth IEEE International Conference on Advanced Learning Technologies, 2008. ICALT '08* (pp. 606 –610). doi:10.1109/ICALT.2008.169

Tanaka, E. H., & Da Rocha, H. V. (2011). Evaluation of web accessibility tools. In *Proceedings of the 10th Brazilian Symposium on on Human Factors in Computing Systems and the 5th Latin American Conference on Human-Computer Interaction* (pp. 272–279). Porto Alegre, Brazil: Brazilian Computer Society. Retrieved from http://dl.acm.org/citation.cfm?id=2254436.2254483

Trifonova, A., & Ronchetti, M. (2003). *A general architecture for m-learning*. Retrieved from http://eprints.biblio.unitn.it/493/

United Nations. (2010). *Factsheet on persons with disabilities*. Retrieved August 6, 2012, from http://www.un.org/disabilities/default.asp?id=18

Uschold, M., & King, M. (1995). *Towards a methodology for building ontologies*. Retrieved from http://129.215.202.23/~oplan/documents/1995/95-ont-ijcai95-ont-method.pdf

Watanabe, T., & Umegaki, M. (2007). Capability survey of user agents with the UAAG 1.0 test suite and its impact on web accessibility. *Universal Access in the Information Society, 6*(3), 221–232. doi:10.1007/s10209-007-0087-7.

Yang, S. J., & Chen, I. Y. (2006). Universal access and content adaptation in mobile learning. In *Advanced Learning Technologies, 2006,* (pp. 1172–1173). IEEE. Retrieved from http://ieeexplore.ieee.org/xpls/abs_all.jsp?arnumber=1652678

Yang, S. J. H., Huang, A. P. M., Chen, R., Tseng, S.-S., & Shen, Y.-S. (2006). Context model and context acquisition for ubiquitous content access in ulearning environments. In *Proceedings of the IEEE International Conference on Sensor Networks, Ubiquitous, and Trustworthy Computing,* (Vol. 2, pp. 78 –83). IEEE. doi:10.1109/SUTC.2006.47

ENDNOTES

1   http://www.w3.org/WAI/
2   http://www.w3.org/WAI/AU/2002/tools.html
3   http://www.w3.org/Amaya/
4   http://www.joomla.org
5   http://www.drupal.org
6   http://www.plone.org
7   https://moodle.org/
8   http://www.adobe.com/br/products/flash/
9   http://www.microsoft.com/brasil/silverlight/
10 Available at http://www.w3.org/TR/WCAG20-TECHS/
11 Synchronized Multimedia Integration Language
12 http://www.w3.org/WAI/ER/tools/complete
13 http://subversion.apache.org/
14 http://www.yiiframework.com/
15 http://www.php.net/
16 http://www.mysql.com/
17 http://protege.stanford.edu/
18 http://www.zend.com/en/
19 http://codeigniter.com/

Chapter 13

Ubiquitous Multi-Agent Context-Aware System for Enhancing Teaching-Learning Processes Adapted to Student Profile

Demetrio Ovalle
Universidad Nacional de Colombia – Campus Medellín, Colombia

Oscar Salazar
Universidad Nacional de Colombia – Campus Medellín, Colombia

Néstor Duque
Universidad Nacional de Colombia – Campus Manizales, Colombia

ABSTRACT

The need for ubiquitous systems that allow access to computer systems from anywhere at anytime and the massive use of the Internet has prompted the creation of e-learning systems that can be accessed from mobile smart phones, PDA, or tablets, taking advantage of the current growth of mobile technologies. The aim of this chapter is to present the advantages brought by the integration of ubiquitous computing-oriented along with distributed artificial intelligence techniques in order to build student-centered context-aware learning systems. Based on this model, the authors propose a multi-agent context-aware u-learning system that offers several functionalities such as context-aware learning planning, personalized course evaluation, selection of learning objects according to student's profile, search of learning objects in repository federations, search of thematic learning assistants, and access of current context-aware collaborative learning activities involved. Finally, the authors present some solutions considering the functionalities that a u-learning multi-agent context-aware system should exhibit.

DOI: 10.4018/978-1-4666-4542-4.ch013

INTRODUCTION

In the last decade, the main contribution that has occurred to virtual university courses development is the adaptation capacity. Diverse kinds of adaptation have been mainly used on the following issues (Brusilovsky et al., 2004): instructional plans (Duque, 2006, 2009), knowledge level assessments, educational contents, student-centered selection of learning objects from repository federations (Rodríguez et al, 2012), among others. In addition, the growth of digital information, high-speed computing, and ubiquitous networks has allowed for accessing to more information and thousands of educational resources. This fact has led to the design of new teaching-learning proposals, to share educational materials, and also to navigate through them.

The context-aware adaptive learning systems, as defined by Wang & Chun-Yi Wu (2011), must actively provide learners with the appropriate learning assistance for their context to complete their e-learning activity. In the traditional e-learning environment, the lack of immediate learning assistance, the limitations of the screen interface or inconvenient operation means the learner is unable to receive learning resources in a timely manner and incorporate them based on the actual context into the learner's learning activities. The result is impaired learning efficiency. Through context aware technology, the system can sense the user's context and automatically adapt it to the known context in order to provide immediate services and applications.

The aim of this chapter is to highlight the advantages of integrating relevant approaches such as ubiquitous computing, context-aware systems, student-centered selection of learning objects, pedagogical intelligent agents, adaptive and collaborative learning, among others, to propose a model of a ubiquitous multi-agent context-aware system for enhancing teaching-learning processes adapted to student profile.

The rest of the chapter is organized as follows: In Section 2, the background that includes the theoretical framework and related works are presented. While Section 3 describes the model proposed, the development methodology, and the system architecture, Section 4 presents the results based on the Ubiquitous Multi-Agent Context-Aware System functionalities. Finally, Section 7 displays the main conclusions and future research directions.

BACKGROUND

This section first provides main definitions about learning planning, adaptive evaluation, multi-agent systems, learning objects, context-aware systems, computer supported collaborative learning, among others. Then, a literature review through related works is presented to demonstrate the relevance on trends on ubiquitous, context-aware, adaptive, and intelligent e-learning system development.

Learning Planning

Learning planning (Duque, 2006, 2009; Arias, 2010) comprises one of the most important tasks within the educational systems allowing students to attain adaptation purposes of their instruction. A learning planning strategy is applied using the virtual course's structure given by (Ovalle et al., 2011) which is composed of following elements: modules, topics, learning activities, learning goals (LGs), learning objects (LOs). In addition, a learning planning strategy is based on the artificial intelligence planning basic concepts described as follows:

- **Problem:** Formulation that expresses the knowledge associated to topics of a specific course that the students try to acquire.
- **Initial State:** The student has basic concepts in the field, which will help him/her to acquire new concepts.

- **Final State:** The student has acquired new knowledge and thus has attained one or several LGs.
- **Learning Activities:** They are specified by the teachers while they build the corresponding virtual course and they must be associated to the LG.
- **Elements:** They are related to the LOs that will be used when a learning activity is performed. Each of them must contain specific metadata allowing to carry out the LO selection in adaptive way.
- **Restrictions:** They can be established at two levels; the first level is related to the structure of the virtual course and are known as "pre-requirements" that indicate what LG must be attained in order to reach another LG. Due to the subdivision of the courses in the previously described components, when a pre-requirement is defined on an LG, such a pre-requirement can also be applied on a topic, on a module and/or on an entire course.

Learning planning is the main component of adaptive virtual courses whose role is to continuously determine the sequence (learning plan) of consistent and coherent learning activities. In addition, the goal of the learning planning is to optimize the learning process for each of the students allowing them to reach their learning goals (LGs) generated dynamically during a virtual learning session.

Adaptive Evaluation

The evaluation process of the student's knowledge level can be considered as important as teaching-learning process; it should be continually executed in order to acts as a self-regulation mechanism that is based on the verification of the accomplishment of the LGs, the measurement of the student's performance and the validation of the pedagogic strategy. From the perspective of active learning environments, the knowledge level assessment takes special importance since it has as responsibility the achievement of the motivation of the students to carry out activities and extends the course content through the solution of questions and practical problems. The evaluation process allows student to be aware of his/her academic state, weakness, and strengths.

Even with access to ICT (Information and Communications Technologies), as well as virtual courses, the evaluation process can be seen limited by static tests or questionnaires that only include the concepts seen in the course and they just serve as a classification instrument of students that approve or reprove the course, the possibility of obtaining any feedback information is not available. With the aim of overcoming the limitations that prevent to take the traditional evaluation at the active learning level, it is important to consider adaptive customized evaluation that facilitates the development of competences and skills corresponding to the knowledge domain for each of the students, which serves as a support for the teaching-learning process.

Multi-Agent Systems

Multi-agent systems (MAS) are composed of a set of agents that operate and interact in an environment to solve a specific and complex problem (Weiss, 2007). This paradigm provides a new way of analysis, design, and implementation of complex software systems and has been used for the development of virtual learning environments (Casali et. al, 2011).

Agents are entities that have autonomy in order to perform tasks by achieving their objectives without human supervision. The desirable characteristics of the agents are as follows (Jennings, 2000):

- **Reactivity:** They respond promptly to perceived changes in their environment.
- **Proactivity:** Agents can take initiative.

Figure 1. Student profile model

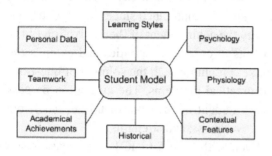

- **Cooperation and Coordination:** They perform tasks communicating with other agents through a common language.
- **Autonomy:** Agents do not require direct intervention of humans to operate.
- **Deliberation:** They perform reasoning processes to make decisions.
- **Distribution of Tasks:** Each agent has definite limits and identified the problems to be solved.
- **Mobility:** They can move from one machine to another over a network.
- **Adaptation:** Depending on changes in their environment they can improve their performance.
- **Parallelism:** Agents can improve performance depending on changes in their environment.

Student Profile

A comprehensive structure that represents the student's information into several categories is considered as the student profile model, choosing among his/her most important or the most significant issues. These categories are: personal data (e.g. name, date of birth, sex, etc.) learning styles (e.g. active, reflexive, sensorial, intuitive, visual, verbal, sequential, global), psychology profile (e.g. dominant brain hemisphere), physiology profile (hearing, vision, etc.) contextual characteristics

(e.g. access device, network state, operating system, etc.), historical issues (activities developed, study times), academic achievements (learning goal approved) and group work performance (Duque, 2009). Figure 1 shows the structure of the student profile model.

LOs, LOR, LOF

According to the IEEE, a Learning Object (LO) can be defined as a digital entity involving educational design characteristics. Each LO can be used, reused or referenced during computer-supported learning processes, aiming at generating knowledge and competences based on student's needs. LOs have functional requirements such as accessibility, reuse, and interoperability (Ouyang & Zhu, 2008; Betancur et al., 2009). The concept of LO requires understanding of how people learn, since this issue directly affects the LO design in each of its three dimensions: pedagogical, didactic, and technological (Betancur et al., 2009). In addition, LOs have metadata that describe and identify the educational resources involved and facilitate their searching and retrieval. Repositories of Los (LORs), composed of thousands of LOs, can be defined as specialized digital libraries storing several types of resources heterogeneous, are currently being used in various e-learning environments and belong mainly to educational institutions (Prieta & Gil, 2010). LO Federations (LOF) serve to provide educational applications of uniform administration in order to search, retrieve, and access specific LO contents available in whatever of LOR groups (Van de Sompel et al., 2008).

Context-Aware U-Learning

As defined in (Hwang et al., 2009) context-aware ubiquitous learning (u-learning) is an innovative approach that integrates wireless, mobile, and context-awareness technologies to detect the situation of learners in the real world and thus provide adaptive support or guidance accordingly.

In the traditional e-learning environments (Wang & Wu, 2011) the lack of immediate learning assistance, the limitations of the screen interface or inconvenient operation means the learner is unable to receive learning resources in a timely manner and incorporate them based on the actual context into the learner's learning activities. The result is impaired learning efficiency. In contrast, ubiquitous computing environments enable users to easily use huge amounts of information and computing services through network connections anytime and anywhere. In addition, a ubiquitous computing environment makes use of sensors, so that the system can sense user information and environmental information from the real world and then provide to the user personalized services accordingly. Such a feature is often called as ''context awareness''.

Computer Supported Collaborative Learning

The computer supported collaborative learning (CSCL) approach derives from the research field of computer-supported cooperative work (CSCW) that refers to a group of people working together at a common working environment, favoring group interaction with the support of computational tools (Collazos, 2003).

Johnson et al. (1991) define collaborative learning as: the "institutional use of small groups in which students work together with the aim of maximizing their learning and that of their mates", identifying five essential components: Positive interdependence, interaction, individual responsibilities, personal, and group abilities. The positive interdependence component as defined by Collazos et al. (2008) is at the heart of collaborative activities. It is important to establish, that it is not enough to get the group to work in a cohesive way to reach positive interdependence. The positive interdependence is the reason by which the group has to collaborate, and in this way the group work becomes a collaborative work.

In collaborative learning, the application of learning strategies is necessary, these are defined as a set of activities, techniques and means that are accordingly planned to the target population needs, the goals they pursue, and the nature of the field domain and courses. Also, learning strategies can be defined as procedures and resources, used by a teaching agent in order to encourage significant learning in students.

Such strategies must implement suitable activities to improve the teaching/learning process, of both the students individually and as a group, thus achieving a better performance in order to reach the proposed goals. This process favors interaction between individuals, because the strategies use methods for performing various activities that can be linked to diverse participants' profiles. These profiles can be obtained through tests, activity monitoring, and other techniques.

RELATED WORKS

A context-aware u-learning environment was developed by Hwang et al. (2009) for guiding inexperienced researchers to practice single-crystal X-ray diffraction operations. The application domain of this research corresponds to science experiments and thus when a student enters a lab or stands in front of an instrument, the sensors are able to detect the location of the student and transfer the information to the server. By analyzing the real time environmental/personal contexts, the profile and the on-line portfolio of individual students, the learning system is capable of guiding the students to learn in the real world by showing them the relevant information in a timely fashion, such as the operating procedure for single-crystal X-ray device, the need-to-know rules for working in the lab, and emergency handling procedures. Experimental results showed that the benefits of applying the context-aware u-learning approach to science experiments can be expected, including the provision of more opportunities for practicing and the saving of manpower in assisting and monitoring the learners. Also this innovative system can be applied to complex science experiments, such as physics, chemistry or biotechnology experiments, for graduate and PhD students in colleges, or research workers in research institutes.

Wang & Wu (2011) applied context aware technology and recommendation algorithms to develop a u-learning system to help lifelong learning learners realize personalized learning goals in a context aware manner and improve the learner's learning effectiveness. In fact, they established that when integrating the relevant information technology to develop a u-learning environment, it is necessary to consider the personalization requirements of the learner to ensure that the technology achieves its intended result. The Sharable Content Object Reference Model (SCORM) platform was used as the basis and integrated with Radio Frequency Identification (RFID) technology to develop an adaptive ubiquitous learning system. Collaborative Filtering (CF) and an association rules mining model was used to develop an adaptive smart ubiquitous learning system. Adaptive learning materials are recommended to lifelong learning learners using this association rules mining model in order to improve the learning motivation and effectiveness of lifelong learning learners. Finally, the adaptive ubiquitous learning system developed in this study offers the following features: (1) Context awareness, (2) Standardized courseware, (3) Personal learning management, and (4) Adaptive course recommendation.

Zervas et al. (2011) established that in order to achieve personalized and ubiquitous learning, those tools showing characteristics of context-aware adaptive learning designs (authoring tools) and context-aware adaptive delivery of learning activities (run-time tools) should follow some design requirements at both the learning design and mobile delivery process. To attain learning design purposes, for instance, the user should be able to: (1) define appropriate content adaptation rules according to the different values of the mobile context characteristics, (2) define context-aware content adaptation rules for each individual learning activity that a learning design incorporates (3) create profiles of content adaptation rules (for certain values of mobile context characteristics), which can be used during the authoring process of a new learning design, (4) graphically design learning designs based on the interconnection of user defined learning activities, among others. Concerning mobile delivery process, for instance, the tool should: (1) be able to automatically detect contextual information such as, place, time, and in some cases physical conditions according to the user situation and it should be able also to let the user input contextual information that it is not possible to be detected automatically, (2) be client-side, so it can be installed to the mobile device and no internet connection should be required during the execution of learning activities, (3) be able to handle the adaptation rules of the delivered learning design and match them with the values of contextual information automatically detected or provided by the user, so as to enable the content adaptation mechanism and deliver adapted educational resources according to the type of user's mobile device, among others.

Chen & Huang (2012) developed a context-aware ubiquitous learning system called CAULS based on radio-frequency identification (RFID), wireless network, embedded handheld device, and database technologies to detect and examine real-world learning behaviors of students in a u-museum in Taiwan. A case study of an aboriginal education course was conducted in classrooms including elementary school teachers and students. The authors designed and used a questionnaire based on the Unified Theory of Acceptance and Use of Technology (UTAUT) theory to measure the willingness for adoption or usage of the proposed system. Moreover, this study also designed learning materials through context-aware interfaces, and subsequently provided personalized learning support for each learner. The experimental results demonstrated that this innovative approach can enhance their learning intention. Furthermore, the results of a posttest survey revealed that most students' testing scores improved significantly, further indicating the effectiveness of the CAULS.

Huang et al. (2011) proposed a meaningful learning-based evaluation method for ubiquitous learning. The method proposed evaluates u-learning along both macro and micro aspects, and in an effort to make u-learning more sustainable. By employing a case study, authors demonstrate the feasibility of the approach by showing the advantages and disadvantages that are common to both u-learning and meaningful learning. Meaningful learning is defined by authors as the ultimate learning status for a learner, regardless of the learning environment. However, both u-learning and meaningful learning must emphasize the authentic and active of the learning activity. The evaluation model used in the method proposed is composed of three levels: the first entails the main goal (i.e. the evaluation of the meaningful and u-learning system), the second entails five dimensions as follows: active, authentic, constructive, cooperative, and personalized, and third entails ten criteria as follows: urgency of learning need, initiative of knowledge acquisition, situation of instructional activity, context awareness, constructivist learning, self-regulated learning, interactivity of learning process, learning community, adaptive learning, personalization service. Finally, they also provide suggestions for instructors and designers so that they can promote the quality of u-learning.

UBIQUITOUS MULTI-AGENT CONTEXT-AWARE MODEL PROPOSED

The model proposed integrate ubiquitous computing-oriented with pedagogical agents in order to build a student-centered context-aware learning system that offers several functionalities as follows:

- Context-Aware Learning Planning.
- Personalized Course Evaluation.
- Selection of Learning Objects According to Student's Profile.
- Search of Learning Objects in Repository Federations.
- Search of Thematic Learning Assistants.
- Access and Management of Current Context-Aware Collaborative Group Activities.

Each of these functionalities are developed through computing modules which interacts among them in order to offer pedagogical personalized services to students based on their profile. For doing so, our u-MAS interacts with two other e-learning MAS systems. The first one is called BROA (Spanish acronym for Learning Object Search, Retrieval & Recommender System) that corresponds to a multi-agent system for searching, retrieving, recommendation and evaluation of learning objects (LO), based on student's profile (Rodríguez et al, 2012). The second pedagogical MAS is called CIA (Spanish acronym for Adaptive and Intelligent Virtual Course Development System) that is an Adaptive and Intelligent Web-Based Educational MAS for developing virtual courses based on learning planning techniques (Moreno et al, 2009).

Development Methodology

There are different kinds of methodologies for modeling multi-agent systems, such as GAIA (Wooldridge et al, 1999) that is one of the first methodologies which is specifically tailored to the analysis and design of agent-based systems. Its main purpose is to provide the designers with a modeling framework and several associated techniques to design agent-oriented systems. GAIA separates the process of designing software into two different stages: analysis and design. Analysis involves building the conceptual models of the target system, whereas the design stage transforms those abstract constructs to concrete entities which have direct mapping to implementation code. The main key concepts of GAIA are the following: roles, which are associated with responsibilities, permissions, activities, and protocols.

Another well-known MAS design methodology is MAS-CommonKADS proposed by Iglesias in his computer science doctoral thesis (Iglesias, 1998) which integrates knowledge and software engineering along with object-oriented protocols. This methodology was developed through the construction of seven models as follows: Agent, Task, Expertise, Communication, Coordination, Organization, and Design.

An integration of both methodologies was used by us in order to model the educational u-MAS. The following is a brief description of each of these models:

- **Role Model (GAIA):** Allows the system designer to identify the expected functions of each of the entities that composes the system. It is necessary to define the goals, responsibilities, capabilities, and permissions for each role.

- **Service Model (GAIA):** Services are coherent blocks of activities undertaken to implement a role. This model identifies all the services associated with each of the roles, its inputs, outputs, pre-conditions, and post-conditions.

- **Agent Model (GAIA and MAS-CommonKADS):** Describes the character-

istics of each agent, specifying name, kind of agent, role, description, skills, services, activities, and goals. In addition, for each of the goals following issues must be specified: input and output parameters, completion condition, successfully condition, and description. According to the GAIA methodology an agent can play several roles as shown in Figure 2, thus, a changing role diagram must be used in this case.

- **Task Model (MAS-CommonKADS):** This model describes all the tasks that agents can perform along with the objectives of each task, its decomposition, procedures, and troubleshooting methods to solve each objective. Figure 3 shows the educational u-MAS's task diagram.

- **Expertise Model (MAS CommonKADS):** Describes the ontologies (knowledge and its relationships) that agents need to achieve their objectives. Figure 3 shows an example of Ontological Model for LOs.

- **Communication Model (MAS-CommonKADS):** Describes main interactions among humans and software agents along with human factors involved for the development of these interfaces, (see Figure 4).

- **Coordination Model (MAS-CommonKADS):** Dynamic relationships among software agents are expressed

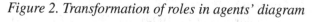

Figure 2. Transformation of roles in agents' diagram

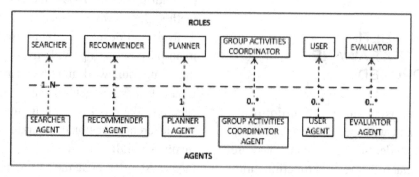

Figure 3. Educational u-MAS's task diagram

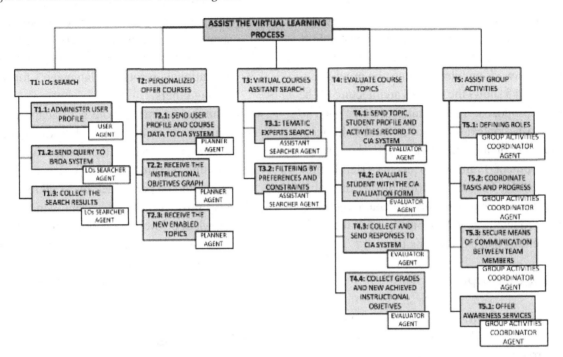

Figure 4. Communication Model

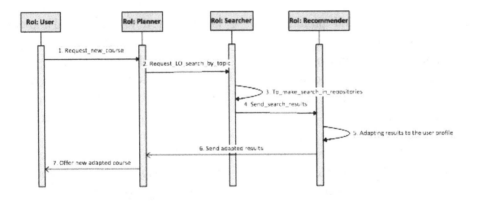

through this model. For doing so, all the conversations among agents must be described: interactions, protocols, and capabilities required. Figure 5 shows the u-MAS's sequence diagram that specifies main interactions among agents.

- **Organization Model (MAS-CommonKADS):** This model aims to de-

scribe the human organization in which the multi-agent system is involved along with the software agent organization structure.

System Architecture

The design phase of MAS-CommonKADS methodology takes as input all the models got from the analysis phase (i.e. role, service, agent, task, expertise, communication, among others) and transforms their specifications for implementation. In addition, the architecture of each agent and the global network architecture must be provided.

Figure 5 shows the u-MAS architecture of the model proposed. This architecture was used to develop the context-aware educational multi-agent system, implemented using JADE (Java Agent Development Framework) agents (Bellifemine et al, 2005). The next Section further describes each of the agents of the student-centered context-aware educational u-MAS along with the main interactions that exist among them.

Agent Description

- **User Agent:** This agent communicates directly with the human user and whose role is representing him within the system along with communications with other agents (Recommender and Planner). Also, the user agent manages the user's profile, enabling the creation and modification of profile's characteristics and preferences. Most of the system's functional scenarios start and finish their execution with this agent whose role is to send requirements and receive their corresponding answers.

- **Recommender Agent:** This is a kind of deliberative agent whose main role is to filter search results coming from searcher agent based on student's profile. In addition, this agent offers to students as a service support the possibility of performing searches of teaching/learning assistants for specific topics of a virtual course that have more knowledge and know-how on certain topics. Those learning assistants can give to the students with advice or answers questions on a particular sub-items or learning activities. This functionality is available from students' mobile devices.

- **Searcher Agent:** This is a reactive kind of agent that is in charge of performing searches of Learning Objects (LO) based on some characteristics such as LO name, educational resource, language, format, among others.

- **Planner Agent:** Its role is to adapt learning plans to students in such a way that the student be guided by the system through a teaching-learning process in the same way as it could be performed by a real teacher.

- **Evaluator Agent:** This agent manages the knowledge level evaluation performed by the system to the learner taking into consideration the topics already learned and the LG attained by the student.

Platform Design

The main framework tools used for the implementation and validation of the u-MAS prototype are described as follows: JADE (Java Agent Development Framework) offers a set of resources to facilitate the development and implementation of multi-agent computational environments which can be used also for building e-learning virtual environments (Bellifemine et al, 2005). For integrating mobile devices, we have chosen JADE-LEAP (http://jade.tilab.com/), a FIPA compliant agent platform.

Protégé is a free, open source ontology editor and knowledge-based framework. The Protégé platform supports two main ways of modeling ontologies via the Protégé-Frames and Protégé-OWL editors. Protegé is based on Java (http://protege.stanford.edu/). ZK is a framework for AJAX web applications developed in Java that allows a user to interface for web applications without using JavaScript (http://www.zkoss.org/product/zk). ZK provides graphical interfaces to communicate with the MAS by means of interface's events.

Figure 5. Context-aware educational u-MAS Architecture

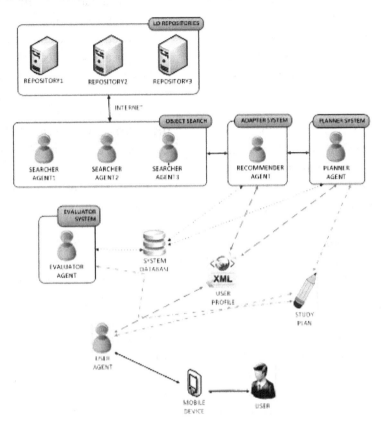

The reasoning mechanism of u-MAS's agent architecture was developed in JAVA, using JDOM for handling XML user's profiles. The local repository manager is stored in the PostgreSQL database that is characterized to be stable, with high performance, and great flexibility. The agent creation and management is made by using JADE platform using FIPA-ACL performatives. The ontology creation was performed by using Protégé and finally, the Web integration was made based on the ZK framework.

SOLUTIONS BASED ON SYSTEM FUNCTIONALITIES

The educational u-MAS mainly offers five functionalities that promote personal learning management, structured and standardized virtual courseware, context awareness solutions, adaptive course recommendations. These functionalities will be further described afterwards.

Functionality 1: The Virtual Course Context-Aware Learning Planning

In order to develop the context-aware planning strategy using a personal learning management approach the following stages should be carried out:

- Teachers must structure and standardize their virtual courses according to the elements specified within the domain model (i.e. Modules, Topics, Learning Goals (LG), Activities, Learning Objects (LO)). When the teacher has defined a course in

247

this way it will be a graph structure that makes relationships between Topics, LG and activities. It is important to remark that there must exist at least one LG without pre-requirements in order that the system can plan the virtual course's initial activities.

- When a student enters to the teacher's virtual course, through his/her mobile device, the system using the pre-requirements must verify which of LGs the student can study in such a way that a listing of topics will be generated to be selected by the student.

- The system thus generates an adapted learning plan tailored to the student's knowledge level and to her/his preferences. This learning plan is formed by one or several LGs that the student can attain carrying out one or several activities.

- The system, based on the specific student profile, guides him/her through the learning plan's activities taking into consideration as context-aware parameter the knowledge level situation (i.e. LGs attained). In addition, it is important to note that each activity can be made by the student using one or several LO. The selection of LO is needed to be done taking into account the student's learning styles previously matched with the metadata that describe them.

- When the student has performed all the activities associated to the learning plan, it is considered necessary to verify if the student actually learned the concepts related to the selected topics, hence a knowledge evaluation is launched by the system for learning validation purposes. The evaluation process will be further described in the next Section.

- The system is in charge of updating the student's knowledge level according to the achieved results (LGs attained by the student) based on the previously learning

plan evaluation. It is important to underline that once the student's knowledge level is updated consequently new virtual course's topics are activated to be pursued and sent to the student's mobile device.

Functionality 2: The Virtual Course Evaluation Process

The virtual course evaluation process is activated by a student using his/her mobile device when a session of the functionality 1 (i.e. virtual course context-aware learning planning) has already been concluded. The evaluation process is performed by means of the selection of questions associated with each of the learning activities that have been made for each of the modules composing the course. In addition, the items that will be part of the evaluation test are looked for in the bank of questions, which covers all the topics of the virtual course. For each topic there are questions of varying levels of difficulty and different kind of presentation (Salcedo et al., 2004).

Concerning the structure of the evaluation questions, as shown in Figure 6, for each question there are one or more answers and each answer has a validity of 1 if it is correct and 0 if not. Questions besides have associated LG, they have respective basic concepts that corresponds to concepts or smallest units of knowledge that are evaluated. This relations because every test must cover most of the content limited by an LG and

Figure 6. Answer-question relationship

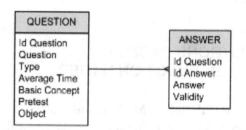

there are not repeated questions about the same concept (Jimenez et al., 2008).

Another parameter of the question is the response time or average time the student takes for answering the question associated to the studied topic. This measure is related largely to the kind of question which may be: MCMA (Multiple Choice - Multiple Answer), MCSA (Multiple Choice - Single Answer), TF (True or False), etc. Likewise, the learning style for each question is specified as described above and a pre-test attribute of binary type, which indicates whether the question is of evaluation (pretest = 0) or if it is pre-test (pretest = 1). These "pretest" questions are created so that the student reinforces the knowledge gained in conducting the activities proposed to achieve the goal, therefore, they are formulated when the content associated to each goal has been studied and covered by the student.

Finally, the attribute with object of binary type states when the question has associated an LO (Learning Object) to facilitate the understanding of the question by the student through images, sounds, etc. Therefore it is defined with object = 1 when there is the respective LO and with object = 0 when there is only the text of the question. This approach selects the questions that most resemble the preferences of each student. For this purpose the values assigned to each dimension of the student are compared with the levels of association of each possible question and the one that shows less difference is the option to be chosen.

When a student has finished reviewing all the activities that were programmed for him in the learning plan, a personalized evaluation is generated taking into account the following steps:

- A set of questions that are related to the activities that are planned is retrieved from the database.
- A filter on the questions, verifying which of these have not already been made to the student.

- The system retrieves the learning style of the student, in order to perform another filter on the set of questions.
- From the remaining set of questions, a question of each basic concept concerning the learning activity is selected.
- An evaluation test is generated with the selected questions form.
- The evaluation is presented to the student and his/her answers are retrieved.

When the student sends the answers of the evaluation test, through his/her mobile device, a request to the system is performed and immediately the following actions are carried out:

- The correct answer for each of the evaluation questions is retrieved from the database.
- The system checks if the answer given by the student agrees with the correct answer of the question. In case when the response is correct the evaluation is stored as correct, otherwise it is stored as incorrect.
- An assessment is performed per question type.
- A total assessment is performed per LG.
- When a LG is not approved, a re-planning of learning activities is made for all the lost LGs.
- The answers of the evaluation test are sent to the student.

It is important to highlight that personalized evaluations are carried through generated tests, presented to the student through his/her mobile device and qualified by the evaluator agent. For the construction of the evaluation question Bank it is necessary that the entire contents of the virtual course be fully structured and defined, taking into consideration that the generated questions emerge from there.

Functionality 3: The Selection Of Los According To Student's Preferences And Limitations

The LOs resulting from the search are recommended based on the student's style of learning and other users' assessments. The Web-based LO search is performed over local and remote repositories, or by using LO repository federations through metadata descriptive LOs. Considering that LORs are distributed, they are different in design and structure, and hence they do not handle the same metadata standards. In our model each agent knows how LOs are stored and how each LO can be searched, accessed, and retrieved. The searcher agent takes care of readdressing queries that the user makes to both the local and the remote repositories. This agent knows the repositories associated with the system and the information that each of them manages. In addition, it can access the user agent's profile to know what characteristics are useful for making a recommendation (learning style, educational level, language preference, among others). This agent recognizes how LOs are stored inside the repositories, under what standard and type of metadata that manages. Also knows the type of search that can be performed within the repository and how to recover a particular LO stored.

Functionality 4: The Search Of Thematic Learning Assistants

Our u-learning MAS offers to students as a service support the possibility of performing searches of learning assistants for virtual courses who have more knowledge and know-how and thus were assigned to help others on certain topics. Those learning assistants can give to the students with advice or answers questions on a particular sub-items or learning activities. This functionality activated anywhere and anytime by students is available through PC servers or their mobile devices as shown in Figure 7.

Functionality 5: The Context-Aware Access Of Current Collaborative Learning Activities Involved

Our virtual courses have within their structure group learning activities as support to the CSCL that are handled by intelligent agents. Thus, the system provides the collaborative learning activities to be performed, the learning/work teams on which a specific student participates, the current state of the group activity, and the schedule of collaborative activities based on a specific collaborative learning context, for a given course and a given student. For each learning activity

Figure 7. U-MAS web based interfaces

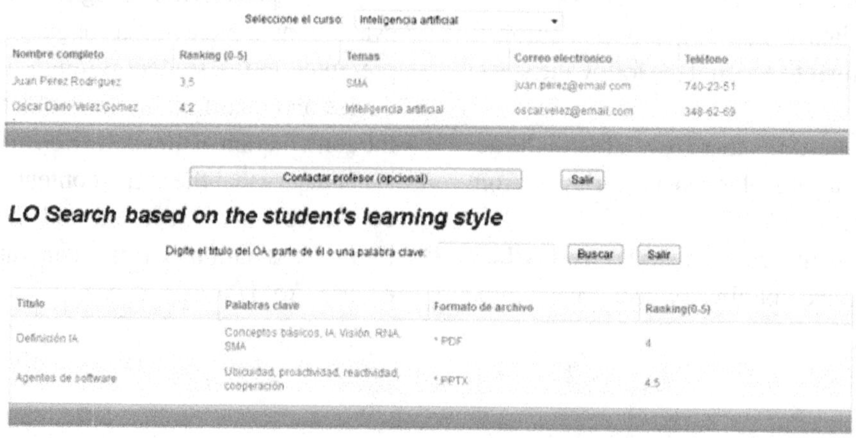

the system shows the subject to be treated, the contents to be used, the members of the formed team, and the student's role. In addition, the system provides forums and chats that can be accessed from student's mobile device.

It is important to highlight that the system provides a set of group awareness services being messages that are triggered and sent to student's mobile device when any activity's uptime will soon expire, or when any commitment established by the student concerning the team's work has failed.

FUTURE RESEARCH DIRECTIONS

Although some advances have already been attained mainly due to the growth of mobile technologies and adaptive virtual educational environments, future research directions concern the enhancement of following features: (1) ubiquitous personalized learning and context awareness, (2) structured and standardized virtual courseware, (3) personal and adaptive learning management, and (4) adaptive and personalized course evaluation and recommendation.

In fact, the system should adaptively consider as much as possible all the characteristics on student´s profile that affect his/her learning process such as: learning styles (e.g. active, reflexive, sensorial, intuitive, visual, verbal, sequential, global), psychology profile (e.g. dominant brain hemisphere), physiology profile (hearing, vision, etc.) and historical issues (activities developed, study times), academic achievements (LG approved) and group work performance. In addition, the system should also consider technological contextual characteristics such as access device, network state, operating system, among other, but also individual and collaborative group learning contextual characteristics. Such contextual characteristics allow the system not only to provide adaptive support or guidance but also immediate learning assistance through student's mobile device, enhancing in this way, his/her teaching-learning process.

CONCLUSION

This chapter presented the advantages brought by the integration of ubiquitous computing-oriented along with distributed artificial intelligence (DAI) techniques in order to build student-centered context-aware learning systems. Based on this model a U-learning Multi-Agent Context-Aware System was developed that offers functionalities as follows: the context-aware learning planning, the course evaluation process, the selection of learning objects according to student's profile, the search of learning objects in repository federations, the search of thematic learning assistants, and the access of current context-aware group activities involved.

In fact, the u-MAS approach was successfully used to integrate the strategies of context-aware learning planning, personalized LO selection, thematic learning assistants search, current collaborative activities access, and to support the adaptive virtual course construction in a modular, structured, distributed, deliberative, proactive, and cooperative way.

ACKNOWLEDGMENT

The research work presented in this chapter was partially funded by COLCIENCIAS through research project entitled: "ROAC Creación de un modelo para la Federación de OA en Colombia que permita su integración a confederaciones internacionales" Universidad Nacional de Colombia, with code 1119-521-29361 and also by project entitled "Mejoramiento de la capacidad académica, visibilidad, contacto e interacción con la comunidad nacional e internacional del grupo de investigación en inteligencia artificial de la Universidad Nacional de Colombia – Convocatoria Nacional 2011 - 2012 - Modalidad 2".with QUIPU code 202010010368.

REFERENCES

Arias, F. (2010). *Multi-agent adaptive model for adaptive virtual courses planning and LO selection*. (MSc Dissertation).

Bellifemine, F., Rimessa, G., Trucco, T., & Caire, G. (2005). *JADE (Java agent development framework) programmer's guide*.

Betancur, D., Moreno, J., & Ovalle, D. (2009). Modelo para la recomendación y recuperación de objetos de aprendizaje en entornos virtuales de enseñanza/aprendizaje. *Revista Avances en Sistemas e Informática, 6*(1), 45–56.

Brusilovsky, P., Karagia-Nnidis, C., & Sampson, D. (2004). Layered evaluation of adaptive learning systems, In *Proceedings of the International Joint Conf. on Engineering Education and Lifelong Learning*, (Vol. 14, pp. 402–421). IEEE.

Casali, A., Gerling, V., Deco, C., & Bender, C. (2011). Sistema inteligente para la recomendación de objetos de aprendizaje. *Revista Generación Digital, 9*(1), 88–95.

Chen, C., & Huang, T. (2012). Learning in a u-museum: Developing a context-aware ubiquitous learning environment. *Computers & Education Journal, 59*, 873–883. doi:10.1016/j.compedu.2012.04.003.

Collazos, C. (2003). *Una metodología para el apoyo computacional de la evaluación y monitoreo en ambientes de aprendizaje cooperativo. (Tesis doctoral)*. Santiago, Chile: Universidad de Chile.

Collazos, C., Alvira, J., Martínez, D., Jiménez, J., Cobos, R., & Moreno, J. (2008). Evaluando y monitoreando actividades colaborativas en dispositivos móviles. *Revista Avances en Sistemas e Informática, 5*(1), 82–93.

Duque, N. (2006). *Adaptive virtual course model using an intelligent planning environment*. (MSc Dissertation).

Duque, N. (2009). *Modelo adaptativo multi-agente para la planificación y ejecución de cursos virtuales personalizados. (Tesis Doctoral)*. Bogota, Colombia: Universidad Nacional de Colombia.

Hwang, G., Yang, T., Tsai, C., & Yang, S. (2009). A context-aware ubiquitous learning environment for conducting complex science experiments. *Computers & Education Journal, 53*, 402–413. doi:10.1016/j.compedu.2009.02.016.

Huang, Y., Chiu, P., Liu, T., & Chen, T. (2011). The design and implementation of a meaningful learning-based evaluation method for ubiquitous learning. *Computers & Education Journal, 57*, 2291–2302. doi:10.1016/j.compedu.2011.05.023.

Iglesias, C. (1998). *Definición de una metodología para el desarrollo de sistemas multiagentes*. Madrid, Spain: Universidad Politécnica de Madrid.

Jennings, N. R. (2000). On agent-based software engineering. *Artificial Intelligence, 117*(2), 277–296. doi:10.1016/S0004-3702(99)00107-1.

Johnson, D. W., Johnson, R. T., & Smith, K. A. (1991). ASHE-ERIC Higher Education Report: Vol. 4. *Cooperative learning: Increasing college faculty instructional productivity*. Washington, DC: George Washington University.

Jiménez, M., Ovalle, D., & Jiménez, J. (2008). Evaluación en línea para cursos tutoriales inteligentes adaptativos usando el modelo de sistemas multi-agente. *Revista Avances en Sistemas e Informática, 5*(1), 20–29.

Moreno, J., Ovalle, D., & Jimenez, J. (2009). CIA: Framework for the creation and management of adaptive intelligent courses. In *Proceedings of 9th World Conference on Computers in Education – WCCE*. Bento Gonçales, Brazil: WCCE.

Ovalle, D., Arias, F., & Moreno, J. (2011). Student-centered multi-agent model for adaptive virtual courses development and learning object selection (2011). In *Proceedings of the IADIS International Conference on Cognition and Exploratory Learning in Digital Age* (CELDA 2011) (pp. 123–130). Rio de Janeiro, Brazil: CELDA.

Ouyang, Y., & Zhu, M. (2008). eLORM: Learning object relationship mining-based repository. *Online Information Review*, *32*(2), 254–265. doi:10.1108/14684520810879863.

Prieta, F. D., & Gil, A. (2010). A multi-agent system that searches for learning objects in heterogeneous repositories. In *Proceedings of Advances in Intelligent and Soft Computing* (pp. 355–362). IEEE. doi:10.1007/978-3-642-12433-4_42.

Salcedo, P., Rojas, M., Manríquez, G., & Gatica, Y. (2004). Curso de UML multiplataforma adaptativo basado en la teoría de respuesta al ítem. *Revista Ingeniería Informática, 10*.

Rodríguez, P., Tabares, V., Duque, N., Ovalle, D., & Vicari, R. (2012). *Multi-agent model for searching, recovering, recommendation and evaluation of learning objects from repository federations*. Paper presented at the 13th Ibero-American Conference on Artificial Intelligence. Cartagena, Colombia.

Van de Sompel, H., & Chute, R. (2008). The aDORe federation architecture: Digital repositories at scale. *International Journal (Toronto, Ont.)*, *9*, 83–100.

Wang, S., & Wu, C. (2011). Application of context-aware and personalized recommendation to implement an adaptive ubiquitous learning system. *Expert Systems with Applications*, *38*, 10831–10838. doi:10.1016/j.eswa.2011.02.083.

Weiss, G. (2007). *Multiagent systems: A modern approach to distributed artificial intelligence*. Boston: The MIT Press.

Wooldridge, M., Jennings, N. R., & Kinny, D. (1999). A methodology for agent-oriented analysis and design. In *Proceedings of the Third Annual Conference on Autonomous Agents*. AGENTS.

Zervas, P., Gómez, S., Fabregat, R., & Sampson, D. (2011). Tools for context-aware learning design and mobile delivery. In *Proceedings of the 11th IEEE International Conference on Advanced Learning Technologies*. IEEE.

Chapter 14
A Learning Object Recommendation System:
Affective-Recommender

Adriano Pereira
Universidade Federal de Santa Maria, Brazil

Iara Augustin
Universidade Federal de Santa Maria, Brazil

ABSTRACT

Emotions play a very important role in the learning process. Affective computing studies try to identify users' affective state, as emotion, using affect models and affect detection techniques, in order to improve human-computer interactions, as in a learning environment. The Internet explosion makes a huge volume of information, including learning objects data, available. In this scenario, recommendation systems help users by selecting and suggesting probable interesting items, dealing with large data availability and decision making problems, and customizing users' interaction. In u-learning context, students could learn anywhere and anytime, having different options of data objects available. Since different students have different preferences and learning styles, personalization becomes an important feature in u-learning systems. Considering all this, the authors propose the Affective-Recommender, a learning object recommendation system. In this chapter, they describe the system's requirements and architecture, focusing on affect detection and the recommendation algorithm, an example of use case, and results of system implementation over Moodle LMS.

DOI: 10.4018/978-1-4666-4542-4.ch014

INTRODUCTION

Student's emotions are inserted in learning process and influence it. A student could even quit learning due to negative feelings, as confusion, frustration or anxiety. In order to avoid these situations, teachers and mentors have to be able to identify emotional reactions, in order to change theirs approaches to improve learning processes (Picard, 1997).

Affective Computing researches try to improve human-computer interactions, through systems able to identify user's affective state, providing automatic responses to it. Affective Computing is the computing that is related to, arises from or influences emotions in human users, providing skills to make decisions, due to emotion's importance in our lives (Picard, 1995) (Calvo and d'Mello, 2010).

Personalization is an important feature in e-learning systems (Kerkiri et al., 2007), as well as, in u-learning, due to distinct students' preferences and experiences. In this way, learning process could be customized to each student, based on his/her learning style and preferences, in order to improve this process. It is based on the idea that individual methods help students to learn more quickly and effectively, improving their understanding about a subject (Jones & Jo, 2004).

Recommendation systems help users providing personalized suggestions, selecting the probable most interesting items, making useful huge data volume (Adomavicius & Tuzhilin, 2005). U-learning allows anywhere and anytime learning, aware to user's context. With the data and mobility explosion, recommendation systems could help students, in u-learning scenarios, choosing and suggesting learning objects in order to customize this process. The customization could be based on student's preferences, and helps them on make decision processes. Recommendation systems are used to delivery courses adaptively, selecting and suggesting the probable most interesting learning objects to each student. (Khribi et al., 2009)

In order to improve recommendation processes, users' context could be used, since states variables usually influence their preferences. In this way, context-aware recommendation systems arise, as systems that use users' situation variables in recommendation process (Hussein, 2009). In u-learning, student's affective state could be used as a context variable, due to its importance in cognitive processes. In this way, we propose Affective-Recommender, a learning objects recommendation system, aware to student's affective state, in an u-learning scenario. Through student's affective states use, the system aims to select and to suggest the probable most interesting objects, as a teacher that change his/her class approach, based on student's affective reactions. Besides, recommendation systems provide personalization, in this case, making learning customized to each student.

This chapter is divided into six main sections: besides Introduction, in Background is made a revision about the main topics discussed in this chapter; in Affective-Recommender System the proposed system is detailed, with its components and way of work; in Results and Analysis, a system implementation is explained, with a scenario of use, a use case and related works; finally, in Future Researches Directions the work's next steps are discussed and *Conclusion* ends this chapter.

BACKGROUND

In this section, the main broad topics treated in this work are present. First, it's made a revision about Affective Computing topics, as Affect Detection and affective models, and affective relation to learning. And after, recommendation systems are exposed, including their operation way and classification.

Affective Computing

Picard (1995) defines Affective Computing as the computing that is related to, is arises from or influences emotions in humans, in order to help them, providing ways to make decisions. It is possible due to emotions' importance in perception and cognition fields. Affective Computing has as objective to construct systems able to recognize user's affective state, responding automatically to them, improving human-computer interaction (Calvo & D'Mello, 2010).

Affective computing systems are divided in (i) those that detect users affective state; (ii) systems that express something that users identify as an emotion; and (iii) system that "feels" emotions (Picard, 1997).

Affect Detection and Affect Modeling

In order to use affect information, it's crucial in Affective Computing Systems to detect users' affective state. This detection doesn't need to be exact, but it's important being the closest possible (Calvo & D'Mello, 2010). Picard (1995) tells that it's important look for users' observables functions, that correspond to their affective states, to identify users' affective state.

Emotions could be defined by six perspectives: (i) as expressions, specially facial; (ii) as embodiments, through physiological signals; (iii) as cognitive approaches, relating emotions to events or objects; (iv) as social constructs, using social analysis to detect them; (v) through neuroscience, relating neurological processes to emotions; and (vi) psychological constructs, accepting that there are different emotional theories, each one treating something different (Calvo & D'Mello, 2010).

Calvo and D'Mello (2010) describe six affect detection modalities:

1. **Facial Expressions:** This approach includes the most part of affect detection researches. In this modality, it's analyzed user's facial expression, captured by some video input device, in order to identify variables that indicate some affective characteristic.

2. **Voice:** It's analyzed what is said and how it is, to find emotional patterns.

3. **Body Language and Posture:** It's checked the relation between emotions and human body positions and gestures.

4. **Physiological Signals:** Using sensors, signals related to emotions, as heart-beat, are captured. Emotions are detected through these signals' analysis.

5. **Brain Imaging:** Trough brain images, neurological circuits are mapped and related to affective-states.

6. **Text Analysis:** People express emotions and feelings in their written text. This modality is based on writing language analyzes to find patters related to users emotions expressions.

Besides these modalities, its possible to detect affective states through users' behavioral data, gained from the interaction with devices; or asking the user how does he/she feel, giving him/her a set of variables to choose, from those the state will be identified (Paiva, 2000) (Broekens & Brinkman, 2009).

Affect detection approaches could be divided into *explicit,* when the system asks user to inform how does he/she feel; and *implicit*, when it uses other kind of data analysis to detect affective state (Broekens & Brinkman, 2009).

Affective Computing in U-Learning

Emotions influences learning processes. A student could event quit his/her studies, due to negative feelings, like frustration. Human-computer interactions are enhanced with users' emotions use, specially in learning scenarios. A good teacher should be able to identify users' affect reactions in his/her classes, to change his/her approaches when necessarily, in order to avoid disappointments and other negative feelings (Picard, 1997).

Attention, memory and decision-making process are affected by our emotions. As these three elements are very important in learning, we could say that emotions influence learning processes (O'Regan, 2003). Intelligence and affection are in constant interaction. Affection could interfer intelligence operation, making acceleration or delay in intellectual development (Piaget, 2005).

Recommendation Systems

Recommendation (Recommender) systems helps users to deal with large amounts of data, selecting and suggesting items that user probably will like most (Adomavicius & Tuzhilin, 2005). These tools uses Knowledge Discovery techniques to make personalized recommendations during an interaction (Sarwar et al. 2001). Recommender systems could use users' profile and necessities to help them making decisions (Ricci, 2010).

Recommendation problem could be defined as the necessity to estimate users' rating to items that he/she doesn't rate yet. Then, it's possible to classify these not-rated items, and to suggest the top-rated to user. This rating could be done with heuristics or estimates (Adomavicius & Tuzhilin, 2005).

Recommender systems are classified in (i) content-based, in which recommended items have similar contents to other well-rated items by a specific user; (ii) collaborative-filtering, recommending items well-rated by users classifieds with similar tastes to current user; and (iii) hybrid approach, that combines both methods.

Context-Aware Recommendation Systems

Context-aware recommendation systems use users' situation variables in recommendation process to improve it. It is possible, because user's interest by an item often is related to his/her specific situation, characterized by context information (Hussein, 2009). These systems aim to act automatically, suggesting items aware to user's context. They use as input, besides possible items to be recommended, context information; and return as output the ranked items (Buriano et al., 2006).

Recommendation in U-Learning

In e-learning and u-learning, recommenders systems could be used to select probable most likely learning objects, indicating them to students. Through recommendation techniques, its possible to adapt the course dynamically, selecting and suggesting items. In this way, a customized learning is possible, improving the process (Kerkiri et al., 2007) (Khribi et al., 2009) (Ghauth & Abdullah, 2009).

Affective-Recommender System

In an u-learning scenario, where students could receive information anytime and anywhere, we propose the Affecttive-Recommender: a u-learning system able to identify users affective state, in order to select probable most interesting learning objects, suggesting them to students in an adaptive way. We use emotion as affective state, once it is a state that changes in time, that could be identified through affect detection techniques (Scherer, 2000). To do this, the system need to be able to model and to detect users' affective state, and to construct student's profile. In this section, we expose system requirements, system architecture and a usual workflow.

Requirements

In order to treat an user individually, a system needs to be able to track user's interaction, gathering information to make his/her profile. Besides, the system has to change its content, organizing the informed data according to users tastes (Cazella, et al., 2010).

Thereby, we constructed a list of system requirements, that have to be treated in order to achieve system's goals. The requirements are described below.

- **Modeling User's Affective State:** It's necessarily to have an way to represent student's affective state (emotion). Through an affective model, the system should know and differentiate these users' states.
- **Detect User's Affective State:** The system needs to identify what is the student's affective state in each interact moment, in order to use it in the recommendation process. The detection have to be aligned to the affective model.
- **Use Only Trivial Devices in Detection:** Detection could be made in different ways. In order to avoid need for sensors or other devices, which aren't the same where recommendation is made, the system needs to use only trivial devices in detection.
- **Define the Set of Items to be Recommended:** Affective-Recommender has to know which learning objects are available to be suggested to students. These learning objects are included and managed by teachers.
- **Construct Students' Profile:** Analyzing student's interaction, their profile need to be constructed to be used in the recommendation process.
- **Recommend Items:** The system has to be able to select and suggest probable most interesting learning objects to student, based on his/her affective state and preferences.

To attain these requirements, we propos a system architecture, exposed as follow.

SYSTEM ARCHITECTURE

The system architecture consists in four components, that interact together:

1. Affective Detector.
2. Recommender.
3. Application.
4. Database.

Figure 1 illustrates the architecture and its interaction. Each component is detailed in sequence.

Affective Detector

In order to model users affective state, Mehrabian (1980) have proposed an approach, classified as multidimensional by Scherer (2000), defining emotions through three dimensions: Pleasure (valence), Arousal and Dominance (PAD). The Pleasure dimension measures "how good" the emotion is. The Arousal, on the other hand, informs "how excited" is the feeling. Lastly, Dominance refers to "user's control" in an emotion. To each dimension, its defined a continuous value, from -1 to 1 (Bales, 2001) (Bradley & Lang, 1994) (Gebhard, 2005). In PAD terms, emotions arises as answers to events, and, in this way, we could determine when it's necessarily to detect users' affective state: whenever there is a context switch,

Figure 1. System architecture

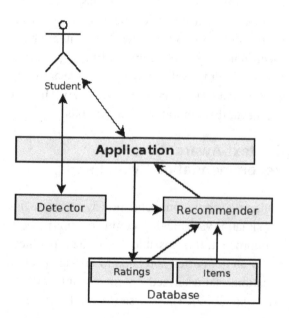

i. e., when the student receive a stimulus from something else.

The affective detector uses Pleasure, Arousal and Dimension model to determine students' affective state. In order to know each dimension value, Lang (1980) have proposed the Self-Assessment Manikin instrument (SAM). Through this tool, users could inform how do them feel, in PAD dimensions. SAM works giving to user three picture scales, one to each dimension: pleasure scales ranges from a happy, smiling picture, to an unhappy; arousal, from an excited, "exploded" wide eyed picture, to a sleepy; finally, dominance scale shows since a large picture, "in control", to a very small. The user have to choose, to each dimension, one picture, or the point between two of them, informing how does he/she feel.

So, in u-learning, its possible to ask the student to inform his/her state, through SAM tool, detecting it in PAD model. In this way, the third requirement is satisfied, once this detection could be done with traditional devices. Through context information analyzes, we could know when the student is affected by some stimulus, that construct an emotion, knowing, in this way, when it is necessary make a detection. The first, second and third system requirements are checked with the affective detector.

Using PAD model, affective states are continuous in the three dimensional space. A discrete set could be gained, considering categories in the continuous space. In our case, it was considered only the valence to each dimension, i.e., the positive or negative sign. In this way, it was considered a space of 8 affective states. Based on Broekens and Brinkman (2009), eight affective states were named, as in the Table 1.

Recommender

In order to create student profile, as expected by fifth system requirement, it's necessarily to get their preferences to each recommended item. As we are using a cognitive approach to model affec-

tive states, which considers emotions are reactions to events, Affective-Recommender treats student preference to an item as the user's reaction to it. In other words, we assume that accessing an item item will provoke some affective change. Then, we detect student affective state after this access, to use the PAD values as student reaction, constructing students' profile.

Collaborative-filtering recommendation techniques try to estimate users' preference to an item based on the preferences of other users with similar tastes (Adomavicius and Tuzhilin, 2005). A two dimensions matrix $U \times I$, that relates Users and Items, is used to represent the preferences to items, in a numeric way. The elements are null in the positions which users' hadn't rate the items (Sarwar et al., 2001). It was used collaborative-filtering technique, instead of based on content, because we believe that suggesting similar content item won't cause different reactions in students.

In order to estimate user's preference to an item not rated yet, usually it is used the aggregated value of similar users' ratings, calculated as follows:

$$r\left(c,s\right) = \sum_{c'=c1}^{cn} sim\left(c,c'\right) \times r\left(c',s\right)$$

In the formula, c refers to current user; s is the interested item; $r(c, s)$ is the preference of user c to item s; $c' \in C$, are the other users' set; $sim(c, c')$ is the similarity between c and c' users; and finally, $r\left(c',s\right)$ is the rating of c' user to s item. The similarity often is calculated based on the cosine of the angles between two vectors, constructed in a m-dimensional space of m items, which each dimension is an available item (Adomavicius and Tuzhilin, 2005). In this way, as closer as the vectors, bigger will be the similarity.

Table 1. Affective-States labels

Affective-State	Pleasure	Arousal	Dominance
Happy	1	1	1
Afraid	-1	1	-1
Surprised	1	1	-1
Sad	-1	-1	-1
Angry	-1	1	1
Relaxed	1	-1	-1
Content	1	-1	1
Frustrated	-1	-1	1

$$sim\left(c, c'\right) = \cos\left(x, y\right) = \frac{\overline{x} \cdot \overline{y}}{|x| \times |y|}$$

$$sim\left(c, c', e\right) = \sum_{s'=s_1}^{sn} \cos(r(c, s', e), r(c', s', e))$$

In order to treat context, the two dimensional matrix (U x I) become a three dimensional, considering the context variables: *U x I x C*. It's possible to use traditional recommendation algorithms, in a context-aware scenario, through matrix reduction techniques, from U x I x C to U x I, selecting only the preferences in determined context (Adomavicius et al., 2005).

In our architecture, the recommender is responsible to select an to suggest learning objects to users, based on their current affective state, as expected by the sixth system requirement. In this way, the matrix relates User, Items and Affective-State. To treat it, we choose the matrix reduction approach, with collaborative-filtering recommendation technique. In this way, a subset of the three dimensional matrix is used, composed only by the ratings of an interested user's affective state.

To estimate user's preference, the above sum is used. As the rating is composed by three values, P, A and D, a similarity calculus was defined: it is calculated using the sum of the cosines between the three-dimensional vectors, constructed by the P, A, D, values of two users' ratings to each rated item, as the following formula:

In that, c and c' are two students; e is the current affective state; sim(c,c',e) is similarity between c and c', in the e affective state; and r(c,s,e) and r(c',s',e) are the PAD vectors, about the reaction of the users c and c' to the item, being in the e state.

Since our approach treats the student's reaction to an item, i.e., the affective state measured after the access, as the rating, it's necessarily to reduce the three PAD values in one, to be used in the sum. The recommender aims to carry student's to more positive – better – states, i.e., states which P, A and D values are positives. To do this, it was defined that student's rating to one learning object is reduced through the formula below:

$$r\left(c, s, e\right) = 2 \times P + A + D$$

In this case, it was considered that Pleasure dimension is heavier than Arousal and Dominance, once it is related to emotion's valence, i.e., how *good* or *bad* is an emotion. So, the recommender is able to select the probable most interesting learning objects, as the items that probably will leave student to a better affective state, based on student's profile, relating others with similar tastes and their reactions to each item. Then, it could suggest these items, in an ordered way, to student.

Application

The application is the kernel of system's architecture. The student interacts directly with the application, using different devices, in an ubiquitous space. In e-learning and, analogously, in u-learning, a Learning Management System (LMS) is used to support learning in an educational environment (Cheng, Safont, Basu, 2010). Both teacher and student use the LMS to put and receive resources, as learning objects, and activities, as evaluations. In Affective-Recommender, the application is a kind of LMS, responsible to monitor users' interaction, triggering other components.

The application must have access to context information. When it's detected a modification in these variables, that could change student's affective state, application calls the detector, as expected in our cognitive model approach. Then, application calls the recommender, in order to get the probably most interesting learning objects, to suggest to student, based on his/her detected affective state. Having the items, the application could suggest them to student and, after his/her accesses a suggested learning object, it could call detector once more, in order to get student's reaction to that item.

In a u-LMS, students could access their courses from different kinds of devices, in different moments and places. The application is the front-end to student. Detecting their affective state, getting and suggesting probable most interesting learning objects, the learning could be personalized to each student, improving this process.

Database

It is necessarily to store data in Affective-Recommender. To do that, we have a database in the architecture, where it is kept (i) users ratings to items, being in each affective state, as expected by U x I x AS matrix; and (ii) items available to be recommended to students.

The Database uses a relational structure to store this data. It is composed by two tables: preferences and items. The preferences table is responsible to store the students ratings, having records composed by (i) student identifier, (ii) learning object identifier, (iii) affective state identifier, and (iv) student's reaction, expressed in PAD values. On the other hand, items table stores the available learning objects to be suggested to students.

Recommender uses both database tables to select items. Through preferences table, student profile is constructed, by application, that manages user interaction and reactions. Items table fills the fourth system requirement, storing the set of available items.

Student Interaction Workflow

A simple student interaction's example in Affective-Recommender starts with the student-LMS interaction. In an ubiquitous environment, application could know that a student is available to receive a recommendation. Each change of context, application triggers detector, in order to identify student's affective state. Then, recommender is fired, also by application, to select the probable most interesting learning objects to current student, with that detected affective state. These items are suggested to student, through application interface. Then, he/she should choose one learning object. After he/she accesses the object, a new detection is made, to check the his/her rating, based on the reaction - change of affective state. Finally, this reaction is stored in database, and the flow could restart.

RESULTS AND ANALYSIS

This section shows work's results, with an implementation of Affective-Recommender system and a scenario of user, and analyzes related works, as follow.

Use Case

In order to validate our approach, Affective-Recommender system was implemented over Moodle platform. Plus, this implementation was used in three classes of undergraduate courses, from Federal University of Santa Maria, in Brazil, in order to check (i) students' impressions about informing how they feel; (ii) if they perceive relations between emotions and education; and (iii) what they think about receive recommendations in this scenario. After an initial period of use, we've applied a questionnaire to students, analyzing their answers, also using in this process data access – related to affect detection. In this section, first we describe the system implementation, and after it use as support tool in these classes.

Affective-Recommender: Over Moodle Implementation

Moodle (Moodle, 2012) is an open-source Learning Management System (LMS) used to create learning environments. We choose using this LMS to implement Affective-Recommender, because it is a well diffused open-source Web application, which could be adapted, in order to fill Affective-Recommender's requirements.

Traditional Self-Assessment Manikin tool needs user's understanding about each dimension, to inform how he/she feels, once he/she has to select one picture by dimension, with semantic features. In order to make this process easier and faster, we used AffectButton (Broekens and Brinkman, 2009), a component that shows a yellow face that changes its expression with mouse movements, allowing student to specify the most appropriated face to his/her current affective state. The selected face in AffectButton indicates its corresponding PAD values, like the SAM tool.

Moodle allows teachers to construct their "virtual classes" using (i) resources, i.e., learning tools used to expose content to students; and (ii) activities: a way to students interact and give feedback to teachers, about worked resources.

Course is the Moodle's unit of learning, where teachers and students are assigned, and in which they could put and access resources and activities. A course could be divided into topics, each one composed by resources and activities, i. e., teachers insert activities and resources in courses' specific topics, from which students access them. Figure 2 illustrates a Moodle course formatted in topics. In our use case, it was defined a topic as the item to be recommend, because teachers could construct it - our learning object – as he/she wises, with resources, like web pages and files; and activities, as forums and questionnaires.

As detector have to be called each change of context, it were defined moments of students' access to do it: (i) each new access in Moodle, after some time; (ii) after they to receive or to send messages to others; (iii) after they finishing some activity; (iv) after they seeing their grades; and (v) after students to access a resource. The last case is used to check the reaction - rating - to each learning object.

It was constructed a new table in Moodle's database, called *Items*, in order to store courses' resources references. A new record is inserted in this table each new resource created by teachers. Affective reaction are stored in another created table, relating previous student's affective state, new affective state, user and item (resource) identifiers.

The recommender algorithm was developed to choose items in the created resources list. After choose, it's looked for its respective course topic, to be recommended. In this way, students always will receive a suggestion composed by all constructed topic.

A recommendation is made always a student access one of his/her courses. Then, he/she could choose the suggested item or see the others available learning objects, clicking in a button, as exposed in Figure 3. If he/she wants to choose another item, a sorted list will appear, with the probable well rated in the top.

Figure 2. Moodle course formatted in topics

Figure 3. Recommendation example in Affective-Recommender implementation over Moodle

Affective-Recommender Use

The system, implemented over Moodle, was used in three different classes of different regular undergraduate courses, which use LMS as learning support tool. The classes (named I, II and III) have 21, 36 and 29 students, respectively. In theses cases, to each worked content, teachers prepared among two or three different learning objects, in order to have options to be recommended. It is important to say that this scenario is not adequate to Affective-Recommender, since there are few object data, few students and few use time. This application, however, was not made to see recommendation quality, but to know students' impressions of the system, as said above. The system was used, initially, over 17 days to classes I and II, and 41 to class III, when it was applied a questionnaire and data access was analyzed.

The applied questionnaire was composed by 11 objective questions and 1 discursive. Those objectives were based on Likert scale, in which sentences was proposed, and students have to choose the degree of concordance to each one. Besides, it was analyzed affect detected states. The analyze is following.

We saw that students can show their emotion, once they agreed that they "can inform how they feel through AffectButton", in a questionnaire question. Further, more than one different state was detected, in average, to each student, what means that they were able to use AffectButton, and that they choose, in some way, the face to inform.

The most detected states were Content (+1, -1, +1), Happy (+1, +1, +1) and Relaxed (+1, -1, -1). All these states have positive valence, what could be justified by students concordance that they "access the LMS when they want to study".

In 64% of the reaction cases, students change their affective state, and they agree that "their affective state changes based on study learning object". They also agreed that "they feel more happy when study objects that they enjoy more". Then, we could support that student reaction, in

terms of affective state change, could be used as preference variable, and that it is interesting recommend learning objects that probably will leave them to more positive states.

Students answered that AffectButton appeared much times. In this way, we have to reanalyze the appropriate moments to show the button, excluding some of them. Also, they disagree that recommended objects are better than others, what were expected.

Finally, they agree that their emotional states influences studying, and that they have doubts about what learning object to choose, seeing a recommendation system as an interesting tool to help in this choose problem. In the discursive answers, some students complain about the number of times that AffectButton appears, and the necessity for Java support, since the component is an applet. Besides, in one answer, it was mentioned that the system could help "teacher-student approximation", because students were informing how they feel.

Through these analyzes, we could perceive that students can inform how they feel, through AffectButton. Plus, we've noticed that changes have occurred in affective states, after their interaction with learning objects; that students identify relations among their emotional states and learning process; and, finally, that a recommendation system could help them in make decision process.

Scenario of Use

As a proof of concept, it was constructed a scenario of use, about Affective-Recommender implementation over Moodle. In this way, five users were created and assigned as students in a fictitious course, called "Summer Computing Course". The course was divided in topics, each one composed by one resource and two activities, about one subject, as a learning object. We made five different learning objects, to be recommended to students.

In order to simplify the understanding, it was defined that all users would be in the state "surprised", which P, A and D values are, respectively, +1, +1 and -1. From this state, we simulated different accesses from students to items, building their profiles. All accesses came from surprised affective state, to simplify the process and understanding, once the User x Item x Affective State will be automatically reduced to User x Item, because there is just one Affective State from students reactions came from. Thereby, we should simulate recommendation process. Table 2 exposes students' reaction to items, in affective states labels; while Table 3 exposes the PAD values to each reaction.

Analyzing the tables, we could see that students 1 and 2 had the same reactions to items 1 and 2 (afraid and angry states, respectively). Plus, student 3 had the same reaction of students 1 and 2 to Item 1 (afraid). Besides, students 4 and 5 had the same reaction to Item 1 (surprised).

In this way, student 1 will receive as recommendation Item 4, due to student 2 is the most similar to student 1, and the reaction of student 2 related to this item was the better possible, leading to happy affective state. As second suggestion, it will be Item 5, that led student 3 to the affective-state happy. As student 1 is less similar to student 3 than to student 2, the order of recommendation will be item 4 and, then, item 3. Analogously, student 2 receive as recommendation Items 3 and 5, because he is more similar to student 1 than student 3, and both reaction lead to happy state.

Student 3 is equally similar to students 1 and 2, then, he/she will receive items 3 and 4 as recommendation. For student 4, Item 4 will be recommended an, then, Item 3. Although students 4 and 5 are more similar than students 4 and 2, the rating value of student 2 to item 4 is much better (4) than the rating's value of student 5 to item 3 (-2). Then, student 4 probably will prefer item 4 instead of item 3. Finally, student 5 will receive both item 5 and 4, with the same rating estimate, because both similarity and users ratings are equals.

Table 2. Students' affective reaction

	Item 1	Item 2	Item 3	Item 4	Item 5
Student 1	Afraid	Angry	Happy	X	X
Student 2	Afraid	Angry	X	Happy	X
Student 3	Afraid	Surprised	X	X	Happy
Student 4	Surprised	Angry	X	X	Angry
Student 5	Surprised	Happy	Afraid	X	X

Table 3. Students' affective reaction in PAD

	Item 1	Item 2	Item 3	Item 4	Item 5
Student 1	-1, 1, -1	-1, 1, 1	1, 1, 1	X	X
Student 2	-1, 1, -1	-1, 1, 1	X	1, 1, 1	X
Student 3	-1, 1, -1	1, 1, -1	X	X	1, 1, 1
Student 4	1, 1, -1	-1, 1, 1	X	X	-1, 1, 1
Student 5	1, 1, -1	1, 1, 1	-1, 1, -1	X	X

RELATED WORKS

There are some similar works to Affective-Recommender. In this section, we describe them, showing the differences between our approach and these related works.

In their work, Shen et al. (2009) expose an affective model, in which detection is made with physiological signals, as heart beats, skin conductibility, blood pressure and brain waves. The model is applied in a pervasive learning management system. It aims to identify how emotions are involved in learning process, in order to detect and to provide responses to these emotional states. Eight states are possible to be detected in this work. The main difference between Shen's approach and ours are related to the affective detection: while them uses physiological signals, that needs specifically sensors to get affective information, we use only the same devices in which students will interact with their classes to check how do them feel, in a cognitive way. In this way, Affective-Recommender doesn't need additional sensors or other devices.

Iepsen et al. (2011) creates a tool to identify students frustration state in Algorithms classes, and propose a way to treat these negative feeling. The tool is composed by an Integrated Development Environment (IDE), where student could write code; and by an alert button, that student could push when he/she feels frustrated. The work have analyzed student's behavioral characteristics before pushing the button, in order to identify which factors lead to frustrated state. From these characteristics, it was added a new button in the IDE, that appears when probable frustration is identified, i. e., when signals which probably will leave to frustration are found. When student clicks in this new button added, teacher's tips and clues are presented, in order to help he/she and avoid frustration. Iepsen's work is specifically to Algorithm's classes, and offers help in form of tips and clues, considering just frustration state. Our approach is generic to any course and

class, considering not only one affective state. Furthermore, in order to help students, Affective-Recommender suggests learning objects, instead of tips and clues.

Jaques (2008) uses OCC Model, a well diffused cognitive model, to detect students affective states in an LMS. Her approach also uses Belief-Desire-Intention model to infer students emotion, from two user profile categories: learning or performance oriented. To classify students, a questionnaire was applied. In this work, student's emotion is detected from a rules set, in the BDI model, and from possible events' desirability, based on OCC model. In her work, its necessarily to apply a questionnaire to classify students, which doesn't occur in ours, since Affective-Recommender constructs students' profiles from interactions. Besides, in Jaque's approach, all the contexts have to be defined in the rules set, what could grow and make the process costly to treat new situations, what isn't necessarily in ours, since collaborative filtering algorithm will get information along students' interaction.

FUTURE RESEARCH DIRECTIONS

Collaborative-filtering recommendation algorithms have issues in cases which there are few data available, as items, users and preferences. In other words, Affective-Recommender system could not be effective if (i) there weren't many learning objects to be recommended; (ii) there weren't many students in a course; and (iii) in the beginning of a course, when each learning object have been accessed by only few students, or even no one.

In order to deal with these problems, first we suggest Affective-Recommender use only in cases where there will be many students and learning objects available. The third problem is a little difficult to be solved. To do it, we propose, as a future work, investigating an way to relate items' content and affective states, considering this relation in recommendation processes. Then, it will be possible to select the probable most interesting items not only based on students profile, but using learning objects content too.

Although Moodle is a well used LMS, we propose as another future work develop a u-LMS, that could be fully integrated with Affective-Recommender. This LMS should be accessed from different devices, monitoring student interactions, in order to identify the best moment to select and suggest items, through analyzing the available context variables.

CONCLUSION

U-learning allows access learning objects anywhere and anytime. Internet and mobility explosion makes available a huge data volume, in which there are many learning information, from that students could obtain knowledge. As personalization is an important feature in learning environments and there are much information available, recommendation systems could be used to select the probable most interesting learning objects, suggesting them to each student.

User's preferences often are related to their interaction context. In this way, context-aware recommendation systems aims to use situation variables to improve the recommendation process. Emotions are related to learning processes, and even should do a student quit classes due to negative feelings. Affective Computing studies try to identify and respond automatically to users' affective state, enhancing human-computer interaction.

These scenario made us to develop Affective-Recommender: a context-aware recommendation system, that selects and suggests learning objects to students, based on their affective state. It was proposed a system architecture, composed by detector, recommender, application and database. The detector uses Self-Assessment Manikins instrument to identify students' affective states,

in the Pleasure, Arousal and Dominance model. Recommendation algorithm proposed is based on collaborative filtering, and it uses students' affective reaction to each item as their ratings. The similarity of two students is calculated by the sum of the cosines between the vectors constructed by each reaction, in P, A, D values.

We implemented Affective-Recommender over Moodle Learning Management System, using Broekens and Briekens AffectButton to identify students' affective state. Through this state, it is possible to select a learning object, defined as a Moodle's course topic, suggesting it to student. In this way, we could prove the system's viability. This implementation was applied in three undergraduate classes, in Federal University of Santa Maria and, through data access and questionnaire analyzes, we saw that the students could inform how they feel, through AffectButton; that affective reaction could be used as a preference variable; and that these users agree a recommendation system helps them to choose learning objects; besides, they mentioned that AffectButton have appeared much times, what means that we need to reanalyze the moments to show it. Finally, it was showed an example of Affective-Recommender scenario of use, in order to explain the system operation.

Technology insertion in learning processes demands new concerns, but provides ways to improve it. As information access is becoming easier and faster along the years, its important look for solutions which are efficient in this new reality. We think that Affective-Recommender is a new learning solution, that could use the over information available to select the best learning objects to each student, in order to customize and improve learning process. Affective-Recommender uses students' affective state in recommendation process, once it is linked with cognitive processes. U-learning environments could be the future in education, providing anywhere and anytime learning, customized to each student.

REFERENCES

Adomavicius, G., & Tuzhilin, A. (2005). Toward the next generation of recommender systems: A survey of the state-of-the-art and possible extensions. *IEEE Transactions on Knowledge and Data Engineering*, *1*(6), 734–749. doi:10.1109/TKDE.2005.99.

Bales, R. F. (2001). *Social interaction systems: Theory and measurement*. New Brunswick, NJ: Transaction Publishers.

Bradley, M. M., & Lang, P. J. (1994). Measuring emotion: The self-assessment manikin and the semantic differential. *Journal of Behavior Therapy and Experimental Psychiatry*, *1*(25), 49–59. doi:10.1016/0005-7916(94)90063-9 PMID:7962581.

Broekens, J., & Brinkman, W. (2009). AffectButton: Towards a standard for dynamic affective user feedback. In R. Dienstbier (Ed.), *Affective Computing and Intelligent Interaction and Workshops, 2009* (pp. 1–8). Amsterdam, The Netherlands: ACII. doi:10.1109/ACII.2009.5349347.

Buriano, L., Marchetti, M., Carmagnola, F., Cena, F., Gena, C., & Torre, I. (2006). The role of ontologies in context-aware recommender systems. In *Proceedings of the 7th International Conference on Mobile Data Management*. IEEE.

Calvo, R. A., & D'Mello, S. (2010). Affect detection: An interdisciplinary review of models, methods, and their applications. *IEEE Transactions Affective Computing*, *1*(1), 18–37. doi:10.1109/T-AFFC.2010.1.

Cazella, S. C., Nunes, M. A. S., & Reategui, E. (2010). A ciência do palpite: Estado da arte em sistemas de recomendação. In R. Dienstbier (Ed.), *Jornada de Atualização de Informática* (pp. 161-216). Rio de Janeiro: PUC

Gebhard, P. (2005). ALMA: A layered model of affect. In *Proceedings of the Fourth International Joint Conference on Autonomous Agents and Multiagent Systems* (pp. 29-36). New York, NY: ACM.

Ghauth, K. I. B., & Abdullah, N. A. (2009). Building an e-learning recommender system using vector space model and good learners average rating. *IEEE International Conference on Advanced Learning Technologies*, *1*(0), 194-196.

Hussein, T., Linder, T., Gaulke, W., & Ziegler, J. (2009). Context-aware recommendations on rails. In *Proceedings of the Workshop on Context-Aware Recommender Systems in Conjunction with the 3rd ACM Conference on Recommender Systems*. New York, NY: ACM.

Iepsen, E. F., Bercht, M., & Reategui, E. (2011). Detecção e tratamento do estado afetivo frustração do aluno na disciplina de algoritmos. In *Proceedings of the Anais do XXII Simpósio brasileiro de Informática na Educação*, (pp. 80-89). IEEE.

Jaques, P. (2008). Avaliando um modelo afetivo de aluno baseado em uma abordagem cognitiva. In *Proceedings of the Anais do XIX Simpósio brasileiro de Informática na Educação*, (pp. 155-165). IEEE.

Jones, V., & Jo, J. H. (2004). Ubiquitous learning environment: An adaptive teaching system using ubiquitous technology. In *Proceedings of the 21st ASCILITE Conference* (pp. 468-474). Perth, Australia: ASCILITE.

Kerkiri, T., Manitsaris, A., & Mavridou, A. (2007). Reputation metadata for recommending personalized e-learning resources. In *Proceedings of the International Workshop on Semantic Media Adaptation and Personalization*, (pp. 110-115). IEEE.

Lang, P. J., Bradley, M. M., & Cuthbert, B. N. (1997). *International affective picture system (IAPS), technical manual and affective ratings*. Gainesville, FL: NIMH Center for the Study of Emotional and Attention.

Martinho, C., Machado, I., & Paiva, A. (2000). A cognitive approach to affective user modeling affective interactions. In *Affective Interactions (LNCS)* (pp. 64–75). Berlin: Springer. doi:10.1007/10720296_6.

O'Regan, K. E. (2003). Emotion and e-learning. *Journal of Asynchronous Learning Networks*, *1*(3), 78–92.

Moodle (2012). Moodle.org: Open-source community-based tools for learning. *Journal of Bibliographic Research, 5,* 117-123. Retrieved October 13, 2012, from http://www.moodle.org/

J. Piaget (Ed.). (2005). *Psicologia cognitiva y educaci*. Buenos Aires: Aique.

Picard, R. W. (1995). *Affective computing*. Cambridge, MA: MIT Media Laboratory.

Picard, R. W. (1997). *Affective computing*. Cambridge, MA: MIT Press.

Ricci, F. (2010). Mobile recommender systems. *International Journal of Information Technology and Tourism*, *1*(12), 205–231. doi:10.3727/1098 30511X12978702284390.

Sarwar, B., Karypis, G., Konstan, J., & Reidl, J. (2001). Item-based collaborative filtering recommendation algorithms. In *Proceedings of the 10th International Conference on World Wide Web* (pp. 285-295). Hong Kong: ACM.

Scherer, K. R. (2000). Psychological models of emotion. In J. C. Borod (Ed.), *The Neuropsychology of Emotion*. Oxford, UK: Oxford University Press.

Shen, L., Wang, M., & Shen, R. (2009). Affective e-learning: Using emotional data to improve learning in pervasive learning environment. *Journal of Educational Technology & Society*, *1*(12), 176–189.

KEY TERMS AND DEFINITIONS

Affective Computing: Computing area that studies affect relation with computer. It is concerned in improve human-computer interactions through affect detection.

Affective State: User state related to his/her affection. Its broadest than an emotion state, because could include moods states.

Collaborative-Filtering: Recommendation technique that uses preferences of users with similar tastes to suggest items.

Moodle: Open-source well used Learning Management System.

Pleasure, Arousal, Model (PAD): Affective model used to express emotions, in three dimensions, given values between -1 and 1 to each one.

Recommendation System: System able to sort a set of items, in order to suggest probable most interesting to users.

Self-Assessment Manikins (SAM): Affect detection instrument, used to identify users affective state in PAD values.

Chapter 15
U–Learning Pedagogical Management:
Cognitive Processes and Hypermediatic Resources Involved in Web–Based Collaborative Workspace

Jocelma Almeida Rios
Instituto Federal de Educação, Brazil

Mary Valda Souza Sales
Universidade do Estado da Bahia, Brazil

Emanuel do Rosário Santos Nonato
Universidade do Estado da Bahia, Brazil

Tereza Kelly Gomes Carneiro
Universidade Estadual de Ciências da Saúde de Alagoas, Brazil

ABSTRACT

The Internet has permitted some changes that may not have been foreseen on its initial design. We started to constitute friendly or professional interactions, and it eventually enabled the emergence of collaborative actions that resulted in cognitive processes in unusual ways, that is, that take place without the physical presence of those involved but with the effective participation of everyone involved in a broad and democratic approach, constituting a collective intelligence. In the professional world, these interactions can turn into significant gains to developed activities. This chapter reviews relevant findings concerning the cognitive aspects related to the knowledge construction developed under the collaborative work approach in Learning Management Systems (LMS). When working collaboratively in a LMS, the subjects engage in cognitive processes mediated by hypermedia resources that potentially have positive impact on their ability to construct, sense, and/or produce knowledge, to the extent that these resources dynamically dialogue with the already markedly multimodal human cognitive ability. In order to support the analysis, the authors present the relationship between cognitive processes and hypermedia and their influence on knowledge production in an LMS. They also present two experiences developed in Moodle, which showed the possibility of using such resources for people prone to collaboration, resulting in a continuous design optimization of the mentioned course.

DOI: 10.4018/978-1-4666-4542-4.ch015

INTRODUCTION

The changes which ark the beginning of the 21st century have deep impact on organization and people's way of living, i.e., the way they deal with each other. The appearance of the computer networks at the late 1970s indicated the potentiality of digital communication hegemony in area of social communication and interaction.

As a result, the new dynamics of the economy grants great importance to information delivered through a variety of media and the construction and diffusion of knowledge which interferes in all aspects of the social life, far beyond the ancient border of the labor world. Such movement promotes changes on the preexisting cultural structures under the influence of new interfaces and digital hypermedia. Certainly, this is a broad and complex phenomenon not entirely understood which lead with computer mediated communication, but not only.

In the context of such transformation, an important aspect is the increase of distance education course proposals in all the educational levels in the last ten years due to the emergence of the so called web 2.0, the improvement of internet connection quality and computer processing capability to home users.

In Brazil, this phenomenon can be testified by the widespread interest of public universities on offering distance education undergraduate courses according to the Brazil's Open University System (UAB – in Portuguese)[1], as such institutions are the most qualified universities in the country. As a centralized federal program, it fails to promote collective and collaborative pedagogical knowledge construction within the institutions, stimulating repetition rather than innovation. Besides the political and bureaucratic issues, there are still technical and cognitive problems. Too often teachers present difficulties in the use of computer systems that support u-learning as well as for those who can't adapt to the use of teaching methodologies appropriate to this type of education. This

context favors the frequent absence of collective involvement and collaborative teaching teams focused on knowledge construction to planning, management and development of these courses, even though with the facilities provided by the support of computers. The non-involvement of the collective management proposal contradicts the collegiate, democratic and participative perspective, important guideline for management education.

In order to fully understand the impacts of such changes and its influence on management and on teaching-learning process in u-learning, this chapter addresses the cognitive aspects related to the Human-Computer-Human Interaction (HCHI) in the knowledge construction process through collaborative work on u-learning pedagogical management, i.e., addressing the relation among cognitive processes, cyberculture and hypermedia and their influence on web-based knowledge production.

This theoretical discussion is addressed in the analysis of the experience of the Post graduation Course on School Management and the Course of Formation for City Educational Department Managers, two u-learning courses on which the theories presented here could be implemented and verified. These empirical experiences permitted the verification of web based professional interaction spaces can provide a opportunity of collaborative intercourse in educational enterprises, allowing teachers and coordinators to easily interact and build a community of practice.

INTERCONNECTIONS IN COLLABORATIVE WORK

In the first half of the twentieth century, the management model used by organizations was inspired by the experiences and ideas of Henry Ford, with production at assembly lines of large scale and the theory of scientific management; Max Weber, with studies on bureaucracy that guides the management by formality, impersonality and hierarchical professionalism to achieve discipline, rigor and confidence; Henri Fayol, with 14 principles of management, including the division of labor, hierarchy, centralization, order and discipline (Maximiniano, 2000). All of these approaches had as main objective to increase productivity, based on strict rules of organization and control, not taking into account aspects related to job satisfaction.

Also in this period, but a little later comes the Theory of Human Relations, by Elton Mayo, that looks at the workers and their needs as an important part of the production process. Other significant contributions were given by Abraham Maslow, with the hierarchy of human needs, and David McClelland who proposed the classification of special needs relying on the theory of Maslow: need of achievement, need of power and need of affiliation or membership (Maximiniano, 2000). However, it is only with the General Systems Theory (VON Bertalanffy, 1950), which emerged in the 1950s, which was a counterpart to the mechanic approach of Scientific Management School and the Human Relations School, that the organization stops being seen as parts, which can be organized according to strict rules, but as a whole composed of parts which are interconnected in communication flows and nonlinear actions. Moreover, the individual is regarded as part of the organizational system and the participatory management approach, proposed by Likert in the 1960s, becomes important.

Collaborative network organizations are a response to the demand to participative management. They are new organizations which suppose mutual engagement of the participants in order to perform their activities and face the challenges together, implying mutual trust in a process which demands time, effort and dedication. The collaborative networks were hugely promoted by the appearance of computer networks, especially the Internet. Camarinha-Matos and Afsarmanesh (2011) define those networks as a variety of organizations and persons whose interaction is supported by computer networks. The integrated entities are normally autonomous, geographically distributed and heterogeneous in the operational environment, culture, social capital and objectives, although they collaborate to achieve common goals.

Besides other variations of collaborative networks, these authors also present the concept of online professional community as a variation of a collaborative network, contributing to building and maintenance of a collaborative organization. Such communities are a mix of virtual community and professional community (Camarinha-Matos; Afsarmanesh, 2005). They assume virtual communities as social systems which use computer technologies to mediate their interactions. As professional communities, they are able to share labor content, technical problems, work values and work related behavior. That is, virtual professional communities can extrapolate the physical environment of an organization.

Camarinha-Matos and Afsarmanesh's concept of Professional community is in line with Lave's and Wenger's (1998) communities of practice. In such environments, individuals are supposed to have a collaborative attitude towards the group which involves self-discipline, autonomy, competence, sense of responsibility, and interpersonal skills. Even though, collaboration only appears when the individuals take part on the decision making process (empowerment), when they feel they belong to the team (membership) and when they feel and are involved and affected by the collective goals.

The failure to involve people on the process may be a result of ineffective leadership, personal reasons (including health), kind of job (dull, repetitive, exhausting etc.), excess charges, lack of autonomy, imbalance between personal and collective aims, bad communication flow, poor technological background of the team, lack of understanding or disagreement about the values, goals and collective goals etc.

The engagement of members of a team is the focus of many working methodologies, like in software engineering, which currently has agile methodologies as protagonists. These methodologies are seeking a self-managed horizontal way to work, valuing people over processes, allowing all team members to discuss on the direction of the project in which they are working (Pressman, 2011).

Socio-cognitive and emotional questions are given regarded as important factors within such methodologies, even if it is not possible to systematize them as controllable and optimizable algorithms due to their inherent complexity. However socio-cognitive and motivational questions are not always considered in such methodologies. This situation can be explained by the distance that separates software designers and engineers from those professionals who study motivation and cognition. Even when a multi-professional team builds up a software, the first professionals normally lead the process.

Social and cognitive components of the software "equation" are not important only during the development of IT projects. Other areas of contact exist in social psychology, cognitive computing, social biology (Maturana, Varela, 1987), etc. Sack (2003; 2006), Duchenaut (2005) and Baarcellini et al. (2008), for example, address the problem of collaborative work of decentralized teams such as free software communities, using Latour's (1987) social-technical approach and the Lave and Wenger's (1998) theory of situated learning. Wenger (2004) also brought another contribution in this area, when he introduced the concept of community of practice, expanding the concept of learning community (Catella, 2011). Since 2000, Carmarinha-Matos' team point to similar questions, investigating cooperation coordination on line companies as a way to face the challenges of globalization (Carmarinha-Matos, Pantoja-Lima, 2001);

Community of practice is a strategy used today in many processes of formation and also in working groups, aiming at collective and collaborative construction of knowledge, and it can be understood as a group of people with a common interest that act together. Carmarinha-Matos' and Afsarmanesh's (2004) collaboration network approach, following Lave's and Wenger's, includes a variety of entities (e.g. organizations and people) that are largely autonomous, geographically distributed and heterogeneous.

At least two things are required so that a group work with actors (people and institutions) and connections (relationships) may be considered a community of practice:

1. Common Interest.
2. Practice of Collaboration.

So, as McDermott (1999) states, communities of practice are groups of people who learn from each other, face-to-face or not, and interact sharing experiences and building better practices to face common challenges. It happens that often, so as in the experiments referenced in this chapter, the problems are solved by a small part of the team, sometimes only one of the team members, what breaks the chain of collaboration.

Wenger, McDermott and Snyder (2002) emphasize three essential elements of a community of practice: *domain*, a *community* and *practice*. *Domain* is the context which starts the collaboration, due to common values and aims. The *community* is the social group itself, united by links of involvement and participation. *Practice* is the accomplishment of the ideas, work schemes, strategies, sharing of documents, information and knowledge, leading to collaborative learning approaches.

People get engaged on cognitive processes mediated by hypermediatic resources, when they work collaboratively in web-based environments. Such event has a potential positive impact on their ability to produce meanings and knowledge, due to the naturally multimodal cognitive abilities of human beings. This characteristic makes multi-task approach manifestly human ability, even in relation to highly complex mental operations (Eysenck, Keane, 2000).

HYPERMEDIA, ONLINE SPACES AND KNOWLEDGE PRODUCTION: REAL POSSIBILITIES

Cyberculture had an impact on human relations with technology and among themselves. Pierre Lévy (1990) defends a close inter-relation between subjectivity and technology. Lévy (1997) states that cyberculture interferes on the way we think and act, changing the basis on which we are. He believes that interconnection is a basic condition to cyberculture due to the emergence of virtual communities and collective intelligences. He argues that connecting knowledge, imagination and spiritual energies of the subject is the best thing to do on cyberspace. However he fails to prove how such emergence influences the cognitive abilities of human beings *stricto sensu*, as he claims, and effectiveness of collective intelligence.

But it is true that the monomidiatic predominance of writing in the West established patterns to the western civilization and mobile hypermediatic artifacts propose a new look for our rationality.

Lev Manovich (1996) argues that the consequences of import analogical conceptions of time and space to the Internet is not appropriate as interactivity is its main characteristics. This category is key to understand internet and is addressed in the academy and the market. It is a kind of main goal for internet, though some aspects must be considered in relation to it, especially its potential like nature, rather than an objective accomplishment to many people on the web. Winner (1997) criticizes cyberspace enthusiasts in relation to their excessive optimism related to

the web, as they seem not to consider the losses and gains, and who loses and who wins.

In relation to knowledge diffusion, technological developments of last twenty years have a deep impact on it, connecting people regardless time and space, what provides the development of cognitive competencies such as autonomy, creativity, discipline, responsibility and collaboration. Such ideas are in line with Vygotsky's (1978) social historic cultural theory. His conception means that higher psychological functions (such as voluntary attention, logical memory, verbal and conceptual conscious thought, complex emotions, divergent thinking, etc.) depend on social interaction as the basis for human knowledge production. Thus, the more we facilitate such interactions, the easier such functions develop.

As past history and culture are integrated on actual history and culture (Macedo, 2006), this cannot mean a determinist process as the individual is actively participant of his cycles of interaction, changing it and transforming it in a collaborative network (Castells, 2000) through communities of practice (Wenger, 2004), web-based or not.

Most organizations, according to Senge (1990), are oriented towards control rather than learning, rewarding people for their ability to obey the rules and established standards rather than for their desire to learn. He also affirms that people tend to expand their creativity on learning organizations, developing new and higher reasoning, leading people to learn continuously how to learn together. Garvin (1993) agrees with Senge when he states that learning organizations create and share knowledge and adapt to new situations easily as a result of a democratic and participative managing pattern in which leaders and employees collaborate in a network structured company (Castells, 2000), i.e., a systemic organization that evaluates continuously its results and improves its processes. It also emphasizes lifelong learning as it promotes key aspects of the subject (in)formation: criticism, creativity and participation.

Under this approach, the web-based work environment may provide the opportunity to create a collaborative environment on which teachers and coordinators may interact more easily.

HUMAN-COMPUTER-HUMAN INTERACTION

Human-Computer Interaction (HCI) is a multidisciplinary field that studies the design, development and implementation of computer systems for human use. It is related to interaction possibilities offered to a user by a software in a particular context of operation in order to perform tasks in an efficient, effective and enjoyable way, according to ISO 9241-11 (ISO, 1998). A software that has good usability, even if it presents some faults in its functionality, it uses to be better accepted.

Jackob Nielsen (1994), precursor of usability studies, considers this aspect as an extension of ergonomic principles for IHC, i. e., the study of interactions among human beings and computing system elements in order to optimize the well being and improve performance in this interaction, seeking goals such as: efficiency, effectiveness, reliability, usefulness, learning and memorization readiness. According to Nielsen, "to some extent, usability is a narrow concern compared to the larger issue of system acceptability, which basically is the question of whether the system is good enough to satisfy all the requirements and needs of the potential users and stakeholders" (Nielsen, 1994, p. 24). Other authors also have recommendations that match or amplify Nielsen's. Shneiderman (2010), for example, defines the golden rules of usability and discusses aspects related to the use of web-based systems, especially those related to collaboration and participation in social media. Among the golden rules of interface software design proposed by Shneiderman, the one which indicates user's control and initiative is noteworthy because the user tends to feel more comfortable when he or she is in control

of the interaction with the system. This feeling favors faster learning through exploration, a very characteristic for both teachers and students in a LMS, as it provides the necessary autonomy in the teaching and learning process.

Bastien and Scarpin (1993) proposed to evaluate usability with interface ergonomic criteria. According to this, interface softwares are considered high qualified as long as their navigational orientations and task execution guides are clear, easily readable, adaptable, simple, allow user's navigation control, provide user's management control, offer several options for performing the same task, have homogenous design – following established standards what eases self-learning – and good error management with clear and objective messages which avoid the occurrence of errors and allow the reversal of actions performed.

Therefore, the concept of usability refers to the speed with which users can learn to use something, their efficiency in using it, their remembrance of it, its inclination to error, how much they enjoy using it, i. e., how are comfortable they feel using the software. This directly implies directly on people's degree of autonomy using computer systems that foster interaction with other people, creating fertile ground for collaboration.

For web-based systems, such as LMS, the ISO 13407 provides guidance on how to achieve quality, user-centric projects that occur throughout the life cycle of interactive computer systems. The guidance provided by this ISO describes an iterative development cycle in which product requirement specifications clarify appropriately the user's requirements and the organization's, as well as it specifies the context in which the product is to be used. Nielsen says that the success of web-based interactive systems is centered on simplicity and usability. In fact, the most widely used LMS, such as Moodle, are chosen for their easiness of use, even by non-computer specialists, and for theirs functional characteristics focused on collaboration. Fernandes (2008) developed a conceptual model to evaluate the human-computer interface, specifically usability and functionality of such softwares, according to both educators and computer professionals with experience in the u-learning. In this work, we studied both LMS functional aspects and data consistency, as well as the ease of adaptation to the task of leading roles, focusing on mechanisms of communication, coordination, interaction and course management.

In any software, interface should facilitate the communication process, helping the user to get a better performance and achieve one's goal quickly and accurately, according to one's cognitive process. But in the case of web-based collaborative softwares, it is necessary that the functional and non-functional requirements, including HCI, are associated with dimensions inherent to their design, represented by administration / coordination, assessment, teaching, research, collaboration, communication / interaction among systems and people, and among people and people, to promote individual and collective (specially) knowledge construction. In other words, the software is not only supposed to provide good usability, allowing the user to be autonomous, effectiveness and speed of navigation and task execution, but also to provide the possibility of Human-Computer-Human Interaction through individual collaboration integrated into the collective network.

COGNITIVE PROCESSES AND HYPERMEDIA

The hypermediatic cognitive processes show that "hypermedia is not only a technique of information manipulation, but a space of knowledge construction and problem solving, a clear example of a cognitive tool" (Matta, 2006, p. 102).

The emergence of IT and its insertion on people's lives, especially on school based knowledge production processes, makes it more important to analyze its impact on human cognitive processes which imply an ethical and social "agreement" among members of such collective process (Lévy, 1994). So, it is important to know how the impacts

caused by IT mediated procedures on autonomy and authorship, to name two of the most important aspects of it.

Firstly, hypermedia points out the anachronism of the way authorship is addressed, according to a notion nurtured in the Modernity. This is a major change on the way people interact and recognize the processes of knowledge production. Here, one must recognize that the lonely and self-sufficient author no longer exists, even if its existence can be disputed et all, due to Bakhtin's (2002) conceptions of polyphony, dialogism and social nature of language of the linguistic sign.

Notwithstanding this linguistic questions, the ubiquitous technologies' popularization leads to the assumption that collaboration is key to knowledge production in a dynamically hypermediatic world and the new ways of knowledge production and diffusion. Hypermedia itself also implies collaboration among cognitive agents to build IT based knowledge: hypermediatic knowledge. There cannot be hypermedia without a multidisciplinary team to produce it, and this necessarily means co-authoring.

Hypermedia not only questions the romantic notion of authoring, but also demands the increase of autonomy as long as the individuals are called to interact collaboratively, developing links towards the others and preserving their subjective authenticity, their autonomy. Paradoxically, the more we collaborate, the more autonomous we get. Without autonomy, one cannot get involved on inter(trans)subjective knowledge construction processes. Thus, collaborative tools only work when autonomous subjects operate them: hypermedia is both autonomy promoter and autonomy dependant, as hypermediatic tools both induce collaboration and depend on collaboration to work.

Autonomy and collaboration are articulated aspects of hypermedia and have a deep relation with ownership and interdependence in the hypermedia production. Hypermedia helps the development of autonomous subjects and depend on such subjects to be well used and actually produced.

U-LEARNING PEDAGOGICAL MANAGEMENT IN PRACTICE

Issues, Controversies, Problems

The Internet is an important vehicle for the promotion of cyberculture. It caused several changes that may not have been foreseen when it was created. It turned to be a place for friendly and professional interactions and also eventually allowed the emergence of collaborative actions that highlighted cognitive processes that take place without the physical presence of those involved, but with the effective participation of all the evoking new modes of broad and democratic participation.

In the professional area, these interactions can result in significant gains of productivity, allowing the transformation of traditional working groups into communities of practice through collaborative networks that operate in web-based geographically dispersed areas.

People who operate collaboratively in web-based workspaces through a human-computer-human interaction approach get engaged in cognitive processes mediated by hypermedia resources, potentially impacting positively on their ability to produce meanings and / or to build knowledge, to the extent that these resources dynamically dialogue with the human markedly multimodal cognitive ability. This cognitive multimodality allows the subject to be multitasking, i.e., he can perform more than one task simultaneously, with little or no interference among them, even when dealing with highly complex tasks and even less when he uses different mental operations (Eysenck, Keane, 2000).

Communities of practice are a very fruitful approach to promote the construction of collective knowledge as they allow people with common interests to exchange information and experiences, permitting the establishment of new connections and the development of new theories within a given area of knowledge. However, the theoretical perspective that supports this approach fails to express all its potentiality to collaboration. There are many obstacles to achieving collaboration among communities of practice that emerge due to the absence of engagement regarding the goals of the community, individualistic or shy personality of certain individuals, competition among members, the disagreements related to authorship, the differences types and levels of training of members, difficulty of dialogue, lack of mutual encouragement, and especially weakness in conducting coordinated common activities. Some of these obstacles were faced in the experiments reported below. Some interventions were demanded in order to minimize the impacts generated by them, as was the case of the teacher training course, creation of collaboration-friendly spaces and contexts, changes in the work organization and hierarchical structure of course management.

Due to its characteristics and its knowledge building potential, communities of practice have gained great attention in the educational sector, both for educational purposes and for management purposes (cf. reports of experiments I and II), especially in u-learning courses, in which not only the students are geographically dispersed but also the teaching staff involved. In such cases, beyond the obstacles mentioned above, one also has to consider the impact of human-computer interaction, due to pervasive mediation and ubiquitous hypermedia resources, poor digital network extent and cultural difficulties even in developed countries. These aspects are important to guarantee the appropriate flow of work processes and also u-learning teaching and management approaches. It is extremely important that digital inclusion, often reduced to a promise, become a fact for everyone.

Thus, autonomy and collaboration should be articulated with ownership and interdependence within the hypermedia knowledge production process, enabling the improvement of collaborative practices while they also contribute to the development and maturation of the autonomy of the individuals involved in these processes of knowledge construction, generating maturation of these cognitive potentialities as a byproduct, as they find fertile ground to grown in hypermedia.

We present now two u-learning course management experiences in which we have applied web-based collaborative work principles according to the previous theoretical basis presented in this chapter (Table 1).

The course was run by multidisciplinary teams whose diversity training, experience and skills represented a positive contribution in both editions. These teams had teaching, administrative and technical assignments that were decided at face-to-face monthly meetings or through computer-mediated meetings. The teams' online interaction was concentrated on the LMS at discussion forums and chats, and also through e-mail and synchronous communication devices and applications not supported by Moodle (Table 2).

The course design followed the guidelines set by MEC with some adjustments dictated by the structural conditions, technical, personal and local institutional relationships sites. Part of the adjustments was accomplished during the first edition. However, even with the changes implemented, there were bureaucratic, structural, curricular, pedagogical, didactic and collective knowledge construction problems, especially pedagogical ones.

Therefore, in the selection of the teaching team for the second edition previous teaching experience in u-learning courses was established as a criterion for selection. Experience as student in the course's first edition was also valid. Even recognizing that all selected teachers had experience with Moodle and u-learning teaching methodologies, it was an important step the promotion of a small formation program in which all team members could share their knowledge and experiences about the issues involved. During these training sessions, the course program was discussed and reformulated. All this promoted interaction and integration among team members and evolved into a democratic and participative collegiate course management experience.

Thus, the pedagogical work was structured based on the interaction through the web-based LMS, distributed in 17 spaces, with 1 to house general discussions on the course operation, called "Coordination Room," and 16 others to address specific issues related to each pole. There were some discussion forums at "Coordination Room", such as: curricular components of the course, especially CBT, institutional assessment, monitoring of teaching assistance, administration, regulatory affairs and technical support. Several documents were also socialized to support administrative and

Table 1. Course Data

	Students	Poles	Cities Achieved	Completed the Course
1st. Edition	400	10	71	235
2nd. Edition	1430	16	229	1030

Table 2. Organization and distribution of the workforce

	Coordination Team	Teaching Team	Technical and Administrative Team
1st. Edition	General Coordinator, Deputy Coordinator, 6 pedagogical coordinators, 2 coordinators of assistance	35 teachers e 20 teachers assistants	1 supervisor and 4 auxiliary administrative technicians
2nd. Edition	General Coordinator, Deputy Coordinator, 6 pedagogical coordinators, 2 coordinators of assistance	64 teachers e 64 teachers assistants	4 coordinators e 10 auxiliary administrative technicians

educational course management as well as tips and information on events of general interest to the group. There were also monthly face-to-face meetings, which aimed to discuss outstanding issues already addressed online. Some meetings, extraordinarily, were happened online, using features such as video conference and web conference.

Experiment: Pradime

The Education City Managers Support Program (Pradime) was proposed by MEC, through its Department of Basic Education (SEB) and in partnership with the Municipal Education Managers Union (Undime) in order to support municipal leaders. Its goals are: to strengthen the role of the leaders at the management of education and educational policies, and to contribute to the advancement of the country in relation to the goals of the National Education Plan (NEP). To do so, it developed professional training courses. From 2009, the courses are now conducted via u-learning 179 hour extension courses in partnership among MEC and federal universities.

In this context, UFBA, through the Faculty of Education, offered this course in the Brazilian States of Alagoas, Bahia, Maranhão and Sergipe in 2010. In this edition, the management of the course was structured with one general coordinator, 1 deputy coordinator, 2 pedagogical coordinators, 16 teachers and 3 technical and pedagogical assistants. The first step to structure the activities was to train the teachers on Moodle (the LMS where the course was offered), and then on the course itself, focusing on the study and analysis of the teaching material and proposed activities in the course design. To ensure the effectiveness of the entire process of interaction in web-based spaces, the first step of course organization was directed to the strengthening of LMS interaction through a space called Virtual Integration Environment (VIE), which was used as an administrative space for the team. In this space we built the main management course tools (project plans, progress reports, manuals, selection and announcement of

default templates for administrative documents), with participation of all team members. Then, there was the space "Teacher Training" where teachers had the opportunity to discuss the course content, the organization of teaching and interaction in the LMS and also administrative issues related to their activities. This process lasted one month long for formation and during all the course for coordination proposes.

The 2012 second edition was developed by the Interdisciplinary Center for Distance Education (NEAD) of the Information Science Institute (ICI)-UFBA. The administrative and teaching structure of the course was greatly expanded and now includes other features not previously established: 1 general coordinator, 5 deputy coordinators, 15 teachers, 7 tutors and 2 technical and administrative assistants. Professionals who had worked at the first edition and others who had experience on u-learning courses based on Moodle LMS were asked to compose the team. Again the LMS was used to teaching and management. A section named "Coordination of Space" at the LMS was created to allow a better structure for management procedures and it was used throughout the course. There were three forums for pedagogical monitoring, (re) construction of pedagogical and didactic approaches and administrative matters). All pedagogical and administrative documents were accessible online on the LMS and also other information such as team assignments, team registration information, schedule of administrative and pedagogical activities. Reports on student monitoring, etc. Such documents were normally collectively produced and accessible on GoogleDocs.

The 2012 edition presented two significant changes: it became a 180 hour course and the both the city educational department chief and an employee of those departments were allowed enrollment in the course, resulting in 555 students.

U-learning course management is different from traditional course management due to its decentralized implementation structure in which the members of the management, pedagogical, technical and administrative teams are geographically dispersed. This geographical dispersion is perhaps the biggest challenge. As it was discussed in the section "Interconnects in collaborative work", people and organizations are still trying to get used to the modus operandi web-based, less hierarchical and more collaborative work. Therefore, the need for engagement was not evident to the group, as well as the need to establish relationships with various actors, the dynamics of asynchronous communication, and the collaborative socially constructed learning model as a prerequisite for the development and management of the administrative and pedagogical courses in collegiate approach.

Thus, perhaps due to the little maturity of the groups in collaborative web-based work, the dynamic of collaboration in early editions of both experiments was insufficient. Suggestions, criticisms and contributions were restricted to some teachers and even those were only related to the course design, evaluation system and activity timetable, even though there were sections in the LMS to promote collective engagement and democratic participative management actions.

In the first editions of the cases presented here, the lack of collective and collaborative involvement of the teaching staff in the planning, development and management of the knowledge construction process was the most relevant fragility more relevant; Such fragility reveals a contradiction between theory and praxis in relation to participatory democratic collegiate management which is a central axis of the courses.

The lack of involvement is partly explained by the practice of centralized planning and decision making, and the feeling of not belonging to the group, what leads to lack engagement of group members (Bastos, Brandao, Pine, 1997). But it cannot be denied the influence that inexperience on web-based interfaces plays in the lack of effective participation of each actor in the collaboration process. This is attested by the frequency and characterization of the demands of support generated by the teaching staff throughout the course, the numerous messages in inappropriate places, which demonstrates a lack of understanding of the dynamics of web based asynchronous communication.

In order to solve some problems identified early, a teacher training process was established for the teaching team of the second edition of Experience I and the first team of Experience II. It was proposed to qualify the pedagogical team to act on a u-learning course. Collective acknowledge of the course project and a collective effort to remake it was the final goal of the training process, as long as the understanding of all the possibilities of existing resources in Moodle, functions in u-learning teaching and the importance of ICT on education. To achieve these goals, this course articulated three dimensions:

1. Rearrange the program content discussed in each curricular component, seeking to meet the specific reality of local educational managing.

2. Strengthen the links among all people responsible for providing the course, from planning team to those responsible for face-to-face student support in the cities.

3. Promote integration among professionals of every polo organized into groups to discuss the concept of u-learning. As a result, we could realize greater integration of teamwork, socialization of the experiences of former students the course's first edition, more homogeneous conception of u-learning in the group and parameterization of proposed monitoring and evaluation.

One of the great aspects of the training course was the promotion of socio-interactive spaces where community members met, exchanged information, ideas and experiences, establishing personal and professional ties in order to overcome typical obstacles to the formation of a web-based community of practice, which become extremely important during the process of collective knowledge construction.

This can be demonstrated by the course content added (videos, articles, manuals etc) that were shared to be disseminated among the students of all classes, as well as reports of academic events, resulting on students and teachers' coauthored academic papers. This interaction also occurred during the planning of face-to-face classes meetings and evaluation, which strengthened the ties among the group members and reinforced the idea of a community of practice. Discussion forums in Moodle and also instant communication software (Google Talk, MSN or Skype), and even web conference (Webconf) were used as support for interaction within the community. This flexibility enhances the idea of a hypermediatic collaborative space of collaborative collective knowledge construction.

In all these areas, the possibility of collective knowledge construction according to network approach was the main objective. In such approaches anyone can become the center of the process at any time in a cyclical collective collaborative process. Such attitude of cooperation was fundamental for (re) construction of Experiments I and II course project, enabling continuous improvement and appropriate understanding of the objectives of the courses by all team members. This continuous development turned possible because of the constant interaction and collaboration clearly demonstrated while the community of practice was being shaped, allowing network knowledge to be produced through hipermidiatic resources which translate complex thoughts and amplify understanding in several areas of knowledge.

These contributions were used to suggest parameters of evaluation of activities, to discuss the course schedule, to define collectively the activities, to prepare the classroom moments, to address the problem of student attendance, etc. The teacher's message socialization process is another noteworthy experience. It increased the capacity of production of the group which is one of the benefits of communities of practice. Knowledge is collectively created, shared an improved resulting into a network collaborative collective participative democratic knowledge management process.

Therefore, experience, training, infrastructure conditions and work organization are preponderant elements for the establishment and strengthening of the community of practice. Moreover, we must emphasize the role of the team manager: he/she must be seen as the leader who works with the group and not as the boss who sets rules and tasks. Thus, u-learning management requires commitment, dedication, creativity and flexibility of all, forcing them to changes during the development of the course.

SOLUTIONS AND RECOMMENDATIONS

The complexity present in human relationships and collaborative working and learning processes allows the establishment of unique patterns to the development of u-learning projects. In each project it is necessary to take into consideration the specificities that permeate it, its target audience, the type of course, the professionals involved, the working infrastructure, the organizational culture, etc. However, there are some basic issues to such projects, if the development of collaborative web-based spaces and communities of practice are concerned. Thus, according to the literature review and experiments reported in this chapter, some strategies are presented below which may contribute to the development of collaborative work environment in u-learning courses.

Strategies for Course's Operation:

- When the course is developed by one institution and implemented by another one, the LMS must be operated by the implementing institution. This is very important in order to avoid difficulties related to expert technical support in a timely manner, if there were performance or usability problems, for example:

  ○ The technical support service for students is an important aspect and it deserves attention, especially when the course is designed to people with little or no experience in u-learning courses, because the learning process can be compromised by operational difficulties. Note also that, whenever possible, it is interesting to provide 24x7 support service, because we know that the public of such courses use up the evening hours and weekends to carry out their activities.

  ○ The LMS is one of the most important aspects for the success of a u-learning course. It must be user-friendly, present clear guidelines for navigation and information organization, have attractive design and objective operational structure. If the LMS does not meet such criteria, LMS access and navigation can become a source of discouragement, undermining the process of individual cognition and collaboration among participants.

• Courses in which a Final Paper is demanded should reduce the number of students per teacher for this activity in particular. This kind of teaching activity requires a more detailed monitoring and more inter-action / mediation, which can get quite impaired when there's a large number of students per teacher. Thus, in order to make it possible to the teacher to act appropriately, assisting in the cognitive construction process of the students, time is necessary: a maximum of ten students per teacher is suggested.

Strategies for Pedagogical Management

• Cultural diversity is to be praised when planning course activities, especially when you want to stimulate collaboration among participants, as each location has its own issues that are specific and directly affect the level of interaction with others.

• One should never forget that cyberculture is still an evolving process. There is a gap between what is planned and what is accomplished both in management and learning processes. It also influences the frequency of participation, the way the activity is to be conducted, along with other relevant factors that may impact the development of the course. So, determining the students' cybercultural profiles is important to prevent possible problems as it allows the teachers to set strategies to face the students' actual conditions which are normal far from ideal ones, as students with extremely poor technological expertise use to enroll themselves on u-learning courses.

• There is still a false expectation that u-learning courses are easier or less rigorous than traditional classroom courses. It is extremely important to face this myth from the early beginning. Instead, u-learning courses require much more dedication, time to study, autonomy and collaboration than expected. There is also the false expectation that teachers and coordinators will need to spend less time doing their pedagogical work. It is important that students' requests are answered in due time.

• In predetermined content u-learning courses, a very common situation in Brazil, namely in courses sponsored by MEC, it is important that everyone involved (coordinators, teachers, tutors and technical and administrative support staff) know the content appropriately. This practice enables team members to become more engaged with the proposed guidelines.

- In order to prevent dispersion among students and teachers, it is important to provide: guideline to the course operation with function description, schedule, guidelines on assessment and certification, etc..; concept maps, mind maps or similar resources which may give a overview of the contents to be addressed; mechanism of monitoring progress and development of the course per student.

Strategies for General Course Management

- The role of the leader is fundamental to let a collaborative web-base process happen. His/her ability to mediate helps the dynamics of collaboration and uncovers possible leaders among the members of the group. The leader must be active and collaborative, making him/herself an example of "not only telling what to do, but also doing things with."
- Expectations related to collaboration and work dynamics should be well explained since the beginning so that all people involved are aware of what to do and how to do.
- Clear selection criteria are to be established regarding formation, experience, theoretical questions such as u-learning methodologies, human-computer interaction, etc in order to determine whether a candidate is adequate to the role to be carried out in the team, rather than only trusting in written résumés.
- The use of asynchronous communication tools such as the Forum should be well explored for administrative questions, be-

cause they allow the discussions to be collective, participatory, collaborative and systematic in a organized way, without requiring that all members are simultaneously present somewhere. It is suggested, therefore, that such spaces are provided in an organized and clear space to ease access, preventing off topic conversations. It is important to avoid dispersion through and loss of time and effort opening several discussions about similar topics.

FUTURE RESEARCH DIRECTIONS

In this chapter, we presented some studies that deal with web-based collaborative work, including those generated from the case study of the experiences described here, which brought many contributions to this field of research, but much remains to be done.

In order to allow future studies to meet the claims related to this area of research, it would be appropriate to develop a framework for u-learning course projects, covering the methodology and tools necessary to ensure that the actors act in a collaborative approach. This is necessarily a multidisciplinary study.

Another possibility, however, in the sense of strengthening the study now developed, is researching what would be the profile of students who favor a more collaborative role in developing the activities of the teaching staff.

CONCLUSION

We have presented the results of researches focused on the cognitive processes involving collaborative work teams working on educational management and administration of geographically distributed web-based u-learning courses. Initially, we discussed how group work became appreciated in recent decades and intensified over the web, due to the possibility of creation of virtual professional community which has its own characteristics that determine its dynamic operation, such as: crucial role of the social actors, maintenance and expansion of the collaboration, and cognitive process whose result is very specific and influenced by resource use hypermedia, resulting in a production of knowledge that is at once individual and collective, that implies and is implied, and that further enhances the learning process and the formation of a collaborative network, creating a positive iterative spiral between cognition and collaboration. The case studies analyzed here, based on theoretical references studied, allowed the proposal of strategies that assist in the management of u-learning courses, which were grouped into three types (operational, pedagogical and administrative).

So, the relation between cyberculture, hypermediatic mechanisms, Human-Computer Human Interaction, and the cognitive processes involved, have a strong influence on the knowledge's production in the areas of web-based work. Therefore, the management of u-learning courses is a great opportunity for the emergence of communities of practice, due to the popularity of ubiquitous and pervasive technologies and the realization that the process of knowledge construction in web-based spaces has real possibilities of collaboration and interaction among individuals. However, it is necessary to recognize that an autonomous behavior of the subjects involved in the process is necessary to the appropriate function of collaborative tools. As a result, hypermedia becomes collaboration promoter and its dependent at the same time.

The experiences presented here show that the creation of communities of practice at the management of a web-base course with several media resources is possible. However, some strategies should be adopted, which should focus on pedagogical and administrative management issues in its operation.

REFERENCES

Bakhtin, M. M. (2002). *Problemas da poética de Dostoiévski* (3rd ed.). (P. Bezerra, Trans.). Rio de Janeiro: Forense Universitária.

Barcellini, F., et al. (2008). A socio-cognitive analysis of online design discussions in an open source software community. *Interacting with Computers, 20*(1), 141-165. Retrieved October 12, 2011, from http://www.sciencedirect.com. ez10.periodicos.capes.gov.br/science/article/pii/S0953543807000793

Bastien, J. M. C., & Scapin, D. (1993). *Ergonomic criteria for the evaluation of human computer interfaces*. Paris: Institut National de Recherche en Informatique et em Automatique. Retrieved November 30, 2012, from http://hal.archives-ouvertes.fr/docs/00/07/00/12/PDF/RT-0156.pdf

Bastos, V., Brandao, M., & Pinho, A. P. (1997). Comprometimento organizacional: Uma análise do conceito expresso por servidores universitários no cotidiano de trabalho. *Revista de Administração Contemporânea, 1*(2). Retrieved June 30, 2012, from http://dx.doi.org/10.1590/S1415-65551997000200006

Camarinha-Matos, L. M., & Afsarmanesh, H. (2005). Collaborative networks: A new scientific discipline. *Journal of Intelligent Manufacturing, 16*(4-5), 439–452. Retrieved May 15, 2012, from http://link.springer.com/article/10.1007%2Fs10845-005-1656-3

Camarinha-Matos, L. M., & Afsarmanesh, H. (2011). Active aging with collaborative networks. *IEEE Technology and Society Magazine, 30*(4), 12–25. doi:10.1109/MTS.2011.943264.

Camarinha-Matos, L. M., & Pantoja-Lima, C. (2001). Cooperation coordination in virtual enterprises. *Journal of Intelligent Manufacturing, 12*(2), 133-150. Retrieved May 15, 2012, from http://link.springer.com/article/10.1023/A%3A1011200526669

Castells, M. (2000). The rise of the network society. In *The information age: Economy, society and culture*. Cambridge, MA: Blackwell.

Catella, H. (2011). Comunidades de aprendizagem: Em torno de um conceito. *Revista Educação, 18*(2), 31-45. Retrieved December 12, 2012, from http://revista.educ.fc.ul.pt/arquivo/vol_XVIII_2/artigo2.pdf

Ducheneaut, N. (2005). Socialization in an open source software community: A socio-technical analysis. *Computer Supported Cooperative Work, 14*(4), 323-368. Retrieved December 14, 2011, from http://www2.parc.com/csl/members/nicolas/documents/JCSCW-OSS.pdf

Eysenck, M. W., & Keane, M. T. (2000). *Cognitive psychology: A student handbook* (4th ed.). Hove, UK: Psychology Press.

Fernandes, G. G. (2008). *Avaliação ergonômica da interface humano computador de ambientes virtuais de aprendizagem*. (Unpublished doctoral dissertation). Universidade Federal do Ceará, Belo Horizonte, Brazil.

Garvin, D. (1993). Building a learning organization. *Harvard Business Review, 71*(4). PMID:10127041.

ISO 9241-11. (1998). *Ergonomics of human system interaction*. Retrieved November 30, 2012, from http://www.it.uu.se/edu/course/homepage/acsd/vt09/ISO9241part11.pdf

Latour, B. (1987). *Science in action: How to follow scientists and engineers through society*. Cambridge, MA: Harvard University Press.

Lave, J., & Wenger, E. C. (1998). *Communities of practice: Learning, meaning, and identity*. Cambridge, UK: Cambridge University Press.

Lévy, P. (1990). *Les technologies de l'intelligence*. Paris: La Découverte.

Lévy, P. (1994). *L'intelligence collective: Pour une anthropologie du cyberespace*. Paris: La Découverte.

Lévy, P. (1997). *Cyberculture*. Paris: Odile Jacob.

Macedo, R. (2006). *Etnopesquisa crítica, etnopesquisa-formação*. Brasília: Liber Livro Editora.

Manovich, L. (1996). *Global algorithm 1.3: The aesthetics of virtual worlds: Ctheory.net*. Retrieved May 15, 2011, from http://www.ctheory.net/articles.aspx?id=34

Matta, A. (2006). *Tecnologias de aprendizagem em rede e ensino de história*. Brasilia: Líber Livro.

Maturana, F., & Varela, F. J. (1987). *The tree of knowledge: The biological roots of human understanding*. Boston: Shambhala Press.

Maximiniano, A. C. A. (2000). *Teoria geral da administração: da escola científica à competitividade na economia globalizada*. São Paulo, Brazil: Atlas.

McDermott, R. (1999). Why information technology inspired but cannot deliver knowledge management. *California Management Review, 41*(4). Retrieved December 01, 2011, from http://www.itu.dk/~kristianskriver/b9/Why%20information%20technology%20inspired%20but%20cannot%20deliver%20Knowledge%20Management.pdf

Nielsen, J. (1994). *Usability engineering*. San Francisco, CA: Morgan Kaufmann. Retrieved November 30, 2012, from http://books.google.com.br/books?id=95As2OF67f0C&printsec=frontcover&hl=pt-BR&source=gbs_ge_summary_r&cad=0#v=onepage&q&f=false

Pressman, R. (2011). *Software engineering: a practitioner's approach* (7th ed.). New York, NY: The McGraw-Hill Companies Inc..

Sack, W., et al. (2003). *Social architecture and technological determinism in open source software development*. Paper presented at 27th meeting of the Society for the Social Studies of Science (4S). Atlanta, GA.

Sack, W., et al. (2006). A methodological framework for socio-cognitive analyses of collaborative design of open source software. *International Journal Computer Supported Cooperative Work, 15*(2-3), 229-240. Retrieved October 12, 2011, from http://dl.acm.org/citation.cfm?id=1149570

Senge, P. (1990). *The fifth discipline: The art and practice of the learning organization*. New York: Doubleday.

Shneiderman, B. et al. (2010). *Designing the user interface*: *Strategies for effective human-computer interaction* (5th ed.). Reading, MA: Addison Wesley.

Von Bertalanffy, L. (1950). An outline of general system theory. *The British Journal for the Philosophy of Science, 1*, 134–165. doi:10.1093/bjps/I.2.134.

Vygotsky, L. S. (1978). *Mind in society: The development of higher psychological processes*. Cambridge, MA: Harvard University Press.

Wenger, E. (2004). *Communities of practice*: *Learning, meaning and identity*. Cambridge, UK: Cambridge University Press.

Wenger, E., McDermott, R., & Snyder, W. M. (2002). *Cultivating communities of practice*. Boston: Harvard Business School Press.

Winner, L. (1997). *Cyberlibertarian myths and the prospects for community*. Retrieved November 30, 2012, from http://www.rpi.edu/~winner/cyberlib2.html

ADDITIONAL READING

Almeida, M. E. (2003). Educação a distância na internet: Abordagens e contribuições dos ambientes digitais de aprendizagem. *Educação e pesquisa, 29*(2). Retrieved Mars 10, 2011, from http://www.scielo.br/scielo.php?script=sci_arttext&pid=S1517-97022003000200010&lng=pt&nrm=iso

L. Camarinha-Mattos, & W. Picard (Eds.). (2008). *Pervasive collaborative networks*. Berlin: Springer. doi:10.1007/978-0-387-84837-2.

Castells, M. (2000). *End of millennium, the information age: Economy, society and culture*. Cambridge, MA: Blackwell.

Cohendet, P., Creplet, F., & Dupouët, O. (2000). Communities of practice and epistemic communities: A renewed approach of organizational learning within the firm. In *Proceedings of WEHIA 2000*. Retrieved December 20, 2012, from http://www.marsouin.org/IMG/pdf/dupouet.pdf

Creplet, F., Dupouet, O., Kern, F., & Munier, F. (2003). *Organizational and cognitive duality on interactions between communities*. Retrieved December 20, 2012, from http://cournot2.u-strasbg.fr/users/egost/papier/Crepelet&all_egost.pdf

Eraut, M. (2000). Non-formal learning and tacit knowledge in professional work. *The British Journal of Educational Psychology, 70*, 113–136. doi:10.1348/000709900158001 PMID:10765570.

Frith, C. D. (2012). The role of metacognition in human social interactions. *Philosophical Transactions of the Royal Society of London. Series B, Biological Sciences, 367*, 2213–2223. doi:10.1098/rstb.2012.0123 PMID:22734064.

D. A. Galeffi, M. A. Modesto, & C. R. Souza (Eds.). (2011). *Epistemologia, construção e difusão o conhecimento: Perspectivas em ação*. Salvador: Eduneb.

Gibson, W. (1984). *Neuromancer*. New York: Ace Books.

Guechtouli, W. (2008). *How do communication structures shape the process of knowledge transfer? An agent-based model*. Retrieved December 20, 2012, from http://halshs.archives-ouvertes.fr/docs/00/34/90/33/PDF/DT2008-55.pdf

Haake, J. (1999). Facilitating orientation in shared hypermedia workspaces. In *Proceeding GROUP '99*. ACM.

ISO 13407. (n.d.). *Human centred design process for interactive systems*. Retrieved November 30, 2012, from http://zonecours.hec.ca/documents/A2007-1-1395534.NormeISO13407.pdf

Lave, J., & Wenger, E. C. (1991). *Situated learning: Legitimate peripheral participation*. Cambridge, UK: Cambridge University Press. doi:10.1017/CBO9780511815355.

Maturana, H. (2001). *Cognição, ciência e vida cotidiana*. Belo Horizonte: Ed. UFMG.

Mork, B. E., Aanestad, M., Hanseth, O., & Grisot, M. (2008). Conflicting epistemic cultures and obstacles for learning across communities of practice. *Knowledge and Process Management*, *15*(1), 12-23. Retrieved December 20, 2012, from http://onlinelibrary.wiley.com/doi/10.1002/kpm.295/pdf

Nielsen, J. (1990). *Hypertext and hypermedia*. Academic Press.

Nielsen, J. (1993). *Usability engineering*. Academic Press.

Nonaka, I., & Takeuchi, H. (1995). *The knowledge creating company*. Oxford, UK: Oxford University Press.

M. Pimentel, & H. Fulks (Eds.). (2011). *Sistemas colaborativos*. Rio de Janeiro: Elsevier.

Primo, A. (2001). *Interação mediada por computador: Comunicação, cibercultura, cognição*. Porto Alegre: Sulina.

Shneiderman, B. (1992). *Designing the user interface: Strategies for effective human-computer interaction*. Reading, MA: Addison-Wesley.

Teles, F. (2010). *Avaliação de ambientes virtuais de aprendizagem na perspectiva da usabilidade de interface*. (Unpublished master dissertation). Pontifícia Universidade Católica de Minas Gerais, Belo Horizonte, Brazil.

Tofler, A. (1980). *A terceira onda*. São Paulo: Bantham Books.

Wang, W. (1999). Team-and-role-based organizational context and access control for cooperative hypermedia environments. In *Proceeding HYPERTEXT '99*. ACM.

Wang, W., Haake, J. M., Rubart, J., & Tietze, D. A. (2000). Hypermedia-based support for cooperative learning of process knowledge. *Journal of Network and Computer Applications*, *23*(4), 357-379. Retrieved December 20, 2012, from http://www.sciencedirect.com/science/article/pii/S1084804500900122

KEY TERMS AND DEFINITIONS

Belonging: Sentiment of the members of a particular group when they feel part of it.

Cognition: It is the human ability of active knowledge construction which occurs in the process of interaction of a person with another and with the environment in which the signs, symbols and language historically and culturally constructed act as mediators of the knowledge construction process, the ability of thought that develops according to the perceptions and emotions of the individual proper to a human being living in society.

Collaboration: Practice of interaction that provides collective experiences and knowledge socialization and mutual help among individuals who are part of this collective group.

Community of Practice: Group of people who have common interests and act together.

Cyberculture: It is s a type of culture characterized by the interaction between society, culture and ICT, marked by the experiences, situations, habits, attitudes, values, behaviors and language of those with whom they interact, whether individuals or institutions.

Cybercultural Profile: Individual characteristics that adhere to the cybercultural behavior standards.

Empowerment: It happens when individuals who constitute a given group are allowed to take part in the decision making process related to collectively and individually activities.

Engagement: Behavior found in individuals who are empowered by the leaders of the group to which they belong, and feel part of that collective.

Human-Computer-Human Interaction: It is the possibility of interaction offered to the users on the web by software in a certain operational context in order to effectively, efficiently accomplish a task.

Hypermedia: Multiple media inserted in a single computing device based on an electronic communication system.

U-Learning: Courses with face to face and distance education activities with web-based hypermidiatic resources available in different kinds of computing devices anytime and anywhere.

ENDNOTES

[1]   This is a federal program directed to the promotion of distance education in Brazilian Public Universities, through the distribution of financial support to the institutions according to the course projects presented to the federal agency that coordinates the process, under certain administrative and pedagogical conditions. Thus, the name Open University of Brazil is misleading as there is no such institution but a project that gathers together proper universities in a project with this name.

Compilation of References

Abowd, G. D., Dey, A. K., Brown, P. J., Davies, N., Smith, M., & Steggles, P. (1999). Towards a better understanding of context and context-awareness. In *Proceedings of the 1st International Symposium on Handheld and Ubiquitous Computing* (pp. 304-307). London: Springer-Verlag.

Abraham, L., & Block, B. (2012). Connected Europe: How smartphones and tablets are shifting media consumption. Reston, VA: comScore.

Abranches, S. P. (2003). *Modernidade e formação de professores: A prática dos multiplicadores dos núcleos de tecnologia educacional do nordeste e a informática na educação. Tese de Doutorado*. USP.

Abreu, J., Claudeivan, L., Veloso, F., & Gomes, A. (2011). *Análise das práticas de colaboração e comunicação: Estudo de caso utilizando a rede social educativa redu*. Retrieved from http://www.br-ie.org/sbie-wie2011/WIE-Trilha1/93028_1.pdf

ACM. (2012). *ACM computing classification system*. Retrieved November 5, 2012, from http://www.acm.org/class/1998

ADL. (2010). *Advanced distributed learning*. Retrieved from http://www.adlnet.org

Adomavicius, G., & Tuzhilin, A. (2005). Toward the next generation of recommender systems: A survey of the state of-the-art and possible extensions. *IEEE Transactions on Knowledge and Data Engineering, 17*(6), 734–749. doi:10.1109/TKDE.2005.99.

Adomavicius, G., & Tuzhilin, A. (2005). Toward the next generation of recommender systems: A survey of the state-of-the-art and possible extensions. *IEEE Transactions on Knowledge and Data Engineering, 1*(6), 734–749. doi:10.1109/TKDE.2005.99.

Aimeur, E., Brassard, G., Fernandez, J., & Mani Onana, F. (2006). Privacy preserving demographic filtering. In *Proceedings of SAC'06*. SAC.

Almeida, M. da G. M. da S. M. E. B. de. (2010). *O cenário atual do uso de tecnologias digitais da informação e comunicação*. Pesquisa sobre o uso das tecnologias de informação e comunicação no Brasil: TIC Educação 2010.

Alves, L. G. P., Kulesza, R., Silva, F. S., Juca, P., & Bressan, G. (2006). Análise comparativa de metadados em tv digital. In *SBC Biblioteca Digital* (pp. 87–98). SBC.

American Society for Training and Development. (2010). *The rise of social media: Enhancing collaboration and productivity across generations*. Retrieved on February 3, 2011 from http://www.astd.org/Publications/Research-Reports/2010/2010-Rise-of-Social-Media

Americo, M. (2010). TV digital: Propostas para o desenvolvimento de conteúdos em animação para o ensino de ciências. Tese de Doutorado, Universidade Estadual Paulista, Bauru, SP., Brazil.

Anderson, R. E., Welch, W. W., & Harris, L. J. (1984). Inequities in opportunities for computer literacy. *The Computing Teacher, 11*(8), 10–12.

Anderson, T., & Dron, J. (2010). Three generations of distance education pedagogy. *International Review of Research in Open and Distance Learning, 12*(3), 80–97.

Andronico, A., Carbonaro, A., Casadei, G., Colazzo, L., Molinari, A., & Ronchetti, M. (2003). *Integrating a multi-agent recommendation system into a mobile learning management system.* Academic Press.

Angelino, L. M., Williams, F. K., & Natvig, D. (2007). Strategies to engage online students and reduce attrition rates. *The Journal of Educators Online, 4*(2), 1-14. Retrieved on October 14, 2011 from http://www.thejeo.com/Archives/Volume4Number2/Angelino-Final.pdf

Arata, L. O. (2003). Reflections on interactivity. In D. Thorburn, & H. Jenkins (Eds.), *Rethinking media change: The aesthetics of transition.* Cambridge, MA: MIT Press.

Arias, F. (2010). *Multi-agent adaptive model for adaptive virtual courses planning and LO selection.* (MSc Dissertation).

Armbrust, M., Fox, A., Griffith, R., Joseph, A. D., Katz, R., Konwinski, A., & Zaharia, M. (2010). A view of cloud computing. *Communications of the ACM, 53*(4), 50–58. doi:10.1145/1721654.1721672.

Augustin, I., Yamin, A., Barbosa, J. L., Silva, L. C., Real, R. A., & Geyer, C. F. R. (2004). ISAM, join context-awareness and mobility to building pervasive applications. In I. Mahgoub, & M. Ylias (Eds.), *Mobile Computing Handbook* (pp. 73–94). New York: CRC Press. doi:10.1201/9780203504086.ch4.

Azuma, R. T. (1997). A survey of augmented reality. *Teleoperators and Virtual Environments, 6*(1), 1–10.

Azuma, R. T., Baillot, Y., Behringer, R., Feiner, S., Julier, S., & MacIntyre, B. (2001). Recent advances in augmented reality. *IEEE Computer Graphics and Applications, 21*(6), 34–47. doi:10.1109/38.963459.

Baek, Y., Jung, J., & Kim, B. (2008). What makes teachers use technology in the classroom? Exploring the factors affecting facilitation of technology with a Korean sample. *Computers & Education, 50*(1), 224–234. doi:10.1016/j.compedu.2006.05.002.

Bailenson, J. N., & Yee, N. (2008). Virtual interpersonal touch: Haptic interaction and copresence in collaborative virtual environments. *Multimedia Tools and Applications, 37*, 5-14. Retrieved on July 25, 2010 from http://vhil.stanford.edu/pubs/2007/bailenson-mm-VIT-CVE.pdf

Bailenson, J. N., Merget, D., Schroeder, R., & Yee, N. (2006). The effect of behavioral realism and form realism of real-time avatar faces on verbal disclosure, non-verbal disclosure, emotion recognition, and copresence in dyadic interaction. *Presence: Teleoperators and Virtual Environments, 15*(4), 359-372. Retrieved September 30, 2009 from http://www.mitpressjournals.org/doi/pdf/10.1162/pres.15.4.359

Bailenson, J. N., Swinth, K., Hoyt, C., Persky, S., Dimov, A., & Blascovich, J. (2005) The independent and interactive effects of embodied-agent appearance and behavior on self-report, cognitive, and behavioral markers of copresence in immersive virtual environments. *Presence: Teleoperators & Virtual Environments, 14*(4), 379-393. Retrieved on May 15, 2011 from http://vhil/stanford.edu/pubs/2005/bailenson-copresence.pdf

Bailenson, J. N., Yee, N., Blascovich, J., Bell, A. C., Lunbald, N., & Jin, M. (2008). The use of immersive virtual reality in the learning sciences: Digital transformation of teachers, students, and social context. *The Journal of the Learning Sciences, 17*, 102-141. Retrieved on August 10, 2010 from http://www.life-slc.org/Bailenson_etal-immersiveVR.pdf

Baker, W. J. (2000). The classroom flip: Using web course management tools to become the guide by the side. In J. A Chamber (Ed.), *Selected Papers from the 11th International Conference on College Teaching and Learning.* Jacksonville, FL: Center for the Advancement of Teaching and Learning.

Bakhtin, M. M. (2002). *Problemas da poética de Dostoiévski* (3rd ed.). (P. Bezerra, Trans.). Rio de Janeiro: Forense Universitária.

Baldauf, M., Dustdar, S., & Rosenberg, F. (2007). A survey on context-aware systems. *International Journal of Ad Hoc and Ubiquitous Computing, 2*(4), 263–277. doi:10.1504/IJAHUC.2007.014070.

Bales, R. F. (2001). *Social interaction systems: Theory and measurement.* New Brunswick, NJ: Transaction Publishers.

Balog, A., Pribeanu, C., & Iordache, D. (2007). Augmented reality in schools: Preliminary evaluation results from a summer school. *International Journal of Social Sciences, 2*(3), 184–187.

Baltrunas, L., Ludwig, B., Peer, S., & Ricci, F. (2012). Context relevance assessment and exploitation in mobile recommender systems. *Personal and Ubiquitous Computing, 16*(5), 507–526. doi:10.1007/s00779-011-0417-x.

Banakou, D., Chorianopoulos, K., & Anagnostou, K. (2009). Avatars appearance and social behavior in online virtual worlds. In *Proceedings of the 13ᵗʰ Panhellenic Conference on Informatics* (pp. 207-211). Corfu, Greece: IEEE Computer Society. Retrieved on January 29, 2012 from http://ebookbrowse.com/avatars-appearance-and-social-behaviors-in-online-virtual-worlds-pdf-d266139551

Bandura, A. (1997). *Self-efficacy: The exercise of control.* New York: Freeman.

Barbosa, D. N. F., Augustin, I., Barbosa, J. L. V., Yamin, A. C., Silva, L. C., & Geyer, C. F. R. (2006). Learning in a large-scale pervasive environment. In *Proceedings of the 2nd IEEE International Workshop on Pervasive Computing (PerEl)* (pp. 226-230). New York: IEEE Press.

Barbosa, J. L. V., Hahn, R., Rabello, S. A., & Barbosa, D. N. F. (2007). Mobile and ubiquitous computing in a innovative undergraduate course. In *Proceedings of the 38th ACM Technical Symposium on Computer Science Education* (pp. 379-383). New York: ACM Press.

Barbosa, J. L. V., Hahn, R., Rabello, S. A., & Barbosa, D. N. F. (2008). LOCAL: A model geared towards ubiquitous learning. In *Proceedings of the ACM Technical Symposium on Computer Science Education* (pp. 432-436). Portland, OR: ACM Press.

Barbosa, D. N. F., Geyer, C. F. R., & Barbosa, J. L. V. (2005). GlobalEdu - An architecture to support learning in a pervasive computing environment. *New Trends and Technologies in Computer-Aided Learning for Computer-Aided Design, 192*, 1–10. doi:10.1007/0-387-30761-3_1.

Barcellini, F., et al. (2008). A socio-cognitive analysis of online design discussions in an open source software community. *Interacting with Computers, 20*(1), 141-165. Retrieved October 12, 2011, from http://www.sciencedirect.com.ez10.periodicos.capes.gov.br/science/article/pii/S0953543807000793

Barnett, C. (1991). Building a case-based curriculum to enhance the pedagogical content knowledge of mathematics teachers. *Journal of Teacher Education, 42*(4), 263–272. doi:10.1177/002248719104200404.

Barret, T., Mac Labhrainn, I., & Fallon, H. (2005). *Handbook of enquiry & problem based learning.* Galway: CELT. Retrieved October 08, 2012, from http://www.nuigalway.ie/celt/pblbook/

Barron, B. J. S., Schwartz, D. L., Vye, N. J., Moore, A., Petrosino, A., & Zech, L. et al. (1998). Doing with understanding: Lessons from research on problem- and project-based learning. *Journal of the Learning Sciences, 7*(3/4).

Barseghian, T. (2011, February 5). Three trends that define the future of teaching and learning. [Blog post]. *KQED Mind/Shift.* Retrieved from http://blogs.kqed.org/mindshift/2011/02/three-trends-that-define-the-future-of-teaching-and-learning/

Bastien, J. M. C., & Scapin, D. (1993). *Ergonomic criteria for the evaluation of human computer interfaces.* Paris: Institut National de Recherche en Informatique et em Automatique. Retrieved November 30, 2012, from http://hal.archives-ouvertes.fr/docs/00/07/00/12/PDF/RT-0156.pdf

Bastos, V., Brandao, M., & Pinho, A. P. (1997). Comprometimento organizacional: Uma análise do conceito expresso por servidores universitários no cotidiano de trabalho. *Revista de Administração Contemporânea, 1*(2). Retrieved June 30, 2012, from http://dx.doi.org/10.1590/S1415-65551997000200006

Batista, J. C. (2010). Os efeitos das políticas industriais para o setor de produtos eletrônicos do Brasil. *Revue d'Economie Politique, 30*(1), 112–123. doi:10.1590/S0101-31572010000100007.

Baylor, A. L. (2009). Promoting motivation with virtual agents and avatars: The role of visual presence and appearance. *Philosophical Transactions of the Royal Society of London. Series B, Biological Sciences,* 3559–3565. doi:10.1098/rstb.2009.0148 PMID:19884150.

Bellifemine, F., Rimessa, G., Trucco, T., & Caire, G. (2005). *JADE (Java agent development framework) programmer's guide.*

Benedek, A. (2009). *Notes on the perspectives of media convergence and the new learning paradigm.* Paper presented at the Meeting of the LOGOS Open Conference New Technology Platforms for Learning Revisited. Budapest, Hungary.

Benyon, D., Turner, D. P., & Turner, D. S. (2005). *Designing interactive systems: People, activities, contexts, technologies*. Reading, MA: Addison-Wesley.

Berelson, B. (1952). *Content analysis in communication research*. Glencoe, IL: Free Press.

Bergmann, J., & Sams, A. (2012). *Flip your classroom: Reach every student in every class every day*. Eugene, OR: International Society for Technology in Education.

Berners-Lee, T., & Hendler, J. (2001). Publishing on the semantic web. *Nature, 410*(6832), 1023–1024. doi:10.1038/35074206 PMID:11323639.

Bessiere, K., Ellis, J. B., & Kellogg, W. A. (2009). Acquiring a professional 'second life': Problems and prospects for the use of virtual worlds in business. In *Proceedings of the 27th International Conference Extended Abstracts on Human Factors in Computing Systems* (pp. 2883-2898). New York: ACM. doi: 10.1145/1520340.1520416

Betancur, D., Moreno, J., & Ovalle, D. (2009). Modelo para la recomendación y recuperación de objetos de aprendizaje en entornos virtuales de enseñanza/aprendizaje. *Revista Avances en Sistemas e Informática, 6*(1), 45–56.

Bez, M. R., Vicari, R. M., & Silva, J. M. Carvalho da, Ribeiro, A., Guz, J. C., Passerino, L., ... Roesler, V. (2010). Proposta brasileira de metadados para objetos de aprendizagem baseados em agentes (OBAA). *Revista Novas Tecnologias na Educação, 8*(2), 1–10.

Biancalana, C., Gasparetti, F., Micarelli, A., & Sansonetti, G. (2011). An approach to social recommendation for context-aware mobile services. *ACM Transaction Intelligent. Systems. Technology, 1*(1). DOI = 10.1145/0000000.0000000

Bickford, L., & del Toro, B. (Producers) & Soderbergh, S. (Director). (2008a). *Che: The Argentine*. [Motion picture]. Los Angeles, CA: IFC Films.

Bickford, L., & del Toro, B. (Producers) & Soderbergh, S. (Director). (2008b). *Che: Guerilla*. [Motion picture]. Los Angeles, CA: IFC Films.

Billinghurst, M. N., & Henrysson, A. (2006). Research directions in handheld AR. *International Journal of Virtual Reality, 2*(1), 51–58.

Billinghurst, M. N., Kato, H., & Poupyrev, I. (2001). The MagicBook - Moving seamlessly between reality and virtuality. *IEEE Computer Graphics and Applications, 21*(3), 6–8.

Black, B., & Wood, A. (2003). Utilising information communication technology to assist the education of individuals with Down syndrome. *Down Syndrome Issues and Information*. Retrieved from http://www.down-syndrome.org/information/education/technology/

Boellstorff, T. (2008). *Coming of age in second life: An anthropologist explores the virtually human*. Princeton, NJ: Princeton University Press.

Bonk, C. J. (2009). *The world is open: How web technology is revolutionizing education*. San Francisco, CA: Jossey-Bass.

Borthick, A. F., Jones, D. R., & Wakai, S. (2003). Designing learning experiences within learners' zone of proximal development (ZPD), enabling collaborative learning on-site and online. *Journal of Information Systems, 17*(1), 107-134. Retrieved on October 12, 2009 from http://www2.gsu.edu/~accafb/pubs/JISBorthickJonesWakai2003.pdf

Boulos, M. N. K., & Wheeler, S. (2007). The emerging web 2.0 social software: An enabling suite of sociable technologies in health and health care education. *Health Information and Libraries Journal, 24*, 2–23. doi:10.1111/j.1471-1842.2007.00701.x PMID:17331140.

Boys, B., Brothers, D., & Jr, C. M. (1989). Paul's boutique. [Audio CD]. Los Angeles, CA: Capitol Records.

Br, C. G. I. (2011). *TIC Brasil: Domicílios e usuários 2011*. Retrieved from http://www.cetic.br/usuarios/tic/2011-total-brasil

Bradley, M. M., & Lang, P. J. (1994). Measuring emotion: The self-assessment manikin and the semantic differential. *Journal of Behavior Therapy and Experimental Psychiatry, 1*(25), 49–59. doi:10.1016/0005-7916(94)90063-9 PMID:7962581.

Brasil. (1998). *Secretaria de educação fundamental: Parâmetros curriculares nacionais*. Matemática: Ensino de quinta a oitava série.

Brasil. 10.098, de 19 de dezembro de 2000., 244 Diário Oficial da União § 1 2 (2000).

Breese, J., Heckerman, D., & Kadie, C. (1998). Empirical analysis of predictive algorithms for collaborative filtering. In *Proceedings of 14th UAI*. UAI.

Broekens, J., & Brinkman, W. (2009). AffectButton: Towards a standard for dynamic affective user feedback. In R. Dienstbier (Ed.), *Affective Computing and Intelligent Interaction and Workshops, 2009* (pp. 1–8). Amsterdam, The Netherlands: ACII. doi:10.1109/ACII.2009.5349347.

Brown, J. S. (2008). *Tinkering as a mode of knowledge production.* Retrieved May 13, 2012, from http://www.youtube.com/watch?v=9u-MczVpkUA

Brown, A. L. (1992). Design experiments: Theoretical and methodological challenges in creating complex interventions in classroom settings. *Journal of the Learning Sciences, 2*(2), 141–178. doi:10.1207/s15327809jls0202_2.

Brown, J. S., Collins, A., & Duguid, P. (1989). Cognition and the culture of learning. *Educational Researcher, 18*(1), 32–42. doi:10.3102/0013189X018001032.

Brown, J. S., Collins, A., & Duguid, P. (1989). Situated cognition and the culture of learning. *Educational Researcher, 18*(1), 32–42. doi:10.3102/0013189X018001032.

Bruner, J. (1991). The narrative construction of reality. *Critical Inquiry, 18*(1), 1–21. doi:10.1086/448619.

Bruner, J. S. (1961). The act of discovery. *Harvard Educational Review, 31*, 21–32.

Brunet, P., Feigenbaum, B. A., Harris, K., Laws, C., Schwerdtfeger, R., & Weiss, L. (2005). Accessibility requirements for systems design to accommodate users with vision impairments. *IBM Systems Journal, 44*(3), 445–466. doi:10.1147/sj.443.0445.

Brusilovsky, P., Karagia-Nnidis, C., & Sampson, D. (2004). Layered evaluation of adaptive learning systems, In *Proceedings of the International Joint Conf. on Engineering Education and Lifelong Learning*, (Vol. 14, pp. 402–421). IEEE.

Buckley, S. J. (2000). Speech, language and communication for individuals with Down syndrome: An overview. *Down Syndrome Issues and Information.* Retrieved from http://www.down-syndrome.org/information/language/overview/

Buckley, S. J. (2001). Reading and writing for individuals with Down syndrome: An overview. *Down Syndrome Issues and Information.* Retrieved from http://www.down-syndrome.org/information/reading/overview/

Buckley, S. J. (2012). *Living with Down syndrome.* Down Syndrome Education International.

Burdea, G., & Coffet, P. (1994). Virtual reality technology (2ª Ed.). Washington, DC: Wiley-IEEE Press.

Buriano, L., Marchetti, M., Carmagnola, F., Cena, F., Gena, C., & Torre, I. (2006). The role of ontologies in context-aware recommender systems. In *Proceedings of the 7th International Conference on Mobile Data Management*. IEEE.

Cable & Satellite Broadcasting Association of Asia. (2009). *Online video in China, Japan & Korea.* Hong Kong: CASBAA.

Calvo, R. (2003). User scenarios for the design and implementation of iLMS. In *Proceedings of the AIED 2003 Workshop, Towards Intelligent Learning Management Systems*. AIED.

Calvo, R. A., & D'Mello, S. (2010). Affect detection: An interdisciplinary review of models, methods, and their applications. *IEEE Transactions Affective Computing, 1*(1), 18–37. doi:10.1109/T-AFFC.2010.1.

Camarinha-Matos, L. M., & Afsarmanesh, H. (2005). Collaborative networks: A new scientific discipline. *Journal of Intelligent Manufacturing, 16*(4-5), 439–452. Retrieved May 15, 2012, from http://link.springer.com/article/10.1007%2Fs10845-005-1656-3

Camarinha-Matos, L. M., & Pantoja-Lima, C. (2001). Cooperation coordination in virtual enterprises. *Journal of Intelligent Manufacturing, 12*(2), 133-150. Retrieved May 15, 2012, from http://link.springer.com/article/10.1023/A%3A1011200526669

Camarinha-Matos, L. M., & Afsarmanesh, H. (2011). Active aging with collaborative networks. *IEEE Technology and Society Magazine, 30*(4), 12–25. doi:10.1109/MTS.2011.943264.

Campbell, M. (2009). Using 3-D virtual worlds to teach decision-making: In same places, different spaces. In *Proceedings ASCILITE*, (pp. 104-109). Auckland, New Zealand: ASCILITE. Retrieved on March 7, 2011 from www.ascilite.org.au/conferences/auckland09/procs/campbell-m.pdf

Campbell, J. (1990). *Transformations of myth through time: Thirteen brilliant lectures from the renowned master of mythology*. New York: Harper & Row.

Campbell, M., & Uys, P. (2007). Identifying factors that influence the success of ICT in developing a learning community: The CELT experience. *Campus-Wide Information Systems, 24*(1), 17–26. doi:10.1108/10650740710726464.

Casali, A., Gerling, V., Deco, C., & Bender, C. (2011). Sistema inteligente para la recomendación de objetos de aprendizaje. *Revista Generación Digital, 9*(1), 88–95.

Casey, D. (2005). U-learning = e-learning + m-learning. In G. Richards (Ed.), *Proceedings of the World Conference on E-Learning in Corporate, Government, Healthcare, and Higher Education 2005* (pp. 2864-2871). Chesapeake, VA: AACE. Retrieved on October 17, 2012 from http://www.editlib.org/p/21634

Castells, M. (2000). The rise of the network society. In *The information age: Economy, society and culture*. Cambridge, MA: Blackwell.

Catella, H. (2011). Comunidades de aprendizagem: Em torno de um conceito. *Revista Educação, 18*(2), 31-45. Retrieved December 12, 2012, from http://revista.educ.fc.ul.pt/arquivo/vol_XVIII_2/artigo2.pdf

Cazella, S. C., Nunes, M. A. S., & Reategui, E. (2010). A ciência do palpite: Estado da arte em sistemas de recomendação. In R. Dienstbier (Ed.), *Jornada de Atualização de Informática* (pp. 161-216). Rio de Janeiro: PUC

Cazella, S. C., Reategui, E., & Behar, P. (2010). Recommendation of learning objects applying collaborative filtering and competencies. In N. Reynolds & M. Turcsányi-Szabó (Eds.), *Key Competencies in the Knowledge Society - IFIP TC 3 International Conference*. Boston: IFIP.

Cazella, S. C., Behar, P., Schneider, D., Silva, K. K. A., & Freitas, R. (2012). Desenvolvendo um sistema de recomendação de objetos de aprendizagem baseado em competências para a educação: Relato de experiências. In *Simpósio Brasileiro de Informática na Educação*. Rio de Janeiro: Anais do Simpósio Brasileiro de Informática na Educação.

Cazella, S. C., Corrêa, I., & Reategui, E. (2008). Um modelo para recomendação de conteúdos baseado em filtragem colaborativa para dispositivos móveis. *Revista Novas Tecnologias na Educação, 6*(2), 12–22.

Cazella, S. C., Silva, K. K. A., Behar, P., Schneider, D., & Freitas, R. (2011). Recomendando objetos de aprendizagem baseado em competências em EAD. *Revista Novas Tecnologias na Educação, 9*, 1–10.

Cebula, K. R., Moore, D. G., & Wishart, J. G. (2010). Social cognition in children with Down's syndrome: Challenges to research and theory building. *Journal of Intellectual Disability Research, 54*, 113–134. doi:10.1111/j.1365-2788.2009.01215.x PMID:19874447.

CETIC. (2012). *Centro de estudos sobre as tecnologias da informação e da comunicação*. TIC Kids Online Brasil 2012 - Pesquisa sobre o Uso das Tecnologias de Informação e Comunicação no Brasil.

CGI.Br. (2010). *A evolução da internet no Brasil*. Revista CGI.Br.

CGPID. C. G. do P. de I. D. (2010). *Plano nacional de banda larga*. Retrieved from http://www.mc.gov.br/publicacoes/doc_download/418-documento-base-do-programa-nacional-de-banda-larga

Charitonos, K., Blake, C., Scanlon, E., & Jones, A. (2012). Museum learning via social and mobile technologies: (How) can online interactions enhance the visitor experience? *British Journal of Educational Technology, 43*(5), 802–819. doi:10.1111/j.1467-8535.2012.01360.x.

Chen, G. D., Chang, C. K., & Wang, C. Y. (2008). Ubiquitous learning website: Scaffold learners by mobile devices with information-aware techniques. *Computers & Education, 50*(1), 77-80. Retrieved on October 16, 2012 from http://www.cbit.soton.ac.uk/multimedia/PDFs/Ubiquitous%20learning%20website%20scaffolding%20learners%20by%20mobile%20devices%20with%20info-aware%20techniques.pdf

Chen, W., Lee, C., Tan, A., & Lin, C.-P. (2012). What, how and why - A peek into the uses and gratifications of ubiquitous computing for pre-service teachers in Singapore. In *Proceedings of the International Conference on Wireless, Mobile and Ubiquitous Technology in Education*, (pp. 182–186). doi:10.1109/WMUTE.2012.41

Chen, W., Seow, P., & So, H. (2010). Extending students' learning spaces: Technology-supported seamless learning. *ICLS, 1*, 484–491. Retrieved from http://ammonwiemers.com/IdetPortfolio/articles/Technology Integration/Extending Students Learning Spaces -- Technology-Supported Seamless Learning.pdf

Chen, Y. S., Kao, T. C., Sheu, J. P., & Chiang, C. Y. (2002). A mobile scaffolding-aid-based bird watching learning system. In *Proceedings of IEEE International Workshop on Wireless and Mobile Technologies in Education (WMTE'02)*, (pp. 15-22). IEEE. Retrieved on October 18, 2012 from http://www.csie.ntpu.edu.tw/~yschen/compapers/bird/pdf

Chen, C., & Huang, T. (2012). Learning in a u-museum: Developing a context-aware ubiquitous learning environment. *Computers & Education Journal, 59*, 873–883. doi:10.1016/j.compedu.2012.04.003.

Chisholm, W. A., & Henry, S. L. (2005). Interdependent components of web accessibility. In *Proceedings of the 2005 International Cross-Disciplinary Workshop on Web Accessibility (W4A)* (pp. 31–37). New York, NY: ACM. doi:10.1145/1061811.1061818

Chiu, P. S., Kuo, Y., Huang, Y., & Chen, T. (2008). A meaningful learning based u-learning evaluation model. In *Proceedings of the Eighth IEEE International Conference on Advanced Learning Technologies*, (pp. 77-81). IEEE. Retrieved on October 14, 2012 from http://ieeexplore.ieee.org/xpl/login.jsp?tp=&anumber=4561631&url=http%3A%2F%2Fieeexplore.ieee.org%2Fxpls%2Fabs_all.jsp%3Fanumber%3D4561631

Chlopak, O. (2003). Computers in Russian schools: Current conditions, main problems, and prospects for the future. *Computers & Education*, (40): 41–55. doi:10.1016/S0360-1315(02)00093-3.

Chou, C. C. (2009). Virtual worlds for organizational learning and communities of practice. In U. Cress, V. Dimitrova, & M. Specht (Eds.), *Learning in the Synergy of Multiple Disciplines (LNCS)* (Vol. 5794, pp. 751–756). Berlin, Germany: Springer. doi:10.1007/978-3-642-04636-0_79.

Chou, C. Y., Chan, T. W., & Lin, C. J. (2003). Redefining the learning companion: The past, present, and future of educational agents. *Computers & Education, 40*, 256–269. doi:10.1016/S0360-1315(02)00130-6.

Chu, H.-C., Hwang, G.-J., & Tsai, C.-C. (2010). A knowledge engineering approach to developing mindtools for context-aware ubiquitous learning. *Computers & Education, 54*(1), 289–297. doi:10.1016/j.compedu.2009.08.023.

Ciurea, C. (2012). The development of a mobile application in a collaborative banking system. *Informatica Economică, 14*(3), 86–97.

Clark, A., Dunser, A., & Grasset, R. (2011). *An interactive augmented reality coloring book*. Paper presented at the meeting of the IEEE International Symposium on Mixed and Augmented Reality (ISMAR). Basel, Switzerland.

Cobo, B. A. L., & Moravec, J. W. (2011). *Aprendizaje invisible*. Livro. Universitat de Barcelona.

Cocea, M., & Weibelzahl, S. (2006). Motivation - Included or excluded from e-learning. In D. Kinshuk, G. Sampson, J. M. Spector, & P. Isias (Eds.), *IADIS International Conference on Cognition and Exploratory Learning in Digital Age, CELDA 2006* (pp. 435-437). Retrieved August 1, 2010 from http://www.easy-hub.org/stephan/cocea-celda06.pdf

Coffman, T., & Klinger, M. B. (2007). Utilizing virtual worlds in education: The implications for practice. *International Journal for Social Sciences, 2*(1), 29-33. Retrieved September 26, 2010 from http://www.akademik.unsri.ac.id/download/journal/files/waset/v2-1-5 1.pdf

Coles, R. (1989). *The call of stories: Teaching and the moral imagination*. Boston: Houghton-Mifflin.

Collazos, C. (2003). *Una metodología para el apoyo computacional de la evaluación y monitoreo en ambientes de aprendizaje cooperativo. (Tesis doctoral)*. Santiago, Chile: Universidad de Chile.

Collazos, C., Alvira, J., Martínez, D., Jiménez, J., Cobos, R., & Moreno, J. (2008). Evaluando y monitoreando actividades colaborativas en dispositivos móviles. *Revista Avances en Sistemas e Informática, 5*(1), 82–93.

Coll, C., & Monereo, C. (2010). Educação e aprendizagem no séc XXI: Novas ferramentas, novos cenários, novas finalidades. In C. Coll (Ed.), *Psicologia da Educação Virtual: Aprender e Ensinar com as Tecnologias da Informação e da Comunicação*. Porto Alegre: Artmed.

Committee, L. T. S. (2002). *IEEE standard for learning object metadata. IEEE Standard 1484*. IEEE.

ComScore. (2012, October 17). *Internet users in Mexico watch more than 14 hours of online video to lead as the most engaged audience in Latin America*. [Press release]. Retrieved from http://www.comscore.com/Insights/Press_Releases/2012/10/Internet_Users_in_Mexico_Watch_More_than_14_Hours_of_Online_Video

Conforto, D., & Santarosa, L. M. C. (2002). Acessibilidade à web: Internet para todos. *Revista de Informática na Educação: Teoria. Prática, 5*(2), 87–102.

Consumer Electronics Association. (2012, May 14). *Consumers view video via more platforms, but HDTVs more popular, CEA study finds*. [Press release]. Retrieved from http://www.ce.org/News/News-Releases/Press-Releases/2012-Press-Releases/Consumers-View-Video-Via-More-Platforms,-But-HDTVs.aspx

Cooper, H. (1982). Scientific guidelines for conducting integrative research reviews. *Review of Educational Research, 52*(2), 291–302. doi:10.3102/00346543052002291.

Copeland, M. T. (1954). The genesis of the case method in business instruction. In M. P. McNair, & A. Hersum (Eds.), *Case Method at the Harvard Business School* (pp. 25–33). New York: McGraw-Hill.

Cornelius, S., & Marston, P. (2009). Toward an understanding of the virtual context in mobile learning. *Research in Learning Technology, 17*(3), 161–172. doi:10.3402/rlt.v17i3.10874.

Costa, R., & Kirner, C. (2012). *Livro interativo de xadrez potencializado com realidade aumentada*. Paper presented at the meeting of the Workshop de Realidade Virtual e Aumentada (WRVA). São Paulo, Brazil.

Cranshaw, J., Toch, E., Hong, J., Kittur, A., & Sadeh, N. (2010). Bridging the gap between physical location and online social networks. *Ubicomp, 10*, 119. doi:10.1145/1864349.1864380.

Creta, G. (2003). *Human computer interaction proceedings*. Hoboken, NJ: Lawrence Erlbaum Associates.

Dabbs, L. (2012, October 25). Mobile learning support for new teachers. *Teaching with Soul!* Retrieved November 15, 2012, from http://www.teachingwithsoul.com/2012/mobile-learning-support-for-new-teachers

Dalgarno, B., & Lee, M. J. (2010). What are the learning affordances of 3-D virtual environments? *British Journal of Education Technology, 41*(1), 10-32. Retrieved on January 15, 2012 from http://edtc6325teamone2ndlife.pbworks.com/f/6325%BLearning%Baffordances%Bof%B 3-D.pdf

Datar, S. M., Garvin, D. A., & Cullen, P. C. (2010). *Rethinking the MBA: Business education at a crossroads*. Boston: Harvard Business School Press.

Davis, A., Murphy, J., Owens, D., Khazanchi, D., & Zigurs, I. (2009). Avatars, people, and virtual worlds: Foundations for research in metaverses. *Journal of the Association for Information Services, 10*(2), 90-117. Retrieved on January 29, 2011 from http://kmcms.free.fr/virtualworlds/AvatarsPeopleandVirtualWorldsFoundationforResearchinMetaverses.pdf

Davis, F. D. (1989). Perceived usefulness, perceived ease of use, and user acceptance of information technology. *Management Information Systems Quarterly, 13*(3), 319–340. doi:10.2307/249008.

de Azevedo, F. L. B. (2009). *Bora ali tomar um café? Concepção de uma experiência ubíqua de suporte à aprendizagem conversacional no ambiente de trabalho. Mestrado*. UFPE.

de Figueiredo, A. D. (2002). *Redes e educação: A surpreendente riqueza de um conceito*. Conselho Nacional de Educação.

de Freitas, S., Rebolledo-Mendez, G., Liarokapis, F., Magoulas, G., & Poulovassilis, A. (2009). Learning as an immersive experience: Using the four dimensional framework for designing and evaluating immersive learning experiences in a virtual world. *British Journal of Educational Technology, 41*(1), 69-85. Retrieved on July 4, 2011 from http://www.sussex.ac.uk/Users/gr20/BJET(2010).pdf

De Lucia, A., Francese, R., Passero, I., & Tortora, G. (2012). A collaborative augmented campus based on location-aware mobile technology. *International Journal of Distance Education Technologies, 10*(1), 55–73. doi:10.4018/jdet.2012010104.

de Oliveira, L. R., & Medina, R. D. (2010). Desenvolvimento de objetos de aprendizagem para dispositivos móveis: Uma nova abordagem que contribui para a educação. *RENOTE, 5*(1). Retrieved from http://seer.ufrgs.br/renote/article/view/14154

Deci, E. L., & Ryan, R. M. (1985). *Intrinsic motivation and self-determination in human behavior*. New York: Plenum. doi:10.1007/978-1-4899-2271-7.

Deci, E. L., & Ryan, R. M. (2000). Intrinsic and extrinsic motivations: Classic definitions and new directions. *Contemporary Educational Psychology, 25*, 54–67. doi:10.1006/ceps.1999.1020 PMID:10620381.

Dede, C. (2005). Planning for neomillennial learning styles: Implications for investments in faculty and technology. In D. Oblinger, & J. Oblinger (Eds.), *Educating the Net generation* (pp. 15.1–15.22). Boulder, CO: EDUCAUSE.

Dede, C. (2009). Immersive interfaces for engagement and learning. *Science, 323*, 66–69. doi:10.1126/science.1167311 PMID:19119219.

Demetriadisa, S., Barbasb, A., Molohidesb, A., Palaigeorgioua, G., Psillosb, D., & Vlahavasa, I. et al. (2003). Cultures in negotiation: Teachers' acceptance/resistance attitudes considering the infusion of technology into schools. *Computers & Education*, (41): 19–37. doi:10.1016/S0360-1315(03)00012-5.

Deshpande, M., & Karypis, G. (2004). Item-based top-n recommendation algorithms. *ACM Transactions on Information Systems, 22*(1), 143–177. doi:10.1145/963770.963776.

Design-Based Research Collective. (2003). Design-based research: An emerging paradigm for educational inquiry. *Educational Researcher*, 5–8.

Dey, A. K., Abowd, G. D., Brown, P. J., Davies, N., Smith, M., & Steggles, P. (1999). Towards a better understanding of context and context-awareness. In *Proceedings of the 1st International Symposium on Handheld and Ubiquitous Computing*, (LNCS), (Vol. 1707, pp. 304-307). Karlsruhe, Germany: Springer.

Dey, A. K. (2001). Understanding and using context. *Personal and Ubiquitous Computing, 5*(1), 4–7. doi:10.1007/s007790170019.

Dey, A. K., Wac, K., Ferreira, D., Tassini, K., Hong, J., & Ramos, J. (2011). Getting closer: An empirical investigation of the proximity of user to their smart phones. *UbiComp, 11*, 163–172.

Dey, A., Hightower, J., Lara, E., & Davies, N. (2010). Location-based services. *IEEE Pervasive Computing / IEEE Computer Society [and] IEEE Communications Society, 9*(1), 11–12. doi:10.1109/MPRV.2010.10.

Diaz, A., Merino, P., & Rivas, F. J. (2009). Mobile application profiling for connected mobile devices. *IEEE Pervasive Computing / IEEE Computer Society [and] IEEE Communications Society, 9*(1), 54–61. doi:10.1109/MPRV.2009.63.

Dickey, M. (2007). Game design and learning: A conjectural analysis of how massively multiple online role-playing games (MMORPG) foster intrinsic motivation. *Educational Technology Research and Development, 55*, 253–273. doi:10.1007/s11423-006-9004-7.

Dikkers, S., Martin, J., & Coulter, B. (2011). *Mobile media learning*. ETC Press.

DiMaggio, P., & Hargittai, E. (2001). *From the digital divide to digital inequality: Studying internet use and penetration increases* (Working paper). Princeton, NJ: Center for Arts and Cultural Policy Studies, Princeton University.

Downes, S. (2010). New technology supporting informal learning. *Journal of Emerging Technologies in Web Intelligence, 2*(1). doi:10.4304/jetwi.2.1.27-33.

Doyle, M. (2009). *Beginning PHP 5.3*. Birmingham, UK: Wrox Press Ltd..

DroidHen. (2012). Shoot the apple. *DroidHen Games.* Retrieved from http://www.droidhen.com/games.html

Duan, L., Street, W. N., & Xu, E. (2011). Healthcare information systems: Data mining methods in the creation of a clinical recommender system. *Enterprise Information Systems, 5*(2), 169–181. doi:10.1080/17517575.2010.541287.

Ducate, L., & Lomicka, L. (2008). Adventures in the blogosphere: From blog readers to blog writers. *Computer Assisted Language Learning, 21*(1), 9–28. doi:10.1080/09588220701865474.

Ducheneaut, N. (2005). Socialization in an open source software community: A socio-technical analysis. *Computer Supported Cooperative Work, 14*(4), 323-368. Retrieved December 14, 2011, from http://www2.parc.com/csl/members/nicolas/documents/JCSCW-OSS.pdf

Dunlap, J. C., & Lowenthal, P. R. (2009). Tweeting the night away: Using Twitter to enhance social presence. *Journal of Information Systems Education, 20*(2). Retrieved March 1, 2010, from http://www.patricklowenthal.com/publications/Using_Twitter_to_Enhance_Social_Presence.pdf

Dunleavy, M., Dede, C., & Mitchell, R. (2009). Affordances and limitations of immersive participatory augmented reality simulations for teaching and learning. *Journal of Science Education and Technology, 18*(1), 7–22. doi:10.1007/s10956-008-9119-1.

Duque, N. (2006). *Adaptive virtual course model using an intelligent planning environment.* (MSc Dissertation).

Duque, N. (2009). *Modelo adaptativo multi-agente para la planificación y ejecución de cursos virtuales personalizados. (Tesis Doctoral).* Bogota, Colombia: Universidad Nacional de Colombia.

Dutra, J. S. (2001). *Gestão por competências.* São Paulo: Editora Gente.

Eccles, J., & Wigfield, A. (2002). Motivational beliefs, values, and goals. *Annual Review of Psychology, 53,* 109-132. Retrieved on September 24, 2010 from http://www2.csdm.qc.ca/SaintEmile/bernet/annexes/ASS6826/Eccles2002.pdf

Edirisingha, P., Nie, M., Pluciennik, M., & Young, R. (2009). Socialization for learning at a distance in a 3-D multi-user virtual environment. *British Journal of Educational Technology, 40*(3), 458–479. doi:10.1111/j.1467-8535.2009.00962.x.

Edwards, P., Dominguez, E., & Rico, M. (2008) A second look at second life: Virtual role-play as a motivational factor in higher education. In K. McFerrin et al. (Eds.), *Proceedings of Society for Information Technology and Teacher Education Internationial Conference 2008* (pp. 2566-2571). Chesapeake, VA: AACE.

Eisenberg, M., & Buechley, L. (2007). *Pervasive fabrication: Making construction ubiquitous in education.* Paper presented at the Fifth Annual IEEE International Conference on Pervasive Computing and Communications. New York, NY.

El-Bishouty, M. M., Ogata, H., Rahman, S., & Yano, Y. (2010). Social knowledge awareness map for computer supported ubiquitous learning environment. *Journal of Educational Technology & Society, 13*(4), 27–37.

Ellet, W. (2007). *The case study handbook: How to read, discuss and write persuasively about cases.* Boston: Harvard Business School Press.

Elliott, E. S., & Dweck, C. S. (1988). Goals: An approach to motivation and achievement. *Journal of Personality and Social Psychology, 54*(1), 5-12. Retrieved on September 26, 2010 from http://www.ncbi.nlm.nih.gov/pubmed/3346808

Emiliy, J. P. R., Edwards, K., & Keller, P. K. (1993). Video see-through design for merging or real and virtual environments. In *Proceedings of the Virtual Reality Annual International Symposium,* (pp. 223-233). VR.

Ersner-Hershfield, H., Bailenson, J. N., & Carstensen, L. L. (2008). *A vivid future self: Immersive virtual reality enhances retirement saving.* Chicago: Association for Psychological Science.

European Commission. (2008). *The use of ICT to support innovation and lifelong learning for all.* Brussels: Author.

Eysenck, M. W., & Keane, M. T. (2000). *Cognitive psychology: A student handbook* (4th ed.). Hove, UK: Psychology Press.

Farhoomand, A. F., & Laurie, J. (2006). *FocusAsia business leaders.* [Video series]. Hong Kong: Asia Case Research Centre, Hong Kong University. Retrieved from http://www.acrc.org.hk/focusasia/focusasia_index.asp

Federal Communications Commission. (2005, Nov. 21). *Making the connections.* Retrieved from http://transition.fcc.gov/omd/history/internet/making-connections.html

Fernandes, G. G. (2008). *Avaliação ergonômica da interface humano computador de ambientes virtuais de aprendizagem.* (Unpublished doctoral dissertation). Universidade Federal do Ceará, Belo Horizonte, Brazil.

Fetch. (2012). Retrieved September 11, 2012, from https://itunes.apple.com/us/app/fetch!-lunch-rush/id469089331?mt=8

Field, J. (2000). *Lifelong learning and the new educational order.* London: Trentham Books.

Finnegan, S. (2012, August 13). *Case study: The importance of production value in new media.* [Blog post]. Retrieved from http://imfinnegan.wordpress.com/2012/08/13/case-study-the-importance-of-production-value-in-new-media/

Fischer, G., & Konomi, S. (2005). Innovative media in support of distributed intelligence and lifelong learning. In *Proceeding of the International Workshop on Wireless and Mobile Technologies in Education.* Los Alamitos, CA: IEEE Computer Society.

Fischer, G., & Konomi, S. I. (2007). Innovative socio-technical environments in support of distributed intelligence and lifelong learning. *Journal of Computer Assisted Learning, 23*(4), 338–350. doi:10.1111/j.1365-2729.2007.00238.x.

Fitzgerald, E. (2012). Creating user-generated content for location-based learning: An authoring framework. *Journal of Computer Assisted Learning, 28*(3), 195–207. doi:10.1111/j.1365-2729.2012.00481.x.

Fleury, A. C. C., & Fleury, M. T. L. (2000). *Estratégias empresariais e formação de competências.* Atlas.

Foster, D. (2002, June 2). Open the labs and set them free? *Los Angeles Times Magazine.* Retrieved from http://articles.latimes.com/2002/jun/02/magazine/tm-44710

Fotouhi-Ghazvini, F., Earnshaw, R. A., Robison, D., & Excell, P. S. (2009). *Designing augmented reality games for mobile learning using an instructional-motivational paradigm.* Paper presented at the Meeting of the IEEE Conference on CyberWorlds. Singapore.

Fox, J., & Bailenson, J. N. (2009). Virtual self-modeling: The effect of vicarious reinforcement and indentification on exercise behaviors. *Media Psychology, 12*, 1-25. Retrieved on October 12, 2011 from http://www.stanford.edu/~bailenso/papers/fox-mp-selfmodeling.pdf

Franceschi, K. G., Lee, R. M., & Hinds, D. (2008). Engaging e-learning in virtual worlds: Supporting group collaboration. In *Proceedings for the 41ˢᵗ Hawaii International Conference on System Sciences,* (pp. 1-10). IEEE. Retrieved on February 16, 2011 from http://www.computer.org/comp/proceedings/hicss/2008/3075/00/30750007.pdf

Franceschi, K. G., Lee, R. M., Zanakis, S. H., & Hinds, D. (2009). Engaging group e-learning in virtual worlds. *Journal of Management Information Systems, 26*(1), 73–100. doi:10.2753/MIS0742-1222260104.

Fraternali, P., Rossi, G., & Sanchez-Figueroa, F. (2010). Rich internet applications. *IEEE Internet Computing, 14*(3), 9–12. doi:10.1109/MIC.2010.76.

Freire, P. (1968). *Pedagogia do oprimido.* Livro. Editora Paz e Terra.

Freire, P. (1977). *Extensão ou comunicação?* Editora Paz e Terra.

Freire, P. (1996). *Pedagogia da autonomia: Saberes necessários à prática educativa.* Editora Paz e Terra.

Galvão, M. A., & Zorzal, E. R. (2012). Aplicações móveis com realidade aumentada para potencializar livros. *Revista de Novas Tecnologias na Educação, 10*(1), 1–10.

Gartner Group. (2007). Gartner says 80 percent of active internet users will have a second life in the virtual world by the end of 2011. *Gartner Group.* Retrieved on June 1, 2010 from http://www.gartner.com/it/page.jsp?id=503861

Garvin, D. (1993). Building a learning organization. *Harvard Business Review, 71*(4). PMID:10127041.

Gazzoni, A., Canal, A. P., Falkembach, G. A. M., Fioreze, L. A., Pincolini, L. B., & Antoniazzi, R. (2006). Proporcionalidade e semelhança: Aprendizagem via objetos de aprendizagem. *Novas Tecnologias na Educação - CINTED-UFRGS, 4*. Retrieved from http://seer.ufrgs.br/renote/article/viewFile/14141/8076

Gebhard, P. (2005). ALMA: A layered model of affect. In *Proceedings of the Fourth International Joint Conference on Autonomous Agents and Multiagent Systems* (pp. 29-36). New York, NY: ACM.

Gee, J. P. (2003). *What video games have to teach us about learning and literacy*. New York: Palgrave Macmillan. doi:10.1145/950566.950595.

Geiger, C., Schmidt, T., & Stocklein, J. (2007). *Rapid development of expressive AR applications*. Paper presented at the meeting of the IEEE International Symposium on Mixed and Augmented Reality (ISMAR). Nara, Japan.

Gerhard, M., Hobbs, D. J., & Moore, D. J. (2004). Embodiment and copresence in collaborative interfaces. *International Journal of Human-Computer Studies, 61*(4), 453-480. Retrieved on October 5, 2009 from http://www.geomobile.de/fileadmin/docs/IJHCS-Paper.pdf

Ghauth, K. I. B., & Abdullah, N. A. (2009). Building an e-learning recommender system using vector space model and good learners average rating. *IEEE International Conference on Advanced Learning Technologies, 1*(0), 194-196.

Girardi, R. (2002). *Framework para coordenação e mediação de web services modelados como learning objects para ambientes de aprendizado na web. (Dissertação de Mestrado). Pontifícia Universidade Católica do Rio de Janeiro*. Rio de Janeiro, Brazil: PUC-Rio.

Giridher, T., Kim, R., Rai, D., Hanover, A., Yuan, J., & Zarinni, F. ... Wong, J.L. (2009). *Mobile applications for informal economies*. Paper presented at the meeting of the IEEE International Multiconference on Computer Science and Information Technology. Mragowo, Poland.

Goffman, E. (1959). *The presentation of self in everyday life*. Woodstock, NY: Overlook Press.

Gomes, A. S., Rolim, A. L. S., & Silva, W. M. (2012). *Educar com o redu*. Recife: Editora universitária da UFPE.

Gomes, F. J. L. (2009). *Explorando objetos de aprendizagem na TV digital: Estudo de caso de alternativas de interação. (Tese Doutorado). Universidade Federal do Rio Grande do Sul*. Porto Alegre, Brazil: UFRS.

Greenberg, J. M. (2008). *From Betamax to blockbuster: Video stores and the invention of movies on video*. Cambridge, MA: The MIT Press.

GSMA. (2012). *mLearning: A platform for educational opportunities at the base of the pyramid*. Retrieved September 20, 2012, from http://www.mobileactive.org/files/file_uploads/mLearning_Report_Final_Dec2010.pdf

Guan, L., Ke, X., Song, M., & Song, J. (2011). *A survey of research on mobile cloud computing*. Paper presented at the Meeting of the IEEE International Conference on Computer and Information Science. Sanya, China.

Guarino, N. (1998). *Formal Ontology in information systems: Proceedings of the first international conference (FOIS'98)*. Trento, Italy. IOS Press.

Guber, P. (2011). *Tell to win: Connect, persuade, and triumph with the hidden power of story*. New York: Crown Business.

Guenaga, M. L., Burger, D., & Oliver, J. (2004). Accessibility for e-learning environments. In K. Miesenberger, J. Klaus, W. L. Zagler, & D. Burger (Eds.), *Computers Helping People with Special Needs* (Vol. 3118, pp. 157–163). Berlin: Springer. Retrieved from http://www.springerlink.com/index/10.1007/978-3-540-27817-7_23

Gulikers, J. T. M., Bastiaens, T. J., & Martens, R. L. (2005). The surplus value of an authentic learning environment. *Computers in Human Behavior, 21*(3), 509–521. doi:10.1016/j.chb.2004.10.028.

Gulz, A. (2004). Benefits of virtual characters in computer-based learning environments: Claims and evidence. *International Journal of Artifical Intelligence in Education, 14*(3), 313-334. Retrieved on September 22, 2009 from http://hal.inria.fr/docs/00/19/73/09/PDF/Gulz04.pdf

Gunkel, D. J. (2010). The real problem: Avatars, metaphysics, and online social interaction. *New Media & Society, 12*(1), 127-141. Retrieved on December 26, 2011 from http://commons.lib.niu.edu/bitstream/10843/13147/1/real_problem_preprint.ped

Gutierrez, J. M., Saorín, J. L., Contero, M., Alcañiz, M., Pérez-Lopes, D. C., & Ortega, M. (2010). Design and validation of an augmented book for spatial abilities development in engineering students. *Journal Computers & Graphics, 34*(1), 77–91. doi:10.1016/j.cag.2009.11.003.

Gutl, C., Chang, V., Kopeinik, S., & Williams, R. (2009). Evaluation of collaborative learning settings in 3D virtual worlds. In *Proceedings of the International Conference of Interactive Computer Aided Learning*, (pp. 6-17). Vienna: iJet. Retrieved on May 17, 2010 from http://dx.doi.org/ijet.v4s3.1112

Hall, T., & Bannon, L. (2006). Designing ubiquitous computing to enhance children's learning in museums. *Journal of Computer Assisted Learning, 22*, 231–243. doi:10.1111/j.1365-2729.2006.00177.x.

Hansen, B. (2012). *Song reader*. San Francisco, CA: McSweeney's.

Harel, I., & Papert, S. (1991). *Constructionism*. Norwood, NJ: Ablex Pub. Corp..

Haughey, M., & Muirhead, B. (2005). Evaluating learning objects for schools. *E-Journal of Instructional Science and Technology, 8*(1). Retrieved April 13, 2011, from http://www.usq. edu.au/electpub/e-ist/docs/vol8_no1/fullpapers/eval_learnobjects_school.htm

Herlocker, J., Konstan, J. A., & Riedl, J. (2004). Evaluating collaborative filtering recommender systems. *ACM TOIS, 22*(1).

Herlocker, J. L., Konstan, J. A., Terveen, L. G., & Riedl, J. T. (2004). Evaluating collaborative filtering recommender systems. *ACM Transactions on Information Systems, 22*(1), 5–53. doi:10.1145/963770.963772.

Herold, D. K. (2010). Mediating media studies - Stimulating critical awareness in a virtual environment. *Computers & Education*, 791–798. doi:10.1016/j.compedu.2009.10.019.

Herrington, J., Reeves, T. C., & Oliver, R. (2007). Immersive learning technologies: Realism and online authentic learning. *Journal of Computing in Higher Education, 19*(10), 65-84. Retrieved on May 18, 2010 from http://ro.uow.edu.au/edupapers/27/

Hew, K., & Cheung, W. (2008). Use of three-dimensional (3-D) immersive virtual worlds in K-12 and higher education settings: A review of the research. *British Journal of Educational Technology, 39*(6), 959–1148. doi: doi:10.1111/j.1467-8535.2008.00900.x.

Hightower, J. L., LaMarca, A. J., & Smith, I. E. (2006). Practical lessons from place lab. *IEEE Pervasive Computing / IEEE Computer Society [and] IEEE Communications Society, 5*(3), 32–39. doi:10.1109/MPRV.2006.55.

Hightower, J., & Borriello, G. (2001). Location systems for ubiquitous computing. *Computer, 34*(8), 57–66. doi:10.1109/2.940014.

Hill, J. R., Reeves, T. C., & Heidemeier, H. (2000). *Ubiquitous computing for teaching, learning and communicating: Trends, issues and recommendations*. Retrieved from http://lpsl.coe.uga.edu/Projects/AAlaptop/pdf/UbiquitousComputing.pdf

Hoareau, C., & Satoh, I. (2009). Modeling and processing information for context-aware computing: A survey. *New Generation Computing, 27*(3), 177–196. doi:10.1007/s00354-009-0060-5.

Hodges, C. (2004). Designing to motivate: Motivational techniques to incorporate in e-learning experiences. *The Journal of Interactive Online Learning, 2*(3), 1-7. Retrieved August 1, 2010 from http://www.ncolr.org/jiol/issues/PDF/2.3.1.pdf

Holben, J. (2011). Time bandit. *American Cinematographer, 92*(11), 32–45.

Hollan, J., Hutchins, E., & Kirsch, D. (2001). Distributed cognition: Toward a new foundation for human-computer interaction research. In J. M. Carroll (Ed.), *Human-Computer Interaction in the New Millennium* (pp. 75–94). New York: ACM Press.

Honan, M. (2007). Apple unveils iPhone. *Macworld*. Retrieved January 2010, from http://www.macworld.com/article/1054769/iphone.html

Huang, Y., Chiu, P., Liu, T., & Chen, T. (2011). The design and implementation of a meaningful learning-based evaluation method for ubiquitous learning. *Computers & Education Journal, 57*, 2291–2302. doi:10.1016/j.compedu.2011.05.023.

Hung, K. H., Kinzer, C., & Chen, C.-L. (2009). Motivational factors in educational MMORPGs: Some implications for education. In Z. Pan et al. (Eds.), *Transactions in Edutainment (LNCS)* (Vol. 5940, pp. 93–104). Berlin: Springer. doi:10.1007/978-3-642-11245-4_9.

Hussain, M., Nakamura, B., & Marino, J. (2011). Avatar appearance and information credibility in second life. In *Proceedings of the 2011 iConference,* (pp. 682-68). Seattle, WA: ACM. doi: 10.1145/1940761.1940868

Hussein, T., Linder, T., Gaulke, W., & Ziegler, J. (2009). Context-aware recommendations on rails. In *Proceedings of the Workshop on Context-Aware Recommender Systems in Conjunction with the 3rd ACM Conference on Recommender Systems.* New York, NY: ACM.

Hwang, G.-J. (2006). Criteria and strategies of ubiquitous learning. In *Proceedings of the IEEE International Conference on Sensor Networks, Ubiquitous, and Trustworthy Computer (SUTC '06)*, (pp. 72-77). IEEE. Retrieved on October 13, 2012 from http://ieeexplore. ieee.org/xpl/login.jsp?tp=&anumber=1636255&url=ht tp%3A%2F%2Fieeexplore.ieee.org%2Fxpls%2Fabs_all. jsp%3Fanumber%3D1636255

Hwang, G.-J., Chu, H.-C., Lin, Y.-S., & Tsai, C.-C. (2011). A knowledge acquisition approach to developing mindtools for organizing and sharing differentiating knowledge in a ubiquitous learning environment. *Computers & Education, 57*(1), 1368–1377. doi:10.1016/j. compedu.2010.12.013.

Hwang, G., Yang, T., Tsai, C., & Yang, S. (2009). A context-aware ubiquitous learning environment for conducting complex science experiments. *Computers & Education Journal, 53*, 402–413. doi:10.1016/j. compedu.2009.02.016.

Iepsen, E. F., Bercht, M., & Reategui, E. (2011). Detecção e tratamento do estado afetivo frustração do aluno na disciplina de algoritmos. In *Proceedings of the Anais do XXII Simpósio brasileiro de Informática na Educação,* (pp. 80-89). IEEE.

Iglesias, C. (1998). *Definición de una metodología para el desarrollo de sistemas multiagentes.* Madrid, Spain: Universidad Politécnica de Madrid.

Illich, I. (1970). *Deschooling society.* New York: Harper & Row.

ISO 9241-11. (1998). *Ergonomics of human system interaction.* Retrieved November 30, 2012, from http://www. it.uu.se/edu/course/homepage/acsd/vt09/ISO9241part11. pdf

Itō, M., Horst, H., Bittanti, M., Boyd, D., Herr-Stephenson, B., & Lange, P. G. et al. (2008). *Living and learning with new media: Summary of findings from the digital youth project.* MacArthur Foundation.

ITU - International Telecommunication Union. (2012). Retrieved from http://www.itu.int/ITU-D/ict/statistics/ at_glance/KeyTelecom.html

ITU, I. T. U. (2010). *The world in 2010: ICT facts and figures.* International Telecommunication Union.

Jackson, P., Walsh, F., Cunningham, C., & Weiner, Z. (Producers) & Jackson, P. (Director). (2012). *The hobbit: An unexpected journey.* [Motion picture]. Los Angeles, CA: Warner Bros. Pictures.

Jackson, P., Walsh, F., Cunningham, C., & Weiner, Z. (Producers) & Jackson, P. (Director). (2013). *The hobbit: The desolation of Smaug.* [Motion picture]. Los Angeles, CA: Warner Bros. Pictures.

Jackson, P., Walsh, F., Cunningham, C., & Weiner, Z. (Producers) & Jackson, P. (Director). (2014). *The hobbit: There and back again.* [Motion picture]. Los Angeles, CA: Warner Bros. Pictures.

Jackson, P. W. (1995). On the place of narrative in teaching. In H. McEwan, & K. Egan (Eds.), *Narrative in teaching, learning, and research.* New York: Teachers College Press.

Jaques, P. (2008). Avaliando um modelo afetivo de aluno baseado em uma abordagem cognitiva. In *Proceedings of the Anais do XIX Simpósio brasileiro de Informática na Educação,* (pp. 155-165). IEEE.

Jarmon, L. (2008). Pedagogy and learning in the virtual world of second life. In P. Rogers, G. Berg, J. Boettcher, C. Howard, L. Justice, & K. Schenk (Eds.), *Encyclopedia of Distance and Online Learning* (2nd Ed.). Retrieved on February 12, 2011 from http://research.educatorscoop. org/Leslie_Jarmon_Second_Life.pdf

Jeng, Y.-C., Lu, S.-C., & Lin, H.-M. (2011). Using e-learning and situated learning theory: Practical lessons from the vocational special education students. In *Proceedings from the e-Business Engineering (ICEBE)*. IEEE. doi:10.1109/ICEBE.2011.70.

Jeng, Y., Wu, T., Huang, Y., Tan, Q., & Yang, S. (2010). The add-on impact of mobile applications in learning strategies: A review study. *Journal of Educational Technology & Society, 13*(3), 3–11.

Jenkins, H. (2002). Game design as narrative architecture. In P. Harrington & N. Frup-Waldrop (Eds.), *First Person*. Cambridge, MA: MIT Press. Retrieved from http://www.web.mit.edu/cms/People/henry3/games&narrative.html

Jennings, N. R. (2000). On agent-based software engineering. *Artificial Intelligence, 117*(2), 277–296. doi:10.1016/S0004-3702(99)00107-1.

Jiménez, M., Ovalle, D., & Jiménez, J. (2008). Evaluación en línea para cursos tutoriales inteligentes adaptativos usando el modelo de sistemas multi-agente. *Revista Avances en Sistemas e Informática, 5*(1), 20–29.

Johnson, D. W., Johnson, R. T., & Smith, K. A. (1991). ASHE-ERIC Higher Education Report: Vol. 4. *Cooperative learning: Increasing college faculty instructional productivity*. Washington, DC: George Washington University.

Johnson, L., Levine, A., Smith, R., & Stone, S. (2010). *The 2010 horizon report*. Austin, TX: The New Media Consortium.

Johnson, S. (2010). *Where good ideas come from: The natural history of innovation*. Riverhead.

Jonassen, D. D., & Hernandez-Serrano, J. (2002). Case-based reasoning and instructional design: Using stories to support problem-solving. *Educational Technology Research and Development, 50*(2), 65–77. doi:10.1007/BF02504994.

Jones, J. G., Morales, C., & Knezek, C. G. (2005). 3-dimensional online learning environments: Examining attitudes toward information technology between students in internet-based 3-dimensional and face-to-face classroom instruction. *Educational Media International, 42*(3), 219-236, Retrieved on June 1, 2010 from http://www.informaworld.com/smpp/content~db=all~content=a714023310

Jones, V., & Jo, J. H. (2004). Ubiquitous learning environment: An adaptive teaching system using ubiquitous technology. In R. Atkinson, C. McBeath, D. Jones-Dwyer, & R. Phillips (Eds.), *Beyond the comfort zone: Proceedings of the 21ˢᵗ ASCILITE Conference* (pp. 468-474). ASCILITE. Retrieved on October 16, 2012 from http://www.ascilite.org.au/conferences/perth04/procs/jones.html

Jones, A., & Issroff, K. (2007). Motivation and mobile devices: Exploring the role appropriation and coping strategies. *Research in Learning Technology, 15*(3), 247–258. doi:10.3402/rlt.v15i3.10934.

Junior, M., & Canuto, A. (2006). Carcara: A multi-agent system for web mining using adjustable user profile and dynamic grouping. In *Proc. IEEE/WIC/ACM IAT'06*. Hong Kong, China: IEEE.

Kafai, Y. B., & Resnick, M. (1996). *Constructionism in practice: Designing, thinking, and learning in a digital world*. Mahwah, NJ: Lawrence Erlbaum Associates.

Kekwaletswe, R. M. (2007). Social presence awareness for knowledge transformation in a mobile learning environment. *International Journal of Education and Development using Information and Communication Technology, 3*(4), 102–109.

Keller, J. (2000). *How to integrate learner motivation planning into lesson planning: The ARCS model approach*. Retrieved on September 26, 2009 from http://mailer.fsu.edu/~jkeller/Articles/Keller%202000%20ARCS%20Lesson%20Planning.pdf

Keller, J. (1987). Strategies for stimulating the motivation to learn. *Performance & Instruction, 26*(8), 1–7. doi:10.1002/pfi.4160260802.

Keller, J., & Suzuki, K. (2004). Learner motivation and e-learning design: A multinationally validated process. *Journal of Educational Media, 29*(3), 229–239. doi:10.1080/1358165042000283084.

Kerkiri, T., Manitsaris, A., & Mavridou, A. (2007). Reputation metadata for recommending personalized e-learning resources. In *Proceedings of the International Workshop on Semantic Media Adaptation and Personalization,* (pp. 110-115). IEEE.

Kim, P., Goyal, A., Seol, S., Dodson, B., & Lam, M. (2011). Pocket school interactive learning ad-hoc network. In *Proceedings of IEEE International Conference on e-Education, Entertainment and e-Management* (pp. 1-14). IEEE.

Kirner, T., Reis, F. M. V., & Kirner, C. (2012). *Development of an interactive book with augmented reality for teaching and learning geometric shapes.* Paper presented at the meeting of the Conferência Ibérica de Sistemas e Tecnologias de Informação. Madrid, Spain.

Klopfer, E. (2008). *Augmented learning - Research and design of mobile educational games.* Cambridge, MA: MIT Press.

Klopfer, E., & Squire, K. (2008). Environmental detectives - The development of an augmented reality platform for environmental simulations. *Education Tech Research, 56,* 203–228. doi:10.1007/s11423-007-9037-6.

Kluge, S., & Riley, L. (2008). Teaching in virtual worlds: Opportunities and challenges. *Issues in Informing Science and Information Technology, 5,* 127-135. Retrieved March 7, 2011 from http://proceedings.informingscience.org/InSITE2008/IISITv5p127-135Kluge459.pdf?q=forming-learning-connections

Koole, M., McQuilkin, J. L., & Ally, M. (2010). Mobile learning in distance education: Utility or futility? *Journal of Distance Education, 24*(2), 59–82.

Korolov, M. (2009). Virtual meeting rush. *Treasury & Risk*: Retrieved on September 22, 2009 from http://www.treasuryandrisk.com/Issues/2009/September%202009/Pages/Virtual-Meeting-Rush.aspx

Kozma, R. B. (1991). Learning with media. *Review of Educational Research, 61*(2), 179–212. doi:10.3102/00346543061002179.

Krippendorf, K. (1980). *Content analysis: An introduction to its methodology.* Newbury Park, CA: Sage.

Krupnick, C. G. (1987). The uses of videotape replay. In C. R. Christensen, & A. J. Hansen (Eds.), *Teaching and the case method: Texts, cases, and readings* (pp. 256–263). Boston: Harvard Business School Press.

Kukulska-Hulme, A., & Traxler, J. (2007). Learning design with mobile and wireless technologies. In H. Beetham & R. Sharpe (Eds.), *Rethinking pedagogy for a digital age: Designing and delivering e-learning* (pp. 180–192). Retrieved April 15, 2009, from http://oro.open.ac.uk/9541/

Kun, G., Zhisheng, L., & Xu, O. (2011). *Technical analysis of mobile learning application in high education.* Paper presented at the meeting of the IEEE International Conference on Computer Science and Education. Shanghai, China.

Laffey, J., Cho, M.-H., Hsu, Y.-C., Huang, X., Kim, B., & Lin, G. Y. Shen, ... Yang, C.-C. (2005). Understanding computer mediated social experience: Implications for CSCL. In T. Koschmann, D. Suthers, & T. W. Chan (Eds.), *Computer Supported Collaboration Learning 2005: The Next 10 Years, Proceedings of the International Conference on Computer-Supported Collaborative Learning 2005* (pp. 617-621). Taipei, Taiwan: International Society of the Learning Sciences.

Laffey, J., Lin, G. Y., & Lin, Y. (2006). Assessing social ability in online learning environments. *Journal of Interactive Learning Research, 17*(2), 163–177.

Lane, N. D., Miluzzo, E., Lu, H., Peebles, D., Choudhury, T., & Campbell, A. T. (2010). A survey of mobile phone sensing. *IEEE Communications Magazine, 48*(9), 140–150. doi:10.1109/MCOM.2010.5560598.

Lang, P. J., Bradley, M. M., & Cuthbert, B. N. (1997). *International affective picture system (IAPS), technical manual and affective ratings.* Gainesville, FL: NIMH Center for the Study of Emotional and Attention.

Lardner, J. (1987). *Fast forward: Hollywood, the Japanese, and the VCR wars.* New York: W. W. Norton.

Lastowka, F. G., & Hunter, D. (2006). Virtual worlds: A primer. In J.M. Balkin & B.S. Noveck (Eds.), *State of play: Law, games, and virtual worlds,* (pp. 13-28). New York, NY: New York University Press. Retrieved December 27, 2011 from hci.stanford.edu/courses/cs047n/readings/virtual-primer.pdf

Latour, B. (1987). *Science in action: How to follow scientists and engineers through society.* Cambridge, MA: Harvard University Press.

Lave, J., & Wenger, E. (1991). *Situated learning: Legitimate peripheral participation.* Cambridge, UK: Cambridge University Press. doi:10.1017/CBO9780511815355.

Lave, J., & Wenger, E. C. (1998). *Communities of practice: Learning, meaning, and identity.* Cambridge, UK: Cambridge University Press.

Law, N., Pelgrum, W. J., & Plomp, T. (2008). *Pedagogy and ICT use in schools around the world: Findings from the IEA SITES 2006 study.* Hong Kong: Springer and Comparative Education Research Centre.

Lemon Team. (2012). Lucky's escape. *Lemon Team Game Development and Porting.* Retrieved from http://www.lemonteam.com/app/luckys-escape/

Lemon, M., & Kelly, O. (2009). Laying second life foundations: Second chance learners get first life skills. *Same Places,Different Spaces: Proceedings Ascilite Auckland 2009,* (pp. 557-565). ASCILITE. Retrieved on December 24, 2009 from http://www.ascilite.org.au/conferences/auckland09/procs/lemon.pdf

Lévy, P. (1990). *Les technologies de l'intelligence.* Paris: La Découverte.

Lévy, P. (1994). *L'intelligence collective: Pour une anthropologie du cyberespace.* Paris: La Découverte.

Lévy, P. (1997). *Cyberculture.* Paris: Odile Jacob.

Lewis, M., Nino, C., Rosa, J. H., Barbosa, J. L., & Barbosa, D. N. (2010). A management model of learning objects in a ubiquitous learning environment. In *Proceedings of the IEEE International Workshop on Pervasive Learning (PerEL 2010)* (pp. 256-261). Mannheim, Germany: IEEE.

Li, S., & Hu, F. (2009). Communication between the RoboCup agents based on the blackboard model and observer pattern. In *Proceedings of the 5th International Conference on Wireless Communications, Networking and Mobile Computing, 2009. WiCom '09* (pp. 1 –5). doi:10.1109/WICOM.2009.5304011

Liedtka, J. (2001). The promise and peril of using video cases: Reflections on their creation and use. *Journal of Management Education, 25*(4), 409–424. doi:10.1177/105256290102500405.

Likert, R. (1932). A technique for the measurement of attitudes. *Archives de Psychologie, 22*(140), 1–55.

Lim, C. P., Nonis, D., & Hedberg, J. (2006). Gaming in a 3D multiuser virtual environment: Engaging students in science lessons. *British Journal of Educational Technology, 37*(2), 211-231. Retrieved on August 9, 2010 from http://edithcowan.academia.edu/documents/0011/5264/BJET__Lim__Nonis___Hedberg_2005_.pdf

Lincoln, Y., & Guba, E. (1985). *Naturalistic inquiry.* Beverly Hills, CA: Sage.

Lindemann, V. (2008). Estilos de aprendizagem: Buscando a sinergia. *Tese (UFRGS).* Retrieved from http://www.lume.ufrgs.br/handle/10183/15352

Lins, W. C.-B., & Gomes, A. S. (2003). Educational software interfaces and teacher s use. In *HCI International 2003.* HCI.

LIP. (2012). *IMS learner information package especification.* Retrieved November 10, 2012, from http://www.imsglobal.org/profiles/index.html

Liu, J., & Gree, J. (2005). *Individulaized selection of learning object.* Paper presented at the International Conference on Inelligence Tutoring Systems. Macei-Alagoas, Brazil.

Liu, G.-Z., & Hwang, G.-J. (2010). A key step to understanding paradigm shifts in e-learning: Towards context-aware ubiquitous learning. *British Journal of Educational Technology, 41*(2), E1–E9. doi:10.1111/j.1467-8535.2009.00976.x.

LOM. (2002). *Learning object metadata.* Retrieved from http://ltsc.ieee.org/wg12/20020612-Final-LOM-Draft.html

LOM. (2012). *IEEE/LTSC/LOM. learning object metadata (LOM) working group 12.* Retrieved November 10, 2012, from http://www.ieeeltsc.org:8080/Plone/working-group/learning-object-metadata-working-group-12/learning-object-metadata-lom-working-group-12

Lombardi, M. M. (2007). *Authentic learning for the 21st century: An overview.* EDUCAUSE Learning Initiative.

LTSC. (2002). Learning technologies standards committee. *IEEE Standard 1484.12.1*. Retrieved from http://ltsc.ieee.org/wg12/files/LOM_1484_12_1_v1_Final_Draft.pdf

Ludi, S. (2007). Introducing accessibility requirements through external stakeholder utilization in an undergraduate requirements engineering course. In *Proceedings of the 29th International Conference on Software Engineering* (pp. 736–743). Washington, DC: IEEE Computer Society. doi:10.1109/ICSE.2007.46

Lui, G.-Z., & Hwang, G.-J. (2010). A key step to understanding paradigm shifts in e-learning: Towards context-aware ubiquitous learning. *British Journal of Educational Technology, 41*(2), E1–E0. doi:10.1111/j.1467-8535.2009.00976.x.

Lyytinen, K., & Yoo, Y. (2002). Issues and challenges in ubiquitous computing. *Communications of the ACM, 45*(12), 63-65. Retrieved on October 14, 2012 from citeseerx.ist.psu.edu/viewdoc/download?doi=10.1.1.135.3184.pdf

Macedo, R. (2006). *Etnopesquisa crítica, etnopesquisa-formação*. Brasília: Liber Livro Editora.

Maier, P., Kinlker, G., & Tonnis, M. (2009). Augmented reality for teaching spatial relations. *International Journal of Arts & Sciences*.

Maldonado, H., & Nass, C. (2007). Emotive characters make learning more productive and enjoyable: It takes two to learn to tango. *Educational Technology, 47*(1), 33-38. Retrieved on November 11, 2009 from http://www.stanford.edu/~kiky/publications.html

Maldonado, H., Lee, J.-Y., Brave, S., Nass, C., Nakajima, H., Yamada, R., et al. (2005). We learn better together: Enchancing elearning with emotional characters. In T. Koschmann, D.Suthers, & T. W. Chan (Eds.), *Computer Supported Collaborative Learning 2005: The Next 10 Years, Proceedings of the International Conference on Computer Supported Collaborative Learning 2005* (pp. 408-417). Taipei, Taiwan: International Society of the Learning Sciences. Retrieved on November 11, 2009 from http://www.stanford.edu/~kiky/publications.html

Malik, O. (2012, January 30). Global broadband zooms, US penetration is over 80 percent. *GigaOm*. Retrieved from http://gigaom.com/2012/01/30/global-broadband-zooms-us-penetration-is-over-80-percent/

Mann, M., & Richardson, J. (Producers) & Mann, M. (2004). *Collateral*. [Motion picture]. Los Angeles, CA: DreamWorks.

Manovich, L. (1996). *Global algorithm 1.3: The aesthetics of virtual worlds: Ctheory.net*. Retrieved May 15, 2011, from http://www.ctheory.net/articles.aspx?id=34

Marçal, E., Andrade, R., & Rios, R. (2007). Aprendizagem utilizando dispositivos móveis com sistemas de realidade virtual. *Revista Novas Tecnologias na Educação, 3*(1), 1–7.

Marshall, C., & Rossman, G. (1995). *Designing qualitative research* (2nd ed.). Thousand Oaks, CA: Sage.

Martinho, C., Machado, I., & Paiva, A. (2000). A cognitive approach to affective user modeling affective interactions. In *Affective Interactions (LNCS)* (pp. 64–75). Berlin: Springer. doi:10.1007/10720296_6.

Maslow, A. H. (1943). A theory of human motivation. *Psychological Review, 50*, 370-396. Retrieved on September 30, 2010 from http://mcv.planc.ee/misc/doc/filosoofia/artiklid/Abraham%20H.%20Maslow%20%20A%20Theory%20Of%20Human%20Motivation.pdf

Mathews, J. (2010). Using a studio-based pedagogy to engage students in the design of mobile-based media. *English Teaching: Practice and Critique, 9*(1), 87–102.

Matta, A. (2006). *Tecnologias de aprendizagem em rede e ensino de história*. Brasilia: Líber Livro.

Mattos, F. A. M., de, , & Chagas, G. J. do N. (2008). Challenges for digital inclusion in Brazil. *Perspectivas em Ciência da Informação, 13*(1), 67–94. doi: doi:10.1590/S1413-99362008000100006.

Maturana, F., & Varela, F. J. (1987). *The tree of knowledge: The biological roots of human understanding*. Boston: Shambhala Press.

Maximiniano, A. C. A. (2000). *Teoria geral da administração: da escola científica à competitividade na economia globalizada*. São Paulo, Brazil: Atlas.

Mayer, R. E. (2004). Should there be a three-strikes rule against discovery learning? *American Psychologist, 59,* 14-19. Retrieved on November 13, 2010 from http://apps.fischlerschool.nova.edu/toolbox/instructionalproducts/edd8124/fall1/2004-Mayer.pdf

Mazman, S. G., & Usluel, Y. K. (2010). Modeling educational usage of facebook. *Computers & Education, 55*(2), 444–453. doi:10.1016/j.compedu.2010.02.008.

Mazur, E. (1991, January-February). Can we teach computers to teach? *Computers in Physics,* 31–38.

McArthur, V. (2010). Professional second lives: An analysis of virtual world professionals and avatar appearance. In *Proceedings of the International Academic Conference on the Future of Game Design and Technology,* (pp. 231-235). doi: 10.1145/1920778.1920814

McArthur, V., & Baljko, M. (2009). Outsiders, interlopers, and employee-identified avatars. In *Proceedings of the 12th Annual International Workshop on Presence,* (pp. 1-8). Retrieved on July 24, 2011 from http://astro.temple.edu/~tuc16417/papers/McArthur_et_al.pdf

McCallum, R. (Producer) & Lucas, G. (Director). (1999). *Star wars episode I - The phantom menace.* [Motion picture]. Los Angeles, CA: 20th Century Fox.

McCallum, R. (Producer) & Lucas, G. (Director). (2002). *Star wars episode II - Attack of the clones.* [Motion picture]. Los Angeles, CA: 20th Century Fox.

McCallum, R. (Producer) & Lucas, G. (Director). (2005). *Star wars episode III - Revenge of the Sith.* [Motion picture]. Los Angeles, CA: 20th Century Fox.

McDermott, R. (1999). Why information technology inspired but cannot deliver knowledge management. *California Management Review, 41*(4). Retrieved December 01, 2011, from http://www.itu.dk/~kristianskriver/b9/Why%20information%20technology%20inspired%20but%20cannot%20deliver%20Knowledge%20Management.pdf

McLuhan, M., & Lapham, L. (1994). *Understanding media: The extensions of man.* Cambridge, MA: The MIT Press.

McPhail, I. P. (1985). Computer inequities in school uses of microcomputers: Policy implications. *The Journal of Negro Education, 50*(1), 3–13. doi:10.2307/2294895.

Melo, C. de A. (2010). *Scaffolding of self-regulated learning in social networks. Dissertação.* UFPE.

Mendonça, A. F., Gomes, A. S., & Montarroyos, E. (2002). *CSCL environment for physics teaching and learning allowing exploratory methodology.* Badajoz: Junta de Extremadura Consejeria de Educación.

Merdes, M., & Laux, G. (2002). Towards mobile computing in transplantation medicine. *Mobile Computing in Medicine, 1*(2), 131–142.

Merriam, S. (1998). *Qualitative research and case study applications in education.* San Francisco, CA: Jossey-Bass Publishers.

Merseth, K. K. (1991). The early history of case-based instruction: Insights for teacher education today. *Journal of Teacher Education, 42*(4), 243–249. doi:10.1177/002248719104200402.

Miller, C. H. (2008). *Digital storytelling* (2nd ed.). Burlington, MA: Focal Press.

Mimio. (2012). MimioSprout early reading. *Mimio.* Retrieved from http://www.mimio.com/en-NA/Products/MimioSprout-Earlyreading.aspx?_id=064914BF5130473EAE50557F1DDE881D&_z=z

Mishra, S. (2012). *Mobile technologies in open schools: Commonwealth of learning 2009.* Retrieved September 20, 2012, from http://www.col.org/SiteCollectionDocuments/Mobile_Technologies_in_Open_Schools_web.pdf

Monahan, T., McArdle, G., & Bertolotto, M. (2008). Virtual reality for collaborative learning. *Computers & Education,* 1339-1353. Retrieved on October 5, 2009 from http://squidguts.org/Portfolio/Subj_use_Technology/virtual_reality.pdf

Moni, K. B., & Jobling, A. (2000). A program to develop literacy in young adults with Down syndrome. *Journal of Adolescent & Adult Literacy, 44*(1), 40–49.

Monteiro, B. S., Prota, T. M., Souza, F. F., & Gomes, A. S. (2008). *Desenvolvimento de objetos de aprendizagem para TVDi.* Fortaleza, Brazil: SBIE.

Moodle (2012). Moodle.org: Open-source community-based tools for learning. *Journal of Bibliographic Research, 5,* 117-123. Retrieved October 13, 2012, from http://www.moodle.org/

Moore, M. (2002). Teoria da distância transacional. *Revista Brasileira de Aprendizagem Aberta e a Distância*. Retrieved from: http://goo.gl/kazuV

Moreno, J., Ovalle, D., & Jimenez, J. (2009). CIA: Framework for the creation and management of adaptive intelligent courses. In *Proceedings of 9th World Conference on Computers in Education – WCCE*. Bento Gonçales, Brazil: WCCE.

Moreno, R. (2004). Decreasing cognitive load for novice students: Effects of explanatory versus corrective feedback in discovery-based multimedia. *Instructional Science*, *32*(1), 99–113. doi:10.1023/B:TRUC.0000021811.66966.1d.

Moreno, R., & Mayer, R. (2007). Interactive multimodal learning environments. *Educational Psychology Review*, *19*(3), 309–326. doi:10.1007/s10648-007-9047-2.

Mostrom, R. N. (1975). *Head mounted displays*. New York: Honeywell, Inc..

Moundridou, M., & Virvou, M. (2002). Evaluating the persona effect of an interface agent in a tutoring systems. *Journal of Computer Assisted Learning, 18*(3), 253-261. Retrieved on October 3, 2009 from http://74.125.155.132/scholar?q=cache:mCpgtGyN3KgJ:scholar.google.com/+Evaluating+the+Persona+Effect+of+an+Interfact+Agent+in+a+Tutoring+Sysem&hl=en&as_sdt=2000

Mülbert, A. L., & Tecnologias, C. N. (2011). *A interação em ambientes virtuais de aprendizagem: Motivações e interesses dos alunos. Revista Novas Tecnologias na Educação*. CINTED-UFRGS.

Murali & Kasif. (2003). Extracting conserved gene expression motifs from gene expression data. In *Proceedings of Pacific Symp. Biocomputing Conf.*, (pp. 77–88). IEEE. Khribi, M.K., Jemni, M., & Nasraoui, O. (2007). Toward a hybrid recommender system for e-learning personalization based on web usage mining techniques and information retrieval. In *Proceedings of the World Conference on E-Learning in Corporate, Government, Healthcare, and Higher Education*. IEEE.

Naidu, S. (2006). *E-learning: A guidebook of principles, procedures and practices*. New Delhi, India: Common wealth Educational Media Center for Asia (CEMCA).

Nakayama, A. M. (2011). *Educação inclusiva: Princípios e representação*. Retrieved from http://www.teses.usp.br/teses/disponiveis/48/48134/tde-07122007-152417/

NCES. National Center for Education Statistics. (2000). *Teacher's tools form the 21st century: A report on teacher's use of technology*. Retrieved from nces.ed.gov/pubs2000/2000102.pdf

Neustaedter, C., & Fedorovskaya, E. (2008). Establishing and maintaining relationships in a social virtual world. *Eastman Kodak Technical Report 344195F*. Retrieved October 10, 2011 from http://clab.iat.sfu.ca/uploads/Main/VirtualRelationships.pdf

New London Group. (1996). A pedagogy of multiliteracies: Designing social futures. *Harvard Educational Review*, *66*(1), 60–92.

New Media Consortium. (2012). Horizon report 2012: Higher education ed. book. The New Media Consortium.

Nielsen (2011, June 15). Cross platform report: Americans watching more TV, mobile & web video. [Blog post]. *NielsenWire*. Retrieved from http://blog.nielsen.com/nielsenwire/online_mobile/cross-platform-report-americans-watching-more-tv-mobile-and-web-video/

Nielsen, J. (1994). *Usability engineering*. San Francisco, CA: Morgan Kaufmann. Retrieved November 30, 2012, from http://books.google.com.br/books?id=95As2OF67f0C&printsec=frontcover&hl=pt-BR&source=gbs_ge_summary_r&cad=0#v=onepage&q&f=false

Nielsen. (2012). *Survey: New U.S. smartphone growth by age and income*. Retrieved from http://blog.nielsen.com/nielsenwire/online_mobile/survey-new-u-s-smartphone-growth-by-age-and-income

Nino, C. P., Marques, J., Barbosa, D. N. F., Geyer, C. F. R., Barbosa, J. L. V., & Augustin, I. (2007). Context-aware model in an ubiquitous learning environment. In *Proceedings of the 3rd International Workshop on Pervasive Learning (PerEL)* (pp. 182-186). New York: IEEE Press.

Noy, N. F., Crubézy, M., Fergerson, R. W., Knublauch, H., Tu, S. W., Vendetti, J., & Musen, M. A. (2003). Protégé-2000: An open-source ontology-development and knowledge-acquisition environment. In *Proceedings of AMIA Annual Symposium*. AMIA.

Noy, N. F., McGuinness, D. L., et al. (2001). *Ontology development 101: A guide to creating your first ontology.* Retrieved from http://er.uni-koblenz.de/IFI/AGStaab/Teaching/SS09/sw09/Ontology101.pdf

O'Brien, L., & Murnane, J. (2009). An investigation into how avatar appearance can affect interactions in a virtual world. *International Journal of Social and Humanistic Computing, 1*(2), 192-202. Retrieved October 10, 2011 from http://inderscience.metapress.com/content/g8267g163k347466/

O'Connor, P., Höpken, W., & Gretzel, U. (2008). Dynamic packaging using a cluster-based demographic filtering approach. In *Proceedings of the International Conference.* IEEE.

OECD. Organisation for Economic Co-Operation and Development. (2001). Learning to change: ICT in schools. Paris: OECD.

Ogata, H., & Yano, Y. (2004). Context-aware support for computer-supported ubiquitous learning. In *Proceedings of the 2nd IEEE International Workshop on Wireless and Mobile Technologies in Education* (pp. 27-34). Los Alamitos, CA: IEEE Computer Society.

Ogata, H., & Yano, Y. (2009). Supporting awareness in ubiquitous learning. *International Journal of Mobile and Blended Learning, 1*(4), 1–11. doi:10.4018/jmbl.2009090801.

Ogata, H., Yin, C., El-Bishouty, M., & Yano, Y. (2010). Computer supported ubiquitous learning environment for vocabulary learning using RFID tags. *International Journal of Learning Technology, 5*(1), 5–24. doi:10.1504/IJLT.2010.031613.

Okawa, E. S., Kirner, C., & Kirner, T. G. (2010). *Sistema solar com realidade aumentada.* Paper presented at the meeting of the VII Workshop de Realidade Virtual e Aumentada (WRVA). Porto Alegre, Brazil.

Oliveira, F. C., & Kirner, C. (2007). *Uso do livro interativo com realidade aumentada em aplicações educacionais.* Paper presented at the meeting of the IV Workshop de Realidade Virtual e Aumentada (WRVA). Porto Alegre, Brazil.

Oliver, M., & Carr, D. (2009). Learning in virtual worlds: Using communities of practice to explain how people learn from play. *British Journal of Educational Technology, 40*(3), 444–457. doi:10.1111/j.1467-8535.2009.00948.x.

Olsson, T., & Salo, M. (2011). *Online user survey on current mobile augmented reality applications.* Paper presented at the meeting of the IEEE International Symposium on Mixed and Augmented Reality (ISMAR). Basel, Switzerland.

Omale, N., Hung, W. C., Luetkehans, L., & Cooke-Plagwitz, J. (2009). Learning in 3-D multiuser virtual environments: Exploring the use of unique 3-D attributes for online problem-based learning. *British Journal of Educational Technology, 40*(3), 480–495. doi:10.1111/j.1467-8535.2009.00941.x.

O'Regan, K. E. (2003). Emotion and e-learning. *Journal of Asynchronous Learning Networks, 1*(3), 78–92.

Oreilly, T. (2007). What is web 2.0: Design patterns and business models for the next generation of software. *SSRN eLibrary.* Retrieved from http://papers.ssrn.com/sol3/papers.cfm?abstract_id=1008839

Orngreen, R. (2004). CaseMaker: An environment for case-based e-learning. *Electronic Journal on e-Learning, 2*(1), 167-180.

Ouyang, Y., & Zhu, M. (2008). eLORM: Learning object relationship mining-based repository. *Online Information Review, 32*(2), 254–265. doi:10.1108/14684520810879863.

Ovalle, D., Arias, F., & Moreno, J. (2011). Student-centered multi-agent model for adaptive virtual courses development and learning object selection (2011). In *Proceedings of the IADIS International Conference on Cognition and Exploratory Learning in Digital Age (CELDA 2011)* (pp. 123 – 130). Rio de Janeiro, Brazil: CELDA.

PAPI. (2012). *IEEE LTSC 1484.2 - Draft standard for learning technology - Public and private information (PAPI) for learners (PAPI learner).* Retrieved November 10, 2012, from http://www.cen-ltso.net/Main.aspx?put=230

Parscal, T., & Hencmann, M. (2008). Cognitive apprenticeships in online learning. In *Proceedings of the 24ᵗʰ Annual Conference on Distance Teaching & Learning*, (pp. 1-4). Retrieved October 21, 2011 from http://pdf.aminer. org/000/270/204/tool_mediated_cognitive_apprencticeship_approach_for_a_computer_engineering_course.pdf

Patrício, M. R., & Gonçalves, V. (2010). *Utilização educativa do facebook no ensino superior*. I Conference Learning and Teaching in Higher Education. Universidade de Évora, Portugal.

Pazos-Arias, J. J., López-Nores, M., García-Duque, J., Díaz-Redondo, R. P., Blanco-Fernández, Y., Ramos-Cabrer, M., et al. (2008). *Provision of distance learning services over interactive digital tv with mhp*. Retrieved from http://portal.acm.org/citation.cfm?id=1342427.1342676

Pea, R. D. (1993). Practices of distributed intelligence and designs for education. In G. Salomon (Ed.), *Distributed cognitions: Psychological and educational considerations* (pp. 47–87). New York: Cambridge University Press.

Peng, H., Su, Y., Chou, C., & Tsai, C. (2009). Ubiquitous knowledge construction: Mobile learning redefined and a conceptual framework. *Innovations in Education and Teaching International*, *46*, 171–183. doi:10.1080/14703290902843828.

Perrenoud, P. (1999). Construir as competências desde a escola. Porto Alegre: Porto Alegre.

Peters, J., Singer, B., & Adler, G. (Producers) & Singer, B. (Director). (2006). *Superman returns*. [Motion picture]. Los Angeles, CA: Warner Bros. Pictures.

Petty, C., Still, K., & Prewitt, J. (2010). Askinosie chocolate: Single-origin or fair-trade sourcing. *Business Case Journal*, *17*(2), 16–30.

J. Piaget (Ed.). (2005). *Psicologia cognitiva y educaci*. Buenos Aires: Aique.

Picard, R. W. (1995). *Affective computing*. Cambridge, MA: MIT Media Laboratory.

Picard, R. W. (1997). *Affective computing*. Cambridge, MA: MIT Press.

Polkinghorne, D. (1988). *Narrative knowing and the human sciences*. New York: State University of New York Press.

Pontes, A. (2010). *Uma arquitetura de agentes para suporte a colaboração na aprendizagem baseada em problemas em ambientes virtuais de aprendizagem. (Dissertação Mestrado)*. Mossoró, Brazil: Universidade Federal Rural do Semi-Árido - UFERSA e Universidade do Estado do Rio G. do Norte - UERN.

Prasolova-Forland, E., & Divitini, M. (2003). Collaborative virtual environments for supporting learning communities: An experience of use. In *Proceedings of 2003 International ACM SIGGROUP Conference on Supporting Group Work* (pp. 58-67). New York: ACM. Retrieved on October 5, 2009 from http://delivery.acm. org/10.1145/960000/958170/p58-prasolova forland.pdf ?key1=958170&key2=9426969521&coll=GUIDE&d l=GUIDE&CFID=65999580&CFTOKEN=24982540

Pressman, R. (2011). *Software engineering: a practitioner's approach* (7th ed.). New York, NY: The McGraw-Hill Companies Inc..

Prieta, F. D., & Gil, A. (2010). A multi-agent system that searches for learning objects in heterogeneous repositories. In *Proceedings of Advances in Intelligent and Soft Computing* (pp. 355–362). IEEE. doi:10.1007/978-3-642-12433-4_42.

Puder, A. (2004). Extending desktop applications to the web. In *Proceedings of the 2004 International Symposium on Information and Communication Technologies* (pp. 8–13). Trinity College Dublin. Retrieved from http:// dl.acm.org/citation.cfm?id=1071509.1071512

Puustjärvi, J. (2007). Syntax and semantics of learning object metadata. In K. Harman, & A. Koohang (Eds.), *Learning Objects: Standards, Metadata, Repositories, and LCMS* (pp. 41–61). Santa Rosa, CA: Informance Science Press.

Quinn, C. (2000). *MLearning, mobile, wireless: In -your-pocket learning*. Retrieved December 05, 2012, from: http://www.linezine.com/2.1/features/cqmmwiyp.htm

Ransome, A. (1909). *A history of story-telling: Studies in the development of narrative*. London: T. C., & E. C. Jack.

Rau, P.-L. P., Gao, Q., & Wu, L.-M. (2008). Using mobile communication technology in high school education: Motivation, pressure, and learning performance. *Computers & Education*, *50*(1), 1–22. doi:10.1016/j. compedu.2006.03.008.

Reategui, E., Epstein, D., Lorenzatti, A., & Klemann, M. (2011). Sobek: A text mining tool for educational applications. In *Proceedings of the International Conference on Data Mining* (pp. 59-64). Las Vegas, NV: Estados Unidos.

Reid, L. G., & Snow-Weaver, A. (2008). WCAG 2.0: A web accessibility standard for the evolving web. In *Proceedings of the 2008 International Cross-Disciplinary Conference on Web Accessibility (W4A)* (pp. 109–115). New York, NY: ACM. doi:10.1145/1368044.1368069

Resnick, M. (2001). *Rethinking learning in the digital age.* Retrieved from llk.media.mit.edu/papers/mres-wef.pdf

Rey-Lopez, M., Diaz-Redondo, R. P., Fernandez-Vilas, A., Pazos-Arias, J. J., Garcia-Duque, J., Gil-Solla, A., & Ramos-Cabrer, M. (2009). *An extension to the adl scorm standard to support adaptivity: The t-learning case-study.* Retrieved from http://portal.acm.org/citation.cfm?id=1460931.14610 76

Ricci, F. (2010). Mobile recommender systems. *International Journal of Information Technology and Tourism*, *1*(12), 205–231. doi:10.3727/10983051 1X12978702284390.

Rice, M. L., & Wilson, E. K. (1999). How technology aids constructivism in the social studies classroom. *Social Studies*, *90*(1), 28–34. doi:10.1080/00377999909602388.

Rigaux, P., & Spyratos, N. (2012). *SeLeNe report: Metadata management and learning object composition in a self elearning network.* Retrieved November 10, 2012, from http://www.dcs.bbk.ac.uk/selene/reports/seleneLRI3.pdf

Ritchie, H., & Blanck, P. (2003). The promise of the internet for disability: A study of on-line services and web site accessibility at centers for independent living. *Behavioral Sciences & the Law*, *21*(1), 5–26. doi:10.1002/bsl.520 PMID:12579615.

Robinson, S. K. (2010). *Bring on the learning revolution!* Retrieved May 13, 2012, from http://www.ted.com/talks/sir_ken_robinson_bring_on_the_revolution.html

Rodrigues, P. G., & Júnior, E. P. F. D. (2010). Middlewares e protocolos para redes sociais pervasivas. *Monografia (PUC-RJ)*. Retrieved from http://www-di.inf.puc-rio.br/~endler/courses/Mobile/Monografias/09/PauloGallotti_MP4PSN-final.doc

Rodríguez, P., Tabares, V., Duque, N., Ovalle, D., & Vicari, R. (2012). *Multi-agent model for searching, recovering, recommendation and evaluation of learning objects from repository federations.* Paper presented at the 13th Ibero-American Conference on Artificial Intelligence. Cartagena, Colombia.

Rogers, E. (2003). *Diffusion of innovation* (5th ed.). New York: Free Press.

Rogers, Y., Price, S., Randell, C., Fraser, D. S., Weal, M., & Fitzpatrick, G. (2005). Ubi-learning integrates indoor and outdoor experiences. *Communications of the ACM*, *48*(1), 55–59. doi:10.1145/1039539.1039570.

Rolim, C. R., Sonntag, N. B., & Barbosa, J. L. V. (2008). A model for the development of location-aware applications. In *Proceedings of the Brazilian Workshop on High Performance Computational Systems (WSCAD)* (pp. 227-234). Porto Alegre: SBC.

Rolland, J. P., & Fuchs, H. (2000). Optical versus video see-through head-mounted displays: Medical visualization. *Presence (Cambridge, Mass.)*, 287–309. doi:10.1162/105474600566808.

Rose, F. (2011). *The art of immersion: How the digital generation is remaking Hollywood, Madison Avenue, and the way we tell stories.* New York: W. W. Norton.

Rosen, L. D., & Weft, M. M. (1995). Computer availability, computer experience and technophobia among public school teachers. *Computers in Human Behavior*, *11*(1), 9–31. doi:10.1016/0747-5632(94)00018-D.

Rovio. (2012a). Angry birds. *The Official Home of Angry Birds.* Retrieved from http://www.angrybirds.com/

Rovio. (2012b). Amazing Alex. *Amazing Alex.* Retrieved from http://teaser.amazingalex.com/

Rovio. (2012c). Bad piggies. *Bad Piggies.* Retrieved from http://www.badpiggies.com/

Rudin, S., Søren, O., Stærmore, S., & Chaffin, C. (Producers), & Fincher, D. (Director). (2011). *The girl with the dragon tattoo.* [Motion picture]. Los Angeles, CA: Columbia Pictures & Sony Pictures Releasing.

Ryang, R. (2005). *The Shining recut.* Retrieved from http://www.youtube.com/watch?v=sfout_rgPSA/

Saccol, A., Schlemmer, E., & Barbosa, J. (2011). *M-learning e u-learning: Novas perspectivas da aprendizagem movel e ubiqua*. Pearson.

Sack, W., et al. (2003). *Social architecture and technological determinism in open source software development*. Paper presented at 27th meeting of the Society for the Social Studies of Science (4S). Atlanta, GA.

Sack, W., et al. (2006). A methodological framework for socio-cognitive analyses of collaborative design of open source software. *International Journal Computer Supported Cooperative Work, 15*(2-3), 229-240. Retrieved October 12, 2011, from http://dl.acm.org/citation.cfm?id=1149570

Saha, D., & Mukherjee, A. (2003). Pervasive computing: a paradigm for the 21st century. *IEEE Computer, 36*(3), 25–31. doi:10.1109/MC.2003.1185214.

Sajadi, S. S., & Khan, T. M. (2011). An evaluation of constructivism for learners with ADHD: Development of a constructivist pedagogy for special needs. In *Proceedings of the European, Mediterranean & Middle Eastern Conference on Information Systems*. IEEE.

Salcedo, P., Rojas, M., Manríquez, G., & Gatica, Y. (2004). Curso de UML multiplataforma adaptativo basado en la teoría de respuesta al ítem. *Revista Ingeniería Informática, 10*.

Salen, K., & Zimmerman, E. (2003). *Rules of play: Game design fundamentals*. Cambridge, MA: MIT Press.

Salmon, G. (2009). The future for (second) life and learning. *British Journal of Educational Technology, 40*(3), 526–538. doi:10.1111/j.1467-8535.2009.00967.x.

Santaella, L. (2010). A aprendizagem ubíqua substitui a educação formal?. *Revista de Computação e Tecnologia da PUC-SP, 17*–22.

Santos, N. dos S. R. S. dos, Lima, J. V. de, & Wives, L. K. (2011). Ubiquidade e mobilidade de objetos de aprendizagem usando o papel como recurso. *RENOTE, 8*(3). Retrieved from http://seer.ufrgs.br/renote/article/view/18067

Santos, O. C., & Boticário, J. G. (2010). Modeling recommendations for the educational domain. In *Proceedings of the Workshop on Recommender Systems for Technology Enhanced Learning* (pp. 2793–2800). ACM Press.

Sarwar, B., Karypis, G., Konstan, J., & Reidl, J. (2001). Item-based collaborative filtering recommendation algorithms. In *Proceedings of the 10th International Conference on World Wide Web* (pp. 285-295). Hong Kong: ACM.

Sarwar, B., Karypis, G., Konstan, J., & Riedl, J. (2000). Analysis of recommender algorithms for e-commerce. In *Proceedings of the 2nd ACM Conference on Electronic Commerce* (pp.158-167). ACM Press.

Satyanarayanan, M. (1996). Fundamental challenges in mobile computing. In *Proceedings of the ACM Symposium on Principles of Distributed Computing* (pp. 1-7). New York: ACM.

Satyanarayanan, M. (2001). Pervasive computing: Vision and challenges. *IEE Personal Communications, 8*, 10–17. doi:10.1109/98.943998.

Satyanarayanan, M., Bahl, P., Cáceres, R., & Davies, N. (2009). The case for VM-based cloudlets in mobile computing. *IEEE Pervasive Computing / IEEE Computer Society [and] IEEE Communications Society, 8*(4), 14–23. doi:10.1109/MPRV.2009.82.

Sawyer, R. (1957). *The way of the storyteller*. New York: The Viking Press.

SBTVD. (2007). *Sistema Brasileiro de TV digital*. Retrieved from http://sbtvd.cpqd.com.br

Schafer, J. B., Konstan, J., & Riedl, J. (2001). E-commerce recommendation applications. *Data Mining and Knowledge Discovery, 5*(1-2), 115–153. doi:10.1023/A:1009804230409.

Schank, R. C. (1990). *Tell me a story: A new look at real and artificial memory*. New York: Charles Scribner's Sons.

Scherer, K. R. (2000). Psychological models of emotion. In J. C. Borod (Ed.), *The Neuropsychology of Emotion*. Oxford, UK: Oxford University Press.

Schmeil, A., & Eppler, M. (2008). Knowledge sharing and collaborative learning in second life: A classification of virtual 3-D group interaction scripts. *Journal of Universal Computer Science, 14*(3), 665-677. Retrieved on February 20, 2011 from http://oaj.unsri.ac.id/files/jucs/jucs_15_03_0665_0677_schmeil_oaj_unscri.pdf

Schmidt, J. P. (2010). *Peer 2 peer university*. Retrieved May 13, 2012, from http://vimeo.com/11158136

Schroeder, R. (2006). Being there together and the future of connected presence. *Presence (Cambridge, Mass.)*, *15*(4), 438–454. doi:10.1162/pres.15.4.438.

Schwartz, N. H. (2008). Exploiting the use of technology to teach: The value of distributed cognition. *Journal of Research on Technology in Education, 40*(3), 389–404.

SCOPEO. (2011). *M-learning en España, Portugal y América Latina*. SCOPEO.

Seale, J. K. (2001). The same but different: The use of the personal home page by adults with Down syndrome as a tool for self-presentation. *British Journal of Educational Technology, 32*, 343–352. doi:10.1111/1467-8535.00203.

Second Life Education. (2010). *Academic organizations in second life*. Retrieved from http://edudirectory. secondlife.com/

Sefton-Green, J. (2004). *Literature review in informal learning with technology outside school*. Bristol, UK: NESTA Futurelab.

Senge, P. (1990). *The fifth discipline: The art and practice of the learning organization*. New York: Doubleday.

Seol, S., Sharp, A., & Kim, P. (2011). Stanford mobile inquiry-based learning environment (SMILE), using mobile phones to promote student inquires in the elementary classroom. In *Proceedings of IEEE World Congress in Computer Science, Computer Engineering, and Applied Computing*. IEEE.

Shadbolt, N., Hall, W., & Berners-Lee, T. (2006). The semantic web revisited. *IEEE Intelligent Systems, 21*(3), 96–101. doi:10.1109/MIS.2006.62.

Shamir, J. (2007). Quality assessment of television programs in Israel: Can viewers recognize production value? *Journal of Applied Communication Research, 35*(3), 320–341. doi:10.1080/00909880701434406.

Shardanand, U., & Maes, P. (1995). Social information filtering: Algorithms for automating word of mouth. In *Proceedings of the SIGCHI Conference on Human Factors in Computing Systems* (CHI '95). ACM Press. DOI=10.1145/223904.223931

Sharples, M., & Taylor, J. (2005). Towards a theory of mobile learning. *mLearn*. Retrieved from http://www. iamlearn.org/public/mlearn2005/www.mlearn.org.za/ CD/papers/Sharples- Theory of Mobile.pdf

Sharples, M. (2000). The design of personal mobile technologies for lifelong learning. *Computers & Education, 34*(3), 177–193. doi:10.1016/S0360-1315(99)00044-5.

Shein, E. (2010). Avatars rising in the enterprise. *Computerworld*. Retrieved on April 20, 2010 from http:// www.computerworld.com/s/article/9174873/Avatars_rising_in_the_enterprise

Shelton, B., & Hedley, N. (2002). *Using augmented reality for teaching earthsun relationships to undergraduate geography students*. Paper presented at the meeting of the IEEE International Augmented Reality Toolkit Workshop. Darmstadt, Germany.

Shen, K. N., Khalifa, M., & Yu, A. Y. (2006). Supporting social interaction in virtual communities: Role of social presence. In *Proceedings of the Twelfth Americas Conference on Information Systems*, (pp. 4461-4469). Retrieved on May 15, 2011 from citeseerx.ist.psu.edu

Shen, L., Wang, M., & Shen, R. (2009). Affective e-learning: Using emotional data to improve learning in pervasive learning environment. *Journal of Educational Technology & Society, 1*(12), 176–189.

Shih, W.-C., Yang, C.-T., & Tseng, S.-S. (2011). Fuzzy folksonomy-based index creation for e-learning content retrieval on cloud computing environments. In *Proceedings of Fuzzy Systems (FUZZ)*. IEEE. doi:10.1109/ FUZZY.2011.6007516.

Shin, W., & Lowes, S. (2008). Analyzing web 2.0 users in an online discussion forum. In *Proceedings of World Conference on Educational Multimedia, Hypermedia and Telecommunications 2008* (pp. 1130–1137). Chesapeake, VA: AACE.

Shneiderman, B. et al. (2010). *Designing the user interface: Strategies for effective human-computer interaction* (5th ed.). Reading, MA: Addison Wesley.

Siemens, G. (2006). *Knowing knowledge*. Retrieved from Lulu.com

Simoes, D., Luis, R., & Horta, N. (2004). Enhancing the scorm modelling scope. In *Proceedings of Advanced Learning Technologies*. IEEE.

Simon, B., Miklós, Z., Nejdl, W., & Sintek, M. (2002). Elena: A mediation infrastructure for educational services. In *Proceedings of the WWW Conference*. Budapest, Hungary: IEEE.

Solis, B. (2010). *Engage! The complete guide for brands and businesses to build, cultivate, and measure success in the new web*. Hoboken, NJ: John Wiley & Sons.

Spelta, L. (2009). *Acessibilidade web: 7 mitos e um equívoco*. Retrieved from http://acessodigital.net/art_acessibilidade-web-7-mitos-e-um-equivoco.html

Spiro, R. J., Feltovich, P. J., Jacobson, M. J., & Coulson, R. L. (1992). Cognitive flexibility, constructivism, and hypertext: Random access instruction for advanced knowledge acquisition in ill-structured domains. *Constructivism and the Technology of Instruction: A Conversation*, 57-75.

Squire, K., & Dikkers, S. (2011). Amplifications of learning: Use of mobile media devices among youth. *Convergence: The International Journal of Research into New Media Technologies*. DOI 10.1177/1354856511429646

Squire, K. (2006). From content to context: Videogames as designed experience. *Educational Researcher, 35*(8), 19–29. doi:10.3102/0013189X035008019.

Squire, K., & Jan, M. (2007). Mad city mystery: Developing scientific argumentation skills with a place-based augmented reality game on handheld computers. *Journal of Science Education and Technology, 16*(1), 5–29. doi:10.1007/s10956-006-9037-z.

Squire, K., Jan, M., Matthews, J., Wagler, M., Martin, J., & DeVane, B. (2007). Wherever you go, there you are: Place-based augmented reality games for learning. In B. Sheldon, & D. Wiley (Eds.), *The Educational Design and Use of Computer Simulation Games* (pp. 265–296). Rotterdam, The Netherlands: Sense Publishing.

Squire, K., & Klopfer, E. (2007). Augmented reality simulations on handheld computers. *Journal of the Learning Sciences, 16*(3), 371–413. doi:10.1080/10508400701413435.

StatCounter. (2012). *Mobile vs. desktop*. Retrieved from http://gs.statcounter.com/#mobile_vs_desktop-ww-monthly-201010-201210

Steinkuehler, C. A. (2004). Learning in massively multiplayer online games. In *Proceedings of the 6th International Conference on Learning Sciences*, (pp. 521-528). Retrieved on November 5, 2009 from http://delivery.acm.org/10.1145/1150000/1149190/p521steinkuehler.pdf?key1=1149190&key2=4767589521&coll=GUIDE&dl=GUIDE&CFID=64891945&CFTOKEN=50934250

StrategyAnalytics. (2008). *Virtual worlds projected to mushroom to nearly one billion users*. Retrieved on June 1, 2010 from https://www.strategyanalytics.com/default.aspx?mod=PressReleaseViewer&a0=3983

Suthterland, I. (1968). A head-mounted three dimensional display. In *Proceedings of the AFIPS Fall Joint Computer Conference*. ACM.

Svensson, M., & Pettersson, O. (2008). Making use of user-generated content and contextual metadata collected during ubiquitous learning activities. In *Proceedings of the Eighth IEEE International Conference on Advanced Learning Technologies, 2008. ICALT '08* (pp. 606 –610). doi:10.1109/ICALT.2008.169

Symeonidis, P., Nanopoulos, A., & Manolopoulos, Y. (2008). Providing justifications in recommender systems. *IEEE Transactions on Systems, Man, and Cybernetics, 38*(6).

Szendrei, J. (1996). Concrete materials in the classroom. In *International handbook of mathematics education*. Dordrecht, The Netherlands: Kluwer. doi:10.1007/978-94-009-1465-0_13.

Takahaski, D. (2010). Free realm hits 9M players, closing in on World of Warcraft. *Gamebeat*. Retrieved on August 18, 2010 from http://games.venturebeat.com/2010/03/05/free-realms-hits-9m players-closing-in-on-world-of-warcraft/

Tanaka, E. H., & Da Rocha, H. V. (2011). Evaluation of web accessibility tools. In *Proceedings of the 10th Brazilian Symposium on on Human Factors in Computing Systems and the 5th Latin American Conference on Human-Computer Interaction* (pp. 272–279). Porto Alegre, Brazil: Brazilian Computer Society. Retrieved from http://dl.acm.org/citation.cfm?id=2254436.2254483

Tang, L., Liu, H., Zhang, J., Agarwal, N., & Salerno, J. (2008). Topic taxonomy adaptation for group profiling. *ACM Transactions on Knowledge Discovery from Data, 1*(4).

Tan, T., Lin, M., Chu, Y., & Liu, T. (2012). Educational affordances of a ubiquitous learning environment in a natural science course. *Journal of Educational Technology & Society, 15,* 206–219.

Tarouco, L. M. R., et al. (2004). Objetos de aprendizagem para m-learning. In *Anais do Congresso Nacional de Tecnologia da Informação e Comunicação (SUCESU)*. Retrieved September 12, 2010, from http://www.cinted. ufrgs.br/CESTA/objetosdeaprendizagem_sucesu.pdf

Tatar, D. E. (2003). Handhelds go to school: Lessons learned. *SRI International Journal Computer, 36*(9), 30–37.

TED. (2011). Salman Khan: Let's use video to reinvent education. *TED Talks*. Retrieved from http://www.ted. com/talks/salman_khan_let_s_use_video_to_reinvent_education.html

Thai-Nghe, N., Drumond, L., Krohn-Grimberghe, A., & Schmidt-Thieme, L. (2010). Recommender system for predicting student performance. In *Proceedings of the Workshop on Recommender Systems for Technology Enhanced Learning*. IEEE.

Thomas, D., & Seeley Brown, J. (2009). Why virtual worlds matter. *International Journal of Learning and Media, 1*(1), 37-49. Retrieved on April 3, 2011 from http://johnseeleybrown.com/virtualworlds.pdf

Thompson, C. (2011, July 15). How Khan Academy is changing the rules of education. *Wired Magazine, 19*(8). Retrieved from http://www.wired.com/magazine/2011/07/ff_khan/all/

Tingen, P. (2005). The Dust Brothers: Sampling, remixing & the boat studio. *Sound on Sound*. Retrieved from http://www.soundonsound.com/sos/may05/articles/dust.htm

Tori, R. (2009). Cursos híbridos ou blended learning. In *Educação a distância: O estado da arte*. São Paulo: Pearson Prentice Hall.

Torraco, R. J. (2005). Writing integrative literature reviews: Guidelines and examples. *Human Resources Development Review, 4*(3), 356-367. Retrieved on April 3, 2011 from http://docseminar2.wikispaces.com/file/view/Literature+review+paper_Torraco.pdf

TrendWatching. (2012). *TrendWatching*. Retrieved May 13, 2012, from http://trendwatching.com

Trifonova, A., & Ronchetti, M. (2003). *A general architecture for m-learning*. Retrieved from http://eprints. biblio.unitn.it/493/

Tu, C.-H., & McIsaac, M. (2002). An examination of social presence to increase interaction in online classes. *American Journal of Distance Education, 16*(3), 131–150. doi:10.1207/S15389286AJDE1603_2.

Tu, C.-H., McIsaac, M., Sujo-Montes, L., & Armfield, S. (2012). Is there a mobile social presence? *Educational Media International, 49*(4), 1–15. doi:10.1080/0952398 7.2012.741195.

Tu, C.-H., Yen, C.-J., Blocher, J. M., & Chan, J.-Y. (2012). A study of the predictive relationship between online social presence and ONLE interaction. *International Journal of Distance Education Technologies, 10*(3), 53–66. doi:10.4018/jdet.2012070104.

Twining, P. (2009). Exploring the educational potential of virtual worlds - Some reflections from SPP. *British Journal of Educational Technology, 40*(3), 496–514. doi:10.1111/j.1467-8535.2009.00963.x.

Tyler-Smith, K. (2005). Early attrition among first-time learners: A review of factors that contribute to drop-out, withdrawal, and non-completion rates of adult learners undertaking elearning programs. *Journal of Online Learning and Teaching, 2*(2). Retrieved September 18, 2009 from jolt.merlot.org/Vol2_No2_TylerSmith.htm

U.S. General Accounting Office. (1996). *Content analysis: A methodology for structuring and analyzing written material*. Washington, DC: GAO.

United Nations. (2010). *Factsheet on persons with disabilities*. Retrieved August 6, 2012, from http://www. un.org/disabilities/default.asp?id=18

Uschold, M., & King, M. (1995). *Towards a methodology for building ontologies*. Retrieved from http://129.215.202.23/~oplan/documents/1995/95-ont-ijcai95-ont-method.pdf

Van de Sompel, H., & Chute, R. (2008). The aDORe federation architecture: Digital repositories at scale. *International Journal (Toronto, Ont.)*, *9*, 83–100.

Vasconcellos, M. (2008). A diferenciação entre figuras geométricas não-planas e planas: O conhecimento dos alunos das séries iniciais do ensino fundamental e o ponto de vista dos professores. *Zetetiké-Unicamp*, *16*(30), 77–106.

Vasileiou, V., & Paraskeva, F. (2010). Teaching role-playing instruction in second life: An exploratory study. *Journal of Information, Information Technology, and Organizations*, *5*, 25-50. Retrieved on March 3, 2011 from http://jiito.org/articles/JIITOv5p025-050Vasileious431.pdf

Vaughan-Nichols, S. J. (2009). Will mobile computing's future be location, location, location? *Computer*, *42*(2), 14–17. doi:10.1109/MC.2009.65.

Venkatraman, S., & Kamatkar, S. J. (2013). Intelligent information retrieval and recommender system framework. *International Journal of Future Computer and Communication*, *2*(2), 85–89.

Vinter, A., & Detable, C. (2008). Implicit and explicit motor learning in children with and without Down's syndrome. *The British Journal of Developmental Psychology*, *26*(4), 507–523. doi:10.1348/026151007X267300.

Vogel, D., Kennedy, D., & Kuan, K. (2007). *Do mobile device applications affect learning?* Retrieved from http://ieeexplore.ieee.org/xpls/abs_all.jsp?arnumber=4076377

Von Bertalanffy, L. (1950). An outline of general system theory. *The British Journal for the Philosophy of Science*, *1*, 134–165. doi:10.1093/bjps/I.2.134.

Vvidis, I. K. (2002). Distributed cognition and educational practice. *Journal of Interactive Learning Research*, *11*, Retrieved from http://go.galegroup.com/ps/i.do?id=GALE%7CA87079467&v=2.1&u=nauniv&it=r&p=AONE&sw=w.

Vygotsky, L. S. (1978). *Mind in society: The development of higher psychological processes*. Cambridge, MA: Harvard University Press.

W3C, W. W. W. C. (2006). *Web Accessibility initiative (WAI)*. W3C.

Wagner, D. (2007). *Handheld augmented reality*. (PhD thesis). Graz University of Technology, Graz, Austria.

Wang, B., Bodily, J., & Gupta, S. (2004). Supporting persistent social groups in ubiquitous computing environments using context aware ephemeral group service. In *Proceedings of the IEEE PerCom*. IEEE.

Wang, S., & Wu, C. (2011). Application of context-aware and personalized recommendation to implement an adaptive ubiquitous learning system. *Expert Systems with Applications*, *38*, 10831–10838. doi:10.1016/j.eswa.2011.02.083.

Warburton, S. (2009). Second life in higher education: Assessing the potential for and barriers to deploying virtual worlds in learning and teaching. *British Journal of Educational Technology*, *40*(3), 414–426. doi:10.1111/j.1467-8535.2009.00952.x.

Warner, R. (2007). *Applied statistics: From bivariate through multivariate techniques*. Thousand Oaks, CA: Sage Publications.

Watanabe, T., & Umegaki, M. (2007). Capability survey of user agents with the UAAG 1.0 test suite and its impact on web accessibility. *Universal Access in the Information Society*, *6*(3), 221–232. doi:10.1007/s10209-007-0087-7.

Weber, R. P. (1990). *Basic content analysis*. Cambridge, UK: Cambridge University Press.

Wei, Z., & Liqiang, S. (2011). *Mobile-learning (m-learning) apply to physical education in colleges*. Paper presented at the Meeting of the IEEE Conference on Circuits, Communications and System. Wuhan, China.

B. Weiner (Ed.). (1974). *Achievement, motivation & attribution theory*. Morristown, NJ: General Learning Press.

Weiser, M., Gold, R., & Brown, J. (1999). The origins of ubiquitous computing research at PARC in the late 1980s. *IBM Systems Journal*, *38*(4), 693–696. Retrieved from http://ieeexplore.ieee.org/xpls/abs_all.jsp?arnumber=5387055 doi:10.1147/sj.384.0693.

Weisner, M. (1993). Some computer issues in ubiquitous computer. *Communications of the ACM*, *36*(7), 75–84. doi:10.1145/159544.159617.

Weiss, G. (2007). *Multiagent systems: A modern approach to distributed artificial intelligence.* Boston: The MIT Press.

Wenger, E. (2004). *Communities of practice:Learning, meaning and identity.* Cambridge, UK: Cambridge University Press.

Wenger, E., McDermott, R., & Snyder, W. M. (2002). *Cultivating communities of practice.* Boston: Harvard Business School Press.

Wesch, M. (2008). *An anthropological introduction to YouTube.* Retrieved from http://www.youtube.com/watch?v=TPAO-lZ4_hU

Wiese, J., Kelley, P. G., Cranor, L. F., Dabbish, L., Hong, J. I., & Zimmerman, J. (2011). Are you close with me? Are you nearby? Investigating social groups, closeness, and willingness to share. *UbiComp, 11,* 197–206.

Wigfield, A. (1994). Expectancy-value theory of achievement motivation: A developmental perspective. *Educational Psychology Review, 6*(1), 49–78. doi:10.1007/BF02209024.

Wiley, D. A. (2000). *Learning object design and sequencing theory. (PhD Tesis).* Provo, UT: Brigham Young University.

Wilson, V. (2004). A standards framework for academic e-advising services. *International Journal of Services and Standards, 1*(1). doi:10.1504/IJSS.2004.005689.

Winner, L. (1997). *Cyberlibertarian myths and the prospects for community.* Retrieved November 30, 2012, from http://www.rpi.edu/~winner/cyberlib2.html

Wlodkowski, R. (1985). *Enhancing adult motivation to learn.* San Francisco, CA: Jossey-Bass Publishers.

Wolske, J. (2012). *Caseworx: Askinosie chocolate.* [Video]. Los Angeles, CA: Caseworx, Inc.

Wood, D. R. (1992). Teaching narratives: A sources for faculty development and evaluation. *Harvard Educational Review, 62*(4), 535–550.

Wooldridge, M., Jennings, N. R., & Kinny, D. (1999). A methodology for agent-oriented analysis and design. In *Proceedings of the Third Annual Conference on Autonomous Agents.* AGENTS.

Wu, T. T., Yang, T. C., Hwang, G. J., & Chu, H. C. (2008). Conducting situated learning in a context-aware ubiquitous learning environment. In Wireless, Mobile, and Ubiquitous Technology in Education, (pp. 82-86). IEEE.

Wyld, D. (2010). A virtual explosion or SNAFU is always better than a real one: Exploring the use of virtual worlds for simulations and training…and developing the leaders of tomorrow. In M. Iskander, V. Kapilla, & M. Karim (Eds.), *Technological Development in Education and Automation* (pp. 73–78). doi:10.1007/978-90-481-3656-8_15.

Yahoo! & Interpret. (2011). Phase 2 of video: Revolution evolution. *Yahoo! Advertising Solutions.* Retrieved from http://advertising.yahoo.com/article/phase-2-of-video-revolution-evolution.html

Yahya, S., Ahmad, E. A., & Jalil, K. A. (2010). The definition and characteristics of ubiquitous learning: A discussion. *International Journal of Education and Development Using Information and Communication Technology, 6*(1). Retrieved on October 17, 2012 from http://ijedict.dec.uwi.edu/viewarticle.php?id=785

Yang, S. J. H. (2006). Context aware ubiquitous learning environments for peer-to-peer collaborative learning. *Educational Technology & Society, 9*(1), 188-201. Retrieved on October 15, 2012 from http://library.oum.edu.my/oumlib/sites/default/files/file_attachments/odl-resources/4479/context-aware.pef

Yang, S. J. H., Huang, A. P. M., Chen, R., Tseng, S.-S., & Shen, Y.-S. (2006). Context model and context acquisition for ubiquitous content access in ulearning environments. In *Proceedings of the IEEE International Conference on Sensor Networks, Ubiquitous, and Trustworthy Computing,* (Vol. 2, pp. 78 –83). IEEE. doi:10.1109/SUTC.2006.47

Yang, S. J., & Chen, I. Y. (2006). Universal access and content adaptation in mobile learning. In *Advanced Learning Technologies, 2006,* (pp. 1172–1173). IEEE. Retrieved from http://ieeexplore.ieee.org/xpls/abs_all.jsp?arnumber=1652678

Yau, S. S., Gupta, E. K. S., & Karim, F. Ahamed, S. I., Wang, Y., & Wang, B. (2003). Smart classroom: Enhancing collaborative learning using pervasive computing technology. In *Proceedings of the II American Society of Engineering Education (ASEE)* (pp. 13633-13642). ASEE.

Yee, N. (2007). Motivations of play in online games. *Journal of Cyber Psychology & Behavior, 9,* 772-775. Retrieved on September 24, 2010 from http://www.cblt. soton.ac.uk/multimedia/PDFsMM09/MMORPG%20 motivation%20for%20playing.pdf

Yee, N., & Bailenson, J. N. (2007). The proteus effect: The effect of transformed self-representation on behavior. *Human Communication Research, 33,* 271-290. Retrieved June 22, 2010 from http://dx.doi.org/doi:10.1111/j.1468-2958.2007.00299.x

Yee, N., Bailenson, J. N., Urbanek, M., Chang, F., & Merget, D. (2007). The unbearable likeness of being digital: The persistence of nonvrebal social norms in online virtual environments. *The Journal of CyberPsychology and Behavior, 10,* 115–121. doi:10.1089/cpb.2006.9984 PMID:17305457.

Yin, C., Dong, Y., Tabata, Y., & Ogata, H. (2012). Recommendation of helpers based on personal connections in mobile learning. In *Proceedings of the International Conference on Wireless, Mobile and Ubiquitous Technology in Education,* (pp. 137–141). doi:10.1109/WMUTE.2012.32

Yin, R. K. (2005). *Estudo de caso: Planejamento e métodos 3.* Brazil: Editora Bookman.

Yoon, C., & Kim, S. (2007). Convenience and TAM in a ubiquitous computing environment: The case of wireless LAN. *Electronic Commerce Research and Applications, 6*(1), 102–112. doi:10.1016/j.elerap.2006.06.009.

Young, J. (2010). After frustrations in second life, colleges look to new virtual worlds. *The Chronicle of Higher Education.* Retrieved on May 19, 2010 from http://chronicle. com/article/After-Frustrations-in-Second/64137

Yu, T. W. (2009). Learning in the virtual world: The pedagogical potentials of massively multiplayer online role-playing games. *International Education Studies, 2*(1), 32-38. Retrieved on July 4, 2011 from http://www. ccsenet.org/journal/index.php/ies/article/view/287/362

Zabriskie, F. H., & McNabb, D. E. (2007). E-hancing the master of business administration (MBA) managerial accounting course. *Journal of Education for Business, 82*(4), 226–233. doi:10.3200/JOEB.82.4.226-233.

Zaina, L. A. M., Bressan, G., Cardieri, M. A. C. A., & Rodrigues, J. (2012). e-LORS: Uma abordagem para recomendação de objetos de aprendizagem. *RBIE,* 20.

Zarifian, P. (2002). La politique de la compétence et l'appel aux connaissances à partir de la stratégie d'entreprise post-fordiste. *Contribuição ao Colóquio de Nantes.* Retrieved December 13, 2002, from http://www.scoplepave.org/ ledico/auteurs/zarifian%20competence%201.htm

Zervas, P., Gómez, S., Fabregat, R., & Sampson, D. (2011). Tools for context-aware learning design and mobile delivery. In *Proceedings of the 11th IEEE International Conference on Advanced Learning Technologies.* IEEE.

About the Contributors

Francisco Milton Mendes Neto received a Ph.D. in Electrical Engineering from Federal University of Campina Grande. He received the MSc degree in Informatics from Federal University of Campina Grande and received the Bachelor's degree in Computer Science from State University of Ceará. He was Software Development Project Manager for Federal Service of Data Processing for several years. In 2006, after an incursion in industry, he joined the Rural Federal University of the Semi-Arid, Brazil, where he is currently an associate professor of the Graduate Program in Computer Science and of the Postgraduate Program in Computer Science. He is currently coordinator of the Research Group in Software Engineering and of the Software Engineering Laboratory. His main research areas are in Knowledge Engineering, Software Engineering, Multiagent Systems, and Computer-Supported Collaborative Learning. Dr. Mendes Neto is a member of the Brazilian Computing Society.

* * *

Shadow W. J. Armfield is an Assistant Professor of Educational Technology in the Department of Educational Specialties at Northern Arizona University. His teaching experience spans over 15 years and includes teaching science at the middle school level as well as teaching technology integration, both face-to-face and online, to pre-service, in-service, and Master-level teachers. His research interests include technology integration in K-12 environments and technology integration in teacher preparation programs.

Lara Augustin has an undergraduate degree in Math from the Federal University of Santa Maria – UFSM (1983), Master in the Computer Science Graduate Program in Federal University of Rio Grande do Sul (1993), and Doctorate in Computer Science by the Federal University of Rio Grande do Sul (2004). Currently, she is a researcher of National Council for Scientific and Technological Development and associated professor I of Federal University of Santa Maria. She was the first coordinator of Computing Graduate Program in UFSM, created in 2006, and currently is substitute coordinator of it. Her experiences are in Computer Science, emphasizing Program Languages, Distributed Systems, and Software Production, acting mainly in Pervasive and Ubiquitous Computing, Mobile Computing, Context-Aware Computing, Healthy Ubiquitous Computing, End-User Programming, and Affective Computing.

Débora Nice Ferrari Barbosa received her BS degree in Information Systems from the Catholic University of Pelotas, Brazil, in 1997. She obtained her MS and PhD degrees in Computer Science from the Federal University of Rio Grande do Sul, Brazil, in 2001 and 2006, respectively. Nowadays, she is a Professor and Researcher at the FEEVALE University, Novo Hamburgo, Brazil. Additionally, she is a

CNPq (the Brazilian Council for the Development of Science and Technology) researcher in Computer Science (scholarship for high productivity). She also is the director of Learningware Educational Technology, a company based in São Leopoldo, Brazil. Her research interests include ubiquitous learning systems, distributed computing, multi-agent systems, and artificial intelligence. She is also a member of the Brazilian Computer Society (SBC).

Jorge Luis Victória Barbosa received his BS degree in Electrical Engineering from the Catholic University of Pelotas, Brazil, in 1991. He obtained his MS and PhD degrees in Computer Science from the Federal University of Rio Grande do Sul (UFRGS), Brazil, in 1996 and 2002, respectively. Today, he is a Professor and Researcher of the Interdisciplinary Postgraduate Program in Applied Computing (PIPCA) at the University of Vale do Rio dos Sinos (UNISINOS), São Leopoldo, Brazil. Additionally, he is a CNPq (the Brazilian Council for the Development of Science and Technology) researcher in Computer Science (scholarship for high productivity) and head of the Mobile Computing Laboratory (MobiLab/UNISINOS). His research interests include mobile and ubiquitous computing and mobile/ubiquitous learning. He is a member of the Brazilian Computer Society (SBC).

Patricia Alejandra Behar is Ph.D. of Computer Science at the Federal University of Rio Grande do Sul. Currently, she is professor and researcher at the Education School and the Post Graduation Programs in Education and Computer Science in Education at the Federal University of Rio Grande do Sul and Coordinator of the Digital Technology Nucleous in Education (NUTED). She has experience in distance education, learning virtual environments, learners and lifelong learning, teaching, and role of teachers in e-learning.

Aquiles Medeiros Filgueira Burlamaqui holds a Doctorate in Systems and Computing Engineering from Federal University of Rio Grande do Norte, graduated in 2003. He is a Professor at the Technologic and Science School of Federal University of Rio Grande do Norte, Brazil. He has published more than 120 papers, including journals, magazine, and conference proceedings. He is advisor of several graduate students (more than 15 former) and also undergraduate students. He has participated in many international events and served in the Program Committee of several conferences, including contributions as Program Chair, General Organizing Chair, and Reviewer. He has done researches in Interactive Digital Television, Virtual Reality, and Robotics. He has coordinated and participated in several projects in the above fields.

Tereza Kelly Gomes Carneiro is finishing her PhD on Knowledge Diffusion at Federal University of Bahia, has Degree on Economics at Federal University of Alagoas (1997), and in Pedagogy at Brazilian Baptist College (2011), and masters on Environment and Development at Federal University of Alagoas (2005). She is an economist at University of Health Sciences of Alagoas, has experience in economics with an emphasis in Economics and Regional Projects Economic and Financial Feasibility, acting on the following areas: professional education, education, public policy, and public management.

Sílvio César Cazella has a PhD and MS degree in Computer Science from the University Federal do Rio Grande do Sul, Brazil. Dr. Cazella works as a lecturer and researcher at the Federal University of Health Sciences of Porto Alegre and University of Vale do Rio dos Sinos, Brazil. His research interests are related to information and health education, artificial intelligence, and recommender systems.

Ana Grasielle Dionísio Corrêa graduated in Computer Engineering from the Universidade Católica Dom Bosco (2002), MSc (2005), and Ph.D. (2011) in Electrical Engineering from the Escola Politécnica of Universidade de São Paulo. She is currently Assistant Professor of Computer Science and Information Systems at Universidade Presbiteriana Mackenzie and researcher at Integrated Systems Laboratory of Escola Politécnica of Universidade de São Paulo (USP), acting on the following topics: interactive electronic systems, virtual and augmented reality, computers in education, health informatics, and assistive technologies.

Néstor D. Duque is Associate Professor from Universidad Nacional de Colombia, campus Manizales and head of the Research Group in Adaptive Intelligent Environments GAIA. He received his master's degree in Systems Engineering from Universidad Nacional de Colombia, and his PhD in Engineering from Universidad Nacional de Colombia, campus Medellin. His PhD thesis was titled "Adaptive Multi-Agent Model for Planning and Execution of Adaptive Virtual Courses" with Cum Laude honors. He is the author of a number of articles in scientific journals and book chapters, speaker at major national and international events, head of the development process of national and international research projects, member of academic committees of a dozen national and international journals, academic review in post-graduate academic programs, and special events. He has also received some meritorious distinction for researching and teaching from School of Administration at Universidad Nacional de Colombia, campus Manizales.

Carlos Evandro de Medeiros Fernandes is a Researcher in Biomedical Engineering. He worked on 2011 as Teacher on College of Science and Technology Mater Chris. He received his M.Sc. in Computer Science from the Federal University of Semi Arid, Mossoró-RN, Brazil, July 2010. He received a Bachelor Degree in Computer Engineering, from Potiguar University, Natal-RN, Brazil, July 2006. Currently, his research activities focus on Biomedical Engineering, Software Engineering, and Embedded Systems.

David J. Gagnon (University of Wisconsin, Madison) is the program manager of the Mobile Learning Incubator, a team of designers, developers, and researchers who are exploring the intersections of place, games, and design through prototyping. David also directs the ARIS Project, an open-source tool and global community that produces locative games and data collection activities. Additionally, David is an instructional designer with the ENGAGE program where he collaborates with faculty to leverage new media for teaching and learning.

Alex Sandro Gomes is Professor at Computer Science Center of Federal University of Pernambuco, Member of Pernambuco Academy of Science, Researcher associated to the Brazilian Research Agency – CNPq. Electronic Engineer by UFPE, Master in Cognitive Psychology by UFPE, and Doctor in Education by Université de Paris v (René Descartes, 1999). He works on Technology Enhanced Learning (TEL). Between the years 2001 and 2012, he coordinated seven research projects in this area and integrated the design team in five others. The LMS Amadeus and the Redu social network—www.redu.com.br—are the most prominent products. The first is distributed by the Brazilian Planning Ministry under GLP2 license. The Redu is a star up at Porto Digital IT cluster. He has published more than 100 papers in specialized periodicals and in conference proceedings. He advised or co-advised more than 35 master's dissertations and PhD theses on TEL.

Christopher L. Holden is an Assistant Professor in the University Honors College at the University of New Mexico in his hometown of Albuquerque. His research focuses on the design and use of place-based mobile games, and the development of the ARIS platform as a tool for these investigations.

Kempes Jacinto graduated as Systems Analyst in College Mater Christi (Mossoró/RN, 2009). He has worked as programmer, system analyst, database administrator, and Web designer in private and multinational companies since 1999. In 2008, he started work in IT technical, first in Federal Rural University of the Semi-Arid (UFERSA) and today in Federal University of Alagoas (UFAL). His main interest areas are in Software Engineering, Assistive Technologies, Real Time Systems, and Unconventional Databases.

Kleber Jacinto received his Master's degree in Computer Science from Federal Rural University of Semi-Arid (2012) and Bachelor's degree in Electrical Engineering from Federal University of Rio Grande do Norte (2004). Since 2006, has been Information Technology Superintendent of Federal Rural University of Semi-Arid, and a professor at School of Exact Sciences in Potiguar University (Laureate International Universities) since 2011. His main interest areas are in IT Governance, Assistive Technologies, and Information Security.

Doris Lee, Ph.D., is a professor at the Training and Development Graduate Program at Penn State University Harrisburg. Dr. Lee's research interests and accomplishments focus on examining learning variables and human and organizational factors involved in different instructional and learning forms.

Cicília R. M. Leite holds a PosDoc Position in Massachusetts Institute of Technology (MIT). She has a doctorate in Computer and Electrical Engineering from the Federal University of Rio Grande do Norte (2011) and a Master's degree in Electrical Engineering from Federal University of Campina Grande (2006) and Bachelor's degree in Computer Science from State University of Rio Grande do Norte (2003). Since 2006, she has been an adjunct professor at State University of Rio Grande do Norte and researcher of the Postgraduate UERN/UFERSA Computer Science Program. Her main research areas are in Software Engineering, Health Informatics, Assistive Technologies, and Real Time Systems.

Breanne K. Litts is a doctoral student in Curriculum and Instruction with an emphasis in Digital Media at the University of Wisconsin – Madison. She currently studies learning and making with the goal of designing learning environments that leverage the affordances of makerspaces. Additionally, she serves as a researcher of the Mobile Learning Incubator exploring the affordances of mobile technologies for learning. Breanne's scholarly interests lie at the intersection of identity, learning, design, and technology, particularly from a learning sciences perspective.

Marina Stock McIsaac is Professor Emerita at Arizona State University where she taught and conducted research in the effective use of educational technologies for over 20 years. Her area of expertise is open and distance learning, specifically in online settings. Her research and teaching interests are in the online use of educational and social networks, particularly Web 2.0 applications for teacher training and professional development. Her publications include more than 50 journal articles and book chapters on distance education, social aspects of online communication, and integration of communication technologies in teaching and learning. Dr. McIsaac has been a recipient of 4 Fulbright Awards to Turkey and Portugal and is Past-President of three National Professional organizations. She has given keynote addresses and workshops in Turkey, Italy, Germany, Cyprus, Taiwan, Hong Kong, Nigeria, and Portugal.

Bruno de Sousa Monteiro graduated in Computer Science in 2006 from the Federal University of Paraíba (UFPB), and obtained a Master's degree in Computer Science in 2009 from the Federal University of Pernambuco (UFPE). He has experience in the areas of computer graphics, development of learning objects, development of applications for mobile and digital TV, and context-aware environments. He is also a professor at the Federal Rural University of the Semi-Arid (UFERSA), since 2011, working in the area of Algorithms and Programming.

Emanuel do Rosário Santos Nonato has degrees in Portuguese and English Languages and Literatures (1998) at Catholic University of Salvador, Specialization in Brazilian Literature (2003) at Catholic University of Salvador, Master Degree on Education (2006) at State University of Bahia, and PhD on Knowledge Diffusion (2013) at Federal University of Bahia. He is an auxiliary professor at Bahia State University, and his main research interest is hypertext and hyperreading.

Demetrio Ovalle is Full Professor at Universidad Nacional de Colombia, campus Medellin. He was head of the Department of Computer Science at School of Mines (2006-2008). He is presently head of GIDIA (Artificial Intelligence Research & Development Group), categorized as A1, maximum category established by Colombian National Science & Technology Bureau. He has published over 150 refereed publications in journals, books and international conferences. He received his Master's and PhD degrees in Informatics, respectively, from Institut National Polythechnique in 1987 and Université Jospeh Fourier in 1991, in Grenoble, France. His research interests are in the areas of Distributed Artificial Intelligence and Multi-Agent Systems (MAS), Virtual Learning Environments, Intelligent Tutoring Systems, Mobile & Ubiquitous Computing, Ambient Intelligence, Autonomic Systems, and Wireless Sensor Networks. He has also received some meritorious distinctions in research from School of Mines at Universidad Nacional de Colombia, campus Medellin.

Adriano Pereira has a bachelor in Computer Science by the Federal University of Santa Maria (2010) and Master in Computer Science in the Computing Graduate Program, also in Federal University of Santa Maria (2012), in Rio Grande do Sul, Brazil. His undergraduate work was about the distributed and scalable data-mining tool Apache Mahout. In Master, he proposed a context-aware recommendation system based on users' affective state. Nowadays, he works as IT Analyst at Data Processing Center in Federal University of Santa Maria with Java Web development. Has experience in Computer Science, emphasizing Distributed Systems, Ubiquitous and Pervasive Computing, Recommendation Systems, and Affective Computing.

João Phellipe de Freitas Pinto is an IT analyst. He works as IT analyst professional at Federal University of Semi Arid since 2012. He received his M.Sc. in Computer Science from the Federal University of Semi Arid, Mossoró-RN, Brazil, January 2013. He has several refereed publications that have appeared in journals, conference proceedings, and book chapters. He received a Bachelor degree in Computer Science, Federal University of Semi Arid, Mossoró-RN, Brazil, in December 2010, and works as professor at the College of Science and Technology Mater Christi, Mossoró-RN, Brazil, since January 2013. Currently, his research activities focus on AI and robotics.

Eliseo Berni Reategui has a PhD degree in Computer Science from the University of London, England, and MS in Computer Science from Universidade Federal do Rio Grande do Sul, Brazil. After finishing his PhD and working in the industry for 5 years, Dr. Reategui held a lecturer position at the University of Caxias do Sul, Brazil, for a few more years. Nowadays, he works as a lecturer and researcher at the Federal University of Rio Grande do Sul. His research interests are related to the use of computers in education, involving areas such as artificial intelligence and human-computer interaction.

Jocelma Almeida Rios is researcher in collaborative knowledge construction, distance education, and management education, has a PhD on Knowledge Diffusion (2013) at Federal University of Bahia, Master in Computer Networks (2007), bachelor on Computer Science with emphasis in Systems Analysis (1996) at University Salvador and on Pedagogy at Brazilian Baptist College (2011). She is currently a professor at the Federal Institute of Education, Science, and Technology of Bahia. She has experience in Computer Science with emphasis in Software Engineering, Information Systems, and Knowledge Engineering, and on Education with an emphasis on management education and educational technology.

Oscar Salazar is a Computer Science Engineer from Universidad Nacional de Colombia, campus Medellin, and he is currently advancing Masters Studies from the Systems Engineering program at the same University. He is also a member of the Artificial Intelligence Research & Development Group – GIDIA, categorized as A1, maximum category established by Colombian National Science & Technology Bureau. The area of emphasis of his research is related to the application of Artificial Intelligence techniques for developing ubiquitous and adaptive virtual courses considering several issues such as user-centered recommendation and adaptation of learning objects, course-planning using learning objects, design and development of strategies for collaborative learning, and construction of teamwork awareness services.

Mary Valda Souza Sales is PhD in Education from the Federal University of Bahia (2013), Master of Education and Contemporary at State University of Bahia (2006), and has degree in Pedagogy at Catholic University of Salvador (1992). She is currently Assistant Professor in the Department of Education (DEDC), Campus I, State University of Bahia. Researcher on teacher training, curriculum, educational technology, virtual learning environments, and distance education with emphasis on the production of educational materials. Nowadays, she works directly with training, distance education, curriculum, and knowledge construction.

Francisco Miguel Silva is an Infrastructure Network Analyst. He worked as an IT professional at Halliburton Energy Services Group from 2001 to 2008. He received his M.Sc. in Computer Science from the Federal University of Semi Arid, Mossoró-RN, Brazil, in March 2012. He has four refereed publications that have appeared in journals, conference proceedings, and book chapters. He received a degree in Computer Networks, from Gama Filho University, Rio de Janeiro-RJ, Brazil, December 2007, and a Bachelor Degree in System Information from College of Science and Technology Mater Christi, Mossoró-RN, Brazil, December 2009. Currently, his research activities focus on telecommunication (quality of service), network services, and infrastructure.

Rafael Castro de Souza is a university student of computer science at the Federal University of Semi Arid. He has published one refereed publication that has appeared in a journal. Currently, his research activities are focused in the area of Software Engineering.

Garrett W. Smith is a doctoral student in the Learning Sciences area of the Department of Educational Psychology at the University of Wisconsin – Madison, as well as a software developer in Academic Technology at the University of Wisconsin – Madison. His research and design activities focus on how emerging technologies provide unique affordances for learning, particularly in coupling aspects of the physical world with digital media.

Laura E. Sujo-Montes holds a Ph.D. in Curriculum and Instruction with emphasis on Learning Technologies and a M.A. in Teaching English to Speakers of Other Languages (TESOL) degree from New Mexico State University. Her teaching experience includes international settings in middle school, undergraduate, and graduate students. Her research interests and work include teaching and researching online learning environments, technology and ESL students, and online professional development. She is a faculty member at Northern Arizona University in Flagstaff, Arizona, USA, where she chairs the Educational Specialties department and teaches undergraduate and graduate online courses.

Raymond Szmigiel is an Instructional Design Consultant for the Marketing Education team at SAP, AG. He designs and develops live virtual training and e-learning courses. Ray has a Bachelor's degree in Communication from Villanova University. In addition, he possesses a Master's degree in Communication Management from the University of Southern California and a Master's degree in Instructional Systems from Penn State University. In the learning and development field, Ray has a particular interest in how Web 2.0 technologies can be incorporated into the training process.

Kamal Taha is an Assistant Professor in the Department of Electrical and Computer Engineering at Khalifa University of Science, Technology & Research (KUSTAR), UAE, since 2010. He received his Ph.D. in Computer Science from the University of Texas at Arlington, USA, in March 2010. He has 30 refereed publications that have appeared (or are forthcoming) in journals, conference proceedings, and book chapters. He worked as an Instructor of Computer Science at the University of Texas at Arlington from August 2008 to August 2010. He worked as Engineering Specialist for Seagate Technology (a leading computer disc drive manufacturer in the US) from 1996 to 2005. His current research interests include information retrieval in semi-structured data, keyword search in XML documents, recommendation systems and social networks, knowledge discovery and data mining, query processing and optimization, and bioinformatics databases (mediators, ontologies). He serves as a member of the Program Committee of a number of international conferences, and he is a reviewer for a number of academic journals and conferences. He was a GAANN Fellow (US Department of Education Graduate Assistance in Areas of National Need) as well as a Texas-STEM Fellow. He is a member of the IEEE.

Chih-Hsiung Tu, Ph.D., is a Professor at Northern Arizona University, Flagstaff, AZ, USA, and an educational/instructional technology consultant with experience in distance education, open network learning, technology training in teacher education, online learning community, learning organization, mobile learning, personal learning environment, MOOCs, and global digital learning. His research interests are distance education, socio-cognitive learning, socio-cultural learning, online learning community, learning organization, social media, personal learning environments, and network learning environments. He has authored many articles, book chapters, edited a book, authored two books, multiple honors as keynote speaker, professional development, professional conference presentations, and others. He has served as an executive board member for ICEM (International Council for Educational Media), SICET (Society for International Chinese in Educational Technology), and International Division at AECT (Association for Educational Communication and Technology). Dr. Tu has global experience with international scholars from Turkey, Portugal, Hong Kong, Singapore, Taiwan, China, Japan, and Cyprus, etc.

Justin Wolske is a Creative/Line Producer working in the entertainment and education media industries. His company Standard|Royal has created features to Web content for companies like MTV, Nike, Sony, eBay, Reebok, Zippo, and many others. He has also been published in *Intelligence & National Security* and *The Journal of Asian Martial Arts*. He is in the development and financing phase for the education media company Caseworx, which re-imagines the business case study for an interactive, global platform. Justin holds a B.A. in History/Philosophy from Indiana University, Bloomington, and an MFA in Film Direction from the University of California, Los Angeles.

Cherng-Jyh Yen is an Assistant Professor of Educational Research and Statistics at Old Dominion University. Previously, he served as a Quantitative Research Methods faculty at the George Washington University. Dr. Yen holds a M.S. in Counselor Education from Indiana University, Bloomington, and Ph.D. in Educational Research from the University of Virginia. His main research interests are in the applications of research designs and statistical analyses in educational studies. In the past, he collaborated with colleagues on research projects of test validation using Structural Equation Modeling (SEM) and multilevel modeling of longitudinal data in the Special Education Elementary Longitudinal Study (SEELS) using Linear Mixed Models (LMM). As a result, various presentations have been made in national conferences, such as the AERA annual conference and AECT annual conference. Papers also appear in different peer-reviewed journals, such as *Journal of School Psychology, International Journal on E-Learning, Quarterly Review of Distance Education,* and *Computers and Education.*

Index

A

AffectButton 260, 262, 265-266

Affective Computing 252-254, 265-267

Affective-Recommender 252-253, 255-257, 259-262, 264-265

Affective States 253-254, 257, 262-265

AGeRA 1-2, 7-16

Android Software Development Kit (SDK) 11

ARToolkit 4-5, 12

Augmented Reality 1-7, 10, 12, 14-23, 25-27, 29, 32-34, 78, 84, 87, 89, 93, 145

Augmented Reality Games on Handhelds (ARGH) 21

authentic learning 51, 163, 165-166, 171-172

Authoring Tool 16, 19, 22, 28, 94-95, 101, 116-117, 202, 221

Authoring Tool Accessibility Guidelines (ATAG) 221

automatic academic advisor 177

Avatars 35-49, 51, 53, 55, 57-58, 206

B

banking model of education 146-147

Beats-Looses 186

biclusters 178-181, 183, 186, 188, 190-191

Biology 75, 271

Brain Imaging 254

C

Caseworx 194-195, 198-199, 211

Cognitive Evaluation Theory 41

Cognitive Process 268, 274, 282

collaboration through the air 21

collaborative filtering 120, 122-124, 126-127, 134-136, 138-139, 142, 174-175, 177-178, 191-192, 240, 264-265, 267

Collaborative Learning

Collaborative Learning 35, 37, 42-43, 45, 47-48, 51-54, 56, 58, 72, 74-75, 84, 88, 92, 138, 143, 153, 155, 174, 204, 235-236, 239, 248, 271

Collaborative Work 10, 239, 268-269, 271, 276, 278-279, 281

Communication Model (MAS-CommonKADS) 242

competence 41, 129, 131-132, 137, 270

computer games 168

Computer-Mediated Communication (CMC) 77, 79, 93

constructivism 45, 161-162, 166, 172-173

Consumer Electronics Association 203, 208

Context-Aware Computing 60, 73, 121, 138, 174

cyberculture 269, 272, 275, 280, 282-283, 286

D

Design-Based Research (DBR) 29

Design Pedagogy 19

Digital Identities 83, 85-86

digital inclusion portal 219

distance education 90-92, 95-96, 114, 117-118, 171, 177, 269, 277, 286

distributed cognition 161, 165-166, 172-173

domain 86, 123, 136, 177, 226, 230-232, 237, 239, 245, 271

Dow Day 27

Down syndrome 160-162, 164-173

E

Eclipse 11

E-commerce 120, 137-138, 174, 177, 220

educational paradigm 2

educational storytelling 194, 199

Education City Managers Support Program 277

Emotional Recommendation 252

Evaluation Metrics 127

Expectancy-Value Theory 40-41, 56